THE GLOBAL GUIDE TO ANIMAL PROTECTION

THE GLOBAL GUIDE TO ANIMAL PROTECTION

Edited by Andrew Linzey

Foreword by Archbishop Desmond Tutu

UNIVERSITY OF ILLINOIS PRESS
Urbana, Chicago, and Springfield

PUBLICATION OF THIS BOOK
IS SUPPORTED BY A GRANT FROM
Figure Foundation

For my son
ADAM,
artist and visionary

CONTENTS

SECTION 6.
CHANGING PERSPECTIVES

SECTION 7.
ANIMAL-FRIENDLY LIVING

EXTENDING JUSTICE AND COMPASSION
ARCHBISHOP DESMOND TUTU

I have spent my life fighting discrimination and injustice, whether the victims are blacks, women, or gays and lesbians. No human being should be the target of prejudice or the object of vilification or be denied his or her basic rights. I could not have lived with myself, as a Christian and a bishop, if I had looked the other way. But the business of fighting injustice is like fighting a multiheaded hydra. As one form of injustice appears to be vanquished, another takes its place. Even if the path of progress seems interminably long, we can content ourselves with the sense that injustices to other human beings are at least on the agenda, or mostly so.

But there are other issues of justice—not only for human beings but also for the world's other sentient creatures. The matter of the abuse and cruelty we inflict on other animals has to fight for our attention in what sometimes seems an already overfull moral agenda. It is vital, however, that these instances of injustice not be overlooked.

I have seen firsthand how injustice gets overlooked when the victims are powerless or vulnerable, when they have no one to speak up for them and no means of representing themselves to a higher authority. Animals are in precisely that position. Unless we are mindful of their interests and speak out loudly on their behalf, abuse and cruelty go unchallenged.

Religious traditions do not, by and large, have a good record on animals. It has taken Christian churches some nineteen hundred years to recognize the immorality of slavery and even longer to recognize that women should not be treated as second-class citizens. Animals have invariably occupied a rather low, sometimes nonexistent place on the moral agenda of the churches. But things are now, slowly but surely, beginning to change. In the same way that sensitivity to race-and gender-based injustice has taken years—even centuries—to develop, so increasing numbers of people are gradually beginning to adopt more thoughtful and compassionate attitudes toward animals.

In many ways, it is odd that my fellow Christians have failed to see the issue of how we treat animals as a Gospel issue. After all, animals are also God's creatures. Christians believe that the world is God's creation. It is a kind of theological folly to suppose that God has made the entire world just for human beings, or to suppose that God is interested in only one of the millions of species that inhabit God's good earth. Our dominion over animals is not supposed to be despotism. We are made in the image of God, yes, but God—in whose image we are made—is holy, loving, and just. We do not honor God by abusing other sentient creatures.

If it is true that we are the most exalted species in creation, it is equally true that we can be the most debased and sinful. This realization should give us pause. So much of our maltreatment of animals stems from a kind of spiritual blindness, a kind of hubris, in which we foolishly suppose that our own welfare is God's sole concern. In fact, God's creation is entrusted to our care and under our protection. There is something Christ-like about caring for suffering creatures, whether they are humans or animals.

Even when faced with urgent human problems, we should not overlook the issue of justice to animals. In fact, an increasing amount of evidence shows that there is a link between cruelty to animals and cruelty to weaker human beings. We know, for example, that violent killers of humans often begin their careers years earlier by practicing on animals. All of us have an interest in the creation of a cruelty-free world. Churches should lead the way by making clear that all cruelty—to other animals as well as human beings—is an affront to civilized living and a sin before God.

This *Global Guide* reflects a growing worldwide sensitivity to animals and a developing sense that—as a matter of justice—they deserve our compassion and respect. It has my warm support.

I

Life on Mars. What was once science fiction may yet become fact. It now seems likely that there is water, an essential prerequisite for the emergence of life, on Mars after all. The possibility emerges that during the lifetime of some of us, or at least our sons' and daughters' lifetimes, human beings will encounter other, nonterrestrial life-forms.

What, we may wonder, would such other life-forms look like? Would they be recognizable in human terms? Would they, for example, have faces or hands or feet? Would they be able to communicate with us, at least in nonverbal ways? Would they be intelligent? Would they be sentient—that is, would they have feelings and be able to experience pain and pleasure? Not least of all, would they have eyes that enable them to look out on the world and actually see us?

We cannot know any of these things for certain, but if the discovery of other such beings were made, it would surely be a groundbreaking event for the human species—an astonishing discovery, no less. The implications—moral, political, and religious—would be profound. It would be the media sensation of all time, even surpassing that of our landing on the moon. History books would have to be rewritten. Philosophical assumptions about how humans are the center of the universe would have to go. Our whole mental view of ourselves as the only intelligent form of life would be changed forever. We would need a great deal more humility about ourselves and our place in the universe.

But consider this: the world in which humans live is already populated with hundreds, thousands, actually billions of other forms of life. And a great many of these life-forms, certainly mammals, already have recognizable human form: they have faces; they have hands or

feet, or both; they are indubitably sentient; they have at least the rudiments of rationality; some (such as whales) have a brain capacity that already exceeds our own; and not least of all, they have eyes through which they see the world and look out on us.

Consider further that if we learned that the Martians we encountered *did* possess intelligence and sentiency, we surely would want to know more about them, to learn of their own ways and history, and to understand their lives. But suppose we then learned that instead of treating these other nonterrestrial beings with respect and understanding, members of our species were actually abusing and exploiting them for humans' own purposes—then, surely, we would be amazed and appalled. Here was an opportunity, we might think, for reciprocal encounter, for mutual understanding, even friendship, and we simply threw it away in an even greater quest for human colonization. We would surely be agog at the ungenerosity, selfishness, and even shortsightedness of the human species.

Yet the truth is that that is precisely what humans now do to most of the terrestrial (and nonterrestrial) nonhuman species we encounter in the world today. We do not look upon the discovery of other life-forms as a source of amazement or wonder, or in a spirit of fraternal respect; rather, we routinely use them for food, for research, and for sport and entertainment. And what is more, most human beings seem perfectly content with our exploiting and harming other species. Indeed, for the most part, it seems that they have not even really thought about it. In the not wholly inappropriate words of Bertrand Russell, "most English people would rather die than think, and most of them actually do."

If we discovered intelligent and sentient Martians, we would surely need to change our perspective; we would have to recognize that ours is not the only way of seeing the world—there would be a Martian perspective as well as a purely human one. And yet the world in which we live is already in fact a many-eyed world. Ours are not the only eyes that look out at the creation around us. In the words of the poet Christina Rossetti,

> And other eyes than ours
> Were made to look on flowers

And once we have grasped this truth, we may also sense the corollary of which Rossetti also speaks:

> The tiniest living thing
> That soars on feathered wing,
> Or crawls among the long grass out of sight
> Has just as good a right
> To its appointed portion of delight
> As any King.
> (*A Nursery Rhyme Book*, 1872, rev. 1893)

The sad fact is that it has taken most of the human species almost three thousand years to recognize the truth of which Rossetti speaks. Generally, we do not see animals as subjects of worth in themselves—that is, if we actually *see* them at all. For far too many of us, animals are the invisible beings in our midst; we live among them (that is, when we have not banished them from their habitats), but we do not stop to gaze in wonder and astonishment at the intricacy, complexity, and beauty of their lives. Too often we are single-eyed people living in a multi-eyed world. A terrible spiritual and moral blindness affects the human species.

And yet, if there is a human blindness to the world—or rather worlds—of animals, there is now a significant awakening, enlightenment no less. Human eyes have begun to move outward to the world of creation and animals, as was inevitable, and have begun to be disturbed by what they see—especially our indifferent and cruel treatment of animal life. Although often trivialized by the media, there is a steady, growing awareness that other life-forms are not just here for us: they are not commodities, machines, tools, resources, here for us. Rather, they are sentient beings with their own intrinsic value, dignity, and rights.

II

This *Global Guide* is part of this new movement of perception, which has begun to take root in countries all over the world. Almost everywhere where animals are exploited and abused, new voices are rising against their maltreatment. For far too long this movement has been thought of as a Western, even European, preoccupation. In fact, it is now truly worldwide; on every continent, in

almost every country, animal protectionists have begun to organize, to make representations, and to ensure that their voices are heard. In short, animal protectionists are making us see animals, sometimes for the first time.

This guide, then, is an invitation to see the world through the eyes of the animals we still ruthlessly exploit for profit and advantage. Sometimes it makes for difficult, even disturbing reading. No book about animals that nowadays avoids the shameful reality of our cruelty toward them could be taken—or should be taken—seriously. There is much to disturb us, much that should rightly disturb us, in this book. It seems that almost everywhere, we have turned what could have been a mutually respectful relationship into a cruel and exploitative one.

But this guide is not just a catalog of horrors, painful though many of the subjects may be. It is also an account of the many heroic attempts made by courageous and selfless people to face the challenge of our unremitting exploitation of the animal world. Almost everywhere we look, we can find cause both for sorrow and for joy—sorrow because of our continued blindness, yet joy that horrors are finally being exposed and that some progress, however small, is being made. Never before has one volume so sought to present, in an accessible form, the worldwide struggle for animal protection waged in many countries and by many hands. Here assembled are many of the major players, the movers and the shakers, who have begun to change the world for animals.

And who are they? They are academics, professionals, and advocates, all of whom have given up part, or even most, of their lives to champion the cause of a more humane world. Seldom has a book brought together such a wealth of knowledge and expertise to bear on an urgent worldwide problem. This, then, is more than a simple factual account, a compendium of terms, or a dictionary of words; this is a volume capable of stirring the heart and refreshing the mind with new perspectives. It is an indispensable aid to seeing the world from the vantage point of those creatures we so readily exploit.

Human beings, we are told, are now suffering from "compassion fatigue." There are so many claims on our attention, so many causes to support, and so many injustices to rectify that people feel overwhelmed and powerless. How can we justify, in this context, giving animals time and space in our already overburdened lives? The answer, if it is not already obvious, is given by many contributors. Human welfare and animal welfare are inextricably related. It is not an either-or matter. We now know that there is a link between cruelty to animals and violence to other vulnerable human beings, notably women and children. A significant proportion of those who commit crimes of violence against humans have histories of violence against animals. One answer to the question "Why are you not more concerned about cruelty to humans?" was given by one of the pioneers of animal protection in the United States, Joyce Tischler of the Animal Legal Defense Fund. She noted that she is concerned about all suffering, and she is "working at the roots." At a time of increasing violence, caring for animals is a practical demonstration of the possibility of a cruelty-free world. Our guide is confirmation of the fact that those countries that care most for human rights care for animal protection as well or, put negatively, that those countries most guilty of disrespecting human rights mostly disrespect animal rights as well.

III

Although animal protection is obviously a matter of global concern, animal protectionists have sometimes been slow in recognizing this fact and have contented themselves with working on an issue-by-issue, country-by-country basis. But what this approach neglects is the need for international strategies to tackle what are global problems. The time has long since gone when we regarded issues of human rights as the concern of solely the government of the country concerned. In the same way, there needs to be recognition that animal abuse transcends national boundaries and should therefore be a matter of international concern.

Representatives of animal protection societies need to assemble regularly on a worldwide basis to consider strategies and measures for reform. We need to create a new worldwide forum that will be a voice for animals globally. Industries responsible for animal abuse and, more importantly, complacent governments have to be made accountable by the international community for their acquiescence in cruelty. The magnitude of the suffering involved—literally billions abused and cruelly treated each year—is so great that international action is now essential. All governments have to take their share of responsibility—and the fact that so many governments seem unaware of their duty and can apparently act without accountability (even, it seems, to their own electorate) must be of concern to all right-thinking people everywhere. It cannot be sufficient to shrug off such culpability as though it was simply part and parcel of the round of politics with which we have become altogether too familiar.

There need to be new, internationally established mechanisms to focus worldwide concern, including two specifically:

The first is an International Cruelty Tribunal (ICT). Humanitarian organizations worldwide should collaborate in setting up an international tribunal to adjudicate on issues of animal cruelty and specifically to assess the culpability of governments. Individuals and groups would be able to bring cases before the ICT where governments have failed to take reasonable steps to prevent systematic and widespread occurrence of cruelty to animals. The ICT would consist of eminent humanitarians drawn from the legal and veterinary professions, together with ethicists, philosophers, theologians, and those accomplished in anticruelty work worldwide. The composition of the ICT would be similar to that of eminent persons groups (EPGs) that undertake investigative and fact-finding work in troubled regions of the world or that study issues of international concern. It would be the ICT's task to hear and assess evidence, to interrogate government representatives, and to produce authoritative reports.

The second is an International Cruelty Register (ICR) that would, subsequent to the findings of the tribunal, name and shame countries whose governments fail to participate in the hearings or fail to take action against cruelty. The register would alert people to those countries whose record on cruelty is outstandingly poor. Like Amnesty International's published list of countries that allow torture, the ICR would focus attention not only on the distressing fact of cruelty itself, but also on the culpability of governments in justifying and supporting cruelty.

The underlying rationale is that people have the right to know the record of governments on the issue of cruelty. Individual citizens should be in a position to make informed decisions about the countries they intend to favor as tourists, as investors, and as consumers. Although the World Trade Organization undoubtedly makes matters more difficult, we need to continue to insist on animal protection exemptions to free trade agreements. In fact, there is ample scope for individual governments to take action on moral grounds. We know from experience that trade embargoes on products that result from animal cruelty are effective. For example, when the European Union banned the import of Canadian seal products in 1983, it had an immediate effect on the number of seals killed, as the figures show: down from 166,739 in 1982 to 57,889 in 1983; 31,544 in 1984; and a record low of 19,035 in 1985. Embargoes are one of the most effective ways of helping governments rethink their support for cruelty.

In addition, there needs to be a massive, globally orientated program of humane education. Although the creation of legislation to protect animals is a priority, it must go hand in hand with a systematic attempt to pursue minimum standards of care for all domesticated and managed animals. Law can take us only so far. Although some incidents of cruelty are the result of deliberate acts, many result from neglect or sheer ignorance of the complex needs of individual animals. This means that in addition to pursuing particular campaigns, animal protection societies need to initiate and coordinate international programs of humane education. Changing ethical sensibility requires change at every level—international, national, and social—but change needs also to take root in the lives of individuals who see the issue of justice to animals.

The preceding proposals are made to animal protection and humanitarian organizations in an attempt to raise the profile of cruelty and to focus international action. The evidence of this book makes clear that new initiatives are necessary if we are to be serious in pursuing the possibility of a cruelty-free world.

IV

This guide has been organized to provide both a macro and a micro view of the state of animal protection worldwide. The first section provides histories and global perspectives, and the entries of subsequent sections address specific concerns relating to particular species in a range of countries. The last three sections address the need for reform, illustrate how perspectives are changing, and detail how protection can be advanced, not least of all by adopting cruelty-free lifestyles. Given the prevalence of animal abuse and the multifaceted nature of animal protection work, it is of course impossible to be comprehensive. We have, of necessity, had to select the major areas of abuse as well as give space to those gross abuses that are seldom publicized. We have sought to strike a balance between including the most known and the more unknown fields of animal cruelty.

There is a growing readership for this guide, which we only began to appreciate as the project evolved. On one hand, there is its potential educational use in schools, colleges, and universities (where the demand for appropriate course materials is great), and on the other, there is a growing body of advocates who want an overall view of the state of animal protection and who are eager to become involved in the struggle for reform. In the middle, there are many who care for animals, either personally or professionally, and who simply want to be better informed.

Since this book seeks to advance ethical perspectives on animals, we also have had to address the language that we commonly use about them. We need to see a connection between our long history of abusing animals and what we think and say about them. Many of the words that we use are derogatory toward animals, such as "beasts," "brutes," "bestial," "critters," "subhumans," "pests," and "vermin"—indeed, even the term "animal"

has become a term of abuse (and not only against animals). It is important to appreciate that our words can convey negative overtones or belittle animals and our relations with them. We have therefore tried to modify some of the usual nomenclature: instead of "pet," we have used "companion animal"; for "owner," we have substituted "caregiver"; and instead of "wild," we have used "free-living." This is not mindless political correctness, but rather an attempt to avoid some of the more obviously prejudicial language about animals, for if we make no effort even to speak of animals without bias, it will be more difficult to treat them fairly.

This guide has been a collaborative venture and has a long history. It has involved corresponding with literally hundreds of animal protection agencies throughout the world. It has been an honor to be in touch with so many people—often in far-flung parts of the globe—who are struggling, oftentimes against the odds, to secure a more humane world. Our project would have been impossible without their support and their preparedness to realize the vision of the book. We are especially grateful to those individuals and organizations that have generously supported the project, including the International Fund for Animal Welfare, the Royal Society for the Prevention of Cruelty to Animals, the Latham Foundation, United Poultry Concerns, Campaign Whale, GREY2K USA Education Fund, and Compassion in World Farming. All contributions are the work of individuals or groups of individuals who take responsibility for their own views, as I alone am responsible here and in my subsequent contributions for my views.

In the midst of compiling this work, I was appointed the Henry Bergh Professor of Animal Ethics at the Graduate Theological Foundation in Indiana. The foundation has an enviable reputation for innovation in the field of theology, ethics, and ministry, and it is a privilege to hold the first post in animal ethics in the world, as well as a special delight to be associated with a post that honors the founder of anticruelty work in the United States. My special thanks to the foundation for leading the way in the academic exploration of this subject.

The University of Illinois Press has been a most supportive publisher, and my particular thanks are due to Kendra Boileau, the original commissioning editor, and Willis Regier, who was enormously forbearing and patient in the face of many delays in delivery of the manuscript. The book is everywhere indebted to his expert editorial hands and those of his colleagues, especially Jennifer Comeau Reichlin and Stephanie Ernst.

This book would have been impossible without the help and support of many fellows of the Oxford Centre for Animal Ethics, who have advised on topics and contributions in addition to writing numerous entries. My special thanks to them all. In particular, I am indebted to Professor Priscilla Cohn, the Centre's associate director, for her guidance and encouragement.

My final thanks are to my wife, Jo, to whom my debt is huge. She has helped sustain me during many a dark night and has been a constant source of help with the editing and proofing of the manuscript. She is the unsung heroine of the book.

ANDREW LINZEY
Oxford Centre for Animal Ethics
director@oxfordanimalethics.com

one

HISTORIES AND GLOBAL PERSPECTIVES

The first subsection of "Histories and Global Perspectives" provides an overview of the emergence of organized animal protection in Europe, the United States, Canada, and Russia.

It would be a mistake to suppose that ideas of animal protection emerged only in the nineteenth century; on the contrary, ideas of respect for life and non-harming emerged in many continents and can be traced as far back as Jainism (*see* Animals in Jainism) and the pre-Socratics. Those who care for animals stand in a long intellectual tradition that has had advocates in every part of the globe. What distinguishes the nineteenth century is that this age-old concern crystallized into organized social movements. From Britain outward to Europe, the United States, and as far as Russia—and within only a few decades—organized movements sprung up as though they possessed an idea whose time had come. By the end of the nineteenth century, that institutionalization of animal concerns had become entrenched in almost every continent.

The second subsection also provides a range of perspectives from around the globe. Readers may be surprised to learn how varied the state of animal protection is worldwide, with some countries making strides while others seemingly remain at something close to a standstill. Consequently, there is much to ponder here about the need for global networking, common strategies, and international collaboration in order to secure even minimal standards for animals worldwide. The spirit of collaboration that so enabled European and North American societies to make progress in the nineteenth century needs to characterize international animal protection in the twenty-first century.

ANDREW LINZEY

HISTORIES OF ORGANIZED ANIMAL PROTECTION

ANIMAL PROTECTION IN BRITAIN

Attempts to protect animals in nineteenth-century Britain were set against broader political projects to build a forward-looking nation that rejected a barbaric past. A new humanity toward animals became a distinctive part of modernity.

The first animals to benefit from parliamentary legislation were animals used in farming. On June 7, 1822, in what became known as "Martin's Act," after Richard Martin, MP, who promoted the bill, it became an offense punishable by fines and imprisonment to wantonly and cruelly "beat, abuse, or ill-treat any horse, mare, gelding, mule, ass, ox, cow, heifer, steer, sheep or other cattle." The rise of organized political discussion—and then societies to protect animals—became a distinctive part of the creation of new political and moral sentiments. Debates on the cruel treatment of animals served to develop and distinguish the character of the developing middle and respectable working classes from that of both the rabble and the dissolute aristocracy.

The Society for the Prevention of Cruelty to Animals (which became the RSPCA) was founded in 1824 initially to implement this first legislation. The SPCA's founding statement was a manifesto of a new rational age, rejecting both bull-baiting and scientific dissection as relics of "rude and obscure ages." In the 1830s and 1840s, the RSPCA, the Animal Friends' Society, and the Rational Humanity Group took upon themselves the propagation of humane treatment toward animals as an indicator of a new age. In the 1860s and 1870s, campaigners' attention shifted to companion animals, particularly dogs and cats. In 1860 Mary Tealby became the first woman to found a British animal welfare organization when she established the Battersea Dogs' Home as a response to seeing dogs dying of "lingering starvation in the streets." In the 1860s, charitable work toward "fallen" dogs (and "fallen women" alike) became distinctive features of the respectable woman.

By the 1870s, animals—primarily dogs and cats—had become the focus of experiments in the hands of scien-tists. The Victoria Street Society, the first organization established to specifically oppose vivisection, had much support from women as well as men. It was led by Frances Power Cobbe, already an experienced campaigner in the political field thanks to her organizing work in the Married Women's Property Committee and in the London Women's Suffrage Society. For Cobbe there was little to distinguish such a scientist from a butcher: "the smooth cool man of science . . . stands by that torture trough." Despite public pressure, the 1876 Cruelty to Animals Act instituted a procedure licensing vivisection and introducing general inspections of laboratories. Scientists conducting animal experiments were now specifically exempt from prosecution for wanton cruelty toward animals. As campaigners had feared, far more experiments were conducted on animals after the 1876 Act was passed: they felt that cruelty had been institutionalized rather than banned. The movement shortly split between those with reforming aspirations and those with abolitionist aspirations. The National Anti-Vivisection Society, led by Stephen Coleridge, advanced gradual reform, whereas the British Union for the Abolition of Vivisection, in which Frances Power Cobbe was the leading light, held out for total and immediate reform.

New organizations campaigning for animals were established in the 1890s. The Our Dumb Friends' League (now the Blue Cross), established in 1897, was primarily philanthropic in its concerns. It funded an animals' ambulance and an animals' hospital for those unable to pay veterinary fees and campaigned against the conditions in which horses were transported from Ireland, as well as against councils asphalting streets since this practice caused injury to horses. The National Canine Defence League (now Dogs Trust), established in 1891, campaigned vigorously and optimistically against both rabies hysteria and vivisection, declaring that once they knew the situation, "all the working class, the masses of voters, will be opposed to vivisection." In a different vein, the Humanitarian League, founded by Henry Salt in 1893, was an explicitly political organization that spanned concerns for animals and for people within a broad organization committed to "prevent[ing] the perpetration of cruelty and wrong—to redress[ing] the suffering, as far as is possible, of all sentient life."

By the twentieth century, there was still evidence of cruelty or neglect carried out by all classes of society, but there was also a mushrooming of different activities in support of animals. Irrespective of whether people ascribed rights to animals or defined them as "dumb creatures," a greater range of animals was receiving legal or charitable protection than had been the case some hundred years before. The organizations established in the nineteenth century—the Battersea Dogs' Home, the National Canine Defence League, the RSPCA, the National Anti-Vivisection Society, the British Union for the Abolition of Vivisection (BUAV), and the Blue Cross—all continue to exist today. The tradition of animal protection in Britain is a long one: the organizations existing to promote animal welfare would also argue vociferously that there is still a pressing need for their existence.

Related articles: Animal advocacy; Animal and human violence; Animals used in research; Cats; Developments in animal law; Dogs; Horses; Live animal exports; Stray animals; The universal charter of the rights of other species; The welfare of cows; The welfare of sheep

Donald, Diana, *Picturing Animals in Britain 1750–1850*, Yale University Press, 2007.
Fairholme, Edward G., and Pain, Wellesley, *A Century of Work for Animals*, Murray, 1924.
Kean, Hilda, *Animal Rights: Political and Social Change in Britain since 1800*, Reaktion Books, 2000.
Kete, Kathleen (ed.), *A Cultural History of Animals in the Age of Empire*, Berg, 2007.
Ritvo, Harriet, *The Animal Estate: The English and Other Creatures in the Victorian Age*, Harvard University Press, 1987.
Turner, E. S., *All Heaven in a Rage*, Centaur Press, reissued 1992.

HILDA KEAN

THE EMERGENCE OF ANIMAL PROTECTION IN RUSSIA

Sensitivity to animals has a long historical provenance in Russia, even giving rise to one of the world's earliest societies for the protection of animals in 1865. This movement was championed by intellectuals, writers, and aristocrats. But it is only comparatively recently that animal protection has again become an organized phenomenon.

The Russian Society for the Protection of Animals was established and supported by czars Alexander II, Alexander III, Nicolas II, and their families. The society published books on humane attitudes toward animals, especially for children, and was instrumental in securing the legal prohibition of cock fighting. Earlier on, Catherine II the Great prohibited, by decree, spring hunting in the Russian Empire in 1763 (Kraev 163–166).

Fyodor Mikhail Dostoyevsky popularized notions of animal protection (*Diary of a Writer*, 1876), and famously, Father Zossima in Dostoyevsky's *The Brothers Karamazov* advised us to

> love all God's creation, the whole of it and every grain of sand . . . Love the animals, love the plants, love everything. If you love everything, you will perceive the divine mystery in things . . . Love the animals: God has given them the rudiments of thought and untroubled joy. Do not therefore trouble [them], do not torture them, do not go against God's intent. (vol. 1, p. 375)

The end of the nineteenth and the beginning of the twentieth century saw the emergence of the "Tolstoy movement," based on the humanistic ideas of the great writer and intellectual Leo Tolstoy. Tolstoy drew the public's attention to the suffering of animals in slaughterhouses, farms, and aquariums. He visited a slaughterhouse, and his experience was reflected in his essay "The First Step" (1892) in which he spoke of vegetarianism as a necessary first step toward spiritual enlightenment.

"Tolstoyans" (as they became known) promulgated ideas of compassion to all living beings and organized vegetarian canteens, kindergartens, schools, and communities. Vegetarian congresses became regular events where vegetarians from Moscow, Kiev, Saint Petersburg, Kishinev, Odessa, and other cities met each other. Magazines and books were published in which various aspects of vegetarianism, including the production of ethical clothes, footwear, and even glue, were discussed (*The Vegetarian Review*, 1913, and *The Vegetarian Journal*, 1914). Along with ideas of compassion to animals, Tolstoyans promulgated pacifism, which is why they were subsequently repressed by the Soviet regime and fully eradicated by the end of the 1930s. Their documents and literature were assigned to virtual oblivion (Braginsky).

In the Soviet period, the movement for the protection of animals was renewed because of the efforts of E. A. Antonova, a teacher, and V. V. Vatagin, an artist. The Moscow-based All-Russia Society for Nature Protection opened a section devoted to animal protection in 1954 (Medkova). The section at first sought to concentrate on the protection of companion animals (*see* Companion Animals) and urban birds but subsequently widened its work to include inspections (under the supervision of Dr. K. A. Semenova) of vivariums, slaughterhouses, and animal farms. The section collected a large volume of material, the most shocking of which concerned the use of animals in experiments without anesthesia. Thanks to their work, the first law regulating the treatment of animals in experiments was adopted in 1977. The rules, which officially prohibited the use of animals without anesthesia, were affirmed by Order of Minister of Health Care and adopted by other ministries and agencies as well.

In the 1980s and 1990s, during the period of perestroika, the first independent organizations for the protection of companion animals and the first private sanctuaries for stray animals were created. The most noticeable among these were the Moscow Society for Animal Protection (chaired by Yu. I. Shvedova) and the Russian Society for Patronage of Animals (chaired by V. I. Maksimova). The Russian Fund for the Protection of Animals, managed by D. S. Taraskina, played an important role in the organization of sanctuaries for animals.

But perhaps the most significant contribution was made by Tatiana Nikolayevna Pavlova (1931–2007), who started the Russian movement for the rights of animals (Novozhilova). Pavlova organized the Russian Vegetarian Society in 1992 (the first one after the revolution of 1917), bringing together the Centre for the Ethical Treatment of Animals and the Scientific-Practical Medical Centre, which became the scientific base of vegetarianism in Russia. Pavlova (who was a linguist and biologist) aroused public opinion through television and radio programs, translated and published foreign literature devoted to the protection of animals, and authored the first learning books in bioethics for schools and colleges approved by the Ministry of Education. She also created the first association of physicians and biologists for the development of alternatives to experiments with animals.

In 1998, Pavlova wrote a federal law for the protection of animals, which was approved by the Russian Parliament and the Council of Federation in 2000 but which sadly failed because President Vladimir Putin refused to ratify it. Pavlova's work inspired the creation of the VITA Animal Rights Center in Moscow in 2003.

At present, animal protection is covered only by article 245 of the criminal code, which mainly concerns companion animals (cats and dogs). The concept of "cruelty" is interpreted in this article as the "infliction of injury to an animal, or death caused by it," and excludes cases of depriving animals of food and water, overheating or overcooling, or subjecting animals to stress. Punishment for cruelty is possible, but it has to be shown that the person behaved cruelly without reason. The civil code includes several clauses about the "humane attitude to animals" that are of a merely declarative nature; other documents have a very low legal status as "orders" or "letters of recommendation." After the first and only attempt at comprehensive federal law failed in 2000, two versions of a

Moscow law for the protection of animals were rejected between 2000 and 2008 as well.

Because of the absence of a comprehensive legal base, the situation is dire for animals in Russia (Committee of the State Duma 41–46). The raising, transportation, and slaughter of animals in meat, dairy, and fur farms are not regulated. In the killing of animals in fur farms, as well as of stray animals, curare preparations are widely used, resulting in tormenting suffocation. Traps are popular in Russia and may be freely purchased in hunting shops. No protection at all is provided for animals used in experiments, which means they may be subjected to painful experiments, used in experiments many times over, kept in inadequate conditions, and killed in inhumane ways. Abuses of animals are still popular, including taking photographs with exotic animals and using them to attract clients' attention in cafes and shops, baiting stations (where free-living animals are used and frequently killed in the training of hunting dogs), and organized animal fights between dogs, roosters, and geese (see Animals in Sport and Entertainment).

But there have been some successes, albeit limited ones. They include the cancellation of a proposed bull fight in Moscow and Yaroslavl in 2000 and 2001, the prohibition of industrial slaughtering of Greenland seal pups in the White Sea in 2009, the substitution of humane alternatives for animal experimentation in ten universities and colleges between 2005 and 2010, the struggle to readopt the rule requiring anesthesia for animals in testing (known as the "ketamine case"), and not least of all, some well-known convictions for cruelty, including for the killing of two Russian dogs named Malchik and Ryzhik.

Related articles: Animal welfare and farming; Animals used in research; The alternatives; Bull fighting; Cats; Cock fighting; Deer hunting; Developments in animal law; Dog fighting; Dogs; Ethical vegetarianism; The ethics of killing free-living animals; Fur farming; The fur trade; Humane research; Hunting with dogs; Live animal exports; Marine mammals in captivity; The pinnipeds; The protection of birds; Shelters and sanctuaries; Slaughter; Stray animals

Braginsky, A. (ed.), *Memoirs of Peasant Tolstoyans, 1910–1930*, Moscow, 1989.

Committee of the State Duma of the Russian Federation on Natural Resources, Environment and Ecology, Roundtable: "Humane Treatment of Animals—The Moral Necessity of Civil Society," verbatim report, June 5, 2009.

Dostoyevsky, F. M., *The Brothers Karamazov*, trans. David Magarshack, Penguin Books, 1958.

———, "January," *Diary of a Writer*, 1876, available at http://www.vita.org.ru/library/philosophy/dostoevskiy-reflection.htm and also at http://az.lib.ru/d/dostoewskij_f_m/text_0480.shtml.

"The First All-Russian Vegetarian Congress," *The Vegetarian Review* (1913), available at http://www.vita.org.ru/veg/veg-literature/veg-viewing1913/55.htm.

Gorbunov, I. I., *The Vegetarian Journal* 1.1 (1914): 1–3, available at http://www.vita.org.ru/veg/veg-literature/veg-vestnik1914/01.htm.

Kraev, N. V., "The History of the Regulation of the Spring Hunting in Russia," *Abstracts of the Third International Symposium "Anseriformes of Northern Eurasia,"* Saint Petersburg, 2005, 163–166.

Medkova, I. L., et al., "All about Vegetarianism," Moscow, 1992, 279, available at http://www.vita.org.ru/veg/veg-literature/vsyo-o-vegetarianstve.rar.

Novozhilova, Irina, "Lifework," *Zoonews* 211 (2006).

Pavlova, T. N., *Bioethics*, Moscow State Academy of Veterinary Medicine, 1997.

Tolstoy, Leo, "The First Step" (1892), in *Recollections and Essays*, 4th ed., trans. Aylmer Maude, Oxford University Press, 1961, 123–135; extract in Linzey, Andrew, and Regan, Tom (eds.), *Animals and Christianity: A Book of Readings*, Crossroad, 1988, and Wipf and Stock, 1990.

"Welcome to the First All-Russian Vegetarian Congress," *Vegetarian Review* (1913), available at http://www.vita.org.ru/veg/veg-literature/veg-viewing1913/55.htm.

IRINA NOVOZHILOVA

EUROPEAN ANIMAL PROTECTION

Societies for the prevention of cruelty to animals, specifically those against vivisection (*see* Animals in Research), were first launched in Europe during the second half of the nineteenth century. Their activity, aimed at raising general sensitivity toward the plight of animals, was characterized by international mutual help, the exchange of information leading to common methods of action, and most of all, the existence of a common cultural framework regarding the relationship between humans and animals. All these elements suggest that a new social movement concerned about animals was born at that time.

These organizations worked to limit animal abuse, specifically "wanton cruelty" against domesticated animals, which was commonplace in slaughterhouses; the use of animals in "sports," such as dog and cock fighting; and the use of mules and horses in urban transport. The opposition to vivisection constituted a distinct stream in the movement.

The mission of the movement was to battle against cruelty, to promote compassion, and more generally, to educate society. The movement's members considered cruel behavior toward animals a form of barbarity and anti-Christian and believed it was likely to develop into antisocial behavior, specifically violence against children and women. Societies for the prevention of cruelty to animals and against vivisection were launched in various parts of Europe over a relatively short period, including in Liverpool (1809); London (1824); Stuttgart (1837); Dresden and Nürnberg (1839); Dublin (1840); Berlin, Frankfurt, and Hamburg (1841); Munich (1842); Berne and Hanover (1844); Budapest, Gorizia, and Paris (1845); Linz (1846); Vienna (1847); Basel (1849); Trieste (1852); Lyon (1853); Zurich (1856); Venice (1858); Lausanne (1860); Lucerne (1866); Geneva (1868); Turin (1871); Florence (1873); Rome (1873); and Milan and Naples (1874).

In this network, some associations represented important points of reference for other newly formed societies: the RSPCA of London—often referred to as the "mother" society—and those of Munich and Paris (called "sister societies") provided a model for international mobilization (via the societies' structure, statutes, and relations with governments) and forms of mobilization (e.g., petitions, campaigns, demonstrations, communications in magazines, scientific treatises).

However, there were differences between associations in different European countries because of the political, economical, and social contexts in which they were grounded. In many Italian states, before the national unification in 1861, freedom of speech, association, and publishing was limited and controlled by the government and the police. After the unification, and therefore with the application of a new common law, there was an increase in the foundation of societies for the protection of animals. Animal protection societies previously launched in the different empires that were to become part of Italy (the Savoy, the Austro-Hungarian Empire, and the Republic of Venice) joined the national society inaugurated by General Giuseppe Garibaldi (1807–1882). In 1871 the Società Protettrice degli Animali contro i mali trattamenti che subiscono dai guardiani e dai conducenti (SPA) was founded thanks to the efforts of British animal protectionist Anna Winter and Timoteo Riboli (doctor and patriot, 1808–1895), with the support of Garibaldi as the SPA's president. The Italian SPA then incorporated other minor societies in 1929, becoming the Ente Nazionale Protezione Animali (ENPA). In 1889, the maltreatment of animals was included in the Italian penal code (the Zanardelli code) as a criminal act against public morality (article 491). However, animal suffering became the central focus of the law per se only when the new penal code was released in 1993 (article 727). The first law regarding the animal protection societies was promoted by Minister Luigi Luzzati in 1913 (law 611) and was replaced by new legislation in 1938. The first law regarding vivisection dates back to 1931.

An international network of cooperation existed among antivivisectionists as well, which was helped by the mobility of upper-class society in Europe at that time, a class to which the majority of animal protection supporters belonged. As a consequence, the circulation of information across countries was facilitated, as were personal relationships between volunteers and representatives from different societies and countries.

At the beginning, British antivivisectionists and public opinion considered vivisection a mere "continental vice." France (with its infamous Alford and Lyon veterinary schools and the vivisectionist Eugene Magnan) and Italy (with the experiments conducted in the hospital of La Specola, Florence) became their primary concern. Nonetheless, the issue would be addressed in Great Britain shortly as well. In France the Société contre la vivisection was founded in 1883 and was distinguished by the support of Victor Hugo (honorary president) and Guy de Maupassant. The Société protectrice des animaux had already started its activity in 1845, and the Grammont Law, the first French law regarding the protection of animals, was formulated in 1850.

The Italian antivivisection movement made its first steps in the 1860s. The British antivivisectionist and women's rights advocate Frances Power Cobbe (1822–1904) of the Victoria Street Society contributed to its foundation while she was in Florence and in contact with animal advocates, such as Lady Walburga Paget (1839–1929, antivivisectionist and vegetarian) and Countess Gertrude Baldelli. Along with other Italian and foreign animal protection campaigners (Mary Somerville among them), they strongly opposed the experiments performed on dogs by Moritz Schiff in 1863 and in 1873–1874. Afterward, Schiff moved to Geneva, where he met Anna Kingsford's fierce opposition. It was Kingsford (1846–1888, vegetarian and women's rights advocate) who promoted the creation of antivivisection societies in France and in Switzerland in the 1980s. The Società fiorentina per la protezione degli animali (SPA in Florence) was founded in 1873, supported by the local aristocracy and British expatriates.

Another example of the mobility of people and ideas at that time was the circulation and translation of books on this subject: it is worth mentioning the case of Marie-Espérance von Schwartz (1818–1899), who moved from Germany to other European countries, dedicating herself to the improvement of children's and animals' conditions of life. In 1875, she read the German translation of *Vivisection* by George Fleming, which inspired her to write the antivivisectionist novel *Gemma oder Tugend und Laster* (translated into Italian, French, and English—as *Gemma or Virtue and Vice* in the latter case) under the

pseudonym of Elpis Melena. In Germany, the novel attracted the attention of Ernst von Weber (1830–1902), who converted to antivivisectionism and founded an organization dedicated to the cause. In 1878 he joined Baroness Schwartz and Ernst Grysanowski (1824–1888, Cobbe's friend) in their battle. Grysanowski, a medical doctor, published the scientific essay *Die Vivisection* (*Die* meaning "The" in English) under the pseudonym of Iatros in 1877. In 1879 *Die Folterkammern der Wissenschaft* ("The Torture Chamber of Science," translated into French and Italian) was published. This pamphlet, written by von Weber, was an immediate success, comparable to Cobbe's *Light in Dark Places*. Von Weber gained Richard Wagner's esteem (1813–1883), and Wagner himself joined the antivivisection movement in Dresden.

The following decades saw many changes within the animal protection and antivivisection movements. As far as animal protection was concerned, the question of animal suffering became central compared to other concerns, such as the link between animal cruelty and violence to humans or the moral judgment of a behavior contrary to religion and God's will. In the twentieth century, the battle against animal abuse was to face other important issues, such as the conditions of animals in factory farming and the extinction of various animal species. During the second half of the last century, a new ethical sensibility sprang from the animal protection and animal welfare branch: more conservative and traditional approaches to the plight of animals were advanced by anti-speciesist principles, which contested not only animal abuse (or "wanton," "unnecessary" cruelty) but also the right of humans to *use* animals for humans' own interests. The current animal liberation or animal rights movement was born.

Within antivivisectionism, two currents animated the debate on animal experiments, one aiming at a regulation of vivisection and the other fighting for its total abolition. The latter prevailed during the twentieth century, opposing vivisection for both scientific and ethical reasons. In Italy, there was a mobilization of scientists and intellectuals against vivisection at the beginning of 1900. Augusto Agabiti (1879–1918), a writer and humanitarian reformer who was also a vegetarian, and doctor Gennaro Ciaburri (1881–1970), founder in 1929 of Unione Antivivisezionista Italiana (UAI, Italian Antivivisection Union), were among them. When the UAI dissolved, a few antivivisection leagues took its place, including the Lega Antivivisezione (LAV—Antivivisection League, the current major organization for animal rights in Italy). LAV was founded in Rome in 1977 by Alberto Pontillo in cooperation with the Swiss antivivisection movement led by Milly Schär-Manzoli (1934–2001) and Hans Ruesch (1913–2007).

In relation to antivivisection in Italy, it is worth mentioning the 1993 law that allows for conscientious objection to animal experiments by doctors, researchers, and students. Before then, in the 1970s, Hans Ruesch's book *Imperatrice nuda* ("Naked Empress") boosted the antivivisection movement in Switzerland and Italy and across Europe. Similarly, Peter Singer's *Animal Liberation* (1975) and Tom Regan's *The Case for Animal Rights* (1984) enlivened the debate about the moral status of animals, resulting in a radical rejection of speciesist ideology. As for Italian animal protection, 1981 is a date to be remembered: the law against straying and the maltreatment of animals (law 281) was promulgated, which, among other features, forbade the killing of companion animals by their caregivers or by animal shelters.

Related articles: Animal advocacy; Animal and human violence; Animal welfare and farming; Animals used in research; Children's relations with animals; Cock fighting; Conservation philosophy; Dog fighting; Ethical vegetarianism; Humane education; Moral anthropocentrism; The moral claims of animals; Shelters and sanctuaries; Slaughter; Stray animals

Burgat, F., *La protection de l'animal*, Presses Universitaires de France, 1997.

Castignone, S., *Povere bestie: I diritti degli animali*, Marsilio, 1997.

Rupke, N. A. (ed.), *Vivisection in Historical Perspective*, Routledge, 1987.

Tonutti, S., "Cruelty, Children, and Animals: Historically One, Not Two, Causes," in Linzey, Andrew (ed.), *The Link between Animal Abuse and Human Violence*, Sussex Academic Press, 2009, 95–105.

———, *Diritti animali: Storia e antropologia di un movimento*, Forum, 2007.

SABRINA TONUTTI

THE HUMANE MOVEMENT IN CANADA

In 1824, almost fifty years before Canada's first humane society was formed, the province of Nova Scotia made cruelty to horses, sheep, and cattle a punishable offense. This was the first Canadian law protecting animals: those convicted had to pay damages to the owner and, at the judge's discretion, were imprisoned or publicly whipped. The Canadian Society for the Prevention of Cruelty to Animals (CSPCA) was formed in 1869, with a mandate to provide effective means for the prevention of cruelty to animals. Believing that most mistreatment was due to ignorance rather than deliberate cruelty, it asked teachers, clergy, and the police to help educate the public about kindness to animals and use punishment only as a last resort. The society produced thousands of circulars in French and English, erected placards, and placed a statement of its object and intentions in newspapers.

On January 1, 1870, an act of the new Dominion of Canada made anyone who wantonly, cruelly, or unnecessarily beat, blinded, ill-treated, abused, or tortured animals used in farming (referred to as "livestock" and poultry), any dog, or any domesticated animal or bird subject to a fine ranging from one to ten dollars or thirty days' imprisonment. By 1873, the CSPCA reported progress: cock fighting had been abolished in Montreal, the killing and trapping of insectivorous birds had been greatly reduced, and the first prosecution had been secured for cruelty to cattle.

Two years later, farmed animals being transported to market were given some legal protection: no animal could be shipped for more than twenty-eight hours without being unloaded and given rest, food, and water (today animals in Canada can be transported for up to fifty-two hours without food, water, or rest—the standard in Europe is twelve hours). But other cruelties remained. The practice of docking horses' tails and use of the check rein (a rein forcing horses' heads to be held uncomfortably high) continued. Despite its name, the Canadian SPCA was a provincial organization formed in Montreal under the Quebec Charter. As the century came to a close, the humane movement developed regionally, and SPCAs sprang up across the country. It was not until 1957 that a national organization was formed—the Canadian Federation of Humane Societies—to improve conditions for animals throughout Canada.

One name often associated with the early humane movement is John Joseph Kelso. A reporter for a Toronto newspaper, Kelso pioneered help for young children employed as cheap labor selling newspapers on city streets. His colleagues, somewhat jokingly, suggested Kelso should also be an advocate for an old, worn-out white horse, then used for transportation. Kelso published a short article advocating a society for the prevention of cruelty and the next day received an anonymous donation of two dollars. Shortly after, he was invited to deliver a paper to the Canadian Institute on the Necessity of a Society for the Prevention of Cruelty in Toronto.

Kelso founded the Toronto Humane Society in 1887, and his lecture marked the beginning of the humane and children's aid movement in Ontario. Five years later, in 1892, the Children's Protection Act formally sanctioned the role of children's aid societies. Because anticruelty laws existed before legislation specifically protecting children, humane societies often took on the role of defending women and children as well as animals. In Nova Scotia, for example, the SPCA's prime function between

1880 and 1900 was providing marriage counseling and legal aid for estranged couples and harassed spouses, usually at the wife's instigation. The Ontario Children's Protection Act gave children protection under the law and allowed them to be removed from an abusive situation or, if appropriate, tried in a juvenile rather than adult court.

The humane movement has spawned many animal protection organizations. In 1944, when Canada introduced a Humane Slaughter Act to reduce killing time in abattoirs, the Association for the Protection of Fur-Bearing Animals (now called the Fur-Bearer Defenders) was formed to seek similar protection for animals used by the fur industry (including free-living fur-bearers). Research to design a more humane trap led in 1958 to the conibear trap, or body-gripping trap. However, this trap was more humane only if the animal entered it correctly; otherwise it proved equally painful to, if not more painful than, steel leghold traps. The Fur-Bearer Defenders and other associations have considerably increased awareness of the cruelty of trapping.

The number of animals trapped in Canada has fallen from more than five million in 1979 to 1980 down to its current level of approximately one million a year (the total figure for North America for 2000 was five to six million). These figures, however, do not include nontarget animals, including birds such as owls and hawks, also caught in traps. Nor do they include the one million animals killed on fur farms.

In the winter of 1976, Brigitte Bardot famously joined other protesters against the annual slaughter of thousands of adult and pup seals, the largest land mammal hunt in the world. Protests against the seal hunt have a long history. As early as 1899, an official representing the American Humane Association condemned its cruelty. More recently, Canadian environmental groups, notably Greenpeace, the International Fund for the Welfare of Animals, and Sea Shepherd have swelled the protests. In 1979, Sea Shepherd crew members saved over a thousand pups by spraying their white pelts with indelible organic dye (hence rendering their fur unsalable). In 1996, however, Canada slaughtered over 250,000 seals, and the slaughter continues to this day.

The Cruelty to Animals sections of the criminal code were written more than a hundred years ago, with only minor modifications in 1954 and 2008. Animals are still classed in legal terms as little more than property. Humane societies have tried from the 1990s onward to change the legal status of animals so that they will be recognized as sentient beings deserving of special protection, despite opposition from farmers, hunters, and trappers. The years since 1824 have been ones of steady, if sometimes uncertain, progress. The humane movement, in Canada and elsewhere, is testimony to the enduring sense that cruelty in whatever form is incompatible with compassionate, just values.

Related articles: Animal welfare and farming; Birds used in food production; Caring for animals and humans; Cock fighting; Developments in animal law; Dogs; Fur farming; The fur trade; Horses; Humane education; Live animal exports; The moral claims of animals; The pinnipeds; The protection of birds; Slaughter; The welfare of cows; The welfare of sheep

Baynger, Janet, *Fanbelt Freddie and Friends: The History of the Kingston Humane Society*, Kingston Humane Society, 2000.

Hodgins, J. George (ed.), *Aims and Objects of the Toronto Humane Society*, Toronto Humane Society, 1888.

Kelso, John Joseph, *Early History of the Humane and Children's Aid Movement in Ontario, 1886–1893*, L. K. Cameron, 1911.

Morris, David B., *Earth Warrior: Overboard with Paul Watson and the Sea Shepherd Conservation Society*, Fulcrum, 1995.

Niven, Charles D., *History of the Humane Movement*, Johnson, 1967.

Savigny, Annie G., *Dick Niven and His Horse Noby: Lantern Slide Lecture Teaching Kindness to Animals*, publisher unknown, ca. 1898.

Sorenson, John, *About Canada: Animal Rights*, Fernwood, 2010.

JANET E. BAYNGER

SOCIETIES AGAINST CRUELTY IN THE UNITED STATES

On February 8, 1866, Henry Bergh spoke before a large crowd at New York City's Clinton Hall. He enumerated the many abuses and cruelties inflicted on animals and called for the formation of a society to protect them. On April 10, 1866, the New York State Legislature granted a special charter for the formation of the American Society for the Prevention of Cruelty to Animals (ASPCA), modeled after the Royal Society for the Prevention of Cruelty to Animals (RSPCA) of England. On April 19, the legislature passed a law that prohibited the mistreatment of animals and authorized the newly formed ASPCA to enforce this law.

The early records of the ASPCA showed Bergh to be both aggressive and inventive in his efforts to protect animals. Although the many horses who pulled the carts, carriages, and trolleys in the city were a major focus, Bergh and the ASPCA also pursued charges related to sea turtles transported for the restaurant trade, animal fighting, pigeon shooting, vivisection (*see* Animals in Research), and the care, transport, and slaughter of animals farmed for food. His efforts soon earned Bergh the nickname "the great meddler" and the ASPCA the enmity of institutional animal abusers. Bergh was a master of public relations, and many of his most famous cases played out in the newspapers and tabloids of the day. These included an extended series of confrontations between Bergh and P. T. Barnum relating to the treatment of the animals at his menagerie and shows.

Barnum would eventually become a grudging admirer of Bergh's dedication to his work. The targets of Bergh's scathing letters and investigative efforts were less forgiving, and several efforts were made to blunt the legal powers of the society. Bergh persevered, however, and he promoted his cause tirelessly.

Henry Bergh was in frequent contact with people around the country, and he encouraged the formation of similar societies. He often provided copies of the ASPCA's charter and model anticruelty laws, and he promoted the use of the SPCA name. In 1867, a second society for the prevention of cruelty to animals was formed in Buffalo, New York (Erie County SPCA), and in 1868, societies were formed in San Francisco, Boston (Massachusetts SPCA), and Philadelphia (Pennsylvania SPCA). By 1874, twenty-five states had formed societies for the prevention of cruelty to animals.

Although these societies drew inspiration from the ASPCA, each was independent in its organization and activities. The leaders of these societies became important figures in the further development of the American animal protection movement. George Angell, founder of the Massachusetts SPCA, was a leading advocate for humane education. Angell had the strong conviction that the most effective way to prevent cruelty to animals was to encourage the development of compassion and empathy in children. He organized the American Humane Education Society as an affiliate of the Massachusetts SPCA in 1889. Likewise, Caroline Earle White was an important catalyst in the formation of the Pennsylvania SPCA. When questions arose regarding the role of women in the management of the society, she helped organize the Women's Branch of the Pennsylvania SPCA. In 1874, the Women's Branch built the nation's first humane animal shelter and took over the management of Philadelphia's animal care and control needs. This included commissioning the design and installation of the first humane euthanasia chamber for use with dogs and cats.

Bergh and the ASPCA also played a significant role in the development of the child protection movement. In 1873, Bergh was approached by a social worker, Etta Wheeler, regarding a young girl named Mary Ellen being abused by her foster parents. Bergh sent one of his agents under the guise of a census worker to verify the girl's condition. Once it was confirmed, he called on

his attorney, Elbridge Gerry, for advice and strategy. Although there were laws protecting children, there were no established protocols for removing a child from an abusive home. Gerry's ingenious interpretation of the writ of habeas corpus resulted in Mary Ellen's removal from the home. The foster mother was arrested and convicted of mistreating the child, and Mary Ellen was placed with a new family in a caring and nurturing home, where she thrived.

Out of this incident grew a myth that Bergh had claimed that if there were no laws to protect children, then he would call on the court to provide Mary Ellen with the same protection afforded a dumb animal. This account was not true and arose from lurid press accounts of the trial. Bergh and Gerry formed the Society for the Prevention of Cruelty to Children in 1874.

Bergh, Angell, White, and the other early leaders of America's animal protection movement anticipated many of the important issues that continue to confront animals and advocates for animals. The societies they helped form and the many hundreds of others inspired by their example are an enduring testimony to their work and vision.

Related articles: Animal advocacy; Animals in circuses; Animals used in research; Children's relations with animals; Cock fighting; Dog fighting; Euthanasia; Humane education; Live animal exports; Pigeon shoots; Roadside zoos and menageries; Shelters and sanctuaries; Slaughter

Lane, M., and Zawistowski, S., *Heritage of Care: The American Society for the Prevention of Cruelty to Animals*, Praeger, 2008.
Shelman, E. A., and Lazoritz, S., *The Mary Ellen Wilson Child Abuse Case and the Beginning of Children's Rights in Nineteenth-Century America*, McFarland, 2005.
Zawistowski, S., *Companion Animals in Society*, Thomson Delmar Learning, 2008.
Zawistowski, S., and Morris, J., "The Evolving Animal Shelter," in Miller, L., and Zawistowski, S. (eds.), *Shelter Medicine for Veterinarians and Staff*, Iowa State University Press/Blackwell, 2004.

STEPHEN L. ZAWISTOWSKI

VEGETARIANISM IN BRITAIN AND AMERICA

Recent research by the International Vegetarian Union historian, John Davis, suggests that the word *vegetarian* was first used in printed form in 1842. However, it was clearly in use prior to that time, at least among a small group of people who were followers of the "sacred socialist" James Pierrepont Greaves and who formed a vegetarian community known as the Concordium at Alcott House, Ham Common in Surrey. The term *vegetarian* at this point, in keeping with the diet of the Concordists, referred to a purely plant-based or vegan lifestyle—eschewing not only animal foods but also woolen clothing—and with much of the diet consisting of raw food. The secular British Vegetarian Society was cofounded by the Concordists and the Bible Christians of Salford, near Manchester, in 1847.

The Bible Christian Church had seceded from the Swedenborgian New Jerusalem Church in 1809 when its founder, the Reverend William Cowherd, influenced by Swedish mystic Emanuel Swedenborg's reputed (if disputed) vegetarianism, preached vegetarianism from his Salford pulpit. In 1817, a year after Cowherd's death, forty members of the Salford Church—a not only vegetarian but also teetotal and pacifist congregation—set sail for America along with two of their ministers, attracted by the possibility of spreading Bible Christianity in a land without an "established" church. One of these ministers, the Reverend William Metcalfe, was successful in establishing a church in Philadelphia. Inspired by their sister churches in North West England, the Philadelphian Bible Christians established a similar organization to the British Vegetarian Society in America in 1850—the American Vegetarian Society.

There had been an earlier, unsuccessful attempt by the Ham Common Concordists to create a vegetarian organization in England in 1843: the British and Foreign Society for the Promotion of Humanity and Abstinence from Animal Food. The American Vegetarian Society had a more successful forerunner in the American Physiological Society, founded in 1837 by Colonel John Benson, which promoted the vegetarian diet based on the lectures and writings of Sylvester Graham and Dr. William Alcott. Although relatively unknown today, Sylvester Graham is considered to be the "father of vegetarianism" in the United States, and American vegetarians in the 1830s and 1840s were usually called "Grahamites" and their diet "Grahamism."

By 1850 the fledgling Vegetarian Society in the United Kingdom had 478 members, with more than half the membership reported as being from the "lower classes," although James Gregory feels that this early plebeian support should not be overstated and that it was always a middle class–led movement with most appeal among the middle and upper working classes. The movement in the United Kingdom also became more London-centric: by the 1870s a number of food reform groups had been established in London, and the London Food Reform Society became the National Food Reform Society in a move that angered the Vegetarian Society's officers.

Tensions between the two organizations were fed by personal conflicts, which led to the establishment of the London Vegetarian Society in 1888. Julia Twigg has noted the cyclic rise and fall of vegetarianism in the United Kingdom in the modern period, which she assessed through consideration of the membership figures of the vegetarian societies as well as the growth or decline in the number of vegetarian restaurants: up in the late 1840s and early 1850s; down in the 1860s and 1870s; up in the 1880s and 1890s; down around World War I and in the early 1920s; up to some degree in the 1930s; down in the 1940s, 1950s, and early 1960s; up in the 1970s, 1980s, and early 1990s. Twigg notes that vegetarianism has a tendency to ride upon the success of other reforms or currents in society.

A distrust of established medicine in the Jacksonian era in the United States led to Grahamism being well received, and the establishment of the American Vegetarian Society in 1850 gave the American movement a structure and official journal. The Civil War led to a decline in interest in vegetarianism, and the death of Metcalfe in 1862 led to the demise of the American Vegetarian Society. Henry Stephen Clubb, a former pupil of Greave's school at Alcott House who had immigrated to the United States in 1853 and become a Bible Christian minister in the 1870s, established the Vegetarian Society of America in 1886, ending a period that Karen and Michael Iacobbo have described as "stagnant and unorganized" for the American vegetarian movement.

The United States experienced something of a golden age of vegetarianism at the start of the twentieth century as it benefited, like the U.K. movement, from the growth of other reforms, such as temperance, antivivisection, and women's suffrage, that were sympathetic to the vegetarian diet. The world-renowned Battle Creek Sanitarium, which was founded by Dr. J. H. Kellogg and which promoted the vegetarian diet among a range of therapeutic treatments, and his brother W. K. Kellogg's venture, the Battle Creek Sanitarium Health Food Company, led to a greater acceptance of the benefits of the vegetarian diet and the invention of many health foods based on Grahamite principles. In the same period in the United Kingdom, the Christian vegetarian organization the Order of the Golden Age had become the most active vegetarian society and was producing much of the vegetarian literature of the time; it also had the capacity to organize a fundraising concert at London's Royal Albert Hall attended by six thousand people and to run a poster campaign on the London Underground.

The counterculture of the 1960s provided another opportunity on both sides of the Atlantic for the growth of interest in the vegetarian movement, with many members of the counterculture espousing vegetarianism among a whole package of New Age beliefs, values, and causes. However, despite the interest in vegetarianism among members of the counterculture, vegetarianism still did not enter the mainstream. The modern vegetarian movement in the United Kingdom began with links to radical groups, and this connection with the margins of society has been a recurrent theme throughout the history of the vegetarian movement. The exception has been in recent years, when vegetarianism has been considered more popular, mainstream, and acceptable to a greater extent than ever before (the Vegetarian Society cited in its "General Statistics from the 1990s" a 1996 NOP survey for Hill and Knowlton/Tesco of 977 adults aged fifteen and over).

In 1969 the London Vegetarian Society and the Vegetarian Society based in North West England merged to form, once again, a united vegetarian society, with headquarters in Altrincham in Cheshire and a London office that was later closed in the 1980s. The North American Vegetarian Society was founded in 1974 by Jay Dinshah and representatives from four other vegetarian groups from North America, to act as host for the World Vegetarian Congress held at the University of Maine in 1975 and attended by fifteen hundred people. The Vegetarian Resource Group was formed by Debra Wasserman and Charles Stahler in 1982 as the Baltimore Vegetarians and produces a newsstand magazine, the *Vegetarian Journal*. In the late twentieth century several new animal rights groups were founded in both the United Kingdom and the United States that now promote campaigns for vegetarianism. Many of these groups, such as People for the

Ethical Treatment of Animals (PETA), Animal Aid, and Vegetarians International Voice for Animals (VIVA!), are ostensibly vegan—promoting a vegan diet through their literature and Web sites—even though the term "vegetarian" is used to describe the diet. As a result we may yet see a return to the early nineteenth-century understanding of the term "vegetarian" to mean a plant-based diet.

Related articles: Animal advocacy; Animals in the Bible; Ethical vegetarianism; Meatout; Plant-based nutrition; Vegan living; Veganic gardening; Vegetarian cooking

Calvert, Samantha Jane, "Ours Is the Food That Eden Knew: Main Themes in the Theology and Practice of Christian Vegetarians," in Muers, Rachel, and Grumett, David (eds.), *Eating and Believing, Interdisciplinary Perspectives on Vegetarianism and Theology*, T. and T. Clark, 2008.

———, "A Taste of Eden: Modern Christianity and Vegetarianism," *Journal of Ecclesiastical History* 58.3 (2007).

Gregory, James, *Of Victorians and Vegetarians: The Vegetarian Movement in Nineteenth-Century Britain,* Tauris Academic Studies, 2007.

Iacobbo, Karen, and Iacobbo, Michael, *Vegetarian America: A History*, Praeger, 2004.

Pushkar-Pasewicz, Margaret (ed.), *The Encyclopedia of Cultural Vegetarianism*, Greenwood, 2010.

Twigg, Julia, "The Vegetarian Movement in England 1847–1981: A Study in the Structure of Its Ideology," unpublished PhD thesis, London School of Economics, 1981, available at http://www.ivu.org/history/thesis/index.html.

Vegetarian Society, "General Statistics from the 1990s" (information sheet), accessed at http://www.vegsoc.org/info/statveg90.html on August 20, 2010.

SAMANTHA JANE CALVERT

PERSPECTIVES FROM AROUND THE GLOBE

ANIMAL ISSUES IN AUSTRALIA

Animal protection issues in Australia fall into three distinct categories. The first relates to the general issue of animal welfare, the second concerns measures taken to protect animals who are farmed and worked in a country where agriculture remains a very significant sector of the economy, and the third concerns the protection and preservation of free-living land animals (*see* Preservation and Killing) and fishes in a fragile environment where biodiversity is under threat and history shows that native fauna are vulnerable to extinction.

General issues of animal welfare and protection are perhaps best seen as primarily the province of the Royal Society for the Prevention of Cruelty to Animals (RSPCA) Australia. The first society was founded in Victoria in 1871 as the Society for the Prevention of Cruelty to Animals (SPCA), and the other states soon acquired their own branches: Tasmania in 1872, New South Wales in 1873, South Australia in 1875, Queensland in 1883, and Western Australia in 1892. The Australian Capital Territory branch was founded in 1955, and the Northern Territory acquired its branch in 1965. In 1923 the SPCAs were granted the Royal Warrant that transformed them into RSPCAs. In

1981 the state branches came together to form a federal RSPCA covering the whole of Australia and designated RSPCA Australia. The first animal protection legislation was introduced in Victoria in 1883 and was designed to ensure that scientists working with animals were licensed (*see* Animals in Research).

In addition to having a general mandate to fight cruelty to animals and to promote animal welfare, RSPCA Australia has also pursued specific campaigns, notably concerning approved farming schemes and the humane food initiative, which enables consumers to choose animal-based food from sources that have reared and slaughtered animals following standards set and monitored by the RSPCA. As in the United Kingdom, RSPCA Australia is a charity driven by community support and public donation.

With regard to animals who are farmed and worked, Australian law has, in the first instance, been conditioned by the underlying assumption of British law that animals are property. Legal measures to prevent unnecessary suffering relate to the treatment of animals on farms and their slaughter, to live export and transport, and to animals used in medical and scientific experiments, where legal measures are supplemented by a Code of Practice drawn up by the National Health and Medical Research Council and revised in 2004. The Australian position is complicated by the existence of statutes at both federal and state levels, so there is variation between provisions at the state level that may not be fully regulated by overarching legislation by the Commonwealth. Legal commentary shows that although there are many laws covering the full extent of animal welfare across the nation, there is relatively little case law and very little that relates to cruelty or omissions in welfare carried out within the agricultural industry.

Australian governments have been reluctant (relative to practice in other developed countries) to legislate on the protection of animals who are farmed, relying instead on a range of industry-sponsored codes of practice requiring only voluntary compliance and of varying degrees of comprehensiveness. A process is currently in progress, via the Australian Animal Welfare Strategy, to develop a series of standards and guidelines for the welfare of animals used in agriculture, and the agreed standards will, it is intended, have statutory force. Much of the material will derive from the existing codes of practice. At the time of writing, the final version is not available. The charity Voiceless acts as a campaigning group to enhance Australian animal law and has many influential supporters.

Since the earliest days of European settlement, the fauna of Australia has been seen as simultaneously a na-tional treasure requiring some protection and a pest or resource requiring control, exploitation, and even extermination. This paradox marks many of the attempts to manage free-living animals, including marine creatures, where, for example, moves to set up national marine parks have frequently clashed with local interests in the fishing industry. Australia has been a staunch supporter of international agreements to limit or ban commercial whaling of various species for many years and hosts an active and militant antiwhaling organization. Most Australian mammals are now protected by law to some degree, but this protection has come too late to prevent the endangerment of many species that, like the Tasmanian tiger, may yet face extinction.

Massive human predation of koalas for their fur and to clear land for farming and building, for example, coupled with ongoing loss of habitat, has meant that these iconic Australian animals are no longer a common sight across their once extensive range. Hunting of the platypus and echidna for scientific research in the later nineteenth century inflicted damage on these populations that has yet to be reversed in spite of strong protection. Although kangaroos are numerous—at least in their main species—they were hunted to the brink of endangerment in the 1970s, and killing for management purposes and meat production still causes controversy.

There are other threats to the fauna too. For example, there is an endemic face cancer at large in the Tasmanian Devil population, which is currently baffling attempts to protect the species and may be related to habitat degradation. Similarly, one of the two populations of the rare white lemuroid ringtail possum in northern Queensland appears to have become extinct as a result of global warming, possibly related to human-caused climate change. Climate change poses a threat to all Australian free-living animals, and so attempts to control it via various legislative initiatives should also be seen as initiatives in animal protection.

Finally, numerous misguided attempts to introduce nonnative animals have often been disastrous. For example, the introduction of the fox to enable hunting has caused a sharp reduction in the dingo population as the native dogs are outcompeted by the introduced creatures. Similarly, rabbits have adversely affected the Australian countryside to various degrees since the late nineteenth century. This has resulted in extermination campaigns involving methods that often are far from acceptable in the context of welfare and protection.

Historically, Australia has witnessed a significant number of mammalian extinctions, most particularly of the megafauna that predominated before and at the time of the initial human settlement of the country. It is widely believed, among indigenous and nonindigenous Australians, that indigenous people had a proud record of environmental responsibility and protected both the lands and animal life until European colonization overrode traditional ways of life, with disastrous effect on both people and animals. However, Professor Tim Flannery has argued that the megafauna's extinction was hastened, if not caused, by the activity of the first Australians both through their techniques for land management and through their activities as hunters. The evidence appears to favor this view, but the argument has caused great anger and offense among both indigenous and nonindigenous Australians.

Related articles: Animal advocacy; Animal agriculture and climate change; Animal welfare and farming; Animals used in research; The big cats; Caring shopping; CITES and international trade; Commercial whaling; Conservation philosophy; Developments in animal law; The ethics of reintroduction; The fur trade; Hunting with dogs; Koalas and their protection; Live animal exports; Marine mammals in captivity; Rabbits; Sea fishes and commercial fishing; Slaughter; The slaughter of kangaroos

Caulfield, M., *Handbook of Australian Animal Cruelty Law*, Animals Australia, 2008.
Flannery, T., *Country*, Text Publishing Company, 2004.
Johnson, C., *Australia's Mammal Extinctions: A 50000 Year History*, Cambridge University Press, 2006.
Parsonson, I., *The Australian Ark*, CSIRO, 1998.
Rolls, E. C., *They All Ran Wild*, rev. annotated ed., Angus and Robertson, 2004.
Sankoff, P., and White, S. (eds.), *Animal Law in Australasia*, Federation Press, 2009.

JOHN SIMONS

ANIMAL PROTECTION IN AFRICA

Summarizing the state of animal protection in Africa, given that this is a continent of incredible diversity, including in its geographical features, its climate, its fauna and flora, and its peoples and their histories and social and religious practices, is a daunting task. Reliable information often cannot be found, and that which does exist may be incomplete or difficult to obtain. In addition to other sources used, animal welfare organizations that are members of the World Society for the Protection of Animals were asked to help with this article by providing information about the problems they experience, legislation in their country, the problems of enforcement, and their hopes for the future.

Organizations concerned with animal protection in Africa

A range of organizations may be involved in some way in animal protection in any particular country and can include, for example, government veterinary services, conservation authorities, and local animal protection societies. Societies for the prevention of cruelty to animals (SPCAs) exist in many countries, including South Africa, Zimbabwe, Kenya, and Tanzania, and in other countries there are organizations that do similar work, examples being the Mozambique Animal Protection Society, the Foundation for Animal Welfare in Cameroon, Animal SOS in Madagascar, and the Liberia Animal Welfare Society. There are more than two hundred welfare societies working in South Africa.

Janet Cox identifies an urgent need to build the capacity of small local organizations and to help them to grow. She explains that "an analysis of African animal protection organizations listed in the World Animal Net Directory covering 54 African countries is an indication of the state of the movement. Of these 54 countries, 34—representing 63%—have just 0–2 animal protection organizations" (4). One problem, it is sometimes argued, is that many animal welfare organizations in Africa are driven by Europeans or expatriates, sidelining locals and presenting a non-African view. However, the situation is much more complicated than it appears because many Europeans have lived in Africa for generations and consider themselves Africans, and also many indigenous African people simply share the desire to help animals in whatever way they can. There is always the danger of this complex situation feeding into racial stereotyping and division and diverting energies away from the real needs.

One interesting approach is taken by Community Led Animal Welfare (CLAW), an animal welfare organization operating in very poor areas of South Africa. In addition to its animal outreach and care activities, it helps people with home-based care and with food parcels and supports child-headed households. Its holistic work finds solid support in the communities it serves, and it points out that animals suffer from poverty too. Alongside welfare organizations, there are animal activist groups such as Animal Rights Africa, Compassion in World Farming, and Beauty without Cruelty that are also often active in welfare-related activities as well as advocacy.

International organizations

International organizations involved in humanitarian relief and "development work" may have animal welfare on their agendas in theory, but it does not appear to be a priority. Nevertheless, these organizations have the potential to play a significant role in animal protection, and the United Nations Food and Agriculture Organization (FAO) has an animal welfare portal on its Web site that carries a range of information, including documents on animal welfare, legislation, training, and scientific reports. It mainly focuses on the welfare of farmed animals, and the site bears the logos of a range of welfare and farming organizations.

The World Organisation for Animal Health (OIE) has developed a range of standards related to the welfare of animals living in different contexts and is continuing to work on developing others, such as those concerning animals used in experimentation. In October 2008, the second OIE Global Conference on Animal Welfare was held in Cairo, and it recommended "the progressive implementation of OIE standards, adapted to the strategies, socio-economic situation, culture and capacities of members. Implementation will be built on regional strategies, and the need to promote scientific research, capacity building, education and communication in the animal welfare area was recognised" (Cox 8).

All OIE members were called on to create or develop animal protection legislation, develop national programs on animal welfare, and promote the adoption of a UN declaration on animal welfare. However, there seems to be no questioning of the implicit assumption that animals exist to be used by humans, and in most cases the need for "animal welfare" is really just another way of using animals more effectively and safely for human wants and desires.

Animal protection laws

Most countries in Africa have laws that pertain to animals and their welfare or protection. In some countries there is no specific legislation dealing with animal welfare, but a mixture of legislation such as "wildlife" and veterinary regulations that have an impact on animal welfare. In a few countries, such as Cameroon, Ethiopia, and Zambia, there appears to be conservation legislation only, although it may be that although welfare legislation exists, people are not aware of it, or it is not applied. This apparent deficiency should, however, not be seen as a lack of commitment concerning animal welfare by the people of these countries.

Legislation is often old and outmoded. For example the main pieces of legislation regarding animal welfare in South Africa are the Animal Protection Act of 1962 and the Performing Animals Act of 1935. One seemingly common problem is that legislation that does exist is frequently not fully enforced, and even when it is, the penalties for its contravention are very small. People also may be unaware even of the existence of such legislation. Overall, animal protection legislation tends to be piecemeal, outdated, inadequate, and poorly enforced, if enforced at all.

There are, however, signs of change. In Tanzania, a new Animal Welfare Act was promulgated in 2008, with animal welfare organizations playing a significant role in its development. The present African National Congress government in South Africa is reexamining laws pertaining to animals, although this is proving to be a long process. Whether the review will result in animals faring better or worse is not certain because there are complex commercial, social, cultural, and religious pressures to consider. The constitution of South Africa, which is one of the most progressive in the world, makes reference to the environment and its protection, but exactly what the legal ramifications for animals are is unclear.

Aquatic life

Africa has a coastline around 26,000 kilometers long, which is home to a wide variety of sea life, and also has a significant number of large internal bodies of water, such as Lake Malawi and Lake Tanganyika. Overfishing and the introduction of exotic species in rivers and lakes are problems, and some species such as crocodile and abalone are farmed. Welfare legislation concerning aquatic life is scant and mainly seems to fall under the free-living "wildlife" banner, if there is any such legislation at all.

Farming, transport, and slaughter

Traditional subsistence farming is practiced alongside large-scale commercial farming in Africa. The FAO puts the number of animals slaughtered for meat at just over 246 million per year, although this figure is acknowledged by the organization as possibly comprising a number of estimates, and so the true figure remains uncertain. Animals are used as a source of traction, food, transport, wealth, and prestige and are slaughtered on such occasions as weddings, funerals, coming-of-age rites, graduations, Christmas, and Eid el Fitr. The slaughter provides food for people but also, in some cultures, is a religious rite that supposedly puts the family in communication with their ancestors. The cry of the animal as he or she is being slaughtered is taken as an indication that this contact has taken place. Animals kept in a traditional way are often relatively free to roam, but with the introduction of intensive farming, this is changing rapidly. It is estimated that 75 percent of all cattle in South Africa end up in feedlots before being slaughtered. In some countries large tracts of farmland are owned by commercial concerns as well as by individual farmers, and in Botswana, a largely dry country, large-scale cattle ranching continues to cause serious concern because of its impact on the environment, including land degradation and water usage. Fences that prevent natural migrations obviously have an adverse effect on free-living animals.

The commercial transport and slaughter of animals is not well monitored or controlled, even if there is relevant legislation in place. Animals may be transported over long distances in extremes of heat and cold and without food or water, and they end their journey badly bruised and with broken limbs or having already died of their injuries. Injured animals may be slaughtered at the point of delivery after violent treatment by their slaughterers. There has been much concern in recent years over the live export of animals by boat, during which they endure appalling cramped and stifling conditions on sea journeys lasting days. Live exports are likely to be carried out to facilitate the cultural or religious practices of the buyers.

In South Africa, the Meat Safety Act requires that animals be slaughtered in an abattoir but makes an exception when the meat is for personal consumption and also when there is slaughter for cultural or religious purposes. In commercial slaughterhouses, if there are any regulations concerning the welfare of animals, they are often not followed; for example, animals might not be stunned before being hoisted up on to the conveyer chain. In some countries many slaughterhouses do not have working stun guns, and other methods, such as hammers, are used on the animals. The practices followed in the numerous small, local slaughterhouses are largely unknown.

Many animals are slaughtered "at home," which might be a village setting but can often be an urban area where the animal is kept in a backyard or garden for a period of time before the slaughter takes place. This may contravene local bylaws, but the right to carry out cultural practices is likely to win the day, and no action is taken. Cattle, goats, sheep, and chickens are moved informally using all sorts of transport. Chickens may be in boxes or may be carried, right side up or upside down, with their feet tied together. They also may be tied to the handlebars of bicycles. Goats and sheep are lashed onto the roofs of vehicles or thrown into the trunks of cars, and cattle are often transported tied down in the back of pickup trucks.

Vegetarian and vegan diets seem to be becoming better known, even popular, although in many places there is a very strong meat-eating culture. In southern Africa much

social life revolves around the braai (barbecue), with the cooking of the meat being a male-dominated activity.

Animal testing

Statistics on the use of animals in laboratories are almost nonexistent. This means the species of animals used and the nature of the experiments carried out are simply unknown. The lack of control, documentation, and regulation may make some countries an attractive destination for companies whose practices fall short of regulations in other countries. Free-living animals are also exported for use in laboratories abroad, but again, little data is available, and at least some of the trade is likely to be "unofficial." According to the British Union for the Abolition of Vivisection, "During 2008–2009 Mauritius supplied over 2,700 monkeys to the UK and over 7,000 monkeys to the USA." Some of these caught monkeys are exported directly, whereas others remain behind to be used for breeding purposes.

Any oversight, if it exists, is likely to be weak, but two developments in South Africa are encouraging. Until very recently there was little protection for animals used in laboratories, but there has recently been an overhaul of regulations relating to experimentation, and the new South African National Standard document, based on Australian and European Union legislation, sets out more stringent conditions.

As part of these conditions, institutions are required to set up ethical committees with a defined composition to examine applications to carry out such work and make decisions about whether it should be allowed. In addition institutions must also permit the SPCA to evaluate compliance. At Rhodes University, the Ethics Committee has embarked on a process of examining the moral questions surrounding the use of animals in research and teaching and whether it is morally right to use them—and if it is, under what circumstances. The committee has produced a document outlining possible arguments and their implications and is opening the debate to a range of interested parties within the university, including researchers and advocates.

Hunting, poaching, and the bushmeat trade

Traditional or informal hunting is done using guns, packs of dogs, and wire snares. Some farmers poison raptors and shoot or trap predators such as leopards. Gin traps, or leghold traps, are common in some places, and in South Africa one company is estimated to be making up to twelve hundred of them a month. The traps are legal in the country, and although they are not supposed to be used against protected species, traps of course do not differentiate. The animals caught in the traps are often discovered dying after being in the trap for days and may have attempted to gnaw off their feet in an attempt to escape. Traditional dress may also include the wearing of animal skins, such as leopard and lion skins.

Commercial hunting or trophy hunting is big business in the region and is surrounded by controversy. Many trophy hunters are from outside Africa and pay large sums of money for the experience of killing (shooting with guns and bow hunting are common methods) a range of animals, including but not restricted to warthogs, lions, rhinos, leopards, oribi, ostriches, cheetahs, baboons, caracals, buffaloes, duikers, elands, giraffes, and elephants. Each species of animal has a specific price allocated for an animal's body. There have been a number of allegations about animals from national parks being lured onto adjoining hunting areas and killed.

Hunting companies offer packages to visitors, and an industry exists around accommodations, guides, transport, permits, clothing, weapons, and taxidermy. The industry maintains that hunting brings in much-needed foreign currency and supports employment. An opposing view maintains that the money mostly flows to the well-off and that live animal tourism brings in vastly more money and provides more employment as well as being more ethical. Canned hunting has received significant exposure recently, where animals, possibly relatively tame and possibly drugged, are hunted in a confined area. The client gets his kill without too much effort and with some certainty. It is a continuing concern that animals sold at "wildlife" or "conservation" sales are being bought by canned hunting operators and are used shortly after purchase for a hunt. Canned hunting has supposedly been banned by the government in South Africa but apparently continues to thrive, bringing in large amounts of money to the operators. The breeding of captive animals, such as lions, may also be linked to this practice. South African hunters have been implicated in illegal hunting in Zimbabwe, where controls are almost nonexistent as a result of the general breakdown of regulation in the country.

Poaching is widespread and ranges from the killing of various animals for meat to the killing of elephants for ivory and rhinoceroses for their horns. Reports suggest that crime syndicates are involved in rhino poaching along with corrupt government officials and politicians and with the alleged participation of some veterinarians. Prevention is costly and often dangerous. Poaching activities range from using local people on foot to high-tech operations with helicopters.

The bushmeat trade is widespread throughout Africa, affecting many different species, including elephants, gorillas, and chimpanzees. New roads into previously isolated areas make the animals easily accessible to poachers on the one hand and the customers easily accessible to the poachers on the other. For some species, such as the mountain gorillas and bonobos, the situation is becoming critical, and they are now on the verge of extinction.

Conservation

Africa has outstanding national parks, including the Okavango Delta, Kruger, Hwange, Lake Malawi, and the Ngorongoro Crater, but there are questions about the management of parks—should they be fenced or unfenced; who should live there, if anyone; and how the benefits from parks should be used. There is ongoing debate about the killing ("culling") of elephants in national parks and the subsequent sale of tusks. For some the animals and plants in parks are resources that generate funds for the upkeep of the park and for profit as well as provide employment. There is a much-touted ideology in conservation that "if it pays, it stays." Others, while recognizing the need to generate funds, see animals and plants as valuable in their own right and argue that humans have a duty to preserve them. Many parks in southern Africa are fully fenced, often creating severe population pressures on some species.

However, transnational frontier parks are a major advance, providing much larger protected blocks of land, which means that animals can more closely follow their normal patterns of migration or some form of migration, easing pressure on resources and allowing a greater chance of genetic mixing. Human encroachment into conservation areas and conflict with animals is an ongoing problem. With growing populations, scarcity of resources, and climate change, this is likely to get worse in the future and has already taken on a political dimension.

Reasons for optimism

Despite the severe hardships faced by many Africans, people find time and resources to be compassionate to animals. Even when cruelty does happen, it is often the result of lack of understanding rather than deliberate cruel intent. Many of the farmed animals remain in a relatively free state, spending much of their lives outside. In South Africa there is an increased interest in purchasing "free-range" products, and governments and other agencies are putting animal welfare on their agendas. Tourism is an important source of revenue that may assist local populations and help to preserve natural areas. Significantly, a growing number of scholars in universities are interested in ethical questions related to animals. The Hunterstoun Centre of Fort Hare University and the University of South Africa hosted major conferences in 2010 and 2011.

Related articles: Animal advocacy; Animal-friendly spirituality; Animal sacrifice; Animal welfare and farming; Animals in circuses; Animals used in research; The big cats; Birds used in food production; Canned hunts; Caring for animals and humans; CITES and international trade; De-snaring in Kenya; Developments in animal law; The ethics of killing free-living animals; Free-living chimpanzees; Live animal exports; Moral anthropocentrism; The moral claims of animals; Perceptions of elephants; Primates worldwide; Religious slaughter; Sea fishes and commercial fishing; Slaughter; Snares and snaring; The trade in primates for research; The welfare of cows; The welfare of sheep

African Conservancy, Wildlife and Conservation Statistics, 2010, available at http://www.africanconservancy.org/about/documents/Facts.pdf.

Animal Protection Act 1962 (South Africa), available at http://www.rattyrascals.co.za/animalprotectionact.html.

Animal Rights Africa, "Key Programmes," available at http://www.animalrightsafrica.org/KeyProgrammes.php.

British Union for the Abolition of Vivisection, "Trading in Cruelty," available at http://www.buav.org/our-campaigns/primate-campaign/buav-primate-trade-investigations/trading-in-cruelty.

Cox, J., "Animal Welfare and Development in Africa—A Wake-Up Call," presentation at World Society for the Protection of Animals, London, 2010.

Meat Safety Act (South Africa), 2000, available at http://www.nda.agric.za/doaDev/sideMenu/APIS/doc/MEATSAFETY.pdf.

National Council of Societies for the Prevention of Cruelty to Animals, South Africa, "Animal Ethics Committees and Protocol Review," 2010, available at http://www.nspca.co.za.

Performing Animals Protection Act 1935 (South Africa), available at http://www.nda.agric.za.

Pickover, Michele, *Animal Rights in South Africa*, Double Storey, 2005.

South African Veterinary Association, "Review of Animal Care Legislation in South Africa," available at http://www.savf.org.za/Documents/Animal%20Care%20Legislation%20Review.pdf.

Standards South Africa, South African National Standard, *The Care and Use of Animals for Scientific Purposes*, SABS Standards Division, 2008.

United Nations Food and Agriculture Organization, "Animal Welfare Web Portal Launched," 2009, available at http://www.fao.org/news/story/en/item/19885/icode/.

World Society for the Protection of Animals, "Education," available at http://www.wspa-international.org/wspaswork/education/Default.aspx.

LES MITCHELL

ANIMALS IN ASIA

One of the biggest challenges facing animal protection organizations operating in Asia is the lack of adequate legislation and, where adequate laws do exist, the lack of enforcement. Corruption also complicates the issue. Even cosmopolitan Hong Kong lags behind most Western countries in its animal protection legislation; it has no laws protecting animals from neglect.

Another major challenge is the lack of awareness among the general population of animals' capacity to feel emotional, or even physical, pain. In fact, China—Asia's most populous country—had no term for "animal welfare" until the late 1990s. Culture plays a big part in the current fate of many endangered species, with rare animals prized for their medicinal qualities, as zoo exhibits (often forced to perform demeaning "tricks"), and as specialty dishes among the very rich.

Sadly, Asia's streets are still home to far too many stray and abandoned dogs and cats who are breeding unchecked, multiplying the problem. These strays suffer terribly, and most who are picked up are killed, many under deplorably cruel conditions, because there is little hope of finding them homes. Meanwhile, the authorities continue to allow unregulated breeding and the import of companion animals for sale in "pet shops," while animal shelters struggle to survive with little or no government support.

Although with rising affluence, companion animals are being welcomed into Asian homes like never before, cats and dogs are also eaten in many Asian countries. Millions of these animals are bred or rounded up, crammed onto trucks, and transported for days in hellish conditions to animal markets, where they are beaten to death, strangled, stabbed and bled out, or boiled alive. The trade in animal fur, including dog and cat fur, is also causing untold suffering to many millions of animals throughout Asia.

Fortunately, this situation is changing rapidly, with animal welfare groups springing up around the region, buoyed by greater freedom of expression and the support of bigger international groups. Organizations such as Animals Asia Foundation are providing funds and practical advice, giving local groups the skills to run their own programs to benefit animals and people alike—these include animal therapy, community projects for street animals such as trap-neuter-release (TNR), engagement of central and provincial authorities in conferences, and education for the young.

International and local welfare groups are helping Asian countries change from within—in Laos, former poachers are hired as forest wardens to protect the animals they once trapped; in Guangdong, known as China's dog- and cat-eating capital, streets are cleaner, and stray cats are healthier because of community-based TNR projects; in the Philippines, local groups working with the authorities are introducing dog registration, neutering, and rabies vaccination programs for street dogs and protecting the human population as well; and throughout Asia, therapy dogs—some rescued from the meat trade—are visiting hospitals, orphanages, and homes for the elderly, changing long-held prejudices against dogs.

Chinese bear bile farmers are offered financial compensation, allowing them to close down their farms. Animal welfare and conservation groups are working with the traditional Chinese medicine community to promote safe and more effective herbal alternatives to animal parts. Local and international animal welfare and conservation groups are lobbying for change at provincial, city, and national levels—and increasingly, they are working with the authorities to introduce community programs and regulations to protect animals and to change people's attitudes.

In the year 2000, a senior official with the China Wildlife Conservation Department in Beijing gave Animals Asia some excellent advice. He said, "Start the debate in China." Since then, animal welfare and conservation groups have started that debate—right throughout Asia. Now the debate is firmly in the public domain, with Asia's internet-savvy youth capturing the urgency of the issue and rallying support for change like never before.

Related articles: Animal pain; Caring for animals and humans; Cats; Confucianism and Daoism; Developments in animal law; Dogs; Dogs as food; The ethics of commercialization; The ethics of zoos; Euthanasia; Feral cats; The fur trade; Humane education; Legal protection of animals in China; Moon bears and bear bile farming; Neutering and spaying; Shelters and sanctuaries; Stray animals

Carson, Lynn, "The Animal/Human Bond: A Prescription for Good Health," *American Journal of Health Education* 37.6 (2006): 361–365.

Jin Pyn Lee, "Asia's Big 5," *Asian Geographic Magazine* (August 2008): 58–68.

Malone, Caroline, "Animal Attraction," *Review Asia* (August 2008): 56–64.

Neale, David, *Dog Breeding—Position Paper*, Animals Asia Foundation, February 2010.

Neale, David, and Yang, Lisa, *Performing Animals in Chinese Zoos*, Animals Asia Foundation, August 2010.

Smillie, Anneleise, *Basic Management Guidelines for Dog and Cat Shelters*, Animals Asia Foundation, 2008.

JILL ROBINSON

ANIMALS IN CHINESE CULTURE

Chinese attitudes toward animals are diverse and complex. With a civilization that has evolved over four millennia and a population that constitutes about one-fifth of the global population, any kind of generalizations or appraisals, positive or negative, risk simplification.

Animals played a crucial role in the formation of early Chinese civilization. The Chinese people were among the first people to domesticate animals such as pigs, horses, cattle, goats, chickens, and silkworms for husbandry, transport, hunting, consumption, clothing, and various other uses. Animals figured as mediums and objects of worship and served as sacrificial victims early in Chinese history. The animal world also provided a rich thesaurus for the expression of fundamental social, moral, religious, and cosmological ideas, according to Roel Sterckx. Besides animals' practical utility, the Chinese people's multifarious attitudes toward animals have also been significantly shaped by the religious traditions of Confucianism, Daoism, and Buddhism, which have interacted with each other and fostered the cultural values of the Chinese people over the past two millennia. These traditions are internally diverse and feature both positive and negative elements concerning humans' relations with other animals.

Confucianism is principally concerned with the moral relations between humans and assumes the superiority of humans over other animals. However, animals are not altogether excluded from its ethical vision. Its emphasis on *ren* (humaneness) and central claim made about human nature—that is, its inability to bear the suffering of others—have been especially expounded on by Mencius (372–289 B.C.E.) and neo-Confucian scholars, such as Wang Yangming (1472–1529 C.E.), to encompass the moral relation between humans and animals. The notion of the union of humanity and heaven (*tian ren he yi*), central to Confucian thought, in a way puts humans and nonhuman animals alike on the same footing in the natural and moral order that is governed by heaven. Humans, animals, and all living things share the same material force and live in harmony with one another in an ideal state. This cosmic vision is also shared by the Daoist tradition, which draws much of its inspiration from the natural order that embodies *dao* (the way). Daoism has been considered especially by contemporary scholars to possess much that could deepen modern ecological thought. Its philosophical system underscores the oneness of all beings and gives vent to the notions of the interconnectedness and interdependence of all living things. Its ideal of living according to the natural order without interference entails a respect for the true nature of animals in humans' dealings with them.

As with other traditions, Buddhism is constituted by various subtraditions and contains diverse sources regarding humans' relations with animals that are often in tension with each other. The concept of rebirth, though it affirms the kinship between humans and animals, reinforces a hierarchical notion of life; beings reborn into nonhuman animals are regarded as suffering from negative karma and belonging to a lower realm than humans in the scale of reincarnation. On the other hand, Buddhism lays emphasis on the equality of all lives and advocates universal compassion. Its first precept of abstinence from killing affirms not only the lives of humans but also the lives of all sentient beings. This tradition of compassion is especially prominent in Mahāyāna Buddhism, the predominant branch of Buddhism in China. Vegetarianism, though generally not practiced in most other countries, is a mandate for monks and nuns in China.

In terms of practical efforts to better the lives of animals, there exists a long tradition of animal release (*fangsheng*) via the liberation of captive animals into their natural habitat in China. Though generally considered to be of Buddhist origin, the practice has also been widely promoted in the Confucian and Daoist traditions. This ritualistic and charitable act has, from time to time throughout history, been encouraged by the state authorities, such as the devoted Buddhist Emperor Wu of Liang (464–549 C.E.), who first decreed against meat-eating in Chinese monasteries. Starting in the late Ming period in the sixteenth century, with encouragement from both the Buddhist and Confucian elites, animal release also became more widely practiced by the general populace and has remained so until this day in many Asian countries. Though originally aimed at the cultivation of compassion and the protection of life, the practice has been criticized for its commercial nature and the harm done to both animals and the environment. Calls for refining this traditional practice are increasing.

Public concern for animal protection grew in the 1920s, when China was desperately searching for a new culture in the face of threats from foreign powers. Publications on the subject increased in number, and an animal protection society was founded by a group of intelligentsia in Shanghai in 1933. In the 1990s, another wave of movement, with a steadily broadening agenda concerned with issues such as stray dogs, cruel sports (*see* Animals in Sport and Entertainment), animal experimentation, and slaughter reform, emerged in Taiwan, Hong Kong, and China. Taiwan passed its first animal protection law in 1998; similar legislative attempts have also been made in China over the past decade.

The rising concern for animals involved influences from both West and East. Western ideas on animal ethics were introduced into China as early as the 1920s, and in recent decades, international collaborations have provided the stimuli for practical change as much as international pressure. At the same time, a clear Buddhist influence can be seen behind the movement for animals since the 1920s in China and since the 1990s in Taiwan. Quests by dedicated reformers and engaged scholars into their own cultural traditions for valuable insights concerning human-animal relations have also been made. From 1929 to 1973, the famous Buddhist artist Feng Zikai (1898–1975) published 450 paintings that drew upon religious traditions as well as Chinese poetry, prose work, folktales, and lore that lauded the virtues of animals and expressed the ideals of union with nature and sympathy for animals. Recent work by scholar Ping Mang and others exemplifies a more comprehensive attempt in a similar direction.

China has long received mixed appraisals with regard to its attitudes toward animals. On the one hand, it is notorious for its atrocious treatment of animals, such as through bear bile farming and shark finning; on the other hand, the Asian traditions have been lauded for being animal-friendly. Whichever is nearer to truth, China still has a long way to go in striving toward an ethical human-animal relationship, and fortunately, it is blessed with a rich cultural heritage that possesses much potential for change.

Related articles: Animal sacrifice; Animal welfare and farming; Animals used in research; Birds used in food production; Buddhist attitudes; The Buddhist case for vegetarianism; Confucianism and Daoism; Ethical vegetarianism; Horses; Legal protection of animals in China; Moon bears and bear bile farming; Shark conservation; Slaughter; Stray animals; The welfare of cows; The welfare of pigs

Kang, Le, *Buddhism and Vegetarianism*, San Min, 2004 (in Chinese).

Lai, Shu-ching, "The Introduction of the Western Animal Protection Movement by Miss Alice Pichen Lee—A Discussion Focusing on *The Light of the West*," *Academia Historica Journal* 23 (2010): 79–118 (in Chinese).

Mang, Ping, et al., *The World of Nature and Self—Chinese People's Faith, Life and View of Animals*, China University of Political Science and Law Press, 2009.

Smith, Joanna F. Handlin, "Liberating Animals in Ming-Qing China: Buddhist Inspiration and Elite Imagination," *Journal of Asian Studies* 58.1 (1999): 51–84.

Sterckx, Roel, *The Animal and the Daemon in Early China,* State University of New York Press, 2002.

Taylor, Rodney, "Of Animals and Humans: The Confucian Perspective," in Waldau, Paul, and Patton, Kimberley (eds.),

A Communion of Subjects: Animals in Religion, Science, and Ethics, Columbia University Press, 2006, 293–308.

CHIEN-HUI LI

ANIMALS IN THE MIDDLE EAST

It is important to define the geographical area referred to as the Middle East. The boundaries appear to change depending on which organization is making the definition and perhaps the geographical distribution of an organization's resources. In this contribution, the Middle East will consist of the Gulf Cooperation Council (GCC) states—Bahrain, Kuwait, Oman, Qatar, the United Arab Emirates (UAE), and Saudi Arabia—as well as Iraq, Israel, Jordan, Lebanon, Palestine, Syria, and Yemen. In addition, Afghanistan and Iran should be included. This list illustrates the immense diversity of wealth, culture, and religion within the region, all of which impact on attitudes toward animals in the Middle East.

Many people are aware of the negative attitude toward dogs held by many Muslims but know little of the various Islamic hadiths or preachings that forbid any deliberate act of cruelty to or mistreatment of animals. In many countries of the Middle East, there is a daily interdependency between species, which is perhaps most apparent between humans and the working equines or camelids. The use of horses, donkeys, mules, and camels in many parts of the region for personal or commercial transportation or for working the lands is still widespread, and in many of the rural villages in Palestine, for example, it can be the only means to reach urban environments.

Generally, there is a distinction made between animals who are perceived as "useful" and those who seem to be a "nuisance" or a "pest." In most Middle Eastern countries, as in many parts of the world, there are many problems with stray dogs and feral cat colonies. In some cases, the populations of these unfortunate animals have become a problem for the human inhabitants. Cats are generally tolerated better than dogs since in some countries there are numerous cultural and historical stories about ancestral and even spiritual relationships with cats. Dogs are not perceived in the same way (at least by most Muslims), and through various interpretations of the Qur'an, they are very often seen as unclean, not to be touched or allowed in the home.

Dogs are seen as more of a threat to the human population than cats because of the greater likelihood of aggressive behavior, because of widespread fear of rabies, and because of their noise and fecal pollutions. Unfortunately, the all-too-common ways of dealing with dogs are by routine shooting with shotguns or high-powered rifles or, even worse, by strychnine poisoning. Where feral cat colonies have become very large, poisoning can often be their fate also.

In some countries, there is a steadily growing status-dog culture, and this is already well established in places such as Israel, the UAE, and Jordan, where pedigree or "purebred" dogs are bred and sought. They are purchased mostly for status or as protection animals but also in some cases as companions. This often leads to a clash of culture, or even conscience, since young people sometimes want to have the same association with their companion animals as many Western cultures do, but the older, more traditional generations prefer to keep the animals outside their property, even as latchkey animals who are allowed to roam while caregivers are away at work. This has led to a population of purebred dogs breeding with local packs of stray dogs.

There are still some countries where keeping companion animals is barely tolerated and even perceived as a Western cultural invasion. This is most notable in Iran, where the keeping of companion animals is discouraged and in some parts prohibited.

Although many working animals are considered important, even essential, there is generally a lack of understanding about the basic needs of the animals and the importance of good veterinary and dietary care. There are a number of international animal welfare organizations working with Middle Eastern governments on school and humane educational programs. There are now animal welfare organizations in most Middle Eastern countries (see, for example, the work of the Middle East Network for Animal Welfare).

Animals who are farmed are of course valued for dairy and meat products, and in some countries of the region, there are some reasonable or good slaughterhouse facilities. However, in others there are very basic methods of handling, restraint, and slaughter, and practically all animals consumed in the region are killed using the halal slaughter method. In most countries, there is insufficient grazing to support the number of animals required to sustain the needs of the population, and consequently large numbers of sheep and cattle are imported, sometimes over extremely long distances, to satisfy that demand. It is unfortunate that the vast majority of the animals slaughtered at the numerous religious festivals are imported and transported alive.

In summary, it is difficult to generalize about the attitudes toward animals by indigenous human populations because many of the countries, particularly the Gulf states, are multicultural and multinational, and in some cases—for example, the United Arab Emirates—expatriates make up the large majority of the population.

A growing number of animal welfare organizations, both indigenous and expat-led, are working with local populations and municipal and central governments to improve the welfare of animals in the region. This is being achieved through the implementation and enforcement of animal welfare legislation, the provision of rehoming and rescue facilities, the work of local veterinarians, and most importantly, humane educational programs, which highlight the needs and sentience of animals and the benefits of living in harmony with other species.

Related articles: Animal pain; Animals and public health; Cats; Developments in animal law; Dogs; The ethics of commercialization; Feral cats; Horses; Humane education; Islam and animals; Live animal exports; Religious slaughter; Shelters and sanctuaries; Slaughter; Stray animals; The welfare of cows; The welfare of sheep

Abbas, Fakhar, *Animals' Rights in Islam*, VDM Verlag, 2009.

Appleby, M. C., Cussen, V., Garces, L., Lambert, L. A., and Turner, J., *Long Distance Transportation and Welfare of Farm Animals*, CABI, 2008.

Appleby, M. C., and Sherwood, Lorna, *Animal Welfare Matters*, WSPA, 2008.

Masri, Al-Hafiz Basheer Ahmad, *Animal Welfare in Islam*, Islamic Foundation, 2007.

———, *Excerpts from the Islamic Teachings on Animal Welfare*, WSPA, 1992.

Middle East Network for Animal Welfare, available at http://www.menaw.net/client/index.html.

TREVOR P. WHEELER

CHALLENGES TO ANIMAL PROTECTION IN SCANDINAVIA

Scandinavia includes Sweden, Denmark, Finland, Norway, and Iceland. Sweden, Denmark, and Finland are members of the European Union (EU). Norway and Iceland are not EU members, but Iceland has applied for membership. Because of the European Economic Area Agreement, most of the animal welfare regulations in the EU are implemented in Norway and Iceland in accordance with EU standards. In addition, national animal welfare acts apply in all the Scandinavian countries (European Free Trade Association Surveillance Authority).

Scandinavian agriculture is still based largely on family farms. Between 1990 and 2000, there was an increase in the number of animals per farm, as well as a decrease in the number of farms. Milk production plays an important role, in addition to pig production in Denmark. Animal welfare problems are related to intensive breeding, housing, transportation, and slaughter and are generally similar to the problems in the rest of Europe. Particularly in Sweden, vegetarianism and veganism have been promoted actively. In particular areas, national legislation ensures stricter practices than does EU law—for example, Danish pigs have access to showers, and in Norway piglets receive local anesthesia and pain relief when they are castrated.

Consumer surveys indicate that Scandinavian citizens are attentive to animal welfare issues and have a higher sensibility toward animal welfare than many other European countries (see European Commission, *Special Eurobarometer*, in this article's bibliography).

Scandinavia is characterized by a strong hunting and trapping culture. Hunting is common and considered "natural," recreational, and traditional. Animal welfare problems include wounding losses but also the specific methods used and the pursuit of the animals. Opposition to hunting so far has been weak in comparison with the antifur movement and criticism of industrial farming. In northern parts of Sweden, Finland, and Norway, there is still reindeer farming, of semi-free-living animals. Animal welfare problems exist both in traditional handling and in the use of new mechanical equipment.

In Norway farmed fishes are the second-largest export product. Aquaculture is an industrial form of animal keeping, and animal welfare problems can be compared to those seen in intensive poultry production. High numbers of dead animals, contagious diseases, and deformities are among the problems reported, in addition to inhumane handling and slaughter methods. The industry works to reduce losses based on economic considerations, with an emphasis on vaccinations and lately also on feeding, light, water quality, and studies of natural behavior in fishes (Institute of Marine Research).

Norway is internationally disparaged for hunting whales and seals, particularly because of the methods of killing. Whereas Norwegian authorities maintain that the methods cause instant death, animal welfare criticism centers on the risk of wounding and prolonged pain. Whaling and sealing have become a matter of nationalist sentiment to Norwegian authorities and political parties. Denmark has jurisdiction over Greenland, where sealing and whaling are defended as traditions of the indigenous people.

Fur farming has been the practice most heavily criticized in Finland, Denmark, Sweden, and Norway. Fox farming has been phased out in Sweden and is due to be phased out in Denmark by 2023. There is considerable public debate about the issue in all the Scandinavian countries.

Animals are used in research in all Scandinavian countries. In Norway a majority of the animals used are fishes, and a considerable number of free-living animals are tagged, monitored, and even subjected to surgery in the field.

Companion animals are common in all Scandinavian countries. So far the keeping of reptiles and amphibians is banned in Norway based on animal welfare considerations. The ban is under debate, and the smuggling of exotic animals seems to be a growing problem. Stray cats are a problem in all of Scandinavia. The attitude toward dogs appears to be different, and stray dogs are rarely seen.

Animals are used in zoos and traveling circuses all over Scandinavia, but national legislation restricts the species allowed, and certain minimum standards have been introduced for the keeping of these animals. For example, with the exception of sea lions, the use of free-living animals is banned in Finland.

Related articles: Animal welfare and farming; Animals and public health; Animals in circuses; Animals used in research; Birds used in food production; Commercial whaling; Ethical vegetarianism; The ethics of killing free-living animals; The ethics of zoos; European animal protection; Feral cats; Fish farming; Fur farming; The fur trade; Hunting with dogs; Legislation in the European Union; Live animal exports; Pig castration; The pinnipeds; Slaughter; Stray animals; The trade in reptiles; Understanding amphibians; Vegan living; The welfare of cows; The welfare of pigs

Danish Ministry of Food, Agriculture and Fisheries, "Animal Welfare," available at http://www.uk.foedevarestyrelsen.dk/AnimalWelfare/forside.htm.

European Commission, *Special Eurobarometer, Attitudes of Consumers towards the Welfare of Farmed Animals*, 2005.

European Free Trade Association (EFTA) Surveillance Authority, "The EFTA Surveillance Authority at a Glance," available at http://www.eftasurv.int/about-the-authority/the-authority-at-a-glance-/.

Finnish Food Safety Authority, "Animals and Health," available at http://www.evira.fi/portal/en/animals_and_health/.

Heinonen, S., "Organic Farming in Finland," 2007, available at http://www.organic-europe.net.

Institute of Marine Research, available at http://www.imr.no.

Jägarnes Centralorganisation, "Hunting in Finland," available at http://www.riista.fi/riistaen.

Law forbidding fox farming (*Lov om forbud mod hold af ræve*), June 12, 2009, available at http://www.retsinformation.dk.

Norwegian Association of Hunters and Anglers, "Hunting in Norway," available at http://www.njff.no.

Norwegian Ministry of Agriculture and Food, "Norwegian Action Plan on Animal Welfare," 2003, available at http://www.regjeringen.no/en/dep/lmd/Documents/Reports-and-plans/Plans/2006/norwegian-action-plan-on-animal-welfare.html?id=456113.

Svenska Jägareförbundet, "Hunting in Sweden," available at http://www.jagareforbundet.se.

Swedish Board of Agriculture, "Animals," available at http://www.jordbruksverket.se/swedishboardofagriculture/animals.

ANTON KRAG AND LIVE KLEVELAND

JAPANESE ATTITUDES TOWARD ANIMALS

Current attitudes toward animals held by the Japanese people are as varied as those held by any other nation. However, they have evolved attitudes based on their unique cultural, religious, political, and economic history. Primary cultural concepts such as *ma*; the religions of Shintoism, Buddhism, and Christianity; and post–World War II politics and the economic realities necessitated by Japan's defeat and subsequent development as an economic world power have all played their part in developing today's attitudes toward animals.

Ma influences all aspects of Japanese culture, including religion, politics, and economics, through its defining of what is appropriate. *Ma* is how the young learn standards of behavior and what attitudes to form. It defines the world as three concentric circles—the inner circle is *uchi*, comprising one's own family, friends, and associates; the middle is *seken*, defined as the public or people; and the outer circle is *soto*, outsiders. As far as behavior and attitudes shown publicly are concerned, the important group is *seken*; there is a very strong imperative kindled in the young to not be shamed before *seken*, and this social obligation is called *giri*. In art, the concept of *ma* results in the "aesthetic of purity" that produces works that seem simple to Western perceptions, but that define their subjects by the space around them. This is particularly significant in the Japanese attitude toward companion animals, free-living species, and the natural world.

Thus, *ma* is a defining and binding force within Japanese culture that until recently has acted as a barrier to the outside world; globalization and Western influences now appear to be having the effect of bringing the rest of the world into the *seken*, where previously they were classified as *soto*. Japan has been taking a more active role in the world politically since the 1990s.

Companion animals are the most protected category of animals in Japan. The 1973 Law for the Protection and Management of Animals was amended in 1999; the name was changed to the Law for the Humane Treatment and

Management of Animals, and the definition of "companion animals" changed from "dogs and cats" to "home animals," which includes those kept at schools and in shelters. Increased keeping of and regard for companion animals, in conjunction with the cultural concept of *ma,* have led to a more public disapproval of their abuse and to a strengthening of the law combined with actual enforcement. Changing population dynamics in Japan are also increasing the interest in keeping companion animals. The population of Japan peaked in 2005.

Many in Japan's younger generation are opting for companion animals instead of children, at least initially. Those who do have children are concerned about youth suicide rates and bullying at schools, and this too has led to increased interest in companion animals as a means to teach children to be more nurturing and respectful, as well as to enable discussions in schools about death.

These situations in combination with acknowledged links between animal cruelty and serial killers have driven public concern and fueled political will to strengthen animal welfare law and enforcement for companion animals; unfortunately, the same cannot be said for other animals.

The welfare of animals on farms is not a significant concern to the Japanese people, except where it impacts on food quality, and this is reflected in the legislation and its monitoring and enforcement. With the nation's defeat at the end of World War II, Japan's economy collapsed, and large-scale starvation was held off only by aid from the United States. This resulted in the industrializing of farm production methods, with rapid proliferation of intensive farming methods obtained from the United States and Germany, including typically housing animals permanently within buildings.

Although technically animals on farms come under the auspices of the Law for the Humane Treatment and Management of Animals 1999, the law has resulted in little noticeable change in ongoing farming practices. After problems in the early 2000s dealing with bovine spongiform encephalopathy (BSE), or mad cow disease, outbreaks in cattle, a food safety committee was formed in the Cabinet Office. This was due to concerns for human health and the public's loss of faith in farm production. Efforts were stimulated primarily after beef consumption in Japan slumped to 40 percent of previous amounts. But although health standards improved, animal welfare enhancements were minimal.

Modern Japan is basically a secular society, with only 25 to 35 percent of the population in 1993 claiming to have a personal religion. However, lack of personal belief does not prevent participation in religious rituals, with about 75 percent of households having family altars and 80 per-

cent of the population participating in religious festivals and visiting shrines. A point to note about religion in Japan is that many people participate (and historically have participated) in the rituals of more than one religion, with the notable exception of Christians.

Aspects of the various religions are significant with regard to animal welfare, such as the biblical concept of human dominion over animals; the Shinto concept of *kami,* spirits that inhabit the natural world, including animal spirits; and the Buddhist proscription against killing terrestrial animals. In the highly technological area of Japan's mainstay industries, rapid advances in knowledge are considered critical, leading to strong support in the business community and the government for research and development. Animals used in research have little protection under Japan's animal welfare legislation and little impact on the perceptions of the Japanese public. It is a literal case of "out of sight, out of mind."

The significance and concern given to free-living animals by the Japanese varies astronomically. Again, the concept of *ma* plays a large role here. Such concerns tend to be limited to select species with either aesthetic appeal or cultural significance. This enables the government ministries and other organizations to formulate policies in relation to free-living species with little regard to animal welfare, not needing to worry about public response. Less than 2 percent of Japanese are members of a conservation or animal-related organization.

The aesthetic of purity defining a minimalist view of beauty allows them to admire cetaceans as magnificent animals while disregarding the suffering they may go through when being killed. Grenade harpoons used in whaling need to strike a restricted target area to immediately immobilize a minke whale and presumably render the animal unconscious while he or she dies. The Japanese tend to ignore, consider irrelevant, or judge unappealing factors that fall outside their valued aesthetic and symbolic boundaries. This focuses their love for nature on specific things in isolation rather than on nature as a whole.

Besides the government's well-publicized endeavors to enable the resumption of commercial whaling through the International Whaling Commission, along with South Africa it is leading the push to lift the ban and resume trade in ivory through the Convention on International Trade in Endangered Species of Wild Fauna and Flora (CITES). The overall attitude of the Japanese toward free-living animals can be seen in the attitude toward Japanese macaques, listed by the International Union for Conservation of Nature (IUCN) as endangered. Legally these monkeys cannot be hunted, but if local governments receive claims from farming communities for damage caused by the macaques, they may grant permission to remove the macaques, and 53,000 have been collected since 1993. The animals taken may then be killed, transferred to a preservation park, or sent to research facilities that currently pay US$1,400 for them. It is not unreasonable to presume that most therefore have gone to research facilities.

In conclusion, although animal welfare law and attitudes are advancing for companion animals because of the increased keeping of companion animals and concerns over child development, little has yet been done to improve the lot of free-roaming animals and those used on farms or for research. If animal welfare groups in Japan could enlist the support of well-known, popular, and respected figures in Japanese society to promote animal welfare issues, it might engender at least the appearance of concern over animal welfare in the public through the operation of *ma*; that would oblige the government to enact stronger laws and businesses that utilize animals to instate more welfare-conscious standards.

Related articles: Animal and human violence; Animal welfare and farming; Animals in the Bible; Animals and public health; Animals used in research; Buddhist attitudes; The Buddhist case for vegetarianism; Cats; Children's relations with animals; CITES and international trade; Commercial whaling; Confucianism and Daoism; Developments in animal law; Dogs; Humane education; Primates worldwide; Shelters and sanctuaries

Cyranoski, D., "Japanese Call for More Bite in Animal Rules," *Nature* 434.7029 (2005).

Isao, K., "The Culture of 'Ma,'" *Japan Echo* 34.1 (2007).

Kishida, S., and Macer, D., "People's Views on Farm Animal Welfare in Japan," 2003, available at http://www.eubios.info/ABC4/abc4335.htm.

McCarney, P., "Japan's Standpoint on Whaling," 2010, available at http://www.helium.com/items/1516632-japans-view-on-whaling.

———, "An Overview of Animal Welfare in Japan," 2007, available at http://www.helium.com/items/553714-an-overview-of-animal-welfare-around-the-world.

Morton, W., *Japan: Its History and Culture*, 3rd ed., McGraw-Hill, 1994.

Reader, I., Andreasen, E., and Stefansson, F. (eds.), *Japanese Religions Past and Present*, University of Hawaii Press, 1993.

PERRY McCARNEY

SOUTH AMERICAN PERSPECTIVES ON ANIMALS

At the risk of portraying South America as a homogeneous entity with a stereotypical culture, one can at least consider it as a region characterized by vast natural resources and serious socioeconomic problems. Despite recent globalization processes, the continent maintains its own particular traits and identity in various areas. Some of these have a significant effect on the condition of animals in this region and explain the South American view of animals' role and value.

The critical importance of South America in terms of animal life is clear: there is no other region on the Earth with such a variety of species. The continent boasts 40 percent of the world's biodiversity. The Amazon rainforest, which stretches across nine countries, has the greatest concentration of living species known to science on the planet. However, South America, just like other continents, faces the same worldwide dilemma—that of how to reconcile economic growth and environmental preservation. The problem has not manifested itself on a larger scale until now because the growth of the region has been relatively slow, and this has prevented a more rapid deterioration of the natural resources. In any case, the myth of the overabundance of nature potentially weakens the notion that nonhuman lives are intrinsically valuable.

The environmental vulnerability of the region also results from its socioeconomic vulnerability. The challenge in South America of producing high levels of human well-being without causing a huge impact on the environment is exacerbated by the fact that this region is made up predominantly of developing countries. Living conditions are of a much lower standard in comparison with the average in countries in the Northern Hemisphere. In rural South America, in particular, a large proportion of the population does not have access to basic sanitation, adequate nutrition, and so on. The strong demand for social justice and essential services tends to deflect moral attention away from the conditions in which animals live. In poor communities, especially, the discourse on protection of animals has less support. In areas where there is a lower quality of life and greater socioeconomic inequality, the argument for giving automatic priority to human well-being, in cases of conflict between human and animal interests, has a greater sway.

Furthermore, South America traditionally has left-wing governments. These governments are inclined to consider the exploration of natural resources for social purposes as politically legitimate. These factors help explain the difficulty in including the animal question on political agendas in South American countries.

As a result of the same social inequality, South American communities are more exposed to violence, in its different degrees and forms, than European or North American communities. This has quite a negative effect on moral sensibility toward animal suffering within these communities.

Roman Catholicism predominates in South America. The influence of the Catholic Church over the region means that religious-type justifications for speciesism (in which animals are discriminated against) are favored among the populations.

South America was colonized by the Hispanics and Portuguese. This largely explains the way of thinking and behaving—including moral attitudes—with respect to animals in the region. In contrast to English-speaking countries, South American psychology is significantly more emotive than rationalist, precisely because of its Iberian heritage. In the place of pragmatic, logical, and analytical tendencies, one finds a passionate and spiritualized perspective. Moral emotions, such as sympathy and pity, are significantly rooted in all spheres of daily life, in private ethics, politics, and activism. Instead of praising the winner, there is a cultural inclination toward compassion for or solidarity with the weakest in society.

As a consequence, in comparison with countries of an Anglo-Saxon origin, the notion of moral rights is much less internalized in the moral psychology of the inhabitants of South American countries. Therefore, the idea that animals are entitled to moral rights is more counterintuitive in South American societies than in countries in the Northern Hemisphere, which are less culturally resistant to it. In other words, the concept of animal rights is less familiar to the Latin mentality. This aspect contributes negatively to the work of animal rights lawyers and nongovernmental organizations. It also helps explain the lower incidence of direct action tactics for the liberation of animals or sabotage of laboratories. Another consequence is mitigation of the polarization of the debate on animal rights versus animal welfare. In philosophical terms, virtue ethics appeal to the moral sensibility of South American societies more than deontological ethics (*see* The Moral Claims of Animals).

Within the field of illicit world trade, the sale of free-living animals lies behind only arms and drug trafficking. In fact, biopiracy is one of the most sensitive areas of all the problems currently involving animals in South America. In Brazil alone, 38 million animals per year are illegally captured and smuggled by dealers (which represents about US$1.5 billion). Monkeys, parakeets, parrots, alligators, snakes, and turtles are some of the most captured species. Despite the unrivaled number of species of free-living animals in the Amazon rainforest (twice the number of bird species as the United States and Canada; fifteen times more fish species than in all the rivers in Europe), there are relatively few specimens within each species. In addition, overhunting and overfishing of species preferred in Amazonian cuisine have resulted in dozens of mammals, reptiles, and fishes being included on the list of species at risk of extinction.

Cattle farming is present on a large scale across the south and center of South America, especially in Brazil, Uruguay, and Argentina. In contrast to other continents, this does not pose significant animal welfare issues because the herds are predominantly kept in an extensive farming system. However, because Brazil has the largest commercial cattle herd in the world, this very system has a devastating consequence: the destruction of the Amazon rainforest.

Related articles: Animal and human violence; Animal-friendly spirituality; Animals in politics; Catholic teaching; CITES and international trade; Conservation philosophy; Moral anthropocentrism; The moral claims of animals; Primates worldwide; Sea fishes and commercial fishing; The trade in primates for research; The trade in reptiles; The universal charter of the rights of other species; The welfare of cows

Aboglio, Ana María, *Veganism* (*Veganismo*), De los Cuatro Vientos, 2009.
Brügger, Paula, *Animal Friend* (*Amigo Animal*), Letras Contemporâneas, 2004.
Levai, Laerte, *Animal Rights* (*Direito dos Animais*), Mantiqueira, 2004.
Lourenço, Daniel, *Animal Rights* (*Direito dos Animais*), Sergio Antonio Fabris Editor, 2008.
Martí, Manuel, *Free Animals* (*Animales Libres*), Grupo Editorial El Vegetariano, 2002.
Naconecy, Carlos M., *Ethics and Animals* (*Ética e Animais*), EdiPUCRS, 2006.

CARLOS M. NACONECY

THE TREATMENT OF ANIMALS IN INDIA

The Indian landmass is one of the globe's top twelve mega-biodiversity regions. India has some of the world's most significant biological diversity since it has only 2 percent of the total landmass of the world but is home to approximately 7 percent of the world's flora and 6.5 percent of the world's known free-living animals. According to the International Union for Conservation of Nature (IUCN) Red List (2008/2010), India harbors 2,530 vertebrate species. Protected areas in India include eighty national parks, among them twenty-eight tiger reserves governed by Project Tiger and 441 wildlife sanctuaries (IUCN category 4 of protected areas).

Project Tiger was launched in 1973 by India's prime minister at the time, Mrs. Indira Gandhi, and the main objective was to ensure a viable population of tigers. At first glance, India has a strong legal and policy framework to regulate and restrict the trade in free-living animals. Trade in more than eighteen hundred species of animals and plants—and in derivatives of them—is prohibited under the Wildlife (Protection) Act, 1972, with the aim of curbing the poaching and smuggling of free-ranging animals and their derivatives. The act actually comprises three parts: one bill, eleven notifications, and one guideline. The Indian government's Ministry of Environment and Forests has also created the National Tiger Conservation Authority, the National Wildlife Board, and the Tiger and Other Endangered Species Crime Control Bureau under various sections of the act.

Unfortunately, the legal policies for conserving the forests and free-living animals have not been very successful, despite the fact that safeguarding the forests has been included in the list of fundamental duties of the citizens of India (article 51(g) of the Indian constitution); India is perhaps the only country in the world that has provided for protection of animals under its constitution. Though the Wildlife Act was amended in 1986, 1991, 2000, 2003, and 2008, the indifferent attitude of some administrators and the lack of implementation are still a major concern.

India has been a member of the Convention on International Trade in Endangered Species of Wild Fauna and Flora (CITES) since 1976. Trade Record Analysis of Flora and Fauna (TRAFFIC) started in 1991 as a monitoring network and a venture of the World Wide Fund for Nature (WWF) India. Since 1987, the IUCN, established in 1976, has worked closely with the national and state governments to monitor and influence action to curb the illegal trade. The Wildlife Institute of India, established in 1982 as an autonomous institute of the Ministry of Environment and Forests, is internationally acclaimed and offers training programs, academic courses, and advice in research and management. The Wildlife Protection Society of India (WPSI), founded in 1994 by Belinda Wright, is one of the most prestigious conservation organizations in India. It has assisted in the arrest of over 375 individuals and in seizures of massive amounts of illegal animal products during the past decade. By the year 2010, the legal program of the WPSI had successfully funded the prosecution of over 151 court cases in 13 Indian states. According to the WPSI, 893 tigers and 3,354 leopards were poached during 1994–2009, and the mortality and poaching figures for 2010 were 41 (tigers) and 248 (leopards).

Trade continues to be a challenge for the anti-poaching teams of forest departments, owing to poor law enforcement and the seemingly uncontrollable interface between officials, smugglers, and aborigines. Hence, it has become necessary for the government to formulate more stringent policies. Common is the killing of animals for hair (mongooses); skin (snakes and monitor lizards); horns (rhinos, for aphrodisiacs); claws, bones, skins, and whiskers (tigers and leopards); tusks (elephants, for ivory); antlers (deer); skin and fur (shahtooshes); shells (turtles); musk pods (musk deer, for cosmetics); skin and gall bladder (bears); and other body parts (pangolins and civets, for traditional medicine). Caged birds such as parakeets, mynahs, ducks, storks, waders, partridges, quails, and munia and peacock feathers are always in great demand for the trade in companion animals (*see* Companion Animals) and for ornamental purposes.

Around 150,000 birds representing 300 indigenous species are captured and traded in India. A large part of the trade is intended for the international market. The international trade in live mammals from India includes blackbucks, giant squirrels, slow lorises, red pandas, golden langurs, hoolock gibbons, and lion-tailed macaques, as well as primates, including rhesus monkeys, for biomedical research. Peregrine and saker falcons are smuggled to West Asia for wealthy sheikhs, who use them for hunting bustard—a critically endangered grassland bird. Birds used in black magic include horned owls, hornbills, egrets, and hoopoes. Following a ban on export, traders are now ironically supported by the "animal release business," since several sects and communities, including the Jains and Hindus, buy birds and snakes to release them back into their natural habitat as part of performing meritorious religious acts.

Pardhis and Bawariyas are the nomadic hunting tribes who work for the traders and travel across the country to poach animals for huge sums of money. They are responsible for killing over a thousand tigers and other endangered species, such as leopards, birds, bears, and ungulates. The hunting parties, which include women and children, are well accomplished at avoiding the dangers and difficulties involved in trapping large mammals. Orders for as many as sixty tigers per year are received by these hunters. According to investigators and insiders of the trade, the hunters use iron traps that close with a great force, capturing and sometimes even cracking the powerful legs of tigers. The hunters immediately arrive on the scene and push a thick bamboo pole with a pointed spear into the tiger's mouth and stuff earth into it to make sure death is quiet. India has two-thirds of the world's tiger population, and with three (Caspian, Bali, and Javan) out of the eight species already extinct, about 250 are killed every year.

Forests and protected areas of the Indian states Rajasthan, Madhya Pradesh, Uttar Pradesh, Orissa, West Bengal, Assam, and Arunachal Pradesh are most susceptible to poachers because they still harbor a large population of tigers and other free-ranging animals. The killing of tigers is currently a burning issue in India since only 1,706 tigers were estimated to be left as of the 2011 census and since more than a thousand were poached between 2001 and 2011. Committed individuals are needed to help enforce antitrafficking laws, to conserve threatened habitats, and to rescue the captured animals. Corruption in this domain is rampant because of the high inflow of quick money. Wardens often risk their lives to enforce laws, only to end up frustrated and face overnight transfers. The sophisticated weapons possessed by the poachers pose a serious threat to the forest department, where one guard is expected to protect fifteen square kilometers armed with just a *danda* (wooden stick). Modern methods to counter poaching are direly needed in India.

India is perhaps the only country in world that provides in its constitution (via article 51) for "compassion to all living creatures." It is well known that India has taught ahimsa (nonviolence) to the rest of the world. Ahimsa emphasizes vegetarianism; bars hunting, killing, or injuring living beings; and is connected with the belief that violence entails negative karmic consequences (derived from Sanskrit, *karma* relates to the principle of retributive justice determining a person's state of life and the state of the person's reincarnations as the effect of his or her past deeds).

Although India has the Prevention of Cruelty to Animals Act (1960), which prohibits the infliction of unnecessary pain or suffering on animals, enforcement is weak. Following its enactment, the Animal Welfare Board of India was formed, and it has been the public face of animal welfare in the country for the last several decades. Although some serious initiatives for the welfare of animals have been taken by the Ministry of Environment and Forests, the government of India has a great deal more to do to ensure enforcement and compliance.

There has been far more animal slaughter in independent India than there was in India under British rule or during the period of Muslim kings. The killing of animals during 1998–2008 broke all previous records. India may now have the largest number of animals used in agriculture in the world. Meat production in India is estimated to be about 2.3 million tons per annum. To catch up with the pace of twentieth-century industrialization, India needed the latest machinery and foreign exchange, and to achieve this goal, it exported resources that were already scarce to the poor population. Meat export actually began quite late, when the government of India issued licenses to big slaughterhouses largely influenced by the Arab markets. The number of slaughterhouses rose from 360 in 1975 to 36,000 in 2010. The Indian leather industry handles approximately 230 million meters of hides and skins annually. According to the Food and Agriculture Organization, 24.3 million cattle, 46.7 million goats, and 16 million pigs were killed in the year 2009. But these figures include only those animals killed in the 3,600 legally operating abattoirs and do not include figures from the 32,000 illegal or unlicensed ones.

A rapid increase in demand for meat and eggs in India, seen especially during the past two decades (1992–2012), has resulted in the development of factory farms. Millions of egg-laying hens are kept in an overcrowded state in tiny cages, which frustrates their natural behaviors. Establishments that confine more than fifty thousand birds in a single shed are increasingly common. In addition, animals such as cows, steers, and camels slaughtered for their meat and skin are transported in abysmal conditions to abattoirs. They are crowded mercilessly in trucks over long journeys without food and water. Sometimes the collapsing animals are severely beaten, and chili and pepper powders are sprayed in their eyes. These and similar actions are performed in order to procure a certificate of their "sickness" on one hand and their "fitness" for slaughter on the other. Since it is illegal to kill healthy young cattle, they are often maimed or poisoned so that they can be declared fit for slaughter. During their ordeal, the animals also suffer unanesthetized castration, tail docking, and dehorning.

There are notorious slaughterhouses in India that often employ inhumane techniques to procure meat and skin. Hundreds of animals in these houses are kept on open ground for days, hungry and thirsty, and then their legs are broken and eyes poked, so that a certificate can be obtained for slaughter. The animals' hunger and thirst cause the hemoglobin to move from blood to fat. This is deliberately done because meat with higher hemoglobin fetches a better price. Then they are pushed into washing showers, where extremely hot water (200 degrees Celsius) is sprayed on them to soften their skins for easy removal. The animals frequently faint at this point, but they are not dead. Then they are hung upside down with one leg on a chain pulley conveyor, and half of the neck is slit. This drains the blood but does not completely kill the animals. This too is deliberate since after death the skin swells thick, which sells for a poor price, but the skin of a live animal is still thin, with better economic value. While the blood is dripping from the neck, a hole is made in the stomach, and air is pumped inside, causing the body to swell and making it easier to peel off the skin. After the skin is removed, the animal is cut into four pieces: head, legs, body, and tail. This is the horrifying picture of abattoirs in modern India.

India's cattle protection laws need to be properly implemented. A central agency with the power to impose stiff fines for animal cruelty could be a solution. With an animal population of more than 500 million, animal cruelty is rampant in India. India's leather industry employs nearly two million people, with another twenty million working in ancillary industries. Even though the cow is considered holy in the Hindu religion, cow slaughter is allowed in two Indian states, West Bengal and Kerala, and as noted previously, healthy cattle who cannot legally be slaughtered are often injured or poisoned so that they can be declared fit for slaughter. The transport of cows across state borders is illegal, but dealers often bribe officials. India's own minimal animal protection laws regarding transport and slaughter are blatantly ignored, and although it claims to have an Animal Welfare Reform Program, the Indian Council for Leather Exports refuses to take any action to prevent leather-selling businesses from obtaining hides and skins from unlicensed, illegal abattoirs. Animals of all ages, including small calves, are brutally killed for the leather trade. The central and state governments issue licenses for "useless" buffalos, sheep, and goats, but there are no agreed-upon criteria for what constitutes a "useless" animal, nor is there any proper monitoring.

Leading animal welfare organizations in Europe and the United States have repeatedly urged Western consumers to boycott Indian leather and leather products. Companies such as Gap, Old Navy, Banana Republic, J. Crew, Liz Claiborne, Fiorucci and Florsheim, Hush Puppies, and Nordstrom have discontinued use of Indian leather. Clarks International, a U.K.-based shoe store, has placed its leather products from India "under review."

"If slaughterhouses had glass walls, everyone in the world would be a vegetarian" is a well-known saying (often attributed to Paul or Linda McCartney). In a country with a rich traditional heritage, where *ahimsa par-modharma* (a Sanskrit phrase meaning "nonviolence is the topmost duty to the extent that it supersedes all other duties") and *vasudhaiva kutumbakam* (a Sanskrit phrase meaning "the whole world is one single family") are the guiding principles, cruelty and butchery should have no place.

Related articles: Animal welfare and farming; Animals in Jainism; The big cats; Birds used in food production; CITES and international trade; Ethical vegetarianism; Facts about bears; The fur trade; Hinduism and animals; Live quail shoots; Moon bears and bear bile farming; Perceptions of elephants; Pig castration; The protection of birds; Slaughter; Snares and snaring; The trade in primates for research; The welfare of cows

Alsdorf, Ludwig, *The History of Vegetarianism and Cow-Veneration in India*, trans. Bal Patil, Routledge, 2010.

Dutta, Ritwick, and Raghuvanshi, Vyom, *Commentaries on Wildlife Law: Cases, Statutes and Notifications*, Wildlife Trust of India, 2007.

Government of India, Ministry of Environment and Forests, "Wildlife" [Wildlife Protection Act, 1972, and Prevention of Cruelty to Animals Act, 1960], available at http://moef.nic.in/modules/rules-and-regulations/wildlife/.

John, Elizabeth, "Identification Sheets for Wildlife Species Traded in South East Asia," *Asian Wildlife Trade Bulletin* 8 (December 2009), publication of TRAFFIC.

Menon, Vivek, and Kumar, Ashok, *Wildlife Crime: An Enforcement Guide*, Wildlife Protection Society of India, 1999.

Menon, Vivek, Sukumar, Raman, and Kumar, Ashok, *A God in Distress: Threats of Poaching and the Ivory Trade to the Asian Elephant*, Wildlife Protection Society of India, 1998.

Mitrá, Avadhútiká Ananda, *Food for Thought: The Vegetarian Philosophy*, Ananda Marga, 2004.

Tansey, Geoff, and D'Silva, Joyce (eds.), *The Meat Business: Devouring a Hungry Planet*, Earthscan, 1999.

Wright, Belinda, *India's Tiger Poaching Crisis*, Wildlife Protection Society of India, 1997.

B. K. SHARMA AND SHAILJA SHARMA

two

AQUATIC AND MARINE LIFE

This section introduces the reader to those aquatic and marine creatures whom we often see least of all, but who inhabit the waters and oceans that make up more than 70 percent of the surface of the Earth.

These creatures live alongside us in their own spheres, but we seldom fully understand them or feel as morally obligated to help them as we may feel to help others. We may be drawn to dolphins, whales, and seals, but other sea creatures evoke less sympathy. As Ross Minett observes in the entry on cephalopods and decapod crustaceans, "historically, animal protection legislation has tended to include only vertebrates . . . and to exclude cephalopods (octopuses, squids, cuttlefishes, and nautiluses) and decapod crustaceans (lobsters, crabs, and crayfishes) on the grounds that the latter are nonsentient and, therefore, incapable of suffering." It seems that the boundaries of sentiency have been too tightly drawn and that some reexamination is in order.

It has to be said, however, that even evidence of sentiency has not prevented the ruthless exploitation of sea mammals, including those creatures to whom we are normally attracted—namely, whales, dolphins, and seals. Articles in this section detail our lack of moral sensibility, as well as the lack of legal protection. Our treatment of fishes, amphibians, and cephalopods and decapods often seems to be morally beyond the pale. We do damage and cause injury, it seems, without really appreciating what we do. This is perhaps clearest of all in this section's first article, which shows the disturbance to marine life caused by human-generated noise.

ANDREW LINZEY

ACOUSTIC IMPACTS ON MARINE LIFE

A growing body of evidence confirms that intense sound produced by human-generated noise in the marine environment can induce a range of adverse effects on marine mammals and other marine organisms. These effects include death and serious injury caused by hemorrhages or other tissue trauma; stranding; temporary and permanent hearing loss or impairment; displacement from preferred habitat; and disruption of feeding, breeding, nursing, communication, sensing, and other behaviors vital to survival. Recent studies show that ocean background noise levels have doubled every decade since the 1940s in some areas.

The primary sources of human-produced noise in the marine environment are shipping, air guns used for oil and gas exploration under the ocean floor, and military sonars. As a result of the masking effects of human-produced ocean noise pollution, the possible communication range of blue whales has decreased from greater than one thousand kilometers to only one hundred kilometers in the noisy Northern Hemisphere. We do not know how this affects the ability of this endangered species to find food and mates.

Mass stranding of whales increased dramatically after 1961, when more powerful naval sonars began to be used (Friedman). In the recent past marine mammal strandings have occurred in Greece (1996), the Bahamas (2000), Madeira (2000), Vieques (1998, 2002), the Canary Islands (2002, 2004), the northwest coast of the United States (2003), and Hawaii (2004). Each stranding has been correlated with the use of high-intensity military sonar. These sonars—both low-frequency (LFAS) and mid-frequency sonar—can have a source level of 240 decibels, which is 1 trillion times louder than the sounds whales have been shown to avoid. One scientist analyzing underwater acoustic data reported that a single low-frequency sonar signal deployed off the coast of California could be heard over the entire North Pacific Ocean.

Necropsies performed on whales stranded in the Bahamas (2000) and the Canary Islands (2002) revealed hemorrhaging around the brain and in other organs, most likely due to acoustic trauma from the use of high-intensity sonar. It appears that the sonar exercise in the Bahamas in 2000 may have either killed the entire population of beaked whales in the area or caused them to permanently move away (Balcomb and Claridge). In December 2004, 169 whales and dolphins died on beaches in Australia and New Zealand after reported military exercises and air gun use in the area.

A report commissioned by the U.S. Navy stated that "the evidence of sonar causation [of whales stranding] is, in our opinion, completely convincing" (Levine et al.). The global magnitude of the problem has not been determined because many fatally injured animals sink in the deep ocean, and not all injured whales strand onto beaches where they can be found. Intense noise generated by commercial air guns used for oil and gas exploration and oceanographic experiments, underwater explosives, and ship traffic also pose a threat to marine life. Air gun use was correlated with whale strandings in the Gulf of California and Brazil in 2002.

High-intensity sonars and air guns not only impact marine mammals but also have been shown to affect fishes, giant squids, and snow crabs. In a study by the British Defense Research Agency, exposure to sonar signals caused auditory damage, internal injuries, eye hemorrhaging, and mortality in commercially caught fishes. Air guns caused extensive damage to the inner ears of fishes and lowered trawl catch rates 45 to 70 percent over a 2,000-square-mile area of ocean (Norwegian Institute of Marine Research). Catch rates did not recover in the five days surveyed after air gun use stopped. This presents the possibility that increasing production of intense underwater noise can significantly and adversely impact already depleted fish stocks in the ocean, the food supply, employment, and the economies of maritime countries.

In his 2005 report to the General Assembly, the secretary general of the United Nations listed underwater noise as one of the current major threats to some populations of whales and other cetaceans. He called for better assessment of the impact of underwater noise on fishes and cetaceans as well as consideration of noise abatement strategies.

Related articles: Animals used in research; The complexity of animal awareness; The declaration of the rights of cetaceans; Intelligence in whales and dolphins; Marine mammals in captivity; Sea fishes and commercial fishing; Stranded marine mammals

Balcomb, K. C., and Claridge, D. E., "A Mass Stranding of Cetaceans Caused by Naval Sonar in the Bahamas," *Bahamas Journal of Science* 8.2 (2001): 1–8.

Engås, A., Løkkeborg, S., Ona, E., and Soldal, A. V., "Effects of Seismic Shooting on Local Abundance and Catch Rates of Cod (*Gadus morhua*) and Haddock (*Melanogrammus aeglefinus*)," *Canadian Journal of Fisheries and Aquatic Science* 53 (1996): 2238–2249.

Fernandez, A., Edwards, J. F., Rodriguez, F., Espinosa de los Monteros, A., Herraez, P., Castro, P., Jaber, J. R., Martin, V., and Arbelo, M., "Gas and Fat Embolic Syndrome Involving a Mass Stranding of Beaked Whales (Family Ziphiidae) Exposed to Anthropogenic Sonar Signals," *Veterinary Pathology* 42 (2005): 446–457.

Friedman, N., *The Naval Institute Guide to World Naval Weapons Systems*, Naval Institute Press, 1989, 380–382.

Hildebrand, J. A., "Impacts of Anthropogenic Sound in Marine Mammal Research: Conservation Beyond Crisis" in Reynolds, J. E., Perrin, W. F., Reeves, R. R., Montgomery, S., and Ragen, T. J. (eds.), *Marine Mammal Research: Conservation Beyond Crisis*, Johns Hopkins University Press, 2005, 101–124.

Levine, H., Bildsten, L, Brenner, M., Callan, C., Flatté, S., Goodman, J., Gregg, M., Katz, J., Munk, W., and Weinberger, P., *Active Sonar Waveform*, JSR-03-200, report from MITRE Corporation, JASON program, for the Office of Naval Research, 2004.

MARSHA L. GREEN

CEPHALOPODS AND DECAPOD CRUSTACEANS

Historically, animal protection legislation has tended to include only vertebrates (such as mammals, birds, reptiles, amphibians, and fishes) and to exclude cephalopods (octopuses, squids, cuttlefishes, and nautiluses) and decapod crustaceans (lobsters, crabs, and crayfishes) on the grounds that the latter are nonsentient and, therefore, incapable of suffering. However, increasingly, scientific understanding of their nervous systems and behavior indicates that these animals are in fact sentient and likely to experience pain and suffering.

Some of these animals are used by humans for food, as fishing bait, and in scientific research. Catching, trapping, handling, holding, transporting, storing, and killing them can cause injury, stress, and suffering. They suffer infections, open wounds, and other lesions, and many may die from starvation, dehydration, overheating, or injuries. The practice of killing lobsters by cooking them alive in boiling water without the use of anesthesia or pre-stunning is of particular concern. The typical method for assessing pain or suffering in nonhuman animals is to assume that an event that is painful or distressing to humans is likely to have the same or similar effect on animals with similar physiology and behavior. This method becomes harder to apply to animals with body and brain structures and behaviors very different from those of mammals, such as invertebrates.

To show that an animal experiences pain and suffering, scientists normally want to be able to show that the animal is, in principle, physiologically capable of feeling pain, behaves in a way that indicates that the animal feels pain or distress, and can behave in ways that show some mental capacity. Decapod crustaceans have a nervous system and a brain. They have a large number of internal and external mechanical and chemical receptor cells and compound eyes that are connected by nerves to the brain. Findings strongly suggest that pain is mediated in crustaceans in a way similar to how it is mediated in vertebrates.

Physiological studies of lobsters show that they are very stressed by humans' process of catching, handling, and transporting them and keeping them out of water. When they are put alive into boiling water to be cooked, they make vigorous efforts to escape. In addition, the behavior of decapod crustaceans shows that they can recognize and remember painful or threatening objects or situations and try to avoid them. They also have the ability to learn, to make discriminations, and to show some understanding and memory both of places and of other individuals.

Cephalopods have a well-developed nervous system and a complex brain, which is relatively larger than the brains of some fishes and reptiles. They have numerous sense organs that rival those found in vertebrates in their complexity. They have good eyesight and an excellent sense of touch. Aspects of their brain functioning have been found to be similar to that of vertebrates. There is good evidence from their behavior that cephalopods can feel pain, and they show signs of fear. Behavioral evidence of learning, memory, special awareness, and decision making suggests that they may have a form of primary consciousness.

The environment and lifestyle of cephalopods mandate that they be capable of complex and flexible behavior. As active predators, they need to explore, understand,

and remember their environment and the behavior of other animals. Studies have shown that octopuses learn easily, including learning by observation of another octopus. They can solve problems, as when they remove a plug or unscrew a lid to get prey from a container. They use rocks and jets of water in a way that could be classified as tool use. They have been found to play with a "toy" and to have individual responses and individual temperaments.

The traditional methods by which these animals are killed for food are now increasingly seen as inhumane. Crabs, lobsters, and crayfishes are killed by a variety of methods, including pithing, boiling, and freezing, or even while people are cutting them up to remove their flesh for meat. Unless one cuts through all thirteen ganglia of a lobster at once, the animal continues to feel pain. When boiled, a lobster will take about three minutes to die (often longer because chilled animals lower the water temperature), and a brown crab can take up to five to six minutes to die. Research suggests that chilling does not anesthetize the animals, and they continue to be sensate.

A preferable stunning method is an electrical stunner that can be used by an unskilled operator. The Crustastun delivers a stun that renders the animal unconscious in less than half a second and dead in up to ten seconds. A large commercial version for processors can kill one to two tons of animals per hour. Three of these are installed in the United Kingdom and one in Ireland. The U.K. supermarket Waitrose requires its suppliers to have killed the animals using the Crustastun. Whole Foods stores in Portland, Maine, stopped selling live lobsters in 2006 but now have a Crustastun, and the stores' suppliers of cooked lobsters also have a unit. Humane euthanasia methods applicable to research laboratories are also being developed, with the aim of avoiding causing pain to the animals.

Certain jurisdictions have already made the decision, on scientific evidence, to include some or all decapod crustaceans and cephalopods within animal protection law. These include New Zealand, Norway, the Australian Capital Territory, and Queensland. The United Kingdom included the common octopus (*Octopus vulgaris*) in the scope of the Animals (Scientific Procedures) Act 1986. A 2005 European Scientific Panel report advised that cephalopods and decapod crustaceans can suffer and thus fall into the same category as other animals currently covered by the directive on the protection of animals used for scientific purposes. The revised directive protects cephalopods but not decapod crustaceans.

In light of the scientific evidence that strongly suggests that decapod crustaceans and cephalopods possess the capacity to experience pain and suffering, it is now necessary to adopt the precautionary principle by giving them the benefit of the doubt in the regulation of all human activities that have the potential to cause them suffering.

Related articles: Animal pain; Animals used in research; The complexity of animal awareness; Euthanasia; Humane education; Legislation in the European Union; Sea fishes and commercial fishing; The trade in reptiles

Advocates for Animals, *Cephalopods and Decapod Crustaceans: Their Capacity to Experience Pain and Suffering*, 2005.
Barr, S., Laming, P. R., Dick, J. T. A., and Elwood, R. W., "Nociception or Pain in a Decapod Crustacean?" *Animal Behaviour* 75.3 (2008): 745–751.
Edelman, D. B., and Seth, A. K., "Review: Animal Consciousness: A Synthetic Approach," *Trends in Neurosciences* 32.9 (2009): 476–484.
Elwood, R. W., Barr, S., and Patterson, L., "Pain and Stress in Crustaceans?" *Applied Animal Behaviour Science* 118.3 (2009): 128–136.
Mather, J. A., "Cephalopod Consciousness: Behavioural Evidence," *Conscious Cognition* 17.1 (2008): 37–48.
Mather, J. A., and Anderson, R. C., "Ethics and Invertebrates: A Cephalopod Perspective," *Diseases of Aquatic Organisms* 75.2 (2007): 119–129.

ROSS MINETT

COMMERCIAL WHALING

Although commercial whaling for large whale species was banned worldwide by the International Whaling Commission (IWC) in 1986, this ban has never been enforced.

Over thirty thousand whales have been slaughtered since the ban was introduced, and every year a growing number of whales are killed. Unfortunately, smaller whale species are not protected by the ban, and around a half-million dolphins and porpoises have been killed in Japan alone since 1986. Japanese fishers still slaughter around twenty thousand of these animals every year.

Currently, Japanese, Icelandic, and Norwegian whalers harpoon over two thousand large whales each year in defiance of the IWC ban, and this number is growing. Meanwhile, the IWC is completing a management scheme for the resumption of commercial whaling. It seems that despite overwhelming public opposition, commercial whaling is set to return.

The history of commercial whaling has seen the systematic destruction of one whale population after another, with some species pushed to the brink of extinction. At first the whalers pursued whales from sailing ships in open boats with hand-thrown harpoons. But the development of steam-powered ships and explosive harpoon cannons meant that whaling ships could pursue and kill the fastest whales, chasing them, literally, to the ends of the earth. The arrival of "factory" ships, massive floating slaughterhouses, meant whales could be processed far out at sea. Catcher boats would harpoon the unfortunate whales and tow them back to the factory ship for rendering into oil. The whalers could now penetrate polar pack ice, stay at sea for months at a time, and slaughter whales by the thousands each year. With this new technology and an insatiable demand for whale oil, the results were catastrophic.

Around two million whales were slaughtered during the twentieth century. Blue whales alone, the largest animals ever to evolve, were harpooned by the tens of thousands each year. The species has never recovered and remains critically endangered, despite more than forty years of protection. As blue whales declined, the whalers switched their attention to the next-largest species, the fin whale, and so the senseless chain of destruction continued. Eventually, only the relatively tiny minke whales were left in any numbers to be worth hunting, and Japanese, Icelandic, and Norwegian hunters have killed many thousands of minke whales during the current whaling ban.

Fearful of wiping out their own "golden goose," the whaling nations agreed to form a self-regulatory body, the IWC, in 1949. However, dominated by whalers, for twenty years the commission presided over the greatest whale slaughter in history. In what became known as the "Whaling Olympics," an average of fifty to sixty thousand whales were killed each year—an average of one whale harpooned every eight minutes. Not surprisingly, whale populations crashed worldwide.

In 1972, concern over the mismanagement of whaling prompted the United Nations to call for an immediate ten-year moratorium on commercial whaling. But it was not until 1986, when enough new countries had joined the organization, that the IWC finally voted for an indefinite ban. However, the whalers have found ways around the ban. Today, Japan kills around fifteen hundred whales each year by claiming the hunting is for "scientific research," and Norway and Iceland have renewed commercial hunting in open defiance of the ban, killing a similar number between them.

Even without whaling, there is growing scientific evidence that whales are under threat as never before. Climate change through global warming, increasing ultraviolet (UV) radiation through the ozone "holes," toxic marine pollution, overfishing, entanglement in fishing gears, ship strikes, chronic noise pollution (including le-

thal military sonar), and the loss of critical feeding and breeding sites—all threaten the future of the world's surviving whale populations.

Global climate change may alter ocean currents, disrupting food availability for whales. Increasing UV radiation is destroying phytoplankton on which the entire marine ecosystem depends. Persistent toxic compounds such as mercury, pesticides, and PCBs are increasingly contaminating whales, undermining their immune and reproductive systems and posing a serious health risk both to the whales and to people who eat them. The extent of the problem is such that stranded beached whales are often treated as toxic waste. Some experts believe that these pollutants could yet cause the extinction of all marine mammals.

Despite modern killing methods, whaling is still appallingly cruel. Laws for the slaughter of domestic cattle, sheep, and pigs call for pre-stunning and killing the animal while he or she is unconscious, but these laws do not apply in the open ocean. The death of a whale is caused by massive internal injuries from an explosive harpoon's shrapnel. The hunted animal must first endure the fear and exhaustion of the chase, the pain of the first harpoon strike, and then being winched by a cable attached to the harpoon, deep within his or her body, to the catcher boat. The unfortunate animal may then be harpooned again or repeatedly shot with a rifle to be finished off. This agonizing process can take from several minutes to well over an hour. A physician aboard a whaling ship once remarked, "The gunners themselves admit that if whales could scream the industry would stop, for nobody would be able to stand it" (Brake, Butterworth, Simmonds, and Lymbery 30).

In 2001, an international workshop of veterinarians and other experts reviewed modern whale killing methods. They reached a truly shocking conclusion: many harpooned whales may still be alive and fully conscious when they are hauled up and butchered on deck. Even the IWC has recognized that the criteria used to determine insensibility and death in whales are "inadequate."

However, even if whaling were humane, the slaughter of such highly sentient creatures merely for profit would still be morally repugnant to many people. Only wealthy developed nations are engaged in, or want to resume, commercial whaling. Whale meat is no longer a nutritional or economic necessity in those countries, and whale products, such as whale oil, have long since been replaced in industry or can be manufactured synthetically. Today, whales are killed for their meat and other edible products, and whale meat has become an expensive gourmet food in Japan. However, whale products have become so contaminated with pollutants such as mercury and other toxins that they pose a serious health risk to people who eat them.

Whale watching is now a global industry worth over US$2 billion, which clearly demonstrates that whales are worth far more alive than dead. We do not need to kill whales anymore, but we still need to save them. The growing threats to these wonderful animals from human activities are such that only by reducing these threats, while strictly enforcing the whaling ban and extending it to protect all whales and dolphins for the foreseeable future, can we ever hope to ensure their survival.

Related articles: Acoustic impacts on marine life; Animal agriculture and climate change; Animal pain; Animals and public health; Challenges to animal protection in Scandinavia; The declaration of the rights of cetaceans; Intelligence in whales and dolphins; Japanese attitudes toward animals; Slaughter; Stranded marine mammals

Brake, Philippa, Butterworth, Andrew, Simmonds, Mark, and Lymbery, Philip (eds.), *Troubled Waters—A Review of the Welfare Implications of Modern Whaling Activities*, World Society for the Protection of Animals, 2004, available at http://www.wdcs.org/submissions_bin/troubledwaters.pdf.
Carwardine, Mark, *Whales, Dolphins, and Porpoises*, Dorling Kindersley, 2010.
Hoare, Philip, *Leviathan*, Fourth Estate, 2009.
International Fund for Animal Welfare, *Whale Watching Worldwide: Tourism Numbers, Expenditures and Expanding Economic Benefits*, 2009.
Kelsey, Elin, *Watching Giants: The Secret Lives of Whales*, University of California Press, 2009.
Morikawa, Jun, *Whaling and Japan*, Hurst, 2009.
Royal Society for the Prevention of Cruelty to Animals, *Report of the First International Scientific Workshop on Sentience and Potential Suffering in Hunted Whales*, 2003.
Wilson, Ben, and Wilson, Angus, *The Complete Whale-Watching Handbook: A Guide to Whales, Dolphins, and Porpoises of the World*, Voyageur Press, 2006.

ANDY OTTAWAY

INTELLIGENCE IN WHALES AND DOLPHINS

Not unreasonably, perhaps, the process of securing recognition that animals have rights has started with nonhuman primates; the intelligence of these animals can be compared with our own relatively easily. But what of animals who live very differently from us—for example, animals swimming in three-dimensional open space with no definable homes or nests, interacting with each other and their environment in ways that we are still striving to understand? This brings us, of course, to whales and dolphins, mammals who lack that vital component of primate (including human) life—the opposable thumb—and whose senses are dominated by sound rather than vision.

For humans to properly understand any animal species, the animals must be studied unobtrusively in their habitat in their natural state. Apes now sit patiently in the company of scientists (or is it the other way around?), allowing their societies to be observed directly. However, dolphins and whales (collectively known as "the cetaceans") offer very few similar opportunities. A fleeting glimpse of a dorsal fin or a tail fluke may be all a field worker gets after hours, days, or even weeks of attempted (and usually expensive) study.

Not surprisingly, our understanding of dolphin and whale behavior is estimated to be more than thirty years behind our appreciation of nonhuman primate behavior. Yet we can already appreciate the keen curiosity and playfulness of the bottlenose dolphin. Tests also show self-awareness ("I think, therefore I am a dolphin"), and field studies reveal excellent examples of advanced group cooperation (for example, when rounding up fish or driving off predators), as well as complex relationships within populations.

In the open ocean, when challenged by predators or otherwise frightened, cetaceans have nothing to hide behind but each other—a factor that has clearly and profoundly shaped the evolution of their behavior and the development of their intelligence and cooperation. Only very recently, as field studies have matured, has it been possible to recognize that some cetaceans have such sophisticated behavior as to warrant the term "culture."

Culture can be identified where patterns of behavior cannot be explained by either genetic transmission or environmental factors. In fact, imitation and teaching are well-established components of the behavior of two of the best-studied cetacean species, bottlenose dolphins and orcas. Indeed, scientists are now suggesting that the complex and stable cultures of orcas have no parallel outside of human societies. Dolphins are known to manipulate and use objects. For example, they use sponges to protect their snouts when probing sediments for food in a bay in Australia. Dolphins have been shown to demonstrate the following scientifically classified abilities:

- tool-using skills
- abstract concept formation
- self-awareness and regulation of behavior
- shared communication and social monitoring
- manipulation, including a high degree of vocal adaptability

Cetaceans are among the few species that form sophisticated, mutually beneficial partnerships with other species, including our own. For example, in Laguna, Brazil, bottlenose dolphins drive mullet toward fishers, and then, with a certain splash of their tails, they tell the fishers precisely when to deploy their throw nets (a case of dolphins having trained people for the reward of fish!). The dolphins then feed on the remaining fish. This has been going on for more than a hundred years on a daily basis whenever the weather is good, meaning three generations of fishers have benefited. Only one group of dolphins in the area does this. Sometimes, they will even search for the fishers and invite them to "go fishing."

News of the intelligence, great behavioral flexibility, and culture of dolphins is probably not a surprise. However, the advanced nature of cetaceans now has strong scientific support. Dolphins are arguably the nearest beings to intelligent aliens we may ever meet. Furthermore, there are actually over eighty cetacean species, with new ones still being discovered. In the case of most, we have little idea about their behavioral repertoires and societies. Even species that we may think we know relatively well, such as the huge and unique Arctic specialists, the bowhead whales, are still surprising us. It has only recently become known that bowheads can live for more than two centuries. This long life may well be an adaptation to the demands of their extreme environment and the need for a culture within which individuals have the time and opportunity to learn the necessary survival skills.

We now need to appreciate that the killing of individual cetaceans is likely to constitute the loss of a member of a family (or part of some other cooperating unit) and, in effect, part of a society. It may, for example, mean the removal of a mother, a mentor, an associate, or even a cetacean team that has learned some particular way to survive in their world. The significance of such losses for these complex species may be difficult to assess precisely, but we can be sure that the losses do harm. Yet, we still hunt such animals for profit, catch them in huge numbers in nets (mainly incidentally, as part of our fishing activities), and dump poisons into their environment.

We need to stand back and think about the significance of what we now know and how it should influence our treatment of these animals and their environment. Animals who possess high intelligence, live in societies, and exhibit culture deserve respect and require careful treatment. New awareness brings a responsibility to protect and conserve them appropriately, and this goal now has to be seen in the context of conserving their cultures and behaving in ways that avoid harm to them as individuals, cultures, and societies.

Related articles: Acoustic impacts on marine life; Animals used in research; Commercial whaling; The complexity of animal awareness; The declaration of the rights of cetaceans; The ethics of killing free-living animals

Dudzinski, Kathleen, and Frohoff, Toni, *Dolphin Mysteries: Unlocking the Secrets of Communication*, Yale University Press, 2008.

Mann, Janet, Connor, R. P., Tyack, P., and Whitehead, H. (eds.), *Cetacean Societies: Field Studies of Dolphins and Whales*, University of Chicago Press, 2000.

Simmonds, Mark P., "Into the Brains of Whales," *Applied Animal Behaviour* 100 (2006): 103–106.

———, *Whales and Dolphins of the World*, New Holland, 2007.

Simmonds, Mark P., and Hutchinson, Judith D. (eds.), *The Conservation of Whales and Dolphins—Science and Practice*, Wiley, 1996.

White, Thomas I., *In Defense of Dolphins: The New Moral Frontier*, Blackwell, 2007.

Whitehead, Hal, *Sperm Whales: Social Evolution in the Oceans*, University of Chicago Press, 2003.

MARK PETER SIMMONDS

THE PINNIPEDS

The pinnipeds (literally meaning feather- or fin-footed) include fur seals and sea lions (family Otariidae), walruses (Odobenidae), and the true seals (Phocidae). Often referred to simply as "seals," they are the aquatic relatives of bears, weasels, dogs, cats, and other terrestrial carnivores (order Carnivora). Thirty-four extant species are currently recognized. Two additional species—the Japanese sea lion (*Zalophus japonicus*) and the Caribbean monk seal (*Monachus tropicalis*)—are now presumed extinct. More than one-third of all seal species are now represented on the IUCN Red List of Threatened Animals as critically endangered, endangered, vulnerable, or near threatened.

The pinnipeds occur mainly in the polar and subpolar regions of both the northern and southern hemispheres. Most are restricted to areas where the water is relatively cold (approximately 20 degrees Celsius or 68 degrees Fahrenheit in the warmest month of the year) and highly productive. They vary in size from the smallest female Galapagos fur seal (*Arctocephalus galapagoensis*), weighing less than 50 kilograms (110 pounds), to the massive adult male southern elephant seal (*Mirounga leonina*), weighing as much as 3,600 kilograms (almost 4 tons). In many species, males are considerably larger than females, but in others, the sexes are of equal size, or females are larger than males. Pinniped bodies are streamlined, and as their name suggests, their limbs are modified as flippers. Although they spend much of their lives in water and feed there, pinnipeds remain tied to land or ice to give birth and nurse their pups and to molt, rest, and avoid aquatic predators, including killer whales (*Orcinus orca*) and great white sharks (*Carcharodon carcharias*).

In the past, commercial sealing for valuable oil and, later, pelts, led to the overexploitation of many pinnipeds. A number of fur seals and sea lions were virtually exterminated by the 1800s. Walruses (*Odobenus rosmarus*) were extirpated from the east coast of southern Canada and the northeastern United States by 1800. A number of true seals were also overexploited, some to very low numbers, including the aforementioned Caribbean monk seal, the gray seal (*Halichoerus grypus*) in eastern Canada, and the northern elephant seal (*Mirounga angustirostris*) on the West Coast of the United States.

Commercial sealing continues for certain species, such as harp (*Pagophilus groenlandicus*), ringed (*Pusa hispida*), and gray seals in the North Atlantic and Cape fur seals (*Arctocephalus pusillus pusillus*) in Namibia. Some modern seal hunts remain completely unregulated; in other cases, government-set quotas appear to be unsustainable. Most of the remaining seal hunts are characterized by unacceptably inhumane killing practices that raise serious ethical questions.

Direct killing by fishers has impacts on both individual seals and populations. In some areas, seals who take fish directly from fisher's nets or who are perceived to be competing for fishery resources are routinely shot. Such killing is usually not reported, and in the case of endangered species such as the Mediterranean (*Monachus monachus*) and Hawaiian (*M. schauinslandi*) monk seals, the removal of even one animal can be detrimental to the population. Globally, the proliferation of scientifically unjustified calls for "culling" seal populations, ostensibly to benefit fisheries depleted by human overfishing, signifies a continuing threat to these animals.

Incidental catches of pinnipeds in commercial fishing gear have animal welfare and conservation impacts on a number of species. Deaths resulting from being caught underwater are typically slow and prolonged in diving mammals such as seals and cause unacceptable suffering. Other potential threats include loss of genetic diversity in small populations; chemical pollution that, among other things, may suppress immune systems; mass mortalities associated with morbilliviruses and other diseases; and entanglement in marine debris. In addition, habitat degradation and loss caused by human activities such as overfishing (which may result in reduced food availability for seals), marine and coastal development (including the proliferation of aquaculture facilities in coastal regions), mass tourism, increasing boat traffic, and noise pollution are also considered serious threats to seals in some locations.

Despite the severe effects of past commercial sealing operations and various indirect threats, global warming now almost certainly poses the most serious threat to pinnipeds. Toward the poles, a reduction in sea ice—particularly in the Northern Hemisphere—represents a loss of critical habitat for a number of pagophilic (that is, ice-loving) seals, including ringed and bearded (*Erignathus barbatus*) seals in Arctic regions and migratory harp and hooded (*Cystophora cristata*) seals who reproduce on sub-Arctic winter pack ice to the south.

For the pinnipeds who live at lower latitudes closer to the equator—for example, Galapagos fur seals and sea lions (*Zalophus wollebaeki*) and Cape fur seals in Namibia—warming air temperatures may well cause overheating (hyperthermia) leading to increases in natural mortality, especially in small pups, during times of the year when they are obligated to be on land. If high ambient air temperatures become limiting, local extirpation of seal colonies or a poleward shift in distribution (which may already be happening in some species) would be expected.

In addition to the direct effects on the seals themselves, climate change is causing additional ecosystem changes that may affect the distribution and abundance of prey species, have impacts on the ability of seals to find food, and expose animals to new diseases. Sea-level rise accompanying global warming also seems destined to reduce available habitat for seals, including haul-out sites on exposed rocks, shoals, or small islands and in caves used by the critically endangered Mediterranean monk seal. Because of their widespread distribution on land and at sea, the conservation of pinnipeds requires coordinated local, national, and international efforts. First and foremost, vulnerable and endangered species require immediate *in situ* legal protection, with adequate enforcement to ensure compliance with the law. There also must be effective protection for currently abundant species to reduce threats that could make them species of concern in the future.

Given that commercial exploitation of free-ranging animals almost always results in overexploitation, it is incumbent on those jurisdictions that permit continued commercial sealing to develop precautionary approaches to the management of hunting activities, including the setting of quotas. There is also an urgent need to make certain that the killing techniques employed comply with accepted twenty-first century standards of "humane" killing. Inherently inhumane seal hunts must be ended based on scientific and ethical considerations.

At a time when some three-quarters of world fisheries are fully exploited, overexploited, or depleted, fishery management plans must also incorporate ecosystem considerations to ensure that adequate food is available for pinnipeds and for other species dependent on marine ecosystems, including humans.

In short, we must learn to manage human activities in a way that minimizes our impacts on individual pinnipeds, their populations, and their critical habitats. Failing that, we may well lose additional species in the not-too-distant future. Leading the list of likely candidates are Mediterranean and Hawaiian monk seals, who seemed destined to follow their Caribbean cousin into oblivion, unless offered dramatic and stringent protection immediately.

Related articles: Acoustic impacts on marine life; Animal agriculture and climate change; CITES and international trade; The ethics of killing free-living animals; The fur trade; The moral claims of animals; Sea fishes and commercial fishing; Shark conservation

European Food Safety Authority, "Scientific Opinion of the Panel on Animal Health and Welfare on a Request from the Commission on the Animal Welfare Aspects of the Killing and Skinning of Seals," *EFSA Journal* 610 (2007): 1–122, available at http://www.efsa.europa.eu/en/scdocs/scdoc/610.htm.

Hansen, S., Lavigne, D. M., and Innes, S., "Energy Metabolism and Thermoregulation in Juvenile Harbor Seals (*Phoca vitulina*) in Air," *Physiological Zoology* 68 (1995): 290–315.

Lavigne, D. M., "Marine Mammals and Fisheries: The Role of Science in the Culling Debate," in Gales, N., Hindell, M., and Kirkwood, R. (eds.), *Marine Mammals: Fisheries, Tourism and Management Issues*, CSIRO, 2003, 31–47, available at http://www.aad.gov.au/Asset/whales/Lavigne%202003.pdf.

Lavigne, D. M., and Kovacs, K. M., *Harps and Hoods: Icebreeding Seals of the Northwest Atlantic*, University of Waterloo Press, 1988.

Learmonth, J. A., MacLeod, C. D., Santos, M. B., Pierce, G. J., Crick, H. Q. P., and Robinson, R. A., "Potential Effects of Climate Change on Marine Mammals," *Oceanography and Marine Biology: An Annual Review* 44 (2006): 431–464.

Linzey, A., *Why Animal Suffering Matters: Philosophy, Theology, and Practical Ethics*, Oxford University Press, 2009.

Rice, D., *Marine Mammals of the World: Systematics and Distribution*, Society for Marine Mammalogy, Special Publication No. 4, Allen Press, 1998.

DAVID M. LAVIGNE

THE REHABILITATION OF DOLPHINS

Many people have a misconception about how captive dolphins are prepared to be returned to their natural state. They think we train or, rather, retrain them. Some people suppose that we teach them to survive in their natural state in the same way that we once taught them to jump through hoops. They think we do it "scientifically." Indeed, many of the people working to readapt and release captive dolphins think that *is* what we are doing. But how can we teach dolphins what they need to know to survive when the main thing they need to know is not to listen to me, or any human being?

What we actually do is so simple that most people do not believe it. In my "Protocol for the Rehabilitation and Release of Captive Dolphins," there are three basic rules: first, assume you know nothing; second, maintain sustained observation; and third, consider the obvious. Briefly, that means that if the dolphins' problems began with what we taught them, the last thing we want to do is teach them something more. In fact, we need to *un*-teach them, which means simply letting them forget what we have already taught them. When preparing captive dolphins to resume their natural life, we do not aim to teach them anything, much less how to live in their natural setting. In fact, it is doubtful whether we could ever teach them that. What we can do, however, is try to understand them in their own situation in the crippled world that we placed them in and then let nature take its course. What we do is not so much a science as a healing art.

What we do should properly be called "un-training." Some trainers do not like that term because it is negative. Trainers themselves are often very strong-willed people. They have to be because they need to be in control. If they lose control, they suppose they have lost everything. Describing what we do as "un-training" implies that we are not doing anything. Some of them have even accused me of simply living with the dolphins for a few months and then turning them loose. There is more to it than that, of course, but not much actually.

What we do in preparing dolphins for life outside captivity is simply allow their previous training to go unreinforced. In fact, we ignore it. And this too is an art, because as we observe the dolphins very closely, day by day, it is possible to see each bit of their previous training progressively falling away. And one day when it is all gone—when it is "extinguished," as the behaviorists would say—they are ready. When the un-training is complete, we also have to perform basic checks—for example, a last health check, to ensure that they have no disease they might transmit to other populations, and a water check to ensure appropriate water quality in the vicinity where they are to be released. Only then are they finally ready to be released and tracked.

In one sense, we do live with the dolphins. We meticulously observe each and every activity, but we are not obtrusive, and we aim not to be known. With each jump, I am there. With each live fish they chase around the pen, I am there too. Every time they dive, every time they surface, with every breath, I am with them—and yet they never know me. To them, I am like a gnarled mangrove tree growing at the edge of the sanctuary, a bush on the bank, or a heron on one leg gazing at the water.

Toward the very end of the rehabilitation process, we keep out of sight as much as possible. We do not talk to the dolphins. We even wear dark glasses when we feed them, so that there is no possibility of eye contact. We do our stealthy business and then steal back to our tent, where we watch them or listen to them breathe and follow them in our mind's eye. We even calculate when the umbilical cord can be cut forever, when they will be thinking not of me or of any other human being, but only of getting on with their lives as dolphins.

Related articles: Animals used in research; The complexity of animal awareness; The declaration of the rights of cetaceans; Intelligence in whales and dolphins; Marine mammals in captivity

Darwin, Charles, *Voyage of the Beagle: Charles Darwin's Journal of Researches*, Penguin, 1989.
Lilly, John C., *Man and Dolphin*, Doubleday, 1961.
McKenna, Virginia, *Into the Blue*, HarperSanFrancisco, 1992.
O'Barry, Richard, and Coulborne, Keith, *Behind the Dolphin Smile*, Algonquin of Chapel Hill, 1988.
———, *To Free a Dolphin*, Renaissance, 2000.
Roth, Hans Peter, and O'Barry, Richard, *Die Bucht*, Delius Klasing, 2010.

RICHARD O'BARRY

SEA FISHES AND COMMERCIAL FISHING

Fishes are aquatic vertebrates covered with scales and equipped with two sets of paired fins and several unpaired fins. They differ from other vertebrates in having no neck between the head and thoracic regions, with important implications for the evolution of brains and forelimbs (pectoral fins).

Humans generally think of fishes as things, not as beings. A change was signaled, however, in 2010 by the European Parliament's adoption of a (nonbinding) resolution recognizing "that target species, as well as nontarget species such as fishes, sharks, turtles, seabirds, and marine mammals, are sentient creatures." The resolution thus "call[ed] on the Commission to allocate support for the development of catching and slaughtering methods that reduce unnecessary suffering of marine wildlife." The Lisbon Treaty, updating the EU statute, also contains a specific provision in its article 13 recognizing that animals are sentient beings and includes fisheries as one of the areas where full regard must be paid to animal welfare requirements.

Fishes are complex animals with full sets of senses and the requisite central nervous systems that serve those senses, coordinate them, and interpret their signals. So fishes feel pain, though we do not yet know whether any of them are self-aware (as are dolphins, elephants, anthropoid apes, and the gray parrot) and therefore suffer when in pain or discomfort—and we do not yet know how they express such sensations.

It is characteristic of a common attitude that when killers of whales, dolphins, seals, and even the giant rodent capybaras are told they are being cruel in their enterprise, the response is "but they are only fishes." One problem in changing human attitudes is that we have only recently learned how to sense energies underwater as we do on land, and as all aquatic animals do. Primates (monkeys, apes, and lemurs) use primarily their visual sense to track their environment; most fishes have prominent eyes but rely largely on the senses by which they detect and analyze vibrations in the water, vibrations that humans would perceive as sound or as shaking or would not perceive it at all—ultrasound or infrasound above or below the detectable frequency range. In fishes the lateral line running along both sides of the body is a detector of vibrations and in some species includes an electric organ and possibly a magnetic detector, perhaps connected with the ability to undertake long-distance migrations.

An organ unique to the bony fishes and possessed by most of them is the swim bladder, which facilitates buoyancy and underwater maneuverability. The olfactory sense, or sense of smell, which gives an ability to identify a huge number of kinds of chemicals at extremely low concentrations, is highly developed in fishes. It is used, for example, by salmons to find their home rivers during migration, by some species to identify other individuals—including sexual partners—and by sharks and others to locate prey. Fishes probably produce pheromones, although the specific organ for detecting them—the vomeronasal organ (Jacobson's organ)—has not been studied in fishes.

It has been shown experimentally that fishes not only feel pain but also experience fear. Experiments in mazes have shown that fishes have spatial memory. The fish brain has no neocortex, but some functions performed in the neocortex of mammals are effectively taken care of by other regions of the brain in other vertebrates.

Like cetaceans, fishes—*pisces* in the old taxonomy—are composed of two distinctly different kinds of animals that, in evolutionary terms, are only distantly related: (1) the bony fishes, class Actinopterygii or teleosts, and (2) the cartilaginous fishes, class Chondrichthyes or elasmobranchs, composed of the sharks and rays. The elasmobranchs appear in the fossil record long before the teleosts. More than half of all vertebrates are fishes. There are 28,000 known extant species of fishes, and 27,000 of them are teleosts. Several more species are discovered every time someone takes a submersible down to a new location.

All the elasmobranchs and over half of the teleosts live in the sea. Several groups of the teleosts are diadromous (migrating between sea and rivers and lakes). Of those some are anadromous, such as salmons (breeding in freshwater, feeding in the sea), and others are catadromous (breeding in the sea, feeding in freshwater), such as gray mullets, eels, and shads. Yet others are confined mainly to the brackish waters of estuaries, marshes, and lagoons. The two classes of fishes differ by much more than the composition of their skeletons and—from the point of view of this article—in two important ways. All extract life-supporting oxygen from the water in which they live using internal gills, but whereas most elasmobranchs must keep moving forward to ensure the passage of sufficient water over the absorbing gills and out through gill slits, the teleosts actively take in water through their mouths and expel it past bony gill covers. The ancestors of freshwater fish species—all teleosts—were marine. They have different metabolic systems from the marine species, especially concerning control of body salt. The fishes have digestive systems distinctly different from those of terrestrial vertebrates, their excretions being mainly ammonia. The elasmobranchs are all carnivores, but among the teleosts are carnivores, herbivores, and omnivores.

It used to be thought that fishes lived only in surface waters and at mid-depths of the ocean, but specialized species have now been found even in the deepest ocean trenches. As fishing methods are developed to operate at greater depths, and market demand escalates, more deepwater species are becoming vulnerable to humans.

Biological diversity among the bony teleost fishes is greater than diversity between elephants and shrews or between the condor and the hummingbird; the smallest is only three millimeters long when full-grown. But in size the elasmobranchs win: whale sharks and basking sharks are as big as whales and are also plankton-eaters. Many of the bony fishes—and not only the biggest species—have naturally long lives, measured in decades rather than in years. Unlike terrestrial and aerial vertebrates, the fishes continue to increase in size throughout their lives, but the average age of individuals in a population—and hence the average size and scale of reproduction—is diminished greatly by intensive fishing, even when that activity is relatively unselective. This is important because not only does the fecundity of teleosts increase in proportion to the weight of the individual female, and hence with the animal's age, but there also is evidence that the eggs and larvae of older fishes are more viable than those shed by younger females.

The reproductive strategies of the two classes of fishes are different. The elasmobranchs produce relatively few young, and commonly those are "laid" enclosed in pouch-like cases (when found washed up on beaches, these are sometimes called "mermaids' purses"), although some species are viviparous. (In several viviparous species the more vigorous larvae eat their siblings or some of the mother's eggs, but most fish larvae in both classes subsist at first on nutrients in attached yolk sacs.) Most teleost species lay very large numbers of eggs, only a few of which survive as juveniles. These two strategies are referred to, respectively, as K-selected and r-selected and have very different consequences for the population dynamics of the species; the K-selected species, with relatively low reproductive rates, are generally considered more vulnerable to extermination by human activities than the r-selected species. Until recently, it has been assumed that the teleost strategy is to ensure adequate survival in a highly variable environment with many predators on larval and young fishes, but Alan Longhurst has recently given a more convincing explanation. He observes that most teleosts are cannibals, feeding on their own young. That is a way of ensuring food supplies for relatively large adults in an environment where practically all the photosynthesizing plants (such as diatoms and coccolithophores), herbivores (such as the crustaceans, euphausids, and copepods), and primary carnivores are tiny but numerous individuals.

Some of the larger, fast-swimming, mostly migratory fish species, such as bluefin tuna, many of the tuna- and mackerel-like species, and several sharks, are warm-blooded (endothermic) creatures, with the entire body, some muscles, or just the eyes and brain being warmer than the ambient temperature. Recent research has indicated that the size of the brain—especially of the area called the telencephalon, which controls movement and use of space—is related to the difference between active foraging and relatively passive feeding behavior.

Until the twentieth century, humans looked at sea fishes almost exclusively as food for ourselves, and that is still so. However, in the twentieth century fishes began to be caught in vast quantities for the production of fish oil and fish meal; this led to the introduction of new kinds of fishing gears and operations and increased the dangers of unsustainable overfishing. That has, in turn, led to two industrial changes in exploitation of these "resources." As fishes have become less abundant, and with restricted geographical range/distribution, vessels have moved further from their home bases, to other regions and further offshore, necessarily being bigger and more powerful for this purpose.

The other change has been an increase in the depth at which many species are caught, and it is this in particular that has new welfare implications for these free-living animals. Fishes caught in shallow waters commonly are brought to the surface alive and left to die on the deck of the boat, though in a few cases they may be brought to market alive or moribund, as are eels and some crustaceans, especially crabs and lobsters. Fishes brought up from great depths are usually dead by the time they reach the surface because of the rapid change of pressure as the gear is hauled in.

Other deaths are caused by crushing. In bottom trawling (called "dragging" in North America) the animals caught near the beginning of a "haul" will be dragged alive for upwards of thirty minutes, having been disturbed on the bottom by weights called "ticklers" strung on the bottom line of the net. But other forms of fishing, aimed principally at small species or juveniles, catch huge quantities of the animals in mid-water, by use of purse seines and mid-water trawls. The catches are inevitably crushed by their own weight and volume, so much so that in some situations, when the catch is hauled to the surface, it arrives practically as a mash.

Another mode of fishing relies on gill nets, which may float near the surface (drift nets) or in mid-water or be laid on the seabed (trammels). The meshes of these nets are adjusted for the species (and sizes) of the desired catch. But the targeted fish die slowly, and while suspended in the nets before they are hauled in, they may be attacked and partially eaten by other predators, such as sharks and toothed cetaceans. Those nets aimed at the capture of large fish species also kill—"incidentally"—other, nontarget species of animals such as dolphins, turtles, and diving seabirds, sometimes in large numbers. Similar so-called bycatches are taken on the hooks of longlines (also at the surface, in mid-water, or laid on the seabed, and as they are hauled in and out of the water), and in these cases the animals caught commonly include seabirds such as albatrosses.

The United Nations Food and Agriculture Organization (FAO) has determined that more than half of all species of fishes exploited commercially are now overfished, so that the global limit of sustainable fish taking has been reached or exceeded. Overfishing has another consequence with respect to protection of fishes. The extreme population depletion of some of the larger fish species and the consequent rising market prices have made it profitable to catch younger animals and to keep them alive and artificially fed in cages suspended in the sea until they are ready for market. This cage-ranching is now extensive in the Mediterranean, in waters around Japan, and elsewhere, and in terms of animal welfare, it is probably comparable with the holding of terrestrial mammals and birds in overcrowded conditions in too-small cages. There are no regulations, anywhere, to provide for the animals' welfare, with respect either to living conditions or to method of transporting and killing, except—of course—insofar as regulations might ensure a better market product. Anyone who has seen huge, live, warm-blooded bluefin tuna lying "panting" on a boat deck, or on a table after being removed from a cage, must feel compassion for the animal. Another downside of mariculture is that the nutrients provided to the captives—whether they are confined in cages or held in lochs/fjords or lagoons—necessarily include a fraction of products from small fish species, a further incentive to overfishing.

The larger species of sharks suffer another kind of abusive treatment—finning, in which the captured animals have their dorsal fins sliced off (to be made into shark fin soup) and are then thrown back into the sea alive. They mostly suffer a slow death: the dorsal fin is not an ornament; it is the fish's stabilizer. Efforts are being made internationally to end this practice or alternatively to require that the entire body be utilized, not "wasted." As with efforts over several decades either to conserve whale populations by using them sustainably or to limit or end whaling because it is regarded as cruel, the international campaigns against shark finning combine two components: compassion for the individual animals and concern that if such marine life is to be used—lethally—this should be done without causing avoidable pain and suffering and without either short- or long-term "waste."

Although many vertebrate species are now legally protected under national and international regulations, usually because they have been reduced to population levels at which they are at risk of extinction, very few species of marine fishes have been granted such a status. Recently a proposal to classify the Atlantic bluefin tuna as an endangered species and to prohibit its capture was quashed in the Conference of Parties to the Convention on International Trade in Endangered Species of Wild Flora and Fauna (CITES), notwithstanding the incontrovertible scientific evidence of its extreme depletion. This is one more case in which governments are very reluctant to agree to list marine species, especially fishes, in CITES Appendix I, which prohibits international trade, reflecting the fear of fishing industries that they will be unduly restrained.

All the marine fishes are vulnerable to some degree and in several ways to many types of ocean pollution, as well as to physical changes in habitat such as destruction of mangroves and coral reefs, runoff of soil from deforestation and construction of buildings near shore, and churning of the seabed by heavy dredges and bottom trawls. The pollutants and contaminants include heavy metals; spills of mineral oil; a great variety of persistent organic chemicals, including especially endocrine disruptors, particularly those affecting reproduction (high-trophic-level carnivorous fishes are particularly vulnerable); persistent solid wastes, including lost fishing nets and lines made of nonbiodegradable synthetic materials ("ghost nets"); carbon dioxide, which is causing the acidity of the ocean to increase and changing the lives of plants and animals with calcareous endo- and exoskeletons, including pteropods (tiny pelagic snails, an important primary food source for many marine animals); and eutrophication by inflow of organic wastes from inland sources, leading to reduced oxygen in coastal waters and increased vulnerability of fishes there to bacterial and viral infections as well as to the creation of sometimes-vast "dead zones." Marine pollution as defined by the United Nations includes additions by human activity of thermal energy and sound; the latter is particularly significant for fishes and other marine vertebrates and possibly for some of the invertebrates too. Finally, global warming, both natural and anthropogenic, by changing the ocean current system, is altering the distribution and migratory patterns of the marine fishes of the open sea, such as the cod, as well as the distribution and abundance of their prey.

Related articles: Acoustic impacts on marine life; Angling for sport; Animal agriculture and climate change; Animal pain; Animals used in research; Cephalopods and decapod crustaceans; CITES and international trade; Commercial whaling; The complexity of animal awareness; The ethics of killing free-living animals; Fish farming; Intelligence in whales and dolphins; Japanese attitudes toward animals; Legislation in the European Union; Perceptions of elephants; The pinnipeds; Primates worldwide; The protection of birds; Shark conservation

Beverton, R. J. H., and Holt, S. J., *On the Dynamics of Exploited Fish Populations*, HMSO, 1957.

Clover, C., *End of the Line: How Overfishing Is Changing the World and What We Eat*, University of California Press, 2008.

Helfman, G., Collette, B. B., Facey, D. H., and Bowen, B. W., *The Diversity of Fishes: Biology, Evolution, and Ecology*, Wiley-Blackwell, 2009.

Longhurst, A., *Mismanagement of Marine Fisheries*, Cambridge University Press, 2010.

Ma, Leung-Hang, Gilland, E., Bass, Andrew H., and Baker, R., "Ancestry of Motor Innervation to Pectoral Fin and Forelimb," *Nature Communications* (2010), doi:10.1038/ncomms1045.

Monbiot, G., "Bluefin Tuna Loses Out Simply Because Scarce Fish Make Profit: Stocks Will Collapse after a Few More Seasons of Fishing at Current Levels, and Investors Will Just Move on to the Next Catch," *Guardian*, March 19, 2010.

Mood, A., *Worse Things Happen at Sea*, Fish Count, 2010, available at http://www.fishcount.org.uk.

Nelson, J. S., *Fishes of the World*, Wiley, 2006.

SIDNEY J. HOLT

SEA TURTLES IN THE MEDITERRANEAN

There are two main threats to the survival of the world's sea turtles. The first is the disruption to the beaches where the turtles come to nest, and the second is the accidental catching of turtles by fishers. Both factors are especially apparent in the Mediterranean. Fishing is, of course, common throughout the region, and often the beaches where tourists delight in spending their hard-earned and much-deserved vacations are the same beaches where these marine reptiles need to come ashore at night to lay their eggs in the sand.

Of the seven species in the world, two nest in the Mediterranean: the greens (*Chelonia mydas*) and the loggerheads (*Caretta caretta*). Of the former, there are only about 339–360 female adults left—the result of intense exploitation for food, oil, and artifacts in the 1950s and 1960s.

Sea turtles have lungs, not gills, and have to surface at regular intervals to breathe. They feed principally on sponges, small fish, mollusks, and squid and browse the sea grass beds. Many of them are caught up in active or discarded fishing gear. In 2001, there was a report of a single fishing boat off the Mediterranean coast of Spain that accidentally caught as many as four hundred turtles in just one day. Trapped in a fishing net, a turtle is unable to surface in order to breathe and quickly drowns. Caught on a hook, the turtle is dragged to the boat, where either the line is cut, leaving the creature to escape with a hook embedded in his or her gullet, or the animal is killed or maimed by the fisher for spoiling his catch. Tens of thousands are caught or killed each year through interaction with fisheries in the Mediterranean. It is not known how many of these survive.

Sea turtles can migrate thousands of miles across seas and oceans to nest and feed. Researchers have fitted sea turtles with radio transmitters and monitored their movements with overhead satellites. Even when the turtles do manage to reach the sandy shore and lay their eggs, their potential offspring are still not safe. Most nesting beaches will, during a season, also accommodate hundreds, even thousands, of tourists who disturb the sand by spreading towels, setting up umbrellas, playing games, and making sand castles. As a result, the eggs incubating beneath the surface of the warm sand may be destroyed unwittingly by people.

Sea turtles are biologically programmed to return to the same region where they hatched to lay their own eggs fifteen to fifty years later, depending on the species. Imagine returning to find yourself in the middle of the grounds of an industrial complex, or under a sun bed, while at the same time battered and confused by the noise from discos or distracted by the lights that will also attract the hatchlings away from the sea, to where they will perish with the sunrise. Small wonder that many females, rather than face the trauma of a trip ashore, abort their eggs on the sea floor where they rot.

To return to their point of origin, turtles may even have to swim through raw sewage or toxic waste, as happened twice in 2001 in Kazanli in Turkey, when the sea was turned red by the spill of toxic waste from the nearby Soda Chrome factory. This is one of the most important nesting beaches for the green turtles in the Mediterranean. Often they emerged from the sea at night encrusted with the residue discharged by the factory, looking like ghostly white apparitions.

While resting on the surface of the water to recover their strength between exhaustive nesting expeditions, they have to run the gauntlet of lethal speedboat propellers and buzzing jet skis. In 1999, a graduate student doing her dissertation on the impact of tourism on the nesting beaches of Laganas Bay sea turtles on the Greek Island of Zakynthos recorded that "the daily location of the turtles in the bay was marked by the six or seven turtle trip boats clustered closely together. They circled the turtles, blocking them in and forcing them to surface for air in the centre of the circle." Persistent reports, campaigns, lobbying, and appeals to the European Commission and to the European Ombudsman resulted in the opening of a case at the European Court of Justice, which led to the presidential decree providing the constitution for the Zakynthos National Marine Park in Laganas Bay in 1999. Eventually, in 2007, the case was closed; however, problems of poor implementation of measures to protect sea turtles persist.

Although it is illegal to kill turtles, in some parts of the Mediterranean they are still eaten as food. Until recently, sea turtles were openly butchered and sold in the fish market of Alexandria in Egypt. Action by the Mediterranean Association to Save the Sea Turtles (MEDASSET) in collaboration with the Friends of the Environment of Alexandria has successfully reduced this trade, but it continues underground.

There can be no future for sea turtles and other sea creatures unless human beings are prepared to think considerately and act generously. In the words of Dr.

Karen Eckert, "regardless of the regulatory framework, sea turtles live or die every day as a result of decisions made by fishermen, coastal landowners, and others, that encounter them. In order for a sea turtle to live another day, the person who encounters it has to live in a world where it makes sense to watch 100 lb of meat swim away."

Related articles: The ethics of killing free-living animals; Legislation in the European Union; Sea fishes and commercial fishing

Bjorndal, K. A. (ed.), *Biology and Conservation of Sea Turtles*, rev. ed., Smithsonian Institution Press, 1995.
Bolton, A. B., and Witherington, B. E. (eds.), *Loggerhead Sea Turtles*, Smithsonian Books, 2003.
Gulko, D., and Eckert, K., *Sea Turtles: An Ecological Guide*, Manual, 2004.
Lutz, P. L., and Musick, J. A., *The Biology of Sea Turtles*, CRC, 1997.
Ripple, J., *Sea Turtles*, Colin Baxter Photography, 1996.
Spotila, J. R., *Sea Turtles: A Complete Guide to Their Biology, Behavior, and Conservation*, Johns Hopkins University Press, 2004.

LILY THERESE VENIZELOS

SHARK CONSERVATION

Sharks are among the most maligned and misunderstood animals on earth. For many, the word *shark* evokes images of fearsome, menacing predators, of "killing machines" who cruise our shores. Sharks are indeed finely adapted predators, sculpted by more than 400 million years of evolution, but most of the roughly four hundred shark species pose no threat to humans. And although shark attacks do occur, they are relatively infrequent and result in very few human fatalities. By contrast, people kill tens of millions of sharks and shark-like fishes each year. Research published in 2006 indicates that between 26 and 73 million sharks are killed annually for the shark fin trade alone.

Sharks are cartilaginous fishes (known as "elasmobranchs"), representing roughly 1 percent of all living fishes. The first shark species pre-date the earliest dinosaurs by 100 million years. Sharks are integral to almost every marine ecosystem on earth. They range in size from the tiny spined pygmy shark (roughly fifteen centimeters in length) to the plankton-eating whale shark, the world's largest fish, which can grow to twenty meters. As top predators, sharks play a crucial role in regulating the marine food chain and keeping other species' populations in balance.

Like many terrestrial top predators, sharks are extremely vulnerable to exploitation. They are slow to mature and reproduce, and they typically produce very few young at a time. The spiny dogfish, for example, reaches maturity around twenty years of age. It has a gestation period of eighteen to twenty-four months and then produces an average of only six to eight pups.

People have long used sharks for food and numerous other purposes, but human pressure on sharks has increased dramatically in recent decades. Today, these ancient predators are threatened by overfishing, indiscriminate fishing technology, and increasing demand for shark products, especially fins. As traditional, commercially valuable fish stocks have declined as a result of overfishing, targeted fishing for sharks has increased. Although precise catch levels or numbers of individuals are difficult to quantify, the United Nations Food and Agriculture Organization (FAO) reported in 2008 that the global shark catch averaged more than 800,000 metric tons per year over the preceding decade. Shark catches, however, are notoriously underreported to the FAO. A 2009 analysis of shark-fin flow through Hong Kong markets indicated significantly higher annual catch levels —perhaps three to four times the FAO estimates.

The globalization of modern, industrial fishing technology has been devastating for sharks. Industrial boats fish for target species with drift nets and longlines that extend for miles. These methods are highly indiscriminate, resulting in the accidental bycatch of millions of sharks each year. The FAO estimates that half of all sharks taken are caught as bycatch in other fisheries. Sharks are ill-equipped to sustain high fishing pressure. Almost all targeted shark fisheries have exhibited a "boom and bust" pattern: increased fishing effort yields initially high catches, followed by population crash and—if stocks are protected—extremely slow recovery. Some populations have declined by as much as 90 percent.

Perhaps the greatest threat to sharks comes from the unsustainable, ever-increasing demand for shark fins, an expensive delicacy in Chinese cuisine. Wealth has increased in Asia since the late 1980s, and the custom of eating shark fin soup, once derided by the Chinese authorities as elitist, has become politically acceptable among China's growing middle class. The resulting demand for shark fin soup has skyrocketed, transforming the shark fin industry into a global gold rush. Shark fins are by far the most valuable part of the shark: a single, high-quality fin may sell for hundreds of dollars, and a bowl of shark fin soup can fetch one hundred dollars. In an effort to maximize profits and conserve hold space, fishers often "fin" sharks at sea, slicing off the fins and tossing the shark—sometimes still alive—back into the ocean. Ninety-five percent of the shark's body goes unused. It is unsustainable, and if the shark is still alive when finned, it is also cruel.

The quest for valuable fins, combined with severe declines in some shark populations, has led to illegal fishing in marine reserves—among the few places where sharks are protected. Fishing operations now illegally target marine reserves for sharks, sometimes virtually extinguishing local populations. Despite mounting pressures, there are virtually no international protections for sharks. As of 2012, only three shark species—whale sharks, basking sharks, and great white sharks—were regulated through CITES, plus all species of sawfishes. Moreover, few countries manage their shark fisheries. A handful of countries have adopted legislation to ban finning in domestic waters—including the United States, the European Union, and some twenty other fishing nations—but the strength of these laws varies, and no international finning prohibition exists. Lack of knowledge about sharks—from basic biology to population levels— further hinders efforts to conserve them.

In 2009, the IUCN estimated that one-third of the world's open-ocean shark species were threatened with extinction, primarily as a result of overfishing. Losing shark populations could have serious ecological and economic implications worldwide, including effects on populations of other marine species and significant impacts on coastal communities. Sharks are also the focus of the growing dive-tourism industry, which brings millions of dollars to coastal and national economies each year, suggesting that sharks are worth more alive than dead. The global shark crisis is a critical test of our ability to manage our exploited marine environment. We must decrease bycatch, cease shark "finning," gather more data, improve enforcement of existing regulations, and implement national and international measures to manage shark fisheries sustainably. Most importantly, we must reduce the demand for shark products—especially fins. Global shark conservation should be of paramount importance to all those who care for these ancient predators on ecological, economic, cultural, or moral grounds.

Related articles: Animals in Asia; Animals in Chinese culture; Animals used in research; The ethics of killing free-living animals; Japanese attitudes toward animals; Sea fishes and commercial fishing

Earle, Sylvia A., *The World Is Blue: How Our Fate and the Ocean's Are One*, National Geographic Society, 2009.
Pew Environment Group, *Navigating Global Shark Conservation: Current Measures and Gaps*, 2012, available at http://www.pewenvironment.org/uploadedFiles/PEG/Publications/Report/Navigating%20Global%20Shark%20

Conservation_Current%20Measures%20and%20Gaps%20 7%206%2012.pdf.

Roberts, Callum, *The Unnatural History of the Sea*, Island Press, 2007.

Terborgh, John, and Estes, James A., *Trophic Cascades: Predators, Prey and the Changing Dynamics of Nature*, Island Press, 2010.

Thorson, Erica, and Wold, Chris, *Back to Basics: An Analysis of the Object and Purpose of CITES and a Blueprint for Implementation*, International Environmental Law Project, 2010.

Watts, Susie, *Shark Finning: Unrecorded Wastage on a Global Scale*, WildAid, 2003.

WildAid, *The End of the Line*, WildAid and Oceana, 2007.

ELIZABETH MURDOCK

STRANDED MARINE MAMMALS

When dolphins, whales, seals, or sea turtles come ashore, they capture our attention. Indeed, for aeons, one of these animals on the beach was considered an economic bonanza for the local community. The stranded animal meant food, oil for heat and light, bones for tools, and skins for warmth. In the last half-century, the response to stranded animals has thankfully changed in many parts of the world. Now the emphasis is on humane care and treatment, with first priority given to returning the animal to the ocean.

In the United States, when dolphins or whales come ashore in numbers, they command massive and sympathetic media attention. Television networks broadcast heartrending images of these deepwater animals floundering on the beach, images that create a stark contrast to our visions of majestic and graceful animals diving in the open ocean. More often, however, marine mammals strand without media attention, as single animals or in small groups. Recreational beach walkers frequently try to care for these animals, unaware that their very presence further jeopardizes the animals' chance of survival. Whether marine animals come ashore singly or in large numbers, they face uncertain futures. Their ultimate fate is often determined not by their condition when they arrived on the beach nor by the people who offer their assistance, but by the lack of appropriate medical facilities for their care.

In many regions of the world, there is a well coordinated response to the report of a stranded marine animal. In the United States, the handling of marine mammals and sea turtles is regulated by the federal government, and only those organizations authorized by the National Marine Fisheries Service may respond to a stranding. In the last three decades, a national network of veterinarians, scientists, people trained in beach response, and

volunteers has developed. Network members are prepared to provide a rapid response and are equipped with medical assessment tools.

Their initial response is best described as a decision tree, a series of questions where different answers mean different subsequent steps: What is the animal's condition—dead or alive? If the animal is dead, network members perform a necropsy (animal autopsy) to determine the cause of death and take tissue samples for more detailed analysis. The animal is then disposed of, often with the skeleton going to a university or museum.

If the animal is alive, the next level of questions determines his or her fate: is the animal well enough to be put back in the water immediately? Or does the animal need medical care before returning to the water? If the animal is well enough for an immediate release, the network staff and volunteers determine the best strategy—for example, transport the animal to a better site for release or attempt to turn the animal around and encourage him or her into deeper water from the stranding site. In either case, before the animal is released, vital statistics about the animal's condition, the stranding site, and circumstances are recorded, and the animal is humanely tagged for identification in case of re-stranding.

If the animal needs medical care, the next step varies with the region of the country and the species of the animal. In the northeastern region of the United States, the major aquariums occasionally accept a seal pup for rehabilitation. A dolphin or small whale might be accepted if the aquarium's largest medical pool is not being used for an aquarium priority (care of its resident population or its breeding program). Staff workload is often the determinant in accepting an animal for medical care. The shortage of appropriate facilities (which must meet federal regulations) often determines an animal's fate as much as the animal's medical condition. If there is no available facility, the animal must be euthanized or, if it is a seal, left on the beach with the hope that the animal will recover on his or her own. Most often, this is not the case.

In Massachusetts, a group of area residents is changing that outcome by creating a facility dedicated to providing medical care for stranded marine animals. The primary mission of the National Marine Life Center (NMLC), a nongovernmental, nonprofit organization, is the rehabilitation and release of stranded marine animals. Education and research are secondary missions. Education programs include public education in a science museum created in the marine animal hospital, programs for school groups, and internships for college students and graduate students specializing in veterinary medicine. Research includes coordinating data from strandings, in itself a relatively new field of endeavor, as well as improving medical care for these animals. The research is noninvasive and entirely benign.

The NMLC, as part of the national stranding network, serves as a regional hospital to the area's highly effective beach response teams. The founders' hope is to add to marine animal conservation programs, both by returning more stranded animals from threatened or endangered species to their breeding populations and by adding to the body of knowledge that can be used in continuing conservation efforts.

If you encounter a stranded marine animal, call your local stranding network hotline or police department or the natural resource officer in your town. Do not attempt to approach the animal. Set up a perimeter to keep people and dogs away until authorized personnel arrive.

Related articles: Animals and the major media; Conservation philosophy; Euthanasia; Intelligence in whales and dolphins; The pinnipeds; Sanctuaries and rehabilitation; Sea turtles in the Mediterranean

Berta, Annalisa, Sumich, James L., and Kovacs, Kit M., *Marine Mammals: Evolutionary Biology*, 2nd ed., Academic Press, 2006.

Evans, Peter G. H., and Raga, Juan Antonio, *Marine Mammals: Biology and Conservation*, Kluwer Academic/Plenum, 2001.

Gales, Nick, Hindell, Mark, and Kirkwood, Roger (eds.), *Marine Mammals: Fisheries, Tourism and Management Issues*, CSIRO, 2003.

Geraci, Joseph R., and Lounsbury, Valerie J., *Marine Mammals Ashore: A Field Guide for Strandings*, 2nd ed., National Aquarium in Baltimore, 2005.

Hoelzel, A. Rus (ed.), *Marine Mammal Biology: An Evolutional Approach*, Blackwell Science, 2002.

Perrin, William F., Würsig, Bernd, and Thewissen, J. G. M. (eds.), *Encyclopedia of Marine Mammals*, 2nd ed., Academic Press, 2008.

Reynolds, John Elliott (ed.), *Marine Mammal Research: Conservation beyond Crisis*, Johns Hopkins University Press, 2005.

SALLIE K. RIGGS

UNDERSTANDING AMPHIBIANS

This class of vertebrate animals includes over five thousand species of frogs and toads, hundreds of species of newts and salamanders, and nearly two hundred species of legless, burrowing creatures called caecilians (no general vernacular name).

The class has existed since the Devonian era, in which the fishes began, but most are post-Jurassic, with many extinct forms. Some scientists think they evolved from the lobe-finned fishes, whereas others think they are of multiple origins, as are the fishes and cetaceans. Most have an aquatic (freshwater) gill-breathing larval stage—the stage of tadpoles—and the adults can live in or out of water and breathe by lungs and through their moist, scaleless skin. The adults are generally carnivorous, as are tadpoles. Reproductive systems vary tremendously; several species care for their eggs after laying them and the larvae, particularly by retaining them inside or outside their bodies. Most lay considerable numbers of eggs at each spawning, but not so many as the bony fishes.

Almost all amphibian species and populations have declined drastically in recent decades, and several are close to extinction. The global causes of this are not well understood, but the use of pesticides in agriculture, the eradication of the insects many of them feed on, water pollution of all kinds, climate change, and the loss of clean aquatic habitat are all certainly involved. The large-scale use of some frogs in medical testing has resulted in the global spread of some lethal diseases affecting amphibians. The species concerned are laboratory-bred, and there is a serious problem of ensuring their well-being in captivity and in experiments. Other factors include increasing "harvesting" of frogs as gourmet food, the home aquarium trade, and the use of common frog species as "type" vertebrate species for dissection by students of biology. The aquarium trade is a particularly serious threat to mostly small tropical species, many of which have spectacular coloration. Overall the amphibians are considered to be the most endangered class of all animals.

Given that they are in a general sense an "intermediate" between fishes and other, mainly terrestrial vertebrates (but not in a direct line), it is reasonable to presume that amphibians have sensory and neural systems as fully capable of feeling pain and experiencing fear as fishes, mammals, and birds. There appears to be little research so far related to the welfare of amphibians, but several Web sites are devoted to this matter regarding frogs, especially those raised in captivity.

Everyone is familiar with the noises made by frogs at certain times, though not all with the variety of sonic communication. It has recently been shown that tadpoles too emit a considerable variety of sounds and ultrasounds, some at least with meanings in their communication with others of the same species. Hence, in terms of animal protection, amphibians deserve the same consideration at least as other vertebrates, together with protection from extinction-threatening environmental deterioration.

ACT Animal Welfare Advisory Committee, "Code of Practice for the Welfare of Amphibians," available at http://www.tams.act.gov.au/.

Canadian Council on Animal Care, *Guide to the Care and Use of Experimental Animals* 1 (1980) and 2 (1984).

Natale, Guillermo S., Alcalde, Leandro, Herrera, Raul, Cajade, Rodrigo, Schaefer, Eduardo F., Marangoni, Federico, and Trudeau, Vance L., "Underwater Acoustic Communication in the Macrophagic Carnivorous Larvae of *Ceratophrys ornata* (Anura: Ceratophryidae)," first record of sound production by Anuran larvae, *Acta Zoologica* (2010).

Reed, Barney T., *Guidance on the Housing and Care of the African Clawed Frog*, Royal Society for the Prevention of Cruelty to Animals, 2005, available at http://www.rspca.org.uk/.

U.S. Department of Agriculture, Animal Welfare Information Center, "Information Resources on Amphibians," available at http://www.nal.usda.gov/awic/pubs/Amphibians/.

SIDNEY J. HOLT

WEST INDIAN MANATEES

West Indian manatees are large, gray-brown, aquatic mammals with bodies that taper to a flat, paddle-shaped tail. They have two flippers with three to four nails on each, and their head and face are wrinkled, with whiskers on the snout. Their closest relatives are the elephant and the hyrax (a small furry animal resembling a rodent). Manatees are believed to have evolved from a wading, plant-eating animal. The West Indian manatee is related to the West African manatee, the Amazonian manatee, the dugong, and Steller's sea cow, which was hunted to extinction in 1768. The average adult manatee is about ten feet long and weighs approximately eight hundred to twelve hundred pounds.

Manatees can be found in shallow, slow-moving rivers, estuaries, saltwater bays, canals, and coastal areas. Manatees are a migratory species. Within the United States, West Indian manatees are concentrated in Florida in the winter, but they can be found in summer months as far west as Texas and as far north as Virginia. They can also be found in the coastal and inland waterways of Central America and along the northern coast of South America, although distribution in these areas may be patchy.

Manatees are gentle and slow-moving animals. Most of their time is spent eating, resting, and traveling. Manatees are completely herbivorous. They eat aquatic plants and can consume 10 to 15 percent of their body weight daily in vegetation. They graze for food along water bottoms and on the surface of the water. They may rest submerged at the bottom or just below the surface, coming up to breathe on average about every three to five minutes. When manatees are using a great deal of energy, they may surface to breathe as often as every thirty seconds.

Manatees have no natural enemies, and it is believed they can live sixty years or more. Many manatee mortalities are human-related, and in the United States, where there are approximately three thousand West Indian manatees left, such mortalities result mainly from collisions with watercraft. Other causes of human-related mortalities include being crushed or drowned in canal locks and flood-control structures; ingestion of fish hooks, litter, and monofilament line; entanglement in crab trap lines; and vandalism. Loss of habitat, however, is the most serious threat facing manatees today.

The reproductive rate for manatees is slow. Female manatees are not sexually mature until five years of age, and males are mature at approximately seven years of age. It is believed that one calf is born every two to five years; twins are rare. The gestation period is approximately thirteen months. Mothers nurse their young for a long period, and a calf may remain dependent on his or her mother for up to two years.

West Indian manatees in the United States are protected under federal law by the Marine Mammal Protection Act of 1972 and the Endangered Species Act of 1973, which make it illegal to harass, hunt, capture, or kill any marine mammal. West Indian manatees are also protected by the Florida Manatee Sanctuary Act of 1978, which states that "it is unlawful for any person, at any time, intentionally or negligently, to annoy, molest, harass, or disturb any manatee." Anyone convicted of violating Florida's state law faces a possible maximum fine of $500 and/or imprisonment for up to sixty days. Conviction on the federal level is punishable by a fine of up to $1,000 and/or one year in prison.

The Manatee Recovery Plan was developed as a result of the Endangered Species Act. It is coordinated by the U.S. Fish and Wildlife Service and sets forth a list of tasks geared toward recovering manatees from their current endangered status.

In October 1989, Florida's governor and cabinet directed the Florida Department of Environmental Protection to work with thirteen "key" manatee counties in Florida to reduce injuries and deaths. These counties include Duval, Volusia, Citrus, Brevard, Indian River, St. Lucie, Martin, Palm Beach, Broward, Dade, Collier, Lee, and Sarasota. Over 80 percent of manatee mortalities have occurred in these counties. The first task of these county governments, working with the state, is to develop site-specific boat speed zones to reduce watercraft collisions. The second task is to develop comprehensive manatee protection plans at the local level.

Other conservation measures deemed important include benign research covering the biology, mortality, population and distribution, behavior, and habitat of manatees; the posting of regulatory speed signs and the levying of fines for excess speeds in designated areas;

manatee education and public awareness programs; and the public acquisition of critical habitat and the creation of sanctuaries.

Related articles: Conservation philosophy; Developments in animal law; The ethics of killing free-living animals; Sanctuaries and rehabilitation

Powell, James, *Manatees*, Voyageur Press, 2002.

Reep, Roger L., and Bonde, Robert K., *The Florida Manatee: Biology and Conservation*, University Press of Florida, 2006.

Reynolds, John E., *Biology of Marine Mammals*, Smithsonian Books, 2007.

Reynolds, John E., and Odell, Daniel K., *Manatees and Dugongs*, Facts on File, 1991.

Ripple, Jeff, *Manatees and Dugongs of the World*, Voyageur Press, 2002.

Tripp, Katie, "Manatees: Ancient Marine Mammals in a Modern Coastal Environment," *Ocean Challenge* 16.3 (2009): 14–22.

KATIE TRIPP

three

FREE-LIVING ANIMALS

The focus in this section is on those free-living (otherwise known as "wild") animals who share the planet with us.

The subject is so broad that we have found it necessary to divide the material into subsections. The first concerns animals in captivity, notably in research centers, aquariums, zoos, and menageries. The second looks at issues of preservation and killing, including the conflicts between animal protection and conservation. The third focuses on sixteen species worldwide, from chimpanzees to beavers, and examines how they fare at the hands of humans. Some of these species are legally protected—others, not so—but it soon becomes clear that even those who are protected are still persecuted or hunted.

The fourth subsection looks at the increasingly important area of international trade. As globalization moves apace, so free-living creatures become increasingly the target of commercial trade, whether they are reptiles, primates, or animals killed for their fur. Although the Convention on International Trade in Endangered Species of Wild Fauna and Flora (CITES) sets down some limits, they are not enough to prevent continued abuse and suffering. The World Trade Organization continues to pose a major threat to animals as markets are opened up and animal protection concerns are marginalized.

ANDREW LINZEY

ANIMALS IN CAPTIVITY

CAPTIVE CHIMPANZEES

In the United States, there are more than 1,600 chimpanzees in biomedical research, and close to a third of them are considered "surplus." There are another approximately 550 chimpanzees in other biomedical research facilities around the world. Approximately 300 chimpanzees are imprisoned in zoos in the United States, and another 1,700 around the world. Estimates of the number of chimpanzees used as companion animals or in the entertainment industry in the United States are difficult to make. One estimate is that perhaps 600 chimpanzees are kept as companion animals or as animals for entertainment.

Around one hundred chimpanzees in the United States and Canada are kept in legitimate sanctuaries where their retirement is permanent. There are more than a dozen sanctuaries in eleven countries in Africa that have over five hundred chimpanzees, and it is estimated that more than fifteen hundred chimpanzees are held illegally as companion animals in these same countries. In Uganda, it is illegal to own a chimpanzee or use him or her in entertainment or research. Therefore, the only two places where chimpanzees can legally exist are their natural environment in forests or sanctuaries where the confiscated chimpanzees are kept. Compare this to the United States, where we continue to use them in life-threatening biomedical research, imprison them in zoos in the name of education, and steal babies from their mothers to sell as companion animals or to force them into demeaning commercial entertainment.

The arc of a chimpanzee life in the United States is neither pleasant nor short, when we bear in mind that they can live more than sixty years. The Fauna Foundation is a legitimate sanctuary in Canada that is refuge for fifteen chimpanzees who came from a biomedical lab that closed. Billy Jo's story is all too common. A biomedical lab purchased him along with another chimpanzee, Sue Ellen, in 1983 after they had been used for fifteen years in the entertainment industry. During those years,

Billy Jo and Sue Ellen had their teeth knocked out with a crow bar. When Billy Jo was sold to the lab, he received a new name: "Ch-447." In the subsequent fourteen years he spent in the lab, he was "knocked down" 289 times, 65 of which times involved four or five men surrounding his small cage, darting him with a dart gun. In addition to several HIV challenges, Billy Jo was the recipient of forty liver punch biopsies, three open wedge liver biopsies, three bone marrow biopsies, and two lymph node biopsies. His present caregivers note that the researchers found no evidence of tangible or practical results from these protocols. Upon waking up alone from one of the knockdowns, he chewed off both his thumbs, and another time, during an anxiety attack, he bit off his index finger. Even today, at his new safe home in Canada, he still suffers from anxiety attacks that leave this handsome adult male choking, gagging, and convulsing, with his persistent fears. There are fourteen other stories like Billy Jo's on the Fauna Foundation's Web site, http://www.faunafoundation.org.

In the name of "progress," we continue to use members of an endangered species in the hope of helping an overpopulated species—namely, humans—become more overpopulated. Babies continue to be stolen from their mothers to be infected with some disease or turned into robots and clowns for the entertainment industry while they are still small and easy to dominate. The training comes from a tradition of domination—namely, physical and mental abuse to control the babies. When they become juveniles, they become too strong, and many are sold into biomedical research or turned into "breeders" so that more babies can be stolen from their mothers. Only a few of them are ever "retired," if a maximum-security prison can even be considered retirement.

The future does not hold much hope for chimpanzees. During the initial HIV panic, the biomedical industry bred chimpanzees in the hope of turning them into profitable tools for HIV research. Their failure has produced a so-called surplus of chimpanzees estimated to be between six hundred and one thousand individuals.

One solution to this problem, published as a minority report by the National Research Council of the United States National Academy of Sciences in 1997, was simply to kill them (the proposed action was referred to in the report as euthanasia, which is a misuse of the term since their deaths would not benefit the chimpanzees, but rather benefit only the financial interests of the organizations holding them). This solution was, thankfully, discarded. The final result was a bill passed in the United States Congress, and signed by the president, to establish alternative places to put the "surplus" chimpanzees. However, these places do not constitute permanent or safe retirement since the animals can be recalled to active research at any time by the biomedical organization that placed them there, and moreover, any babies born there must be returned to be used in research. Because of these requirements, no legitimate sanctuaries will be able to take the chimpanzees.

The only hope left for captive chimpanzees is their release as compatible social groups into large, protected, legitimate sanctuaries. There are a few successful sanctuaries in Africa, where social groups of twenty or more are provided areas of five hundred acres enclosed by electric fences. In the United States, there are few signs that this path is going to be followed, though a few people are directing a great deal of effort to improve conditions for chimpanzees. One legitimate sanctuary, Save the Chimps (http://www.savethechimps.org), actually brought a lawsuit against the United States Air Force and was able to settle for the release of twenty-one of the chimpanzees used in the U.S. space program. Others continue to work on gaining legal status for captive apes, to remove them from entertainment and prevent private enslavement.

Related articles: Animals in circuses; Animals used in research; The ethics of zoos; Euthanasia; Free-living chimpanzees; The legal rights of great apes; Primates worldwide; Sanctuaries and rehabilitation; The trade in primates for research

Cavalieri, P., and Singer, P. (eds.), *The Great Ape Project*, St. Martin's Press, 1994.

Corbey, R., and Theunissen, B. (eds.), *Ape, Man and Apeman: Changing Views since 1600*, Lieden University, 1995.

Fouts, R., "Apes, Darwinian Continuity and the Law," *Animal Law* 10 (2004): 99–124.

Fouts, R. S., and Fouts, D. H., "Chimpanzees," in Bekoff, M., and Meaney, C. (eds.), *Encyclopedia of Animal Rights and Animal Welfare*, Greenwood, 1998, 105–107.

Fouts, R. S., and Mills, S. T., *Next of Kin*, William Morrow, 1997.

Siddle, S., and Cress, D., *In My Family Tree: A Life with Chimpanzees*, Grove Press, 2002.

ROGER FOUTS AND DEBORAH FOUTS

THE ETHICS OF ZOOS

Two central ethical questions arise from the consideration of zoos: First, do they succeed or fail in meeting the needs of the captive animals on display? And second, do they or do they not provide the human spectator with a valuable experience?

Concerning the animal needs question, one might argue (as do many zookeepers and patrons) that zoos provide better care than what animals might expect if they were living free in nature: veterinary care, a stable food supply, protection from predators. Breaking down the overly large category of "animals" into specific species and even individual animals, one might argue that some animals (injured animals, perhaps, or smaller animals or animals who naturally live in a climate similar to that of a given zoo) would fare better than animals who are accustomed to a larger range or who have habitats more obviously irreproducible in captivity.

Against this proposition, consider that freedom is generally considered ethically and practically preferable to captivity—certainly this is true for human beings, and it would seem intuitively true for other animals as well. Although some animals might seem more comfortable than others in a cage (or what zoos sometimes paradoxically refer to as "cageless enclosures," designed to make the human spectators more comfortable, if not the inmates themselves), we could easily find aspects of the captive experience that are different from and inferior to what any animal, no matter how small or docile, would experience in his or her natural life.

Another strand of the animal needs question concerns zoos' activities on behalf of endangered species. Supporters claim that zoos protect groups of animals whose existence has become precarious as a result of habitat degradations and that zoo programs rescue species that might be near extinction. Skeptics respond that such rescue programs serve mainly to appeal to zoo audiences' desire to see themselves as being involved in important conservation work, but actually do little good.

Expenditures on conservational programs tend to be small proportions of zoos' operating budgets, and the motivation behind the selection of species in such programs often seems to be based less on actual ecological urgency and more on the animals' popular cultural appeal: "charismatic megafauna" (as zoo professionals describe the blockbuster animal attractions—e.g., panda bears) are disproportionately represented. And finally, zoologists warn that it is very difficult to breed many species in captivity and especially difficult to preserve wide and healthy gene pools. When zoos undertake such conservation programs, critics argue that the point is mainly to sustain the animals' availability on the zoo circuit for a few more generations; ironically, the animals' appeal may be enhanced since their species is rare and possibly soon to vanish.

The real value of captive breeding programs would be the ultimate reintroduction of species to their natural state, and this is a rare occurrence (habitat restoration is much more difficult—and expensive—than breeding a few specimens for display). Zoos frequently describe their conservation activities using the trope of Noah's ark, but the allegory breaks down when one considers that the story of Noah describes the release of the animals back into nature after the dangers have passed.

For spectators, zoos are promoted as educational and entertaining. Those who support zoos presumably believe that these benefits come with no negative consequences to the animals; those who oppose zoos argue that the spectacle is inherently demeaning—in the tradition of circuses, organ grinders, piano-playing chickens, and painting elephants—and that the power dynamics of free human visitors outside the cages observing trapped, displaced, decontextualized animals inside the cages reinforce ecologically oppressive symbolism about human supremacy and the subaltern inferiority of other species.

If zoos were effective venues of education, presumably the hundreds of millions of annual zoo visits would result in an enlightened ecological concern for animal rights and conservation, which is unfortunately not apparent in contemporary society. Critics see zoos as "greenwashing": making it seem as if people care about animals, but in reality representing a token and insubstantial ethical commitment to trans-species living that makes it possible for us to go about our highly consumptive and unsustainable habits without reckoning the toll this takes on animal populations and habitats. Zoos offer an opportunity for people to observe animals conveniently: on our own terms and in our own neighborhoods. It may be argued that this constitutes miseducation—a delusory vision of how other animals really live in our world.

Related articles: Animals in circuses; Conservation philosophy; The ethics of reintroduction; Humane education; Roadside zoos and menageries; The scientific claims of zoos

Acampora, Ralph (ed.), *Metamorphoses of the Zoo: Animal Encounter after Noah*, Lexington, 2010.

Baratay, Eric, and Hardouin-Fugier, Elisabeth, *Zoo: A History of Zoological Gardens in the West*, Reaktion, 2002.

Jaschinski, Britta, *Zoo*, Phaidon, 1996.

Malamud, Randy, *Reading Zoos: Representations of Animals and Captivity*, Macmillan and New York University Press, 1998.

Mullan, Bob, and Marvin, Garry, *Zoo Culture*, University of Illinois Press, 1998.

Rothfels, Nigel, *Savages and Beasts: The Birth of the Modern Zoo*, Johns Hopkins University Press, 2002.

RANDY MALAMUD

MARINE MAMMALS IN CAPTIVITY

One of the most popular groups of animals in the world is the order of mammals known as cetaceans: dolphins and whales. These aquatic animals with large heads, nearly hairless fishlike bodies, and paddle-shaped forelimbs have earned a place in the hearts of millions of people worldwide. The majority of cetaceans kept captive in aquariums today belong to the families Delphinidae (bottlenose dolphins and killer whales) and Monodontidae (beluga whales). In nature, most cetaceans live in social groupings called pods that consist of a number of individuals of varying ages who play, feed, and travel together. Family bonds are so strong in some species, such as killer whales, that certain pod members will remain together for their entire lives.

Cetaceans were first exhibited in captivity in the 1860s, when London's Westminster Aquarium put dolphins on display. Their popularity with the public soon led others to follow suit. One of the biggest boosts to the popularity of cetaceans in captivity occurred in 1962 when the movie *Flipper* was released. Thereon, dolphin shows became immensely popular. Hundreds of dolphins were captured to satisfy an ever-increasing public demand, but few survived very long. Since that time, hundreds of cetaceans have been captured for aquariums around the world. And over the years, public concern about the capture and confinement of these animals has also grown.

When cetaceans are captured from the ocean, they are removed from their natural social structures and forced into artificially controlled groupings. The normal sex ratio, age makeup, number of animals per pod, and space they inhabit are vastly different from what they would experience in the ocean environment. Both wild-caught and captive-born cetaceans face numerous problems in captivity, including boredom, frustration, restriction of normal activities, and sensory deprivation. This severely restricted lifestyle can lead to psychological and social disturbances, including the development of stereotypic (meaningless mechanical repetition of a movement or series of movements) swimming patterns, aggressiveness toward other cetaceans and people, establishment of unnatural pecking orders, excessive masturbation, and a range of other aberrant behaviors.

The space, depth, and complexity that cetaceans experience in a natural setting cannot be duplicated in aquariums. Bottlenose dolphins have been known to swim more than twenty-five miles in a single day, and killer whales have been recorded traveling more than one hundred miles. Both can dive to depths exceeding five hundred feet. The physical activity experienced by captive cetaceans falls far short of what each animal would experience in a natural setting. Even the chemical quality of the water can be a matter of concern. Many facilities housing cetaceans chlorinate their pools by adding sodium hypochlorite to the water or by bubbling chlorine gas into the water. This helps decrease the levels of bacteria and nitrogenous waste from the animals' excrement, urine, and uneaten food, but it can be irritating, or even damaging, to cetacean eyes and skin.

The acoustic environment provided for captive cetaceans can also be problematic. Most cetaceans live in a world of sound, utilizing a very sophisticated system of echolocation for hunting and navigating. The confined conditions of captivity make much of the acoustical repertoire of dolphins and whales redundant.

Public education is often cited as a justification for the continued confinement of cetaceans in aquariums. Advocates of captive facilities claim that aquariums play a significant role in educating the public about cetacean welfare and conservation issues, but they have provided virtually no evidence to support their claim. Educated critics believe aquariums do little, if anything, to educate the public. According to Erich Hoyt, in his 1992 report *The Performing Orca: Why The Show Must Stop*, "a number of marine parks world-wide also seem to be jumping on the bandwagon, trying to increase their educational content—from almost nothing, to at least something" (60). Further, Hoyt says, "the educational materials produced as hand-outs, or for sale, by marine parks vary considerably. Most are rather poor in content and quality" (62). In my visits to aquariums around the world, it has not appeared as though a lot has changed since that time.

Captive breeding is repeatedly offered as another justification for keeping cetaceans in captivity, but close examination reveals an unmitigated failure in that regard. Legitimate captive propagation for conservation is far more than breeding animals for zoo and aquarium displays. The goal of captive propagation should be the production of a genetically viable, self-sustaining population of a particular species, with the surplus from that population being reintroduced back into the wild as soon as possible. That has not happened for cetaceans, nor is it even necessary. According to Hoyt, "neither orcas (killer whales) or [*sic*] bottlenose dolphins—the captive

breeding successes that have received most of the attention as well as veterinary expertise and financial backing—are reduced to levels that would normally justify an early start to captive breeding" (58). With more than 100,000 individuals still existing in the wild, the same is true for beluga whales, who now seem to be the preferred choice for aquarium displays.

Author and zoologist Dr. Ronald Orenstein, who has examined beluga breeding in captivity, and commented in 1990, "In twenty three years, breeding success—in biological terms, meaning the production of breeding age adults in captivity—has been zero. In fact, even if young were produced, given that almost a third of the captured animals are now dead, how long will it be before the programme even breaks even in terms of adding to, and not subtracting from, the total beluga population?" It is not much better today. Cetaceans continue to be captured from their natural state to replace those who have died in aquarium tanks around the world. There have been few, if any, captive-bred cetaceans returned to their natural state as part of aquarium industry–sponsored captive propagation programs. For the most part, captive breeding of cetaceans is not successful, but even if it were, it would not help address the challenges faced by cetaceans in the wild.

Cetaceans tend to be far-ranging, deep-diving, highly social predators with biological and ethological needs that are difficult, if not impossible, to satisfy in captivity.

Related articles: Acoustic impacts on marine life; Animals used in research; Commercial whaling; The declaration of the rights of cetaceans; The ethics of zoos; The intelligence of whales and dolphins; The rehabilitation of dolphins

Biting the Hand That Feeds: The Case against Dolphin Petting Pools, Whale and Dolphin Conservation Society and the Humane Society of the United States, 2003.

Brower, Kenneth, *Freeing Keiko: The Journey of a Killer Whale from Free Willy to the Wild*, Gotham Books, 2005.

Davis, Susan G., *Spectacular Nature: Corporate Culture and the Sea World Experience*, University of California Press, 1997.

Hoyt, Erich, *The Performing Orca—Why the Show Must Stop: An In-Depth Review of the Captive Orca Industry*, Whale and Dolphin Conservation Society, 1992.

Jenkins, Leesteffy, *Stopping the Use, Sale and Trade of Whales and Dolphins in Canada: How Protection Is Consistent with WTO Obligations*, Zoocheck Canada, 2003.

Kirby, David, *Death at SeaWorld: Shamu and the Dark Side of Killer Whales in Captivity*, St. Martin's Press, 2012.

Orenstein, Ronald, *The Thin Line: Zoos, Animal Organizations and Conservation* (lecture), conference of the Canadian Association of Zoological Parks and Aquariums, 1990.

Rose, Naomi, "The Well-Being of Captive Marine Mammals:

Concerns and Conflicts," in *The Well-Being of Animals in Zoo and Aquarium Sponsored Research*, Scientists Center for Animal Welfare, 1996.

Rose, Naomi, Farinato, Richard, and Sherwin, Susan, *The Case against Marine Mammals in Captivity*, the Humane Society of the United States and the World Society for the Protection of Animals, 2006.

Williams, Vanessa, *Captive Orcas, "Dying to Entertain You"—The Full Story*, Whale and Dolphin Conservation Society, 2001.

ROB LAIDLAW

ROADSIDE ZOOS AND MENAGERIES

The word *zoo* typically conjures up images of large zoological institutions, such as national zoos located in the centers of major cities. These zoos and a handful of others like them have created the erroneous perception that most zoos are focused on the preservation of endangered species, usually through captive breeding, and conservation education. The public has been led to believe that zoos are modern arks—an important lifeline for vanishing species threatened with extinction. But those claims do not stand up to scrutiny, and few zoos make more than a token contribution in that regard. Many zoos do nothing at all.

Throughout North America, hundreds—perhaps thousands—of amateur zoos, roadside menageries, and "wildlife" displays exhibit captive representatives of free-ranging animals to the public. Some of these displays are little more than a few caged animals used to attract potential customers to a commercial business, whereas others are more like traditional zoos. Commonly referred to as "roadside zoos," these displays are estimated to constitute up to 90 percent of all zoos in North America.

Often started by well-meaning but ill-informed people, many roadside zoos fail to provide even the basic necessities of life to their animals. Their common features are striking: barren, poorly designed cages that are so small they provide almost no opportunity for natural movement or exercise; improper floor surfaces; lack of shelter and privacy; poor-quality feed; filthy water containers; cages littered with feces, candy wrappers, rotting food, and other garbage; and lack of appropriate veterinary care.

Even when roadside zoos are kept clean, and the animals are fed an appropriate diet, psychological and emotional suffering still occurs. The absence of adequate physical and mental stimulation causes many animals to develop abnormal and sometimes self-destructive behaviors. Extreme lethargy; endless pacing, rocking, or head-turning; the pulling out of hair or feathers; tail-biting, leg-chewing, and head-bashing; hyperaggressiveness; and other aberrant behaviors are easily observed in many roadside zoos.

Human safety is also seriously compromised. Zoo staff and the general public are often placed at risk because of poorly constructed cages and enclosures, unlocked doors and gates, lack of facilities to isolate animals during exhibit cleaning, absence of perimeter fencing to discourage escaped animals from leaving zoo property, lack of security and emergency plans, and absence of zookeeper training. Further, many zoos fail to utilize standoff barriers to keep visitors a safe distance from the animal cages.

Conservation education and the preservation of endangered species through captive breeding are the two most commonly cited justifications for the existence of modern zoos. Whether any zoos actually meet these criteria is highly debatable, but we can be confident that roadside zoos make no contribution to either. Basic educational strategies such as interpretive literature, guided tours, meet-the-keeper sessions, school outreach programs, and other educational activities are almost always absent. Even explanatory signs on animal exhibits are often negligible or nonexistent, so the public has little or no information about the animals they observe. The public is often left to view distressed animals they know little about. Roadside zoos present a distorted and diminished view of free-ranging animals and are therefore educationally counterproductive.

Virtually every roadside zoo operator claims to be helping save endangered species, but few of them participate in, and many are not even aware of, recognized captive breeding programs. Most breeding in roadside zoos consists of unplanned births of relatively common animals of whom there is already a surplus in captivity. Eventually, they are dumped into the exotic companion animal trade, the entertainment industry, or other roadside zoos. Many of the animals have an unknown genetic history or are hybrids, so they cannot be assimilated into organized endangered species breeding programs.

Why, then, do roadside zoos proliferate in North America? A patchwork of laws governing the captivity and treatment of animals from free-ranging species is found throughout North America. Unfortunately, many of them fail to address basic animal welfare issues, few contain specific accommodation and care standards, and most are not seriously enforced, if they are enforced at all. National zoo-industry associations in the United States and Canada administer voluntary accreditation programs for member institutions, but there is little incentive for roadside zoos and menageries to join and meet the association's rather minimal standards. And the associations do little if anything to force substandard zoos to close.

As long as zoos exist, efforts must be made to ensure that they place the physical, psychological, and social well-being of animals as their highest priority, and government agencies should enact zoo licensing laws that incorporate tough animal welfare provisions, the ability to conduct comprehensive annual inspections, the right to revoke licenses and shut down substandard zoos, and the establishment of a guaranteed closure fund into which all zoos must pay. Keeping animals from free-living species as companion animals, partly a by-product of the inappropriate disposition of zoo surplus in past years, should also be prohibited. But legislators and the industry have been slow to act.

Related articles: Animal pain; The complexity of animal awareness; Conservation philosophy; Developments in animal law; The ethics of zoos; The scientific claims of zoos

Animal Protection Institute, *A Life Sentence: The Sad and Dangerous Realities of Exotic Animals in Private Hands in the U.S.*, 2006.

Batten, Peter, *Living Trophies: A Shocking Look at the Conditions in America's Zoos*, Thomas Y. Crowell, 1976.

Cowan, Karen, Long, Jennifer, and Laidlaw, Rob, *The State of the Ark: Investigating Ontario's Zoos*, World Society for the Protection of Animals, 2002.

Green, Allan, and the Center for Public Integrity, *Animal Underworld: Inside America's Black Market for Rare and Endangered Species*, Public Affairs, 1999.

International Fund for Animal Welfare, *Fatal Attractions: Big Cats in the USA*, 2006.

Laidlaw, Rob, *Wild Animals in Captivity*, Fitzhenry & Whiteside, 2008.

Zoocheck Canada, *A Review of Zoos in Ontario: Has Anything Changed?*, Zoocheck Canada, 2010.

Zoocheck Canada and WSPA, *Wild Neighbours: The Safety and Security of Ontario's Wildlife in Captivity Facilities*, Zoocheck Canada and World Society for the Protection of Animals, 2010.

ROB LAIDLAW

THE SCIENTIFIC CLAIMS OF ZOOS

Many questions arise from an ethical critique of the practice of science in zoos. Fundamental is when and why the practice arose. For this we have to look back to the 1820s, when scientists of the day decided that it would be useful to hold a collection of animals in London with the stated aim of, as presented in a royal charter granted by King George IV, "the advancement of Zoology and Animal Physiology and the introduction of new and curious subjects of the Animal Kingdom" (Mitchell 38–43). The current stated objective of the world's zoos is "to support animal care and welfare, environmental education and global conservation" (World Association of Zoos and Aquariums).

In the United Kingdom, the Zoo Licensing Act of 1981 requires zoos to be involved in conservation work in order to be licensed and to operate. Determination of compliance with the act relies on inspections by those who "shall have experience of animals of kinds which are kept in zoos or which in the Secretary of State's opinion might be so kept" (Zoo Licensing Act). This is a useful starting point from which to look at the ethics of science in zoos because people who fulfill this criterion cannot be considered objective. That the zoo industry had a major role in the formulation of the act also indicates that it is not an objective regulatory tool.

Zoo activities considered to be scientific include the exchange of information, veterinary care, nutrition, environmental enrichment, animal behavior, captive breeding, reintroduction, conservation, and education. All of these are open to subjective interpretation—for example, "the exchange of information" can simply mean attending a conference on zoo management, an activity far removed from the conservation of animals in their natural state.

Veterinary medicine in zoos is, in the majority of cases, applied to the treatment of infectious diseases, the treatment of physical injuries, the collection of biological samples to support therapies or to aid research, and advice on diets. It can be argued that the diseases and the injuries arise as a result of animals being held in captivity and that the diets that zoo animals are given lack many of the features of food that drive their choices in their natural state—the qualities of smell, texture, color, and manipulation are removed from the process when artificial and prepared food is their only choice.

The study of the behavior of captive animals is just that. An animal behaves according to the condition in which he or she lives; therefore, if animals in zoos suffer less than they would in their natural state, then the behaviors that these animals would undertake to protect themselves from such suffering will be missing in captivity. Also, the three-dimensional environment that an animal has evolved to live in is totally different from the environment found in a zoo. The animal's interaction with the captive environment will therefore make it difficult, if not impossible, for such an animal to be introduced to his or her natural habitat and survive. In order to convince the public that it is committed to the physical and psychological well-being of the animals it holds, the zoo industry hoists the flag of environmental enrichment. In fact environmental enrichment is necessary only because the animals are held in unnatural conditions. It is used more to reduce the guilt felt by zoo staffs and the public than to improve the lives of the captive animals or prepare them for release.

The arguments against zoos and for habitat and ecosystem protection are nowhere better made than in *Extinction: The Causes and Consequences of the Disappearance of Species* (Ehrlich and Ehrlich 207–241). The arguments address the issue from the viewpoint of wanting to ensure that free-living animals remain free in their natural state. It is clear from reading this critique that zoos offer nothing to the cause of conserving species. The breeding of animals in such places is more a publicity-generating activity than it is a conservation one. It is very common to find articles in newspapers and other media covering amusing stories about zoo animals—especially when baby animals are born. This attention is designed to encourage people to visit zoos; it has nothing to do with protecting the planet's animals.

An audit of *in situ* (in the natural habitat) conservation projects supported by the world zoo and aquarium community showed that for the 113 evaluated projects that are attempting to help the conservation of high-profile threatened species and habitats, the "investment made by zoos and aquariums" is "suggestive of an appreciable contribution to global biodiversity conservation" (World Association of Zoos and Aquariums). It is interesting to note the words "suggestive" and "appreciable contribution" in this statement. They imply that the zoo community itself is not prepared to say categorically that it is helping significantly to conserve the planet's animals. Field conservation forms a very small part of what zoos do, and most of their income is spent on maintaining the functions of the zoos—their infrastructure, staff costs, press machinery, and veterinary care.

In 1998 I calculated that, based on the cost of maintaining the Niokolo-Koba National Park in Senegal, the $1 billion per year taken from zoo visitors in the United States would protect 200,000,000 square miles of natural habitat—2 percent more than the surface area of the planet. This is a very simplistic comparison but shows how little the zoo industry contributes to real conservation—preferring instead to maintain its commercial base.

In a 2004 article on zoos in *The Biologist*, the journal of the Society of Biology, Dr. Brian Bertram admits that zoos are a recognized part of the tourism industry, making reference to "providing a good day out for visitors" (199–206). It can be argued that this is the overriding reason most people visit zoos. The zoo environment is designed more for the pleasure of the public than for the benefit of its captive animals. In reality, beyond appearances, things have not changed since the 1820s—the days when "walking in the zoo [was] the OK thing to do" ("Walking in the Zoo," a music hall song made famous by the Great Vance in the 1800s). Having worked in a major U.K. zoo, I strongly believe that zoos are designed more to please the public than to conserve animals or educate.

The overriding conclusion that can be drawn from a close look at the scientific work carried out in zoos is that it has achieved and is achieving nothing of importance in relation to zoos' major claim of conserving the planet's animals for the benefit of future generations—or for the animals' own sake. Conservation is not a zoo issue, but a political one, and making the public believe that zoos are protecting species from extinction masks the enormity of the problem that species face in their natural state, especially from human beings. It means that members of the public believe that they need do nothing to ensure that natural places are protected because zoos are doing it for them, allowing politicians and global businesses to carry on destroying habitats and species unhindered.

Related articles: Conservation philosophy; The ethics of reintroduction; The ethics of zoos; Humane education; Roadside zoos and menageries

Bertram, Brian, "Misconceptions about Zoos," *The Biologist* 51.4 (2004): 199–206, available at http://www.biaza.org.uk/resources/library/images/biologist.pdf.

Ehrlich, Paul, and Ehrlich, Anne, *Extinction: The Causes and Consequences of the Disappearance of Species*, Gollancz, 1981.

Mitchell, P. Chalmers, *Centenary History of the Zoological Society of London*, Zoological Society of London, 1929.

World Association of Zoos and Aquariums, "About WAZA," available at http://www.waza.org.

———, "Conservation through Zoos and Aquariums," available at http://www.waza.org/en/site/conservation.

The Zoo Licensing Act (U.K.), 1981, chapter 37, section 8, subsection 2, available at http://www.legislation.gov.uk/ukpga/1981/37.

DAVID SPRATT

PRESERVATION AND KILLING

ANIMAL PROTECTION AND ENVIRONMENTALISM

It is widely assumed that protecting animals and protecting the environment are one and the same thing. And indeed, both concerns have a lot in common. Both the animal liberation movement and the environmental movement became popular in the 1970s; both are opposed to a blunt anthropocentrism or humanocentrism that deprives the nonhuman natural world of any intrinsic value or dignity. Moreover, in public controversies and campaigns, both animal liberationists and environmentalists frequently act together.

On closer examination, though, there are some significant differences between the ethics of animal protection and environmental ethics, differences that have been the subject of both fierce controversies and academic attempts at mediation and reconciliation. (The subsequent description of their respective views depicts "ideal types," to use Max Weber's term, which most of the time are not as clear-cut in reality.)

First, animal protection is based on a sentiocentric or pathocentric ethics that holds that all sentient creatures—those who are capable of feeling pleasure and pain—have interests or rights and are therefore to be treated accordingly. Nature devoid of sentience does not deserve the same consideration and respect. A mouse, as Peter Singer argues, does have an interest in not being kicked along the road, because he will suffer if he is treated this way. A stone, on the other hand, does not have interests, because it cannot suffer. By contrast, environmentalism is generally based on a biocentric ethics that accords dignity to all living beings, including trees and other plants, or an ecocentric (physiocentric, holistic) ethics, according to which not only individual living beings (e.g., a particular human or nonhuman animal or a particular plant) but also minerals, soils, waters, species, entire ecosystems, and the biotic community as a whole are intrinsically valuable.

Second, animal welfare and animal rights focus on the well-being of individual animals. By contrast, the primary ethical goal or principle of a holistic environmentalism such as Aldo Leopold's land ethic is the preservation of the integrity, stability, and beauty of the biotic community.

Third, whereas animal protection focuses on reducing animal pain and on minimizing animals' premature deaths as moral evils, pain and death are frequently regarded by environmentalists as part and parcel of the process of life or the order of nature with no ethical relevance.

The philosophical differences between animal protection and environmentalism entail practical conflicts in several areas. Environmentalists frequently have no moral qualms about eating meat, hunting, and fishing as long as ecosystems are not jeopardized in the process. Whereas animal advocates are in favor of letting free-living animals be, environmentalists are more interested in controlling and managing nature with the objective of enhancing the common ecological good. In the interest of the so-called whole, they appear to be prepared to inflict considerable suffering on individual animals and to kill (or "cull") them at will. The notion of sacrificing an individual nonhuman (or even human?) animal for the greater biotic good has prompted Tom Regan to accuse holistic environmentalists of advocating "environmental fascism."

Yet like several other ethicists (Gary E. Varner, Mary Anne Warren, Paul Taylor, Mary Midgley, Ted Benton, and ethologist Marc Bekoff), Regan also tried to find a common ground between the two divergent approaches, for in the final analysis, the good of the whole and the good of each individual being are closely interconnected: Because habitat is so important to animals, sound ecosystems are a condition for their thriving. Because the good of the whole is dependent on the good of all and of each individual, individual (sentient) beings must not be used merely as means to an end and rather should be treated with respect. The good of individual free-living animals cannot be divorced from the existence of adequate ecosystems, and the good of a so-called whole cannot be ensured at the expense of individual animals. This is the normative guideline and the practical challenge.

Related articles: Animal pain; Conservation philosophy; Ethical vegetarianism; The ethics of killing free-living animals; The ethics of reintroduction; Moral anthropocentrism; The moral claims of animals; The universal charter of the rights of other species

Bekoff, Marc, "Minding Animals, Minding Earth: Old Brains, New Bottlenecks," *Zygon* 38.4 (2003): 911–941.

Light, Andrew, and Rolston, Holmes, III (eds.), *Environmental Ethics: An Anthology*, Blackwell, 2003.

Linzey, Andrew, *Creatures of the Same God: Explorations in Animal Theology*, Winchester University Press, 2007, Lantern Books, 2009.

Meyer-Abich, Klaus Michael, *Aufstand für die Natur: Von der Umwelt zur Mitwelt*, München, Hansa, 1990.

Sapontzis, Steve, "Environmental Ethics versus Animal Rights" in Bekoff, Marc, and Meaney, Carron A. (eds.), *Encyclopedia of Animal Rights and Animal Welfare*, Greenwood Press, 1998, 161–162.

Taylor, Angus, *Animals and Ethics: An Overview of the Philosophical Debate*, 3rd ed., Broadview Press, 2009.

KURT REMELE

CONSERVATION PHILOSOPHY

Humans are all over the place. When we interact with nature, we usually redecorate landscapes and the living rooms of animals for our own ends, with little or no thought to their needs. Humans are very much a part of nature, and our widespread intrusions and big brains carry with them enormous responsibilities as nature's supposed and self-professed stewards. We are the only species that can "save the planet." Although we may have dominion over nature, we are obliged not to dominate her selfishly. Researchers agree that the most serious problems facing numerous species (many of which are perilously close to extinction) and the efforts to conserve and to protect them are too many humans, unsurpassed overconsumption, and too little critical habitat (areas where individuals can thrive undisturbed).

The basic questions faced in conservation are similar to those encountered whenever humans and animals meet. Often there are personal agendas that involve trade-offs among biological, political, economical, sociological, and ethical factors. Important general questions include what role humans should play in managing and controlling nature, whether we should even try to restore or recreate ecosystems, and whether it is reasonable to try to maintain or increase the number of species (biodiversity) on the planet. Is it better, or might it be better, to have fewer species, in which individuals have a higher quality of life? "Better" needs to be assessed from the animals' points of view.

There are other questions: Can we do whatever we please to animals? Do animals have rights, and if so, what responsibility does this entail for humans? Should we let animals be and never intentionally interfere in their lives, even if it means some species will become extinct and some conservation projects will be abandoned? Should we interfere in animals' lives when we have spoiled their habitats or when they are sick, provide food when there is not enough food to go around, or move (translocate) them from one place to another? Are native species more valuable than nonnative species? Should human interests trump animal interests? Should we be concerned with individuals, populations, species, or entire ecosystems?

In conservation biology, often the interests (and rights) of individuals are put aside for the perceived benefits that accrue to higher levels of organization—populations, species, or ecosystems. Individuals often are kept in zoos or in other captive situations to reproduce or to await release into their natural state "for the good of their species," despite the lack of evidence that zoos or other captive programs contribute much to conservation efforts. Renowned zoo administrator Terry Maple comments, "Any zoo that sits around and tells you that the strength of zoos is the SSP [Species Survival Plan] is blowing smoke" (qtd. in Croke 171). Individuals are also moved about, despite predictions that some will die but that the species will hopefully thrive.

Patient and proactive planning is essential to accomplish the challenging and often daunting goal of saving individuals, species, and their homes. This is the aim of the growing field of compassionate conservation, which involves preserving critical habitat, assessing public attitudes toward the animals themselves, and protecting individuals from exploitation so that sustainable populations can flourish. When animals are translocated, it is important to assess psychological and physical impacts that result from stress and the breaking up or re-forming of social (family) groups. Stress can influence survival and reproduction. There are also cascading and unpredictable effects when ecosystems are changed. In Yellowstone National Park, Wyoming, reintroduced wolves killed about 50 percent of the resident coyotes in one area, the effects of which influenced many other animals.

Nature is very complex. Interrelationships among humans, animals, and habitats are multidimensional and complicated. Thus, there are few quick solutions for most conservation problems. Successful proactive planning takes time. Asking difficult questions and calling attention to conservation programs that include compromising individuals for the good of their species are useful forms of compassionate activism. Although many conservation programs have been successful, in some cases it may be impossible to regain what was lost. In the end, perhaps we are simply faking nature by trying to reinvent rather than improve nature.

Emotions and passions run high, especially in highly visible projects involving such charismatic species as wolves, grizzly bears, and black rhinoceroses. It is often because conservation issues become so personal that it is difficult to reach solutions that are readily agreeable to all human parties. What is important is that people agree that ethics is an essential element in any discussion of conservation and that ethical issues are not traded off against other agendas. Giving animals priority in conservation programs will allow us to expand our compassion footprint to numerous diverse species.

Related articles: Animal protection and environmentalism; The ethics of reintroduction; The ethics of zoos; The scientific claims of zoos; The universal charter of the rights of other species

Bekoff, Marc, *The Animal Manifesto: Six Reasons for Expanding Our Compassion Footprint*, New World Library, 2010.
———, *Animal Passions and Beastly Virtues: Reflections on Redecorating Nature*, Temple University Press, 2006.
———, *The Emotional Lives of Animals: A Leading Scientist Explores Animal Joy, Sorrow, and Empathy—and Why They Matter*, New World Library, 2007.
——— (ed.), *Ignoring Nature No More: The Case for Compassionate Conservation*, University of Chicago Press, 2013.
Croke, V., *The Modern Ark: The Story of Zoos: Past, Present, and Future*, Scribner, 1997.
Marino, Lori, Lilienfeld, Scott O., Malamud, Randy, Nobis, Nathan, and Broglio, Ron, "Do Zoos and Aquariums Promote Attitude Change in Visitors? A Critical Evaluation of the American Zoo and Aquarium Study," *Society and Animals* 18 (2010): 126–138.

MARC BEKOFF

DE-SNARING IN KENYA

Some years ago, near my home in Kenya's Maasai Mara, I noticed a number of animals (primarily giraffes and elephants) with life-threatening injuries caused by wire snares. In order to alleviate their suffering, I worked with the Kenya Wildlife Service to bring veterinarians to the Mara to remove these snares, thereby saving the animals from an excruciating slow death. Wanting to improve the chances for these animals, I then decided to take it a step further and received permission from the authorities to run a community de-snaring program.

The bushmeat trade has reached epic proportions throughout many African countries. TRAFFIC, the "international wildlife trade monitoring program," reports that bushmeat is as much as 75 percent less expensive than domestic meat in many countries. Free-living animals also come under even greater threat during times of economic hardship because of the burgeoning population. In addition, there is now a full-scale commercialized trade in bushmeat. Fortunately, the Maasai Mara Game Reserve and the surrounding area have a highly developed tourism industry, and the local Maasai communities recognize that without the free-living animals, there would be no income. They themselves do not consume the meat from such animals, and now, through our project's conservation education, they also realize the importance of not tolerating the poachers who come in from afar.

The de-snaring team consists of five young people. The two team leaders are college graduates from Nairobi. The other members are drawn from the local Maasai youth on a rotational basis. We attempt to operate ten two-week sweeps each year, working with the armed rangers provided by the local authorities. We are able to provide the team with a vehicle and full camping and safety equipment. They are able to patrol deep into areas where poachers previously had free rein. As a result the poachers have been forced to abandon their camps, which in some cases housed up to fifty people on a semipermanent basis.

Our team spends two days of every sweep teaching the value of conservation in the local schools. The schoolchildren now collect snares on a regular basis while in the field herding their cattle. We also help the community by installing water catchment systems in areas where schools and communities have no clean source of water—or no water at all. We provide textbooks and supplies in eight schools, and we organize field trips for the children to go into the Maasai Mara Reserve so that they can enjoy and appreciate the animals from the safety of a vehicle. We encourage the communities to plant trees and develop their own nursery.

The young people are so excited about being involved in protecting their heritage that during the weeks when we do not have organized sweeps, they organize themselves into teams to keep the pressure on the poachers. In our first two years of operation, our team, along with the rangers, confiscated close to one thousand snares; confiscated hundreds of kilograms of dried meat, leopard and lion skulls, elephant tusks, skins, spears, and arrows; and assisted in the arrest of ten poachers. In the poachers' camps, and from evidence from field patrols, we documented a total of 117 animals killed by poachers' snares. Scientific estimates of the number of animals killed each year by poachers in the Serengeti/Mara ecosystem indicate that the number could easily exceed 20,000 animals.

Snaring is indiscriminate and results in the death of many nontarget animals, such as leopards, lions, hyenas, and elephants. We have documented the startling and distressing death of twelve lions and have helped rescue six others caught in snares. We also have documented twelve elephants with trunks severed by the wire snares and have started a photographic file of these individuals in order to track their survival rate.

By removing the snares, we are helping to save many animals from an excruciating death. But although individual action is important, the problem needs to be tackled at a national level. Subsistence poaching, for example, is clearly driven by economics, and this was sadly demonstrated when we caught a sixteen-year-old boy who was snaring in order to earn money to attend school. He, like most of the poachers we encounter, is a part of a highly developed system that moves hundreds of thousands of kilos of bushmeat into local markets.

The underlying difficulty is that local people often see very little direct benefit from the existence of animals. We still have a long way to go to help people see that the animals' preservation is in the interests of everyone, including the very poor. To reinforce this point, a proportion of the money we raise through my tourism business goes to the local community. Donations come directly from visitors whom we introduce to the local people so that the latter can see a direct correlation between economic prosperity and appreciating free-living animals.

In the long term, it should be the duty of the government to make sure that the local people are themselves involved with the protection of the area and receive the economic benefits that preservation can generate. We need to find imaginative ways of generating sustainable income for the communities whose lives are impacted (often negatively) by free-living animals, so that they are not tempted to make their living illegally by assisting the poachers. It is critical that we find some long-term resolution to the conflict between a burgeoning population on one hand and the need to preserve free-living animals on the other. Whatever solution is proposed, we need to realize that human welfare and animal welfare are intertwined and, not least of all, that the cruelty of snaring should become a thing of the past.

Related articles: Animal protection in Africa; The big cats; Caring for animals and humans; Conservation philosophy; Developments in animal law; Free-living chimpanzees; Perceptions of elephants; Primates worldwide; Snares and snaring

Grante, Viktor T., and Williams, Horace O. (eds.), *Illegal Trade in Wildlife*, Nova Science, 2009.

Green, Alan, *Animal Underworld: Inside America's Black Market for Rare and Exotic Species*, Public Affairs, 2006.

Hosking, David, and Withers, Martin, *Traveller's Guide: Wildlife of Kenya, Tanzania and Uganda*, Collins, 2007.

Hoyt, John A., *Animals in Peril: How "Sustainable Use" Is Wiping Out the World's Wildlife*, Avery, 1996.

Krapf, Daniel, *Wildlife of Kenya*, Novum, 2009.

TRAFFIC, information available at http://www.traffic.org/.

White, Rob, *Crimes against Nature: Environmental Criminology and Ecological Justice*, Willan, 2008.

ANNE KENT TAYLOR

THE ETHICS OF KILLING FREE-LIVING ANIMALS

Attempted justifications for the killing of free-living animals usually include the notion that there are "too many" animals—too many bears, deer, geese, squirrels; the list is almost endless. The solution, some say, is to control the animals' numbers, and this means killing by one means or another, usually with guns, bow and razor-tipped arrows, trapping, or poison. It is said that their numbers must be controlled because they are a danger to us, or they frighten us, or they are just an annoying nuisance. Black bears, known to be docile, are shot and killed in the United States because they get into unsecured garbage cans, raid bird feeders, and frighten people.

Deer are killed because they are said to destroy their own habitat—one wonders how they survived for millions of years without our help in controlling their numbers; because they cause vehicle accidents, which is especially true during hunting season, when they try to flee from hunters; and because they are said falsely to spread Lyme disease. Geese leave droppings on golf courses and foul ponds in parks, which is claimed—without evidence—to spread disease to humans. Despite the fact that the tactic is ineffective, gray squirrels are killed in the United Kingdom because they are outcompeting red squirrels.

These are some of the excuses given when it is said that free-living animals must be killed. No one questions, or at least very few people question, whether there really are too many bears, deer, or other animals. Similarly, it is seldom asked whether there are nonlethal means of reducing the number of animals or whether killing these animals actually leads to a decrease in their numbers or even to a decrease in the harm they are said to cause.

What does it mean to say that there are too many animals? Too many for what? And to whom? "Wildlife" agencies often assert that the number of animals has exceeded the carrying capacity, supposedly a scientific expression defined as the number of animals who can survive in a given area. Two points must be noted: First, according to this definition, carrying capacity cannot be exceeded because the number of animals who survive is the number that the area can support. For this reason, a qualifying phrase is usually added to this definition: the number of animals who can survive in excellent condition or who can survive indefinitely or without damaging the habitat, such as the understory or certain species of plants or trees. The second point to remember is that the carrying capacity, even when defined with these additional phrases, is never a constant number. The amount of rain, the severity of a winter, the presence of other animals competing for the same food, disease, parasites, insects, and so on can all influence the number of animals who can survive in a given area. It is simply misleading to claim that the carrying capacity refers to a specific number that is valid for years or even for months. Perhaps for these reasons, it has been said that "it appears that 'carrying capacity' is a Holy Grail for deer managers—highly desirable, frustratingly elusive, and of questionable authenticity" (Bunnell 158). Despite these facts, "game managers" refer to unvarying carrying capacity numbers year after year.

*"Too many" defined as exceeding
the cultural carrying capacity*

Sometimes the notion of cultural carrying capacity is employed as if this were a scientific notion endorsed by biologists. The cultural carrying capacity, however, refers only to the number of animals that a given culture will tolerate, and since culture is not monolithic in the developed world, there is rarely widespread agreement in any community. If even two people complain, it can be said that the cultural carrying capacity has been exceeded.

The absence of natural predators

Game agencies often assert that since we have killed off all the predators who formerly limited the number of prey animals, human hunters must now do the job that natural predators once did. It is not at all clear that the agencies really believe this assertion, for it has been amply documented that predators do not control prey numbers. The reverse is true: prey animal numbers control predator numbers, for animal populations are ultimately governed by their food supply, and prey animals are predators' food. This does not mean that predators have no effect on prey: predators may keep population levels below some maximum number, and they may exert enough pressure to prevent "disease, starvation and other regulatory forces associated with poor nutrition" from taking effect (Schaller 404), but they do not limit populations in the way that some game agencies would have us believe.

If game agencies really believe that predator pressure kept prey at very low levels in the past and that prey animals are now so numerous that they are causing environmental damage or spreading disease, then one wonders why these very same agencies encourage—or even permit—the killing of predators. In Pennsylvania, for example, it is said that we are overrun with deer and that only lethal means can control their numbers, but at the same time it is legal to kill an unlimited number of coyotes all year long ("Furbearer Hunting Season"). Just as illogical are the vehement protests over the introduction of wolves into some areas in the western United States despite the fact that the U.S. government promised to compensate any farmer who suffered losses due to wolves. Apparently hunters do not appreciate predators killing the animals whom the hunters themselves want to kill.

Scientists have pointed out that even if they wanted to, humans could not compete with natural or biological predators. We know that predators primarily kill the old and infirm as well as newborn or very young animals. George Schaller asserts that predators "bring a discernment that cannot be matched by man; the predators weed out the sick and old, they keep herds healthy and alert"(407). Most hunters or cullers do not want to kill immature or sick animals, and apparently even if they so desired, they could not discern which animals are debilitated or ill.

People do not ask whether hunting or killing ("culling") deer, for example, will reduce numbers because it seems so self-evident that if you kill a deer, you have one less deer. Such an assumption is mistaken, however, and reveals a basic lack of knowledge concerning population dynamics. For example, if a portion of a deer herd is killed, there are fewer deer but only for the moment. The following spring, the herd will contain the same number as or even more deer than before the kill because deer numbers, like those of every other animal, are primarily controlled by their food supply. Statistics for the Great Swamp in New Jersey provide just one example of this natural phenomenon, which is often called compensatory reproduction. Sometimes this increase is explained in terms of density. "Quite simply, many populations which have reached a density at which they constitute a problem as a pest are probably suffering reduction in recruitment and survival due to the effects of that same density. If population figures are lowered artificially, the density-dependent brake on population growth is released: reproduction increases, mortality declines" (Putman 171).

A "Wildlife Note" of the Pennsylvania Game Commission acknowledges this fact: "The age and health of a doe influence her reproductive capacity. Females from the best range produce more fawns than those from poor range" (Fergus). If the food supply remains constant but there are fewer deer, each animal will have more food (better nutrition) and will reproduce more than if food were limited. This is a natural or innate mechanism that has evolved. It is easy to understand: if a severe winter or a disease killed off a number of animals, they would be more likely to survive as a species if they could increase their offspring. For example, deer and foxes accomplish this by increasing the number of young, so that instead of a single birth, a deer may produce twins or even triplets, and foxes may have larger litters. Both female foxes and deer will also breed at an earlier age, thus increasing the population. These facts show why hunting or "culling" is not effective.

Furthermore, if hunting or culling removes a large number of animals, something like a vacuum is created; other animals of the same species may move into this less densely populated area. When we are told that there are too many and that if the killing does not commence immediately, we will soon be inundated by these animals, we are being asked to believe in a myth: animal numbers do not increase indefinitely; they cannot increase beyond their food supply.

If all the usual excuses for killing free-living animals are just that—excuses—one might be led to ask whether killing is ever ethical. Most people would assert that if our life were threatened, we could with moral impunity kill an animal just as we are entitled to kill another human in self-defense. Excluding this exception, it is difficult to justify killing animals, although many people have tried to do so with the excuses mentioned here. Claims of justification make sense only if it is assumed that human fears and even the most frivolous of human desires have an exalted status. Yet even then, when killing is ineffective and completely useless, it is absurd to argue that it is morally justified. The existence of nonlethal alternatives, such as contraceptives, that reduce numbers reveals the falsity of the claim that killing is the only choice. Similarly, the existence of various means that eliminate or decrease the so-called damage or harm done by animals, such as fencing, netting of trees, and chemical and physical deterrents, further reveals the vacuity of the claim that killing is necessary. Certainly killing for recreation (see Animals in Sport and Entertainment) cannot be justified on any rational terms.

Related articles: Animal protection and environmentalism; Conservation philosophy; Deer hunting; The ethics of reintroduction; Facts about bears; Immunocontraception; The protection of birds; Snares and snaring

Bunnell, F. L., "Reproductive Tactics of Cervidae and Their Relationship to Habitat," in Wemer, C. M. (ed.), *Biology and Management of the Cervidae*, Smithsonian Institution Press, 1987.
Cohn, P. N., "Exploding the Hunting Myths" in Cohn, P. N. (ed.), *Ethics and Wildlife*, Edwin Mellen Press, 1999.
———, "Wildlife Contraception: An Introduction" in *Animal Law Seminar*, Pennsylvania Bar Institute, 2003.
Cohn, P. N., Plotka, E. D., and Seal, U. S. (eds.), *Contraception in Wildlife*, Edwin Mellen Press, 1996.
Fergus, Chuck, "White-Tailed Deer," Wildlife Note 28, Pennsylvania Game Commission.
"Furbearer Hunting Season," adopted November 2010, Pennsylvania Game Commission, State Wildlife Management Agency.
Putman, R., *The Natural History of Deer*, Cornell University Press, 1988.
Schaller, G. B., *The Serengeti Lion: A Study of Predator-Prey Relations*, University of Chicago Press, 1972.

PRISCILLA N. COHN

THE ETHICS OF REINTRODUCTION

Reintroduction, or "rewilding" as it is sometimes known, is the process of reintroducing free-ranging species into a given area where they have become extinct. Species now reintroduced include the wolf, beaver, bison, and boar, and there are ambitions to introduce many more (Rewilding Symposium). The process is undertaken in the interests of biodiversity and is often a well-intentioned attempt to redress the balance of nature, which humans themselves have previously disturbed through overhunting or by causing the rapid depletion of resources or the environment on which the species depend.

As described, reintroduction sounds like a benign process. But in fact the process bristles with difficulties—ecological, philosophical, and ethical. In the first place, ecology is a dynamic. It is forever changing. The danger of appeals to biodiversity is that they can motivate an attempt to freeze a once-upon-a-time ecological system of the past. The point is that once released we cannot control reintroduced species. There is no such thing as a containable reintroduction. There can never be, for example, just one or two beavers—if they can survive, they will change the entire ecology of a country since they fell trees, create wetlands, and dam up rivers. All species populate in relation to the food and environment available. By reintroducing species, we can do immense ecological harm by disrupting rather than complementing the existing ecosystem.

Second, species have become scarce or gone extinct in a given area because people have not tolerated them and have killed them by poisoning, trapping, snaring, or shooting. It is ethically questionable to reintroduce species unless humans are now prepared to tolerate them. For example, many cattle farmers are understandably not prepared to tolerate wolves. Indeed, people now hunt the boars who have been reintroduced, which makes one wonder whether sporting interests were not themselves the impetus for reintroduction at the outset. The question has to be asked: what good does it do the released animals if one is only setting up new conflicts between the animals and humans whereby the animals will always be the losers?

Third, the philosophical problem is that human beings, who have been so inept at controlling their own population, now presume to know how many other species there should be, where they should live, and how large their populations should be. But humans do not always know best. Indeed, people now defend so-called conservation efforts on the grounds that—because we have made so many bad judgments in the past—we now have to act to mitigate their adverse effects. But the problem may be the very idea that we always know better than nature. Reintroductions may be yet another display of human hubris, pride. Moreover, the notion of biodiversity, so loved by conservationists, is philosophically contestable, if not vacuous. There never was a pristine biodiversity.

In sum, reintroductions need to be subject to ethical scrutiny. First, the likely ecological disruption, both short and long term, needs to be taken more rigorously into account. Second, there must be a genuine and demonstrable tolerance toward reintroduced species to prevent the repetition of previous attempts at extermination. Third, species should not be reintroduced into environments where they will inevitably be subject to harm from human beings. More fundamentally, the idea that we have untrammeled rights to manipulate, dominate, and control the natural world must be questioned.

Related articles: Animal protection and environmentalism; Conservation philosophy; The ethics of killing free-living animals; The moral claims of animals

Foreman, Dave, "Rewilding North America" (extract), the Rewilding Institute, available at http://rewilding.org/rewildit/what-is-rewilding/.

Linzey, Andrew, "Against Harming," *BBC Wildlife* (January 1996): 46.

———, "Letting Be" (guest editorial), *BBC Wildlife* (October 1990): 6–7.

———, *Why Animal Suffering Matters: Philosophy, Theology, and Practical Ethics*, Oxford University Press, 2009.

Lorimer, Jamie, and Driessen, Clemens, "Return to the Wild," Project at King's College, London, available at http://www.kcl.ac.uk/sspp/departments/geography/research/epd/ReturntotheWild.aspx.

Rewilding Symposium, "Pleistocene Rewilding—Lions and Elephants in U.S.A.," available at http://rewilding-symposium.weebly.com/index.html.

ANDREW LINZEY

IMMUNOCONTRACEPTION

Human contraceptives were first tested on animals and then later used to control fertility in animals. Starting in the 1960s, hormonal contraceptives were tested on a large number of animals, including, among others, dogs, lions, deer, horses, rats, and birds. Delivery of these compounds was comparatively simple for zoo animals, where much of the early research occurred, but difficult for free-ranging animals, because large and frequent doses were necessary and also because baits were often avoided by the target animals. In addition, social behavior was sometimes adversely affected. A major disadvantage concerned passage of these steroid hormones through the food chain, whereby other, nontargeted species, such as predators or even humans, might ingest them. By 1987, data clearly revealed that hormonal contraceptives were causing health problems in at least some animal species (Vollset and Jakobsen).

Since the late 1980s, much of the research has been directed toward immunocontraception, a method whereby an individual animal is injected with a substance that causes the animal to produce antibodies that interfere with a process necessary for reproduction. Several different kinds of immunocontraceptives are possible. Vaccinations could counteract the effect of hormones that are necessary for reproduction and made by the brain (gonadotropin-releasing hormone or GnRh) or by the pituitary gland (luteinizing hormone or LH and follicle-stimulating hormone or FSH) and so forth (Massei et al.). The vaccine that has been most widely tested and developed is porcine zona pellucida (PZP).

The zona pellucida is the noncellular membrane that surrounds the mammalian egg. When the proteins from the zona pellucida from pig eggs are inoculated into an animal from a different species, that animal produces antibodies that prevent sperm from penetrating the animal's own zona pellucida, thus preventing fertilization and reproduction (Dunbar et al.).

There are a number of practical advantages, some of which translate into ethical advantages, to using PZP. It is, on average, approximately 90 percent effective and does not pass through the food chain. Since only a small amount of the vaccine is needed, it can be delivered remotely by a dart, thus avoiding the stress of capture or anesthesia. PZP does not significantly affect social behavior and, so far, has not been found to cause any serious health problems. It is safe for pregnant animals, is reversible, and is effective on a broad range of species. The vaccine itself is very inexpensive. Costs for an immunocontraceptive program vary largely according to personnel expenses. All these positive aspects of PZP are a reflection of the mechanism of action and the extreme "downstream" point of action—that is, nothing else in the reproductive system (or the remainder of physiology) is affected except fertilization.

In general, then, there are many advantages to PZP immunocontraception. It is humane for animals, since it causes neither death nor discomfort. It represents no danger to humans, since it does not involve guns or razor-tipped arrows. It is effective since there is no rebound reproduction, a phenomenon that occurs when large numbers of animals are suddenly removed. Bizarre and often troublesome animal behavior is avoided, since the young are not orphaned, and social structure is not affected. Genetic diversity is not lost, since it is reversible. Lethal methods such as hunting and killing ("culling") offer none of these advantages (Kirkpatrick et al.).

Immunocontraceptives in general, and PZP in particular, seem to be desirable, if they are used as an alternative to killing or hunting or if they are used to limit the reproduction of zoo animals so that so-called surplus animals are not born.

Hunters, of course, do not view immunocontraception as desirable for they fear that its use threatens their "lifestyle" (see Animals in Sport and Entertainment). They are, however, not alone in their criticism of PZP. Some animal rightists have also raised ethical objections, claiming that immunocontraception is simply one more example of human domination and manipulation of the natural world, one more way in which we control nature for our own ends, and with our own welfare as the primary criterion. This criticism is valid, but it would also apply to our habitual ways of treating free-living animals, which include shooting, poisoning, and gassing them, manipulating their habitat, and so on. Seen within this context, immunocontraception appears benign, even if it does not represent the ideal of noninterference with, and respect for, all nonhuman animals.

Another objection concerns the fact that PZP is a slaughterhouse product made from pig ovaries. It is claimed that purchasing these ovaries only increases slaughterhouse profits and encourages more slaughter. This objection is not valid. If these ovaries were not bought by the makers of PZP, they would be purchased by pharmaceutical companies that use various hormones derived from them and even by Chinese restaurants. Thus, making PZP does not increase slaughterhouse profits. Furthermore, whether or not their ovaries were sold, pigs would still be slaughtered for their meat. Eliminating the use of PZP would not lessen the number of pigs killed. Pig ovaries will not need to be utilized in the future if the ongoing research that is directed at genetically engineering PZP is successful.

A third, although infrequently heard, objection to PZP is that the development of this vaccine inevitably leads to more animal experimentation. Many scientists, but not all, believe it is a necessary part of the scientific method to kill and necropsy animals in order to prove that PZP is harmless. According to this view, the fact that PZP-vaccinated horses have lived longer and been in better condition than those who were not treated does not militate against this necessity.

A fourth objection is the ease with which PZP can be misused. It is one thing, critics assert, to use PZP as an alternative to killing and quite another to control the number of predators to protect their prey so that hunters or fishers can kill them. Actual instances of such misuses have already occurred. Denying that they had overfished, Canadians wanted to use contraception on seals because they claimed that the seals were responsible for the lack of fishes. Similarly, PZP was used in Canada to reduce the number of wolves to prevent them from preying on caribou herds that hunters wanted to exploit.

Scientists continue their research, not only on PZP to make it effective for a longer period, but also on other kinds of immunocontraception, such as GonaCon, a GnRh vaccine developed by the United States Department of Agriculture specifically for deer. Scientists are also working to produce a sterilant for domestic cats and dogs that is as effective as, but easier and less invasive than, surgical spaying and neutering (Grimm).

Immunocontraception: ethically desirable or the opening of Pandora's box? The jury is still out.

Related articles: Animals used in research; Deer hunting; The ethics of killing free-living animals; The ethics of zoos; Neutering and spaying; Slaughter

Dunbar, B. S., Kaul, G., Prasad, M., and Skinner, S. M., "Molecular Approaches for the Evaluation of Immune Responses to Zona Pellucida (ZP) and Development of Second Generation ZP Vaccines," *Reproduction* Supplement 60 (2001): 9–18.

Grimm, D., "A Cure for Euthanasia," *Science* 325 (2009): 1490–1493.

Kirkpatrick, J. F., Rowan, A., Lamberski, N., Wallace, R., Frank, K., and Lyda, R., "The Practical Side of Immunocontraception: Zona Proteins and Wildlife," *Journal of Reproductive Immunology* 83 (2009): 151–157.

Massei, G., Cowan, D. P., Coats, J., Gladwell, F., Lane, J. E., and Miller, L. A., "Effect of the GnRH Vaccine GonaCon on the Fertility, Physiology and Behaviour of Wild Boar," *Wildlife Research* 35 (2008): 540–547.

Turner, J. W., Rutberg, A. T., Naugle, R. E., Kaul, A. M. A., Flanagan, D. R., Bertschinger, H. J., and Liu, I. K. M., "Controlled Release Components of PZP Contraceptive Vaccine Extend Duration of Infertility," *Wildlife Research* 35 (2008): 555–562.

Vollset, I., and Jakobsen, G., "Feline Endocrine Alopecia-Like Disease Probably Induced by Medroxyprogesterone Acetate," *Feline Practice* 16 (1986): 16–17.

PRISCILLA N. COHN

PRESERVING ANIMALS IN MADAGASCAR

Madagascar is a veritable treasure trove for nature enthusiasts: thanks to an estimated 165 million years of isolation from Africa and about 80 million years from India, the "Great Red Island" is classified by Conservation International (among others) as one of our planet's "megadiversity hotspots."

Approximately 150,000 of the 200,000 animal and plant species estimated to exist there are found nowhere else in the world. Other contributing factors to this extraordinarily high rate of species endemism include the country's enormity—Madagascar is the world's fourth-largest island—and its tropical location. Although Madagascar was one of the last habitable landmasses to be colonized by human beings, its natural assets have suffered more at the hands of people than is the case in many other countries. Aside from natural climatic cycles, reasons for the chronic environmental degradation—and the wave of animal extinctions that took place there—include inappropriate agricultural techniques, rural poverty, and land hunger.

Madagascar is one of the world's great conservation priorities. Many international agencies are hard at work trying to save what remains of its remarkable plant and animal life. A quick look at some statistics is enough to set any naturalist's pulse racing. Roughly 83 percent of the island's animals are endemic—that is, they exist nowhere else on earth. And if you exclude birds, of which 42 percent are endemic, the total shoots up to an astonishing 97 percent. In other words, almost every animal marooned on this giant life raft is found only in what remains of its ancient and fragile ecosystems, which vary from permanently humid rainforests to an unworldly spiny desert.

But less than 20 percent of the original forests remain intact. And although only some 2 percent of the forests fall into protected areas, it must be said that some sizable tracts still support much of their full complements of animal and plant species. Some of these—high-profile examples, including rainforest national parks such as Masoala and Ranomafana—have become the mainstay of Madagascar's flourishing ecotourism industry, a vital source of revenue for one of the world's dozen poorest nations.

Many of the animal groups still thriving in Madagascar have long since died out on the continents, where they were replaced by more "evolved" fauna. This "primitive" aspect is perfectly illustrated by Madagascar's flagship animals, the lemurs. Only in Madagascar are lemurs, who belong to a primate suborder known as the prosimians, able to have a diurnal lifestyle. Elsewhere, they have been forced into a nocturnal existence by the more successful, dominant, and aggressive monkeys and baboons. In time, the lemurs proliferated into some 103 extant species, varying from the baboon-sized indri to the Madame Berthe's mouse lemur, which at forty-four grams is the smallest of all primates.

Unfortunately, a drawcard of many Malagasy animals is an unenviable one: rarity. Too many of the island's animals are vulnerable, threatened, or endangered. Although there have been few known extinctions during the last century, there is a long list of species dangerously close to the edge. Habitat destruction aside, frenzied collecting for the insatiable animal trade (*see* Trade) and, to a much smaller extent, hunting for bushmeat are also to blame. Although there have been erratic attempts at implementing protection of some forests, illegal logging and animal collecting remain increasingly problematic in almost all the country's protected areas. The aesthetic appeal of some Malagasy animals has certainly led to their being highly sought-after in the exotic companion animal trade.

This applies especially to Madagascar's incredibly diverse herpetofauna, in which trade has exploded during the last two decades. In just one year, the number of brightly colored, poisonous mantella frogs exported escalated from 230 individuals to a staggering 11,058. And that is the known statistic—not accounted for are the illegally exported individuals (or "specimens") and the mortalities prior to, and during, exportation. (Mortality rates are extremely high among amphibians—up to

90 percent—and among reptiles, such as chameleons, who do not handle well the trauma of the usually brutal smuggling process.)

Certain localized animals, such as the indri, survive only in their natural habitat. So they may be seen nowhere else but where they belong—in the fragile Malagasy rainforests. Fortunately, the indris, being impressive as they are, have become the star attraction in at least one protected area, Andasibe-Mantadia National Park. The park's success has led to economic opportunities for many local people involved in its management, as well as spurring on the development of the hospitality industry. (The more a locality becomes a tourist draw-card, the more local people are employed to staff and manage the infrastructure, which is developed around it.) Thus, the resident troops of indris—along with the rainforest's other denizens—receive protection because local people understand increasingly that it is better to have animals roaming free than cooking in a pot fueled by wood taken from their forest home.

People come to Madagascar because of the possibility of close contact with endangered life-forms. The majestic Madagascar fish eagle is a good example: critically endangered, it is one of the world's six rarest raptors. At Lake Ravelobe in Ankarafantsika National Park, it is standard fare to be able to observe these birds for extended periods. There is definitely something to be said for making that "eye-to-brain" connection with a member of a species in which there are a mere two hundred individuals.

With more than 80 percent of all tourists coming primarily to see the island's animals, Madagascar's government has long been aware of the importance of protecting animals in their natural habitats. Consequently, support has been lent to the conservation agencies involved, but following the political events of 2009, the withdrawal of all except some humanitarian aid to the donor-dependent nation has had many negative effects on conservation programs there.

In the first decade of the twenty-first century, there have been some commendable conservation successes, but in the field of animal protection, much remains to be achieved. There are very few centers in the country able to receive and protect free animals who have been illegally taken into captivity and then either confiscated by the Ministry of Environment and Forestry or abandoned, after people have realized that they actually do not make suitable companion animals.

All species of lemurs, for instance, are officially protected under CITES Appendix I, but there is very little enforcement of this protection in practice. Consequently, centers such as Parc Ivoloina, commendably managed by the Madagascar Fauna Group (MFG) in conjunction with

DREF Atsinanana, receive an ever-increasing stream of "private donations" of such animals: some are brought in by concerned tourists or by Malagasy, who buy the animals along the roadside or at markets, whereas others are confiscated at ports, airports, or holding pens. Well-placed sources cite the operating of international flights between Antananarivo and Asia—notably the route to Bangkok, from where flights continue on to China—as one of the major reasons for a marked increase in the smuggling of illegally caught free animals out of the country. Now more than ever, there is an urgent need for the government to muscle in, particularly when it comes to stamping out the growing illegal trade in animals.

Related articles: Animal protection in Africa; CITES and international trade; Conservation philosophy; Free-living chimpanzees; Primates worldwide; The protection of birds; Sanctuaries and rehabilitation; The trade in primates for research; The trade in reptiles; The treatment of animals in India; Understanding amphibians

Bradt, H., Schuurman, D., and Garbutt, N., *Madagascar Wildlife: A Visitor's Guide*, 3rd ed., Bradt Travel Guides, 2008.

Glaw, F., and Vences, M., *A Field Guide to the Amphibians and Reptiles of Madagascar*, 3rd ed., Vences and Glaw Verlags, 2007.

Goodman, S. M., and Benstead, J. P. (eds.), *The Natural History of Madagascar*, University of Chicago Press, 2004.

Jolly, A., *Lords and Lemurs: Mad Scientists, Kings with Spears, and the Survival of Diversity in Madagascar*, Houghton Mifflin, 2004.

Mittermeier, R., et al., *Lemurs of Madagascar*, 2nd ed., Conservation International Tropical Field Guide Series, 2006.

Schuurman, D., and Ravelojaona, N., *Globetrotter Madagascar Guide*, New Holland Books/Struik, 2012.

DEREK SCHUURMAN

SANCTUARIES AND REHABILITATION

By definition, sanctuaries for free-living animals offer a safeguard, or haven, for these animals, protecting them from danger in an undisturbed environment. As the development of human society increases its demands on the natural environment, the number of animals displaced from their natural habitats increases. Individual animals are continually being placed into crisis situations as a result of human activities; the range of species, and the manner in which they are affected, is vast. The concept of sanctuaries for free-living animals ("wildlife sanctuaries") has been developed not only as a means of rescuing these individuals, but also to actively address the root cause of these problems.

Human nature, including our inherent empathy with animals, has dictated that we simply cannot allow animals to suffer needlessly. There is a will to intervene and a feeling of responsibility, especially if the problem is deemed to have been caused by humans. Furthermore, rehabilitation work can play a critical role in the conservation of threatened species. A fine example is provided by the rescue and rehabilitation of over 20,000 African penguins impacted by the Treasure oil spill in South Africa in July 2000.

The scope and range of sanctuary work undertaken worldwide is vast, and examples include the following:

- The rescue and rehabilitation of animals impacted by oil spills.
- The rescue and relocation of animals from cruel confinement, such as substandard zoos, circuses, and the entertainment industry; the rescue of companion animals; and the rescue of bears in China from farms in which they are "milked" for their bile.
- The confiscation of endangered or threatened animals from illegal trade (according to the Convention on International Trade in Endangered Species of Wild Fauna and Flora, CITES). Illegal trafficking of endangered species is the third-largest illegal trade in the world after trade in drugs and weapons.
- The rescue of orphaned animals. As adults are hunted or poached for commercial or sporting value, infants may be left defenseless or sold as companion animals. Some of the most disturbing examples of this are seen with the chimpanzee and gorilla orphans of the bushmeat trade in central Africa.
- Human-animal conflict situations. As humans encroach on natural habitats, animals are forced into human-inhabited areas where they are viewed as "pests" or as a potential danger. Such individuals may be relocated to another more suitable site; if no such site is available, they unfortunately are taken into captivity.
- Rehabilitation of sick or injured animals or animals affected by natural disasters (e.g., floods, hurricanes, earthquakes, droughts, and blizzards).

The centers that have developed can generally be viewed as either providing permanent sanctuary care or focusing on rehabilitation and return of the animals to their natural state. Rehabilitation as a science is still very much in its infancy, and although developments are progressing at a rapid rate, there is still much to be learned. It is, however, an unfortunate fact that many animals within sanctuaries cannot be released because of the sheer scale of habitat destruction or failure to provide them with appropriate protected environment. Alternatively, the individuals may be deemed unsuitable for release if their experiences in captivity have rendered them permanently incapable of adapting to their natural life or if they have contracted diseases while in captivity that would potentially threaten free-living populations.

By adopting an integrated approach to conservation, many sanctuaries are in effect attempting to shut themselves down, since if they are successful in preventing free-living animals from entering crisis situations, then the need to rescue and rehabilitate individuals will dramatically reduce. The conservation roles played by sanctuaries include the education of local schoolchildren; outreach programs to local communities to raise awareness and the possible provision of alternative employment opportunities; training of local animal caregivers, veterinarians, and officials (for example, CITES confiscation officials); and raising public awareness and lobbying governments. In addition, some sanctuaries are directly involved with facilitating poaching patrols or snare removal patrols, and some have brought about the creation of new protected areas. Other sanctuaries that are actively involved in programs aimed at releasing endangered or threatened species back into their natural state run captive breeding programs. The ethics of such programs are often disputed by animal protectionists.

Sanctuaries are essentially run by caring and dedicated staff who are prepared to commit twenty-four hours a day, seven days a week, to the animals in their care. Although the work that most centers undertake deserves full recognition and applause, especially given that most operate on very tight budgets, usually relying on donations, it must be remembered that the term "sanctuary" should not earn instant respect. Very few countries inspect or license their sanctuaries and rehabilitation centers; consequently, the relative standards of animal care vary dramatically.

Related articles: Animals in circuses; CITES and international trade; Conservation philosophy; De-snaring in Kenya; The ethics of reintroduction; The ethics of zoos; Free-living chimpanzees; Moon bears and bear bile farming; The moral claims of animals; Primates worldwide; Shelters and sanctuaries

Berkner, A. B., "Wildlife Rehabilitation Techniques: Past, Present and Future," *Proceedings of the U.S. Fish and Wildlife Service Pollution Response Workshop*, Environmental Contaminant Evaluation Program, U.S. Fish and Wildlife Service, Washington, DC, 1977, 127–133.

British Wildlife Rehabilitation Council, "Ethics," 2010, available at http://www.bwrc.org.uk/.

Clumpner, C., and Wasserman, J., "Creating a Wildlife Rehabilitation Facility," *Wildlife Journal* 14.3 (1991).

International Wildlife Rehabilitation Council, "Minimal Standards for Wildlife Rehabilitation," 2010, available at http://theiwrc.org/resources/guidelines-for-wildlife-rehabilitation/.

Norman, Richard, "Why Rehabilitate Oiled Wildlife?," available at http://www.ibrrc.org/pdfs/Why_rehab_paper_Norman.pdf.

Wildlife Information Network, "Electronic Encyclopaedia," available at http://www.wildlifeinformation.org/About/ElecEncyclopaedia.htm.

JOANNE FIELDER

SNARES AND SNARING

The use of snares to trap animals dates from the development of plant fiber and cordage use in the Upper Paleolithic period, before the use of bows and arrows. There are numerous references to snares in ancient texts, including the Hebrew Bible. Today, snares remain prevalent around the world. They are used in subsistence and commercial hunting (including the fur trade), poaching (including the bushmeat trade), recreational bushcraft, population control, predator and "pest" species control, and occasionally research.

The basic design of the snare is an anchored noose, originally made of vine or plant fiber and nowadays usually made of steel cable. It is positioned where an animal will walk into it and become trapped by the neck, abdomen, or leg. Snares are suspended above the places where animals run or browse, in order to catch them around the neck, or placed down low so that the animal will step into the trap and be held around the leg. Some operators attach the noose to a bent sapling or treadle mechanism so that it will spring up when triggered and the animal will be hanged more quickly.

A snare is often classed as a restraining trap rather than a killing trap. However, the struggles of the captured animal cause the wire to twist and tighten, leading to strangulation or severe injuries. Sites where animals have been caught in snares tend to show signs of extreme disturbance to the surrounding ground and vegetation—known as a "doughnut" in the United Kingdom—where the animal has tried to run, jump, or scrabble its way out of the trap, often for a period of several hours or more.

Although operators use skill in identifying the signs of the species they wish to catch and in setting their traps accordingly, snares are inherently indiscriminate. In 2005, the report of the U.K. Independent Working Group on Snaring (IWGS) set the proportion of nontarget captures between 21 and 69 percent in the United Kingdom.

In African countries, including Kenya, Zimbabwe, Sudan, Tanzania, Uganda, Zambia, Malawi, and Guinea, the indiscriminate use of snares by poachers has been identified as threatening the viability of the safari industry and the revenues that should accrue to the community. Snares are set for small "game" animals such as antelopes (duikers), bushpigs, and porcupines but also exact a heavy toll on giraffes, zebras, chimpanzees, elephants, and other animals. Governments and animal protection groups carry out targeted de-snaring operations. The David Sheldrick Wildlife Trust in Kenya estimated that 1,000 snares—the number that one team would typically lift in just a few days—would otherwise account for up to 18,250 animals in a year. The trust also notes that "these cruel devices are non-selective in that a wire snare set for a small antelope can cause the slow and agonizing death of an elephant as the noose tightens and cuts deeper into a limb or trunk, sometimes severing it entirely" ("Desnaring Project").

The devastating effect of snares on endangered populations is graphically illustrated by the plight of the saola in Vietnam: this small forest bovine was only discovered in 1999 and is now thought to be nearing extinction because of the introduction of wire snares for hunting in the 1990s. Surveys in northeast China found that snares set for ungulates were also killing tigers and leopards, and even the cherished mountain gorillas in Congo, Rwanda, and Uganda fall victim to snares. In Bossou, Guinea, however, chimpanzees have been seen to deactivate, and sometimes even destroy, snares set out in the forest.

For many critics, it is the prolonged suffering of the individual in the snare that makes it an unacceptable technique for the twenty-first century. The IWGS report identified a number of animal welfare impacts associated with snare use in the United Kingdom: these ranged from the stress of restraint and fear of predation or capture to painful injuries inflicted by the snare, thirst, hunger and exposure, infections arising from injuries, and the pain and injury associated with killing by the snare operator.

Animal welfare standards in killing and restraining traps were examined by researchers at the University of Bristol, who highlighted the paucity of research and the lack of proper standards for assessing the welfare of trapped mammals. The researchers also stressed the risk of pressure necrosis and ultimate death in released animals, little of which is observed. Researchers at the University of Cambridge found that snaring had such extreme effects on an animal's welfare that, regardless of the potential benefits, its use as a "pest" control method was never justified.

Differing attitudes toward conservation and animal welfare around the world have led to the development of regulatory regimes ranging from outright bans on snares to more complex rules about their use. In Australia, for example, neck snares are illegal, but leg snares are permitted. In the United States, the trapping of animals for their fur, as well as for nuisance and damage control, is highly regulated by state wildlife agencies. A survey in 2007 found that snares (defined as "any trap using a cable to trap a furbearer") were permitted in thirty-eight states and prohibited in nine.

A number of European member states, including Austria, Cyprus, Czech Republic, Denmark, Estonia, Germany, Greece, Hungary, Lithuania, Luxembourg, and Malta, either prohibit the use of snares or have no tradition of using them. Switzerland, which is not an EU member state, also has a complete ban on the use of snares. Other European states strictly limit snaring, to comply with European conservation and habitats legislation, which restricts the use of nonselective traps. However, snares are still generally permitted in five member states (Belgium, France, Ireland, Latvia, and the United Kingdom).

The use of snares in the United Kingdom is consistently controversial, with animal welfare campaigners pointing to continued evidence of extreme suffering and nontarget capture. Proponents of snaring argue that the traps are essential to protect quarry species (mainly free-living grouse and reared pheasant) for sport shooting (*see* Animals in Sport and Entertainment) and that rigorous predator control benefits biodiversity, although this is debatable. In Scotland, recent legislation on free-ranging animals has provided complex regulations intended to improve practice among gamekeepers. All snares must now be tagged with the user's identification number, which is issued on completion of operator training.

The use of snares against so-called exotic species, such as elephants and giraffes, as well as gorillas in one part of the world, causes horror, but elsewhere snares are claimed as useful management tools against predation and nuisance. But the point is that the suffering of the individual in the snare is the same, regardless of whether the animal is valued by society or labeled as a "pest."

Related articles: Animal protection in Africa; Animals used in research; The big cats; Conservation philosophy; De-snaring in Kenya; The ethics of killing free-living animals; Free-living chimpanzees; The fur trade; Legislation in the European Union; Perceptions of elephants; Primates worldwide

Batcheller, Gordon, *Summary of Trapping Regulations for Fur Harvesting in the United States*, Furbearer Conservation Technical Work Group, 2007.

Boddicker, L., "Snares for Predator Control," in Marsh, R. E. (ed.), *Proceedings Tenth Vertebrate Pest Conference*, University of Nebraska, 1982.

David Sheldrick Wildlife Trust, "Desnaring Project," available at http://www.sheldrickwildlifetrust.org/desnaring/index_new.asp.

Iossa, G., Soulsbury, C. D., and Harris, S., "Mammal Trapping: A Review of Animal Welfare Standards of Killing and Restraining Traps," *Animal Welfare* 16 (2007): 335–352.

Kirkwood, James (ed.), *Report of the Independent Working Group on Snaring*, Department for the Environmental, Food and Rural Affairs, 2005.

Ohashi, G., and Matsuzawa, T., "Deactivation of Snares by Wild Chimpanzees," *Primates* 52 (2011): 1–5.

Rochlitz, I., Pearce, G., and Broom, D., "The Impact of Snares on Animal Welfare," *Report on Snaring*, OneKind, 2010.

LIBBY ANDERSON

FOCUS ON SPECIES WORLDWIDE

THE BIG CATS

Of the thirty-eight species of free-living cats left on this planet, the most endangered include the Andean mountain cat, cheetah, Iriomote cat, jaguar, kodkod, lion, snow leopard, Spanish lynx, and tiger and many of the subspecies of most of the other twenty-nine species. All the big cats are included in this list because their size, larger territorial range, loss of habitat, and apparent value as body parts have resulted in their reduction worldwide. Currently, for example, there may be fewer than 800 snow leopards and 4,200 tigers left in their natural state.

All the members of the cat family have been persecuted since human beings evolved on our planet. Seen as a threat to life, as a source for clothing or body part jewelry, and as a source of raw materials for "medicines," their numbers have been systematically depleted. Many have died simply as a result of competition with human beings for land or food. Habitat loss has caused many species to travel vast distances into unfamiliar terrain to find food, where hunters and poachers have found it easier to track them. Competition for prey species, also hunted by humans, has resulted in the starvation and death of many cats. The larger the cat, the easier the animal is to track, and therefore the more susceptible the cat is to death by starvation.

Tigers have provided poachers with huge incomes from the sale of pelts for tourists, claws and teeth for jewelry, and body parts for supposed medicines and aphrodisiacs. DNA tests on these so-called medicines show that the bones of other animals, quite often cattle, are frequently substituted because the scarcity of real tiger bones cannot meet the demand. Yet these substitute "medicines" are still claimed to be efficacious and also provide huge profits for the trade. The shortage of tigers has put pressure on other large cats, such as the lion and snow leopard.

Loss of habitat is by far the biggest single killer of big cats. It will also ultimately be the single most important killer of all species, including human beings. As we lose more productive land to desert, pollution, minefields, and disease, we simultaneously lose species, soil, surface water, farmland, and forest. Loss of vegetation makes soil vulnerable to erosion. Loss of soil produces desert and thus more land incapable of providing sustenance to all of us. Bare land, particularly in the tropics, forces life-giving moisture-laden clouds higher into the atmosphere. These clouds then escape the tropics, which were designed to absorb this moisture, into temperate zones where they invariably produce flooding and landslides. The more these "tropical" cloud formations escape their natural environments, the more cloud cover there will be at higher latitudes. Ultimately, this will cool these areas and could trigger another ice age.

Why are cats so important in the general design of our ecosystem? Ironically, all carnivores help alleviate suffering. Old, injured, and infirm members of prey species would experience long lingering deaths, and population explosions of prey species could result in overgrazing and threaten all living species if numbers are not controlled. Life is tough out there in nature, and it is not just cats and their prey who suffer. As a natural regulatory system, the virgin environment is a perfect design. Sadly, the one animal on this planet who threatens all life has no natural predator, and although an occasional human is lost to a big cat, human beings are by far the most dangerous animals on this planet.

The preservation of big cats is as important as the preservation of every living animal and plant with which we share our fragile planet. Since carnivorous animals are highly susceptible to imbalances in the Earth's ecosystem, they are good indicators of the general health and well-being of our common environment. The ex-ploitation and destruction of any species on our fragile planet will threaten the survival of all of us. The balance of nature has evolved over millions of years. Human beings are the one species capable of destroying this balance and, with it, almost all life.

Originally founded to promote the conservation of big cats by breeding them in captivity and releasing them into their natural habitat, the Cat Survival Trust now concentrates on conserving the entire habitat where cats live because it is both more cost-effective and more environmentally beneficial. The trust rescues cats from bankrupt zoos and illegal collections and cares for big cats with long-term veterinary problems. It currently cares for about forty cats at its headquarters in Hertfordshire, England, many of whom are rescued animals. The cats are not on public view, but trust members and educational groups can visit by appointment.

Perhaps the Cat Survival Trust's biggest contribution to cat preservation is the purchase, following a public appeal, of ten thousand acres of virgin tropical forest in northeast Argentina, home to five cat species. In protecting this natural habitat at a cost of thirty pounds per acre, the organization now protects seventy cats from five species, five million trees, billions of insects and plants, and hundreds of thousands of other birds, mammals, reptiles, fishes, and primates.

Related articles: Cats; Conservation philosophy; The ethics of killing free-living animals; The ethics of zoos; Sanctuaries and rehabilitation; South American perspectives on animals

Ewer, R. F., *The Carnivores*, Cornell University Press, 1997.
Gittleman, John L., Funk, Stephan M., MacDonald, David W., and Wayne, Robert K., *Carnivore Behavior, Ecology and Evolution*, vols. 1 and 2, Cornell University Press, 1989 and 1996.
Kitchener, Andrew, *The Natural History of the Wild Cats*, Cornell University Press, 1997.
MacDonald, David W. (ed.), *The Princeton Encyclopedia of Mammals*, Princeton University Press, 2009.
MacDonald, David W., and Loveridge, A. J. (eds.), *Biology and Conservation of Wild Carnivores*, Oxford University Press, 2010.
Vargas, Astrid (ed.), *Iberian Lynx Ex Situ Conservation*, Fundacion Bioversidad, 2009.

TERRY MOORE

COEXISTING WITH COYOTES

Coyotes and humans shared the same environment long before European settlers arrived in North America. To many Native American cultures, coyotes were powerful mythological figures endowed with the power of creation and venerated for their intelligence and mischievous nature. The Aztec name for the coyote was *coyotyl*, which loosely translates to "trickster," whereas Navajo sheep and goat herders referred to the coyote as "God's dog." European settlers, however, viewed coyotes as a threat to livestock and as a competitor for game species, a view that unfortunately still persists in many areas of North America. As a result, the coyote remains the most persecuted native carnivore in the United States.

Coyotes typically weigh twenty to thirty pounds, are similar to a tan-colored shepherd-type dog, and are able to crossbreed with dogs and wolves. Native to the grasslands and prairies of North America, coyotes have expanded their range threefold since the 1850s, largely in response to human alterations of the environment and the eradication of larger predators including wolves, cougars, and grizzly bears. At least nineteen coyote subspecies now roam throughout North America, from California to Newfoundland, and from Alaska to Panama, occupying a broad range of habitats, from grasslands to deserts, from eastern woodlands to boreal forests, and from agricultural lands to urban parks.

Coyotes occupy the biological niche between foxes and wolves and play an integral role in their environment by helping to maintain healthy ecosystems and species diversity. As opportunistic omnivores, coyotes feed on a wide variety of mammals, insects, and fruits, though rodents are their main food source. Indeed, the success of coyotes is a testament to their ability to survive—and even thrive—on whatever food is available. Coyotes generally fear people; however, those who associate humans with food may become habituated. Habituated coyotes now frequent suburban areas, taking advantage of abundant food, water, and shelter. Unsecured garbage, unfenced gardens, and unattended domesticated animals become easy targets. Documented cases of coyotes biting humans, however, are rare and most often caused by humans feeding coyotes.

Historically, conflicts between humans and coyotes have been addressed through lethal means. Between 1916 and 2000, the U.S. Department of Agriculture's Wildlife Services program (formerly Animal Damage Control) killed nearly six million coyotes, largely at taxpayers' expense, for the benefit of a small number of sheep and cattle ranchers. In addition, hundreds of thousands of coyotes are killed each year for their fur, for "sport" (*see* Animals in Sport and Entertainment), and in "body count" contests where prizes are awarded for killing the most coyotes. Most states in America have no laws regulating by what means, or how many, coyotes may be killed, and some states still offer bounties to encourage

coyote killing. Despite decades of systematic poisoning, trapping, and shooting campaigns aimed at eradicating coyote populations, there are more coyotes in North America today than ever before.

The coyote's remarkable success appears to be directly related to lethal attempts to reduce its populations. Years of intense persecution have selected coyotes who are more adaptable, resilient, and wary of people. They have learned to spring traps without being caught, to avoid poison baits, to hide their dens from prying human eyes, and to hunt during times of little human activity. To further avoid humans, coyotes have become more active during the night.

Widespread attempts to control coyote populations have had little long-term impact because coyotes' strong compensatory responses—such as increased litter size and pup survival—allow them to replenish their numbers and reoccupy vacated habitat. Further, although lethal control may produce a short-term reduction of coyotes in a particular area, the vacuum is soon filled by coyotes emigrating from surrounding areas and by shifts in neighboring packs.

Despite clear scientific evidence demonstrating the futility and counterproductive nature of indiscriminate lethal coyote control, many state and federal "wildlife managers" continue to promote killing as the best method to address conflicts. An increasing number of scientists, however, have begun to speak out against lethal control. Their studies show that coyotes, as well as other large carnivores, play a vital ecological role, and their removal can have a negative impact on species diversity and the health and integrity of native ecosystems.

But scientific evidence is not enough. What is needed is a new paradigm for the way we treat native carnivores—indeed, all free-living animals—one that recognizes the ecological importance of these species, as well as their intrinsic value as individuals. If the money and efforts used to kill coyotes and other predators were redirected toward cost-effective, nonlethal methods, such as public education, better landscape development, improved fencing, and guard animals, conflicts could be significantly reduced without the need to kill. Ultimately, it will be the public that pressures managers to make this ethical shift, as communities across North America demand that conflicts be addressed with humane solutions that do not involve killing.

Related articles: Conservation philosophy; Dogs; The ethics of killing free-living animals; Facts about bears; The fur trade; Humane education; The moral claims of animals; Snares and snaring

Fox, C. H., "An Analysis of the Marin County Strategic Plan for Protection of Livestock and Wildlife: An Alternative to Traditional Predator Control," master's thesis, Prescott College, Arizona, 2008.

———, "Predator Control and Ethics," in Bekoff, M. (ed.), *Encyclopedia of Animal Rights and Animal Welfare*, 2nd ed., Greenwood, 2010.

———, "Trapping in the United States" in *Animals and Their Legal Rights*, rev. ed., Animal Welfare Institute, 2010.

Fox, C. H., and Bekoff, M., "Ethical Reflections on Wolf Recovery and Conservation: A Practical Approach for Making Room for Wolves," in Musiani, M., Boitani, L., and Paquet, P. (eds.), *The World of Wolves: New Perspectives on Ecology, Behaviour and Policy*, University of Calgary Press, 2010.

Fox, C. H., and Papouchis, C. M., *Coyotes in Our Midst: Coexisting with an Adaptable and Resilient Carnivore*, Animal Protection Institute, 2005.

——— (eds.), *Cull of the Wild: A Contemporary Analysis of Wildlife Trapping in the United States*, Animal Protection Institute, 2004.

CAMILLA H. FOX

FACTS ABOUT BEARS

There are eight species of bear living in habitats as varied as the tropical rainforests of Indonesia and the icy Arctic wastes. Polar bears (*Ursus maritimus*) are the only bear species living in the cold Arctic regions, and brown bears (*Ursus arctos*) live in temperate forests of the Northern Hemisphere from North America (where they are often called grizzlies) through parts of Europe and on through Asia and China, to the northern island of Hokkaido in Japan.

American black bears (*Ursus americanus*) inhabit North America, and Asiatic black bears (*Ursus thibetanus*) are found from Pakistan through Southeast Asia and into China and Japan. Sloth bears (*Melursus ursinus*) are found mainly in the forests of India, and the small sun bear (*Helarctos malayanus*) inhabits the tropical forests of Southeast Asia. The only bear species to inhabit South America, living in the cloud forests of the Andes, is the spectacled bear (*Tremarctos ornatus*). The giant panda (*Ailuropoda melanoleuca*) is the eighth bear species, of which only around two thousand are left in central China, surviving on a diet consisting almost entirely of bamboo shoots.

Not only have bears suffered massive habitat loss over the past century, but they also continue to be abused and exploited throughout the world. Bears are hunted for sport (*see* Animals in Sport and Entertainment), shot as "pests," caught as cubs for the exotic companion animal trade, incarcerated in pitiful enclosures in zoos, and forced to perform unnatural acts in circuses. They are killed for their body parts, especially for their teeth, skin, body fat, and flesh. Bear paws are an expensive delicacy in Asian restaurants. Bear gall bladders fetch thousands of dollars for their supposed medicinal qualities in the Far East.

China has more than ten thousand bears in "bear farms," where they are kept in cramped cages and their bile is drained daily through a tube inserted into their gall bladders. Chinese bear farms are believed to produce more than ten thousand kilos of bear bile each year for Chinese medicines, despite the fact that there are herbal and synthetic alternatives. Another six thousand bears are kept in Vietnamese and South Korean bear farms.

In Pakistan, bears are pitted against fighting dogs in vicious bear-baiting events, and in India the biggest threat to bears is their capture to be trained as dancing bears. Dancing bears used to be a common sight in Turkey and Greece, but the practice was eradicated by 1996. A few hundred dancing bears were still being used in Pakistan and India in 2009, but the practice is gradually being banned through concerted efforts of the relevant authorities supported by specialist nongovernmental organizations (NGOs).

Bears in zoos often show abnormal behaviors, such as continual pacing, head weaving, or lethargy. This is the result of environmental deprivation, where the intelligent creatures are kept in sterile captive conditions with no outlet for their natural behavior. The worst example of bears in captivity is in Japan, where more than a thousand are kept in seven bear (zoo) parks, with possibly fifty or more bears held in each concrete enclosure. The unfortunate captive animals spend their day begging and fighting over tidbits from tourists who believe the animals' aggressive fighting over the food, space, and mates is normal. Investigators from the World Society for the Protection of Animals (WSPA) have witnessed bears with horrendous injuries at these Japanese parks, including multiple lacerations around the neck and flaps of skin hanging off and left untreated.

Hunting of bears for sport is legal in many countries, including North America, where hunters use bows, crossbows, guns, and hunting dogs in pursuit of their quarry. Many bears escape, only partially wounded, and die a slow death. Even mother bears are legally hunted when they emerge from their winter dens after hibernation. In many cases, their orphaned cubs are left to die.

Despite this catalog of abuse, there are some signs of hope. Pakistan has now banned bear-baiting. Bear dancing is diminishing. The Vietnamese government is now working with NGOs to prevent the escalation of bear farming in its country, but in China, where bear farming is a legal business, the number of caged bears used for bile extraction is increasing. In 1991, WSPA launched its Libearty Campaign to raise consciousness about the plight of bears in their natural state and in captivity. WSPA has funded investigations, lobbied for legislation, put pressure on governments, and pioneered bear sanctuaries for rescued or orphaned bears—for example, in Pakistan, in Romania, and in the U.S. state of Idaho.

Bears urgently need international legal protection. The trade in bear products must be curtailed. People need to appreciate that inappropriate captive zoo conditions can inflict great harm on bears. Not least of all, people need to be educated to see bears for who they are: intelligent, sensitive, even graceful creatures who have a claim on our moral concern.

Related articles: Animals in Asia; Animals in Chinese culture; Animals in circuses; The complexity of animal awareness; Developments in animal law; The emergence of animal protection in Russia; The ethics of killing free-living animals; The ethics of zoos; Hunting with dogs; Japanese attitudes toward animals; Moon bears and bear bile farming; The moral claims of animals; Sanctuaries and rehabilitation

Breiter, Matthias, _Bears: A Year in the Life_, Firefly Books, 2009.
Brown, Gary, _The Bear Almanac_, Globe Pequot Press, 2009.
Brunner, Bernd, _Bears: A Brief History_, Yale University Press, 2009.
Masterson, Linda, _Living with Bears: A Practical Guide to Bear Country_, Pixyjack Press, 2006.
Ward, Paul, _Bears of the World_, Facts on File, 2003.
Watkins, Victor, _Bear Sanctuary_, Bear Sanctuary, 2010.

VICTOR WATKINS

FREE-LIVING CHIMPANZEES

When I began my chimpanzee research in 1960, in Tanzania's Gombe national park, there must have been well over one million free-living chimpanzees in Africa. It is estimated that there are now 300,000 at most, and they are spread through twenty-one nations, many in small fragmented populations that have little hope of long-term survival (they are already extinct in four countries). And for other primates the situation is even more alarming. One species, Miss Waldron's red colobus, was declared extinct in 2000.

The exploitation of natural resources through poverty, ignorance, or greed is the root cause of catastrophic environmental problems along with human population growth. How incredible to learn that the number of people born throughout the world _each day_ is greater than the current number of all the great apes (chimpanzees, bonobos, gorillas, and orangutans) combined.

It was not until 1986, when most of the scientists working in different study sites across Africa met at a conference, that I suddenly realized how serious was the plight of chimpanzees in their natural state. The time had come for me to leave my forest paradise and try to raise awareness about what was going on—chimpanzee numbers plummeting as a result of habitat destruction and hunting. I began traveling around the world, giving talks about the situation and gradually realizing the massive harm we humans are inflicting on nature everywhere. Wilderness areas and the animals living there are imperiled, we are losing biodiversity, and it is desperately important that we learn to live in greater harmony with the natural world.

The survival of chimpanzees is threatened as a result of deforestation as land is cleared for animal grazing, growing crops, and building homes and as trees are felled for firewood and the lucrative charcoal business. Also, many chimpanzees are caught in wire snares set to catch other animals for food—and though the chimpanzees can usually break free, they cannot remove the cruelly tightened wire noose. Eventually they lose a hand or foot or die of gangrene.

But it is the bushmeat trade—the _commercial_ hunting of free-living animals for food—that is the greatest threat to chimpanzees today. In these animals' last stronghold in the Congo Basin, foreign logging companies make roads deep into previously inaccessible forests. This provides access for hunters who camp along the roads and shoot every kind of animal they see, including elephants, gorillas, monkeys, antelopes, pigs, and even birds and bats—any animal who can be killed, smoked, and transported to the cities, where the urban elite pay more for this flesh than for that of chickens or goats because it satisfies a cultural preference for free-living animal flesh. Huge truckloads—and even planeloads—of bushmeat regularly cross international borders. In addition, traditional pygmy hunters not only catch animals to feed themselves, but also are paid to supply meat for the logging companies' employees and their families in the huge settlements.

None of this is sustainable: unless a concerted effort is made to control the bushmeat trade, it will soon result in the virtual extinction of the great apes—and countless other species—in many parts of Africa. Moreover, the bushmeat trade almost certainly contributes to the spread of disease. Chimpanzees and humans can be infected with the same diseases. Human handling of sick chimpanzees may have led to the Ebola epidemic. The chimpanzee form of the Simian AIDS retrovirus almost certainly jumped the species barrier as a result of humans butchering the meat of infected animals and then mutated into HIV1 and HIV2, leading to the human AIDS pandemic.

There is still some illegal trafficking in chimpanzees—including the shooting of mothers to steal infants as companion animals and entertainment, though chimpanzees used in this way, like those used in medical research, mostly are bred in captivity. At the aforementioned 1986 conference we learned a great deal about the conditions that many captive chimpanzees were forced to endure, and it became obvious that it was desperately important to improve conditions in zoos and research labs. It is estimated that the number of captive chimpanzees worldwide is between 4,000 and 6,000, with about 1,500 in the United States. This figure includes those kept in zoos, labs, and sanctuaries and those kept as "pets." It is because they are so like us biologically that chimpanzees may be used as substitute humans in biomedical research, sometimes imprisoned for life in cages only five feet by five feet. It is unethical to treat chimpanzees in these ways. Nor should they be used for entertainment or bought as companion animals. By the time a chimpanzee is five or six years old, he or she is already as strong as most humans. The cute infant who could be dressed up and treated as one of the family suddenly becomes potentially dangerous and must be locked up or, in Africa, tied with chains.

Chimpanzees, along with the other great apes, are our closest living relatives. Chimpanzees differ from us genetically, in the structure of the DNA, by only just over 1 percent. The anatomy of chimpanzee and human brains is almost identical—though ours is bigger. Not surprisingly, chimpanzees show intellectual performances once thought unique to us. Studies have revealed countless similarities in social behavior. We are not the only beings on the planet with personalities, minds, and emotions, as once was thought. There is, after all, no sharp line dividing us from the rest of the animal kingdom. How will we be judged, by future generations, if we allow the great apes to vanish along with the last of the great rainforests?

Related articles: Animals and public health; Animals used in research; Captive chimpanzees; CITES and international trade; The complexity of animal awareness; Conservation philosophy; The ethics of killing free-living animals; The ethics of zoos; The future of free-roaming orangutans; The legal rights of great apes; Primates worldwide; Snares and snaring; The trade in primates for research

Goodall, Jane, *The Chimpanzees of Gombe: Patterns of Behavior*, Belknap Press of the Harvard University Press, 1986.
———, *In the Shadow of Man*, Houghton Mifflin, 1971, and Mariner Books, 2010.
———, *Through a Window: 30 Years Observing the Gombe Chimpanzees*, Houghton Mifflin, 1990, and Mariner Books, 2010.
Goodall, Jane, and Bekoff, Marc, *The Ten Trusts: What We Must Do to Care for the Animals We Love*, Harper San Francisco, 2002.
Goodall, Jane, and Peterson, Dale, *Visions of Caliban*, Houghton Mifflin, 1993.

JANE GOODALL

FREE-RANGING HORSES

Their hoofprints were barely visible as we stood on the edge of the water hole. The free-ranging horses had recently been there but had left a narrow path without disturbing the vegetation. We stood there and imagined them returning at dusk to get the last drink of the day, the mares and foals cautiously approaching the cool water under the watchful vigilance of the band stallion. The peaceful silence of the moment was suddenly broken by the sound of a bulldozer. Just over the hill, a housing development was taking shape, and this water hole would soon be gone. The joy we had felt for those minutes turned to sadness. Where would these horses go?

This question of loss of habitat has profoundly affected the fate of millions of free-ranging horses over the last five centuries. In the rush for more space, humans have squeezed the horses onto ever-shrinking and increasingly rugged areas of land, decimating their numbers and upsetting sensitive genetic balances, through governmental removal and adoption policies. Begun in the nineteenth century, these polices have their origin in the desire to remove Native Americans from ancestral lands. To corral the nomadic tribes, the government allowed the wholesale slaughter of their food source, the buffaloes, and their transportation, the mustangs. Thus began the descent toward near extinction for the free-ranging horse.

But it was not always so for these magnificent animals. Their ancestors evolved in North America before mysteriously disappearing about eight thousand years ago. During the fifteenth century, the Spanish explorers brought with them today's modern horse, inadvertently reintroducing Equus to its original indigenous territory. Horses had returned to their native land. The Spanish horses soon began to flee human confinement, eventually forming herds that freely roamed the western plains, sharing the grasses with the buffalo and transforming the lives of the Plains Indians.

Today, they can still be found in most western states, with the majority in the high deserts of Nevada. They are normally dark bay in color, but paints, duns, buckskins, and horses of other colors can be found. A few display the primitive striping on their legs, taking us back to a time before humans domesticated the horse. In some states there are just a handful of free horses left, hanging on despite the continued loss of habitat. At the beginning of the twentieth century, there were as many as two million free-ranging horses roaming throughout the west. But by the 1960s they were almost wiped out by those who rounded them up to be processed into food for companion animals; killed them outright because they were competition for the precious grass needed for millions of cattle; or sold them as war mounts for the Boer War and World War I, when over a million free-ranging horses were rounded up and sent to war—not a single one returned home.

It was a woman from Nevada who came to be known as "Wild Horse Annie" who began to protest the treatment of America's free-ranging horses. She galvanized an entire nation. It was her courage and dedication, together with enormous pressure from the American people through their letters to governmental officials, that helped bring about the Wild Free Roaming Horse and Burro Act passed by Congress in 1971. Responsibility for this new protection of free-ranging horses and burros was assigned to a reluctant Bureau of Land Management, which before the 1971 act had allowed these very same horses to be killed. This was the same agency that had been created in the 1930s to oversee cattle grazing in vast areas of the west.

Unfortunately, since the act was passed, many of the horses have still remained unprotected from abuse and slaughter. Hundreds have been shot while peacefully grazing. Over the years, free-living horses have been stolen by "mustangers" and shipped to slaughter. Thousands of others are rounded up each year by the Bureau of Land Management to be adopted for a mere 125 dollars by any qualified person—the Bureau's way of managing the number of free-ranging horses competing with cattle for grazing. Many of the adoptions are not successful, and the horses end up in deplorable situations. After caring for an adopted mustang for one year, the adopter receives an ownership title to the horse. For a good many of the horses, the transfer of title means a trip straight to the slaughterhouse, where the horses' flesh is sold in European and Asian markets, a sad end for animals who are revered for their freedom and beauty.

As with other free-ranging animals, the horse has faced difficulties and a reduction of numbers when competing for space with humans. As the planet grows smaller and open space more precious, the future of free-ranging horses will be dependent on humans learning to share space with other creatures.

Related articles: Conservation philosophy; Developments in animal law; Horse slaughter; Horses

American Society for the Prevention of Cruelty to Animals, "Wild Horses," 2010, available at http://www.aspca.org/fight-animal-cruelty/equine-cruelty/wild-horses.html.
Clarke, Barbara, "Wild Horses—Symbol of the West Moving East?," *San Francisco Chronicle*, March 12, 2010, available at http://articles.sfgate.com/2010-03-12/opinion/18386540_1_wild-horses-manifest-destiny-rancher.
James-Patton, Valerie, and MacDonald, Cindy, "America's Wild Horses, Critical Crossroads," *True Cowboy Magazine*, October 2010.
Ryden, Hope, *America's Last Wild Horses*, Lyons Press, 2005.
Stillman, Deanne, *Mustang*, Houghton Mifflin, 2008.
Wuerthner, George, and Matteson, Mollie (eds.), *Welfare Ranching: The Subsidized Destruction of the American West*, Island Press, 2002.

DEBORAH ELLSWORTH AND BARBARA CLARKE

THE FUTURE OF FREE-ROAMING ORANGUTANS

The tropical rainforests of Southeast Asia, considered one of the world's biologically richest ecosystems, are a refuge for some of the world's most endangered species, including orangutans. However, the future of these forests and the species these forests harbor is under tremendous threat. If the onslaught of habitat destruction is not halted, experts predict that by the 2030s, biologically viable populations of Asia's only great apes will no longer exist.

Orangutans were one of the first great apes known to the Western world, yet for many years, they were the least understood. Often called the "neglected ape," orangutans were rarely seen in their natural habitat—the great rainforests of Borneo and Sumatra in Southeast Asia. In the Malay language, *orang hutan* means "people of the forest." In recent years, the behavior and ecology of these remarkable apes have become better known. However, time is short. Today, there are probably no more than fifty thousand free-ranging orangutans remaining, and their numbers are declining daily. The exploitation of tropical rainforests for timber coupled with the establishment of massive palm oil plantations, as well as poaching and strip-mining for gold and zircon, has put the continued existence of orangutan populations into question.

Orangutans—unlike their gregarious African cousins, chimpanzees, bonobos, and gorillas—live a semi-solitary existence high in the forest canopy. They are truly "people of the forest"; no other great ape spends so much time in the trees. Recently, two distinct species have been classified: the Bornean orangutan (*Pongo pygmaus*) and the Sumatran orangutan (*Pongo abelli*). With the exception of mature Bornean males, both species seldom venture onto the forest floor. Orangutans are almost entirely dependent on the forest for their survival, subsisting on over four hundred different kinds of fruit, young leaves, bark, and vines, as well as the occasional insect. Anatomically, the body of an orangutan is well adapted to this lifestyle. Orangutans have short trunks, long arms, and hook-like fingers that are particularly suited to hand-over-hand movement, called brachiation, as well as climbing and clambering in the forest canopy. At night orangutans are dependent on the forest for shelter. They sleep in tree nests, which they construct on a daily basis in the evening or late afternoon, bending large branches to create a strong platform and breaking and flattening smaller branches and leaves to provide bedding.

Since the 1990s, Southeast Asia has become one of the world's leading sources of tropical timber. Recently it was estimated that as much as 70 percent of the timber exported from Indonesian Borneo (Kalimantan) was harvested illegally. Illegal and commercial logging operations reduce the area covered by forest, erode the soil, and expose the remaining forest fragments to the risk of fire. In addition to sheltering orangutans, many forests also constitute the last refuge for endangered species such as the Sumatran rhinoceros, proboscis monkey, and species of hornbills.

Land clearing for palm oil plantations and timber estates not only annihilates the forest but also fragments forests and confines orangutans to small, restricted areas. Gold mining, in particular, often takes place within or near protected areas of forest. Independent miners, using pans and sieves, extract small deposits of gold from the sandy soils beneath the forest. Although in many instances, these operations are small in scale, the damage done to the forest is immense. Areas of pristine rainforest are quickly transformed into barren moonscapes; rivers become devoid of life, polluted by heavy metals such as mercury that are used to separate gold from the soil.

The greatest threat to orangutans is land clearance for permanent commercial agriculture. Palm oil plantations are particularly popular as a cash crop because the palms grow rapidly and produce a greater income than logging. Large tracts of rainforest are cleared to establish plantations. Crops are then planted in orderly rows of one species, also termed monocultures. This practice is disastrous for orangutans and drastically reduces biodiversity, destroying what was once habitable primary rainforest for numerous species, including orangutans.

In addition, orangutans are caught or killed in plantations as agricultural "pests." If the victim is a mother, her infant is captured and sold as a "pet." Some infants are subsequently confiscated and taken to rehabilitation centers. There, an attempt is made over a number of years to reintroduce the ex-captive orangutans back into the forest. Although essential to the welfare of individual orangutans, the rehabilitation and release process is difficult and time-consuming, and this process will not be enough to save orangutans as viable populations in nature. Free-ranging orangutan populations will survive in perpetuity on this planet only if large tracts of rainforest in Borneo and northern Sumatra are preserved and protected.

Tropical rainforests are of global importance. They are a storehouse of plants, fungi, and microorganisms, many of which could be important sources for medicines, materials, and even foods in the future. Rainforests also help regulate global climate and protect fragile soils and watersheds, helping prevent flooding. Species such as orangutans also coexist and interact with other rainforest plants, animals, and insects, in a multitude of intricate ways (many still yet to be unraveled).

Orangutans inadvertently play an important role in shaping and preserving the forests they inhabit through branch breaking (a type of pruning), snag pushing, and seed dispersal. The disappearance of orangutan populations may have profound consequences for remaining tropical rainforests and thousands of other animals and plants that inhabit this fragile environment—consequences that as yet cannot be fully evaluated.

Related articles: Animals in Asia; Conservation philosophy; Free-living chimpanzees; Primates worldwide; Sanctuaries and rehabilitation

Galdikas, Biruté Mary, *Great Ape Odyssey*, Harry N. Abrams, 2005.
———, *Orangutan Odyssey*, Harry N. Abrams, 1999.
———, *Reflections of Eden*, Little, Brown, 1995.
Gallardo, Evelyn, *Among the Orangutans*, Chronicle Books, 1995.
MacKinnon, John, *In Search of the Red Ape*, Ballantine Books, 1975.
Nadler, R. D, Galdikas, B. M., Sheeran, L. K., and Rosen, N. (eds.), *The Neglected Ape*, Springer, 1996.

BIRUTÉ MARY GALDIKAS

KOALAS AND THEIR PROTECTION

Koalas are loved the world over for their gentle demeanor and teddy bear–like features. They are one of the living icons of Australia. They live naturally only on the island continent and have evolved with the eucalypts to take a unique place among Australia's flora and fauna.

Often called bears, koalas are in fact marsupials, like most of the mammals of Australia. Their young are born after approximately thirty-five days of gestation; the jelly bean–like baby koala makes his or her way unaided from the mother's cloaca to her pouch where the baby attaches to a teat and spends the next six to seven months slowly developing. Around then, the young koala is ready to make the transition from a milk diet to that of eucalyptus leaves. In order to digest the fibrous and otherwise poisonous gum leaves, the young koala must eat pap—a form of runny feces produced by his or her mother—which provides the young koala with the intestinal gut flora he or she needs to survive on a diet of gum leaves. Once the young koala—called a joey—begins to eat gum leaves, the animal grows quickly into a furry, fluffy bundle and, inquisitive like most young animals, begins to explore his or her treetop home.

Eucalyptus trees provide both food and shelter to koalas, and although koalas have been known to browse on several other species, eucalyptus leaves form their staple diet and are essential to their survival. Koalas live within hierarchically structured breeding groups where each animal has his or her own home range or territory. A koala's home range comprises a number of key trees that act as boundary markers, bedrooms, pantries, and sometimes battlegrounds. Home ranges vary in size depending on a number of factors, including habitat quality, sex, age, social status, and the carrying capacity of the habitat.

The home range of a koala in a socially stable population is of a size that contains enough trees of the right species to provide adequate food and shelter for that particular individual throughout his or her entire life. Unless there is a disturbance (for example, tree clearing) to their habitat, koalas will occupy the same home range all their life. Koalas regularly move between their home range trees to feed, to shelter, and to maintain social contact with other koalas. This allows for regeneration of leaves, which provide the animal's food, and for the regular scenting or marking of home range trees to indicate ownership. Koalas remain in a tree until they have exhausted its food supply unless there is something wrong in the greater environment, such as isolation or fragmentation of remaining habitat resulting from land clearance.

Since the European settlement in Australia, koalas and people have had what could be described as a schizophrenic relationship. During the late 1800s and early 1900s, they were hunted for their fur, and estimates suggest that as many as ten million koalas were shot during those years. In the early 1900s, koalas began to enjoy adoration as the little teddy bears of the bush. Popular children's books, such as those featuring the character Blinky Bill, were written, and koalas were identified as a symbol of national pride. But although people love koalas, they also pose the greatest threat to the species' survival. Roughly 80 percent of the koala's original habitat has been cleared, and of what remains almost none is protected. The koala has been a protected species since the late 1930s, but the animals' actual habitat has never been protected. There is a well-known slogan in Australia today that sums it all up: "No tree . . . no me."

Many people are concerned about the future of koalas; they nurse sick, injured, and orphaned koalas back to health and fight to protect their habitat. There are also various sanctuaries around the country where captive koalas can be visited by members of the public, who come in droves to watch and hold these beloved animals. A 1997 study estimated that koalas contribute over one billion dollars to Australia's economy each year in terms of foreign tourism. Unfortunately, very little of that is returned to bolster efforts to protect the species.

The Australian Koala Foundation has nominated the koala as a vulnerable species because the animals are threatened in many parts of their range. Australia has one of the highest land-clearing rates in the world, and koalas, along with many other precious native species, are losing food and shelter as a result. Those who live in or near koala habitat can do many practical things to help. For example, they can drive carefully, especially at night (thousands of koalas are killed on the roads every year), and keep companion dogs inside at night (thousands of koalas are also killed by dogs, often in the dog's own backyard, which may also be within the koala's home range). They also can plant trees and keep a sturdy rope dangling in swimming pools so that if koalas fall in, they can climb back out.

Related articles: Animal issues in Australia; The fur trade; Sanctuaries and rehabilitation

Australia Koala Foundation, "The Koala: Endangered or Not?," available from https://www.savethekoala.com/koalasendangered.html.

Moyal, Ann, *Koala: A Historical Biography*, CSIRO, 2008.

Schaller, George B., *The Last Panda*, University of Chicago Press, 1993.

Sharp, Anne, *The Koala Book*, Pelican, 1995.

Wilson, Edward O., *Consilience: The Unity of Knowledge*, Knopf, 1998.

DEBORAH TABART

MOON BEARS AND
BEAR BILE FARMING

Of the eight bear species in the world, the Asiatic black bear (*Ursus selenarctos thibetanus*) is perhaps the most maligned. Affectionately named the "moon bear," originating from the Latin, because of the yellow moon-shaped chest crescent, this species suffers widespread exploitation and abuse in every country throughout its range.

The moon bear is believed by scientist Daniel Taylor-Ide to be the original yeti, and the animal's habitat extends from Iran to Japan and across Southeast Asia. Listed under the Convention on International Trade in Endangered Species (CITES) Appendix I, the surviving moon bears number as few as 25,000, estimates indicate. Their numbers continue to diminish as a result of habitat loss, population fragmentation, nuisance animal control measures, exploitation for entertainment, and the commercialization of bear parts and bile juice for use in traditional medicine. Capable of destroying forty trees in one night in Japan, the moon bear has become a favorite "nuisance" target of hunters, while the practice of logging and the subsequent habitat reduction across the bears' range further compounds their fragile status as an endangered species.

As the most bipedal of all the bear species, the ease with which moon bears stand on their hind legs is a characteristic often cruelly exploited for entertainment. Dancing bears in India, baited bears in Pakistan, and circus bears in Vietnam, China, and other parts of Asia are frequently subjected to the painful removal of teeth and claws, in order to facilitate a safer training environment.

Undoubtedly, one of the most significant impacts on their population is the demand for their whole gallbladders and bile juice, which is used in traditional Oriental medicine Asia-wide and in Asian communities throughout the world. In South Korea, where a single gallbladder can fetch US$10,000, the once-abundant moon bear has been hunted almost to extinction. With the trade expanding across Asia, countries such as Cambodia (which have historically seen minimal usage of bear parts) are now hosts to an industry that is supplying gallbladders for medicine and bear paws for restaurants. Bear parks in Japan keep moon bears in pits for public entertainment, and once the animals die, their gallbladders fuel a booming pharmaceutical industry.

In the early 1980s, despite the available herbal and synthetic alternatives, countries such as Korea, China, and Vietnam began to search for a still animal-based alternative to taking animals from their natural state and killing them for the sake of a two-ounce organ. The first, North Korea, subsequently announced that it had developed a unique method of obtaining this "liquid gold"—and the practice of bear farming was born. Bears were taken as cubs, caged, and surgically implanted with metal catheters, so that bile could be extracted on a regular basis while the animal was kept alive.

A few years later, Chinese scientists adopted the same procedure, and by the early 1990s, there were nearly 500 bear farms in operation, holding more than 10,000 bears. There are officially 7,002 farmed moon bears on 67 farms in China, and such farming has created a host of welfare problems: with a stimulated demand, bears are still poached for their whole gallbladders by illegal hunters and are also often taken as an illegal source of new stock for the farms. In Vietnam, the situation for moon bears is literally out of control. With fewer than 100 thought to be surviving in their natural habitat, the number on bear farms exploded from a few hundred in 1999 to over 4,000 by mid-2000. As of 2013, the number has lowered to approximately 2,000. Although South Korea banned the practice of bear farming in 1992, just over 1,000 bears remained on the defunct farms as of 2012. Additionally, breeding has not been disallowed, and a relaxation of the law now sees bears over the age of ten slaughtered and their gallbladders sold.

Conditions on bear farms are unbelievably cruel. In China, moon bears are confined for up to thirty years in cages the size of their own bodies and milked daily for their bile through rusting metal catheters implanted deep into their gall bladders. A new so-called humane technique called "free dripping" uses no implant, but also involves a high mortality rate as a result of bile leakage, widespread infection, and peritonitis. In Vietnam, bile is extracted with the aid of ultrasound, which detects the location of the gallbladder in an anesthetized bear, before a four-inch spinal needle is punched into the abdomen, and bile is then "pumped" into a receptacle.

However, there is hope for this magnificent species. In July 2000, Chinese government officials signed an agreement with the Animals Asia Foundation, pledging to rescue five hundred moon bears from the worst farms and work toward the total elimination of bear farming. Between October 2000 and 2012, over 40 bear farms were closed by the government, with 277 confiscated bears turned over to the care of Animals Asia, to live in a sanctuary that has won the Global Federation of Animal Sanctuaries award. In a similar initiative, from 2006 to 2012 over 110 bears in Vietnam were confiscated from the farms and now reside at Animals Asia's second rescue center near Hanoi. Other groups working to end the bear farm industry in Vietnam include Education for Nature Vietnam, Free the Bears, Wildlife at Risk, and the World Society for the Protection of Animals. The program is seen as a wake-up call for protecting the beautiful moon bear before it is too late—and for promoting animal-free, traditional Oriental medicine.

___

Related articles: Animals in Asia; Animals in Chinese culture; Animals in circuses; Animals in the Middle East; CITES and international trade; Facts about bears; Japanese attitudes toward animals; Legal protection of animals in China; Slaughter; The treatment of animals in India

Animals Asia Foundation, "End Bear Farming," 2011, available at http://www.animalsasia.org/index.php?UID=2J0NIOGTVCWA.
BBC Science and Nature, "Asiatic Black Bear, Tibetan Black Bear, Himalayan Black Bear, Moon Bear," 2008, available at http://www.bbc.co.uk/nature/wildfacts/factfiles/10.shtml.
Born Free Foundation, "Moon Bears," available at http://www.bornfree.org.uk/animals/moon-bears/.

JILL ROBINSON

PERCEPTIONS OF ELEPHANTS

Elephants are widely considered some of the world's most magnificent animals on account of their intelligence, beauty, size, and strength. New discoveries are continually made about this species since the animals' complexity leaves a seemingly endless line of questions for scientists to tackle. Congruently, the management and conservation issues surrounding these animals are also many and complex. The massive reduction in wilderness areas available for free-living animals, a process associated with the resource demands of increasing human populations, is a major threat to the elephant. As the largest terrestrial mammal, the elephant requires immense open spaces for survival. Only recently have conservationists realized the dangers of confining this and other species, whose ecology necessitates freedom of movement.

Another primary threat to this species is insatiable demand for ivory, which has been a driving force behind the rapid decline of this species. Recently, this decline reached terrifying rates. Between 1979 and 1989, poaching for ivory halved Africa's elephant population from 1.3 million to 609,000. Central and eastern Africa were the most seriously affected areas, with some country's populations being locally extirpated and other experiencing over 75 percent declines. Responding to the predicted imminent elephant extinction, the 1989 Convention on International Trade in Endangered Species (CITES) agreed to ban ivory trading. Consequently, elephant poaching largely ceased. Today, many elephant populations are beginning to recover, but an uncontrolled trade in ivory remains a serious threat, as demonstrated by recent upsurges in ivory poaching in relation to increased global demand for such commodities.

Studies of elephant society have uncovered an intricate world where the core family unit of elephant society is an almost inseparable group, serving as the foundation to greater hierarchical delineations in elephant society. Regularly associating family units have been termed kinship or bond groups, which interact with other groups of families to form clans. In undisturbed populations, elephant society is believed to be a great, extended family that serves as the basis for spatial use and interactions. In populations that have experienced heavy human disturbance, unrelated individuals will join to re-form the basic structure of elephant society despite the lack of kin. Their degree of cognitive ability supports the well-known proverb "elephants never forget," as do physiological studies of elephant brains. Field studies demonstrate that old matriarchs lead their families through a vast social network where relations and dominance have been worked out among hundreds of individuals. Research on elephants' cognitive spatial knowledge also demonstrates an incredible understanding of the spatial aspects of their environment.

The stories about the gentleness of elephants, often represented by the image of the huge beast running from a mouse, are also based on reality. A dominant male elephant, weighing upwards of six tons, will balk and avoid a tiny, obstinate bird protecting her nest. With their incredibly sensitive trunks, elephants can shell a peanut. At the same time, that trunk can break the neck of a cow with a single swipe, and the power of elephants has been demonstrated many times when they devastate human structures in an attempt to get crops or crush a four-wheel-drive truck with little effort. The basis for reverence and fear is well founded.

Most scientists who study individual elephants can share tragic tales demonstrating the sensitivity of elephants and their ability to mourn. Mothers who have lost their calves will stand over their dead babies for days, and some, while trying to raise the dead to their feet, will break their tusks before giving up. Though elephant graveyards exist only where humans have massacred large numbers of elephants in a single location, one of the most remarkable and inexplicable elephant behaviors is their interaction with the bones of their kin. Entire families have been seen gathering around and smelling the remains of an individual. During such instances, elephants toss bones into the air, move their feet just slightly above the remains without touching anything, place ribs and tusks into their mouths, and eventually scatter the bones widely throughout the bush. The reasons for this ritual are unknown, though the behavior has been repeatedly seen and is specific to the bones of elephants.

In many cultures around the world, the bond between elephants and humans is ancient and close. Elephants have been valued in ways that are not solely economic. Unfortunately, the stories regarding elephants increasingly focus on negative interactions between the two species, largely in relation to the increased degree of overlap in human- and elephant-dominated landscapes. However, elephants hold a cultural significance for many traditional communities in African and Asian countries. The Maasai and other pastoralist people in Africa have myths that link elephants and humans in original creation. Consequently, elephants are believed to hold sacred value, which has resulted in coexistence and mutual respect for centuries. In some areas, as a result of rapid human population growth, human encroachment into elephant areas results in conflict over resources between the two species. Seeking positive solutions that benefit both humans and elephants under these circumstances will ultimately determine the fate of elephant populations in Africa and Asia.

Related articles: Animal protection in Africa; Animals in Asia; CITES and international trade; The complexity of animal awareness; Conservation philosophy; De-snaring in Kenya; Snares and snaring

Blanc, J. J., Barnes, R. F. W., Craig, C. G., Dublin, H. T., Thouless, C. R., Douglas-Hamilton, I., and Hart, J. A., *African Elephant Status Report, 2007: An Update from the African Elephant Database*, IUCN/SSC African Elephant Specialist Group, Gland, Switzerland, 2007.

Douglas-Hamilton, I., "African Elephants: Population Trends and Their Causes," *Oryx* 21 (1987): 11–24.

Moss, C. J., *Elephant Memories: Thirteen Years in the Life of an Elephant Family*, William Morrow, 1988.

Owen-Smith, N., *Megaherbivores: The Influence of Very Large Body Size on Ecology*, Cambridge University Press, 1988.

Shoshani, J., "Understanding Proboscidean Evolution: A Formidable Task," *Trends in Ecology and Evolution* 13 (1998): 480–487.

Wittemyer, G., Okello, J. B. A., Rasmussen, H. B., Arctander, P., Nyakaana, S., Douglas-Hamilton, I., and Siegismund, H. R., "Where Sociality and Relatedness Diverge: The Genetic Basis for Hierarchical Social Organization in African Elephants," *Proceedings of the Royal Society B-Biological Sciences* 276 (2009): 3513–3521.

GEORGE WITTEMYER

THE PERSECUTION OF BADGERS

Badgers are among Britain's most popular mammals and are now protected by law. Yet badgers have been persecuted for hundreds of years—and still are. In many towns and villages, it was a traditional part of a weekend's entertainment to go badger digging. The Protection of Badgers Act 1992 was enacted to protect badgers from baiting and other forms of intentional cruelty. It also sought to protect badgers and their setts from the adverse effects of development—for example, road building and housing. But the pressures on badgers have never been greater. Indeed, such is the current level of persecution that badger crime is now a U.K. wildlife crime priority.

Hundreds of badgers still die agonizing deaths each year. An estimated ten thousand are dug from their setts and cruelly baited with dogs, in the name of so-called sport (*see* Animals in Sport and Entrainment). Many suffer horrendous injuries and are killed in snares—both accidentally and intentionally. Others are poisoned or shot, or their setts are damaged or destroyed.

Hunting for foxes with dogs was a serious threat to badgers before the introduction of the Hunting Act 2004. In particular, "sett stopping" involved the blocking of badger setts to prevent foxes seeking refuge underground. This led in some cases to badgers being suffocated underground or driven from their setts. Other abuses involved hunts "digging out" foxes, resulting in setts being damaged or destroyed and badgers being injured or killed. Digging for foxes has for many years been one of the most common covers used by badger diggers.

The 2004 act has greatly improved badger protection by banning most forms of hunting with dogs and the stopping of setts. However, the use of dogs below ground has not been completely banned, and this gives cause for continued concern. Building development alone destroys many setts and vital feeding areas. An estimated fifty thousand badgers are killed on the roads. Not least of all, badgers remain threatened by unscientific government policies on controlling bovine tuberculosis in cattle. Despite an increasing body of scientific evidence showing that killing badgers is ineffective and that cattle-based measures are key to controlling the disease, the Cameron government in England is licensing farmers to shoot badgers as of this writing, with the killing set to start in June 2013. And in Wales, despite a successful legal challenge by the Badger Trust, the government was pursuing plans for an annual cull of badgers over a five-year period as of 2012.

More than thirty years of government-orchestrated badger killing has failed to control bovine tuberculosis in cattle. Occurrences of numerous infectious diseases of cattle are increasing in the United Kingdom, including pneumonia and diarrhea. A sustainable solution to the problem must therefore be based on improving cattle-focused measures such as tighter movement controls, more rigorous TB testing, improved diagnostic tests, and the development of a cattle vaccine.

Illegal persecution, usually associated with hunting with dogs, continues to be a major problem. Badgers continue to be persecuted largely because of weaknesses in the Protection of Badgers Act 1992. This is part of a wider problem affecting wildlife legislation, and steps are being taken to secure improvements to such laws. The Countryside and Rights of Way Act 2000 has addressed many weaknesses, but problems remain, such as low penalties and weak police powers.

The United Kingdom's Home Office routinely records crimes against badgers, along with such crimes as theft and vehicle offenses. However, crimes against free-living animals are frequently considered a low priority by the police force. With a few notable exceptions, most forces do not have full-time dedicated wildlife liaison officers (WLOs), and most WLOs carry out their work in their own time, with little or no financial support. Each police force should have at least one full-time WLO and a network of professionally trained WLOs available twenty-four hours a day, and all should be provided with the support required to carry out their work effectively.

After twenty years, it is clear that concessions made to the pro-hunting lobby to prevent its sabotage of the Protection of Badgers Act 1992 have made the legislation often unworkable and unenforceable. Those who commit badger offenses have been subject to arrest since 2005, but enforcement of the act is weakened because there are no powers to access property and land or to interview suspected offenders. Consequently, suspected offenders frequently hamper police investigations by refusing to be interviewed. Investigations are inevitably frustrated when access to land is denied, as frequently occurs if the landowner knows about, is sympathetic to, or is actually involved in the offenses.

Specific loopholes in the legislation result in unacceptable suffering to badgers. Free-running snares can be used legally to capture foxes and rabbits, yet hundreds of badgers are injured and killed in both legal and illegal snares. The obvious solution would be to ban the manufacture, possession, and use of all snares. Neither is the 1992 act an effective deterrent. The maximum penalty in England and Wales is currently up to six months' imprisonment or a 5,000-pound fine, or both. However, maximum penalties are rare, with many offenders receiving only a fine, usually significantly less than 1,000 pounds. Occasionally, offenders are sentenced to just two or three months' imprisonment. In Scotland, the law has improved, with unlimited fines and up to three years' imprisonment. However, increased sentences might act as a real deterrent to potential offenders.

Badgers are an important part of Britain's natural heritage. They are a symbol of a flourishing countryside. Like all Britain's free-living creatures, badgers should be cherished as a vital part of our past and our future.

Related articles: Animals and public health; Hunting with dogs; Snares and snaring

The Forestry Commission, *Forest Operations and Badger Setts*, 1995.

Independent Scientific Group on Cattle TB, Department of the Environment, Food and Rural Affairs, *Bovine TB: The Scientific Evidence*, 2007.

National Federation of Badger Groups, *The Case for a Ban on Snares*, 2002, available at http://www.badger.org. uk/_Attachments/Resources/43_S4.pdf.

Neal, Ernest, and Cheeseman, Christopher, *Badgers*, Poyser Natural History, 1996.

Report of the Committee of Inquiry into Hunting with Dogs in England and Wales, chaired by Lord Burns, 2000, available at http://www.huntinginquiry.gov.uk/mainsections/report.pdf.

Roper, Timothy J., *Badger*, New Naturalist Library, Collins, 2010.

Scottish Natural Heritage, *Scotland's Wildlife: Badgers and Development*, 2001.

ELAINE KING

PRIMATES WORLDWIDE

Nonhuman primates are the animals closest to human primates on the evolutionary tree. Everyone reading this article is a primate! In the course of evolution, species developed with increasing intelligence, forward-looking eyes that help with depth perception, greater manual dexterity than other animals, and a long period of mother-infant dependency. These animals are known as the primates.

There are over 250 primate species living in Africa, Asia, South and Central America, and Gibraltar. Many primate species are well known to the public, especially gorillas, chimpanzees , and orangutans. Others are less well known, but highly endangered, such as the drill, the Kloss's gibbon, and the golden lion tamarin. The most widespread primates are the macaques of Asia and North Africa and the baboons of Africa and parts of the Arabian Peninsula.

Our nonhuman primate cousins are exploited in many ways.

Primates as food

In many primate habitat countries, these animals are eaten, but use of primates as food in traditional cultures did not jeopardize the survival of primate species. Also, some cultures have a taboo on eating animals who greatly resemble humans—at Boabeng-Fiema in Ghana, colobus monkeys are so revered that when one dies, the animal is given an elaborate funeral. However, there is now a large-scale commercial trade supplying cities with bushmeat from rainforest primates. This trade is inhumanely conducted and is pushing many ape and monkey species toward extinction.

Primates as companion animals

There is a large, mainly unregulated trade in baby primates in the United States, European nations, and other countries. Baby monkeys, caught from their natural state, are traded when their mothers are shot. Breeders who kidnap them from their mothers soon after birth sell other baby monkeys as well. Baby primates cling to their mothers from birth, and if removed, they will also cling to human beings, and human keepers often dress baby primates in diapers and human clothing. But when these infants grow up and mature, they often attack and injure humans. Some of these primates are killed; some end up in substandard menageries. Only a few are turned over to primate sanctuaries.

Primates in entertainment

Some people find the resemblance between humans and other primates, especially chimpanzees, amusing. Chimpanzees are often used in movies, television commercials, and circuses. These uses of primates all involve training them to perform behaviors that are unnatural and stressful. When the animals mature, they become surplus. Many former performing chimpanzees have ended up in research laboratories.

Primates in biomedical research and testing

Because of their similarity to humans, nonhuman primates are often used in biomedical research and testing. Many would argue that for this reason they should not be used. In the United States, more than fifty thousand primates are used annually. Among the uses are experimental medicine and surgery and vaccine production and testing. Thousands of primates have been infected with an illness resembling, but not identical to, human AIDS and have suffered horrible deaths.

Primates maintained for biomedical research are often kept in tiny cages for years on end. In the United States it is legal to keep monkeys alone in tiny cages 6 feet square (0.56 meters square) and 32 inches (81.28 centimeters) high and chimpanzees in cages 25.1 feet square and 7 feet (213.86 centimeters) high. Primates are also used in production of Chinese traditional medicines.

Zoological exhibition

Zoos often exhibit primates, with great apes always being star attractions. Some zoos try to provide adequate facilities for primates, especially for popular species, such as gorillas. But there are also hundreds of substandard zoos and menageries in which primates are incarcerated, sometimes alone, in miserable conditions, with nothing to keep their brains and bodies active.

Primates in trade

Besides the internal companion animal and meat trade in habitat countries, primates are often exported to countries to which they are not native. This trade is ugly, with many primates dying during capture, in initial holding, in the cargo holds of jet planes, and in holding centers in importing countries.

Among the African species victimized by international trade are baboons and vervet monkeys (for research), chimpanzees (for exhibition, as companion animals, and for research), and gorillas (for exhibition). There are several sanctuaries in Africa that provide a home for primates rescued from trade. They include Limbe and Sanaga Yong in Cameroon, Tacugama in Sierra Leone, and Chimfunshi in Zambia.

The macaques of Asia have always been in high demand for medical research and drug testing. The species most sought after are the rhesus and long-tailed macaques. Macaques often undergo horrific pain and suffering in experiments. This does not arouse the same public concern as the suffering inflicted on chimpanzees, who are better known to the public. There are a few rescue centers in Asia for primates, especially orangutans.

The most commonly traded South American monkeys are the squirrel, capuchin, spider, and woolly monkeys. All these species are much sought after for the companion animal trade.

Smuggling

The trade in primates is regulated by the Convention on International Trade in Endangered Species of Wild Fauna and Flora (CITES). Under CITES, primates are listed in either Appendix I (endangered; commercial trade banned) or Appendix II (may become threatened unless trade is strictly controlled). Unfortunately, many Appendix I species, such as gorillas, orangutans, and chimpanzees, are smuggled internationally by criminals. Often they are concealed in small containers for transport. This leads to the deaths of many animals from asphyxiation or stress.

One notorious shipment was the famous "Bangkok Six" case. Six baby orangutans and two gibbons were stuffed into coffin-like crates and smuggled out of Singapore. The animals were going to a Russian animal trader but were confiscated in appalling condition at Bangkok Airport. Three of the babies had been shipped upside down. One individual went to prison for his role in this crime, and several other smugglers were indicted.

With the tropical rainforests of the world under heavy pressure, the future for the world's primates looks grim. The Miss Waldron's colobus monkey is now almost extinct. Over forty species are listed as being in serious danger of extinction by the International Union for Conservation of Nature. The lives of most captive primates worldwide are bleak. Massive efforts by compassionate humans are needed so that we can keep more primates in their natural habitat—and improve the lives of captive primates.

Related articles: Animal protection in Africa; Animals in Asia; Animals in Chinese culture; Animals in circuses; Animals used in research; Captive chimpanzees; CITES and the international trade; The complexity of animal awareness; The ethics of zoos; Free-living chimpanzees; The future of free-roaming orangutans; The legal rights of great apes; Roadside zoos and menageries; Sanctuaries and rehabilitation; South American perspectives on animals; The trade in primates for research

Brewer, Stella, *The Chimps of Mount Asserik*, Knopf, 1978.

Cleveland, Will, *The Baboons of Dawn*, Guild Book, 2010.

de la Bedoyere, Camilla, *No One Loved Gorillas More*, National Geographic Society, 2005.

Mahoney, James, *From Elephants to Mice: Animals Who Have Touched My Soul*, Wiley, 2010.

Reynolds, Vernon, *The Chimpanzees of Budongo Forest*, Oxford University Press, 2005.

Weisman, Alan, *The World without Us*, St. Martin's Press, 2007.

SHIRLEY McGREAL

THE PROTECTION OF BIRDS

The modern-day protection of birds began in the United Kingdom and had its origins in the Sea Birds Protection Bill of 1869, which provided a closed season for killing seabirds when they were on their breeding cliffs. This bill came about because of widespread repugnance at shooting parties whose pleasure was to slaughter seabirds sitting on nests in the colonies of Flamborough Head in Yorkshire. During the 1880s, there was also a marked increase in the import of bird skins to make hats for women, with millions of herons and egrets being killed to meet demand. This requirement for skins led to the virtual extinction of the great crested grebe in Britain. Several pressure groups were formed to fight the trade, and their amalgamation resulted in 1889 in what is now known as the Royal Society for the Protection of Birds (RSPB). It was a change in fashion, however, rather than the actions of pressure groups, that caused a decline in the trade, which did not become illegal until 1921.

Similar concerns in the United States led to the incorporation in 1905 of the National Audubon Society, named after the famous ornithologist and artist John James Audubon, who published his *Birds of America* between 1827 and 1838. The National Audubon Society consists of many voluntary societies that are affiliated to the national body and has more than half a million members. The protection of birds in the United States is divided between the national government and the state governments. Some species, mainly game birds and wildfowl, can be hunted (*see* Animals in Sport and Entertainment) during the open season, but it is illegal to sell them.

Other early nongovernmental organizations concerned with bird protection were the Bombay Natural History Society of India, formed in 1883, and the Netherlands Society for the Protection of Birds, formed in 1899. Bird protection societies were founded in many other countries in the first half of the twentieth century. By the second half of the twentieth century, emphasis had switched to conservation—the maintenance of sustainable populations of birds and their habitats and ecosystems.

In the United Kingdom, the Protection of Birds Act of 1954 was the most significant piece of legislation to affect birds, superseded in 1981 by the Wildlife and Countryside Act. Under the latter act, all free-living "wild birds" and their nests and eggs in the United Kingdom are protected by law. Rare birds are on Schedule 1, and harming them incurs higher financial penalties. A relatively small list of species, mainly birds labeled game birds and wildfowl, can be hunted outside the closed season, for up to five months during autumn and winter. Another small group of species, considered "pests," either to agriculture (for example, woodpigeons) or because they take the eggs and young of "game" birds (for example, crows), can be killed at any time of year with the authority of a landowner.

The United Kingdom's Countryside and Rights of Way Act of 2000 strengthened the bird protection laws by including a new offense, reckless disturbance of species on Schedule 1, which overcame the problem of proving that disturbance was intentional. It also introduced harsher fines—and indeed potential prison sentences—for serious crimes against birds. The U.K. government's Biodiversity Action Plan, aiming to reverse severe declines in populations of individual species, is recognized in law, and "Sites of Special Scientific Interest" are given greater protection. The European Community Birds Directive deals with bird protection throughout the European Union (though some countries, such as Malta, openly flout it). Special protection areas are designated to protect bird populations of significance.

In the United Kingdom, more than fifty years of legislation, together with education, have led to a generally enlightened attitude toward birds, and the RSPB now boasts considerably more than one million members. But how effective has this legislation been? The reduction in the number of "quarry species" and the development of networks of protected areas have well served the nation's wading birds and waterfowl, the majority of which species have shown steady increases in numbers since the 1970s. Many of the rarer birds of prey have also increased in numbers because of the banning of toxic chemicals in agriculture and because of protection. Unfortunately, there is still much illegal persecution of birds of prey in areas managed intensively for game, the rare hen harrier being especially targeted on grouse moors.

Those birds who have to cross the Mediterranean in order to reach their winter quarters run the gamut of traps, birdlime, and guns, much of it illegal, but laws are poorly enforced. It is estimated that some 500 million migrant birds are killed annually in southern Europe, species that in northern Europe have the full protection of enforced laws. Even in northern Europe, declining species that are considered game often receive no additional protection to help reverse population declines. For example, in the United Kingdom, both snipes and woodcocks have suffered declines of more than 60 percent between the 1970s and 2010s, but their shooting seasons have not been closed or shortened, there is no bag limit, and shot birds can be offered for sale.

The majority of land in the United Kingdom is farmed, and agricultural intensification has removed both habitat and feeding opportunities for birds, with dire consequences. Eighteen species of once-common birds have declined in numbers by more than 50 percent since 1970—in the case of the tree sparrow, by 95 percent. Gardens are now refuges for once-common species such as the song thrush and blackbird. Even the once-ubiquitous starling and house sparrow are giving much cause for concern. Taxpayer-funded habitat enhancement schemes on farmland have been largely unsuccessful in reversing population declines, probably because they have been too general and insufficiently targeted at the needs of individual species. More carefully implemented schemes should be more successful, though undoubtedly more expensive.

The very fact that many bird species cross continents during their annual migrations requires international cooperation for their conservation. BirdLife International, with its headquarters in Cambridge, England, is a partnership of nongovernmental organizations in more than one hundred countries worldwide—the RSPB and National Audubon Society are key players. BirdLife International aims to conserve birds, birds' habitats, and global biodiversity. One of its key programs is to identify and protect a global network of sites, important bird areas (IBAs), for the conservation of birds.

Conservation, including that of birds, is generally seen as maintaining sustainable populations of species for future generations to enjoy or exploit—a largely anthropocentric focus. It also needs an ethical dimension. For example, those few species in the United Kingdom that nowadays are still hunted may be killed in large numbers. Some thirty-five million pheasants, most of them reared for the purpose and often in conditions that would be illegal for poultry, are gunned down for fun every year. In an ethical society, in the twenty-first century, can such senseless slaughter of sentient birds be any more justified than the killing of breeding seabirds in the nineteenth century?

Related articles: Animals used in research; Birds used in food production; Cock fighting; Conservation philosophy; Developments in animal law; The fur trade; Humane education; Legislation in the European Union; Live pigeon shoots; Live quail shoots; Moral anthropocentrism; The moral claims of animals; Pigeon racing; The production of foie gras; The treatment of animals in India; The welfare of mute swans

Collar, N. J., Long, A. J., Gil, P. R., and Rojo, J., *Birds and People: Bonds in a Timeless Journey*, BirdLife International, 2007.

Donald, P., Collar, N., Marsden, S., and Pain, D., *Facing Extinction: The World's Rarest Birds and the Race to Save Them*, T. and A. D. Poyser, 2010.

Doughty, R. W., *Feather Fashions and Bird Preservation: A Study in Nature Protection*, University of California Press, 1974.

Lovegrove, R., *Silent Fields*, Oxford University Press, 2007.

MacLean, N. (ed.), *Silent Summer*, Cambridge University Press, 2010.

Samstag, T., *For the Love of Birds: The Story of the Royal Society for the Protection of Birds*, Royal Society for the Protection of Birds, 1988.

CHRISTOPHER F. MASON

THE SLAUGHTER OF KANGAROOS

All over the world, free-living animals are being driven to the point of extinction. The usual reasons are habitat loss, hunting, and the export trade. In Australia, the killing of seven species of kangaroo and wallabies is encouraged by the government, and the products of this massacre—meat and skin—are aggressively marketed around the world by the nation's embassies and high commissions.

The killing is done mainly by rifle-toting part-timers. They roar through the outback at night in four-wheel drives fitted with powerful spotlights. The Code of Conduct states that animals are supposed to be "head shot," but frequently it is a neck or body shot, and still-living animals have their legs sliced open and a hook inserted, and they are then hauled up on to the trucks to gasp their life away.

Footage by the International Fund for Animal Welfare (IFAW) Australia of an experienced shooter shows that the majority of kangaroos targeted are shot in the throat and do not die instantly. The only government-funded research examining the accuracy of the shooters was undertaken by the Australian RSPCA, which stated that 15 percent of animals are killed inhumanely—however, the authors warned that the results were distorted because the shooters knew they were being tested and were on their "best behavior." The Australian RSPCA is opposed to the killing because "the incidence of cruelty is too high to be justified."

When a female is shot, the shooter searches her pouch and, if he feels a baby inside, pulls the baby out. The shooter is then supposed to issue a "heavy blow" to the head, but older, ex-pouch joeys hop away to die a slow and lonely death from predation, cold, or starvation. Again, footage from IFAW Australia shows a joey being pulled from his dying mother's pouch and tossed to the ground. The ten-year-old son of the shooter twists his foot on the joey's head, but the animal is still alive after these crude attempts to kill him or her. Veterinary scientist and agronomist Dr. John Auty has studied the killing of kangaroos in all Australian states. He maintains, "Shooters often have a thorough contempt of the law. They commit cruelty on a regular basis" (National Kangaroo Campaign).

Kangaroos (mainly reds, eastern and western grays, and wallaroos) are slaughtered by the millions, including, males, females, and baby joeys. The official adult kill quota for 2005 was 3.9 million, but to this must be added a million or so baby joeys, the by-products of this mass slaughter. With unofficial and illegal kills, the total may be as high as a staggering nine million animals. Unsurprisingly, the Australian government's Department of Environment and Heritage reports a severe drop in kangaroo numbers. The population for the hunted species was 51 million in 2000 and 25 million in 2004. The number of red kangaroos dropped from 17 million to 8 million during this period.

Two main reasons have been advanced by the kangaroo industry for the killing. The first is that kangaroos are a major wheat crop "pest." However, a four-year study of gray kangaroos in Western Australia by the Commonwealth Scientific and Industrial Research Organisation (CSIRO) found that kangaroos never visit 95 percent of wheat crops. The study concluded that kangaroos have virtually no impact on the country's crops and even recommended that farmers, who have natural bushland on their property, encourage its growth to help keep the kangaroos fed.

Dr. Graham Arnold, formerly of CSIRO, studied the impact of kangaroos on croplands and stated in 1998, "Most kangaroos did not like to eat farm crops and would only thrive if given access to their natural foods . . . Unless the community manages remnant vegetation to minimise degradation and enhance the regeneration of native plants, kangaroos, and some other native species, will disappear from much of Western Australia over the next 100 years . . . Today, five species of kangaroo are extinct throughout the wheatbelt and four species are found only in a few locations." Despite this, the Australian government regularly refers to kangaroos as "pests." Dr. Arnold responds, "Pests is an emotive word. It conjures up visions of animals destroying crops. I can think of no situations where this is likely to be true for kangaroos" (National Kangaroo Campaign).

The second main reason given for slaughtering kangaroos is that they compete for resources with cattle and sheep. A six-year study by Dr. Steven McLeod at the University of New South Wales is the most comprehensive of its type. It found that "there was no evidence of a competitive effect of red kangaroos on sheep" (McLeod). The study concluded that red kangaroos do not affect the body mass, wool growth, or reproductive output of sheep or the growth and survivorship of lambs.

Another myth propagated by the Australian government is that kangaroos breed "out of control." However, the work of Amanda Bilton of the University of New South

Wales, at Fowler's Gap, shows this notion has no basis. Fowler's Gap is unique in that it runs a large commercial sheep station but has not killed kangaroos for more than thirty years. Bilton determined that on average only one-third of joeys survive to weaning. Furthermore, the average number of joeys weaned in a single female's lifetime is only 3.26. Given that many weaned young do not survive to breed, recruitment into the adult population may be as low as 6 to 8 percent a year. This means that the current rate of extermination is greater than the kangaroos' reproduction rate.

Perhaps the most bogus claim of all is that killing helps to ensure the kangaroos' survival by placing a value on them. In fact, by targeting only the biggest and fittest animals of greatest value, the kangaroo killing industry is destroying the process of natural selection. Dr. David Croft, a biologist at the University of New South Wales, states that the kill may effectively take close to 100 percent of large males, forcing smaller and younger males, who are genetically weaker, to breed (National Kangaroo Campaign 70–73). Dr. Ian Gunn, of the Animal Gene Storage Centre of Australia, warns that this process has the potential to cause the extinction of a number of remaining species (National Kangaroo Campaign).

Australia has the worst conservation record in the world. Since the settlement of Europeans 210 years ago, eighteen species of mammals have become extinct, and another forty-five are threatened. Six species of kangaroo are already extinct (and a further four on the mainland), and seventeen other species are now classified as endangered or vulnerable. It is therefore difficult to trust the government's claims that the number of remaining kangaroos being killed is "sustainable."

The final claim against kangaroos is that they destroy the environment, when in fact it is the hard hooves of 160 million cattle and sheep that are doing the most damage and are relentlessly turning vast tracts of Australia into desert. Kangaroos are merely the scapegoat to divert attention from the destruction caused by livestock farming. Destruction of the world's animals has continually been supported by claims that it is necessary—even vital—and with assurances that it is all "strictly controlled." It is important to stop Australia's destruction of its unique animals—and not just for the sake of the kangaroos. Australia is one of the few countries capable of maintaining large protected wildernesses without strong human population pressures on their boundaries.

Related articles: Animal issues in Australia; CITES and international trade; The ethics of killing free-living animals; Koalas and their protection; Slaughter

Arnold, Graham, "Can Kangaroos Survive in the Wheatbelt?" (1998), in National Kangaroo Campaign, *The Kangaroo Betrayed*, Hill of Content, 1999.
Ben-Ami, Dror, "A Shot in the Dark: A Report on Kangaroo Harvesting," 2009, available at http://www.kangaroo-protection-coalition.com/support-files/a_shot_in_the_dark.pdf.
Gellatley, J., *Born to Be Wild*, Women's Press, 2000.
———, *Under Fire: A Viva! Report on the Killing of Kangaroos for Meat and Skin*, Viva!, 2007.
Gellatley, J., and Wardle, T., *The Silent Ark*, Thorsons, 1996.
McLeod, S., *The Foraging Behaviour of the Arid Zone Herbivores the Red Kangaroo* (Macropus rufus) *and the Sheep* (Ovis aries) *and Its Role on Their Competitive Interaction, Populations Dynamics and Life-History Strategies*, PhD thesis, University of New South Wales, February 1996.
National Kangaroo Campaign, *The Kangaroo Betrayed*, Hill of Content, 1999.
Sutterby, N., "Kangaroo, the Extinction of An Australian Icon!," 2008, available at http://www.kangaroo-protection-coalition.com/kangaroo-extinction.html.

JULIET GELLATLEY

THREATS TO THE BROWN HARE

It is hard to envisage a mammal whose fortunes have been greater influenced by the vagaries of human behavior than the brown hare. Hares have been moved around the world so extensively that no one is sure of their original range. The brown hare evolved on the open steppes of Asia and spread into agricultural habitats throughout Europe during the postglacial period. How much of this spread was natural, as forest landscapes were cleared, and how much was due to deliberate releases for hunting remains unclear. Certainly, brown hares were introduced to many of the Mediterranean islands between two and three thousand years ago and to Britain, probably before Roman times, for coursing. From Britain, brown hares were then introduced to Australia, Canada, the Falklands Islands, New Zealand, large parts of South America, and eastern parts of the United States of America.

Most of these introductions were to supply populations to hunt for "sport." In fact, following the decline in hare numbers in Europe, there is now an extensive return trade—for example 150,000 to 200,000 hares are imported to Italy each year, principally from central Europe and Argentina, for hunting.

Despite this restocking, hare numbers are declining throughout much of Europe, probably because of patterns of agricultural change, although hunting pressure may also be playing a role. The hare population in Britain today is only 20 percent of what it was one hundred years ago. Because of this dramatic decline, the brown hare was one of the first species to be given a Biodiversity Action Plan in 1995. Although the goal of the action plan was to double the spring population of hares by 2010, this target was missed, and hare numbers probably declined rather than increased.

Despite the problems facing hares in Britain, there has been very little attempt to implement measures to protect the species. Virtually every other member state of the European Union and the Council for Europe has a closed season for hares, generally allowing hunting only from October to December. This is because hares breed from January to September or October. The brown hare is the only game species in Britain without a closed season. In the early 1990s, over five million hares were shot in Europe each year, with around 300,000 (40 percent of the entire population) shot in Britain. Most are killed in driven shoots in February and March after the game bird season. For driven hare shoots, many people surround a large area of land and then walk inward, shooting all the hares they see. Over 90 percent of the hares can be killed. Since hares start breeding in January, pregnant females are shot and orphaned leverets left. Many shot hares are sold to game dealers and then exported.

Until 2005, when the U.K. Hunting Act 2004 came into effect, hares were also hunted in Britain with a wide variety of dogs: bassets, beagles, harriers, greyhounds, and lurchers. The first three are pack dogs who hunt by scent, and the hares were subjected to an extended chase in these hunts. Up to two thousand hares were killed each year by packs of hounds. Prior to around 1550, there was no clear difference in the types of hounds used to hunt different prey, but thereafter hound breeds became classified according to the size of their quarry. Smaller hounds used for hunting rabbits and hares were called *bègle*, which was anglicized to become "beagle." Harriers are larger hounds and were used to hunt both foxes and hares, primarily in west and southwest Britain. Early harriers were followed on foot, but modern harriers are faster and were followed on horseback; beagles and bassets were followed on foot. Bassets were developed in the sixteenth century from genetic freaks—puppies of normal-sized staghounds who had developed retarded limbs. A hundred years later, they arrived in Britain and were used to hunt hares. Although hunting hares with hounds is currently illegal in Britain, it continues in Ireland and Europe.

Coursing was also made illegal by the Hunting Act 2004. For formal coursing prior to the act, two greyhounds were matched against each other, and points were awarded for the skill demonstrated during the chase. Around 8 percent of coursed hares (250 per season) were killed by greyhounds, and this often involved the two greyhounds engaging in a tug of war over the live hare. However, the most frequent type of coursing was with lurchers. There are around 200,000 working lurchers in Britain, that is, roughly one per three hares. This posed a potentially high hunting pressure, especially when coursing with lurchers was generally undertaken to catch and kill the hare. This was often a clandestine activity undertaken without the landowner's permission. Though now illegal, it remains to be seen whether the practice will die out.

There also remains the problem of coursing gangs that operate in eastern England. Here groups of people, sometimes many hundreds, descend on private land to course hares, and prior to the Hunting Act 2004, there was little that the landowner or police could do to combat these acts of mass trespass. Damage to land and crops was often extensive and threats to landowners frequent. The only way that farmers could keep these gangs off their land was to shoot all the hares so that there were too few left to attract the lurcher gangs. So hunting with lurchers put a dual pressure on hares, and this had a dramatic impact on hare numbers in parts of Britain. Fortunately, the additional powers under the Hunting Act 2004 made it easier for the police to target coursing gangs, and so this activity may also be brought under control.

Related articles: The ethics of killing free-living animals; Greyhound racing; Hunting with dogs; Legislation in the European Union

Harris, S., and Yalden, D. W., *Mammals of the British Isles: Handbook*, 4th ed., the Mammal Society, 2008.

Hutchings, M. R., and Harris, S., *The Current Status of the Brown Hare* (Lepus europaeus) *in Britain*, Joint Nature Conservation Committee, 1996.

Jennings, N., Smith, R. K., Hackländer, K., Harris, S., and White, P. C. L., "Variation in Demography, Condition and Dietary Quality of Hares *Lepus europaeus* from High-Density and Low-Density Populations," *Wildlife Biology* 12 (2006): 179–189.

Smith, R. K., Jennings, N. V., and Harris, S., "A Quantitative Analysis of the Abundance and Demography of European Hares *Lepus europaeus* in Relation to Habitat Type, Intensity of Agriculture and Climate," *Mammal Review* 35 (2005): 1–24.

Smith, R. K., Jennings, N. V., Robinson, A., and Harris, S., "Conservation of European Hares *Lepus europaeus* in Britain: Is Increasing Habitat Heterogeneity in Farmland the Answer?," *Journal of Applied Ecology* 41 (2004): 1092–1102.

Stott, P., Harris, S., and Wight, N., "Fertility and Infertility in the European Hare *Lepus europaeus* in Australia," in Alves, P. C., Ferrand, N., and Hackländer, K. (eds.), *Lagomorph Biology: Evolution, Ecology, and Conservation*, Springer, 2009, 225–240.

STEPHEN HARRIS

UNDERSTANDING BEAVERS

Beavers may be the most misunderstood animals of Europe, Asia, and North America, yet also the most important—most important because their habit of building dams on streams creates wetlands, the "rainforests of the North" that are the land's best life support system. Although the enormous environmental benefits of beavers were not known soon enough to stop their widespread extermination in the past, nature's engineers are now reclaiming some of their historic territory in North America and Europe.

Even the beavers' scientific name, the genus "Castor," arose because of a misunderstanding: early Europeans believed that because beavers had no visible sexual organs, they were somehow castrated. Both castoreum, an aromatic product of beaver glands, and their lustrous fur so attracted trappers and traders that beavers were almost wiped out before people realized their true value.

Grey Owl, an Englishman who lived in indigenous fashion in the Canadian wilds during the early 1900s, helped popularize beavers worldwide. His best-selling book *Pilgrims of the Wild* tells how he abandoned trapping after adopting two beaver kits and began promoting the protection of this keystone species and wilderness. Relentless hunting and trapping for "brown gold" had already extirpated beavers in most of the United States and southern Canada and the majority of Asian and European countries by 1900. During the twentieth century, beaver advocates, including Europeans and Americans inspired by Grey Owl, began to protect remnant populations and restore beavers.

At least sixty million beavers (*Castor fiber*) once lived throughout Eurasia. By 1900, only about 1,200 Eurasian beavers survived in half a dozen countries. Thanks to restoration programs, however, there are now over 600,000 beavers in Europe—a tiny percentage of the original number, but a great comeback from the remnant populations of 1900. Asian populations of *Castor fiber* still remain very small and urgently need protection.

In Europe, attitudes toward beavers and their treatment vary greatly, from Scandinavia, where they can be shot as a game species, to certain central European countries where they are highly protected. In 2009, eleven beavers were released in Scotland, the first free-ranging ones in the United Kingdom in four hundred years. As more people become aware of the paddle-tailed animals' charming responsiveness and environmental benefits, public support for the species is growing. Beavers, along with their ponds, are ideal for watchable "wildlife" and tourism.

About twelve million beavers (*Castor canadensis*) now reside in North America. (Although the American and Eurasian beavers are similar in their basic behavior and appearance, they have different numbers of chromosomes and cannot interbreed.) Beaver restoration in North America is well ahead of programs elsewhere. Yet an estimated 60 to 200 million beavers were present in North America prior to European colonization, whereas only about 10 percent of that population survives today. More education about the benefits of nature's engineers and modern methods of coexistence is vital.

Native Americans called the beaver "the sacred center" because their dams create rich habitats teeming with fishes and other animals. Each family typically builds several dams that maintain many acres of freshwater wetlands. Such wetlands have been rated as the land's most valuable ecosystem in terms of benefits, such as water cleansing, water storage, flood control, and increased biodiversity. An international team of thirteen ecologists and economists in 1997 estimated these natural services to be worth about $20,000 per hectare ($8,000 per acre) per year. Human construction of wetlands in the United States regularly costs from $25,000 to $250,000 per hectare ($10,000–$100,000 per acre), whereas a beaver will create and maintain several acres of wetlands at no charge.

Hydrologists blame the uncontrolled trapping of North America's beavers during the 1700s and 1800s, followed by intensive drainage for agriculture, for today's major environmental problems. Such problems include water pollution, massive erosion, and rising species extinction along with escalating damage costs from major floods and droughts. Beavers build leaky dams that slow the flow of streams, which creates quiet water nurseries for fishes and allows time for wetlands microorganisms to detoxify pollutants, such as pesticides. In addition, beaver dams accentuate the normal filtering function of wetlands by collecting silt, and there can be 90 percent less sediment in the water downstream. This means that less costly treatment is required at plants that produce drinking water.

The presence of many beaver dams in the headwaters of rivers moderates the flow and keeps water on the land longer. This, in turn, alleviates both droughts and major downstream floods, extreme weather events that are becoming more frequent as a result of climate change. Marshy beaver wetlands already are, or will become, peatlands, as dead vegetation accumulates underwater. Peatlands are the best ecosystem for carbon sequestration, but draining them allows the peat to oxidize and release carbon dioxide, the major greenhouse gas. Beavers are our allies in combating climate change.

Biologists worldwide warn that we are losing species at an alarming rate. In some countries, such as Lithuania, beaver ponds create the only available places for rare amphibians to spawn. According to the U.S. Environmental Protection Agency, 43 percent of endangered and threatened species rely on wetlands at some stage in their life cycles. Beavers can help correct the growing problem of extinction—and they work for free.

Relocating beavers can be stressful for them, and not all animal protectionists judge the practice ethically acceptable, but when beavers are likely to be killed as "nuisances," they can be humanely live-trapped and transported to improve degraded ecosystems. For example, the Sho-Ban Indians of Idaho have used beavers to restore trout and willow habitat on their land. In parts of the U.S. West, nature's engineers are being relocated to naturally manage water. Beavers could be put to work solving problems with water quality and quantity in Europe and Asia too.

Although most North American governments endorse policies to protect wetlands, managers may still consider beavers primarily as furbearers and/or nuisance animals and prefer the traditional solution of trapping. Tens of thousands of acres of vital beaver wetlands are needlessly drained annually in North America when beavers who flood roads are killed with governmental approval—despite proven, long-term methods to prevent this. Removing beavers is a short-term and environmentally destructive solution, since studies show that where good habitat remains, resettlement of empty habitats regularly occurs.

Instead of considering the presence of beavers as the problem, identifying and solving specific problems (road flooding, tree cutting, and so on) gives the best, most lasting solutions. For example, protecting trees with wire fencing prevents damage, and installing water-level control devices stops unwanted flooding. Modern beaver flow devices are cost-effective and environmentally sound, as has been shown in many studies and by the thirty-year history of installations at Canada's 36,100-hectare (88,000-acre) Gatineau Park. Similar flow devices have been used to prevent road flooding, while saving wetlands, on 52,610 hectares (130,000 acres) of Penobscot Indian Nation lands in Maine for fifteen years. Since the early 2000s, the Snohomish County Public Works Department in Washington has not had to remove any beavers from road sites in that 541,308-hectare (1,337,600-acre) county, thanks to a successful, economical flow device program. More education is needed to help both those entrusted with management and the public understand modern methods of coexisting with this keystone species.

Most beaver trapping is done with conibear traps, the purportedly "quick kill" traps. In fact, quick kills very often do not occur, since a conibear works efficiently only when the victim enters at the right position and at the right speed. Drowning traps are especially cruel for beavers since these animals can hold their breath for ten minutes or more, and they die of agonizing oxygen deprivation—not carbon dioxide narcosis as was once assumed. Leghold traps and snares are other nonselective devices that leave their victims helpless against predators and may cause suffering for days. Beavers are known to mate for life and mourn lost mates.

As the artificial barriers that have separated humans from other species are progressively overcome, the exploitation of such reasoning, sensitive, and environmentally beneficial animals becomes impossible to justify. Beavers plan ahead in their activities, have often been observed to use reasoning, and may even show a sense of humor in the form of practical jokes, as they interact with humans and one another.

All animals play a role in the web of life, but beavers are unique as the keystone species that restores wetlands, the land's most valuable ecosystem.

Related articles: The ethics of reintroduction; European animal protection; The fur trade; The humane movement in Canada; Snares and snaring

Brown, S., and Brown J., *How to Control Beaver Flooding*, Beavers: Wetlands and Wildlife, 1999.

Brown, S., Shafer, D., and Anderson, S., *Control of Beaver Flooding at Restoration Projects, WRAP Technical Notes Collection*, U.S. Army Engineer Research and Development Center, 2001, available at http://el.erdc.usace.army.mil/elpubs/pdf/tnwrap01-1.pdf.

Costanza, R., d'Arge, R., de Groot, R., Farber, S., Grasso, M., Hannon, B., Limburg, K., Naeem, S., O'Neill, R., Paruelo, J., Raskin, R., Sutton, P., and van den Belt, M., "The Value of the World's Ecosystem Services and Natural Capital," *Nature* 387 (May 15, 1997): 253–260.

Muller-Schwarze, D., and Sun, L., *The Beaver: Natural History of a Wetlands Engineer*, Cornell University Press, 2003.

Owl, G., *Pilgrims of the Wild* [1935], Charles Scribner's Sons, 1971.

Simon, L., "Solving Beaver Flooding Problems through the Use of Water Flow Devices," in Timm, R., and O'Brien, J. (eds.), *Proceedings of the 22nd Vertebrate Pest Conference,* University of California, 2006, 174–180.

SHARON TAYLOR BROWN

THE WELFARE OF MUTE SWANS

The mute swan, *Cygnus olor* (derived from two words meaning "swan," the former being the Latin and the latter apparently derived from an old Celtic name for the species of bird), is found in many parts of the world and is known in Britain as a "royal bird." It is protected by a law known as the Royal Prerogative. That means that it is a criminal offense to harm the birds, disturb their nests, or steal their eggs. But despite their privileged legal status, there are continuing concerns about their welfare and the preservation of their habitat.

Mute swans may be seen in large groups or flocks across the countryside, but when they breed in Britain, they are mainly solitary pairs. Once ready to leave the parents, the young look to join a flock, where they learn social behavior during the following three years of life. When people see large flocks, they often find it hard to believe that these birds need continuing protection if their numbers are not to decrease to dangerously low levels.

Swans have few natural enemies. They are vegetarian and generally show aggression only when defending their young. Almost all the threats to their survival and welfare come from human beings. In the 1970s swan numbers were drastically declining, and one of the likely factors was lead poisoning caused by fishing weights used by anglers. Since the 1990s the use of lead in fishing has been banned, and there have been fewer mortalities, probably as a direct consequence. There are still some deaths from lead poisoning, but that is probably due to the existence of some lead lying just beneath the surface of river mud, which is swallowed by foraging birds, or environmental lead in the water areas caused by "road runoff"—namely, petrol (gasoline). Careless fishing that causes "hooked" or "tackled" birds also poses a continuing problem.

A major concern is the number of birds who die each year from collisions with overhead power cables. This has been recognized as a problem for decades, and thankfully, some power companies have finally started to take positive action, especially EDF Energy, which is pioneering in this respect. Other companies still pay lip service to the protection of these birds when what they should be doing is simply marking these lines with brightly colored balls or shiny disks, which would largely eliminate the threat. Swans are large, heavy birds; when flying at speeds of thirty to fifty miles an hour, they have difficulty swerving and also have poor forward vision. Whole flocks, as well as individuals, frequently collide with power lines. If they are not killed outright by electrocution, they suffer burns and broken wings. Countless smaller birds also hit lines but probably go unnoticed because they are not large and white.

Pollution is another factor in high mortality. It may take the form of human sewage leaks, diesel oil, refined oil, or general litter. A swan who is caught in an industrial diesel spill is at risk of death not only by drowning (because the animal's feathers become waterlogged), but also because, when ingested, diesel causes burning and subsequent destruction of vital organs. Death in such cases may take several weeks and cause untold suffering. The guardians of waterways, such as the U.K. Environment Agency, are active in investigating such disasters and have the necessary authority to act against offenders.

Loss of natural habitat is an ever-growing problem. As the demand for roads and housing increases, there is an inevitable loss of suitable nesting and feeding grounds. Planning authorities need to exercise careful, enlightened management of key areas that can impact adversely on swan habitat and welfare. For instance, it is obviously necessary for water authorities to dredge river areas, but care needs to be taken to provide slopes rather than steep, straight sides to the banks. If habitat declines, so will future generations of swans.

Sadly, it is not uncommon for swans to be shot, their nests vandalized, and eggs stolen. Unfortunately, air rifles and crossbows were not covered in the amendments to the British law regulating and licensing firearms.

The most taxing time is when the young cygnets take to the water at two to three days old. Pikes, herons, crows, and even minks in some areas may take the unwary young. Foxes, the only natural land predator, are known to take on healthy, full-grown swans as well as weak or sick birds who are obviously more at risk. The minks, who have increased in numbers over the years, are also an increasing threat to swans. Botulism, a natural organism found in slow-running water areas in warm weather, has been known to kill large flocks when the birds feed on decaying green matter. When this occurs, an expert needs to spot symptoms in the first few hours and provide suitable treatment immediately; otherwise it will be too late.

The mute swan is possibly the most beautiful living ornament of the United Kingdom's lakes and rivers, but continued vigilance is needed to ensure the birds' welfare and protection. Such vigilance is also vital if future generations are not to be deprived of seeing and knowing these birds. They have been associated with the United Kingdom for more than a thousand years, perhaps even longer, but if we are not careful, they could be just a memory a hundred years from now.

Related articles: Angling for sport; Conservation philosophy; The protection of birds

Birkhead, Mike, *Population Ecology and Lead Poisoning of the Mute Swan*, Oxford University Press, 1982.

Birkhead, Mike, and Perrin, Christopher, *The Mute Swan* (Helm Field Guides), Christopher Helm, 1988.

Hibbert, A., *Animal Welfare: Read All about It*, Franklin Watts, 2004.

Sears, J., *Lead Poisoning in Mute Swans in the Thames Area during 1989*, Nature Conservancy Council, Information and Library Services, 1990.

Strod, D. A., Mudge, G. P., and Pienkowski, M. W., *Protecting Internationally Important Bird Sites: A Review of EEC Special Protected Area Network in Great Britain*, Joint Nature Conservation Committee, 1990.

White, Rob, *Crimes against Nature: Environmental Criminology and Ecological Justice*, Willan, 2008.

DOROTHY BEESON

TRADE

CITES AND INTERNATIONAL TRADE

Planet Earth is home to over 13,000 known species of mammals and birds; thousands of reptile, amphibian, and fish species; some 250,000 flowering plant species; and millions of insect and other invertebrate species. Together these animals and plants form part of the great natural wealth of the world with which we are entrusted, both for present generations and for generations to come. Yet many thousands of species are under pressure because of human activities such as habitat destruction, pollution, and unsustainable use.

International trade, both legal and illegal, has grown dramatically over the past few decades as improved transport has made it easier to ship animals and plants, and their products, anywhere in the world. It is big business: commercial fishing and the timber trade aside, this international trade is estimated to be worth billions of dollars annually and to involve more than 350 million live plants and animals every year. Much of this trade aims to satisfy the demand for exotics and ornamental plants. Parts and derivatives such as furs and skins, traditional medicines, extracts, and oils are also traded commercially in large quantities. Concerned about the overexploitation of many vulnerable species through the then-unregulated international trade, governments adopted the Convention on International Trade in Endangered Species of Wild Fauna and Flora (CITES) in 1973. The treaty entered into force in 1975 and had 175 member states in 2010.

The convention prohibits most commercial international trade (and regulates noncommercial trade) in an agreed-upon list of plant and animal species that are threatened with extinction and that are, or may be, adversely affected by trade. These species are listed in the so-called Appendix I, which includes the snow leopard, the tiger, and other big cats; many rare primates, such as the chimpanzee and the gorilla; almost all large parrots; most crocodiles; all sea turtles; slipper orchids; and many cacti—in total 655 animal species and 298 plant species.

CITES also regulates commercial international trade in plant and animal species that are not threatened with extinction but that could become so if their trade is not strictly regulated. These species are listed in Appendix II, which includes all other big cats, primates, cetaceans, parrots, crocodiles, cacti, and orchids, plus several carnivorous plants—in total 4,399 animal species and 28,679 plant species.

A third list, Appendix III, includes species subject to regulation within a particular member country, and for which the cooperation of other member countries is sought to help regulate trade. There are 160 species of animals and 10 plant species in Appendix III. As trade impacts and population levels change, animal or plant species can be added to the CITES appendices, deleted from them, or transferred from one appendix to another. These decisions are based on the best scientific information available and the likely effectiveness of different types of regulation.

Where trade is allowed, CITES regulates the export, re-export, import, and introduction of listed species through a system of permits and certificates that may be issued only if certain conditions are met, and which must be presented when leaving or entering a country. For species listed on Appendices I and II, one important requirement is that international trade in specimens of these species must not be detrimental to their survival in their natural habitat. Another requirement is that the animal or plant must have been legally obtained.

The conditions, consultations, and inspections under which permits are issued and accepted are at the core of how CITES regulates international trade in listed species. Properly issued permits represent the end result of a chain of legal verifications, biological and ecological considerations, and considerations regarding sustainability and management that have to be made before a permit is issued.

CITES also addresses health and welfare concerns for live specimens. The transportation of any living being must conform to transport requirements, so as to minimize the risk of injury, damage to health, or cruel treatment. In exceptional cases, where trade in specimens of Appendix I species is authorized, the CITES Scientific Authority of the state of import must be satisfied that the proposed recipient is suitably equipped to house and care for the animal or plant. In the case of live animals who have been confiscated, the member states have adopted detailed guidelines, including the option of relocating animals to rescue centers.

With human population and economic activity continuously expanding, the pressures facing plants and animals will only become greater. CITES is helping to make species conservation and the satisfaction of human needs mutually supportive, by ensuring that plant and animal species are not subjected to unsustainable exploitation because of international trade.

———

Related articles: The big cats; Conservation philosophy; Free-living chimpanzees; The fur trade; Primates worldwide; The trade in primates for research; The trade in reptiles; The World Trade Organization

CITES Secretariat, *Activity Report of the CITES Secretariat 2008–2009*, 2010, available at http://www.cites.org/eng/disc/sec/ann_rep/2008-09.pdf.

The Conference of the Parties, *CITES Appendices I, II and III*, 2010, available at http://www.cites.org/eng/app/appendices.shtml.

———, *CITES Strategic Vision: 2008–2013*, 2007, available at http://www.cites.org/eng/res/all/14/E14-02.pdf.

UNEP-WCMC (comps.), *Annotated CITES Appendices and Reservations*, 2008, CITES Secretariat, Geneva, and UNEP-WCMC, Cambridge, 2008, available at http://www.cites.org/eng/resources/pub/checklist08/index.html.

——— (comps.), *Checklist of CITES species* (CD-ROM), CITES Secretariat, Geneva, and UNEP-WCMC, Cambridge, 2008, available at http://www.cites.org/eng/resources/pub/checklist08/index.html.

STEPHEN V. NASH

(ON BEHALF OF THE CITES SECRETARIAT)

THE FUR TRADE

Historically, fur has always been associated with status and excess. Twelve thousand squirrel and eighty ermine skins were used for just one of Henry IV's robes, and the types of fur that could be worn depended on the rung of the social ladder a person occupied. Fur is still seen as a status or fashion statement. Animals have been exterminated from many of their territories by the trade in fur. As early as 1526, the last beaver was killed in the United Kingdom, and subsequently, in many parts of Europe, target species, such as the much-prized marten, were progressively "hunted out." Because of this, many of the animals became commercially extinct, so that it was simply no longer worth hunting them.

The early explorers of North America provided a solution to this shortfall. Fur trappers became an integral part of British colonization, and the Hudson Bay Company, established by royal charter in 1670, actually owned most of the land that was later to become Canada. The overexploitation of free-living animals now began in another continent, and the beaver, one of North America's most common mammals, was almost exterminated. Indeed, it was only a change in fashion, away from felt beaver hats, that saved the species. The sea mink was not so lucky and became extinct in 1894. By the beginning of the last century, the economics of fur trapping and the difficulty in finding sufficient fur had led to the development of fur farming.

The main trapping nations are the United States, Russia, and Canada. Information about the exact numbers and the types of animals being trapped is very hard to obtain from the two larger trapping nations—the United States and Russia—although Canada does publish annual statistics. Around five million free-living animals are still trapped each year. The British Fur Trade Association says that only about 15 to 20 percent of the global fur trade comes from free-living animals, but since the world trade accounts for more than fifty million animals each year, that amount is still considerable. According to the Fur Commission U.S.A., based on statistics released annually by Oslo Fur Auctions, there was a worldwide "harvest" of 50.5 million mink pelts in 2010 alone.

One of the most commonly used traps used to catch animals for their fur is the steel-jawed leghold trap—a device whose use has been banned throughout Europe. In fact it was outlawed in England and Wales in 1958 by the Pests Act (1954), and Scotland followed a little later. When the steel jaws of the leghold trap slam shut on the victim's leg (an action similar to the slamming of a hand in a car door), injuries such as torn flesh and broken bones are frequently inflicted. Animals then often go to great lengths to escape, some even chewing off or wearing through their trapped limbs.

The two other common trapping methods involve the conibear (invented by trapper Frank Conibear) and the snare. The conibear trap is sometimes referred to by the fur trade as an "instant kill trap," and indeed, if an animal of the right size enters the trap's jaws at the right speed and angle, he or she may be killed quickly. But as with the leghold trap, neither the conibear nor the snare can discriminate, and all too often, animals are held crushed or with severe injuries for hours or even days. Ironically, it is still legal for furs from animals caught in leghold traps to be imported into Britain and within the European Union, where the use of such traps is illegal.

Indeed, all traps are inherently indiscriminate since they are triggered by the first animal unfortunate enough to step into them. Endangered species are caught in them, as are companion animals.

Related articles: The emergence of animal protection in Russia; Fur farming; The humane movement in Canada; Snares and snaring; Understanding beavers

British Fur Trade Association, "Farmed and Wild Fur," available at http://www.britishfur.co.uk/index.php/farmed-and-wild-fur/farmed-and-wild-fur/.

Dolin, Eric Jay, *Fur, Fortune and Empire: The Epic History of the Fur Trade in America*, Norton, 2010.

Fur Commission U.S.A., "Production Statistics," available at http://www.furcommission.com/farming/production/.

Fur Free Alliance, "Facts about the Fur Trade," available at http://www.infurmation.com/facts.php.

Linzey, Andrew, "Fur Farming," in *Why Animal Suffering Matters: Philosophy, Theology, and Practical Ethics*, Oxford University Press, 2009, 97–114.

———, *Public Morality and the Canadian Seal Hunt*, Respect for Animals and the Humane Society of the United States, 2005.

Respect for Animals, "Trapping," 2012, available at http://www.respectforanimals.co.uk/facts-and-reports/trapping/2/.

MARK GLOVER AND ANDREW LINZEY

LIVE ANIMAL EXPORTS

A wide variety of animals, including pigs, sheep, cattle, poultry, and horses, are transported across countries, across continents, and in some cases across the open sea for slaughter, further fattening, or breeding purposes.

Being loaded onto a truck is likely to be a disturbing experience, especially for animals who are unused to travel. They are removed from the environment they know and are likely to suffer considerable fear from human handling and a range of unfamiliar stresses. They may be mixed with animals they do not know, which may lead to aggression. If the truck is crowded, the driving jerky, or the floor uncomfortable, the animals may well try to remain standing during a journey that in Europe may legally last up to twenty-eight hours in the case of sheep, with a one-hour break in the middle. After a twenty-four-hour rest, they can legally be transported for another twenty-eight hours, and so on.

Across Europe, sheep and lambs are exported from Hungary, Romania, and Spain for slaughter in Greece and from these same countries as well as Poland for slaughter in Italy. At the beginning of a journey, sheep remain standing. After four to ten hours, they lie down in increasing numbers if there is space to do so. If they are overcrowded or the journey is really rough, they remain standing, leading to exhaustion. Sheep normally feed throughout the day but are unlikely to do so on a crowded lorry. After twelve hours they can be very hungry. On long journeys they can be subjected to extremes of heat or cold. Long journeys in hot conditions can lead to severe stresses, including thirst and dehydration, particularly if the animals are crowded close together, making it hard for them to cool down.

Cattle are transported from the cooler pastures of Ireland to be fattened in the confines and heat of a Spanish feedlot. From Spain they may be transported for slaughter in Italy on journeys longer than 2,000 kilometers. Journeys can be as long as 1,200 kilometers in Argentina and as long as 2,500 kilometers in the United States and Brazil. Cattle naturally lie down to rest, but in transporters they may remain standing for very long periods. In one study the first animals started to lie down only after twenty hours of transport (Knowles et al., cited in Scientific Committee on Animal Health and Animal Welfare 80). This does not mean that they were standing because they were comfortable. Cattle transported in pairs in stock crates often lie down after two to three hours. But in the conditions of long-distance commercial transport, cattle stand up to avoid the risk of being trampled and to avoid being thrown around on a bumpy journey and when the vehicle accelerates, breaks, or corners.

Transport is even more stressful for other species. Pigs travel very badly and are very prone to travel sickness. Food is often withdrawn for four or more hours before a journey to reduce the likelihood of the animals vomiting. Pigs are transported from the Netherlands to Spain, Italy, and eastern Europe for slaughter or further fattening. Since pigs have simple digestive systems with little storage capacity, they are likely to suffer severely from hunger and thirst on such long journeys.

Fifty thousand horses are transported to Italy each year, mostly from Poland and Romania, but also from

Spain and France. Most of these journeys take more than eight hours, and some exceed 2,000 kilometers. Some of these horses have been bred for meat; others have been used as beasts of burden. All are likely to suffer considerably on journeys of this length.

Very young animals are even less able to cope with the stresses of transport. Dairy calves are routinely separated from their mothers within a few days or even hours of birth. Female calves are often kept for future milk production. Male dairy calves, if they are not shot at birth, are reared for beef or veal. The Netherlands is a major center for veal production, even though the Dutch eat little of this meat. Each year, 700,000 calves are imported into the Netherlands, many from as far away as Ireland, Poland, and Lithuania.

Calves are particularly poorly adapted to cope with transport. They wish to suckle but are deprived of the comfort and protection of their mothers. They cannot properly regulate their body temperatures and are susceptible to heat and cold. Their immune systems have not properly developed, and they can succumb to infection as a result of their inability to respond to the stresses of transport. Death rates from 1 percent to as high as 23 percent have been reported (Knowles, cited in Stevenson). Although the veal crate has now been banned in Europe, calves reared for veal in the Netherlands are generally kept in barren conditions in slatted pens without bedding. Until the recent tuberculosis outbreak, calves were also exported to the Netherlands from the United Kingdom despite the fact that Dutch farmers rarely provide the bedding that would be required by British welfare legislation.

Journeys throughout the world can be up to 2,500 kilometers long in the United States, Brazil, and China and as long as 4,000 kilometers in Australia. The world's longest journeys are by sea. In the year ending June 2010, more than three million sheep and just under one million cattle were exported from Australia to the Middle East and Southeast Asia. The sheep are first transported by lorry from the farms on which they are reared to the ports. These journeys can be as long as 2,000 kilometers. This is followed by a sea journey that can last eleven to twenty-five days, longer if the ships stop at more than one port. Mortality rates can be high. In 2009, 31,850 sheep died on voyages from Australia, approximately 1 percent of the 3.5 million sheep carried.

At sea, animals can be subject to rough weather and extremes of temperature. They are usually kept in pens with access to food and water, but it does not follow that the food will be consumed. Australian sheep are kept free-range on pasture. Many do not adapt to eating the pellets of food that are provided during the sea journey, despite a prescribed introductory period of shipboard rations before boarding. Approximately half the animals who die on the voyage perish because of "inanition" or a "persistent failure to eat"—they starve to death.

Those lucky enough, or unlucky enough, to survive the rigors of the journey are likely to face methods of slaughter, without stunning, that would be illegal in the country of origin. Severe cruelty has been documented on a number of occasions (see the Animals Australia Web site on live export: http://liveexport-indefensible.com/investigations/).

Transport stress causes suffering and suppresses the immune system. Tired, frightened animals are especially prone to disease, and transporting animals can spread such diseases. In the mid-1990s, the export of calves from Britain was temporarily banned to prevent the further spread of bovine spongiform encephalopathy, commonly called "mad cow disease." Exports from Britain were again suspended during the foot-and-mouth disease outbreak of 2001, but not before sheep exported from the United Kingdom transmitted the infection, it is believed, to calves imported from Ireland at a holding point in France. The calves in turn transmitted the virus to the Netherlands, where a vaccination program followed by a major cull was required to contain the disease. More recently, calves from Britain infected with bovine tuberculosis were exported to the Netherlands, leading to a voluntary ban on imports from the United Kingdom. There has also been concern in the United Kingdom that imports of cattle might increase the risk of another outbreak of the bluetongue virus.

The stresses of transport are, unsurprisingly, bad for meat quality, producing flesh that is either very damp or very dry. Short periods of stress can result in PSE meat (pale, soft, and exudative), caused by a buildup of lactic acid in the animal's muscle. This is particularly a problem in pigs. Long periods of transport-induced stress cause the opposite effect—DFD meat (dark, firm, and dry)—as the muscles run out of energy and acid levels fall too low. This is particularly a problem in cattle. Long periods without sufficient food and water also cause animals to lose condition and body weight, and many become injured or die during the journey. Death rates among chickens rise significantly if the journey lasts longer than four hours.

Despite these obvious economic disadvantages, the trade continues. This may be the result of slaughterhouses and meat processors looking for animals to slaughter and process. It may be due to concentrations of particular industries—for example, factory-farmed veal production in the Netherlands or beef feedlots in Spain. The practice may be supported so that meat can be sold as locally killed, perhaps misleading local consumers into thinking it was also locally produced. Live export is sometimes defended on the grounds of a lack of local slaughterhouses near the point of production or a lack of refrigeration capacity where the meat is sold and consumed. Sometimes live transport is driven by market distortions caused by subsidy. Most usually, long-distance transport and live export are defended on the grounds of free trade. But animals are not mere products—they are sentient beings, a point now recognized by the Amsterdam Treaty of the European Union in 1997. We should not be free to do with them as we wish or to leave their welfare to the unchecked vagaries of the market.

Transport causes suffering. So long as people, whether rightly or wrongly, continue to eat meat, animals must be reared, transported, and slaughtered in the most humane way possible. This means better handling and transport and the shortest distances possible. At a minimum, this should require maximum journey times of eight hours for mammals and four hours for poultry. With the arguable exception of small island production, sea journeys add additional welfare risk and should not be required or permitted.

Related articles: Animal issues in Australia; Animal welfare and farming; Animals and public health; Birds used in food production; Legislation in the European Union; Slaughter; The welfare of cows; The welfare of pigs; The welfare of sheep

Amsterdam Treaty of the European Union, 1997, available at http://www.europlarl.ecin/topics/treaty/section2_en.htm@ chap8 (for discussion, see Linzey, Andrew, *Why Animal Suffering Matters*, Oxford University Press, 2009, 140–141).

Appleby, M. C., Cussen, V., Garcés, L., Lambert, L. A., and Turner, J. (eds.), *Long Distance Transport and the Welfare of Farm Animals*, CABI, 2008.

Australian Livestock Export Corporation Limited, *Livecorp Annual Report, 2009–10*, 2010, available at http://www.livecorp.com.au/Public%20Files/Publications/Annual%20 Report%2009-10%20Final.pdf.

European Food Standards Agency, *Welfare of Animals during Transport: Scientific Report of the Scientific Panel on Animal Health and Welfare on a Request from the Commission related to the Welfare of Animals during Transport*, adopted March 30, 2004, available at http://www.efsa.europa.eu.

Scientific Committee on Animal Health and Animal Welfare of the European Commission, *Report on the Welfare of Animals during Transport* (details for horses, pigs, sheep, and cattle), adopted on March 11, 2002.

Stevenson, P., *Long Distance Transport in Europe: A Cruel and Unnecessary Trade*, Compassion in World Farming, 2008, available at http://ciwf.org/publications.

PHIL BROOKE

THE TRADE IN PRIMATES FOR RESEARCH

The trade in nonhuman primates for research is a global industry. It is an industry responsible for inflicting immense cruelty and suffering on tens of thousands of primates every year, during their capture, caging, holding, and transportation to laboratories worldwide. The major importers and users of primates in research are the United States, China, the European Union, and Japan.

Primates traded are Old World species, in particular macaques (*Macaca* sp.), but African green monkeys (*Chlorocebus aethiops*) and baboons (*Papio* sp.) are also used. The trade in New World species includes squirrel monkeys (*Saimiri sciureus*), marmosets *(Callithrix* sp.), and tamarins *(Saguinus* sp.). All these primates are listed under Appendix II of the Convention on International Trade in Endangered Species (CITES)—the species could become endangered if trade is not controlled.

The main exporting regions of the world are those where the primate species are indigenous, such as Southeast Asia, Africa, and South America. There are also countries where primate species were introduced hundreds of years ago and subsequently established themselves as free-living populations. Such countries include Mauritius—a major supplier of long-tailed macaques (*Macaca fascicularis*)—and Barbados and Saint Kitts, suppliers of the African green monkey.

China has established itself as the world's largest supplier of primates for research, in particular the long-tailed macaque, despite the fact that the species is not indigenous. Companies within China are also financers of primate farms in countries in Southeast Asia, and they import macaques from these farms in large numbers to populate their own supply and research facilities.

Historically, the global trade has been one in free-living animals. Over the years, many hundreds of thousands of primates have been torn from their natal groups and habitat and transported to laboratories. The capture of primates from their natural state unavoidably inflicts substantial suffering on them and is inherently cruel (BUAV, *Paradise Lost*; *Cambodia*). The substantial negative impact caused by trapping is universally recognized by relevant organizations and official bodies (e.g., the European Commission in 2002).

Primates taken from their natural habitat continue to be exported from Mauritius (long-tailed macaques), Guyana (squirrel monkeys), Barbados and Saint Kitts (African green monkeys), Tanzania and Suriname (baboons), Guyana and Suriname (capuchins), and Peru (owl monkeys, also called night monkeys).

In recent years, some source countries have responded to international pressure by breeding and exporting primates who are captive-born (the offspring of formerly free-living parents) or captive-bred (the offspring of parents who themselves were bred in captivity). Nevertheless, free-living populations continue to be trapped to establish and maintain the breeding facilities. There are concerns regarding the validity of captive breeding programs and the mislabeling of "wild-caught" animals as captive-bred animals. Field investigations have also found appalling and unacceptable conditions for primates in both holding and breeding facilities (BUAV, *Cambodia*; *Indonesia*; *Laos*).

The most widely traded primate species used to be the rhesus macaque (*Macaca mulatta*) from India. Free-living populations were decimated by the trade in the 1960s and 1970s, and following international pressure, an export ban was implemented (IPPL). The long-tailed macaque has now become the most widely traded species (Environment News Service)—260,384 individuals were traded globally between 2004 and 2008 according to CITES. The long-tailed macaque is indigenous to Southeast Asia; major exporting countries in the region include Vietnam, Indonesia, Cambodia, and Laos. Some countries, including Thailand and Malaysia, have banned their export. The world's largest exporters of the long-tailed macaque are two countries where the species is not native: China and Mauritius.

Since 2004, there has been an exponential increase in the numbers of these animals traded. This increase is due to the rapid acceleration of large-scale breeding facilities in Southeast Asia, in particular in countries such as Cambodia and Laos, where macaque farming has become a big industry and where a largely unregulated trade has resulted in the indiscriminate and intensive trapping of primates to establish and maintain the numerous breeding and supply farms within the region.

Primatologists are questioning the conservation status of the long-tailed macaque. One recent study concluded that data are deficient for native populations of the long-tailed macaque in the Indochina region, particularly in Cambodia, and concluded that "it is imperative that the conservation status of M. fascicularis be reassessed, particularly taking into account the impact of trade on the species, requiring as such a careful assessment by the CITES Secretariat" (Eudey).

Primates are packed into small wooden crates and transported to destinations around the world in the cargo holds of passenger and cargo airplanes. This causes immense stress and suffering. Transit, by air and road, can take days to complete. During that time, the primates may have to endure inadequate ventilation, noise, extreme temperature fluctuations, and delays. Statistics for primate deaths and illnesses either during transportation or subsequent to it are not always made public. There have been, however, many examples of primates found dead on arrival, often as a result of distress and shock due to the conditions on board.

Nonhuman primates are used in research because of their similarities to humans. Yet it is precisely these similarities that make their suffering so unjustifiable. Humans' continued trade in and use of these animals raises profound ethical questions. The animal welfare costs associated with every stage of their capture, forced confinement on farms, transportation, and eventual use in the research laboratory are unacceptable.

Related articles: Animals used in research; Captive chimpanzees; CITES and international trade; Conservation philosophy; The fur trade; The legal rights of great apes; Legislation in the European Union; Live animal exports; Primates worldwide

BUAV (British Union for the Abolition of Vivisection), *Cambodia: The Trade in Primates for Research*, 2008.

———, *Indonesia: The Trade in Primates for Research*, 2009.

———, *Laos: An Investigation into the Trade in Primates for Research*, 2010.

———, *Paradise Lost: The Trade in Primates for Research*, 1992, UNEP-WCMC Cites Trade Database, available at http://www.unep-wcmc.org/citestrade/.

Environment News Service, "New Online Tool Monitors Endangered Species Trading," 2010, available at http://www.ens-newswire.com/ens/aug2010/2010-08-25-01.html.

Eudey, Ardith A., "The Crab-Eating Macaque (*Macaca fascicularis*): Widespread and Rapidly Declining," *Primate Conservation* 23 (2008): 129–132.

Health and Consumer Protection Directorate-General of the European Commission, "The Welfare of Non-Human Primates Used in Research," Report of the Scientific Committee on Animal Health and Animal Welfare, 2002, available at http://ec.europa.eu/food/fs/sc/scah/out83_en.pdf.

IPPL (International Primate Protection League), "India Bans Export of Rhesus Monkeys," *IPPL Newsletter* 5.1 (1978): 2–4, available at http://www.ippl.org/newsletter/1970s/014_v05_n1_1978-04.pdf#page=2.

SARAH KITE

THE TRADE IN REPTILES

Many, if not most, people view the decline of the dinosaurs as something of a tragedy, at least if interest in the animals' fossilized remains is anything to go by. The "golden age of reptiles" met with rapid and near-global extinction, a major catastrophe marking the end of a long and successful reign. If we could step back in time, we would see our "prehistoric greats" living in harmony with the near-identical forefathers of modern-day crocodiles and turtles—who are still as ancient and yet as up-to-date as ever. With about nine thousand described species, reptiles outweigh mammalian diversity by around 40 percent, divided between four main groupings: crocodilians (crocodiles and alligators), turtles (sea turtles, terrapins, and tortoises), lizards, and snakes.

Currently, however, instead of a giant asteroid-Earth collision (a popular theory to explain dinosaur extinctions), present-day reptiles endure a Chinese water torture–like scenario that is almost as pervasive as an asteroid impact and almost certainly more cruel. Using devious means, destructive practices, and daft excuses, hunters, marketers, enthusiasts, "companion" animal keepers, wearers of reptile skins, and culinary connoisseurs of reptile bodies form an inhumane conspiracy against reptile life. These exploiters probably know that most people will not bother to stand up for reptiles. Reptilian evolutionary success must now contend with the pathology of human exploitation—and it is not pretty.

Culinary passions, largely in Asia, involve many reptiles. Added to harsh handling, treatment, and storage are the appalling methods of slaughter, including decapitation, which involves a slow death for the severed head over more than an hour. While a client consumes a snake's body, the animal's head may still be alive in a bucket in the kitchen. In China alone, estimates suggest that hundreds of millions of turtles are used annually for the culinary, traditional medicine, and companion animal industries. When turtles are sold as food, to prove the stock's "freshness" to buyers, stallholders will slice off the underside of the turtles' shells to show the beating heart. Once purchased, turtles may be boiled alive—an extreme and far from instantaneous death. The slaughter of sea turtles can take days as, following capture and incapacitation, they are carved up alive and sold piecemeal.

Probably the most commonly seen reptile skin products are derived from crocodiles, pythons, and rattlesnakes. Although a lot of what appears to be reptile hide is actually fake, the inhumanities of the "natural" skin trade are real. Snakes are nearly all "wild-caught," and many, if not most, are skinned alive or decapitated and then skinned. Crocodiles are typically bred on ranches, but often breeders, like hunters, take from free-ranging populations. Intensive rearing, involving spatial restrictions, is highly stressful, with co-occupant aggression and infections making for an unhealthy environment. Often, and especially for snakes, confinement is blatantly unsanitary, and the treatment of the animals is harsh. None of this would help skin retailers if it were generally known, at least not if people harbored respect for these normally unpopular animals.

For reptiles kept as companion animals, captive existence commonly amounts to what may be described as a drawn-out series of prequels to death. That is not so surprising considering that even zoo-maintained reptiles regularly manifest serious signs of captivity-stress and die from related traumas. Exotic companion animal keepers, zoos, local and national authorities, supposed experts, and even animal welfare groups often readily accept the imprisonment of reptiles in transparent cages that are no larger than a television set. These same people might complain, protest, or even riot if a puppy were confined to a dried-out fish tank until he or she died. But reptiles also need space, natural habitat, appropriate climate, natural diet, and diverse biological, behavioral, social, and psychological stimulation. In fact, it is arguably worse to entrap a reptile in a vivarium than it is to cage a puppy.

Modern biology has recognized that reptiles are highly sensitive to their physical environments and to physical treatment, pain, stress, and psychological trauma and that they have complex needs that only nature can provide. Habitat and species degradation (both of which may involve poor welfare) could be reduced dramatically through adoption of the so-called green, or "reverse-list," principle in which no animals are traded until standards are verifiably assessed. The destruction of countless abused, shipped, and caged animals, worldwide, could be alleviated if even basic safeguards were implemented. The only practicable and just regulatory solution remains the complete abolition of spurious industries, such as the companion animal, culinary, and skin trades. For now, the devastation of biodiversity and the (at best) palliative care of the millions of should-be free-ranging animals trapped in captivity goes on.

Related articles: Animals in Asia; Animals in Chinese culture; The complexity of animal awareness; The ethics of killing free-living animals; The ethics of zoos; Sea turtles in the Mediterranean; Slaughter

Broom, D. M., and Johnson, K. G., *Stress and Animal Welfare*, Chapman and Hall/Kluwer, 1993.
Drayer, M. E. (ed.), *The Animal Dealers: Evidence of Abuse of Animals in the Commercial Trade 1952–1997*, Animal Welfare Institute, 1997.
Gutzwiller, K., and Knight, R. (eds.), *Wildlife and Recreationists*, Island Press, 1994.
Macphail, E. M., *Brain and Intelligence in Vertebrates*, Oxford Scientific, 1982.

Ristau, C. A. (ed.), *Cognitive Ethology: The Minds of Other Animals*, Erlbaum, 1991.

Warwick, C., Frye, F. L., and Murphy, J. B. (eds.), *Health and Welfare of Captive Reptiles*, Chapman and Hall/Kluwer, 1995.

CLIFFORD WARWICK

THE WORLD TRADE ORGANIZATION

The World Trade Organization (WTO), with 153 member states, plays a central role in the negotiation, establishment, and enforcement of rules on international trade based on the principle of nondiscrimination, which requires that all equivalent goods be treated equally for the purpose of trade, no matter which country they come from.

The WTO was established in 1995 by a series of intergovernmental agreements arising out of the General Agreement on Tariffs and Trade (GATT). In addition to trade in goods (including nonhuman animals), WTO agreements also encompass trade in services and the regulation of intellectual property. In the context of globalization, international agreements governing trade increasingly impinge on the production processes of individual countries and include prohibitions on legislation construed as interfering with free trade. This means that if one WTO member state creates a domestic law that, for example, protects animals against harm, under the WTO dispute settlement process, other member states may lodge a complaint against that law if they believe it creates a trade barrier. The WTO's enforcement mechanisms, such as economic sanctions, give teeth to adverse rulings and in practice may mean that a country is forced to repeal the legislation in dispute.

For its advocates, the WTO provides a mechanism through which trade conflicts can be managed peacefully and constructively with reference to agreed-upon rules, fairly applied and enforced. In this view, such an approach ensures that consumers and economies will benefit from optimally efficient trade arrangements, and the world economy will grow through expansion of trade—growth that is crucial in enabling the development of the poorest economies.

For critics of the WTO, free trade principles too often result in a "race to the bottom" in which the most efficient (cheapest) means of production are effectively given preference, no matter the cost to animals—both human and nonhuman—and the environment. In the view of these critics, the WTO primarily represents the interests of the richest states and their powerful business sectors, who seem to benefit most from the economic orthodoxies the WTO promotes. These corporate/state interests also have the best access to the WTO's enforcement mechanisms and have the most influence in setting the rules, which critics say points to a democratic deficit in the operation of the WTO.

Reflecting economic orthodoxy among trade economists and experts, WTO agreements and instruments generally presume that barriers to trade are tempting to governments for domestic political reasons, but are also destructive. Consequently, barriers are permitted under WTO rules only when no other approach can achieve a "legitimate objective." Barriers may be tariffs or, increasingly, requirements that imports conform to technical specifications. Legitimate objectives may relate to issues such as national security considerations; prevention of deceptive practices; human health and safety; or animal and plant health (Barton, Goldstein, Josling, and Steinberg 138). There has been an assumption that technical trade barriers should focus on the direct impact of the product on consumers—for example, the risk of disease or injury from the product—not on "incidental harms" from the production process. Therefore, health and safety of workers is not deemed a legitimate objective (Barton et al. 138–139), nor is animal welfare. The exclusion of animal welfare considerations has "led to the mobilization of animal welfare advocates, who have since demanded to participate in trade policymaking processes and criticized the WTO's rules and mission" (Barton et al. 139). These activists point out that the problems posed by the WTO rules are not only direct, in terms of disallowing domestic rules banning trade in goods negatively affecting animal welfare; they also have a chilling effect, where fear of WTO sanctions may cause some governments to retreat from a strong position in defense of animals.

The WTO and many of its member states tend to argue that issues such as occupational health and safety and animal welfare are not trade concerns and are best dealt with by other agencies, such as the International Labour Organization (ILO) or the World Organisation for Animal Health (OIE). However, the WTO is the only international body capable of enforcing its rules, which means that activists see little value in turning to less influential organizations such as the OIE to address their concerns.

Because the WTO rules are established by agreement between member states and effectively require consensus, it is impossible to change them when some states oppose reform. For example, in response to domestic pressure, in 2000, the European Union proposed animal-friendly trade measures to the Doha Round of trade negotiations conducted under the WTO's auspices. These included the establishment of a new multilateral agreement on animal welfare; a labeling regime pertaining to animal welfare standards for imported foods; and compensation to enable producers to meet the additional costs of producing food to EU animal welfare standards. Those proposals met strong opposition, in particular from developing countries, with a number of member states asserting that the WTO was not an appropriate forum in which to pursue an animal welfare agenda (Hobbs, Hobbs, Isaac, and Kerr). Those proposals did not advance.

However, although animal welfare is not explicitly provided for in trade agreements as a legitimate state objective, some animal welfare issues attain legitimacy when they are treated as environmental matters. There is also provision for moral exceptions in the GATT (rule XX[a]]) that can be used to legitimate constraints on trade for animal protection purposes (Thomas).

In the well-publicized shrimp-turtle case, the WTO dispute settlement process upheld a complaint by India, Malaysia, Pakistan, and Thailand against U.S. laws prohibiting the importation of shrimps harvested by methods (such as using purse seine nets) that harm sea turtles. Although the shrimp-turtle case has been viewed as an example of the WTO blocking animal protection, the final decision of the WTO did find that the protection of the endangered sea turtles (based on environmental principles) was legitimate grounds for a trade barrier. The complaint was nonetheless upheld because it was determined that the United States was discriminating against the complainant countries by helping some Latin American countries, but not the complainants, develop turtle-friendly fishing methods that met with U.S. domestic environmental standards (Lane). The shrimp-turtle case demonstrates the importance of animal protection instruments being designed carefully to avoid any appearance of discriminatory treatment between states.

Following the "Battle for Seattle" in 1999 (Wilkinson), in which attempts to negotiate a new Multilateral Agreement on Investment under the WTO's auspices were derailed in the face of mass protests, the WTO has sought to improve some of its processes, including more engagement with nongovernmental organizations (NGOs). Although transparency has been enhanced, critics would still like to see more open policy and rule formulation, more democratic governance, and better incorporation of "non-economic" issues, such as human and animal rights and environmental protection, into trade processes and standards (Paterson). Moreover, although labor and environmental issues are now engaged with by the WTO, animal protection is not on the agenda to the same degree.

As production processes that cruelly exploit some animals become increasingly globalized, reform of the WTO, so that principles of animal protection can be established as legitimate trade concerns, is increasingly important. Although there is scope under the current GATT for animal protection to provide a basis for laws affecting trade (Archibald), such laws face considerable technical hurdles to implement and survive the WTO dispute settling process. Removing barriers to regulating trade in pursuit of animal protection is not a simple process. Changes to the WTO rules must ultimately be agreed on by all member states. Animal protection concerns all too often appear to be culturally specific to rich countries and are easily portrayed as merely another means of blocking economic development in poor countries through the erection of trade barriers. Therefore, building a constituency of support for animal protection in the developing world will be crucial in achieving WTO adoption of trade rules that allow more effective regulation of production processes to safeguard animals.

Related articles: CITES and international trade; Developments in animal law; The fur trade; Live animal exports; The trade in primates for research; The trade in reptiles; The universal declaration on animal welfare

Archibald, Catherine Jean, "Forbidden by the WTO? Discrimination against a Product When Its Creation Causes Harm to the Environment or Animal Welfare," *Natural Resources Journal* 48.1 (2008): 15–51.

Barton, J. H., Goldstein, J. L., Josling, T. E., and Steinberg, R. H., *The Evolution of the Trade Regime: Politics, Law, and Economics of the GATT and the WTO*, Princeton University Press, 2006.

Hobbs, A. L., Hobbs, J. E., Isaac, G. E., and Kerr, W. A., "Ethics, Domestic Food Policy and Trade Law: Assessing the EU Animal Welfare Proposal to the WTO," *Food Policy* 27 (2002): 437–454.

Lane, Katie A., "Protectionism or Environmental Activism? The WTO as a Means of Reconciling the Conflict between Global Free Trade and the Environment," *University of Miami Inter-American Law Review* 32 (2001): 103–136.

Paterson, B., "Realising or Preventing the Democratization of the World Trade Organization," paper presented at the 5th ECPR General Conference, Potsdam, September 10–12, 2009.

Thomas, Edward M., "Playing Chicken at the WTO: Defending an Animal Welfare–Based Trade Restriction under GATT's Moral Exception," *Boston College Environmental Affairs Law Review* 34 (2007): 605–637.

Wilkinson, R., *The WTO: Crisis and the Governance of Global Trade*, Routledge, 2006.

SIOBHAN O'SULLIVAN AND SANDY ROSS

four

COMPANION ANIMALS

Millions of people worldwide have companion animals. Some are lavishly treated; many are not. Some are neglected (largely because of ignorance) or placed in unsuitable environments, abandoned, or euthanized when caregivers tire of them.

The first subsection of "Companion Animals" begins with the essential information about caring for the most common of our companions, such as dogs, cats, guinea pigs, hamsters, horses, and rabbits. It is important that everyone who cares for such animals be familiar with the essentials of proper care, including housing, feeding, and the need for veterinary care. The second subsection includes a range of articles focusing on the responsibilities of caring for companions, including how to enrich their environments, teach them humanely, provide for them in times of emergency, and microchip them so that they can be identified and rescued when lost, as well as how we should envision ourselves in relation to these animals who are wholly dependent on us.

The third subsection looks at the sensitive issues of health, loss, and bereavement. It is important that caregivers be attentive to the issues surrounding their companion's health needs, including health care, first aid, and insurance to cover veterinary bills. In order to prevent further unwanted companions, it is vital that caregivers arrange for their animals to be neutered or spayed. Since humans often form close emotional bonds with their companions, the experience of bereavement can be especially distressing. Our articles on euthanasia, burial, and bereavement are meant to provide helpful information for those going through this experience.

The final subsection focuses on the various abuses that companion animals endure worldwide—for example, through cosmetic mutilation, pound seizure, selective breeding, and thoughtless abandonment. Underlying these abuses is the way in which animals are still frequently regarded as commodities or consumable goods for sale. The commercialization of companion animals causes great suffering, as demonstrated by puppy mills and the killing of dogs as food. The widespread, unregulated breeding and sale of companion animals worldwide inevitably leads to homelessness or killing since there are not enough good homes available.

ANDREW LINZEY

CARING FOR INDIVIDUAL SPECIES

CATS

In many surveys, cats are commonly described by their caregivers as "close friends." Most of us accept that our cat companions are as aware of our moods as we are of theirs. Mechanistic descriptions of animal behavior are being replaced by an understanding of "emotionality"— how all animals, including humans, are emotionally complex beings. This enables us to examine not only our own mood states better, in terms of assessing our general well-being, but also those of our cats.

Most caregivers in Europe allow their cats the freedom of the great outdoors to behave as they wish and then care, feed, and enjoy social interaction with them when they return home. Only about 10 percent of cats are believed to live permanently indoors in the United Kingdom, but the figure is higher and rising in the United States. Cats kept in city apartments may be unable to reach ground level, and some caregivers choose to keep them indoors anyway because of concerns about their safety outdoors. Indoor cats are less likely to catch diseases and suffer injuries and are far less likely to contract parasites. Moreover, expensive pedigree cats (4 percent of the 7.5 million cats in the United Kingdom in 2002) are most unlikely to be stolen if kept indoors. Indoor cats live longer and safer lives and are likely to be physically healthier than cats allowed to go hunting and exploring outdoors. But what of their mental welfare?

The cat evolved as a solitary predator *at the top of the food chain*. This means that each one is designed to move through a hunting environment, avoiding danger and detecting and catching prey. To do this, cats have evolved astonishing sensory capabilities and are super-sensory compared with social hunter-gatherers (such as human beings) and hunter-scavengers (such as dogs), who find food as part of a team and can rely on one another to detect and respond to danger.

Supersensory, yet increasingly kept in unchanging and unchallenging physical environments (and sometimes subjugated to their caregiver's fears or demands),

indoor cats may fail to receive sufficient attention to their social and predatory needs. This can lead directly to emotional dysfunction and result in behavioral problems. General mood state is a particularly crucial factor for the cat because it is largely determined by the environmental and social lifestyle in which the cat is maintained. It is difficult to identify accurately or treat any particular behavior problem, such as indoor urine spraying or inter-cat aggression, based solely on a cat's emotional responses at the time without analyzing the animal's general mood state beforehand and adjusting his or her care to improve it.

This attention to cats' mood states is necessary because cats, being able to detect so much more of what is going on around them, actually *need* to have their senses stimulated and to express the behaviors associated with detecting, stalking, and catching their prey. Some cats also need to have contact with other cats, and all will certainly need to have frequent contact with their caregivers to retain a mood of contentment in a domestic setting.

The challenge of keeping a cat content indoors is similar to the challenge of keeping other captive animals happy in a small and unchanging environment where most aspects of their lives, including feeding and physical health, are managed for them. The key is often to introduce animals to the emotion of frustration in their day-to-day lives. This is just as vital to well-being as the love and attention that caregivers can offer. If there is never anything problematic to resolve in terms of social interaction and acquiring food, and there is little or no access to novel items, then a cat may become bored or obsessed with some minor aspect of life as a compensatory mechanism. It is the relief of mild frustration by overcoming little difficulties and exploring new things that produces a mood of well-being. Indoor cats can otherwise become lazy and unfit, and they may sleep even more than the two-thirds of life that cats normally sleep away anyway, as simply another means of recycling the neurotransmitters that are associated with feelings of well-being.

The following suggestions may help keep a cat, whether allowed outdoors or confined indoors, psychologically healthy:

Play predatory games

The opportunity to express the innately rewarding predatory sequence of "eye-stalk-chase-pounce-bite" in organized games can make up for the lack of opportunity to hunt real prey. Instigating chase games with a range of moving toys to simulate different types of prey is necessary up to thirty times per day for solitary indoor cats. This is because cats are designed to catch about ten mice a day for survival but would perhaps catch a mouse only one time in three initiations of their hunting sequence, so dangling a fishing rod–type toy and rolling balls of paper past a domesticated cat's line of vision—and then up and over furniture for the cat to chase and pounce on—are activities caregivers need to engage in frequently.

Offer the right social contact

Indoor cats in particular tend to coincide their time of activity with the presence of their caregivers—and rest and sleep when they are alone—so it is important to "be there" when they need you. One Swiss study showed that the more the caregivers responded to their cat, the more likely the cat was to respond to them; and the more interactions initiated by the cat, the longer these interactions lasted. Indoor cats should never be kept singly if at all possible, so that they have this vital social contact even when caregivers are away. Some cats may be very territorial and prefer to live alone, but if they can be kept in pairs or greater numbers, they will not only hopefully enjoy being affectionate with each other but also practice their hunting behaviors in gentle form on each other. This means that the number of chase games that you need to instigate with each cat can be reduced.

Increase territorial complexity

The amount of space available to a cat is less important than the complexity and degree of novelty within the territory. Free-ranging cats encounter a changing environment every time they go out, and so to compensate for that lack of stimulation indoors, it is essential to provide as changing an environment as possible for indoor cats (or for outdoor cats during prolonged bad weather or in old age, when they may elect to stay indoors). This can be achieved by bringing in lots of new objects, such as tree branches, rocks, folded newspapers, and cardboard boxes to explore and run through, as well as providing commercial activity centers and toys to help ensure that they use their senses and engage their emotions fully.

Make feeding a challenge

Providing food in bowls reduces a cat's natural active foraging time to just a few minutes a day compared with the hours that he or she would need to spend hunting for food. Provide dry food in foraging toys that he or she must manipulate for the food to fall out—these are available from all good companion animal supply stores. Divide the daily recommended ration into as many refills as possible and hide the toys in different places every time, including in and around the new objects that are brought in for the cat to explore. Divide the rest of the daily ration into portions to be hidden around the home for the cat to seek out before eating.

With daily attention to their diet, health care, and physical—and psychological—well-being, cats should enjoy a long and healthy life. As ever, the more effort the caregiver makes to understand how to keep and react with cats, the more rewarding their lives will be, indoors or out.

Related articles: Animals used in research; The big cats; The complexity of animal awareness; The concept of guardianship; Dogs; Feral cats; Humane education; Kennels and catteries; A lifelong responsibility; Neutering and spaying; Understanding companion animals

Bessant, Claire, *The Cat Manual: The Complete Step-by-Step Guide to Understanding and Caring for Your Cat*, Haynes, 2009.
Edney, Andrew, and Taylor, David, *Caring for Your Cat: 101 Essential Tips*, 2nd ed., Dorling Kindersley, 2003.
Humane Society of the United States, "Cats," 2011, available at http://www.humanesociety.org/animals/cats/.
Nevile, Peter F., *Do Cats Need Shrinks? Cat Behaviour Explained*, Book Sales, 1994.
Royal Society for the Prevention of Cruelty to Animals, "Cats," 2011, available at http://www.rspca.org.uk/allaboutanimals/pets/cats.

PETER F. NEVILLE

DOGS

Originally, the ancestors of the domesticated dog were often bred specifically for a job, for work. Most are now kept as companion animals, and the contemporary challenge is how to provide optimum care while respecting the animals' natural, instinctive behaviors. To keep a domesticated dog healthy and happy, caregivers should follow a basic set of guidelines to ensure that the dog is integrated into the home environment while at the same time being allowed to develop his or her own personality.

Housetraining is probably the most important aspect of dog keeping to get right from the outset. Dogs live in packs in their natural state and therefore have a set of behaviors when it comes to urinating, some of which may seem strange to humans. They have a natural instinct to keep their living area clean, but when nature calls, and they do not have access to the outdoors, they will relieve themselves on the spot. This habit obviously needs to be modified, but the companion animal cannot do it alone and needs help. Rescue dogs in particular may need retraining to get back into the routine even if they have already been housetrained, since events from their past may cause them to urinate out of fear or uncertainty.

Dogs' desire for company derives from their original "pack mentality" when they lived and hunted in packs. One school of thought suggests that unless persuaded otherwise from the outset, a domesticated dog will perceive his or her caregiver as a subordinate member of his or her "pack." Problems can therefore occur when the dog is left alone since the dog will be worried about the absent pack member and be anxious for that person's return, so that he or she can regain control.

Although dogs should never be left on their own for a long period of time, it is important that caregivers feel able to leave for short periods of time when necessary. Again, this is an area in which rescue dogs in particular often require behavioral modification. They have a tendency to suffer acute anxiety, and this can lead to problems, such as destructive behavior, messing, or barking in the house. Dogs always benefit from a routine, and it is important to establish a routine that settles the animal when the caregiver is preparing to go out, to prevent the dog from becoming unduly anxious. Ensuring that plenty of items are available to keep him or her occupied—such as toys and chews—will help. These should always be removed from the dog's sight immediately upon the caregiver's return, to ensure that they are viewed as a positive treat and so that a good association begins to develop with the dog's period alone.

Since dogs originally lived in hierarchical packs, it is natural for the individual dog to accept, and feel secure in, his or her allotted place in the "pecking order." But sometimes a dog may attempt to challenge this with attention-seeking behavior. Dogs are highly intelligent creatures, and many will try out new behaviors when entering a new environment as their confidence grows. Popular tactics include barking, jumping up, mouthing, and chewing treasured household items. The key thing to remember is that attention-seeking problems stem not from a lack of attention per se, but from the dog actually receiving the attention he or she craves for unwanted behaviors. Initially, the caregiver should simply ignore a dog engaged in any of these problematic activities and calmly take any "props" out of reach. Once the dog turns his or her attention to another more acceptable activity, such as going to his or her bed, enthusiastic praise should be offered. Over time, the bad behaviors should begin to cease as the dog begins to realize what will produce attention.

The practice of training dogs is obviously a by-product of dogs' current position in a society created by humans, and as such, training can be alien to dogs' natural instincts. However, some basic training techniques are always necessary—aside from the general embarrassment and inconvenience of having a badly behaved dog, it is important for caregivers to ensure that dogs do not pose a threat to themselves or members of the public. Training classes can provide an excellent framework, but caregivers can implement the following with ease at home:

- Teach a "sit" to ensure control over the dog at all times. This is particularly useful when meeting new people or visiting the veterinarian.
- Establishing a good recall will avoid any potentially dangerous situations on walks.
- Lead training is essential as a general courtesy to other pavement users. Use a lead at all times when walking a dog in public areas, especially where there is traffic, because no matter how well behaved a caregiver may insist a dog is, a sudden sight or sound may cause the animal to take fright and potentially cause an accident.
- Encourage proper play. Most domesticated dogs find interaction with their caregivers both fun and stimulating, but it is essential that dogs learn how to return toys happily without any confrontation. Play also helps to build a bond, burns off energy, and can be a useful reward when teaching other commands.
- Training should always be consistent. Many dogs become confused if teachers, or rules, chop and change. Any visitors to the house should be aware of the ground rules relating to the canine of the house, and caregivers should be vigilant to ensure that well-meaning visitors are not tempted to break them. The best that any person who has a dog can do for that dog is to adhere to the rules of responsible dog caregiving. Investing time in training and exercise and feeding the right way to ensure a healthy mind and body are the most effective ways of ensuring that a canine companion is happy.

Grooming is also an essential part of a domesticated dog's daily routine because it plays a major part in building a bond between the dog and his or her caregiver. This ritual also provides an ideal opportunity to check for fleas, ticks, or any matted fur, while keeping the coat clean and healthy.

Identification is imperative. All dogs should both be microchipped and wear an identification tag—and contact details should be updated in the event of a house move. All responsible dog caregivers should carry a supply of poop scoops when walking, and it is worth remembering that it is a legal requirement in the United Kingdom to keep dogs on leads in public places.

Finally, regular visits to a veterinarian are essential in order to ensure good health and to detect any early signs of disease. Any person who cares for a dog needs to be vigilant with regard to the animal's general well-being.

Related articles: Animals used in research; Canine profiling; The complexity of animal awareness; The concept of guardianship; Dog fighting; Dogs as food; Enhancing a dog's environment; Greyhound racing; Humane education; Hunting with dogs; Kennels and catteries; A lifelong responsibility; Microchipping; Neutering and spaying; Pound seizure; Puppy mills; Selective breeding; Shelters and sanctuaries; Stray animals; Teaching animals humanely; Understanding companion animals

Abrantes, Roger, *Dog Language: An Encyclopedia of Canine Behaviour*, 3rd ed., Dogwise, 2010.

Clothier, Suzanne, *Bones Would Rain from the Sky: Deepening Our Relationship with Dogs*, Grand Central, 2002.

Coppinger, Raymond, *Dogs: A New Understanding of Canine Origin, Behavior and Evolution*, University of Chicago Press, 2002.

Donaldson, Jean, *Culture Clash*, 2nd ed., James and Kenneth, 1996.

Royal Society for the Prevention of Cruelty to Animals, "Dogs," 2011, available at http://www.rspca.org.uk/allaboutanimals/pets/dogs.

Scholz, Martina, *Stress in Dogs: Learn How Dogs Show Stress and What You Can Do*, First Stone, 2006.

ALI TAYLOR

GERBILS

In their natural state, gerbils live in groups called colonies. As social animals, same-sex pairs or groups of gerbils can live happily together, but they should be introduced to one another before the age of seven to eight weeks to prevent fighting. Gerbils are agile and are very good diggers and gnawers, so their housing should be constructed to provide continual opportunity for these behaviors. They are active during the day.

Gerbils have the following requirements:

- Companionship with other gerbils.
- Daily feeding of a rodent diet of a commercial pellet or seed-based mix, with a small amount of fresh fruit and vegetables and occasional sunflower and pumpkin seeds.
- A constant supply of clean drinking water, changed daily, in a drip-feed bottle with a metal spout.
- A large home called a gerbilarium—a big aquarium tank with a close-fitting wire mesh cover.
- Plenty of burrowing material (peat, sawdust, woodchips) and shredded paper, paper tissues, and hay for bedding. Do not use cotton, wool, or similar fluffy bedding products.
- Items such as cardboard boxes, tubes, wooden chew blocks, flowerpots, and glass jars to help provide a complex and interesting environment.
- Tidying of the gerbilarium by the caregiver every day and thorough cleaning of the gerbilarium every few weeks.
- Some quiet time every day to allow for rest.
- Prompt veterinary care if they are stressed, ill, or injured.
- Arrangements for another suitable person to look after your gerbil(s) on your behalf if you are unable to care for them at any time.

Gerbils should be handled with care and in a way that does not cause distress. Using food, caregivers can teach gerbils to walk onto the caregiver's outstretched hand, while the caregiver limits the gerbil's movement with the other hand over the animal's back. It is important to never catch or pick up a gerbil by his or her tail because this can lead to degloving, where the skin of the tail is shed. Care should also be taken when choosing items for the gerbilarium. Where tail injuries occur, veterinary advice should be sought.

Care should be taken to ensure that the gerbilarium is never left in direct sunlight or near any sources of heat, since the gerbils may suffer heat exhaustion. In the case of heat exhaustion, veterinary advice should be sought immediately.

Diseased gerbils generally are less active, show a loss in body weight, and have a hunched posture and ruffled fur. A common disease to affect gerbils is Tyzzer's disease. Symptoms include tiredness, huddling in a hunched position, lack of appetite, and diarrhea. This can lead to death within three days, so you should seek veterinary advice straightaway. If you have any concerns about your gerbils' health or behavior, always ask your veterinarian for advice.

Related articles: The complexity of animal awareness; The concept of guardianship; Humane education; A lifelong responsibility

Harper, Don, _Hamsters and Gerbils_, Smithmark, 1996.
Humane Society of the United States, "Gerbils," 2011, available at http://www.humanesociety.org/animals/gerbils/.
Royal Society for the Prevention of Cruelty to Animals, "General Pet Care," 2011, available at http://www.rspca.org.uk/allaboutanimals/pets/general.
———, "Measuring Animal Welfare in the U.K., 2005–2009," 2011, available at http://www.animalwelfarefootprint.com.

JOHN ROLLS

GUINEA PIGS

Guinea pigs are traditionally thought of as good first "pets" for children; however, it should always be an adult who takes responsibility to ensure guinea pigs are properly handled and cared for. Caregivers must ensure that they meet their guinea pig's welfare needs.

Environmental and behavioral needs

Guinea pigs are active animals and need the opportunity to perform species-typical behaviors, including running, digging, standing fully upright on their back legs, and stretching out when lying down. Guinea pigs need a secure living environment that is large enough for them to exercise in and high enough for them to stand up fully on their back legs.

Accommodation for guinea pigs should be escape-proof and provide protection both from predators (such as foxes, cats, dogs, ferrets, and birds of prey) and from extremes of weather and temperature. Caregivers should ensure their guinea pigs have constant access to safe hiding places, pipes, and shelters. In the case of more than one guinea pig, there must be enough places for all guinea pigs to hide at the same time.

All areas of a guinea pig's living environment should be well ventilated, dry, and draft-free and protected from extremes of heat and cold—temperatures above 26 degrees Celsius (79 degrees Fahrenheit) can cause heat stroke, and temperatures below 15 degrees Celsius (59 degrees Fahrenheit) can cause guinea pigs to become chilled. If a guinea pig is housed outdoors, the accommo-

dation should be sheltered from direct sunlight and the prevailing wind direction. Ideally, when temperatures drop to below 15 degrees Celsius, guinea pigs should be housed indoors. If not, they must be provided with sufficient bedding throughout their accommodation to enable them to keep warm. Indoors, the accommodation should be away from direct sources of heat, such as radiators and sunny windows, and protected from drafts. A room temperature of 17 to 20 degrees Celsius (63 to 68 degrees Fahrenheit) is ideal.

Bedding should be safe for guinea pigs to eat, such as dust-free straw or hay. Products made from softwood, such as pine, should not be used because they can make guinea pigs ill. Caregivers should clean their guinea pig's accommodation regularly, to ensure he or she has clean, dry bedding.

Guinea pigs should be provided with safe toys for playing and chewing and regular opportunities to play with other friendly guinea pigs and people. Caregivers should provide untreated wooden toys to chew, such as fruit tree or willow sticks; toys made of plastic should be avoided. Guinea pigs should also be provided with suitable materials that allow tunneling behavior.

If a guinea pig changes his or her behavior, the animal could be distressed, bored, ill, or injured. Signs that a guinea pig may be suffering from stress or fear can include hiding most of the time, chewing cage bars, overgrooming, overdrinking or playing with the water bottle, sitting hunched, displaying altered feeding or toilet habits, reluctance to move, or repeated circling of his or her enclosure. If a guinea pig's behavior changes, caregivers should seek advice from a veterinarian or clinical animal behaviorist.

Social needs

Guinea pigs are naturally sociable and normally prefer to be with another guinea pig. Guinea pigs who are brought up together will usually get along with each other, but males introduced for the first time as adults may fight. Therefore, guinea pigs should be kept with at least one other friendly guinea pig, unless a veterinarian or clinical animal behaviorist advises otherwise. A good combination is a neutered male and one or more females. Two females can also live together. Litter brothers who are neutered may also successfully live together, if they have been brought up together.

Guinea pigs kept together will naturally form a pecking order, with some animals being more dominant than others. A caregiver should ensure that each guinea pig has places he or she can go to get away from companions if he or she wants to. Unfamiliar guinea pigs should be introduced gradually and under supervision, preferably in a space that is new to both guinea pigs. Guinea pigs should be handled gently every day from an early age, and if a guinea pig has to be kept on his or her own for some reason, the caregiver must provide the animal with daily companionship.

Dietary needs

Fresh, clean drinking water should be provided at all times, and the supply should be checked twice a day. The guinea pig's digestive system needs lots of grass or hay in order to function properly. Guinea pigs have special dietary needs and must have sufficient vitamin C in their diet.

Good-quality hay should make up the majority of a guinea pig's diet and should be available at all times. Grass-based pellets designed for guinea pigs should also be available daily—this will provide essential vitamin C. This vitamin is destroyed over time and quickly with exposure to the air, so caregivers must give a fresh portion of pellets each day.

Fresh grass and leafy greens such as kale and broccoli are excellent sources of vitamin C. Washed fresh grass and some washed, safe leafy greens or weeds should be offered to guinea pigs every day. Some plants are poisonous to guinea pigs, so caregivers should find out which plants are safe to feed guinea pigs. Root vegetables such as carrots or fruit such as apples should be given only in small amounts, such as an apple quarter, as a treat. Citrus fruits should not be fed to guinea pigs.

Caregivers should check that their guinea pig is eating every day, monitor the amount their guinea pig eats and drinks, and check that he or she is passing plenty of dry droppings. If a guinea pig's eating or drinking habits change, the number of droppings decreases or stops, or there are soft droppings, caregivers must speak to a veterinarian immediately.

Health needs

Guinea pigs are not good at showing outward signs of pain and so may be suffering a great deal before anything is noticed. A change in the way a guinea pig normally behaves can be an early sign that he or she is ill or in pain, so these animals should be checked for signs of illness or injury every day.

In warm weather the fur and skin around a guinea pig's rear end and tail area should be checked twice a day, as urine staining or droppings that are stuck will attract flies, which can lay eggs and cause fly-strike, which is often fatal. Guinea pigs should be taken at least once each year for a routine health check by a veterinarian, who will advise on treatments for external and internal parasites (e.g., mites and worms). Front teeth and nails should be checked at least once a week because these can grow quickly—only a veterinarian should correct overgrown or misaligned teeth.

Caregivers should groom their guinea pig's coat regularly to keep it in good condition, which is especially important in long-haired guinea pigs, who will need daily grooming. A small amount of white discharge around the eyes is commonly seen when guinea pigs groom themselves—if this discharge increases or decreases, or there is a discharge at other times, it may be a sign that a guinea pig is ill and needs veterinary attention.

Male guinea pigs should be neutered unless they are intended for breeding and provisions have been made to care for both parents and offspring.

The information in this article was produced using RSPCA-owned information on guinea pigs' welfare needs, put together by a panel of experts. Details of the experts who contributed to this information are available at http://www.rspca.org.uk/sciencegroup/companionanimals/reportsandresources/expertcontributors.

Related articles: Animal pain; Animals used in research; Children's relations with animals; The concept of guardianship; A lifelong responsibility; Neutering and spaying

Department of Food, Environment and Rural Affairs, *Animal Welfare Act for England*, 2006, available at http://www.defra.gov.uk/foodfarm/farmanimal/welfare/act/index.htm.

Kaiser, S., Krüger, C., and Sachser, N., "The Guinea Pig," in Hubrecht, R., and Kirkwood, J. (eds.), *The UFAW Handbook on the Care and Management of Laboratory and Other Research Animals*, 8th ed., Wiley-Blackwell, 2010.

Royal Society for the Prevention of Cruelty to Animals (RSPCA), "Guinea Pig Welfare Needs Information," 2009, available at http://www.rspca.org.uk/allaboutanimals/pets/rodents/guineapigs (see the five welfare needs—environment, diet, behavior, company, and health and welfare—listed on the left-hand side of the page).

Welsh Assembly Government, *Animal Welfare Act for Wales*, 2006, available at http://wales.gov.uk/topics/environmentcountryside/ahw/animalwelfare/animalwelfareact2006/?lang=en.

JOHN ROLLS

HAMSTERS

In their natural state, hamsters make underground homes, building nests within them. They are generally nocturnal, which means they are active at night and should be left alone and quiet during the day. In winter they may go into a deep sleep, or hibernation. The Syrian hamster is solitary and should not be kept in pairs or groups. Other species can be sociable—for example, the Campbell's dwarf hamster and the Russian winter white dwarf hamster—but great care is needed when introducing them, or they may fight.

Hamsters have the following requirements:

- Daily feeding of a rodent diet of a commercial pellet or seed, grain, and nut mix, with a small amount of fresh fruit and vegetables.
- A constant supply of clean drinking water, changed daily, in a drip-feed bottle with a metal spout.
- A large home that is kept indoors, out of direct sunlight and away from direct sources of heat.
- A nest box inside their home. Hamsters need somewhere they can burrow, go out of sight to sleep, and hoard food.
- A deep layer of shavings or a peat/shaving mix on the floor of their home. Shredded paper, paper tissues, and hay should be provided for bedding. Do not use cotton, wool, or similar fluffy bedding products.
- Plenty of exercise. A solid exercise wheel (no open rungs) should be fixed to the wall of the hamster's home.
- The provision of items such as cardboard boxes, tubes, wooden chew blocks, flowerpots, and glass jars to help provide a complex and interesting environment.
- Tidying of their home every day, with thorough cleaning every week, by their caregiver.
- Regular brushing by their caregiver, especially if they have long hair.
- Lots of quiet time during the day.
- Prompt veterinary care if they are stressed, ill, or injured.
- Arrangements for another suitable person to look after your hamster(s), on your behalf, if you are unable to care for them at any time.

Hamsters should be handled with care and in a way that minimizes distress. They should be picked up very gently using both hands as a scoop. It is always best to handle them close to the ground, or over a flat surface, in case they become frightened and jump.

It is important to check your hamster daily, and if you have any concerns about his or her health or behavior, always contact your veterinarian for advice. For example, the development of skin sores or fur loss could indicate parasites or fungal disease, which will require treatment.

Hamsters' cheek pouches can become impacted, which can lead to swellings on one or both sides of the face. If any material becomes lodged in the pouches, or a swelling persists, seek veterinary advice straightaway. Wet tail is a potentially fatal disease that is highly infectious. If a hamster is tired, loses his or her appetite, and has watery diarrhea, do not hesitate to seek veterinary advice straightaway. If your hamster becomes too cold and goes into hibernation, you can revive him or her by raising the temperature of the room. Hamsters may suffer from overgrown teeth and claws. Check teeth and claws regularly, and take the hamster to the veterinarian for trimming if necessary.

Related articles: Humane education; A lifelong responsibility

Humane Society of the United States, "Hamsters," 2011, available at http://www.humanesociety.org/animals/hamsters/.
Royal Society for the Prevention of Cruelty to Animals, "Hamsters," 2011, available at http://www.rspca.org.uk/allabout animals/pets/rodents/hamsters (see the five welfare needs—environment, diet, behavior, company, and health and welfare—listed on the left-hand side of the page).
———, "Measuring Animal Welfare in the U.K., 2005–2009," 2011, available at http://www.animalwelfarefootprint.com.
———, "Veterinary Care," 2011, available at http://www. rspca.org.uk/in-action/whatwedo/vetcare/-/article/ EM_VeterinaryCare.

JOHN ROLLS

HORSES

Caring for a horse or pony is not something to be entered into lightly. Contrary to popular opinion, they are not animals who can just be turned out in a field and visited once or twice a week. A field, with just grass to eat, may not be enough for some to survive, let alone live healthy lives. Of the many horses and ponies suffering from neglect, starvation, or abuse who come into the care of World Horse Welfare (WHW; previously the International League for the Protection of Horses) every year, very few of them have caregivers who are intentionally cruel. Most of their suffering is caused by ignorance.

Anyone contemplating looking after a horse or pony needs to learn about his or her care and welfare needs. Without appropriate care, these animals cannot live happy, healthy lives. It is important to understand, for example, that an animal may be thin for a variety of reasons, not necessarily because of lack of nourishment. All horses and ponies need to have their teeth checked every six months and rasped (filed) as required because the constant chewing required to grind up their food can wear the teeth so that they form sharp edges. These edges can damage the inside of the mouth, and any resulting wounds can easily become infected. The animal may be reluctant to eat for no other reason than his or her mouth hurts, or the animal may swallow food too quickly without chewing properly.

Another reason horses or ponies may not put on weight, even if they are eating well, is worms in their intestines. The developing worms can be picked up in the field when animals are grazing, which is why horses' droppings should be removed from their paddocks daily if possible but at minimum twice a week. Obviously, the more animals on the field, the more important the regular removal of droppings becomes. All horses out on grass need to be on a carefully managed program to minimize worm infestation. How often an individual should be dewormed depends on circumstances, and veterinary advice should be sought. Generally, it is important to use a dewormer that will kill a broad spectrum of worms and to follow the instructions carefully, always ensuring that the correct dose is given for the size of the animal; otherwise, the treatment could be ineffective. If a horse is never dewormed and is on a small field with lots of animals who are similarly poorly managed, chances are that the horse will have a heavy worm burden. He or she will become thin and listless, with dull coat and eyes. Moreover, worms may migrate through the walls of the animal's intestines, which can be fatal.

Good pasture management not only involves the regular removal of droppings; it also involves regular fence checks to make sure that there are no gaps from which the animals can escape, no loose strands of wire in which they can become entangled, and no rabbit holes down which they could break a leg. It also means maintaining a good supply of clean water and removing poisonous plants. If well fed, most horses would not touch poisonous plants in their fields. But this does not mean that we should allow such plants to thrive or plant poisonous trees as hedging. Yew, laurel, and conifers are deadly, as is the apparently innocuous plant the ragwort, with yellow flowers in July and recognized in the spring by a rosette of frilly leaves. Ragwort should be dug up carefully (using gloves), with attention to ensure that no roots remain in the soil, and burned.

Both feet and teeth should be checked regularly. All horses and ponies should have their hooves trimmed by a registered farrier (a blacksmith who specializes in shoeing horses) every six to eight weeks. Those ridden on the roads would normally be shod and need to have their feet picked out daily to remove stones or nails, which might make them lame. Unshod ponies turned out in a field

with no hard surfaces to wear down their feet cannot just be left unchecked. The hoof horn will grow until it turns up at the front like Turkish slippers. As well as being uncomfortable and painful, it puts stress and strain on the legs, and if the problem is left unattended, the pony may well have to be euthanized. All horses and ponies "living out" in fields should be checked daily for injuries, signs of distress, or off color. They can also pick up a form of lice (similar to that which sometimes affects schoolchildren). If the lice infestation goes untreated, the itchiness will cause the poor animal to rub and rub, removing not just hair but skin as well.

In the winter, native ponies and cold-blooded animals develop thick coats, full of natural oils, that will protect them from the harshest climates, but thoroughbreds, part-thoroughbreds, and warm-blooded animals are not so lucky. If they are to live outside in the winter, then they will need the protection of thick waterproof rugs to keep them warm. Adequate shelter must also be provided in the winter so that they can seek protection from the wind, the wet, and the cold. Their water source should be checked twice a day to make sure that it has not frozen over because horses, like humans, cannot survive long without water. Care should be taken to ensure that rugs are fitted correctly. They should be straightened if they have slipped, changed if they are wet through, or replaced by a warmer one if the horse is cold (or non-waterproof rug should be added under the outer one). In the winter months, when the grass does not contain adequate nutrients, all horses and ponies, whether living in stables or outside, use up more than usual amounts of energy to keep warm. To help them conserve their energy, caregivers need to feed them more hay and greater quantities of "hard" feed, depending on their workload and the weather.

But it is not just the cold, bleak winter months that cause suffering. With the onset of spring, when the grass produces lush new growth, there is a risk that ponies, and even horses, will contract laminitis. This is extremely painful. The laminae inside the animal's feet begin to swell but are constricted by the horny hoof growth. The result is lameness and agony for the poor animal. Horses and ponies suffering from laminitis can sometimes be seen adopting a peculiar stance, with one front leg, or both, sticking out as they attempt to take their weight back onto their heels. It is important that an animal with laminitis be removed from his or her field and put in a stable and that the veterinarian be called immediately. If the condition is left undiagnosed, the animal may well have to be euthanized.

As one can see, caring for horses is fraught with difficulties and dangers; it involves a lot of time, hard work, and not inconsiderable expense. Only those who understand the day-to-day dietary and veterinary needs of horses and ponies should even contemplate looking after them. It may be every child's dream to have a pony, but in reality, it is an adult responsibility.

Related articles: The complexity of animal awareness; The concept of guardianship; Euthanasia; Free-ranging horses; Horse slaughter; Jumps racing; A lifelong responsibility; Rodeos

Auty, Islay, and Batty-Smith, Jo, *BHS Complete Manual of Horse and Stable Management*, Kenilworth Press, 2008.

Bishop, Ruth, *The Horse Nutrition Bible: The Comprehensive Guide to the Correct Feeding of Your Horse*, David and Charles, 2005.

Pickeral, Tamsin, *The Horse Lover's Bible: The Complete Practical Guide to Horse Care and Management*, Caroll and Brown, 2008.

The Pony Club, *The Manual of Horsemanships: The Official Manual of the Pony Club*, 13th ed., 2007.

Ranelagh, Elizabeth O'Beirne, *Managing Grass for Horses: The Responsible Owner's Guide*, J. A. Allen, 2005.

LYNDA FREEBREY

RABBITS

The welfare needs of rabbits are often poorly understood by potential and existing caregivers, and the Royal Society for the Prevention of Cruelty to Animals (RSPCA) is concerned that this lack of knowledge, together with many inappropriate traditional housing and husbandry practices, has a detrimental impact on rabbit welfare.

Rabbits are traditionally thought of as good first "pets" for children; however, the RSPCA does not recommend them as suitable companion animals for young children because rabbits have complex needs and are not easy to look after well—they can also be easily injured if not handled correctly. Caregivers must ensure that they meet the welfare needs of rabbits who depend on them.

Environmental and behavioral needs

Rabbits are active animals who need the opportunity to perform normal species-typical behaviors, including hopping, running, jumping, digging, standing fully upright on their back legs, and lying down fully outstretched. Caregivers should provide their rabbits with a secure living environment that is large enough for them to exercise in and stand up fully on their back legs. Rabbits need opportunities to exercise every day to stay fit and healthy. They should be provided with a dry, well-ventilated, draft-free, escape-proof shelter (where they can rest and feel safe) as well as a large exercise area. They should be protected from predators (such as foxes, cats, dogs, ferrets, and birds of prey) and extremes of weather and temperature. Caregivers should make sure their rabbits have access to safe hiding places, pipes, and shelters, where they can go to be alone if they want to or to hide, if they feel afraid. There must be enough places to allow all rabbits to hide at the same time.

Rabbits should be given regular access to an appropriate place to eliminate, which should be separate from where they eat and sleep. Sufficient bedding that is safe to eat, such as dust-free straw or hay, should be provided to keep rabbits warm. The housing and toilet areas should be cleaned regularly.

Rabbits are highly social, playful, and inquisitive animals, and they should be provided with safe toys to play with and chew and regular opportunities to interact and play with other friendly rabbits and people. Suitable materials should be provided to allow rabbits to perform digging behavior, and areas should be provided to allow rabbits to mark their territory with chin secretions, urine, and droppings as well.

Caregivers should be observant; if their rabbit's behavior changes or becomes an ongoing problem, or he or she shows regular signs of stress or fear, caregivers should seek advice from a veterinarian or clinical animal behaviorist. Signs that a rabbit may be suffering from stress or fear can include hiding, chewing cage bars, overgrooming, overdrinking or playing with their water bottle, sitting hunched, and demonstrating altered feeding or toileting habits, reluctance to move, or repeated circling of his/her enclosure.

Social needs

Rabbits should be handled gently every day from a young age. They are naturally social animals and normally prefer to be with another rabbit. If a rabbit has to be kept on his or her own for some reason, the caregiver must interact with him or her in a positive way every day. Neutering reduces the likelihood of fighting in both male and female rabbits—a good combination is a neutered male and a neutered female or neutered littermates of the same sex.

Rabbits kept together will naturally form a pecking order, with some animals being more dominant than others. A rabbit can be bullied and may suffer if unable to get away from other rabbits that he or she does not like. Caregivers should ensure each rabbit has a place he or she can go to get away from companions, if necessary. Advice should be sought from a clinical animal behaviorist if caregivers are unsure about how to introduce rabbits.

Dietary needs

Fresh, clean drinking water must be provided at all times, and the supply should be checked twice a day.

Good-quality hay and grass should make up the majority of a rabbit's diet and should be available at all times. A small amount of commercial rabbit pellets or cereal mix can be fed, but hay or grass is much more important. Feeding the correct diet of mainly hay, grass, or both will help prevent a lot of common diseases such as dental and gut disease.

Safe, washed leafy greens or weeds should be offered to rabbits every day. Some plants are poisonous to rabbits, so caregivers should find out which plants are safe to feed rabbits. Lawnmower clippings should not be fed because these can upset a rabbit's digestive system and make him or her ill. Root vegetables such as carrots and fruits should be given only in small amounts as a treat. No other treats should be fed because they may be harmful. No sudden changes should be made to a rabbit's diet because this could upset the rabbit's digestive system and make him or her very ill.

Rabbits produce two types of droppings—hard dry pellets and softer moist pellets (called caecotrophs) that they eat directly from their bottom and that are an essential part of their diet. Caregivers should check that their rabbit is eating every day, monitor the amount their rabbit is eating and drinking, and check that he or she is passing plenty of dry droppings. If a rabbit's eating or drinking habits change, caregivers must speak to a vet immediately because their rabbit could be seriously ill.

Health needs

Rabbits are not good at showing outward signs of pain and so may be suffering a great deal before anything is noticed. A change in the way a rabbit normally behaves can be an early sign that he or she is ill or in pain, in which case a veterinarian must be consulted immediately.

In warm weather the fur and skin around a rabbit's rear end and tail area should be checked twice a day, given that urine staining or droppings that are stuck will attract flies; these flies can lay eggs and cause fly-strike, which is often fatal. Rabbits should be taken to a veterinarian for a routine health check at least once a year. Front teeth and nails should be checked at least once a week because these can grow quickly. Only a vet should correct overgrown or misaligned teeth.

Rabbits are vulnerable to many infectious diseases and other illnesses, especially dental disease, and they can catch deadly infectious diseases from free-living rabbits. Rabbits should be vaccinated regularly against myxomatosis and viral hemorrhagic disease (VHD), as advised by a veterinarian. Domesticated rabbits should be prevented from having contact with free-living rabbits or areas where these rabbits have been. Treatment should be given for external and internal parasites (e.g., fleas and worms) as necessary, as advised by a veterinarian. Caregivers should groom their rabbit's coat regularly to keep it in good condition—long-haired rabbits will need daily grooming.

Rabbits should be easily identifiable, ideally via a microchip, because they will be more likely to be reunited with their caregivers if lost and to receive prompt veterinary care if injured. Companion animal insurance should be considered by rabbit caregivers, to ensure their rabbit is covered if he or she needs veterinary treatment.

If a rabbit's caregivers are going away, they should try to find someone to care for, and meet all the welfare needs of, their rabbit within his or her familiar home.

The information in this article was produced using RSPCA-owned information on rabbits' welfare needs, put together by a panel of experts. Details on the experts who contributed are available at http://www.rspca.org.uk/sciencegroup/companionanimals/reportsandresources/expertcontributors.

Related articles: Animal pain; Animals used in research; Children's relations with animals; The complexity of animal awareness; The concept of guardianship; Humane education; Insurance; A lifelong responsibility; Microchipping; Spaying and neutering; Toxicity testing

Campbell-Ward, M., and Meredith, A., "Rabbits," in Meredith, A., and Johnson-Delaney, C. (eds.), *BSAVA Manual of Exotic Pets*, 5th ed., British Small Animals Veterinary Association (BSAVA), 2010.

Department of Food, Environment and Rural Affairs, 2006, *Animal Welfare Act for England*, available at http://www.defra.gov.uk/foodfarm/farmanimal/welfare/act/index.htm.

Mullan, S. M., and Main, D. C. J., "Survey of the Husbandry, Health and Welfare of 102 Pet Rabbits," *Veterinary Record* 159 (2006): 103–109.

Royal Society for the Prevention of Cruelty to Animals, "Rabbit Welfare Needs Information," 2009, available at http://www.rspca.org.uk/rabbits (see the five welfare needs—environment, diet, behavior, company, and health and welfare—listed on the left-hand side of the page).

Schepers, F., Koene, P., and Beerda, B., "Welfare Assessment in Pet Rabbits," *Animal Welfare* 18 (2009): 477–485.

Welsh Assembly Government, *Animal Welfare Act for Wales*, 2006, available at http://wales.gov.uk/topics/environmentcountryside/ahw/animalwelfare/animalwelfareact2006/?lang=en.

JOHN ROLLS

RESPONSIBLE CARE

CHILDREN'S RELATIONS WITH ANIMALS

Current statistics indicate that many people share their lives with companion animals. This relationship between people and animals is best documented for modern Western countries, and available statistics indicate that between almost half of all households (47 percent in the United Kingdom) and nearly three-quarters (63 percent in Australia; 67 percent in the United States) include companion animals. Of particular relevance, the statistics indicate that companion animals are most common in households with children. This is not surprising when one considers the nature of children's relationships with companion animals.

As a social species, our need for interpersonal attachments and social relationships is strong. Feeling connected to others through the formation of social attachments is fundamental to our physical and psychological health. Indeed, so important is the need to belong that the presence of close social bonds is of more significance than the types of bonds that one has. Although the majority of research demonstrating the importance of human bonds is restricted to humans' relationships with other humans, there is growing empirical evidence that the strong human tendency toward social bonds extends to nonhuman species and that these bonds are associated with benefits similar to those documented with human-human bonds. Moreover, such benefits to physical and mental well-being extend across the life span and apply to children, adolescents, and adults. There is also indication that the relationships children have with companion animals differ fundamentally from the relationships they have with adults and that the benefits provided by such relationships may be of particular significance for children's well-being.

Although the child's family environment is generally considered to be central to a child's development of social competencies and valued traits, including empathy and emotion regulation, the cultivation of such traits through their relationships with companion animals is being increasingly recognized. Thus, relationships with

companion animals can constitute a vital part of the healthy emotional development of children. Through caring for companion animals, children learn important developmental tasks. They develop a sense of responsibility and competence in their interactions with others, an understanding of others' feelings (i.e., empathy), and achievement of a sense of autonomy, importance, and worth. Developmental lessons can be more powerful when provided by companion animals, given children's fascination with and attraction to animals.

When directed at animals, children's attention tends to be more sustained (as opposed to distracted) and consequently more likely to lead to improved behavioral control. Such focused attention may result from the fact that interactions with animals are characterized by unpredictability, fascination, wonder, and awe at animals' natural beauty and complexity. Moreover, in contrast to relationships with other humans, children's relationships with animals provide an opportunity for emotional investment and expression that is free of negative evaluation and criticism or rejection (otherwise referred to as unconditional positive regard).

Because nonhuman animals accept us unconditionally and without judgment, they provide an opportunity for emotional investment that is nonthreatening and consequently perceived to be safe, particularly by children. Indeed, such unconditional positive regard may be the key factor in the positive relationships that children have with their animal companions. Given such a predominantly accepting nature, companion animals can serve as a source of unconditional social support for children, often with clear advantages over human support. Other important characteristics of the child-animal bond include the devotion and loyalty that companion animals provide. Children consider their animal companions to be attentive and empathic listeners and see them as a source of solace during times of stress, loneliness, or boredom.

Highlighting the powerful effect that the presence of nonhuman animals can have on children's social behavior is the work of American psychologist Boris Levinson.

In the 1950s, Levinson was having difficulty establishing even a preliminary relationship with a particularly withdrawn young boy he had been working with over some months. Although Levinson was usually accompanied by his dog Jingles at work, it was his common practice to remove the dog from his consulting room before his clients arrived. However, on one particular occasion, the boy arrived for his appointment early, and for the first time, Levinson noticed the boy behaving quite differently, apparently quite fascinated by the dog.

Consequently, in subsequent sessions with this boy, Levinson kept his dog with him. It was not long before the boy began talking to the dog and eventually to Levinson. Jingles consequently became an integral part of Levinson's work. He found that the presence of the dog enabled him to more rapidly establish rapport with his clients. Levinson referred to this process as "social facilitation." Since Levinson, others have demonstrated the therapeutic role of children's interactions with animals, and animal-assisted therapy has been adopted by increasing numbers of child workers, particularly for children with disabilities.

Thus, it seems that the benefits provided for children's well-being through their interactions and bonds with companion animals are best described as socioemotional benefits. In modern times, particularly in the Western, industrialized world, a cultural way of behaving that has been referred to as individualism (a way of life in which members of a given society are motivated to pursue individual and independent success) predominates. There are concerns that increasing individualism is resulting in an erosion of collective concern and an alarming increase in psychopathology, to such an extent that living in the late twentieth and early twenty-first centuries has itself been nominated as a risk factor for the development of depression.

It may be that the evolution of our culture, now dominated by economic rather than biological forces, no longer provides optimal avenues for meeting our hardwired belongingness and connectedness needs. It may also be that in such a cultural climate, companion animals can provide buffering and health-promoting support for all—and most particularly for those more dependent and vulnerable members of society, our children and the elderly. Thus, although living in modern times is a risk factor for psychopathology, it is becoming increasingly clear that sharing our lives with companion animals constitutes a protective or buffering factor against psychopathology.

Related articles: Animal and human violence; Caring for animals and humans; Dogs; The experience of loss; Humane education; A lifelong responsibility

Baumeister, R. F., and Leary, M. R., "The Need to Belong: Desire for Interpersonal Attachments as a Fundamental Human Motivation," *Psychological Bulletin* 117 (1995): 497–529.

Diener, E., Oishi, S., and Lucas, R. E., "Personality, Culture, and Subjective Well-Being: Emotional and Cognitive Evaluations of Life," *Annual Review of Psychology* 54 (2003): 403–425.

Fawcett, N. R., and Gullone, E., "Cute and Cuddly and Whole Lot More? A Call for Empirical Investigation into the Therapeutic Benefits of Human-Animal Interactions for Children," *Behaviour Change* 18 (2001): 124–133.

Gullone, E., "A Lifespan Perspective on Human Aggression and Animal Abuse," in Linzey, Andrew (ed.), *The Link between Animal Abuse and Human Violence*, Sussex Academic Press, 2009, 38–60.

Levinson, B. M., "Pets, Child Development, and Mental Illness," *Journal of the American Veterinary Association* 157 (1970): 1759–1766.

Melson, G. F., "Child Development and the Human-Companion Animal Bond," *American Behavioral Scientist* 47 (2003): 31–39.

Robin, M., and ten Bensel, R., "Pets and the Socialization of Children," *Marriage and Family Review* 8.3–4 (1985): 63–78.

ELEONORA GULLONE

THE CONCEPT OF GUARDIANSHIP

One of the most exciting recent developments in the animal protection movement is the campaign to elevate the status of animals beyond that of property, commodities, and things. Historically, humanity has regarded our relationship with other animals in terms of ownership. This conception of animals as property is the basis of both our legal relationship with animals and our everyday thinking about their place in our lives. Because almost all animal abuse and exploitation stems from viewing animals as property, the animal protection movement is becoming unified in challenging this demeaning, cruel, and unjust perspective.

The language of ownership has long played a vital role in movements seeking social change. Abolitionists, suffragists, and child advocates have challenged language to end the oppression of people as property. Now animal advocates are addressing the same concern, challenging the belief that it is appropriate for people to "own" animals. Viewing another being, human or animal, as property allows us to discount that individual's interests and disregard his or her desires. It allows us to act toward other beings in the same manner we would act toward property—we can neglect, mistreat, abandon, exploit, and destroy them because it is our right to do so as owners of the "property."

There are two major contexts in which animal protectionists are currently pursuing the campaign to elevate animals from the status of property—in codified and everyday language and in the courts. First, the campaign challenges the use of terms such as "owner," which subtly but consistently reinforce perceptions of animals as property. Not only have hundreds of animal organizations and shelters replaced the term "owner" with the more equitable and responsible term "guardian," but local and state governments are also making the change. By 2002, Boulder in Colorado, West Hollywood and Berkeley in California, Sherwood in Arizona, and the state of Rhode Island had passed ordinances and legislation recognizing the concept of guardianship.

At the same time these important changes in language are occurring, the U.S. court system is addressing a number of groundbreaking cases concerning the concept of animals as property. Time after time, the courts have given animals back to "owners" even after those same people severely abused them, because of the strength of property rights and at the expense of the needs of individual animals. However, these events are becoming less commonplace as courts recognize the interests and rights of animals. For example, in the late 1990s, a Vermont court disregarded a man's will directing that his horses be killed after his death. According to the court, the horses should be treated not as mere property to be killed as the "owner" had wished, but rather as individuals with needs and interests of their own.

One of the most promising signs for the future of this work is how greatly it has resonated within the movement, gaining support from a diverse set of organizations and individuals. Authors and advocates, as well as city shelters and national animal advocacy organizations, now recognize the concept of animal ownership as the root of the injustice they are collectively fighting against. By 2002, nearly two hundred organizations had endorsed the campaign. As a result, the campaign is acting as an organizing principle that promises to foster greater cooperation within the movement, as more and more cities and states codify the guardianship concept.

As a veterinarian, I have witnessed firsthand the effects of the property status of animals, including the insensitivity of people who have euthanized their companion animals for blatantly frivolous reasons, such as scratching, shedding, or barking too much. It is this insensitivity that is responsible for the millions upon millions of animals who are abandoned, mistreated, neglected, abused, and exploited, every year the world over. With regard to companion animals alone, the benefits of choosing guardianship over "ownership"—of always adopting and rescuing animals rather than buying or selling them—are far-reaching. From helping end the deaths of millions of animals in our nation's shelters to curtailing the horrors of the puppy mill trade, to strengthening laws that would truly punish and deter animal abusers, to raising children to respect all animals and treat them with dignity—these are but a few of the benefits that will accrue to millions of animals around the world.

As our language and laws begin to support this new relationship, people will take more responsibility in their actions toward animals and grant them greater protection and respect. By working at the roots of injustice, instead of the symptoms, we hasten the day when a new ethic is achieved for all beings—human and nonhuman alike.

Related articles: Animal advocacy; Animal and human violence; Caring for animals and humans; Developments in animal law; Euthanasia; Humane education; Moral anthropocentrism; The moral claims of animals; Puppy mills; Shelters and sanctuaries; The universal charter of the rights of other species

In Defense of Animals, "The Guardian Campaign," available at http://ida.convio.net/site/PageNavigator/Guardian_Survey.
Institute for Humane Education, 2007, "What Is Humane Education?," available at http://www.humaneeducation.org/.
Kind Planet, "Guardianship: Changing Consciousness," available at http://www.kindplanet.org/guardian.html.
Linzey, Andrew, and Cohn, Priscilla N., "Terms of Discourse," *Journal of Animal Ethics* 1.1 (2011): vii–ix.

ELLIOT M. KATZ

DISASTER PLANNING

Natural disasters, such as tornadoes, hurricanes, and floods, displace thousands of families from their homes every year. On a smaller but no less serious scale, fires, illnesses, accidents, and sudden death can have terrible consequences for companion animals who depend on their human families to protect them and provide for their daily needs. Historically, companion animals have not been included in traditional disaster planning or relief services. But the tragic events in New York City and Washington, DC, on September 11, 2001, demonstrated to the whole world the important role animals play in rescue efforts and in the comforting of survivors and the families of victims. Among the media and the general public, awareness increased of the importance of rescuing animals who were caught as innocent victims, trapped, injured, or displaced by the events of that terrible day.

Local, national, and international humane societies have traditionally assisted in animal rescue in response to disasters. In 1992, when Hurricane Andrew devastated a large section of Miami, Florida, it was discovered that disaster planning for companion animals required a sophisticated and professional response. In 2005, when Hurricane Katrina decimated Louisiana and the Gulf Coast, more than 1.5 million people were evacuated from just the state of Louisiana. However, many people using emergency evacuation services—or arriving at shelters—were told that they had to leave their companion animals behind. Tens of thousands of companion animals were separated from their caretakers; many died before they could be rescued or were rescued by local and national animal welfare groups but never reunited with their families because of lack of identification. Thousands of volunteers came to help with the rescue and care of animals after Katrina, but some were turned away, and others were hindered in their efforts by the scope of the disaster on the ground. As a result of Hurricane Katrina, the U.S. Congress passed the Pets Evacuation and Transportation Standards Act of 2006, requiring states to include disaster planning for animals in their emergency evacuation plans. It has made a substantial difference in how animals are treated during an emergency situation.

In October 2012, when Hurricane Sandy battered the East Coast, public officials and nonprofit animal organizations began spreading the word days in advance, asking residents to evacuate with their companion animals. Preparations were made to accommodate animals in many shelters, and arrangements were made for animal care at sites in Connecticut, Delaware, New York State, New Jersey, Pennsylvania, Virginia and Washington, DC. All of New York City's evacuation shelters accepted animals.

The Federal Emergency Management Agency provides specific information on evacuating with your companion animals (http://www.ready.gov/caring-animals), and newspapers, Web sites, and social media networks provide the locations of specific shelters that will accept both animals and people. Some national animal protection organizations have published special training materials and developed training programs for volunteers; among these are the American Humane Association, the Humane Society of the United States, Noah's Wish, United Animal Nations, and the Veterinary Medical Assistance Team. However, the most vital preparation and planning can be accomplished by animals' caretakers or guardians. In other words, a companion animal's best chance of survival in a disaster rests in the hands of those closest to the animal—his or her human family members.

Emergency personnel agree that nothing guarantees a successful evacuation more than planning and practice. Regular fire and evacuation drills are mandatory for many large buildings and for private residences. In the event of a disaster, when evacuating your home, always take your companion animals with you to ensure their safety. Even when people do not anticipate being away for more than a few hours, it is safest for the companion animals to be evacuated at the same time. Do not wait until the last minute to leave the premises. Evacuate as soon as possible. In the case of mandatory evacuation by emergency personnel, companion animals may not be permitted to leave with their human family. If they must be left behind, there may not be an opportunity for people to return to the area until a much later time. In such a case, leave a supply of water and dry food available.

Further safeguarding of companion animals includes providing them with some form of permanent identification, such as microchipping, in case of separation. Packing a small box of supplies (a waterproof container is ideal) in an easily accessible place is another important step in ensuring the animal's welfare and safety should disaster strike. Suggested items for the kit include the following:

- A sturdy carrier and/or collar and leash set up and ready for each of your animals in case of sudden evacuation. In an emergency, these items are essential to ensure a passage to safety. Each animal's name and your name, address, and telephone numbers should be safely secured to both the inside and the outside of the carrier.
- A copy of your companion animal's most recent veterinary records. The veterinarian's name, address, and telephone number should be included in this information.
- A recent photograph of your animals. It is also recommended that you keep photos of yourself posing with your animals in a safe place other than your own home. These can be invaluable in proving guardianship should your home and its contents be destroyed.
- Any medications that the animal requires.
- Leashes, collars, and harnesses, as needed.
- A week's supply of nonperishable food and bottled water.
- Towels, blankets, and other appropriate bedding and comfort items, such as toys.
- Litter trays, garbage bags, bleach, and paper towels. The bleach is used to decontaminate animal living areas (carriers, crates, and so on), which can be especially important in a flood situation where there has been contact with contaminated water.

Although policies may evolve, currently most emergency shelters for people do not allow companion animals. It is also unlikely that local humane societies or animal shelters will have sufficient resources to house those animals who have families to protect them. It is recommended, however, to contact these groups to ask whether they have special facilities or can recommend emergency resources. It is important to know in advance where a companion animal can be housed in case of an emergency.

It is recommended that families of companion animals make arrangements with family or friends who live outside their immediate area to serve as a safe place for their animals to stay in case of emergency evacuation. Veterinarians and local boarding facilities may also be contacted ahead of time for information on policies and costs. It should be noted, however, that in the case of widespread disaster, these facilities are often the first to become full. For families who do not wish to be separated from their companion animals, hotels that permit animals should be identified. After investigating these options in advance, animal guardians should create and keep accessible a list of names, addresses, and telephone numbers of temporary housing resources for companion animals.

Even the best-laid plans do not always go as anticipated. Sometimes evacuation orders are carried out while many people are not at their homes. In case of such circumstances, it is recommended that caregivers arrange contingency plans in advance with friends or neighbors who can evacuate companion animals in the caregivers' absence. The designated friends and neighbors should have access to keys and be familiar and comfortable with all the companion animals.

Disaster preparedness checklists are available free of charge from a number of animal protection and veterinary medical organizations. Although not all disasters can be prevented, advance planning and preparation increases the odds that our best friends will remain safe and by our sides.

Related articles: Animals and the major media; Caring for animals and humans; The concept of guardianship; Humane education; A lifelong responsibility; Microchipping; Shelters and sanctuaries

American Red Cross, "Pet and Disaster Safety," 2009, available at http://www.redcross.org.
American Veterinary Medical Association, "Disaster Preparedness and Response," 2008, available at http://www.avma.org.
Federal Emergency Management Agency, "Information for Pet Owners," 2010, available at http://www.fema.gov.
Humane Society of the United States, "Disaster Preparedness for Pets," 2010, available at http://www.hsus.org.
National Anti-Vivisection Society, *Companion Animals and the Law: A New Perspective*, 2008.
Pets Evacuation and Transportation Standards Act of 2006, Public Law 109-308 (2006).

PEGGY CUNNIFF
AND THE STAFF OF NAVS

ENHANCING A DOG'S ENVIRONMENT

Environmental enrichment is concerned with improving the environmental welfare of animals. Providing a positive, rewarding, and stimulating environment based on trust and affection, rather than force and compulsion, helps our companions to be both healthy and happy.

Dogs are a classic example of a species whose welfare can be dramatically improved by environmental enrichment. When we allow dogs to burn off calories in a safe and natural way, they are likely to behave more naturally in a restricted environment and are less likely to be stressed by handling and restraint. Breed differences and husbandry requirements should obviously be borne in mind when considering enrichment options.

Most dogs, kept as companions, spend a considerable portion of their time in enforced idleness, whereas, as opportunists, they are adapted to seeking a wide variety of rewarding situations in unpredictable locations. A predictable and limiting environment makes these inactive periods boring and is often a cause of stress. The average dog is a very adaptable animal, and a healthy adult can cope with a range of conditions, particularly if he or she has access to areas with different microclimates.

Animals have emotionally complex lives and need appropriate environments and stimulation. Good housing should allow the dog to exercise an element of choice, allow him or her to manipulate or chew safe objects, and provide opportunities for human and canine socialization, which satisfies their behavioral needs.

It is important to provide stimulation through a system of rewards. Rewards include food, water, foraging, sniffing/scenting, attention, grooming, coolness (when body temperature is high), and warmth (when the body temperature is low). Knowing what a dog likes—and will work for—is essential in creating a stimulating environment, especially if the animal spends most of the time looking at four walls, and food is provided independent of his or her behavior. In their natural state, dogs are hunter-scavengers; it is natural for them to spend a large amount of their daily energy looking for food. Companion dogs' needs are similar, so one of the worst things we can do is feed a dog once a day. When the food is gone in seconds, we wonder why the dog is bored or understimulated and now has extra time and energy to devote to those misbehaviors!

Companion dogs' problematic behaviors may include chewing or other destructive actions, barking or howling, pacing or behaving hyperactively, and introverted behaviors, such as sucking, licking, biting, and even self-mutilating. Paws, wrists, and flank areas seem to be favorite spots to work on, although sometimes the root of the tail seems to be a target. Whether the dog is bored or anxious, behavioral enrichment is required to keep the dog happy and healthy.

Food dispensers (and there are quite a few on the market) offer several advantages over conventional feeding methods. For example, food is distributed over a longer period of time. For example, a food dispenser filled with thirty pieces of kibble lasts about half an hour, whereas the same amount of food is normally consumed within thirty seconds to three minutes when given all at once. That means that with a dispenser, the dog's time spent foraging (looking for food) increases. The food is available only randomly, and this very unpredictability increases the dog's vigilance. Maintenance is also easy and does not require any additional time. The food dispenser can be given to the dog to play with and can be refilled at any time. Even small amounts of food delivered by the dispenser have a strong effect on the behavior of the animals. This is important because all enrichment activities related to food have to be incorporated into the feeding schedule; this is much easier when the amount of food needed for enrichment is low. And finally, such dispensers are inexpensive.

These rather simple interactive toys can help enrich the dog's foraging experience and thus reduce boredom and monotony. Any food or drink enrichment that requires extra manipulation and prolongs consumption time is a good thing because it provides mental stimulation.

As part of the dog's behavioral enrichment program, scenting and tracking should be encouraged. Many homes have a grassy enclosed exercise area where a dog can be let off the lead for a free run. Caregivers should give their dog every opportunity to search using their nose. Searching and tracking exercises have proved an excellent remedy for both understimulated and overactive dogs. If dogs could not hunt, track, and catch their quarry, for most of history, they would not have survived. Dogs use their nose to pick up scent particles in the air, on the ground, or both, depending on the overall environmental factors.

Caregivers can provide much needed stimulation for their dogs by providing simple scenting and tracking "games." For example, caregivers can lay a scent (by mak-ing foot markings or dropping small amounts of food) leading to hidden treats or toys in the garden. Scattering food around the exercise area and letting the dog go find it is another great way to allow the dog to use his or her nose. The garden (or yard) area should include a digging area, approximately three feet square, with sand added to the soil to make digging easier. Bury tidbits, toys, bones, and chews in the permitted digging area and let the dog find them.

All these programs should, of course, be in addition to regular exercise. All adult dogs require at least one hour of freedom off the lead every day. A day without a walk can be a very boring day indeed. In addition, grooming each day promotes mutual trust and affection and also allows caregivers to check for early signs of ill health.

_____

Related articles: Caring for animals and humans; The complexity of animal awareness; Dogs; Humane education; A lifelong responsibility; Teaching animals humanely; Understanding companion animals

Burch, M. A., and Bailey, J. S., *How Dogs Learn*, Wiley, 1999.

Coppinger, Raymond, and Coppinger, Lorna, *Dogs: A New Understanding of Canine Origin, Behaviour and Evolution*, Crosskeys Select Books, 2004.

King, Stephen G., *Ready Steady Click!*, Crosskeys Select Books, 2000.

King, Stephen G., and Davies, Claire L., *Ready Steady Click! Workbook*, Crosskeys Select Books, 2002.

Pryor, Karen, *Don't Shoot the Dog! The New Art of Teaching and Training*, 3rd ed., Ringpress Books, 2002.

Serpel, James, *The Domestic Dog: Its Evolution, Behaviour and Interactions with People*, Cambridge University Press, 1995.

STEPHEN G. KING

KENNELS AND CATTERIES

Many people who have companion animals are understandably anxious about leaving their animals when going away on holiday or vacation. Sometimes the problem can be resolved by finding a neighbor or relative to "pet sit," or live in the house. There are also professional agencies that offer pet-sitting arrangements. Sometimes, however, boarding a companion animal at a kennel or cattery is the only solution. Once this decision has been made, it is important to select the best cattery or kennel, so that you can go away on holiday without worrying about the safety or welfare of your animals.

The first thing is to find your local licensed premises. You can ask your veterinarian, look in local directories, and ask people you know for recommendations. The best policy is to visit several and have a good look around the whole premises. If you are not allowed to do this, then it is probably best to choose somewhere else, since it is your right to know as much as possible about the place (including its facilities) that you are going to entrust with your companion animal.

When you are looking around, always check that the facility is clean and tidy everywhere. The materials used in the construction of floors, walls, and other surfaces should be easy to clean, and there should be no bad smells as you enter the building. Make sure there are at least two doors or gates between your animal and the outside; you do not want him or her to escape. All animals should have access to a clean, full water bowl. Check in the kitchen to see whether there is enough storage for food and whether each animal's dietary requirements are taken care of. There should also be plenty of clean, dry bedding and heating and cooling, as well as ample ventilation to prevent disease. Allow enough time to visit the premises and make sure you book your animal into the boarding home well in advance, just as you would with a good hotel. The better places are more likely to fill up quickly, particularly during holiday periods.

When you arrive, make sure to give the owner of the boarding home all your animal's details, including age, sex, habits, dietary requirements, likes and dislikes, and medical history, as well as the veterinarian's contact details. Always check that the details you are passing on are correct, and remember to leave a phone number where you can be reached while away or a number of a trusted friend.

Your cat must be vaccinated against feline upper respiratory disease (cat flu) and feline infectious enteritis. Annual boosters need to be given three weeks prior to boarding, and the cattery staff will need to see the vaccination certificate. Dogs must also be fully vaccinated against distemper, viral hepatitis, leptospirosis, and parvovirus and must have a valid vaccination certificate. For some kennels, especially during peak season, dogs will need to be vaccinated against kennel cough (Bordetella) as well because this illness can be highly contagious. You should be aware that staff members have the right to examine your animal, and if he or she is in poor health, boarding may be refused. It is always good policy to bring along your animal's favorite toy or bedding.

For cats, check that the building or cattery units are well maintained and that each cat has access to an exercise area with fresh air and daylight. Both indoor and outdoor catteries should have heating facilities, and the sleeping areas should be warm and dry with sufficient bedding. Check that there is mesh over any windows to prevent escape. Litter trays should be clean, with sufficient litter. Shelves, toys, scratching posts, and an interesting view to keep them amused are also desirable.

For an indoor dog kennel, there should be an exercise area where the dogs are let out regularly. A quick calculation of the number of dogs using that area will tell you how much time they are likely to spend there. Ask the kennel staff how much exercise the dogs actually get. If each kennel has a run attached, check that the exercise areas are clean and droppings are picked up immediately. There should be enough clean, dry bedding available, and the sleeping area should be warm with ample ventilation.

Kennel or cattery owners should hold a license issued by their local authority in the United Kingdom, which must be displayed on the premises. It is also important to check the premises' insurance coverage. You need to find out whether your animal will be covered if he or she falls ill, or whether you will have to pay when you return. It is also advisable to check with the veterinary practice they will use should your animal become ill, or find out whether they will call your own veterinarian. It is a good idea to put your animal in for boarding a few days before you go away just in case there are any problems. You will feel much better when you go on holiday if you know your companion animal has already settled in quickly and easily.

Finally, you need to be entirely satisfied that you have left your companion animal in the best place that will care for his or her safety and welfare. Companion animals are entirely dependent on us; they trust us and love us unconditionally. It is important that their trust not be abused by sheer thoughtlessness. By your conscientious example, you can ensure that only the very best kennels and catteries are promoted and supported.

Related articles: Cats; The concept of guardianship; Dogs; Enhancing a dog's environment; A lifelong responsibility; Shelters and sanctuaries

Bailey, Gwen, *Clever Dog*, Collins, 2009.
——, *How to Train a Superdog*, Dorling Kindersley, 2009.
——, *What Is My Cat Thinking? The Essential Guide to Understanding Your Pet*, Hamlyn, 2010.
——, *What Is My Dog Thinking? The Essential Guide to Understanding Your Pet*, Hamlyn, 2010.
Key, David, and Key, Kay, *Cattery Design: The Essential Guide to Creating Your Perfect Cattery*, David Key Kennel and Cattery Design, 2006.
——, *Kennel Design: The Essential Guide to Creating Your Perfect Kennels*, David Key Kennel and Cattery Design, 2008.

GWEN BAILEY

A LIFELONG RESPONSIBILITY

In Australia, 85 percent of people live with a companion animal at some point in their lives, providing a unique opportunity to nurture, to learn from, and to interact with another living creature. We Aussies often talk of our affection for animals, both our native free-living "wild-life" and our domesticated companions. With one look at our numerous shelters caring for thousands of surrendered dogs and cats, however, we may begin to question our nation's supposed devotion. Similar situations exist all over the world. Cute puppies and kittens readily find homes, only to end up unwanted and homeless when the going gets tough. We really ought to regard the human-animal relationship as a privilege—one that comes with many responsibilities.

Selecting an appropriate companion to fit our lifestyle is the beginning of the human–companion animal partnership. Cat, dog, rabbit, or goldfish: the choice depends on personal preference, but our decision should also take into account our experience, our available time and space, and not least of all, the financial cost. The animal's breed, age, sex, and temperament also determine the extent to which we may bond with that individual.

In choosing to live with a companion animal, we have a duty to fulfill his or her needs. In Australia, the Prevention of Cruelty to Animals Act requires that the person in charge of an animal exercise reasonable care, control, and supervision of the animal, prevent any acts of cruelty, and alleviate any pain and suffering. Desexing of companion animals (also known as neutering or spaying) is strongly recommended by authorities, and registration and microchipping of dogs and cats is required in some states. Our commitment to our companions must extend beyond these fundamental requirements, however, if we are to truly meet the needs of our animal companions.

Companion animals, as this term suggests, need companionship. When given the opportunity to interact, many companion animals form close emotional attachments to their human companions. Young animals, in particular, need many positive socialization experiences to prevent future behavioral problems from developing. Sadly, many of our canine companions find themselves alone for a great part of each day, an unnatural situation for a pack animal. The Australian belief that a big backyard is enough to satisfy a dog or cat is an outdated one, especially if that backyard offers no opportunity for socialization.

Responsibility for a companion's needs continues throughout the animal's life, and this requires some understanding of his or her behavior, both the animal's instinctive drives and the behavior that he or she learns while living with us. Unfortunately, many animals are denied the opportunity to behave in a natural manner, resulting in problems for their caregivers. Australian working dog breeds, such as cattle dogs, are regularly surrendered to urban pounds and shelters as a result of chasing children or cyclists or simply being too difficult to handle. Cats instinctively hunt, but in Australia we frown on felines who are allowed to roam freely overnight because of the dangers they pose to the native Australian fauna; many councils now impose a dusk-to-dawn curfew. Terriers who dig too enthusiastically, toy dogs who become overly dependent, Persian cats whose long hair becomes matted—these are all common problems for many human companions.

Lack of stimulation, insufficient exercise, and failure of people to provide positive forms of training may also result in animals displaying antisocial activities. Our companions want to please us. They are not deliberately seeking ways to annoy us. Behavior problems can be cured, or at least managed, but prevention is a far better option. Many pounds and shelters are dealing daily with the failure of human–companion animal relationships. Many of these sad situations could have been avoided had the caregiver gained a little more knowledge and accepted a lot more commitment.

Responsible practice does not begin and end with individual caregivers. Commercial businesses and nonprofit organizations all have a duty to aid responsible, caring behavior toward companion animals. Breeders, shops that sell animals, companion animal food companies, kennels, dog walkers, groomers, animal shelters, and all other companion animal–oriented enterprises have a responsibility to educate themselves, their clients, and their customers about companion animal needs. Without this commitment we may simply perpetuate a cycle of ignorance, which inevitably results in problems, adoptions, surrenders, and ultimately euthanasia.

When we choose to share our life with a companion animal, we have a responsibility to care for that individual throughout his or her entire life. Wherever possible, we should strive to give that animal a full and rewarding existence. If we fulfill our responsibilities, then we not only will enhance an individual animal's life, but also will be promoting the true value of animals in society as well as helping others to reap the rewards of the human-animal relationship.

Related articles: Animal issues in Australia; Animal pain; Cats; Children's relations with animals; The concept of guardianship; Developments in animal law; Dogs; Enhancing a dog's environment; The ethics of commercialization; Euthanasia; Humane education; Kennels and catteries; Microchipping; Neutering and spaying; Rabbits; Shelters and sanctuaries; Teaching animals humanely; Understanding companion animals

Australian Companion Animal Council, *Contribution of the Pet Care Industry to the Australian Economy*, 2010, available at http://www.acac.org.au/ACAC_Report_2010.html.

———, *The Power of Pets*, 2009, available at http://www.acac.org.au/pdf/PowerOfPets_2009_19.pdf.

New South Wales Government, Prevention of Cruelty to Animals Act, 1979, available at http://www.legislation.nsw.gov.au/maintop/view/inforce/act+200+1979+cd+0+N.

Righetti, Joanne, "Responsible Pet Ownership," 2010, available at http://petproblemsolved.com.au/blog/2009/05/responsible-pet-ownership-tired-old-phrase-or-is-it-alive-surviving-thriving/.

JOANNE RIGHETTI

MICROCHIPPING

Thousands of companion animals are lost every year, even to the most careful and loving caregivers. Sadly, many of these animals and caregivers are never reunited. The best way to ensure that an animal will be found if he or she goes missing is to have the animal microchipped—implanted with a special microchip "tag." The Royal Society for the Prevention of Cruelty to Animals (RSPCA) supports the national microchip identification databases for animals. It is the quickest, surest way of getting any lost animal back to his or her caregiver, safe and sound.

Once an animal has been microchipped, the animal has his or her own unique code number. The caregiver's name and address are entered next to this number on the national computer database. If a lost or stolen animal is found, a scanner passed over the implanted microchip immediately reveals the number. It then takes just a short while to check the number with the database to find details of the caregiver, who can then be contacted.

The microchipping scheme provides a fast, foolproof means of identifying an animal wherever he or she is found nationwide. The RSPCA and many other animal welfare organizations, veterinarians, and local authority dog wardens have scanners that can read the microchip's details and access the databases.

Microchipping is no more complicated than a normal injection. A tiny microchip—the size of a grain of rice—is inserted under the animal's skin, usually at the base of the neck, between the shoulder blades. Once inserted, it does not move about and cannot be seen, but it can be read by the scanner through the skin. Most animals can be microchipped, but microchips are mainly used for dogs and cats. More and more horses are now being microchipped too.

The system is also comparatively cheap. A one-off payment of less than thirty pounds in the United Kingdom (prices vary in different areas) or ten to seventy-five dollars in the United States will enable an animal to be microchipped and remain in the database for life. The caregiver's details can be quickly amended if an address changes. Simply contact your local RSPCA branch or veterinarian, who will be able to advise.

Some people say that because their animal already has a collar tag, microchipping is unnecessary. By law all dogs in the United Kingdom have to wear a collar with a tag showing the name and address of the caregiver, but accidents do happen. Collars sometimes break, and identification tags fall off and get lost. There is always a chance that even the most reliable and well-cared-for animal will go missing or be stolen. Home-loving companion animals are often the most vulnerable because they do not know their way around the local area. Microchips identify an animal permanently and harmlessly.

More than 4.2 million animals have already been microchipped in the United Kingdom, where the government has recently announced plans to legally require the microchipping of dogs. It is the policy of the RSPCA, as well as many other animal welfare organizations, to microchip all dogs and cats they rehome.

Related articles: Cats; The concept of guardianship; Dogs; Horses; Humane education; A lifelong responsibility; Shelters and sanctuaries

Avid Microchips, available at http://www.avidplc.com.

British Small Animal Veterinary Association, 2011, "Microchip Advisory Group Code of Practice," available at http://www.bsava.com/Advice/MicrochipAdvice/tabid/154/Default.aspx.

idENTICHIP, 2011, available at http://www.identichip.co.uk.

Petlog, available at http://www.petlog.org.uk.

RSPCA, "Microchipping Your Pet," 2010, available at http://www.rspca.org.uk/allaboutanimals/pets/general/microchipping.

ALASTAIR MacMILLAN

SHELTERS AND SANCTUARIES

Shelters and sanctuaries, as defined in the English language, are places of safety, offering protection from danger (or the elements) and freedom from disturbance. Throughout the world, hundreds of sanctuaries have been developed to deal specifically with domesticated animals. Animals are placed into these centers for a variety of reasons, and the way in which they are looked after, as well as the eventual fate of the animals concerned, often varies greatly.

Most sanctuaries have to cope with homeless or unwanted animals, including, for example, stray animals living on the streets of towns and cities—dogs and cats who have been abandoned by previous caregivers, who have escaped or become lost, or who are the result of uncontrolled breeding within stray or feral populations. Companion animals may also be victim to natural disasters, separated from their homes and caregivers by the effects of flooding, tornadoes, hurricanes, and earthquakes.

Some of the common reasons dogs and cats are relinquished to shelters include the financial burden associated with keeping them, whether through relatively expensive dog licensing schemes (the cost of obtaining a dog license in Beijing, China, is currently approximately five hundred dollars), expensive veterinary fees, or costs incurred by meeting sometimes-ravenous appetites. Behavioral reasons are also frequently cited; aggression, destructive tendencies, or house soiling often push caregivers into either giving their animals to sanctuaries or abandoning them.

Although dogs in some communities are adequately cared for, forming an integral part of the local society, these so-called community dogs are in the minority. Unfortunately, most cats and dogs living on the street have to cope with inadequate supplies of food and are under immense pressure to survive. Some simply cannot stand the competition. With the risk of disease, road traffic accidents, fights with other animals, and general mistreatment at the hands of human beings exacerbating their plight, weaker individuals finish their days in solitude and suffering. Uncontrolled reproduction within stray populations only worsens this situation.

In some countries, it is government policy to catch these animals and "cull" them by lethal injection or electrocution. Such draconian measures do not provide a lasting solution to the problem. Although the number of animals may be reduced temporarily, nature has provided dogs and cats with a prolific ability to reproduce, and the situation will soon recur. Education is the foremost tool to address the problem. Only fundamental changes in attitude and behavior will effect a long-term solution. In the immediate term, however, the most humane and effective solution is to prevent excessive reproduction through surgical sterilization. Merely providing housing, care, and adoptions for needy animals through shelters will not address the root of the problem. Shelter programs should include education and sterilization programs in order to assist the battle against overpopulation.

The majority of shelters in the Western world aim toward relocating the animals in their care, to suitably appropriate homes, through adoption. In other countries where attitudes toward companion animals vary, shelters are often looked upon to provide permanent sanctuary care for homeless animals. For example, in Thailand unwanted dogs are frequently abandoned at Buddhist temples, where the monks are expected to care for them. Meanwhile, the excessively high demand on some shelters to continually accept new arrivals has forced euthanasia policies to be adopted.

Caring is an essential ingredient in an animal shelter, and although many shelters are started by people who care deeply, their facilities are not always managed appropriately. All too often, shelters have a difficult time refusing an animal. But when too many animals are accepted, or animals of a species for which the shelter does not have appropriate facilities are accepted, the end result is poor animal care, poor quality of life for the animals sheltered, overstretched staff, and a poor image within the local community. Efficiently managed shelters should have fully developed policies on the type and number of species that can be accommodated, veterinary treatment, euthanasia, and adoption requirements.

Most shelters provide basic veterinary care services, including deworming medication and vaccinations, and may perform, stipulate, or recommend surgical sterilization. An increasing number of shelters offer animal training classes for community caregivers and will conduct behavioral assessments and training of animals under their care. Addressing behavioral issues increases the chances of a successful adoption; if existing behavioral problems are resolved and the acquisition of new problems is prevented, the animal is less likely to be returned to the shelter. Other education programs often run by shelters concern issues of animal care, welfare, cruelty, and overpopulation.

Efficient and caring sanctuaries are playing a vital role in the global advancement of animal welfare. However, the term "sanctuary" should not command instant respect; any center worthy of this name must be capable of offering the highest standards of care and should, with equal vigor, be seeking long-term solutions to the problems faced by cats and dogs, especially overpopulation.

Related articles: Buddhist attitudes; Cats; The concept of guardianship; Disaster planning; Dogs; Feral cats; Humane education; A lifelong responsibility; Neutering and spaying; Pound seizure; Stray animals

American Sanctuaries Association, "Sanctuary Criteria," available at http://www.asaanimalsanctuaries.org/sanctuary_criteria.htm.
The Dogs Trust, "How Rehoming Works," available at http://www.dogstrust.org.uk/rehoming/howrehomingworks/default.aspx.

Royal Society for the Prevention of Cruelty to Animals, "Education and Animals: Guidance for Educational Establishments in England and Wales," available at http://www.rspca.org.uk.

———, "Guidelines for the Design and Management of Animal Shelters," available at http://www.rspca.org.uk.

JOANNE FIELDER

TEACHING ANIMALS HUMANELY

We have all seen it. A caregiver gets angry or frustrated and lashes out at his or her dog. Perhaps such actions, when they happen in rage or anger, are at least understandable. But there are many people who keep companion animals and regard themselves as good caregivers who still use force or violence to teach their animals. Among some "trainers" or "behaviorists," such violence is still accepted as commonplace, even moral.

An example of how far this tendency has gone can be found in the phenomenon of electric collars. These are devices strapped to a dog's neck that are capable of giving a severe electric shock. These collars are legal in the United Kingdom, the rest of Europe, the United States, and elsewhere and are frequently used by caregivers and trainers—and even advocated by behaviorists. Shock collars are an illustration of how aggressive and violent "training" of animals is accepted, even by some animal welfare organizations.

Our humane instincts should recoil from the use of such devices and indeed from all attempts to subdue animals by force or violence. There are good moral and philosophical reasons for thinking that such actions are unacceptable. Consider that all companion animals are absolutely, or nearly absolutely, dependent on us; they look to us for sustenance, companionship, comfort, and kindness. For the most part, they would not exist if it were not for our deliberate intervention through breeding or buying. They are almost entirely within our control and completely vulnerable to our actions. These circumstances mean that we should exercise special care and attention in relation to them. Their very vulnerability places on us a very special obligation of trying to understand the world through their eyes.

Second, although people who keep companion animals often speak of the need for "punishment," the reality is that if the idea of punishment is appropriate at all, it can be logically applied only to those who are moral agents—that is, beings who have free will and are morally responsible for their actions. Although caregivers sometimes speak as though their dog or cat were morally responsible ("he did a bad thing today"), a moment's reflection will make us appreciate that animals are not morally responsible agents (cats cannot choose not to hunt birds, since hunting instincts lie deep within their nature), and therefore, the whole notion of punishment is inappropriate. In the words of C. S. Lewis, "animals are incapable of sin or virtue; they can therefore neither deserve pain nor be improved by it."

It is also important to remember what companion animals give us: among other things, unconditional love, companionship, and emotional support. Yet the phenomenon of our relationship with companion animals is often a mixed blessing for the animals concerned. Some caregivers do indeed care for their animals and lavish attention on them (which can, in itself, be the cause of problems), but not all. Despite the fact that Britain is known as an animal-loving country, up to a thousand unwanted, neglected, or abandoned dogs are destroyed every week—at least some of whom may be killed for "behavioral problems" not of their own making. Indeed, figures from the Royal Society for the Prevention of Cruelty to Animals (RSPCA) show that reported cases of cruelty to animals are at a record high: complaints of cruelty investigated by the RSPCA have risen year by year, from 137,245 in 2007 to 159,686 in 2010. In the light of what companion animals give us, they deserve better.

We need another model of how we should behave toward companion animals. Instead of acquiescing to the use of violence toward them, we should rather extol—and educate keepers of animals in—the value of humane teaching. This does not mean simply allowing our companions to do as they like or failing to act in the case of an animal who is aggressive. On the contrary, what is needed is a new attitude in which we try to understand the sometimes confusing (to us) behavior of companion animals and especially the ways in which their human companions often induce fear, trauma, anxiety, stress, and aggression through unsuitable handling and rearing and, most centrally, through a failure to understand their basic behavioral needs.

Developing a positive, reward-based environment for our companion animals is not difficult. It takes a little imagination and preparedness to look at our own actions and ask whether we are being really fair to them. For example, there is a clear behavioral need for all animals to associate with their own kind and to enjoy freedom. Yet so often, even in safe, open spaces, dogs are constrained on leads, which produces high levels of anxiety, stress, and even aggression. The very act of confining animals is nearly always the direct cause of frustration and aggression between them.

In order to bring about a new attitude toward the teaching of animals, it is important to challenge the regular violence meted out to animal subjects. Specifically, people who have "problem" animals need to obtain advice from individuals who are really committed to animal welfare. Do not assume that all those who call themselves "trainers" or "behaviorists" are on the side of animals or care about their welfare. Ask about the methods used; be present when the teaching is carried out; and most importantly, object to coercive or violent "training." In many cases, it is only because the caregivers acquiesce to the supposed need for violent training that such training becomes the norm.

When caregivers are tempted to react out of frustration or anger to their companion animal, they should take a good step back and begin to contemplate the world through the eyes of the companion animal. The key question to ask is why the animal may be behaving in the way he or she is. There is a great deal of truth in the old adage that "what a dog most wants to do is to please you." Moments of conflict are invariably a sign that the companion animal has not understood or has simply suffered too much or that his or her basic needs are not being adequately met.

_____

Related articles: Animal and human violence; The concept of guardianship; Dogs; Enhancing a dog's environment; The ethics of commercialization; Humane education; A lifelong responsibility; Reporting cruelty in the United Kingdom; Understanding companion animals

Donaldson, Jean, *The Culture Clash*, 2nd ed., James and Kenneth, 1996.
Masson, Jeffrey, *When Elephants Weep: The Emotional Lives of Animals*, Vintage, 1996.
Swartz, Barry, and Robbins, Steven J., *Psychology of Learning and Behavior*, 2nd ed., Norton, 1984.
Whitehead, Sarah, *Hands Off: Simple, Gentle Ways to Teach Your Dog at Home*, Alpha, 1999.

ANDREW CONSTANT

UNDERSTANDING COMPANION ANIMALS

How many caregivers of domesticated cats and dogs have asked themselves how their companions view them? With a little knowledge and imagination, it is possible to glean insight into the way companion animals see their world and the role their human caregivers play therein.

In their natural state, kittens are social animals, happily sharing their territory with their littermates and mother. As they reach maturity, however, adolescent cats leave their family group to search for their own territory, where they will lead a solitary life. Unlike their undomesticated counterparts, domesticated cats often live happily with others for their whole lives. This is because although domesticated cats reach physical maturity at around eighteen months, psychologically, they remain kittens for their entire lives, viewing other companion animals as they would their littermates and viewing their human caregiver as parent. When a cat purrs and "pads" with his or her front paws, the cat is mimicking the behavior of suckling from his or her mother. Similarly, a cat may also purr when frightened or in pain. Purring in times of stress does not indicate contentment though. Rather, this purring is a cat's appeal to be "protected" by his or her mother or, in the human family, his or her caregiver. In these instances, stroking a cat can often offer comfort and reassurance, which is an important element in emulating the parental role.

In order to provide a feline companion with all he or she needs for a happy and healthy life, a caregiver needs to embrace the role of "mother cat." Grooming a cat is an important element in strengthening the bond between companion and caregiver and simulates a mother washing her young in order to keep them clean and free from parasites. For the caregiver, grooming also provides the opportunity to check a cat for lumps and bruises that cannot otherwise be seen through the animal's fur.

Play is also an important element in the role of the caregiver. Mother cats teach their kittens to hunt. Caregivers can simulate this activity by encouraging their feline companion to chase small soft toys or a small ball. A favorite hunting game of many domesticated cats can be simulated by tying a soft toy to the end of a bamboo cane and allowing the companion cat to chase after the toy, periodically letting the cat catch his or her prey.

Domesticated dogs do not view their human caregivers in the same way domesticated cats do. Dogs are naturally pack animals and so are at home living as part of a human family. Unlike cats, companion dogs do not remain in a psychological state of puppyhood throughout life and therefore do not see their human caregivers as parents, but see them rather as pack leaders (or heads of the family).

If a dog is unsettled or afraid—for instance, because of a thunderstorm or fireworks—and the caregiver wants to help the dog feel more secure, rather than acting as a "mother" and grooming him or her as with a cat, a caregiver can be much more reassuring by allowing the dog to see that his or her leader is absolutely calm and unconcerned by these external events. If the dog's leader is behaving in an abnormally physically affectionate way, then to the dog it seems his or her leader must also be afraid and in need of the *dog's* reassurance. The dog will deduce from this scenario that the thunderstorm or firework noises that frighten him or her must be even more dangerous than the dog first thought. Although loving caregivers may instinctively wish to hug and reassure their companion when he or she is stressed, it can be counterproductive. In times of stress or fear, the role of the "leader" is to lead by example. By remaining calm, caregivers can communicate to their companions that they have nothing to fear.

As animals naturally adapted to living in a family group, dogs often become stressed when left on their own. From a historical canine perspective, a dog abandoned by his or her pack would have little chance of survival because dogs in natural packs rely on their pack for the majority of their hunting as well as for their protection. When a canine's viewpoint is considered, it is easy to understand why many companion dogs suffer a degree of separation anxiety when left alone.

Although it is not ideal for dogs to be left alone, it is often impossible for caregivers to be with their companions twenty-four hours a day. The caregiver as "leader" can, however, take steps to reduce any anxiety experienced by the companion dog when the dog is left on his or her own. It is important for caregivers to ensure their companions have had the opportunity to burn off some energy via a walk or active play prior to being left. The caregiver can mitigate any boredom the dog may experience once alone by providing "food toys" that allow the dog to exercise his or her scavenging skills. Also, because

dogs relieve stress by chewing, it is important to provide an appropriate "chew toy," which can allow a safe outlet for any nervous tension.

By reading and observing, caregivers can develop insights into the way companion animals view their world and specifically their human caregivers. These insights are invaluable in understanding our companion animals and our place in their lives.

Related articles: Animal pain; Cats; The concept of guardianship; Dogs; Enhancing a dog's environment; A lifelong responsibility; Teaching animals humanely

Abrantes, Roger, *The Evolution of Canine Social Behaviour*, Wakan Tanka, 2010.

Beaver, Bonnie B., *Feline Behaviour*, Saunders, 2003.

Hough, K. A., *Domestic Animal Behaviour for Veterinarians and Animal Scientists*, Iowa State University Press, 1991.

Serpell, J. A. (ed.), *The Domestic Dog: Its Evolution, Behaviour and Interaction with People*, Cambridge University Press, 1995.

Smith, Abbey A., "Utilitarianism for Animals, Kantianism for Humans? A Discussion of the Status of Animals," master's thesis, University of Exeter, 1998.

Tabor, Roger, *Understanding Cat Behaviour*, David and Charles, 2003.

ABBEY ANNE SMITH

HEALTH, LOSS, AND BEREAVEMENT

ANIMAL BURIALS

Human beings often form close emotional bonds with their companion animals; indeed, for some people—usually but not exclusively children and the elderly—companion animals are the "significant other" relationship in their lives. The death of a companion animal can occasion deep emotional trauma, shock, disorientation, and feelings of guilt—all the usual experiences associated with other kinds of bereavement. But such bereavement is accompanied by two practical issues—namely, how to properly mark closure and how to respectfully dispose of the body of a loved companion. It is those two issues I want to address.

It is psychologically important that there be a "closure" moment, an explicit recognition of the death of the loved companion accompanied by a formal farewell and

pause for thanksgiving. This can assist the bereavement process and help the individual to move on. For people who have built up a close bond over many years, even decades, it is inconceivable that the body of a companion should be disposed of like garbage. Sadly, however, religious traditions have been slow to recognize the spiritual significance of the animal-human bond; they provide little or nothing to help individuals move through the grieving process or say farewell. More directly, there are few religious rites for people to use for animal burials.

When our beloved dog Barney died, we decided to bury him in our garden but found that we had no form of words to use or to assist us at that poignant moment of closure. Christians inherit two thousand years of spirituality and scholarship, and yet the religion is silent—at least liturgically—about the deaths of millions of other species, even those who share and enrich our lives. A tradition that has even countenanced the blessing of cars and whaling ships has never, it seems, even registered a pastoral need in relation to the death of companion animals. Because of this lacuna, I subsequently wrote the book *Animal Rites: Liturgies of Animal Care* (1999), which comprised a range of animal-friendly and animal-inclusive rites, including a specific rite for animal burial.

Many people, when their companion animal has to be euthanized, leave their animal with the veterinarian, and it is usually the veterinarian who disposes of the body. But it is a far more wholesome way of saying goodbye to allocate a small area in the garden and say appropriate words of farewell. Some people, of course, do not have gardens or yards and use (especially in the case of large animals) a local animal cemetery, or an area usually set aside in a local animal sanctuary or shelter. But wherever possible, it makes sense to use the person's own garden or yard and to choose words that rightly and properly reflect a sense of loss and mark the life of the sentient creature who has died.

Skeptics sometimes ask, "Well, what are you doing in such a burial service for animals?" My answer is that, as a Christian priest, I am doing what I also do in the case of human burials—giving thanks for the life of the individual and committing his or her life into the hands of Almighty God.

But what words should we use precisely? Following are two sets of burial prayers in *Animal Rites* that people have found most helpful:

(i) Holy Father
your Son, Jesus Christ
taught us that not one sparrow
is forgotten in your sight;

we ask you now to remember
our friend and companion (*Name*)
whose life was blessed
by the gift of your Spirit
and whose life among us
on earth has ended.

Receive now we pray the
life of (*Name*)
which we commit into your hands.

Take pity, dear Lord, on this innocent creature
whose life, like ours, was burdened
with suffering and pain,
and grant us with *him/her*
a share in your eternal kingdom.

Eternal Father, we know that nothing
can finally separate us from those we love

and that in another place and another time
we shall be reunited with all those earthly faces
whom we have loved
and for whom we now mourn.

We ask these prayers
through Jesus Christ
your Son, Our Lord.
Amen.

———

(ii) Pilgrim God
who journeys with us
through the joys and shadows
of this world

be with us
in our sorrow
and feel our pain;

help us to accept
the mystery of death
without bitterness
but with hope.

Among the shadows
of this world,
amid the turmoil of life
and the fear of death

you stand alongside us,
always blessing, always giving,
arms always outstretched.

For this we know:
every living thing is yours
and returns to you.

As we ponder this mystery
we give you thanks
for the life of (*Name*)
and we now commit *him/her*
into your loving hands.

Gentle God:
fragile is your world,
delicate are your creatures,
and costly is your love
which bears and redeems us all.
Amen.

Some people may be surprised to find such confident statements of a future life for animals. The line that caused the most controversy in *Animal Rites* was its dedication: "To Barney, still wagging his tail in heaven" (in fact, following Martin Luther, who once spoke of his dog Fido still wagging his tail in heaven). In fact, the redemption of all things is wholly orthodox Christian belief. Christians have simply forgotten that the God who creates all things is also the same God who redeems all things, even and especially animals. That, for example, is the clear teaching of Saint Paul in Romans (8:18–24) where he likens suffering creation to a state of childbirth awaiting deliverance. He writes, "The creation itself will be set free from its bondage to decay and obtain the glorious liberty of the children of God" (Romans 8:2, RSV).

Such prayers obviously meet a deep psychological and pastoral need, especially if the companion animal concerned has had to be euthanized (as in our case with Barney). The taking of any life is a deeply serious matter and should never be undertaken thoughtlessly, but there are times when the suffering of animals is so great that no other alternative seems open to us. We have a duty to protect and honor life, but an even stronger one to prevent and alleviate suffering. No one in these circumstances can feel anything other than a sense of guilt and sorrow, even if the decision was properly made in the best interests of the animal concerned. Burial services help us to celebrate a life once lived, to express gratitude, and to share our sorrow.

They also serve another important function, and that is to remind others and us that there is a strong Christian duty to care for animals. Baptist preacher Charles Spurgeon once recounted the view of Rowland Hill that a person "was not a true Christian if his dog or cat were not the better off for it" and commented, "That witness is true" (Spurgeon 559). Christians have so often neglected animals that it is high time that they began to find appropriate ways of respecting and caring for them. Including animals in our prayers is not enough, but at least it is a beginning.

Related articles: Animal-friendly spirituality; Animals in the Bible; Catholic teaching; Children's relations with animals; Dogs; Euthanasia; The experience of loss; Shelters and sanctuaries

Ironside, Virginia, *Goodbye Dear Friend: Coming to Terms with the Death of a Pet*, Robson Books, 1994.
Linzey, Andrew, *Animal Rites: Liturgies of Animal Care*, SCM Press/Pilgrim Press, 1999.
———, *Animal Theology*, SCM Press/University of Illinois Press, 1994.
———, *Creatures of the Same God: Explorations in Animal Theology*, Winchester University Press/Lantern Books, 2007 (see especially chapter 8, "On Being an Animal Liturgist," 135–151).
Spurgeon, Charles H., "First Things First," *The Metropolitan Tabernacle Pulpit*, vol. 31 (1885).
Webb, Stephen H., *On God and Dogs: A Christian Theology of Compassion for Animals*, Oxford University Press, 1998.

ANDREW LINZEY

EUTHANASIA

The literal meaning of "euthanasia" is a good death, or an easy death. It describes a planned death that is painless and relatively stress-free. Properly understood, the euthanasia of animals is a compassionate act that allows them to die peacefully, rather than in great pain or prolonged distress. It is indicated in cases of severe injury, untreatable conditions that impair the quality of life, and terminal illness.

Veterinarians have the responsibility of putting an end to the suffering of animals in their care. There are ethical dilemmas, however, when caregivers are unwilling to let their companion animals go and persist in trying to keep them alive in circumstances when death would be the kindest option. In some countries where euthanasia is not commonly practiced, veterinarians may be obliged to give prolonged palliative care, even when there is little or no chance of recovery.

To be sure the death is easy, the method must be appropriate and carried out with competence and compassion. The person doing the killing need not always be a veterinarian, but he or she must be completely focused on inducing a peaceful and humane death. The handling must always be done in a way that reassures the animal and avoids stress.

For each species of animal there are appropriate recommended methods of euthanasia designed to minimize suffering. For cats and dogs and some other mammals, the most acceptable method is the intravenous injection of a concentrated barbiturate solution. Animals who are frightened (as some are when approached by strangers or veterinarians) may be sedated first. Large animals, such as horses and farmed animals, also may be injected or may be killed humanely with a gun, either free bullet or captive bolt, but the operator must be familiar with the proper use and positioning of the gun.

The word "euthanasia" is also commonly used to describe the humane destruction of healthy animals in situations where it is less than clear that death is in the best interests of the animal concerned, and this presents serious ethical dilemmas for those involved in veterinary or shelter work. There are various reasons that healthy companion animals are presented for euthanasia—for example, homeless animals competing for limited resources. Where conditions are grossly inadequate, a quick, painless death may be preferable to a slow death from starvation and disease. Changes in a caregiver's circumstances, such as illness or a move between homes, or death of a caregiver may mean that the animal can no longer stay with his or her family. There are also many unwanted animals as a result of uncontrolled breeding, and animals may be abandoned or rejected because of unfulfilled, unrealistic expectations or unforeseen problems with keeping companion animals. Animals may have persistent behavioral problems with which caregivers cannot cope.

Veterinarians are not usually obliged to kill healthy animals against their better judgment and may be able to suggest other options, such as referral to specialists in behavioral therapy or rescue and fostering organizations. However, if an animal is known to be dangerous, then he or she should be humanely destroyed. There are now neutering programs that limit the production of unwanted animals and education programs to promote responsible caring. Caregivers who have realistic expectations and understand their animals' needs are more likely to make an effort to help their animals rather than reject them. The guiding moral principle is that animals should be euthanized only when it is in their own individual interest.

Even though euthanasia can immediately end the suffering of a beloved animal, having to make that difficult decision puts caregivers in a great dilemma. How does a person come to terms with what amounts to imposing a death sentence on his or her best friend? In many cases, the animal concerned has been a devoted companion, and a bond of some moral or even spiritual significance has developed between them. It may be that they have been working partners, as with mountain rescue, sheepherding, and assistance dogs. These precious relationships do not end easily, and the emotional trauma accompanying the prospect of imminent death may be intense.

Complete confidence in the judgment of the veterinarian is necessary in order to avoid overpowering feelings of guilt and uncertainty about the decisions being made. The caregiver must be reassured that euthanasia is the only compassionate and realistic option and that the timing is right. Caregivers should fully understand the procedure, be permitted to remain with the animal, and be reassured by the peaceful death that they have made the right decision. Every detail of those few minutes will be permanently etched on the caregiver's memory, and whether the experience is devastating or acceptable will to a great extent depend on the compassion and skill of the veterinary team.

Even while accepting that they did the right thing and feeling grateful that the euthanasia went smoothly and the suffering has ended, people who have greatly loved a special animal may be overwhelmed by the loss, and deep grief may remain for a long time. Through the grief, however, it usually helps them to remember that they gave their animal an easy death.

Related articles: Animal burials; Animal pain; Animal-friendly spirituality; Animal welfare and farming; Cats; The concept of guardianship; Dogs; The ethics of killing free-living animals; The experience of loss; Horses; Neutering and spaying; Slaughter; Veterinary ethics

Adamec, Christine A., *When Your Pet Dies*, Time Warner International, 1996.
Kay, William J., Cophen, Susan P., Fudin, Carole E., Kutscher, Austin H., Nieburg, Herbert A., Grey, Ross E., and Osman, Mohammed M. (eds.), *Euthanasia of the Companion Animal*, Charles Press, 1988.
Nakaya, Fujimoto Shannon, *Kindred Spirit, Kindred Care: Making Health Decisions on Behalf of Our Animal Companions*, New World Library, 2005.
Stewart, Mary F., *Companion Animal Death: A Practical and Comprehensive Guide for Veterinary Practice*, Butterworth Heineman, 1996.
Walker, Kaetheryn, *The Heart That Is Loved Never Forgets: Recovering from Loss—When Humans and Animals Lose Their Companions*, Bear and Company, 1998.
Wolfelt, Alan, *When Your Pet Dies: A Guide to Mourning, Remembering and Healing*, Companion Press, 2004.

MARY F. STEWART

THE EXPERIENCE OF LOSS

The loss of a companion animal can be a traumatic experience. It marks the end of a partnership that may have lasted many years, sometimes more than a decade. Companion animals often provide significant benefits: friendship, unconditional love, physical activity, and social contact. In the case of animal-assisted partnerships, companion animals will have enabled everyday tasks and even freedom of movement. When an attachment is severed, either through death or through another form of enforced separation, the experience of loss can be profound.

The grieving process varies from individual to individual, even for the same individual, and may be different for different animals. Whatever the nature of the grieving process, it is a normal and appropriate response to the loss of a loved companion. For some people, the loss of an animal is marked by sadness and tears, which may be transient or last for several days. Other symptoms may include loss of appetite, fatigue, headaches, and inability to sleep. For some, it may feel as if they have lost a member of their family, and their grief may have a similar pattern to that following a human bereavement, which may include all or some of the following stages of grief.

The initial reaction may be one of shock and disbelief, where perception is altered, and it may be difficult for the person to comprehend what is happening, even if the death was expected. This may be followed by a period of sadness and grief, when events leading up to the loss are relived, and the full pain of the loss is experienced, sometimes resulting in physical pain. The need to apportion blame is also common, and anger may be directed at others for their part in the loss or for their reaction to it. This anger may be interspersed with a deep yearning and longing to see the loved one again and to feel his or her presence. Bereaved people may also experience depression, a sense of helplessness and hopelessness, or even a feeling that life is not worth living. There also may be an overwhelming sense of responsibility and guilt, particularly when an animal was involved in an accident or a decision was made to euthanize an animal.

A person grieving for a much-loved animal may experience some or all of these phases of grief. The feelings will normally pass over time, but the length of time may vary from a few days or weeks to several or many months. In some cases grieving may take many years. The intensity is also affected by several factors. These include the nature of the attachment, the length of the association, the circumstances surrounding the loss, and the emotional and practical support that is available to the grieving person. The loss of a long-standing partnership, or of an animal who was rescued or raised as an orphan, or who had some kind of link with a person who has died, may result in an intense grief lasting several months.

The important thing to remember is that grieving is a natural process. It is psychologically normal to experience pain and grief after bereavement—in the same way that it is normal to experience pain after an accident or injury. Grieving is the way in which the human psyche begins to heal itself after the shock of loss. Despite this, there is a general tendency on the part of the public and even well-meaning friends to minimize the extent of the pain and dismiss the grief with statements such as "it was only an animal." This, together with an expectation that mourners should quickly readjust, may result in feelings of isolation.

Our society still has a long way to go in recognizing companion animal loss as a legitimate form of grief. Yet several avenues of support have opened up over the past few years, including support services over the telephone and the internet, as well as face-to-face counseling. In addition, some veterinary practices send condolence cards and letters and sometimes make follow-up calls to owners who are adversely affected by their loss. There are also an increasing number of helpful books, offering insights into the grieving process as well as helpful hints on what to expect and how to cope. These forms of support can bring much comfort and reassurance to those who are living with bereavement.

Related articles: Animal burials; Animal-friendly spirituality; Euthanasia

Barton Ross, C., *Pet Loss and Children*, Routledge, 2005.

Grey, R., *Coping with Pet Loss*, Sheldon Press, 2006.

Ironside, V., *Goodbye, Dear Friend: Coming to Terms with the Death of a Pet*, JR Books, 2009.

Lambert. A., *Missing My Pet*, BGFT, 2006 (suitable for use with primary school–age children).

Lee, L., and Lee, M., *Absent Friend: Coping with the Loss of a Treasured Pet*, Ringpress Books, 1992.

Society for Companion Animal Studies, *Death of an Animal Friend*, 10th ed., 2006 (originally published 1990).

NIGEL K. WALTON
AND JO-ANN FOWLER

FIRST AID

"Not to hurt our humble brethren is our first duty to them, but to stop there is not enough. We have a higher mission—to be of service to them whenever they require it." These words of Saint Francis of Assisi should inspire all those who want to offer first aid to animals in distress.

It is important to appreciate that animals, like humans, suffer pain and stress and have their own complex emotional lives. They have similar systems for perceiving pain and reacting to stress. Even fishes have special nerve endings that detect painful injuries. Humans are not the only sensitive beings on earth. More than one hundred years ago, Charles Darwin remarked, "We have always underestimated the richness of the mental lives of animals." He believed animals experience terror, anticipation, and fear, as well as pain and pleasure. He said they love their offspring and can grieve. They can be kind, jealous, self-complacent, and proud.

Stress is a more difficult concept than pain. There are many stressors, and some are necessary for development and keeping the body functioning properly, whereas some cause pathological changes.

Companion animals

A companion animal's health and well-being depends on diet; physical needs, such as exercise and play; and emotional needs, such as companionship, affection, and touch, summed up in the phrase "tender loving care" (TLC). Prevention is better than cure, but accidents and diseases can occur. Some will need urgent veterinary attention, whereas others can be treated with first aid and may even be dealt with at home.

Injuries

ROAD ACCIDENTS

May result in shock, fractures, hemorrhage, and wounds, all of which will need veterinary attention. If the animal is in shock and unconscious or semiconscious, move the animal carefully onto a towel to carry him or her, to avoid making any fracture or hemorrhage worse. Keep warm, quiet, and in dim light. Stop any serious bleeding with a clean cloth or a tourniquet. Clean dirt gently from open wounds and cover with a clean cloth. If the bowels are exposed, wash them with warm water that has first been boiled (and then allowed to cool enough that it will not cause burns) and cover with a clean wet cloth, and take the animal to a veterinarian.

CUTS, BITES, AND SCRATCHES

If superficial, wash with boiled, then-cooled water and apply antiseptic powder. Puncture wounds often go septic, so veterinary attention is needed. If the wound is gaping open, it needs to be sutured.

STINGS

Treat bee and wasp stings with antihistamine cream. If antihistamine cream is not available, rub in baking soda or washing soda. If an allergic reaction occurs, antihistamine by injection or by mouth is needed quickly.

BURNS

If not severe, apply a cold pack to relieve the pain. Do not burst the blister. If severe, take the animal to a veterinarian at once.

LAMENESS

Look for a stone in the hoof of a horse. In a dog or cat look for a thorn or a wound in the paw.

CHOKING

Attempt to remove the foreign body, such as a bone or needle. If the animal has swallowed a foreign body, take him or her to a veterinarian.

CONSTIPATION

Liquid paraffin, or mineral oil, is safe for all animals. Amount depends on size—for example, a tablespoonful for a cat, a liter for a horse.

POISONING

Do not attempt first aid. Consult a veterinarian.

FEVER

Following are normal temperatures for select animals: cats and dogs, 38.4°C; horses, 38°C; rabbits, 40°C; guinea pigs and hamsters, 39.4°C. If the temperature is raised more than one degree for a day, consult a veterinarian. Temperature is taken inside the rectum.

CONVULSIONS AND FITS

Comfort the animal in a quiet place with subdued light. If convulsions persist more than an hour or so, consult a veterinarian. If the episode is caused by heat stroke, bathe the animal in cold water or wrap in a cold wet towel to bring the temperature down.

PARASITES

Fleas, lice, ticks, and worms are all treatable with over-the-counter products. Infestation with fleas and lice and ticks can be prevented by products such as Frontline. Heartworm can be prevented by a monthly treatment with a heartworm preventive.

CAR SICKNESS

Use human treatments scaled down for size.

Free-living animals

Free-living animals abound in urban areas as well as the countryside. Every roadside bank, wood, field, and garden is home to many species. Prey animals are genetically adapted to being preyed upon; when they are not quickly killed, they escape and rapidly resume their normal behavior. Unfortunately, humans cause injuries, either accidentally or deliberately, to which free-living animals are not adapted, and they suffer horribly. They may be accidentally struck by a car, poisoned by chemicals, contaminated with oil, or deliberately shot, trapped, or poisoned. Much suffering results from ignorance.

People come across injured or sick animals and wonder what will happen to them. You may accidentally strike a bird with your car. The animal drops to the ground, feathers awry, beak open, eyes closed, but still breathing, and you wonder what to do. Should the bird be treated and where? Should the bird be put to sleep to end his or her suffering? The primary intention should be to help the animal recover so that the animal can be returned to his or her natural state.

One of the major problems in embarking on the care and treatment of a free-living animal is that the vast majority of these animals do not take kindly to it. Never expect gratitude or cooperation, and understand that you may even get injured. It is better to call the experts and carefully mark the spot where you found the animal. There are, of course, exceptions, such as hedgehogs and small birds, who can be taken to a sanctuary.

First aid

Free-living animals are usually stressed by handling and proximity to humans. To provide rest, peace, and quiet, you should put them in a box (chew-proof and with air-holes) or a covered cage where they can feel safe and stay warm (25 degrees Celsius). Offer water in a small flattish lid (a saucer can be tipped if the animal stands on the edge) and some food (tinned cat food, grated hardboiled egg, and grain). If the animal is a bird, and you do not know whether the bird is a seed-eater or insect eater, offer a selection and keep him or her warm. Giving a small bird some water with a pinch of glucose with an eye-dropper administered at the hinge of the beak will help. It is unwise to attempt treatment. Take him or her to a sanctuary—addresses can be found in local directories.

A hedgehog hibernates between October and March, so if one is found during that period, it is likely to be asleep rather than dead. Put the animal back in his or her nest unless a dog has found the animal, or put him or her in a cardboard box with plenty of dry straw, hay, or leaves, in a shed or garage. If the hedgehog is awake, feed him or her tinned dog or cat food and water.

Some other points to remember: A rabbit does not need extra heat. Feed rabbits cereal plus grass or hay. Most of the other mammals can be dangerous. Squirrels, foxes, and badgers bite, and deer have a powerful kick. It is best to call an expert. If you come across an orphaned bird, it is wise to leave him or her alone—normally the parents are nearby and will feed the young bird. A baby deer left alone while his or her mother feeds is not an orphan, so do not disturb him or her.

There is one important thing to remember: it is always advisable to seek veterinary advice. First aid can only be that—first aid. Veterinary advice and treatment should then be sought.

Related articles: Animal pain; The complexity of animal awareness; Enhancing a dog's environment; Euthanasia; Holistic health care; Rabbits; Reporting cruelty in the United Kingdom; Reporting cruelty in the United States; Shelters and sanctuaries

Beyval, A. C. D., Rahman, S. A., and Gavinelli, A. (eds.), *Animal Welfare, Global Issues, Trends, and Challenges*, International des Epizootics, 2005.

Hunter, Francis, *Before the Vet Calls*, Thorsons, 1984.

Jordan, W. J., *A–Z Guide to Pet Health*, Constable, 1986.

Jordan, W. J., and Hughes, John, *Care for the Wild*, Jordan, 1983.

———, *Care for the Wild: First Aid for Wild Creatures*, University of Wisconsin Press, 1983.

Molineaux, Elizabeth, *Manual of Wildlife Casualties*, British Veterinary Association, 2003.

Pitcairn, Richard H., and Pitcairn, Susan Hubble, *Dr. Pitcairn's Complete Guide to Natural Health for Dogs and Cats*, Rodale Press, 2005.

W. J. JORDAN

HOLISTIC HEALTH CARE

In recent years, there has been a rekindling of interest in holistic health care and a desire to use natural products and medicines. Not only people but also their animal companions are experiencing the benefits of holistic care. Holistic medicine (sometimes spelled "wholistic") is the art of natural healing. It is not so much a discipline as a concept in the care and treatment of individuals.

The concern of holistic practitioners is to assist in the healing process of the animal. They treat the whole animal, not just the disease. They believe there is a central life force, variously termed as chi, prana, or ki, that protects and keeps the body in balance and allows it to heal. There is a strong belief in the body's own innate ability to heal itself given the right circumstances. The holistic practitioner employs different healing disciplines that help balance and support the body in healing.

Holistic approaches are concerned with the whole system of the animal and all the various factors, both emotional and physical, that may influence it. For example, the holistic practitioner is concerned with the relationship between the animal and his or her caregiver, as well as physical symptoms of health or disease. It is important that all the energies—physical, emotional, spiritual, and environmental—work together to manifest wellness. Disease occurs when these energies are out of synchronization within themselves and with each other.

Frequently, people, including medical professionals, are confused by the terms used in holistic medicine. "Alternative medicine" refers to disciplines used instead of conventional, or allopathic, medicine. "Complementary medicine" refers to disciplines used in conjunction with conventional or allopathic medicine. The term most often incorrectly used for holistic medicine is homeopathy, which is in fact a distinct discipline that may or may not be employed in holistic treatments.

The American Veterinary Medical Association (AVMA) defines holistic veterinary medicine as "a comprehensive approach to health care employing alternative and conventional diagnostic and therapeutic modalities. In practice it incorporates, but is not limited to, the principles of acupuncture and acutherapy, botanical medicine, chiropractic, homeopathy, massage therapy, nutraceuticals, physical therapy as well as conventional medicine, surgery and dentistry." The holistic practitioner will explore all disciplines, including conventional medicine, and integrate those healing disciplines needed to achieve optimum well-being.

Conventional medicine, however, is not necessarily the first discipline of choice. The integrative holistic practitioner's medical toolbox comprises many medical disciplines. Usual veterinary approaches will look for the root cause of an illness. Thus, if an animal presented an operable cancer, the conventional veterinarian would cut it out, and the animal would, in most cases, be considered cured. The integrative holistic veterinarian would additionally seek to understand why the tumor occurred in the first place and attempt to remove the causes so that the tumor does not return.

The primary focus in holistic medicine is to support wellness and prevent illness. Good nutrition is paramount to good health and is the cornerstone in the prevention of illness. From a holistic perspective, there is no more vital factor than the food that we feed our companion animals. In today's market, we are barraged with commercially prepared foods, which often provide less than adequate nutrition. They are prepared under high pressure and high temperatures, and the food's natural vitamins and enzymes are frequently destroyed. Many of these foods contain preservatives, additives, by-products, and other inedible or less than nourishing elements. Years of poor nutrition have taken a toll on our animals, as they have on humans. Today, for example, we are seeing more cancers and skin diseases than ever. The holistic practitioner will recommend feeding our animal companions as naturally as possible. This may include a natural raw food diet. Dr. Ian Billinghurst introduced the Biologically Appropriate Raw Food (BARF) diet, which has been popular among holistic health practitioners since the early 1990s. Improving nutrition for our animal companions can improve all aspects of their health.

Integrative holistic care encompasses many different disciplines, including acupuncture, chiropractic, homeopathy, and herbal medicine. There are also dozens of esoteric fields, such as flower essences, essential oils, aromatherapy, glandulars, massage, physical therapy, Bowen technique, TTouch, reiki, kinesiology, magnetic therapy, ayurvedic medicine, environmental medicine, and many more. Frequently these disciplines are looked at as "New Age" medicine, but nothing could be further from the truth. Though some disciplines may be new, many of these disciplines have been around for hundreds, even thousands, of years. They have proven themselves as effective healing modalities throughout the ages.

Treating our animal companions holistically can both add to the quality of their lives and prevent disease. Because caregivers are a part of the healing process, our lives can be enriched as well.

Related articles: Animal-friendly spirituality; The concept of guardianship; Homeopathy

Broadfoot, Paula Jo, Palmquist, Richard E., Johnston, Karen, Wen, Jui Jia, and Fougere, Barbara, with Roman, Margo, *Integrating Complementary Medicine into Veterinary Practice*, ed. Robert Goldstein, Wiley-Blackwell, 2007.

Dodds, W. Jean, *The Canine Thyroid Epidemic*, Dogwise, 2011.

Flaim, Denise, *The Holistic Dog Book*, Howell Book House, 2003.

Goldstein, Martin, *The Nature of Animal Healing*, Knopf, 1999.

Pitcairn, Richard H., and Pitcairn, Susan Hubble, *Dr. Pitcairn's Complete Guide to Natural Health for Dogs and Cats*, Rodale Press, 1995.

Schwartz, Cheryl, *Four Paws, Five Directions*, Celestial Arts, 1996.

Stein, Diane, *Natural Healing for Dogs and Cats*, Crossing Press, 1993.

SUSAN MARINO

HOMEOPATHY

Homeopathy is a system of medicine that was developed by a German doctor, Samuel Hahnemann, in the late eighteenth and early nineteenth centuries. Two spellings of the term are used; the original "homoeopathy" is still used widely, but increasingly, modern practice is to ignore the original diphthong, and hence the form "homeopathy" is seen most often.

Since its initial development, homeopathy has been expanded and refined, with its use spreading around the world. It has been used to treat animals from its very early days. Its basic philosophy differs from that of conventional Western medicine in that functional upsets in the body are regarded as the true origin of disease, with pathology arising as a result of those upsets. The homeopathic view is that if a person or animal has a lump, it is because the individual is ill, as opposed to the conventional view that the individual is ill because he or she has a lump. Symptoms are viewed as the result of the body's attempt to correct the underlying functional upset, and treatment is aimed at helping the system to correct the true underlying cause of the disease rather than concentrated primarily on the removal of the presenting symptoms. Working through the body's own immune system, the therapy assists nature to work the whole disease process out of the body. Because of this approach, it is possible to obtain cures in some situations that conventionally are regarded as chronic and incurable.

The therapy's use, however, is not limited to the "hopeless" cases. It can be employed successfully in cases of acute illness where, by assisting the natural defense mechanisms of the body, it facilitates a cure without any of the longer-term weakening effects on the system that may occur with some modern drugs and that can lay the foundations for future illness.

The substances used in treatment (usually called

"remedies" rather than "medicines") are derived from many sources, and there is no intrinsic reason that any substance cannot provide a remedy. Homeopathy is often confused with herbalism because many homeopathic remedies (roughly 50 percent) are derived from plants, but herbalism is a valid and distinct medical system in its own right.

Usually, the basic principle of homeopathy is expressed as "let like be cured by like." However, it is described more accurately as "let similar be cured by similar," in contrast to modern linguistic usage, which equates "like" with "same." In practice this means that during illness the patient receives in the form of a homeopathic remedy a substance that is known to produce similar symptoms in a healthy body. In the diseased body this remedy reinforces and supports the innate defense mechanisms of the patient in the exact areas where support is needed and hence accelerates the curative process.

Many of the substances used as sources for homeopathic remedies are, in their raw state, toxic to the body; indeed, many of the most poisonous substances known make the most powerful healing agents when subjected to the homeopathic manufacturing process. This process involves stages of great dilution, and it is this that has given rise to the idea that homeopathy is merely the use of very small, extremely dilute doses. Although this dilution stage is important to homeopathy, it is not by any means its fundamental principle. Allied to the dilution are stages of severe but controlled agitation, termed "succession," through which energies are released into the remedies, energies that are unacknowledged by basic physics but widely recognized in the fields of quantum physics and mathematics.

All testing of remedies on healthy bodies in order to provide the necessary knowledge of their action is carried out on human volunteers, and the results have been shown to be valid for animals. In practical terms dosage is usually by mouth, although other routes are used sometimes with farmed animals. The important requirement is that the remedy be absorbed via one of the mucous surfaces of the body, such as the mouth or nose. In acute disease the speed of response can amaze those not used to the system, but at the other end of the scale, chronic, long-standing conditions can take a long time to clear and require prolonged treatment. With homeopathy it is the speed at which the body can respond that determines the effectiveness of the treatment.

Homeopathy is a holistic approach to health and disease, and therefore, the consideration of the whole animal/person is an integral part of the system. All aspects of the patient are taken into account in the selection of an appropriate remedy. Because of the individual nature of every prescription, two patients suffering from the same conventionally named condition may receive different remedies.

There are no side effects, in the conventional sense, associated with the use of remedies. This means that even in cases that are incurable, control of the illness using homeopathy is potentially safer than treatment with conventional medications. The two medical systems are not inevitably incompatible, and there are situations where the two can be used together to the greater benefit of the patient.

In many countries homeopathy is available from within the veterinary profession, with training and qualifications available. The Faculty of Homeopathy (U.K.) supervises training of veterinarians and offers a qualification that is available in many countries around the world. The designation "Vet MF Hom" indicates a homeopathically qualified veterinarian. In addition the International Association for Veterinary Homeopathy offers the international qualification of "Cert IAVH," and other countries have their own national qualifications.

In spite of much adverse publicity from some quarters, homeopathy is a scientifically plausible and clinically validated therapy that offers opportunities to provide a natural, safe, and effective means of treating both animals and people.

Related article: Holistic health care

Bellavite, P., and Signorini, A., *The Emerging Science of Homeopathy*, North Atlantic Books, 2002.

Hamilton, D., *Homeopathic Care for Cats and Dogs*, North Atlantic Books, 1990.

Owen, D. (ed.), *Principles and Practice of Homeopathy*, Churchill Livingstone/Elsevier, 2007.

Saxton, J. G. G., *Bowel Nosodes in Homeopathic Practice*, Saltire Books, 2008.

———, *Miasms as Practical Tools*, Beaconsfield and Narayana, 2006.

Saxton, J. G. G., and Gregory, P. A., *Textbook of Veterinary Homeopathy*, Beaconsfield, 2005.

J. G. G. SAXTON

INSURANCE

All caregivers want to give their animal companions the best medical attention if the need arises. That is why insurance should feature on the checklist of every responsible caregiver. Sadly, only 7 percent of cat caregivers and 14 percent of dog caregivers in the United Kingdom have taken this step so far. So how can insurance help your animal companion?

Veterinary fees

Veterinary fees are increasingly expensive. Being sure that one can pay the bill when the need arises is essential to responsible care. Veterinary fee coverage is therefore one of the main planks of insurance for companion animals, and it is doubly important. Not only is it there to pay for routine treatments; it is also vital because huge advances are being made in the treatments available to enhance quality of life and alleviate suffering in ill or injured animals, but such treatments can be very expensive. Insurance is often the only way a caregiver can ensure that these treatments are available to his or her animal companion. Be cautious, however. Some insurance plans limit payout for a treatment to twelve months. If a companion animal suffers from a long-term illness—diabetes, for example—he or she will need treatment for some years. It is important to determine whether an insurer would cover this.

Death by accident or illness and loss by theft or straying

Money can never compensate for the loss of a dear companion, but most insurance companies will pay out the money value of your companion animal if the worst does happen.

Public liability

Caregivers, who are legally responsible for their companion animals, run the risk of liability if, for example, a dog runs off and causes a bad road accident. That is especially true in today's "compensation culture." Thus, insurance usually provides public liability coverage. It is important to check the precise amount of coverage provided, since personal injury claims can be huge where loss of earnings are recovered by the injured party. Again, caution is required: many U.K. policies limit cover to one million pounds; others offer double this.

Holiday or vacation cancellation

If a caregiver's holiday has to be canceled because his or her companion animal suddenly requires treatment, then the caregiver may lose substantial sums. Some insurance policies cover holiday cancellation.

Advertising and reward

If a companion animal goes missing, then the insurance may include advertising and reward coverage.

Boarding fees

Provisions need to be made if the caregiver is ill or requires hospital treatment. Insurance often gives some coverage for the cost of kennel and cattery fees at such a time.

Here are some pointers to help you get the best coverage:

- Cost of premiums: Some insurers rate their premiums according to postcode, or zip code, so cheap offers may not universally apply. Also, consider whether the premium is different for a pedigree or purebred animal versus a crossbreed or mixed-breed animal. Different levels of coverage obviously require different premiums, so it is wise to select appropriately and with care.
- The cost of making a claim: Every insurance policy carries an "excess," or deductible. That is the sum the caregiver will be responsible for when a claim is made. If the excess is fifty pounds, the caregiver will have to pay the first fifty pounds of any claim. It is therefore obviously important to check what excess or deductible a caregiver may be liable for.
- Age of the companion animal: Some insurers will take only animals up to eight years old. And beware that some insurers will "load" a premium by adding an extra amount onto the basic premium once a companion passes that age.

Related articles: Cats; Dogs; The experience of loss; Kennels and catteries; A lifelong responsibility

Bower, John, and Bower, Caroline, *The Cat Owner's Veterinary Handbook*, Crowood Press, 2009.

Christensen, Wendy, and staff of the Humane Society of the United States, *Complete Guide to Cat Care*, St. Martin's Press, 2004.

Fogle, Bruce, *Dog: For the Complete Care and Understanding of Your Best Friend*, Mitchell Beazley, 2010.

Gerstenfeld, S. L., *The Cat Care Book*, 2nd ed., Da Capo Press, 1989.

Kenney, Doug, *Your Guide to Understanding Pet Health Insurance*, Philosophia, 2009.

Riley, M., *The Truth about Pet Insurance*, Espino Enterprises, 2010.

CHRISTOPHER FAIRFAX

NEUTERING AND SPAYING

There are a staggering 2,500,000 stray dogs and cats in the United Kingdom. Thousands of unwanted animals are abandoned or destroyed every day. Countless animals struggle to survive on our streets, cold, hungry, frightened, and often sick or injured. Responsible care of companion animals means not adding to the problem. If caregivers allow their companion animals to breed, then even if they find good homes for the puppies or kittens, they are using up homes that the animal rescue charities desperately need for the animals they already have waiting to be adopted. There are simply not enough good homes to go around.

Female cats and dogs

If a female cat is mated every time she comes into season, and all her kittens survive, she could be responsible for no less than 21,000 surplus cats in just seven years. Similarly, a female dog can be responsible for up to 4,500 puppies during the same period.

There is a mistaken belief that a female cat or dog should have a litter before being spayed. In fact, there is no benefit to the animal in allowing this to happen, and dogs and cats should be spayed or neutered as soon as they are old enough, at around five months, although they can, of course, be sterilized at any older age.

There are health benefits to having a female companion animal spayed. She will be less likely to develop mammary tumors, cystic ovaries, endometriosis, and a pyometra; the latter is a potentially life-threatening infection of the uterus and is very common in unaltered middle-age female dogs. It is important that female cats kept inside be spayed because a high percentage develop pyometras, and many of these cats, unless they have an emergency hysterectomy, will die of peritonitis. It is also cruel to keep unspayed cats confined in flats since they constantly come into season and remain in an almost permanent state of frustration.

Male cats

Unneutered male cats are unlikely to be acceptable in most households. Once they become adults, their urine becomes very pungent, and they develop the habit of "spraying" their territory, including their caregiver's homes. They spend most nights fighting other male cats and chasing females. This means they often disappear for days at a time and can reappear with appalling fight injuries and abscesses. Male cats are not "playing" or "bluffing" when they fight; their aim is to maim and incapacitate other cats, and many of the injuries they inflict on each other can be life-threatening without veterinary treatment. Male cats can also infect other cats with FIV, the feline equivalent of HIV, during these terrible battles. FIV cannot be passed from cats to humans, but the dis-

ease significantly reduces the life expectancy of infected cats. In short, a neutered male cat is more likely to be happy as a family companion animal, less likely to stay out at night, and less prone to FIV infection, and he will no longer feel the need to mark his territory by spraying.

Male dogs

Anyone who has tried to control a male dog when there is a female dog in season close by is aware of these dogs' strong instinctive urges. Male dogs enter a state of high sexual tension and can become quite aggressive. Through sheer frustration, they often try to masturbate (or relieve themselves) on cushions or even children's legs. In an excited state, they also tend to urinate all over the house and can be aggressive to other dogs they encounter. It is cruel to allow them to endure this type of frustration when neutering can make them happy, well-behaved, family animal companions.

There are also important health benefits associated with neutering male dogs—for example, a reduction in the incidence of hormone-dependent tumors. Retained testicles must always be removed since they can become malignant. Neutered dogs are less likely to fight with other dogs and are therefore less at risk from injury.

In summary, the most important contribution that caregivers of companion animals can make to the cause of animal welfare is to have their own animals neutered and spayed in order to reduce the number of unwanted animals. There are numerous health and social benefits to both companion animal and caregiver alike. Most importantly, neutering and spaying animals is the only humane solution to the tragic problem of companion animal overpopulation.

Related articles: Caring for animals and humans; Cats; Dogs; The ethics of commercialization; Immunocontraception; A lifelong responsibility; Stray animals

Alderton, David, Edwards, Alan, Larkin, Peter, and Stockman, Mike, *The Complete Book of Pets and Pet Care: The Essential Family Reference Guide to Pet Breeds and Pet Care*, Lorenz Books, 2006.

Edney, Mark, *Complete RSPCA Cat Care Manual*, Dorling Kindersley, 2006.

The Official RSPCA Pet Guide—Care for Your Dog, 2nd ed., Collins, 1994.

RSPCA Pet Guide—Care for Your Cat, Collins, 2005.

Sands, David, and Sands, Amanda Jane, *Caring for Your Pet Kittens and Cats*, 2nd ed., Interpet, 1999.

CELIA HAMMOND

ISSUES OF CONCERN

CANINE PROFILING

Newfoundlands, German shepherds, Saint Bernards, Dobermans, and rottweilers share a common problem: over the years these breeds of dogs have been subject to breed discrimination. Today, American pit bull and Staffordshire terriers along with mixed-breed dogs who share their physical characteristics are the target of breed-discriminatory laws (BDL) throughout the world. In an effort to protect citizens from so-called dangerous dogs, some jurisdictions define all "pit bulls" as dangerous per se based purely on their breed and then either ban them or impose strict limitations on their "ownership." However, upon studying the matter, these jurisdictions have found that these laws are ineffective, inefficient, and unfair.

Studies throughout the world, including the United Kingdom, Spain, the Netherlands, and the United States, have indicated that breed-discriminatory laws are ineffective in that they fail to protect citizens from dog bites or attacks. For example, in Spain, researchers compared reports of dog bites to the public health department of Aragon, Spain, for five years before and five years after the legal ban on pit bull–type dogs and concluded that the law was "not effective in protecting people from dog bites in a significant manner" (Rosado et al. 172).

Breed-discriminatory laws are also costly. For example, Prince George's County, Maryland, established a task force to study the effectiveness of its pit bull ban. The task force reported that over a two-year period, the ban cost the county approximately $560,000. The costs were traced to the impounding of hundreds of pit bulls a year, housing and caring for a large percentage of them during the lengthy hearing process, and eventually killing them because of their appearance, thus incurring cost of euthanasia and disposal of their bodies. Meanwhile, hundreds of other dogs brought to the shelter were killed because there was no room for their care. To better analyze the costs associated with such laws, Best Friends Animal Society commissioned a study to develop a model to estimate the costs of a breed ban by locality.

According to the model, if the United States were to enact a national ban on pit bull–type dogs, it would cost the country $459,138,163 annually to enforce.

Finally, breed-discriminatory laws are unfair and may be unconstitutional. Targeting a dog because of breed rather than behavior is fundamentally flawed. Each dog is an individual and should be judged based on his or her behavior, not breed. Dog caregivers have challenged these laws for decades on a number of constitutional grounds, including procedural and substantive due process. Generally, the laws are upheld by courts, although in recent years some courts have begun to side with pit bull caregivers. The most successful challenges are those that claim the laws are unconstitutionally vague and violate the caregiver's procedural due process by failing to provide adequate procedures for identifying the breed of dog and by denying caregivers the ability to challenge the breed designation by local authorities. Further, with the relatively recent scientific advances in canine DNA, the actual breed or breeds of a dog can be more accurately determined. Studies comparing visual identifications of breed with DNA testing of dogs have shown that the visual identification is very often inaccurate. This, in turn, results in arbitrary enforcement of the law.

Caregivers have also challenged BDL as irrational. They argue that breed does not determine a dog's temperament or expected behavior, and thus, targeting a breed does not effectively protect the public from harm. In fact, pit bulls are noted for being highly obedient animals who strive to please their caregivers and make excellent family companions. Factors other than breed are far more predictive of dangerous behavior. A study of fatal dog attacks noted the following commonalities among the attacks: (a) 97 percent of the dogs had not been neutered; (b) 84 percent involved caregivers who abused, neglected, chained, or failed to constrain their dog or left their dog unsupervised around children; and (c) 78 percent of caregivers kept the dog not as a companion but rather to guard, breed, or fight. Thus, banning a dog based purely on breed does not rationally relate to protecting the public.

The more effective, efficient, and fair approach to protecting the public from dog bites or attacks is to target reckless human caregivers. Progressive jurisdictions are instituting a variety of regulations to address the problem of reckless humans, including allowing convicted felons to own only sterilized dogs, prohibiting humans cited more than once for animal abuse or neglect from keeping a companion animal, restricting the chaining or tethering of dogs when unattended, mandating that dogs be leashed when off the caregiver's premises, promoting public education, and imposing stiff fines on humans who violate the laws. By regulating the culpable party and addressing the factors that generally lead to dangerous behavior by dogs, jurisdictions can better protect their citizens and treat dogs and their caregivers fairly.

Related articles: Animal and human violence; The concept of guardianship; Dog fighting; Dogs; Euthanasia; Shelters and sanctuaries; Spaying and neutering

Delise, K., *The Pit Bull Placebo: The Media, Myths and Politics of Canine Aggression*, Anubis, 2007.

———, "Types of Dog Bites," National Canine Research Council, available at http://nationalcanineresearchcouncil.com/dog-bites/types-of-dog-bites/.

Dias v. Denver, 567 F.3d 1169 (10th Cir. 2009).

John Dunham and Associates, *The Fiscal Impact of Breed Discriminatory Laws in the United States*, 2009, available at http://www.guerrillaeconomics.biz/bestfriends/.

"License Required," Dangerous Dog Ordinance, Saint Paul, Minnesota, Code of Ordinances §200.02 (2009).

"Possession of Unsterilized or Vicious Dogs by Felons Prohibited," 720 ILCS 5/12–36 (2010).

Report of the Vicious Animal Legislation Task Force, 2002, available at http://www.understand-a-bull.com/BSL/Research/PGCMD/PGCMTOC1.htm.

Responsible Pet Ownership Bylaw, Calgary, Alberta, Bylaws 23M2006, amended by 48M2008, 49M2008, 61M2011.

Rosado, B., et al., "Dangerous Animals Act: Effect of the Epidemiology of Dog Bites," *Journal of Veterinary Behavior* 2.5 (2007): 166 (in Spanish).

Schaffner, Joan E. (ed.), *A Lawyer's Guide to Dangerous Dog Issues*, American Bar Association, 2009.

Voith, Victoria L., et al., "Comparison of Adoption Agency Breed Identification and DNA Breed Identification of Dogs," *Journal of Applied Animal Welfare Science* 12 (2009): 253.

JOAN E. SCHAFFNER

COSMETIC SURGERY

Although many countries have either stopped or banned cosmetic surgeries, otherwise known as "non-veterinary mutilations"—such as ear cropping and tail docking of canines—these practices remain legal in the United States. Regrettably, the American Kennel Club (AKC), many breed associations, a large section of the public, and a fortunately decreasing number of veterinarians still view these surgical procedures, done only to alter a dog's appearance and not for her or his health, as acceptable, even desirable.

Tail docking involves removing a segment of the dog's vertebral column, which may constitute as much as one-quarter to one-third of the total body length. It is usually done with scissors and without the benefit of anesthesia on puppies, who are usually two to five days old. Ear cropping is usually performed on dogs nine to twelve weeks old and involves cutting and reshaping the ears so that they stand up straight rather than grow naturally. Although anesthesia is used for this latter procedure, it is traumatic, and the puppy must undergo follow-up visits to a veterinarian in which the ears are handled, stretched, and retaped.

Tails are present in the overwhelming majority of vertebrate species, proving their evolutionary importance for balancing and maneuvering, as well as for intra-species communication. Similarly, the ear pinnae (flaps) provide a means of communication by their positioning and serve to focus incoming sounds into the ear canal. The hanging ear flaps also protect the ear's inner structures.

Excuses for performing these cosmetic surgeries often appeal to the idea that they somehow benefit a particular dog breed. Tail docking supposedly prevents tail injuries, even though many breeds used in the field are typically undocked. Ear cropping is rationalized as a prevention for ear infections, even though many breeds, notorious for developing ear inflammation, are never cropped.

There are some welcome signs that the United States will at some point ban these practices. For example, some breed clubs have changed their standards to allow undocked and uncropped dogs to be shown. Some breeders are refusing to dock the tails of their litters of puppies and discourage ear cropping when selling them. Some shelters discourage, or even prohibit, the practice in their contracts with individual adopters.

The American Veterinary Medical Association (AVMA), the largest veterinary association in the world, changed its position statement on this issue in 1999. The previous statement did not ask veterinarians to take any responsibility for these procedures, but rather placed the matter in the hands of the AKC. Now the AVMA clearly states that these procedures, when done for cosmetic purposes, are not medically justifiable and are of no benefit to the patient. The statement goes on to say that these procedures cause pain and distress and, as with all surgical procedures, are accompanied by inherent risks, such as those associated with anesthesia, as well as blood loss and infection. It recommends that veterinarians advise caregivers about these procedures before agreeing to perform them.

The World Small Animal Veterinary Association recently took aim at the United States by saying that it is the "Last Frontier" of needless, cruel, cosmetic animal companion surgery and is requesting that veterinary associations sign its petition against these practices in order to start a positive trend toward banning them altogether.

Dogs are highly revered in the United States and are considered by many caregivers to be members of their human family. However, our relationship to them, in many cases, remains one in which the dog is used as a symbol of status or elegance and is therefore cosmetically altered—"mutilated" as the Royal College of Veterinary Surgeons firmly asserts—to suit the whim of the human caregiver. It goes without saying that true dog lovers would never subject a beloved companion to the pain and fear inherent in cosmetic surgery, remodeling their friend to suit a capricious and illogical fashion standard.

Related articles: Animal pain; The concept of guardianship; Dogs; Selective breeding; Veterinary ethics

Bennett, P., and Perini, E., "Tail Docking in Dogs: A Review of the Issues," *Australian Veterinary Journal* 81.4 (2003): 208–218.

Durr, A., and Freudiger, U., "Ear-Cropping as a Prevention against Otitis Externa?" *Schweiz Arch Tierheilkd* 188.6 (1976): 239–248.

Gumbrell, R. C., "Canine Ear Cropping," *New Zealand Veterinary Journal* 32 (1984): 119.

Juarbe-Diaz, S. V., "Assessment and Treatment of Excessive Barking in the Domestic Dog," *Veterinary Clinics of North America Small Animal Practice* 27.3 (1997): 515–532.

Morton, D., "Docking of Dogs: Practical and Ethical Aspects," *Veterinary Record* 131.14 (1992): 301–306.

Tobias, K., "Feline Onychectomy at a Teaching Institution: A Retrospective Study of 163 Cases," *Veterinary Surgery* 23.4 (1994): 274–280.

HOLLY CHEEVER

DOGS AS FOOD

In 1998, ten Saint Bernard dogs from Europe and the United States were exported to China for dog meat trials, along with Great Danes and Tibetan mastiffs. As a result, the Chinese government declared the Saint Bernard to be "the meat dog of choice," advertising the animal's supposed aphrodisiac qualities in business brochures designed to encourage the farming of these highly intelligent animals. Large breeding farms were set up, supported by Web sites detailing rearing and housing requirements and spelling out the financial benefits of farming Saint Bernards for table meat.

Dog-eating had died out during the Cultural Revolution of 1966–1976, when Red Guards rampaged through the country killing dogs, even those raised for food, because they were regarded as a bourgeoisie extravagance. Since that era, the importation of the Saint Bernards has prompted a resurgence of dog meat farms.

There are now an estimated 25,000 Saint Bernards in China, plus thousands of German shepherds, Dalmatians, Newfoundlands, and Leonbergers, being bred for food and fur. It was reported in 2002 that Chinese dog farmers believed that in a few short years, Saint Bernards would become as prolific as sheep and cattle. Dog farms are springing up all over China. In one area, Peixian, 300,000 dogs are slaughtered annually. One dog farmer raises 100,000 dogs a year, almost all for slaughter at about six months of age. Crossing a Saint Bernard or Dalmatian with a locally bred dog produces two litters of eight to ten puppies a year. Each crossbred puppy grows to about fifty kilograms in five months.

Historically, there have been commercial breeders of cows and pigs in China but not dogs, until Saint Bernard breeders appeared on the scene. They have proliferated, partly due to government funding. These farms are also setting up Web sites asking for investors from the United States and other countries to help them expand their operations. Because of Western abhorrence of the practice of eating dogs, Chinese businessmen have had difficulty in procuring financial support. This has led them to negotiate with foreign companies to import stud dogs.

Buyers of the Saint Bernards include farmers and small businessmen who come from all over China, hoping to make some money on the side by breeding dogs. They are drawn by advertisements boasting a high rate of return; it is claimed that raising dogs is three times as profitable as raising poultry and four times as profitable as raising pigs.

There are no animal welfare organizations in China, and the dogs are subjected to the most inhumane treatment imaginable. Videos show slaughter methods that are too horrific for general release to the media. Some methods include the following:

- Pouring boiling water over the live animal to increase the adrenaline production. The throat is then cut and the flesh left to dry.
- Cutting holes in the paws. The animal is then left to bleed to death, which takes at least ten

minutes. This procedure supposedly makes the meat taste better.

- Breaking the animal's legs the night before slaughter and then skinning the dog alive the following morning.
- Beating with sticks, slowly strangling, or blow-torching the animal.

The Food and Agriculture Organization of the United Nations (FAO) keeps a complete list of all livestock and, through its member countries, has the power to classify dogs as inappropriate for human consumption. Dogs do not appear on the FAOSTAT list, yet China (a FAO member country) has unilaterally classified them as livestock. A petition asking that the dogs be classified as not for human consumption, signed and supported by over four and a half million people worldwide, was presented to the FAO in Rome on November 2, 2001. A reply received stated, "There are no rules at an international level that prohibit the commercialisation of dogs as slaughter animals. Codex Alimentarius defines meat as the edible part of any slaughter animal slaughtered in an abattoir and includes edible offal." There are no commercially run "abattoirs" for dogs in China; they are slaughtered in backyards.

This is not an acceptable response, and the FAO has not even alerted its member countries to the fact that the world's largest petition for animals has been received. The FAO has stated that a member country can discuss such matters at an FAO council or conference, yet member countries have failed to address this situation despite many requests, including from the New Zealand government.

Australia is one country that has taken the lead on this issue. Through the Australian National Kennel Council, it has formally legislated against the export of dogs from Australia to any country where they are consumed as food. Dogs can be sold only to registered members of kennel clubs for showing or for breeding, to enhance the breed for shows only.

Governments are quick to cite cultural reasons for failing to address this issue. However, the first secretary of the Chinese embassy in Wellington, New Zealand, stated in an interview on June 18, 2002, that this new venture with the Saint Bernards and other Western/European dog breeds has nothing to do with "culture"; it is purely a commercial venture.

Never before in the history of this world have domesticated dogs been exported from one country to another as food, and it is now clear that China has no intention of stopping this trade. The logical solution is for each country to impose its own ban on all dogs going to any country where they are bred and consumed as food. We owe dogs this protection, given the close relationship that has developed between dogs and humans over thousands of years. Dogs have provided human beings with friendship, companionship, protection, and service as working animals over the decades. Will the twenty-first century be remembered as the time when domesticated companion animals were turned into livestock?

Related articles: Animals in Chinese culture; Dogs; The ethics of commercialization; The fur trade; Legal protection of animals in China; Live animal exports; Puppy mills; Slaughter

Blunt, Elizabeth, "Swiss SOS for St Bernards," *BBC News*, February 6, 2001, available at http://sirius.2kat.net/BBC.html.

Chang, Emily, "Inside the Cat and Dog Meat Market in China," *CNN World*, March 9, 2010, available at http://articles.cnn.com/2010–03–09/world/china. animals_1_dog-meat-cats-and-dogs-number-of-pet-owners.

Gallagher, Ian, "The Cat Meat Trade in China," 2001, available at http://sirius.2kat.net/cats.html.

Sirius Global Animal Charitable Trust, "China's Dog Meat Farms," available at http://www.siriusgao.org/Peixiun.html.

Watts, Jonathan, "Chinese Legal Experts Call for Ban on Eating Cats and Dogs," *Guardian*, January 26, 2010, available at http://www.guardian.co.uk/environment/2010/jan/26/dog-meat-china.

ELLY MAYNARD

THE ETHICS OF COMMERCIALIZATION

There are thousands, if not millions, of neglected, abandoned, or abused companion animals worldwide who live on the streets or who are waiting for adoption or rehoming in shelters and sanctuaries. Many advocates for animals adopt or rehome these animals to the extent that they can, but there are simply too many animals around and too few good homes available. That is why euthanasia is still the lot of many of these animals.

An ethical approach must, therefore, ask critical questions about the commercialization of companions. In the first place, there are few legal controls on breeding and selling worldwide. Puppy mills in the United States, Canada, and the United Kingdom are a prime example. These are wholly commercial enterprises predicated on selling animals as commodities or products for humans who want to "own" them. Again with "pet shops," the aim is to make a business at the selling of companion animals, and they frequently do so without even providing rudimentary information about how these animals should be cared for. Encouraged by well-meaning children who are attracted to cute creatures, many families take on animals without realizing that caring for an animal is a lifelong responsibility. The result is an ever-increasing number of animals who are abandoned, ill treated, or euthanized. Animal protection organizations are frequently left with the unenviable task of having to take responsibility for animals when caregivers have themselves failed to do so.

Second, many caregivers fail to understand the full behavioral, social, and environmental needs of the animals they acquire. Many home environments are simply inappropriate for companion animals, especially "exotic" animals. The result is inevitably neglect, sometimes willful, but in most cases simply resulting from ignorance and misunderstanding. Easy selling and buying of animals means that huge responsibilities are incurred without much long-term thought or planning. In addition, companion animals are also easy targets of abuse, as the rise of complaints regarding cruelty to animals in the United Kingdom indicates.

Third, there is the question of food. It is not easy to provide adequate nutrition for carnivorous companions without providing meat, which means in practice that a high companion animal population can be sustained only by the killing of other species, such as kangaroos, horses, fishes, farmed animals, and even whales. Thus, caregivers of companions are often unwittingly complicit in the slaughter of many thousands of other animals every year, not to mention the by-products of slaughter. The so-called pet food industry helps feed some species of animals at the expenses of others. Whether it is possible to feed dogs or cats adequately on a vegetarian diet is still the subject of debate (Knight).

These considerations mean that animal advocates and organizations need to be more proactive in the following areas:

- Seeking to curtail the breeding of, and trade in, companion animals. As long as there are few or no controls on breeding animals and selling them, there can be no solution to the problem of overpopulation. Overbreeding at one end leads inexorably to euthanasia at the other.
- Making it illegal for people to purchase or adopt companion animals without education in their basic welfare needs and dissemination by the seller or adopting organization of appropriate species information. Without this, abuse through neglect or ignorance is inevitable.
- Ensuring neutering and spaying. This simple measure is the only way to guarantee that caregivers are contributing to the solution rather than creating a problem for others to solve.

- Identification through microchipping is also essential, as is a system of licensing, in order to ensure that caregivers can be traced and held accountable.
- Supporting courses in humane education in the curriculum of schools and colleges worldwide, including information about how to properly care for companion animals.
- Encouraging those who wish to acquire animals to do so only from shelters or sanctuaries. Buying from breeders or shops only perpetuates the problem by rewarding those people who want to make money out of trading in animals.

Doubtless, there will always be homeless animals who need our care. It needs to be more widely recognized that such caring is not only a potentially enjoyable experience but also a work of service that involves many responsibilities, not to mention forethought, planning, and finance. The legal requirement of caregivers to have a "duty of care" in the Animal Welfare Act of 2006 in the United Kingdom is a welcome first step in the right direction, and similar legislation needs to be introduced in other countries. But it needs to go hand in hand with a more critical approach to the commercialization of animals that is the cause of neglect, abandonment, and euthanasia.

Related articles: Cats; Dogs; Euthanasia; Humane education; A lifelong responsibility; Puppy mills; Stray animals

Carpenter, Edward, et al., "The Animals Man Uses as Pets," *Animals and Ethics*, Watkins, 1980, 25–28.
Grier, Katherine C., *Pets in America: A History*, University of North Carolina Press, 2009.
Knight, Andrew, "Vegan Animals," 2005, available at http://www.andrewknight.info/publications/vegetarianism/vegan_animals/vegan_animals.html.
Linzey, Andrew, *Christianity and the Rights of Animals*, SPCK/Crossroad, 1987, 133–138.
———, "Pet and Companion Animals," in Reich, Warren T. (chief ed.), *Encyclopaedia of Bioethics*, rev. ed., vol. 1, Macmillan Reference Library, Simon and Schuster, and Prentice-Hall International, 1994, 180–184.
Tuan, Yu-Fu, *Dominance and Affection: The Making of Pets*, Yale University Press, 1984.

ANDREW LINZEY

FERAL CATS

A feral cat is simply a cat who lacks human socialization. Feral cats are often the product of unaltered domesticated cats who have been allowed to roam free or have been turned out by their caregivers to live on their own. Feral cats are found around the globe, with the largest known colonies existing in Rome. The group Friends of Roman Cats estimates that 300,000 feral cats live in Rome in approximately two thousand colonies. Feral cats are found in cities, in suburban areas, and in rural areas of many countries. It is estimated that the feral cat population in the United States exceeds fifty million cats.

Feral as well as domesticated cat ancestry can be traced back to the African wildcat. Cats were first domesticated thousands of years ago. To the ancient Egyptians they were sacred. Cats have played a significant role in the control of rodents and the diseases spread by them throughout human history (Engels).

However, cats are prolific reproducers, and two unaltered cats and their offspring can produce up to 420,000 cats in seven years. Some environmentalists argue that cats decimate other free-ranging animal populations, particularly songbirds. Various approaches have been undertaken to control the population of feral cats. Feral cat population control approaches range from eradication through trapping, shooting, and poisoning to the development of trap-neuter-release (TNR) and low-cost spay/neuter programs.

The Italians have declared cats a part of their "bio-heritage." Thousands of feral cats live in the ancient Roman ruins, in cemeteries, and in various public places throughout Rome. Both the cats and the "cat ladies" who feed them are protected by law; it is a crime in Rome to harm a cat or the cat ladies. The Torre Argentina cat sanctuary is located in the same place where Caesar was assassinated. Friends of Roman Cats sponsors "cats and culture" tours that allow tourists to see how the Italians handle their feral cat population.

Likewise, the Parliamentary Cats of Canada have long been permitted to live on Parliament Hill in Ottawa. Canadian tradition traces their existence to a British garrison of 1850. The cats are fed by volunteers and receive donated veterinary services. Recently, cat structures were built to provide the cats shelter from the elements. At the opposite end of the spectrum, eradication has been employed in many island communities, and most recently, in its preparations for hosting the Olympics, China eradicated its cat population through roundup and starvation. The Chinese government was able to obtain the cooperation of its citizens through a propaganda program that convinced citizens that cats were carriers of disease.

In most Western countries, heightened awareness of animal cruelty and scientific research support TNR programs. Volunteer nonprofit organizations such as Alley Cat Rescue and Alley Cat Allies in the United States and British organizations such as Romney House and the Royal Society for the Prevention of Cruelty to Animals have developed such programs, which trap feral cats, spay or neuter them, vaccinate them, treat them for fleas, tip the left ear to indicate that they have been altered, and then release them back to their colonies, where food is supplied by a colony caretaker.

TNR programs have proven to be a humane way of dealing with feral cat populations. TNR programs stabilize the population at a manageable level, are more effective and less costly than eradication, and deal with the issue of feral cat population control in a more humane way. Current research suggests that eradication necessarily fails because of the vacuum effect. The vacuum effect states that if food and shelter are present, cats will return to an area. The research also suggests that altered and vaccinated feral cats can live a long and healthy life with the aid of a caretaker who provides them with food.

As more research is done, it is likely that our improved understanding of feral cats will debunk many of the myths surrounding cats and result in the adoption of more TNR programs and less attempts at eradication through hunting, starving, or poisoning.

Related articles: Animals in Chinese culture; The big cats; Cats; Euthanasia; Humane education; Immunocontraception; Neutering and spaying; The protection of birds; Stray animals

Engels, D., *Classical Cats: The Rise and Fall of the Sacred Cat*, Routledge, 1999.
"Feral Cats All Over the World," 2001, available at http://from-feral2domestic.com.
Hartwell, S., "The Great Australian Cat Dilemma," 1994, available at http://feralcat.com.
———, "Why Feral Eradication Won't Work," 1996, available at http://feralcat.com.
Holton, L., *Feral Cat Colony Management and Control: Facts and Myths about Feral Cats*, Alley Cat Rescue, 2009.
Winograd, N., *The Myth of Pet Overpopulation and the No Kill Revolution in America*, Alamaden, 2007.

FAITH BJALOBOK

POUND SEIZURE

Many regional and local authorities in the United States have laws that require local pounds, or give local pounds the option, to turn over to laboratories on demand those animals who remain unclaimed for a specified time after their arrival (typically five days). "Pound seizure" is the legally sanctioned or voluntary release of animals from pounds and shelters to laboratory animal dealers and to research and educational facilities for the purpose of animal experimentation.

The ultimate fate of these animals is nearly always death. However, before these animals reach their end, they may suffer horribly as research subjects. Cats and dogs are most commonly the objects of pound seizure, especially former companion animals, because their trust and friendliness to human touch make them more manageable than strays.

There are also pounds and shelters that voluntarily supply their animals to research facilities or schools as a source of income. Many animals are supplied after they have been euthanized and are sold as dissection specimens. Because these animals would have been put down anyway, the objection arises not so much from the use of their bodies as from the conflict that arises when a shelter has a monetary disincentive to pursue a campaign of reuniting lost animals with their families or to make them available for adoption. If providing dissection specimens (or live animals for research or terminal labs) is a source of income for these facilities, there is a serious risk that these shelters, pounds, and animal care facilities will cater to the interests of the institutions providing that funding. Many people would argue that this constitutes an inherent conflict of interest and a violation of public trust for shelters whose primary responsibility should be protecting the interests of the animals by promoting adoption and responsible care of companion animals.

Although some researchers support pound seizure because it provides relatively cheap and easy access to an apparently unlimited supply of specimens for testing, most scientists feel that such a "random source" of mixed breeds (and unknown histories) provides, at the very least, uncertain subjects for most experiments. Although there is compelling evidence that no nonhuman animal is a suitable model for research on human diseases and physiological functions, the unknown health and genetic backgrounds of random source animals make them especially misleading sources of credible data.

The World Health Organization recommends against the use of random source animals, and the National Institutes of Health, the U.S. agency that funds most biomedical research, has testified before Congress that companion animals are "not a good or desirable research animal." It has also been argued that the system of subjecting pound animals to practice surgeries could be replaced by cooperative programs that make animals available for surgeries that spay or neuter the animals and then return them to the shelter to be adopted—a viable option that benefits both the surgical student and the animal.

Because pound animals are relatively cheap and easy to come by, pound seizure provides experimenters with no incentive to replace their use of animals with humane alternatives. Yet alternatives, such as cell and tissue cultures, realistic mannequins, "virtual reality" simulators, computer models, and other advanced technologies, are available and continue to be developed and validated.

On October 1, 2012, the National Institutes of Health implemented a plan to limit funding to researchers for the use of cats from Class B (random-source) animal dealers, as recommended in a 2009 report issued by the Institute for Laboratory Animal Research. That report found that random-source dogs and cats are not necessary for use in biomedical research because there are adequate numbers of animals available from other sources. In 2011, the NIH implemented a forty-eight-month pilot project to reduce the number of dogs obtained from Class B dealers and to give researchers time to find alternative sources for their dogs.

Although the NIH decision may help to eliminate the use of animals from Class B animal dealers, it is not likely to have an effect on animals taken directly from shelters or on the use of euthanized shelter animals for dissection. It also impacts only federal facilities and federal funding, not state or privately owed entities.

In the United States, Minnesota and Oklahoma require pound seizure of animals in government-run facilities. Seventeen states and the District of Columbia prohibit pound seizure; those states are California, Connecticut, Delaware, Hawaii, Illinois, Maine, Maryland, Massachusetts, New Hampshire, New Jersey, New York, Pennsylvania, Rhode Island, South Carolina, Vermont, Virginia, and West Virginia. Most other states leave regulation of pounds and government-owned shelters to local authorities. Some states, such as Michigan, regulate the selling of animals on a county-to-county basis. In Michigan only one county still permits the sale of pound animals for use in research. There is no federal U.S. law on pound seizure; however, pound seizure is illegal in England, Denmark, Sweden, and Holland.

Animal advocates strongly object to the practice of pound seizure. They maintain that the public should be able to rely on animal shelters to provide ethical, humane treatment for lost or unclaimed animals. They consider it a "double blow" of betrayal against an animal who may have once been a treasured companion and who, for whatever reason, now finds himself separated from his family and caged in a strange environment. Families experience the anguish of wondering whether their lost animal, or one they gave up, may have suffered in a painful experiment. People who can no longer care for their animals may choose to abandon them in fields or by roadsides rather than taking them to a shelter, falsely believing that an animal has a better chance of surviving on his or her own. This merely aggravates the problem of homeless strays, many of whom populate pounds and animal shelters.

Related articles: The alternatives; Animals used in research; Cats; Developments in animal law; Dogs; Euthanasia; Humane research; Shelters and sanctuaries; Stem cell research; Stray animals

Bernard, Neal D., "Pound Seizure," Physicians Committee for Responsible Medicine, available at http://pcrm.org/search/?cid=524.

Groves, Julian McAllister, *Hearts and Minds: The Controversy over Laboratory Animals*, Temple University Press, 1997.

International Institute for Animal Law, "Prohibition on Pound Seizure," 2010, available at http://www.animallaw.com/poundseizuremodellaw.htm.

National Anti-Vivisection Society (U.S.), "Class B Dealers: Who Are They and Why Should They Be Eliminated?," 2011, available at http://www.navs.org/page.aspx?pid=446.

National Anti-Vivisection Society (U.S.), "Pounds Seizure Puts Shelter Dogs in Jeopardy," 2012, available at http://www.navs.org/pages/legal/more-legal/legal—pound-seizure-lm.

National Research Council, Committee on Scientific and Humane Issues in the Use of Random Source Dogs and Cats for Research, *Scientific and Humane Issues in the Use of Random-Source Dogs and Cats in Research*, National Academies Press, 2009, available at http://dels.nas.edu/Report/Scientific-Humane-Issues/12641.

Phillips, Allie, *How Shelter Pets Are Brokered for Experimentation: Understanding Pound Seizure*, Rowman and Littlefield, 2010.

Reitman, Judith, *Stolen for Profit: How the Establishment Is Funding a National Pet-Theft Conspiracy*, Pharos, 1993.

PEGGY CUNNIFF, MARCIA KRAMER, AND ALEXANDRA BERNSTEIN

PUPPY MILLS

Each year, millions of dogs are killed in animal shelters while at the same time "puppy mills," also known as "commercial breeders" in the eyes of the U.S. government, breed thousands of puppies a year for sale to "pet shops" across the United States, Canada, Asia, and Europe. A puppy mill is a place where several breeds of dogs are raised, and the breeder always has puppies for sale; dogs are bred solely for financial gain, with little or no regard for breed integrity. Most of the dogs are forced to live their entire lives in dark warehouses, in tiny, crowded, and indescribably filthy conditions. Females are bred continuously until they die, or until they can no longer produce "profit" for the mills. Puppy mills exploit pregnancy for profit.

Most puppies sold in stores come from these breeding farms. The female dogs (bitches) and male dogs (studs) spend lonely lives in small, barren cages, producing one litter after another. Most cages have wire floors, allowing the urine and feces to fall through and into the cage directly below. There is little protection from the hot summers or the cold winters and little or no veterinary care. Crusted, oozing eyes; ear infections; mange that turns skin into a mass of red scabs; abscessed feet from the wire floors—all are common sights.

Such appalling conditions inevitably lead to serious problems. By the time puppy mill puppies are shipped to stores, many are suffering from ear infections, bronchial illness, and serious congenital health conditions, such as hip deformities, epilepsy, and vision or hearing deficiencies. People who pay hundreds of dollars for puppies often find that they must spend thousands more on veterinary care.

After World War II, when farmers were desperately seeking alternative methods of making money after traditional crops had failed, the United States Department of Agriculture (USDA) encouraged the raising of puppies as a crop. Retail outlets grew in number as the supply of puppies increased. However, the puppy farmers had little knowledge of canine husbandry and often began their ventures with little money and already-rundown facilities. They housed their dogs in chicken coops and rabbit hutches, provided little socialization, and often eschewed veterinary care because they could not afford to pay.

The appalling conditions that existed in puppy mills were a major force behind the passage of the U.S. Animal Welfare Act of 1966. However, as so often happens, the intention of the legislation was weakened, and the appellation was widened to include any breeder who breeds lots of dogs, no matter what the conditions of the kennel or the health of the puppies. The USDA licensed more than 4,600 animal dealers in 1991. There are almost 11,000 facilities licensed in the United States. Animal shelters nationwide euthanize around eight to twelve million unwanted dogs annually. The care, feeding, and ultimate euthanasia of otherwise healthy, throwaway dogs in public and private nonprofit animal shelters involve considerable public expense. The expense constitutes a massive public subsidy for the so-called pet industry as it persists in breeding puppies by the hundreds of thousands each year.

What, then, should be done to remedy this sad situation? We need to educate the general public about the conditions in puppy mills, the complicity of retail stores, and the risks they are running when they buy such animals. The number of puppy breeding farms that wholesale their "products" to USDA-approved brokers, which in turn sell the puppies to stores, is growing. Mills use female dogs repeatedly for breeding, without any regard for their well-being or quality of life. The illusion is created that the store consumer is receiving a well-bred, healthy puppy, which constitutes nothing less than a fraud on the buying public. In fact, breeding is frequently indiscriminate, and little thought is given to eliminating breed-specific genetic disorders. The puppies are bereft of adequate socialization, which is the cause of many subsequent behavior problems.

It is essential that people adopt their canine companions from the many shelters or rescue groups that have given these dogs another chance at life by rehabilitating them and providing them with veterinary care. Only by encouraging people not to buy animals in stores will we begin to curb the trade and stop the suffering.

_____

Related articles: The concept of guardianship; Dogs; The ethics of commercialization; Euthanasia; Humane education; Selective breeding; Shelters and sanctuaries

American Society for the Prevention of Cruelty to Animals, "What Is a Puppy Mill?," 2010, available at http://www.puppymills.com/.

Humane Society of the United States, "Puppy Mills," 2011, available at http://www.humanesociety.org/issues/puppy_mills/.

O'Neil, Jacqueline, *Second Start: Creative Rehoming for Dogs*, Simon and Schuster, 1997.

Patterson, Shirley, "What Is a Puppy Mill and How Can You Stop Them?," 2010, available at http://www.puppymills.com/.

United Hearts for Animals, "Puppy Mills Breed Misery," 2010, available at http://www.hua.org/about-puppy-mills.html.

Walker, Joan Hustace, *Dog Adoption: A Guide to Choosing the Perfect "Preowned,"* Ics Books, 1997.

CAROL B. JOHNSON

SELECTIVE BREEDING

"Selective" dog breeding involves breeding only from animals who have specific "desirable" traits. For centuries, dogs were primarily bred to work and so were bred for fitness and health rather than appearance. In the nineteenth century, this changed, largely because of the growing popularity of dog showing. By the beginning of the twenty-first century, there were over thirty thousand people showing dogs as a hobby in the United Kingdom and hundreds of thousands doing so worldwide.

Breeding to produce show dogs has had a profound effect on the appearance and well-being of the animals. Each breed has a "breed standard" that provides a template of the "perfect" physical specimen, resulting in dog breeders selectively breeding based on the physique of the animal, with less consideration given to the health and temperamental stability of the dog. In many breeds, the animals' anatomical features are now so exaggerated that the animals' general health and welfare are damaged.

For several decades, animal welfare organizations worldwide have been concerned that this type of selective breeding is responsible for the suffering of many pedigree dogs. In 2006, Advocates for Animals and the Companion Animal Welfare Council both undertook reviews to examine the extent of the suffering these breed practices caused. In 2007, the Royal Society for the Prevention of Cruelty to Animals (RSPCA) commissioned an independent review of such practices. The review took two years to complete, and when published, the findings were damning. The study examined both the primary problems caused by breeding for specific exaggerated physical features and the genetic "side effects" of breeding animals to conform to the "ideal" physical specimen.

The review found that exaggerated physical traits were causing welfare issues, and all breeds were negatively affected to some degree. One type of exaggerated anatomy causing particular suffering is brachycephalic abnormality (dogs with a disproportionately flat face and broad skull). Examples of affected breeds are the English bulldog, pug, and bullmastiff. In affected breeds, many animals were found to be suffering from breathing difficulties and abnormality of the tear ducts. In addition, pregnant dogs often required surgical intervention when whelping because the pups' skulls were too large to be delivered naturally. Joint, ophthalmic, gastric, skeletal, and skin disorders were also identified as direct results of dogs being bred with exaggerated physical features.

Moreover, it was concluded that the breeding of exaggerated anatomical traits could also cause behavioral and interactional problems. Dogs communicate primarily with body language and posture, and some breeds now have such abnormal physical features that their ability to communicate with other dogs is negatively impacted.

A secondary effect of breeding dogs primarily for their morphology is an increased prevalence of genetic susceptibility to a huge range of diseases, as well as temperament problems. Breeding for specific physical traits, by its nature, reduces the genetic diversity of any given breed. The reduction of the gene pool is often made worse by the practice of "line-breeding," which involves breeding related dogs over many generations to preserve "desirable" physical traits. Over generations, the reduction in genetic diversity within a breed becomes so great that almost every individual dog is related at the genetic level. The agreement of most national kennel clubs to register puppies born from first- and second-degree relatives mating, but refusal to register "outcrossed" dogs who have been bred to a different breed and then bred back to their own to increase genetic diversity, compounds this problem.

Because of selective breeding practices, every breed has an increased susceptibility to genetic disorders, with a high risk of recessive conditions (where both parents have to carry the defective gene for their puppies to develop the disease). Although on average each breed is affected by between four and eight genetic conditions, in the most inbred breeds, this figure can be significantly greater.

Causing harm to animals for the purpose of breeding specific types is ethically unacceptable. The RSPCA has put forward a range of steps that must be taken in order to improve the health and help safeguard the welfare of pedigree dogs. A critical first step must be taken by kennel clubs globally—refusal to register the progeny of matings between first- and second-degree relatives. Further, they must set limits on the number of times any one dog is allowed to stand at stud. Additionally, they need to encourage improvement of genetic diversity by opening their stud books to allow outcrossing, thus significantly expanding the gene pool and reducing the prevalence of genetic disorders.

It is vital that dog breeders act responsibly, breeding only from healthy, temperamentally sound dogs whose lineage is as diverse as possible. Breed clubs should work alongside the kennel clubs to ensure that breed standards are amended to actively discourage exaggerated morphology and include health and temperament requirements. Breed clubs are also ideally placed to oversee the implementation of testing among the breeding population for breed-specific diseases and to organize further studies of such diseases. Welfare organizations and veterinary professionals can also improve the situation by monitoring the health of pedigree dogs and by educating the public about the health and welfare problems associated with the selective breeding of dogs.

Unless all parties concerned with pedigree dog welfare act together, the future well-being of many pedigree breeds cannot be assured.

Related articles: Cosmetic surgery; Dogs; The ethics of commercialization; A lifelong responsibility

Advocates for Animals, *The Price of Pedigree: Dog Bred Standards and Breed-Related Illnesses*, 2006.

Companion Animal Welfare Council, *Breeding and Welfare in Companion Animals*, 2006.

Gough, A., and Thomas, A., *Breed Predispositions to Disease in Dogs and Cats*, Blackwell, 2004.

McGreevy, P. D., "Breeding for Quality of Life," *Animal Welfare* 16 (2007): 125–128.

McGreevy, P. D., and Nicholas, F. W., "Some Practical Solutions to Welfare Problems in Dog Breeding," *Animal Welfare* 8 (1999): 329–341.

Rooney, Nicola, and Sargon, David, *Pedigree Dog Breeding in the U.K.: A Major Welfare Concern?*, commissioned review, Royal Society for the Prevention of Cruelty to Animal, 2009.

ABBEY ANNE SMITH

STRAY ANIMALS

Italy, like most European countries, has a considerable stray animal population, and it is this particular country's situation on which this discussion focuses. There are nearly seven million dogs and eight and a half million cats in Italy, of which over a million and a quarter are stray cats and over 800,000 are stray dogs. According to the organization Animalisti Italiani, approximately 150,000 dogs and 200,000 cats are abandoned every year. It is worth focusing on the situation in Italy because it is the one European country that both has a huge problem and has made serious attempts to remedy it.

Until 1991, animal advocacy organizations such as the National Institute for the Prevention of Cruelty to Animals, the National League for the Defense of the Dog, and the Anti-Vivisection League were the main agencies dealing with stray animals. On their shoulders rested the care of strays and the management of shelters, adoption, education, and rehoming, as well as neutering and spaying programs. The small number of state pounds kept animals for only a few days before euthanizing them.

In 1991, the Italian government passed the Defense of Pets and Stray Prevention Act. The routine euthanasia of strays was outlawed. A dog registration program was introduced. For the first time, caregivers became legally responsible for their companion animals. Caregivers who abandoned their animals, or who did not microchip their animals to establish identity, were subject to prosecution and could be fined. The law obligated local and regional authorities to collect strays, to establish animal shelters or support existing ones, to pioneer neutering and spaying programs, and to provide education for caregivers of companion animals.

Despite these welcome—and indeed radical—measures, the outcome was not entirely positive. Within a short period of time, there was a massive overcrowding of shelters. A government fund was set up to help establish private shelters, but this has resulted in the proliferation of poorly run establishments often managed by people whose interest is wholly commercial and who have little care for, or understanding of, animal welfare. Ten years later, the health minister, Umberto Veronesi, issued a circular seeking to address some of the problems associated with the implementation of the 1991 act. In response to campaigning from animal associations, he made clear that future financial support for shelters should be based on animal welfare criteria, rather than purely economic criteria.

Figures produced by the police and the health ministry show that there has been considerable abuse of strays in shelters, including even cruelty. According to data provided by the Anti-Vivisection League and NAS (the "anti-sophistication" branch of the Italian police, the duty of which is not only to control the quality of food, but also to investigate cruelty against animals and so on), of 78 private shelters that were inspected, 14 were deemed unsatisfactory, and out of 133 state-sponsored shelters, 30 were also judged unacceptable. Unsatisfactory shelters were engaged in either administrative irregularities or criminal activity.

Specifically, strays are often used for dog fighting, which has become a major problem throughout Italy. Although dog fighting is illegal, criminal organizations continue to organize underground fights where huge sums of money are bet on the outcome. Criminal activity involving animals is known in Italy as "zoomafia," and it includes not only dog fighting but also a range of other activities, such as illegal horse racing and the sale of exotic species. The zoomafia has profited from the abundance of stray animals in shelters, who are now regularly sold for dog fighting throughout Italy.

So Italy has to contend not only with a huge stray animal population, but also with an increasingly profitable and well-organized zoomafia that has been assisted by the growth of well-meaning but, in practice, often rather unscrupulous government-funded animal shelters. It seems that even as we deal with one form of abuse, another one—equally, if not more, abhorrent—emerges. One welcome result, however, is that the animal protection community in Italy has at last begun to realize the scale of the problem and the need for urgent action. Animal organizations are now better organized than ever before with the support of mailing lists, Web sites, and an active system for reporting abuse. Certainly, it will take time—probably years—to rectify the present situation, but the increasing sensibility of the Italian government, along with its preparedness to enforce animal welfare legislation, heralds a better future for the cause of animals.

The Berlusconi government initiated various measures in the field of animal protection. In particular, the Ministry of Health has considerably enlarged its site, adding a part on animal rights, protection of animals, defense of animal welfare, abandonment, and stray animals, as well as traveling with animals. The undersecretary for health, Francesca Martini, has signed many ordinances, including an important ordinance on August 6, 2008, calling for "the identification and registration of the canine population," nationally regulating the regional canine registry, microchipping, and the control of stray animals. A December 18, 2008, ordinance—containing "standards on the prohibition of the use and possession of bait or poisoned treats"—is designed to counter the poisoning of stray animals.

On May 21, 2010, a task force was created to combat the stray animal problem and the private kennels where dogs are severely ill-treated and for the defense of diseased animals; the task force consists of ten veterinarians and four officials and operates in collaboration with the Carabinieri (police force) and with all authorities and associations responsible for enforcing animal protection laws in the territory. Unfortunately, there are still areas in Italy, particularly in the south, where stray animals constitute a very serious problem; in some areas remedy is sought by killing strays with poisoned treats or with rifles, both of which are officially banned. The minister of tourism, Michela Vittoria Brambilla, has created a government site titled "Four Legged Tourists," offering lots of useful information for caregivers of companion animals who want to go on vacation, as well as a current list of all facilities available to house animals.

The well-intentioned laws need to be strictly policed and enforced. They need to impact those who have no regard for animals (as well as those who do), who may comply if only for fear of facing the appropriate penalties.

Related articles: Cats; CITES and international trade; The concept of guardianship; Developments in animal law; Dog fighting; Dogs; The ethics of commercialization; European animal protection; Euthanasia; Feral cats; Humane education; Jumps racing; Microchipping; Neutering and spaying; Shelters and sanctuaries; The universal charter of the rights of other species

Amministrazione Provinciale di Savona (ed.), *Atti della giornata di studio su: Il randagismo degli animali. Aspetti sanitari, legali, ecologici e zoofili*, 1988.

Boitani, L., and Fabbri, M. L., *Censimento dei cani in Italia con particolare riguardo al fenomeno del randagismo*, Ricerche di Biologia della Selvaggina, 1983.

Luciano, Menini, *Una città per tutti*, ULSS n. 25 della Regione Veneto, 1994.

Marchesini, Roberto, *Il canile come presidio zooantropologico. Da struttura problema a centro di valorizzazione del rapporto con il cane*, Edizioni Medico-Scientifiche, 2007.

Mazziotti, Anna, *Voci di canili*, Helicon, 2002.

Meyer, Edgard Helmut, and Apuzzo, Stefano, *Qua la zampa. Breviario legale e pratico per cani, gatti ed altri animali*, Edizioni Stampa Alternativa, 2006.

BRUNO MANZINI

five

AREAS OF WORLDWIDE CONCERN

This section concentrates on three areas of global concern: animals in farming, animals in research, and the use of animals for "sport" and recreation.

By far the most significant (numerically) are the animals utilized in agriculture. Billions of land animals and aquatic animals are raised and slaughtered every year for human consumption worldwide. Yet securing even minimal welfare standards for these animals is an immense global challenge. Through the intensification of farming since the 1960s, animals have been crowded into smaller and smaller units, where their behavioral needs cannot be adequately met, which causes stress, frustration, abnormal behaviors, and both mental and physical suffering. Our first subsection examines the plight of farmed animals worldwide—from fishes to sheep—and highlights the most problematic uses.

The second subsection focuses on animals used in research. Accurate figures are not available for the numbers used worldwide, but the total number is around 500 million. Animal testing is a global cause of concern, and the various articles detail the kinds of species used and the range of experiments in which they are used, including product testing, tests for toxicity, cloning, genetic manipulation, and military purposes. Most welcome is the advent of reliable alternatives to traditional testing and perhaps the emergence of stem cell research, but without accurate, publicly accessible information, it is not always easy to scrutinize the effectiveness of experiments. In any case, the ethical issue of whether it is right to inflict suffering on animals cannot be avoided.

Our third subsection catalogs the uses of animals for entertainment and for "sport." "Sport" is by definition a game between equally or nearly equally matched partners, but that can hardly be said to be the case in the practices detailed here, in which animals are unevenly matched against their human persecutors. Killing for entertainment is surely one of the least justifiable things we do to animals, and the catalog of cruelty in this subsection is disturbing.

ANDREW LINZEY

ANIMALS IN FARMING

ANIMAL WELFARE AND FARMING

One of the first things that should strike anyone who thinks about animal welfare is the low level of concern for farmed animals compared with the concern for companion animals (*see* Companion Animals) or even free-living animals (*see* Free-Living Animals). In most of the developed world, for example, a pregnant sow—an intelligent and social animal—can be immobilized in a stall so short and narrow that it almost touches her for four months of pregnancy. Such treatment would be unthinkable (and illegal) for a canine companion. But farmed animals, in most humans' view, exist to provide us with food and thus are often destined for an early death. And the numbers are huge. In the United Kingdom alone, nearly 28 million mammals (cattle, sheep, and pigs) and 870 million poultry are slaughtered annually.

And how do farmed animals live before slaughter? Some, mostly sheep and cattle, still live much of their lives grazing on free-range farms. But the vast majority of farmed animals (especially pigs, poultry, and now also fishes) are in intensive (or "factory") farms. When it began, the intensification of animal production was seen as essential to national food security and a better diet for all. Increased production of meat, milk, and eggs resulted, but the animals have paid a high price. For our convenience, and in the name of cheap food, farmed animals were shoehorned into what were seen as efficient production systems.

In the name of efficiency, we invented narrow veal crates for calves, in which they could not turn around; battery cages for laying hens, in which they could not stretch their wings; narrow stalls for pregnant sows; concrete pens for the fattening of piglets; and barren sheds for tens of thousands of chickens raised for meat. This "efficiency" often means housing animals on slatted wire or concrete floors, without bedding, daylight, or fresh air. These production systems often prevent exercise and many aspects of natural behavior, such as exploration, foraging, and social interaction.

Confinement and crowding inevitably lead to frustration, aggression, injury, and disease. Laying hens in battery cages, for example, cannot build a nest, which is one of their basic behavioral needs. Sows kept in narrow stalls suffer from chronic stress and from lameness. Hens used for egg laying often develop osteoporosis and suffer broken bones. Overcrowded piglets have their tails cut off (without anesthetic) to discourage them from biting each other. The production of specialized animals who have ever more offspring or yield more muscle, milk, or eggs can put an enormous strain on the animals' bodies. Chickens raised for meat, bred to grow unnaturally fast, suffer from deformed legs and heart failure. Fifty years after the advent of intensification, such farming now looks more and more like the problem rather than the solution. Because intensification invariably increases stress, farmed animals are more liable to disease. There has been public dismay over bovine spongiform encephalopathy (BSE, commonly referred to as mad cow disease), foot-and-mouth disease, swine fever, and avian influenza (bird flu) in the United Kingdom, in Europe, and worldwide. All this has coincided with more and more evidence of the mental and emotional complexity of animals' lives and the welfare problems caused by intensification.

In the United Kingdom and Europe, there has been legal progress toward dismantling some of the worst aspects of intensive farming. The European Union has banned narrow veal crates for calves, some forms of cages for laying hens as of 2012, and sow stalls (gestation crates) for most of the pregnancy of breeding sows starting in 2013. Several U.S. states have now legislated along the same lines, and some important food companies have stopped using eggs and other products from these very intensive systems, as a result of consumer concerns.

But there is still much that needs to be changed. Fundamentally, we need to recover a new sense of responsibility for animals raised for food, animals who are totally under our control. Animals are not just economic commodities; they are sentient individuals. We must ensure that they have the best life possible. Specifically, there should be a fundamental recognition that all farmed animals require access to the outdoors, enough space for exercise and exploration, comfortable bedding, and the social interaction natural to their species. They should not be made to grow or produce at a rate that damages their health. These changes alone will require a radical reform of animal farming.

Farmed animal welfare needs to become a priority, for consumers especially. Many farmers now say they would prefer to farm in a more animal-friendly way, if consumers would be willing to pay a little more for higher-welfare products. We can all help by educating ourselves, persuading others, and crucially, using our purchasing power.

Related articles: Animals and public health; Birds used in food production; Caring shopping; The complexity of animal awareness; Fish farming; Humane education; Legislation in the European Union; Slaughter; The welfare of cows; The welfare of pigs; The welfare of sheep

Broom, D. M., and Fraser, A. F., *Domestic Animal Behaviour and Welfare*, 4th ed., CABI, 2007.
Compassion in World Farming, *Stop, Look, Listen: Recognising the Sentience of Farm Animals*, 2006, available at http://www.ciwf.org.uk.
Keeling, L. J., and Gonyou, H. W. (eds.), *Social Behaviour in Farm Animals*, CABI, 2001.
Turner, Jacky, *Animal Breeding, Welfare and Society*, Earthscan, 2010.
Webster, John, *Animal Welfare: Limping towards Eden*, Blackwell, 2005.
Young, Rosamund, *The Secret Life of Cows*, Farming Books and Videos, 2003.

JACKY TURNER

BIRDS USED IN FOOD PRODUCTION

Chickens, turkeys, and ducks have a zest for living and enjoying the day. Treated with respect, they are friendly, sociable birds with an appealing sense of independence. At a distance, turkeys look like otherworldly visitors moving gracefully through the grass. Up close, one sees their large, dark, almond-shaped eyes and sensitive fine-boned faces. Chickens enjoy being together in small flocks, sunning, dustbathing, and scratching in the soil for food. A mother hen will fiercely protect her young brood, driving off predators and sheltering her little chicks beneath her wings. The rooster keeps watch over the flock. He calls the hens if he senses danger, and when he finds a tasty morsel for them to share, he lets them know—"chook-

chook-chook-chook-chook!" The hens flit, fly, and race through the grass to see what banquet awaits them.

Ducks are creatures who have evolved to eat, swim, dive, clean, and play in the water. They need to dunk their heads in water frequently for the health of their eyes. At our bird sanctuary in Virginia, in the United States, running the hose and filling the swimming pool each day is a ritual that elicits shrieks of delight from our white Pekin ducks, who quack a quite different tune if this ritual is delayed too long. As the hose starts running, the ducks move in, sucking up food from the watery mud with their bills and smacking their feet in it. The chickens wade in and scratch for the food the water churns up in the grassy pools. The turkeys, who by nature are water-loving birds who can swim, sip deeply and pipe their flute notes, while following the rivulets through the grass along with the chickens.

These birds are not "wild." They are modern "food production" birds who were rescued from the barren factory conditions to which they were said to be "behaviorally adapted" and "genetically suited"—that is, after they were locked up in buildings and cages full of toxic excretory ammonia fumes from which they could not escape.

Chickens were the first farmed animals to be permanently confined indoors in large numbers in automated systems based on intensive genetic selection, antibiotics, and drugs. Until World War II, chickens were raised in towns and villages and on farms, and many city people kept chickens in back lots. Following the war, the U.S. chicken industry became the model for poultry production throughout the world. Chickens were genetically divided into two distinct types—broiler chickens for meat production and laying hens for egg production. Battery cages for laying hens—identical units of confinement arranged in rows and tiers—and confinement sheds for broiler chickens (a "broiler" chicken is a six- to seven-week-old baby bird) came into standard use in the 1940s and 1950s.

The turkey and duck industries took a similar course. Whereas the domesticated chicken derives from the jungle fowl of southeast Asia, and most farmed ducks (primarily Pekins) are descended from the free-living mallard duck, the domesticated turkey derives from imported Bronze and Black turkeys from Europe who were crossed with the "wild" turkeys of America at the beginning of the nineteenth century. As the poultry industry expanded, birds genetically selected for breast meat and fast growth had mating problems, which led both to the adoption of artificial insemination, which is now the sole method of mass-producing turkeys for human consumption, and to "skip-a-day" diets for chickens used for breeding. Modern "meat-type" birds are susceptible to heart and breathing problems and to painful lameness so severe that, in scientific studies, chickens choose food laced with pain-relieving drugs over nonmedicated food.

To date, there are no welfare laws for poultry in the United States, and Canada's weak welfare laws, mandatory in only a few provinces, are poorly enforced. A California law, scheduled for implementation in 2015, may or may not eliminate battery cages for egg-laying hens in that and other states. The U.S. Humane Methods of Slaughter Act excludes birds, even though 99 percent of animals slaughtered for food in the United States each year are birds, mainly chickens—conservatively, nine billion of ten billion total land animals slaughtered in 2009. In the United Kingdom, where some poultry companies gas the birds to death or into a reputed state of unconsciousness during the slaughter process, the majority of birds are administered painful pre-slaughter electric shocks, as they are in the United States; these shocks are intended to induce muscular paralysis rather than stun the fully conscious birds, so that their feathers can be pulled out more easily after they are dead, and to prevent "unsightly" hemorrhage in the meat sold to consumers. Laying hens in the United States are debeaked and deprived of food or vital nutrients for up to two weeks in order to manipulate the economics of egg production, and millions of "spent" hens are buried alive, shipped to live poultry markets and spent fowl plants, or trucked to Canada at the end of their laying cycles for destruction. Egg-type male chicks are destroyed throughout the world as soon as they hatch for lack of commercial value.

The only sure way of avoiding such exploitation is for people to remove poultry and eggs from their diet and discover the variety of vegan alternatives to animal products. Welfare reforms can do only so much given the huge number of birds involved in a global industry that slaughters more than forty billion chickens for meat each year and given that the poultry industry, even in countries where welfare laws may exist, is for all practical purposes ungovernable. Compassion over cruelty and killing is in the hands of each person; each of us determines the fate of these animals at the cash register and in the kitchen.

Related articles: Developments in animal law; Live animal exports; Live pigeon shoots; Live quail shoots; Pigeon racing; The production of foie gras; The protection of birds; Sanctuaries and rehabilitation; Slaughter; Transgenic animals; Vegan living

Davis, Karen, "Chicken-Human Relationships: From Procrustean Genocide to Empathic Anthropomorphism," in Bradshaw, G. A., and Cater, Nancy (eds.), "Minding the Animal Psyche," special issue, *Spring: A Journal of Archetype and Culture* 83 (2010): 253–278.

——, *The Holocaust and the Henmaid's Tale: A Case for Comparing Atrocities*, Lantern Books, 2005.

——, *More Than a Meal: The Turkey in History, Myth, Ritual, and Reality*, Lantern Books, 2001.

——, *Prisoned Chickens, Poisoned Eggs: An Inside Look at the Modern Poultry Industry*, Book Publishing Company, 2009.

——, "Procrustean Solutions to Animal Identity and Welfare Problems," in Sanbonmatsu, John (ed.), *Critical Theory and Animal Liberation*, Rowman and Littlefield, 2011.

——, "Thinking Like a Chicken: Farm Animals and the Feminine Connection," in Adams, Carol J., and Donovan, Josephine (eds.), *Animals and Women: Feminist Theoretical Explorations*, Duke University Press, 1995, 192–212.

KAREN DAVIS

FISH FARMING

Tucked along remote coastlines, or discreet river valleys, lies one of the fastest-growing sectors of intensive animal rearing—fish farming. Up to fifty thousand salmon can be crowded into a single sea cage, where they often swim in constant circles, like caged zoo animals. Often suffering blinding cataracts, fin and tail injuries, body deformities, alarmingly high mortality, and infestation with parasites, the "king of fish" is now raised intensively in factory farms under the sea. And the situation can be even worse for farmed trout, who are often packed into tanks or ponds up to three times more tightly than salmon.

Major farmed salmon–producing nations worldwide include the United States, Norway, Scotland, Canada, Chile, Japan, Iceland, and New Zealand.

Caged and crowded

Fish farms can be as intensive as anything found on terra firma. Crowding and confinement can cause fishes to suffer stress, leading to greater susceptibility to disease. Wave after wave of serious disease outbreaks has caused the deaths of millions of farmed salmon. Official figures have shown overall death rates of 10 to 30 percent. Such high mortality would raise alarm bells in other types of animal farming.

Infested with parasites

Intensive farming has led to serious infestation with parasitic sea lice, which can cause considerable suffering and death in affected fishes. These small crustaceans feed on the host salmon. Lice damage can be so severe around the head that the living fish's skull is exposed—a condition known as the "death crown."

Current treatments include the use of strong nerve toxins. The fishes are crammed together and bathed in organophosphates, or synthetic pyrethroids, or they receive chemical treatments in their feed. Other methods include bathing fishes in the irritant hydrogen peroxide or using another type of fish, the wrasse, as a "cleaner" to literally eat the lice off the backs of the salmon. Mortality for the wrasse can be as high as 50 percent, partly because of the stress of capture and transport. Others die from bullying or being eaten by salmon cage-mates, or through starvation in the winter at the low point of the sea-louse life cycle.

Trout

About 125 million trout are raised and killed in Norway each year. Other big European trout farming countries include Italy, Denmark, Germany, Finland, Spain, and the United Kingdom. Trout are often crammed—even more tightly than salmon—into freshwater ponds or concrete tanks called "raceways" with fast-flowing water. They can be stocked at thirty to sixty kilograms of fish per cubic meter of water. Such high stocking densities lead to high levels of fin and tail injuries.

Starvation and slaughter

About 35 million salmon and roughly the same number of trout are slaughtered annually in the United Kingdom. That is more animals than almost all the pigs, sheep, cattle, and turkeys put together. They are often starved for about three to ten days before slaughter.

Slaughter methods for trout include the suffocation of fishes in air or on ice. The cooling effect of the ice prolongs the time it takes for suffocating fishes to become unconscious. They can still be conscious as long as fifteen minutes after their removal from the water. Another inhumane slaughter method often used for both salmon and trout is carbon dioxide stunning. The fishes are placed in a bath of carbon dioxide–saturated water, which causes them to thrash around. After thirty seconds, they stop moving, but they do not lose consciousness for four to nine minutes. The danger is that when their gills are cut with a knife as part of the slaughter process, the fishes may be immobile but still conscious as they bleed to death.

There have been some moves to improve welfare at slaughter. U.K. retailers surveyed now insist that salmon be killed using more humane percussive stunning techniques, whereby a single blow to the head kills the fishes, and that trout be stunned this way or be electrocuted.

The World Organisation for Animal Health (OIE) is developing guidelines for the humane killing of fishes.

Declining salmon

It is often claimed that fish farming takes the pressure off unfarmed fishes by providing an alternative. However, the reverse is true. Farmed fishes are fed free-ranging fishes in the form of fish meal. Over three tons of free-caught fishes are needed to produce one ton of farmed salmon. Salmon farming has been blamed for declines of free-living populations. Competition from fish farm escapees for food and breeding, together with the transmission of diseases and parasites to free-living fishes, has been linked to population crashes of unfarmed salmon in areas with large numbers of fish farms.

Intensive fish farming has resulted in salmon and trout being readily available at the supermarket checkout. However, the true cost includes suffering fishes and a damaged environment. Consumers can help stop the "cage rage" of factory fish farming by avoiding farmed fishes.

Related articles: Angling for sport; Animals and public health; Sea fishes and commercial fishing; Slaughter

Ashley, P. J., "Fish Welfare: Current Issues in Aquaculture," *Applied Animal Behaviour Science* (2006), available at http://www.flinders.edu.au/about_research_files/Documents/Info%20for%20Research/Ethics%20and%20Biosafety/AWC/AquacultureWelfare.pdf.
European Food Safety Authority, "General Approach to Fish Welfare and to the Concept of Sentience in Fish," *EFSA Journal* 954 (2009): 1–27.
Huntingford, F. A., Adams, C., Braithwaite, V. A., Kadri, S., Pottinger, T. G., Sandoe, P., and Turnbull, J. F., "Review Paper: Current Issues in Fish Welfare," *Journal of Fish Biology* 68.2 (2006): 332–372.
Stevenson, P., *Closed Waters: The Welfare of Farmed Atlantic Salmon, Rainbow Trout, Atlantic Cod and Atlantic Halibut*, Compassion in World Farming and World Society for the Protection of Animals, 2007, available at http://www.ciwf.org/publications.

PHILIP LYMBERY

FUR FARMING

More than fifty million minks (*Mustela vison*) and three million foxes (mostly Arctic fox, *Alopex lagopus*) are bred to meet the worldwide demand for their skins. According to fur trade sources, European countries—especially

Denmark, the Netherlands, Finland, and Norway—head the list of producers, but China is rapidly catching up. Other fur farming countries include Russia, the Baltic States, Poland, Argentina, Canada, and the United States.

The methods used in this form of intensive husbandry are essentially uniform across the globe. Minks and foxes are kept in rows of barren wire cages in open-sided sheds. A typical mink cage measures 85 centimeters long, 40 centimeters wide, and 45 centimeters high, and a cage for two Arctic foxes typically measures 110 centimeters square. A mink cage is never longer than a person's arm, and the conditions in which the animals are kept meet the operators' demands for efficiency rather than the animals' needs. The killing is carried out immediately after the animals' first winter's molt, when their fur is at its prime. The main methods used are gassing (for minks) and electrocution (for foxes).

Confining such animals in battery-like cages drives them to perform repetitive, stereotyped behavior; self-mutilation; and even cannibalism. The Farm Animal Welfare Council, a U.K. government advisory body, registered its disapproval as early as 1989 on welfare grounds and described minks and foxes as still "essentially wild" creatures. Subsequent research by A. J. Nimon and D. M. Broom has reinforced the view that fur-farmed animals suffer from poor welfare ("Welfare of Farmed Mink" 205, 222; "Welfare of Farmed Foxes" 223, 241–244).

The Scientific Committee on Animal Health and Animal Welfare of the European Union concluded that areas of concern, with respect to the welfare of minks, include gastric ulcers, kidney abnormalities, tooth decay, self-mutilation, and stereotypies. And foxes do not fare any better, since they suffer from abnormal behaviors such as "exaggerated fear responses, infanticide, stereotypies and pelt-biting." The report concluded that "current husbandry systems cause serious problems for all species of animals reared for fur" (71, 84–88, 185). The fact is fur farming imposes suffering on the animals concerned and for relatively trivial purposes.

Nevertheless, some commentators have sought to justify fur farming and the fur trade. Richard D. North, for example, holds that fur is a luxury and tries to defend it, arguing that "the need for luxury is one of the most fundamental human urges, as it is one of the most powerful well-springs of activity in the whole animal kingdom" (23). But in the face of the suffering of millions of animals every year, it is difficult to take such claims seriously. Even from a utilitarian cost-benefit perspective, the argument fails and spectacularly so.

An increasing number of European countries are legislating against fur farming. The Westminster Parliament banned it in England and Wales in 2000 on the grounds of "public morality." Scotland soon followed. Austria has also banned fur farming, and fox farming is banned in the Netherlands and Sweden. Similarly, Italy imposed new welfare standards in 2001 (which came into force in 2008) that are so stringent that it is doubtful that fur farming can survive. But elsewhere fur farming remains big business, and the fur trade continues to expand.

Related articles: Animals in Chinese culture; Challenges to animal protection in Scandinavia; The emergence of animal protection in Russia; The fur trade; The humane movement in Canada; Legislation in the European Union; The moral claims of animals; Progress in animal welfare; Slaughter; South American perspectives on animals

Linzey, Andrew, *The Ethical Case against Fur Farming*, Respect for Animals, 2002.
———, "Fur Farming," in *Why Animal Suffering Matters: Philosophy, Theology and Practical Ethics*, Oxford University Press, 2009, 97–114.
Nimon, A. J., and Broom, D. M., "The Welfare of Farmed Foxes *Vulpes vulpes* and *Alopex lagopus* in Relation to Housing and Management: A Review," *Animal Welfare* 10 (2001).
———, "The Welfare of Farmed Mink (*Mustela vison*), in Relation to Housing and Management: A Review," *Animal Welfare* 9 (1999).
North, Richard D., *Fur and Freedom: In Defence of the Fur Trade*, Institute of Economic Affairs, 2000.
Scientific Committee on Animal Health and Animal Welfare, *The Welfare of Animals Kept for Fur Production*, European Commission, Health and Consumer Protection Directorate-General, 2001.

ANDREW LINZEY AND MARK GLOVER

HORSE SLAUGHTER

Horse slaughter refers to the practice of killing horses to use their meat for human consumption. People in many countries consider horse meat a delicacy. However, in countries such as Kazakhstan and Mongolia, horse meat is a staple of the population's diet. Horses are slaughtered and eaten in a variety of countries, including Japan, the Netherlands, Germany, France, Canada, Mexico, Chile, Poland, Senegal, Spain, and Italy.

Horse meat is not eaten in the United States largely because of the iconic status Americans afford the horse. American and Canadian horses destined for slaughter are sold by their owners at auctions, where kill buyers bid against private individuals. Horses purchased by kill buyers are loaded onto trailers and shipped to slaughter facilities. In other countries such as the Netherlands, some horses, much like cattle, are raised for meat. In Kazakhstan the horse's throat is slit by the local butcher. In countries utilizing assembly-line slaughter, the most widely used method of killing is the captive bolt. This instrument shoots a rod into the horse's brain. The goal is to render the horse unconscious before the dismemberment process begins.

However, recent videos released by U.S.-based Animals' Angels, GAIA (Global Action in the Interests of Animals), and the Canadian Horse Defence Coalition have shown conscious horses being dismembered and other instances of abuse at horse slaughtering facilities in Mexico, Canada, and South America. In response to the airing of these videos, several Belgian markets have pulled horse meat from their stores' shelves. Worldwide, animal organizations are pushing for bans on horse slaughter because of the inherent cruelty. Many of them argue there is no humane way to mass-slaughter horses for human consumption.

Currently, there are no operating horse slaughter facilities in the United States. However, it is estimated by the Equine Welfare Alliance that during 2012, a total of 176,223 American horses were shipped across the border to be slaughtered, primarily in Canadian and Mexican slaughter facilities. In response to the issue of tainted horse meat being found in the European food supply, early in 2013 legislation was introduced in both the U.S. Congress and Senate to ban horse slaughter and end the export of American horses for slaughter. The Safeguard American Food Exports (SAFE) Act is backed by the Humane Society of the United States, the American Society for the Prevention of Cruelty to Animals, and equine advocate groups and is gaining bipartisan support in both the House and Senate.

In addition to the humane issues raised by horse slaughter, the *Journal of Food and Chemical Toxicology* recently published a report on the use of bute (phenylbutazone) in American horses. Because American horses are not raised for food, the use of bute, an equine anti-inflammatory that is also known to be a human carcinogen, is basically unrestricted. The study suggested that the likelihood of horses having been administered bute and other substances banned for use in food animals, such as equine dewormers, reaching the slaughterhouses is high. In response to the potential for adverse human health effects, the European Union has instituted guidelines for determining that horses headed for slaughter have not been administered substances known to be harmful to humans. This is problematic for Americans who wish to sell their horses to a kill buyer because the United States has no mechanism in place to guarantee the removal of horses who have been administered banned substances from the slaughter pipeline.

As more and more equine advocates and humane organizations worldwide continue to expose the reality of horse slaughter, the demand for horse meat continues to decline. An increased public awareness of the conditions in horse slaughter facilities coupled with scientific studies suggesting that horse meat, at least in the case of horses not raised for meat, poses a threat to public health will likely result in the elimination of or severe restrictions on the mass slaughter of horses.

Related articles: Animals and public health; European animal protection; Free-ranging horses; Horses; The humane movement in Canada; Japanese attitudes toward animals; Jumps racing; Legislation in the European Union; Live animal exports; Slaughter; South American perspectives on animals

Bjalobok, F., "The Requirements of Justice," 2010, available from http://animallawcoalition.com.

Blondeau, N., and Marini, A., "Association of Phenylbutazone Usage with Horses Bought for Slaughter: A Public Health Risk," 2010, available at http:www.sciencedirect.com/science.

Dodman, N., "Horse Slaughter," 2009, available at http://vets forequinewelfare.org.

Heller, B., *After the Finish Line: The Race to End Horse Slaughter in America*, Bowtie Press, 2005.

Holland, J., "Horse Slaughter Trends 2006–2009," 2010, available at http://equinewelfarealliance.org.

———, "Perfect Time to End the Slaughter of American Horses," 2010, available at http://equinewelfarealliance.org.

FAITH BJALOBOK

PIG CASTRATION

In most countries, male piglets are castrated before being fattened for slaughter. Castration is supposedly performed in order to prevent a small proportion of male pigs from developing a distinct odor called "boar taint." Some sexually mature male pigs develop boar taint as a result of the naturally occurring chemicals androstenone and skatole. Flesh tainted by these chemicals is considered unpleasant by some meat consumers. To avoid any risk of dissatisfied customers, piglets around the world are routinely castrated by the meat industry.

In castration of piglets, an incision is made between the hind legs with a scalpel. The opening allows the testicles to be pulled out and cut away. The whole procedure is usually performed by the pig farmer without veterinary assistance or any form of pain relief. Intuition should convince most people that surgery on animals without pain relief causes excruciating pain. Indeed, a number of behavioral and physiological studies have conclusively shown that castration without anesthesia involves great suffering and long-term distress in piglets. Despite this evidence, the pig industry claims that castration without anesthesia is not a serious welfare problem.

Norway is the first country in the world to introduce a law making it illegal for the pig industry to routinely castrate male piglets. Norwegian animal advocates contributed to this legislative victory for pigs, first by gaining a thorough understanding of the practice of pig castration and then by collaborating with scientists and other experts to bring about an end to the suffering. Evidence from the Norwegian veterinary authorities and testimony from scientists resulted in a documentary on Norwegian television. The program created a public outcry and initiated a broad political debate.

In view of the public concern, the Norwegian government was forced to contemplate a ban on castration. The powerful pig industry and its allies immediately lobbied intensely to prevent any proposals that might restrict castration. They argued that the costs of a ban would be astronomical, citing figures in the tens of millions of euros. They claimed that pigs would not benefit from anesthesia since administering the pain relief would cause as much distress as the castration itself. The pig industry was determined to delay a ban on castration indefinitely.

Pressured by the pig industry, the Norwegian government sent a proposal involving only minor reforms to the Parliament for approval. Animal advocates appealed to the members of Parliament to reject the proposal. The heated debate culminated in a parliamentary hearing on the issue. Norwegian animal advocates argued that the pig industry's claims were vastly exaggerated and unreliable. They were able to show that the Danish pig industry had voluntarily stopped castrating pigs without encountering any significant practical or financial difficulties. In Denmark it was found that through improvements to the living conditions of pigs, the incidence of boar taint could be dramatically reduced. Chemical techniques for detecting the offending odors were also devised in Denmark in order to exclude tainted meat from the market.

In view of the new evidence, the Norwegian Parliament finally decided on March 8, 2002, to forbid all castration of pigs by January 1, 2009. Until the ban was in force, only veterinarians would be permitted to castrate piglets, and only when appropriate anesthesia was administered.

During the transition period the pig industry made great efforts to overturn the ban. Despite protests from the animal protection movement, a new farmer-friendly Norwegian government decided to postpone the ban indefinitely in November 2008. At present the most promising option for reinstating the ban on pig castration is with the introduction of immunovaccination against boar taint. However, in the meantime it is forbidden to castrate piglets without anesthesia and prolonged pain relief. Only veterinarians are allowed to perform the procedure, and tissue must be cut, not torn apart.

***

Related articles: Animal pain; Animal welfare and farming; Challenges to animal protection in Scandinavia; The welfare of pigs

Bonneau, M., "Use of Entire Males for Pig Meat in the European Union," *Meat Science* 49, Suppl. 1 (1998).

Danish Meat Research Institute, *Skatole and Boar Taint*, 1998.

Fredriksen, B., and Nafstad, O., "Surveyed Attitudes, Perceptions and Practices in Norway regarding the Use of Local Anaesthesia in Piglet Castration," *Research in Veterinary Science* 81 (2005): 293–295.

Godt, J., Kristensen, K., et al., *Consumer Evaluation of Meat from Danish Entire Pigs: Skatole and Boar Taint*, Danish Meat Research Institute, 1998.

Haga, H. A., and Ranheim, B., "Castration of Piglets: The Analgesic Effects of Intratesticular and Intrafunicular Lidocaine Injection," *Veterinary Anaesthesia and Analgesia* 32.1 (2005): 1–9.

Jaros, P., et al., "Effect of Active Immunization against GnRH on Androstenone Concentration, Growth Performance and Carcass Quality in Intact Male Pigs," *Livestock Production Science* 92 (2005): 31–38.

Lagerkvist, C., et al., "Immunocastration of Male Pigs by Immunization against Gonadotrophin-Releasing Hormone as an Alternative to Surgical Castration or No Castration: A Choice Experiment with Swedish Consumers," *AgBioForum*, 2006.

Prunier, A., "A Review of the Welfare Consequences of Surgical Castration in Piglets and the Evaluation of Non-Surgical Methods," *Animal Welfare* 15 (2006): 277–289.

ANTON KRAG

THE PRODUCTION OF FOIE GRAS

Foie gras livers come from ducks and geese who have been force-fed so that the excessive quantities of feed are transformed into fat stored in the liver. Ninety-five percent of foie gras comes from ducks, and 5 percent from geese. The liver grows to ten or twelve times the normal weight; in ducks it increases from 60 grams to 550 or 600 grams; in geese from 80 grams to 1 kilo.

France is the leading producer of foie gras in the world, producing more than eighteen thousand tons a year; a further three to five thousand tons of foie gras is produced outside France. It has been calculated that more than 43 million ducks around the world are subjected to force-feeding, 36 million of these in France, mainly in the southwest. The animals are raised and force-fed under conditions that are quite barbaric and contrary to basic animal welfare. When they are four months old, the ducks are trained to eat increasing quantities, administered in a single daily feeding session. This lasts for ten days, during which the feed increases from 180 to 380 grams a day.

Then comes the final stage, the force-feeding, lasting two to three weeks. On most farms, ducks are kept in small individual cages where it is impossible for them to move normally, and most live in darkness. The calorie content of the feed (mainly corn mixed with fat) is dramatically increased. This feed is administered twice a day, with first a gradual and then a substantial increase in quantity: the first day of force-feeding starts with 190 grams per feeding session, and by the last day the birds are being force-fed 450 grams.

Twice a day, the bird is held down to be fed: the handler grasps the bird's neck and inserts a tube twenty to thirty centimeters long down the animal's gullet. Pneumatic force then propels the food at high speed down the tube in just two or three seconds—even amounts of more than one pound of feed toward the end of the force-feeding period. The handling rate can be 350 or more ducks an hour. Force-fed geese are kept in group cages or enclosures, but the technique for force-feeding geese is similar, with three daily feeding sessions and larger quantities of feed, reaching 700 grams per session by the end of the force-feeding period.

The whole system produces considerable suffering. Naturally gregarious animals are isolated and deprived of their normal eating patterns. Without light, they are unable to follow their normal behavior—for example, foraging or satisfying natural curiosity. Force-feeding causes both pain and physical damage to the esophagus, with sometimes fatal tearing of tissue. A large percentage of force-fed ducks kept in individual cages have injuries to the sternum and fractured bones. The birds often have their beaks cut by the severing of the hook on the upper beak. The liver grows and expands to such a size that it distends the abdomen, causing shortness of breath. The huge amount of feed ingested through the tube causes an increase in body temperature, and feces are semi-liquid.

Foie gras is a diseased liver, suffering from steatosis. Both the structure and the function of the organ are acutely pathological: for example, the size of liver cells expands by a factor of seventy, bile secretion is abnor-

mally low, and there is a tenfold increase in fat levels and half the normal water content, along with various other anomalies detectable by biochemical analysis. If force-feeding were to last even two or three days more, it would cause fibrosis, damage to vessels, local hemorrhages, and jaundice, with fatal consequences.

To defend the practice, foie gras producers maintain that such fat livers are found naturally in migratory birds, who need to store energy. This is patently untrue for two reasons: first, the energy supplies of migratory birds are not stored in the liver but are spread under the layer of skin and throughout the body, and second, foie gras ducks are hybrids bred from Barbary ducks and have no migratory instinct.

The foie gras industry also argues that eating foie gras is "good for human health" because it contains 1 percent free cholesterol. However, in digestion of one hundred grams of foie gras, the body absorbs fifty or sixty grams of fats containing 95 percent triglycerides. Consuming a product with such high fat content and high triglyceride levels causes health damage. In fact, eating foie gras is not "good" for anyone's health. It is also relevant that each force-fed duck produces two thighs and two breast fillets—that is, a total world production of 72 million thighs and 72 million breast fillets every year. The consumption of duck legs and magret or preserved goose or duck is morally indistinguishable from eating the liver, given the violation of basic animal welfare.

The only rational conclusion is to put an end to the force-feeding of geese and ducks, and the best way to do that is to ban the production, trade, import, and sale of foie gras. Every humane person reading this article will be able to see the moral of the story and should make a resolution never to buy or eat foie gras again because of the suffering of ducks and geese tortured solely for commercial and culinary interests.

Related articles: Animals and public health; Birds used in food production; The protection of birds

Comiti, Antoine, *L'INRA Au Secours du Foie Gras*, Éditions Sentience, 2006.

Coulon, Jean-Marie, and Nouët, Jean-Claude, *Les Droits de L'animal*, Éditions Dalloz, 2009.

Fondation Ligue française des droits de l'animal, *Analyse critique du rapport du Comité scientifique de la santé et du bien-être animal sur la protection des palmipèdes "à foie gras,"* 2000.

———, *Le Gavage des Palmipèdes et le Foie Gras*, 2006.

Scientific Committee on Animal Health and Animal Welfare, European Commission, *Welfare Aspects of the Production of Foie Gras in Ducks and Geese*, 1998.

JEAN-CLAUDE NOUËT

RELIGIOUS SLAUGHTER

Religious slaughter (also known as "ritual slaughter"—a term rejected by its supporters) is the method of slaughtering animals by a single cut to the throat without pre-stunning. The practice has caused considerable controversy and is banned in many countries, including Switzerland, Sweden, Norway, and Iceland. In 2011, the Dutch parliament voted by 116 to 30 to prohibit it. The European Directive on slaughter allows member states to make exceptions to pre-stunning, and religious slaughter is legal throughout most of the world, including many member states of the European Union, the United States, and the United Kingdom. Supporters of the practice say that it is humane, whereas animal advocates claim the reverse. In addition, advocates oppose the non-labeling of kosher meat, which they argue helps maintain the practice and prevents informed consumer choice.

The difficulty principally arises within Judaism because orthodox teaching requires animals to be free from injury before slaughter. Since stunning practices, such as electrocution or a captive bolt to the brain, obviously injure the animal (in order to secure unconsciousness), such animals are deemed unfit (*trefar*) for slaughter. Within Islam, the difficulty is that animals must be alive at the time of slaughter, and so although stunning is allowable in principle, the methods must not entirely kill the animal.

Because the controversy has sometimes descended into rhetoric that appears to be anti-Semitic or xenophobic in tone, it is important to try to determine the issue of relative humaneness on the basis of scientific evidence. A report by the British government's Farm Animal Welfare Council (FAWC; not an animal protection organization but a body of farmers, business owners, scientists, and welfare representatives) showed that animals who are killed by the *shehita* method are liable to have 14 to 35 seconds more consciousness during the act of slaughter itself than through the captive bolt system (*On the Welfare* 19, 25). This conclusion is further refined in a more recent FAWC report, which explained,

> Loss of sensibility post-cut can be detected by observing brain function through electroencephalographic methodology—a lack of response indicating certain insensibility or death. The scientific evidence shows that sheep become insensible within 5–7 seconds of the cut (3–7 seconds in goats). Adult cattle, however, may take between 22 and 40 seconds to become insensible. This period may be extended should occlusion occur of the carotid arteries take place [*sic*]. Work done on calves has shown a variation in period to insensibility from 10–120 seconds depending on the extent of occlusion of the carotid arteries or ballooning in blood vessels. Furthermore, a separate study of brain response after Shechita slaughter of cattle compared to that after captive-bolt stunning indicated responses for up to 60 seconds in the former and no response in the latter. (Farm Animal Welfare Council, *Report* 25, para. 198)

Both reports recommended that the current exemption concerning religious slaughter in the United Kingdom be rescinded.

It seems, therefore, that religious slaughter causes more suffering than the alternative methods that involve pre-stunning, especially the captive bolt system. And of course there is the additional problem of shackling, hoisting, or rotating (as in the Cincinnati pen), which inevitably causes stress. That said, of course it is important to compare like with like. Conventional slaughter can itself cause great suffering—for example, if the captive bolt is misapplied or if the electricity current in electrical pre-stunning is less than the voltage required. Similarly, in religious slaughter the knife must be exceptionally sharp to avoid more than one cut, and there must be facilities to enable an immediate exsanguination (rapid blood release). But comparing like with like, it does seem that religious slaughter makes animals more liable to suffering.

Religious authorities, of course, reject this conclusion and frequently claim that believers would not inflict unnecessary suffering on animals (e.g., Homa). The tragedy is that both Jewish and Muslim methods aim to provide the most painless death possible. Muhammad's insistence that the sharpest knife be used for slaughter and the fact that both methods require professional training testify to this. One of the greatest of rabbinic expositors, Moses Maimonides, himself explicitly said that the clear purpose behind *shehita* was to minimize suffering. Moreover, at the time of its instigation, *shehita* and *halal* were the most humane methods compared with their alternatives—namely, hammering, poleaxing, and strangulation. The difficulty for both traditions is that during the last fifty years, we have learned more about humane slaughtering techniques than ever before.

It seems that both these religious traditions have been far too defensive. Given that the aim of slaughter in both traditions is to kill with a minimum amount of pain, there should be a more open discussion about how their religious teachings should apply in a different context. For example, some Muslim authorities, such as the European Council of Fatwa and Research, have recognized stunning as permitted, as long as the animal is not killed prior to slaughter, and some rabbis accept that after *shehita* has been performed, the captive bolt system can be used. Two Jewish and Christian theologians point out,

Our hope for a resolution of this issue lies in a recognition (by non-Jews) of the historic Jewish commitment to animal welfare on the one hand, and a renewed appreciation (by Jews) that since the intention of the tradition is to ensure humane killing, any reassessment of Jewish practice in this regard may be properly viewed as a reinforcement, rather than an abandonment, of the tradition itself, on the other hand. (Linzey and Cohn-Sherbok 56)

One way forward may be efforts such as the DIALREL (Encouraging Dialogue on Issues of Religion Slaughter) project initiated by the European Union, which supports the dissemination of scientific evidence, dialogue, and exchange.

Related articles: Animal-friendly spirituality; Islam and animals; Judaism and animal life; Legislation in the European Union; Slaughter

DIALREL, "Religious Slaughter: Encouraging Dialogue between Stakeholders and Interested Parties as well as Gathering and Dissemination of Information," available at http://www.dialrel.eu/introduction.
FAWC (Farm Animal Welfare Council), *Report on the Welfare of Farmed Animals at Slaughter or Killing, Part 1: Red Meat Animals*, HMSO, 2003.
———, *On the Welfare of Livestock When Slaughtered by Religious Methods*, HMSO, 1985.
Homa, Bernard, "The Jewish Method of Slaughter," *Humane Killing and Slaughterhouse Techniques*, Universities Federation for Animal Welfare, 1971.
Linzey, Andrew, *Animal Theology*, SCM Press/University of Illinois Press, 1994.
———, *Creatures of the Same God: Explorations in Animal Theology*, Winchester University Press/Lantern Books, 2007.
Linzey, Andrew, and Cohn-Sherbok, Dan, *After Noah: Animals and the Liberation of Theology*, Mowbray/Continuum, 1997.

ANDREW LINZEY

SLAUGHTER

By virtue of numbers alone, the slaughter of animals for food represents the most compelling animal welfare concern worldwide. According to the United Nations Food and Agriculture Organization (FAO), the number of land animals killed for food in 2008 exceeded 59 billion, including 57 billion birds, 1.3 billion pigs, 925 million sheep and goats, and 298 million cattle. Nearly one-half of the world's total were killed in slaughterhouses in just three countries—Brazil, China, and the United States.

Welfare laws governing slaughter require that animals be rendered insensible to pain before killing. Humane slaughter laws originated in Europe, with Switzerland leading the way in 1874. Between that time and the mid-1930s, several additional European nations adopted humane slaughter legislation. In 1951, New Zealand and parts of Australia passed laws governing slaughter, and in 1958, the United States Congress enacted the Humane Methods of Slaughter Act. The Council of the European Community enacted a directive on stunning of animals before slaughter in 1974, which was replaced in 1993 with a directive on the protection of animals at the time of slaughter or killing. By 2010 a European Convention for the Protection of Animals for Slaughter had been signed and ratified by twenty-five nations.

Animals are typically rendered insensible to pain prior to slaughter by one of three primary methods—mechanical (captive bolt or gunshot), electrical (current applied to the head or body or both), or chemical (carbon dioxide and/or inert gases such as nitrogen or argon). The captive bolt is used on grown cattle, and electrical stunning is utilized for smaller animals. Gas is used to anesthetize hogs prior to bleeding and can also be used to render birds unconscious. A majority of birds, however, are stunned—they are hung upside-down by their legs on conveyor belts, and then their head and upper body are dragged through an electrically charged water bath. After the animals have been rendered unconscious, their throats are cut, either as they stand upright or after they have been shackled by a leg and hoisted, and they ultimately die from blood loss.

Welfare concerns associated with slaughter are numerous. Transportation to slaughter is stressful to animals because of rough handling during loading and unloading, loss of balance, lack of food and water, and exposure to noise, wind, exhaust, and temperature extremes during transit. At the slaughtering plant, animals may be subjected to abusive treatment, including excessive use of prodding devices and the beating and dragging of conscious, nonambulatory animals by an extremity or the neck. Animals may be held for extended periods in overcrowded pens with no access to food, water, or shelter from the elements.

The most serious welfare problems encountered during the slaughter process itself are inadequate stunning, inadequate bleeding, too long an interval between stunning and bleeding, and the absence of stunning altogether, as occurs in religious slaughter.

Inadequate stunning can result from malfunctioning or poorly maintained equipment, the use of too little electrical current or for too short a time, or the application of the stunning device to the wrong part of the body. Audits conducted in recent years by major international restaurant companies reported that the average percentage of cattle stunned correctly on the first shot was similar for slaughter plants in Australia, Canada, and the United States, with approximately 75 percent of plants reaching 99 to 100 percent stunning accuracy. However, investigations conducted by animal advocacy organizations suggest that industry and third-party audits may not always provide an accurate assessment of stunning practices in the absence of outside observers.

Inadequate bleeding, as well as too long a time interval between stunning and bleeding, may result in the animal regaining consciousness before being dismembered in the case of cattle or before being scalded in the case of pigs and poultry. In the United States, there is no requirement that birds be stunned prior to slaughter. Although poultry plants in the United States submerge birds to be killed in tanks of electrified water, the current may be set too low to adequately stun, and millions of laying hens receive no stunning at all because their bones are so brittle that immersion in an electrified water bath would cause them to shatter.

It has been estimated that more than half of the billions of animals killed for food annually in developing countries are slaughtered without the benefit of stunning. In 2005, the World Organisation for Animal Health (OIE), with its 176 member countries and territories, adopted its international Guidelines for the Slaughter of Animals for Human Consumption. In addition, animal protection organizations, in collaboration with the FAO in some cases, are working to provide humane slaughter training and equipment to countries in Asia and Latin America, with Brazil and China identified as key targets. Because they desire to export their meat products, humane slaughter has become a starting point for promoting animal welfare in these countries. In 2008 humane slaughter was officially written into China's regulations on the killing of pigs, a first for the world's largest meat producer.

With approximately 20 percent of the world's population belonging to the Muslim or Jewish faiths, religious slaughter is an issue of special concern (see Changing Religious Perspectives). It is the position of many, but not all, individuals of these faiths that animals should not to be stunned prior to bleeding. Without stunning, animals must endure pain and distress for a prolonged period of time between throat-cutting and loss of brain responsiveness. In addition to being bled without the benefit of stunning, animals killed through religious slaughter may be shackled and hoisted while still conscious. In 2010, the European Union debated mandatory labeling of meat from animals slaughtered without pre-stunning. Many countries—Iceland, New Zealand, Norway, Sweden, and Switzerland—do not allow religious exceptions for stunning, and it is hoped that other nations will incorporate this change into their own humane slaughter legislation.

Related articles: Animal protection in Africa; Animals in Chinese culture; Birds used in food production; Horse slaughter; Legal protection of animals in China; Legislation in the European Union; Live animal exports; Religious slaughter; South American perspectives on animals; The treatment of animals in India; The welfare of cows; The welfare of pigs; The welfare of sheep

Appleby, M. C., Cussen, V., Garces, L., Lesley, L. A., and Turner, J. (eds.), *Long Distance Transport and Welfare of Farm Animals*, CAB International, 2008.

Chambers, P. G., Grandin, T., Heinz, G., and Srisuvan T., *Guidelines for Humane Handling, Transport and Slaughter of Livestock*, United Nations Food and Agriculture Organization and Humane Society International, 2001.

Eisnitz, G., *Slaughterhouse: The Shocking Story of Greed, Neglect, and Inhumane Treatment inside the U.S. Meat Industry*, Prometheus Books, 1997.

Grandin, T., *Humane Livestock Handling: Understanding Livestock Behavior and Building Facilities for Healthier Animals*, Storey, 2008.

Jones, D., *Crimes without Consequences: The Enforcement of Humane Slaughter Laws in the United States*, Animal Welfare Institute, 2008.

Trent, N., Ormel, P., Garcia de Siles, J. L., Heinz, G., and James, M., "The State of Meat Production in Developing Countries: 2002," in Salem, D. J., and Rowan, A. N. (eds.), *The State of the Animals II*, Humane Society Press, 2003.

DENA M. JONES

THE WELFARE OF COWS

The dairy cow surely has pride of place among farmed animals. Historically, she has been revered, and she is frequently portrayed as a symbol of maternal nurturing. The life of the majority of cows used for dairy, however, is very harsh.

The young female, or heifer, can produce her first calf at around two years of age. In a natural environment, she would let her calf suckle several times a day—in between, she would leave him in a sheltered, safe area, probably with some other calves, and wander off to graze, thus fueling her own milk supply. After a couple of weeks, the calf would start eating grass as well, and over the next eight months or so, he would gradually wean himself off his mother. The maternal bond is very strong. There are records of cows traveling several miles on their own to find calves who have been taken from them and sold to other farms. In all cases they somehow manage to scent out their own calf in completely unknown territories.

In the high-tech dairy industry, the calf is taken away from his mother at just a day or two old. This causes apparent anguish to both. The cow is then milked to capacity, often producing ten times as much milk as her calf would have suckled from her, had he been allowed to do so. In North America and Europe, traditional breeds of cattle have lost out to such breeds as the big black and white Holsteins, specifically bred to have huge udders and produce vast quantities of milk.

Although many cows do have summer-season access to grass, others are kept in "zero grazing" systems, never going out to grass at all. In 2009, the European Food Safety Authority (EFSA) published an important report on the welfare of dairy cows. It had this to say about zero-grazing:

> If dairy cows are not kept on pasture for parts of the year, i.e. they are permanently on a zero-grazing system, there is an increased risk of lameness, hoof problems, teat tramp, mastitis, metritis, dystocia, ketosis, retained placenta and some bacterial infections. (European Food Safety Authority, *Scientific Opinion on Welfare of Dairy Cows*)

Most cows have their milk production boosted by processed "concentrates," feeds based on soybeans, grains, fish meal, and sometimes animal wastes—all foods that these herbivorous ruminants would never naturally choose to eat. These unnatural foods can provoke an acid condition in the cow's gut leading to discomfort and sometimes to a general acidic condition. This makes the cow more likely to go lame. Lameness is a huge problem for cows. In modern dairy farms, around a quarter of cows go lame every year. If they are not treated swiftly and well, the pain can be severe and enduring.

The other major problem for dairy cows is mastitis, inflammation of the udder and teats. According to a 1997 report published by the Farm Animal Welfare Council, an advisory body to the U.K. government, over a third of cows get mastitis every year. Filthy flooring, excessive pulsating from milking machines, and the fact that the cow is being pushed all the time to her physiological limits predispose the cow to infection by the bacteria that cause this highly painful condition.

Perhaps the most telling statistic about the modern dairy cow is that she is usually killed by the time she is five or six years old. By then, at what may be less than a quarter of her natural life span, she will be worn out. She will fail to conceive or get recurring bouts of mastitis or lameness. It is not economic to keep her anymore, so she will be sent for slaughter. Even so, some cows are actually pregnant when they are sent to slaughter. The 2009 EFSA report summed up the situation:

> Genetic selection for high milk yield with insufficient emphasis on other traits relating to fitness increases the risk of suffering from metabolic and reproductive prob-

lems. This risk is greater when housing, nutrition and management are unable to compensate for the adverse effects of genetic selection. The increased inbreeding of recent years may lead to, or be associated with, increased reproductive problems, reduced lifetime milk production and a reduction in breeding performance if it continues. Excessive or prolonged negative energy balance in dairy cows is more likely to occur in the highest producing animals and has been found to be associated with reduced fertility, digestive, metabolic and infectious disease, especially mastitis. (European Food Safety Authority, *Summary of Scientific Opinion*)

The catalog of hardships we inflict on the dairy cow is increasing. Many top-quality cows are now induced to "super-ovulate" (produce extra egg cells) on a regular basis. After impregnation by artificial insemination, their multiple embryos are extracted and implanted into cows of lower quality, who carry the embryos to term. The procedure is usually performed via the cervix rather than surgically. However, it can be painful; in some parts of the world—for example, in the European Union—an epidural anesthetic must be used, whereas in other countries no such relief is mandatory.

Some countries, such as the United States, also allow the use of bovine somatotrophin (BST)—a genetically engineered version of the cow's growth hormone that is injected fortnightly into cows to increase milk yield. The European Union has banned the use of BST because it is associated with even higher levels of mastitis and a range of other health problems.

There is still one more sad side to the modern dairy industry—the fate of the male calves as well as some female calves. Because Holsteins do not produce great steaks, being the wrong shape, the calves are not wanted for beef. In the United States, most will end up in narrow wooden veal calf crates, unable to turn around for the rest of their lives and fed a low-iron liquid-only diet to keep their flesh pale. The end product is so-called white veal for the gourmet market. Veal crates have been banned in the European Union, on cruelty grounds, since 2007.

Globally, many cattle reared for meat live more natural lives than dairy cows and are allowed to roam on grassland or are kept outdoors in fields. But in intensive farms they too often end their lives indoors, sometimes on straw, sometimes on harsh concrete slats, being fed a booster diet to put on those precious kilograms. Others end up in barren mud yards, called "feedlots." Often, as in the United States, hormones are administered to increase and speed up the animals' muscle (meat) growth. Animal breeders have developed breeds in which the animals develop double the normal muscle, the most notorious being the Belgian Blue breed. These massive creatures are very profitable in terms of meat yield, but the females have great difficulty delivering their large calves, and cesareans are usually inevitable, with the related stress and discomfort.

Cattle used to be dual-purpose—bred both for meat and for their milk. They were kept in natural conditions, and they usually suckled their calves, ate a natural diet, and could live for many years. Through selective breeding we have developed breeds with characteristics that are unsustainable on welfare grounds and that subject the dairy cow to such physiological stress that her body cannot sustain the punishment for more than a few years. It is surely time to reverse direction and develop kinder ways to keep cattle.

Related articles: Animal pain; Animal welfare and farming; Animals and public health; Legislation in the European Union; Slaughter; The treatment of animals in India

Broom, D. M., and Johnson, K. G., *Stress and Animal Welfare*, Chapman and Hall, 1993.
D'Silva, Joyce, and Webster, John (eds.), *The Meat Crisis: Developing More Sustainable Production and Consumption*, Earthscan, 2010.
European Food Safety Authority, *Effects of Farming Systems on Dairy Cow Welfare and Disease*, 2009.
———, *Scientific Opinion on Welfare of Dairy Cows in Relation to Leg and Locomotion Problems*, 2009.
———, *Summary of Scientific Opinion on Welfare of Dairy Cows in Relation to Metabolic and Reproductive Problems*, 2009.
Webster, John, *Animal Welfare—A Cool Eye towards Eden*, Blackwell, 1993.
———, *Animal Welfare—Limping towards Eden*, Blackwell, 2005.

JOYCE D'SILVA

THE WELFARE OF PIGS

The popular perception of pig farming is of contented pigs roaming and rooting in the soil. This could not be further from the truth for many of the world's pigs. In the Western Hemisphere, most pigs are factory farmed. Large numbers of animals are crammed into small pens, confined in cages or crates, and subjected to an array of routine mutilations, such as tail docking and castration. Every stage of pig rearing on these farms is geared toward maximum production, often causing considerable suffering. This intensive pig industry has been spreading around the world.

The sheer scale of global pig production can be glimpsed from the following figures. Every year, around 250 million pigs are raised for slaughter in the European Union, along with 130 million in the United States and Canada and nearly 700 million in China.

Caged production machines

Female breeding pigs—sows—are perhaps the most abused animals on the factory farm. As soon as a young female reaches breeding age (six months old), she is made pregnant. She will often spend her four-month pregnancy caged in a narrow sow stall or chained in a row by a heavy tether around her neck. The stall is just bigger than the sow herself, and it prevents her from exercising or even turning around. She is forced to stand or lie on a stark concrete and slatted floor. She is kept like this for pregnancy after pregnancy.

Factory-farmed sows also spend motherhood behind bars. When the time to give birth nears, the heavily pregnant sow is moved to another narrow metal contraption known as the farrowing crate. Here she will stay until her piglets are weaned at three to four weeks old. This archaic system, which pins the sow down to one place, is supposedly used to protect piglets from being crushed by their mother but is actually quite unnecessary. Sows kept in a more natural outdoor environment are perfectly able to rear their piglets without crushing them. At the end of the cycle, the piglets are taken from the mother at about a month old. The sow is made pregnant again, and the cycle of confinement repeats itself.

Born to run, root, and play

Pigs are active, inquisitive, and social animals, renowned for being as intelligent as dogs. They will naturally spend most of their day rooting in the soil, foraging, or exploring their world. These behaviors are usually rendered impossible on the factory farm. Crated and caged sows commonly carry out meaningless, repetitive motions, known as stereotypies. Experts regard these stereotypies as outward signs that the animals are under stress and suffering. These are the only means available for the desperately frustrated sow to attempt to cope with her confinement. Stereotypic behaviors for a sow include bar-biting, sham-chewing (chewing the air), shaking her head from side to side, repeatedly nosing in the empty feed trough, and attempting to root at the concrete floor.

Fattened for slaughter

On many intensive pig farms, young pigs being fattened for slaughter are forced to spend their lives on bare concrete or slatted floors. Bedding material is often nonexistent. Barren conditions cause boredom and frustration, which in turn can lead to problems with so-called vices, such as piglets biting each other's tails. Factory farm problems are solved using factory farm ways. Tail docking is used in this case. Here, the piglets' tails are cut with pliers or a hot docking iron without the use of an anesthetic. Scientific evidence shows that when the animals are kept in better conditions, the "need" for tail docking can be eliminated.

In many countries, castration also is routinely carried out on male piglets. This severely painful mutilation is often performed without anesthetic. In the United Kingdom, farmers generally no longer engage in this practice, but castration is still carried out widely in other countries because of fears of "boar taint," an unpleasant odor that can be found in the meat of sexually mature boars. Piglets are usually castrated when they are just a few days old, and their squeals can be almost deafening.

Signs of change

The European Union recently agreed to ban sow stalls for pregnant pigs, except for the first four weeks of pregnancy, starting January 2013, with the equally cruel system of sow tethering being banned from 2006. As a result, increasing numbers of breeding sows in Europe already spend their pregnancies in more humane systems, either outdoors or indoors in groups, where they can exercise and carry out natural behaviors. Some European countries have enacted their own unilateral bans on sow stalls and tethers, including Finland, Sweden, and the United Kingdom. In the Philippines, where about 24 million pigs a year are produced, legislation prohibits the use of sow stalls for more than six weeks at a time.

These are highly welcome steps for animal welfare. They come against a backdrop of increasing recognition that animals are sentient beings who feel pain and suffer. These strides must be followed by many more if we are to see an end to the suffering of countless millions of pigs in the world's factory farms.

Related articles: Animals in Chinese culture; The complexity of animal awareness; Pig castration; Progress in animal welfare; Slaughter

Arey, D., and Brooke, P., *Animal Welfare Aspects of Good Agricultural Practice: Pig Production*, Compassion in World Farming, 2006.

European Food Safety Authority, "Scientific Report on Animal Health and Welfare Aspects of Different Housing and Husbandry Systems for Adult Breeding Boars, Pregnant, Farrowing Sows and Unweaned Piglets," *EFSA Journal* 527 (2007): 1–107.

———, "Scientific Report on Animal Health and Welfare in Fattening Pigs in Relation to Housing and Husbandry," *EFSA Journal* 564 (2007): 1–100.

———, "Scientific Report on the Risks Associated with Tail Biting in Pigs and Possible Means to Reduce the Need for Tail Docking," *EFSA Journal* 611 (2007): 1–98.

Pickett, H., *Welfare of Pigs in the European Union*, Compassion in World Farming, 2009.

Webster, J., *Animal Welfare: Limping towards Eden*, Blackwell, 2005.

PHILIP LYMBERY

THE WELFARE OF SHEEP

Sheep are farmed and herded over a wide range of climates, landscapes, and human farming systems, from pastoralists in Asia, South America, Africa, and the Middle East to the commercial sheep farmers of Europe, New Zealand, and Australia. There are estimated to be around one billion farmed or herded sheep in the world.

The European Union slaughters nearly 170 million sheep and lambs a year, nearly half of them reared in the United Kingdom and Spain. Australia and New Zealand keep around 113 million sheep between them, and there are estimated to be 136 million in China. During the past fifty years of intensification of animal farming, sheep farming has retained its image as a green, peaceful, and natural form of farming. So it is ironic that because of their convenient size, lack of aggression, and relatively short gestation period (five months), sheep have been much used by high-tech genetic engineers and cloners.

In traditional farming, sheep are kept to produce milk, meat, hair, or wool, whereas in commercial farming in developed countries, an individual sheep now has little commercial worth. This fact, unfortunately, impacts on welfare. To be profitable, sheep have to be mass-produced, and often they are specialized for a particular function. Most of the nearly seventeen million sheep slaughtered annually in the United Kingdom are used to provide lamb meat, and their wool is now often not worth the cost of shearing.

Are meat, milk, and wool from sheep welfare-friendly products? Not as much as the free-range and natural image would suggest. The creeping intensification of sheep farming has led to a number of welfare problems. The best-known problem is the long-distance transport of sheep for sale and to slaughter. Even within a small country such as England, sheep are forced to travel long distances to slaughterhouses and frequently have to suffer the stress of travel and sale at markets. Not only among ewes and their lambs but also more generally, sheep recognize each other and develop bonds within a stable flock. These bonds are often broken and ignored in commercial sheep trading.

Internationally, sheep are mass-transported over huge distances for slaughter. Several million live sheep are transported to ports each year and exported by ship from Australia and New Zealand to the Middle East in journeys that can take nearly a month from farm to final destination. Up to two million sheep and lambs are transported annually across Europe to markets and slaughterhouses. On these journeys, sheep and lambs can suffer from crowding, trampling, dehydration, hunger, heat, and cold, as well as the stress of mixing with unfamiliar animals. Rules on journey times, rest periods, and slaughter methods are often ignored or unenforced. At some slaughterhouses where the sheep are taken, they are roughly handled, and some have their throats cut without stunning. When there are unexpected delays in sea or truck journeys, hundreds of sheep may die from heat stress or disease.

The most common health and welfare problems suffered by sheep in developed countries are probably a result of our selective breeding and management practices. We have bred sheep to be much heavier and to have thicker wool, which has to be sheared rather than being shed like a coat. Sheep now suffer commonly from painful foot problems and from parasitic problems, such as scab and blowflies. These issues are controlled by sheep-dipping and footbaths, which are also likely to be stressful or painful for the sheep. For reasons of convenience or tradition, young lambs are subjected to mutilations such as castration and tail-docking without anesthetic, mutilations that are routinely performed in the United Kingdom with the use of rubber rings that cut off the blood supply to the tail or testicles. Breeding for copious wool encourages fly-strike (which can result in sheep being eaten alive by maggots). To reduce fly-strike, the industry subjects many Merino wool sheep in Australia to mulesing (cutting off folds of skin and flesh on the animal's rear) without anesthetic, although consumer concern is encouraging the industry to develop ways to phase out this practice.

In spite of the "natural" image of sheep farming, the industry is under pressure to get higher productivity from the animals. Breeding for large lambs and multiple lambs leads to higher mortality for both ewes and lambs during pregnancy and at lambing time. Internationally, the death rate of lambs is high and does not appear to be decreasing in spite of modern veterinary knowledge. In the United Kingdom, an average of up to 15 percent of lambs die (and sometimes the percentage is much higher), and 75 percent of all ewe deaths take place around the time of lambing.

If sheep farming is to be protected as an extensive and welfare-friendly undertaking, urgent reforms are needed. In Britain and Europe, long-distance transport and multiple journeys to market should be ended. On welfare grounds, sheep should be slaughtered only in local slaughterhouses. Alternative management methods must be found to mutilations such as castration and docking. Sheep breeding should aim to develop positive health and natural resistance to parasites, rather than focus on breeding for maximum meat, milk, or wool production. Any public subsidies for sheep farming should be tied to high standards of animal welfare and environmental sustainability.

Most importantly, there is a major welfare cloud on the horizon—the prospect of the mass genetic engineering of sheep. Biotech companies are aiming to produce pharmaceutical and industrial proteins in sheep milk, as well as breeding or genetically engineering sheep for faster growth or heavier muscles. Such developments are unlikely to remain issues just for the Western world. Biotechnologists are aiming to use embryo transfer, genetic engineering, and cloning to increase the productivity of China's hundreds of millions of sheep and goats.

Related articles: Animal issues in Australia; Animal protection in Africa; Animals in Asia; Animals in Chinese culture; Animals in the Middle East; Cloning animals; Developments in animal law; Live animal exports; Pig castration; Religious slaughter; Slaughter; South American perspectives on animals; Transgenic animals

Broom, D. M., and Fraser, A. F., *Domestic Animal Behaviour and Welfare*, 4th ed., CABI, 2007.

Compassion in World Farming, *Stop, Look, Listen: Recognising the Sentience of Farm Animals*, 2006, available at http://www.ciwf.org.uk.

Keeling, L. J., and Gonyou, H. W. (eds.), *Social Behaviour in Farm Animals*, CABI, 2001.

Turner, Jacky, *Animal Breeding, Welfare and Society*, Earthscan, 2010.

Webster, John, *Animal Welfare: Limping towards Eden*, Blackwell, 2005.

Young, Rosamund, *The Secret Life of Cows*, Farming Books and Videos, 2003.

JACKY TURNER

ANIMALS IN RESEARCH

THE ALTERNATIVES

An "alternative" or "replacement" to an animal test can be defined as "any scientific method employing non-sentient material which may, in the history of animal experimentation, replace methods which use conscious living vertebrates" (Russell and Burch). Animal-based methods that have been refined to cause the animals less pain or distress or that use fewer animals (see discussion of the 3Rs in Russell and Burch) are also sometimes referred to as alternatives. However, not everyone is comfortable with an "improved" animal test being called an "alternative," and therefore the term "replacement" is often preferred for clarity.

The development of alternatives to animal experiments is an ever-expanding field and is now seen as a useful research area in its own right. Centers for the development of alternatives now exist in most major chemical and drug companies and within most governments. There are also centers for the validation of alternative methods in Europe (ECVAM), the United States (ICCVAM), and Japan (JAVAM). It is generally accepted that alternative methods not only spare animals from suffering in laboratories but also save the company time and money and importantly produce more reliable and accurate results. For example, reconstituted human skin models have been shown to be more predictive of skin irritation in humans than the rabbit test that they now replace (Jirova et al.).

Alternative techniques include tests based on chemistry (*in chemico*), computers (*in silico*), and cells and tissues (*in vitro*, literally meaning "in glass"—i.e., in a test tube) and ethical human studies (*in vivo*). In vitro techniques commonly use bacteria, fresh human or animal cells, or permanent cell lines. Examples of in vitro replacement tests include the following:

- the Ames test to detect whether a substance will cause damage to genes (genotoxicity), which uses bacteria instead of live mice who are fed the chemical and then killed to look at their tissues

- the embryonic stem cell test to detect whether a substance will damage the unborn fetus (reproductive toxicity), which uses established cell lines instead of live rats or rabbits who are force-fed the chemical and killed one day before they would have given birth

- the monocyte activation test to detect contaminants in injectable drug solutions, which uses donated human blood in a simple test tube test instead of live rabbits who are injected into their ears, with their temperature monitored rectally for up to eight hours at a time

- reconstituted human epidermis tests to test for whether chemicals will irritate the skin, which is a 2D layer of skin cells derived from human skin donated from plastic surgery, instead of the rabbit Draize test in which rabbits are shaved and then smeared with a potentially corrosive substance

- colonogenic assays to detect whether a substance might cure cancer, which uses cancer cells taken from human patients instead of live mice who are genetically modified to have cancer and are then injected with a potential drug

Future in vitro replacement techniques are likely to involve the combination of individual cell-based tests to mimic a more complete "whole body" response. Simple cell-based tests can even be combined within a mini "bioreactor," which allows researchers to see the direct effects of a substance on different organs of the body after it has been metabolized by liver cells. The creation of 3D mini organs is also developing, such as a mini liver to test the safety of drugs. Many researchers now think the way forward may be toxicogenomics, which looks at the effects of substances on genes as an indicator of effects even before they have occurred.

In silico techniques include computer models that work out whether a chemical is likely to be toxic based on whether it has a similar structure to another more understood chemical. Computers can also be used to build up pictures of entire systems such as the human heart and predict what effect a drug might have on the circulation.

In chemico techniques are chemistry-based tests and can be extremely powerful and fast methods. They work on the basis that a toxic reaction might be predicted based purely on the chemistry of the chemical of interest. For example, the peptide reactivity assay is based on the extent to which a chemical binds with proteins in skin cells, which is a key determinant of whether these new proteins will cause an allergic reaction called skin sensitization. Other chemical techniques include high-tech chromatography devices that identify toxins within a mixture. This technique is now a replacement for the detection of toxins within shellfish, a test that currently requires the death of 50 percent of the mice injected with the shellfish mixture to prove contamination.

It is also possible to use human volunteers in ethically designed studies in vivo that replace animals, often primates. For example, the development of noninvasive brain imaging scanners such as functional magnetic resonance imaging machines, or MRIs, enable researchers to "see" activity in the human brain, rather than using nonhuman primates in invasive brain or pain experiments (Langley et al.). Similarly, the development of accelerated mass spectrometers allows researchers to inject volunteers with microdoses of drugs to track their metabolism in the body because they measure such minute quantities that volunteers are never at risk.

Replacement can be considered "absolute" if the method does not depend on any animal material, but unfortunately, many replacements are "relative" in that they still depend on the use of animal tissues or use animals of lower neurophysical sentience (such as insects and worms). Currently, many in vitro cell-based replacement systems rely on primary (freshly killed) animal tissues or animal-derived proteins, such as the Ames test, which uses proteins experimentally derived from rats; tests using fetal bovine serum, which is obtained directly from the still-beating hearts of calves taken out of their mothers at the slaughterhouse; and the bovine corneal opacity and permeability test for eye irritation, which uses the eyes of cows slaughtered for food. There are increasing efforts to move away from these relative replacements in the interests of sound science and animal welfare.

As a consequence of the development and use of alternatives, the number of animals used in laboratories is thought to have decreased significantly from the 1970s. However, it is still at a very high estimate of 115 million animals every year (Taylor et al.) and is currently, in Europe at least, no longer decreasing. This is particularly disappointing when we consider that since 1986 Europe has had legislation in place (previously called 86/609/EEC and now 2010/63/EU) that prohibits the use of an animal when a suitable alternative is "reasonably and practically available." (No such mandate to use alternatives exists in the United States or most other countries around the world.) In addition, the cosmetics industry has been forced to develop alternatives because of a ban in Europe on the testing of cosmetics after 2009, which resulted from considerable public pressure.

Unfortunately, the development of alternative methods is limited by inadequate investment, the speed at which validation projects proceed, reluctant regulatory acceptance following validation, and the obvious problems with comparing a potentially superior method with an outdated, highly variable gold standard (the old animal test), which would in all likelihood fail itself if it were to go through the same validation process (Balls and Combes). Many alternative methods are vastly cheaper than the animal test they replace—a good example is the in vitro cell transformation assays that cost twenty thousand euros and take three weeks to complete, compared to the rat cancer bioassay that costs one million euros and takes two years. Unfortunately, alternatives can cost a lot of money to develop in the first place. L'Oreal, for example, claims it has spent 200 million euros developing the skin model to replace the Draize skin irritation test performed on rabbits.

Related articles: Animal pain; Animals used in research; Humane research; Legislation in the European Union; Primates worldwide; Stem cell research; Toxicity testing

Balls, M., and Combes R., "The Need for a Formal Invalidation Process for Animal and Non-Animal Tests," *Alternatives to Laboratory Animals* 33.3 (2005): 299–308.

Balls, M., van Zeller, A.-M., and Halder, M., *Progress in the Reduction, Refinement and Replacement of Animal Experimentation*, Developments in Animal and Veterinary Science series, vols. 31A and B, Elsevier Science BV, 2000.

Jirova, D., Liebsch, M., Basketter, D., Spiller, E., Kejlova, K., Bendova, H., Marriott, M., and Kandarova, H., "Comparison of Human Skin Irritation and Photo-Irritation Patch Test Data with Cellular In Vitro Assays and Animal In Vivo Data," in Proceedings of the 6th World Congress on Alternatives and Animal Use in the Life Sciences, August 21–25, 2007, Tokyo, Japan, special issue, *AATEX 14* (2008): 359–365.

Langley, C., Aziz, Z., Bountra, Q., Gordon, C., Hawkins, N., Jones, P., Langley, G., Nurmikko, T., and Tracey, I., "Volunteer Studies in Pain Research—Opportunities and Challenges to Replace Animal Experiments. The Report and Recommendations of a Focus on Alternatives Workshop," *NeuroImage* 42 (2008): 467–473.

Russell, W. M. S, and Burch, R. L., *The Principles of Humane Experimental Technique*, Methuen, 1959.

Taylor, K., Gordon, N., Langley, G., and Higgins, W., "Estimates of Laboratory Animal Use in 2005," *Alternatives to Laboratory Animals* 36.3 (2008): 327–342.

KATY TAYLOR

ANIMALS USED IN RESEARCH

Cats

Cats are favored by animal researchers for a wide variety of scientific experiments, and they remain one of the best-documented animal subjects in the laboratory. Researchers favor cats because they are easy to obtain, fairly uniform in size, and convenient to maintain in the laboratory because of their fastidious habits. Most cats are bred by animal dealers and then sold to laboratories, although some in the United States are obtained from local pounds or shelters.

Because the anatomy of the cat's sensory system has been studied so thoroughly, the animals are used extensively in research involving the nervous system, including spinal cord research. Cats are used to discover how humans recover from strokes and traumatic injuries and to study gangliosidosis, a disorder that causes skeletal abnormalities and developmental disabilities in humans. Cats are also utilized in the study of vision, speech, and hearing functions. In particular, cats have been the subjects of studies on such eye disorders as glaucoma and amblyopia, commonly known as "lazy eye," and hearing disorders such as tinnitus, a condition that causes chronic, high-pitched hearing in the ears of humans.

Another significant area is the study of AIDS. Animal researchers are convinced that the same methods and technology used in the attempt to develop a feline AIDS (FIV) vaccine can be applied to the HIV virus that causes AIDS in humans. However, the feline immunodeficiency virus (FIV) does not resemble the human immunodeficiency virus (HIV), making a feline AIDS model inapplicable to humans. Additional research where cats are currently used include studies in alcohol and drug abuse, Alzheimer's disease, narcolepsy (excessive daytime sleepiness), digestive disorders, diabetes mellitus, toxoplasmosis, and sleep deprivation.

Cats are poor models for human disease. Even the casual observer will note that cats' hearing is much more sensitive than humans' hearing, and their ability to jump great distances far exceeds that of humans. Anatomically and functionally, the cats' brain and spleen are very different from that of human beings. Additionally, drugs affect different species in different ways. For example, the antibiotic chloramphenicol is tolerated by dogs but can kill a cat. Histamine affects a cat's brain arteries in exactly the opposite way that it affects primates. In 1982, the antidiarrheal Clioquinol was removed from the market after it caused paralysis and blindness in human patients. Yet it had passed animal testing, which included cats. And although millions of people every day rely on pain medications containing acetaminophen, this drug causes renal failure and death in cats.

Dogs

Dogs are obtained from a number of different sources. Some of the research dogs come from biological supply companies that purpose-breed them specifically for research. Purpose-bred beagles are a popular choice for researchers because of their small size. Other dogs are obtained from local pounds and shelters. Racing greyhounds, obtained from dog racing tracks, are also popular with researchers because their lack of body fat makes it easy to reach their internal organs. In addition, greyhounds are easy to manage in the laboratory because they are accustomed to being handled in the racetrack environment.

Dogs have been used extensively in many areas of research, including the cardiovascular, respiratory, and circulatory systems; emphysema; amyotrophic lateral sclerosis (ALS, commonly known as Lou Gehrig's disease); the gastrointestinal system and the effects of radiation; diabetes; and testing for the toxicity levels of pharmaceutical drugs. Dogs are also favored as experimental subjects in the study of trauma and shock, including post-shock infections, and in research on the skeletal system, such as repairing fractured bones, reattaching limbs, and developing artificial limbs. In the operating room, doctors in training practice their surgical techniques on dogs. These are commonly known as "dog labs." However, many prestigious medical schools in the United States have eliminated dog labs from their curriculum. Some of these include Harvard, Stanford, Columbia, and Yale.

Dogs are also used in the development of new surgical techniques, including microsurgery. Dogs are extensively used in the development of cardiovascular surgical techniques and in organ transplantation experiments. Anesthesia techniques are also evaluated on dogs. Behavioral research is another area where dogs are seen by animal researchers as appropriate stand-ins for humans. Dogs are often the subject of studies on alcohol and drug addiction and have been used to study phobic behavior, the nature of panic disorders, and the effect of caffeine on the nervous system. Two drugs used to treat heart arrhythmia, encainide and flecainide, were proved to be safe and effective in dogs but caused heart attacks in humans. Blood clotting is a common side effect of oral contraceptives in human females but does not occur in dogs—in fact, contraceptives have the opposite effect.

It seems especially ironic that an animal whom humans have domesticated and given the title "man's best friend" is used as a research tool, a victim of biomedical research.

Farmed animals

Among the most extensive and controversial uses of farmed animals—in this instance, pigs—is in xenotransplantation. Xenotransplantation is the surgical replacement of organs, tissue, and cells from one species with body parts from a different species. Scientists have been experimenting with transplanting pig organs into baboons and other species for some time, and many believe that transgenic, or genetically engineered, pigs will serve as the ultimate factory for human spare parts. Yet there has been little if any progress since 1984 when a twelve-day-old baby girl, "Baby Fae," received a baboon's heart and died three weeks later. Transgenic pigs have their genes altered to prevent the human body from rejecting their organs, cells, and tissue. Xenotransplantation has sparked widespread ethical and scientific debate. Many scientists are concerned about the risks of transmitting deadly diseases from one species to another.

Other research involving pigs includes the healing process of burn victims, the development of new techniques in heart surgery and anesthesia, and the exploration of nonsurgical treatments for heart attack patients.

Other farmed animals have been used in genetic research as well, the best-known example being Dolly the sheep, the first clone made from an adult animal. Sheep are also used extensively to study problems that occur in human pregnancy and in human neonates (infants who have just been born). The arteriovenous shunt, which allows patients with kidney failure to be connected to a dialysis machine, was tested on sheep. Sheep have also been used in military research to test weaponry and the effects of nuclear explosion and radiation, as well as in "wound labs," where they are purposely shot so that battle surgeons can practice treating their wounds.

Like sheep, goats have been used in military research as living targets for studying the effects of gunshot wounds on the battlefield. They have also had nuclear bombs detonated near them in order for researchers to study the effects of nuclear explosions and radiation fallout.

Marine life

All manner of marine life are used by researchers in experiments, from rainbow trout to sharks and tropical fishes. As with land animals, marine creatures are poor laboratory models for human beings. Researchers use sharks to study cancer, concentrating on their immune cells, because it is believed they are virtually immune to cancer. In addition, scientists are studying the reproductive biology of nurse sharks for application to human reproductive systems. Goldfish are used in vision and neurological studies. Electric eels are used to study bioelectrical and chemical spheres of the nervous system. Lobsters are used in the study of motor coordination to learn more about treating diseases of the nervous system, such as Parkinson's disease and Huntington's chorea. Rainbow trout are used in the study of liver cancer. Tropical fishes are used in the study of skin tumors.

Skates, a relative of the shark, are kept in captive breeding colonies to create a steady supply of these creatures for experimental purposes. Researchers are studying reproductive hormone cycling in skates, as well as artificial insemination and sperm storage. In addition, they are studying the embryonic development aspects of skate corneas, lens, olfactory organs, and membrane transport in developing cardiac muscle cells.

Researchers are increasingly relying on a relatively new model organism, the zebra fish, for a variety of scientific investigations. Zebra fishes are frequently used to study vertebrate development and physiology, as well as the pathogenesis of human disease at the cellular and molecular levels. This organism is small, reproduces quickly, and has transparent eggs and embryos. It is easy for scientists to maintain zebra fishes in the lab, as well as manipulate and observe them. Despite many documented limitations of the zebra fish model, they are used as models for a number of human diseases, including cancer, heart disease, glaucoma, and neuromuscular diseases.

Primates

Chimpanzees are humankind's closest living relatives, sharing more than 98 percent of our genetic code. They are highly intelligent and social beings who have language and distinct cultures. They use tools, teach their young, and plan for the future. Chimpanzees in captivity have been taught American Sign Language, and their proficiency shows that they can understand and use abstract symbols in their communication. Chimpanzees can even pass these acquired language skills on to their children.

Our close genetic kin have suffered terrible exploitation in the name of science. Historically, chimpanzees have been used in all manner of invasive experiments, from head injury, venereal disease, and sex change experiments to space research in which they were spun in giant centrifuges and placed in decompression chambers to induce unconsciousness. In fact, a chimpanzee named Ham became the first U.S. astronaut when he was launched into space in 1961. The U.S. military has also used primates for research on the effects of radiation.

Today, chimpanzees are used in a small number of studies focused on infectious disease experiments and monoclonal antibody therapies. Because chimpanzees are the only known nonhuman animals who can become infected with HIV, they have been used extensively for AIDS research, although the infections seldom develop into full-blown AIDS. Despite years of research, the chimpanzee model for AIDS has been a failure. The "necessity" of chimpanzees in other areas of biomedical and behavioral research has recently come under tremendous scrutiny in the United States. In December 2011, the Institute of Medicine (IOM) Committee on the Use of Chimpanzees in Biomedical and Behavioral Research released a report indicating that the scientific necessity of chimpanzee research is very limited. The director of the National Institutes of Health accepted the report, and a working committee was tasked with deciding how to implement the IOM report. It has been estimated that a number of current protocols involving chimpanzees may be phased out in light of the findings of the working committee, which was due to release its report in early 2013.

Apes and monkeys are favorite subjects in psychological studies. Of all nonhuman species, they are the ones whose behavior most closely resembles that of humans. Monkeys, especially rhesus monkeys, are used more often than their chimpanzee cousins in experiments because they are smaller and less expensive to breed and maintain. Neurological testing includes experiments on the brains of living animals, including cutting, coagulating, and removing brain tissue, and stimulating the brain by electrical and chemical means. Many common experiments are designed to find out how animals react to different kinds of negative stimuli through the administration of intense, inescapable shock to various parts of the body and deprivation of social contact, sleep, and/or nourishment. In order to create a model for human depression to test antidepressants and other drugs, researchers conduct maternal deprivation experiments, in which baby monkeys are taken from their natural mothers and encouraged to "bond" with an artificial surrogate made of cardboard and fabric. In a typical scenario, a baby monkey searching for the gentle reassuring touch of his or her mother returns again and again to the surrogate, which is specifically wired to jolt the baby with an electrical shock every time he or she clutches it.

Primates have also been used in alcohol and drug addiction studies. The practice of creating animal addicts to study as models for human behavior is particularly unsound, given the dramatic physiological and metabolic differences between humans and animals. Further, there is no shortage of human addicts who could participate in these clinical studies.

Baboons are among the largest of all monkeys. One disturbing role they are forced to play is in xenotransplantation, where they are used as if they are a collection of spare parts. Baboons have been unwitting donors of their kidneys, livers, hearts, and bone marrow. Cross-species transplants have been conducted since 1963 with dismal results. Apart from the moral argument against xenotransplantation, if it were proven successful, there is strong evidence that it could create more problems than it potentially solves. Virulent infections could cross the species barrier, and new diseases could be introduced into the human population.

Rodents

Rodents—mice, rats, and guinea pigs—represent the vast majority (about 90 percent) of all animals used in scientific research in the United States. The United States' Animal Welfare Act of 1966 does not protect rodents, and it does not even require specific accounting of the number used. Therefore, there is no way to know conclusively just how many millions of rodents suffer and die each year in laboratories, although estimates are in the tens of millions. Although the term "lab rat" is used as a catch-all term for rodents, mice are used far more than rats because they are smaller, and more of them can be kept in the laboratory. They also breed faster and are less expensive.

Despite abundant evidence that rodents are poor models for humans, experimentation on mice and rats spans virtually the entire field of biomedical research. This research encompasses cancer, genetics, immunology, and virology, as well as the behavioral sciences. Rodents are also used to study the effects of aging and exposure to radiation. They are used in research on Alzheimer's disease, AIDS, alcoholism, and drug addiction. Mice and rats are typically used to test new pharmaceutical drugs before they are tested on humans. These tests are designed to evaluate the effectiveness of the drugs, to measure toxicity levels, and to identify possible adverse reactions.

Mice used in laboratory research are commonly descendants of an abnormal albino species bred under controlled conditions. However, since the 1980s, the number of genetically engineered "transgenic" animals used in research has been growing rapidly. Reports from Great Britain in 2010 revealed that genetically modified animals now represent the majority of animals used in experimentation. Transgenic mice and rats are genetically engineered animals—mutants who have selected human genes in their bodies. The human genes make these animals more susceptible to certain human diseases. Researchers can now select mice and rats who mimic specific human diseases and conditions ranging from diabetes to cancer. There are even those who have been genetically engineered to be obese.

Guinea pigs were among the first animals used widely in the medical laboratory, giving rise to the use of the term "guinea pig" to mean anyone, human or nonhuman, used in a test or experiment. When it was discovered that they were susceptible to many human diseases, guinea pigs were used to test treatments for tuberculosis. Because of guinea pigs' rapid reproductive rate and high resistance to disease, they are considered valuable laboratory animals and are used for testing serums and antitoxins and for experiments in genetics and nutrition. Today, mice and rats have largely replaced guinea pigs, although these animals are still used in many behavior, heredity, and nutrition studies. New pharmaceutical drugs are also tested on guinea pigs.

Although there is currently no legislation pending in the United States Congress that would amend the Animal Welfare Act to specifically include rats, mice, and birds under the act's definition of "animal" and thus the protections and regulatory terms of this act, it is likely that animal welfare advocates will pursue such changes in the future—and just as likely that biomedical research interest groups will strongly oppose those efforts.

***

Related articles: Animals and public health; Captive chimpanzees; Cats; Cloning animals; The complexity of animal awareness; Dogs; The ethics of testing; Guinea pigs; The legal rights of great apes; Military experiments; Pound seizure; Primates worldwide; The trade in primates for research; Toxicity testing; Transgenic animals

Greek, C. Ray, and Greek, Jean Swingle, *Sacred Cows and Golden Geese,* Continuum, 2000.

———, *Specious Science: Why Experiments on Animals Harm Humans*, Continuum, 2002.

———, *What Will We Do If We Don't Experiment on Animals?*, Trafford, 2004.

Hajeri, Vinita A., and Amatruda, James F. "Studying Synthetic Lethal Interactions in the Zebrafish System: Insight into Disease Genes and Mechanisms," *Disease Models and Mechanisms* (January 2012).

Institute of Medicine and National Research Council. *Chimpanzees in Biomedical and Behavioral Research: Assessing the Necessity*, National Academies Press, 2011.

LaFollette, Hugh, and Shanks, Niall, *Brute Science: Dilemmas of Animal Experimentation*, Routledge, 1996.

Malakoff, David, "Activists Win Big on Rodent, Bird Rules," *Science*, February 7, 2000.

National Anti-Vivisection Society (U.S.), "Animals in Scientific Research," 2012, available at http://www.navs.org.

———, *Law in the Laboratory: A New Perspective*, 2008.

———, "The Scientific Case against Animal Experimentation," *Expressions* 5 (2002).

Shanks, Niall, and Greek, C. Ray, *Animal Research in Light of Evolution*, Rodopi, 2009.

PEGGY CUNNIFF AND PAMELA OSENKOWSKI

CLONING ANIMALS

Cloning is one of society's most complex, misunderstood, and controversial science topics. It has sparked fears of "Frankenstein" science although proponents claim that this technology holds the promise of cures for a host of human ailments. Cloning has sparked ethical debates and government intervention. On February 22, 1997, when newspaper headlines announced the successful cloning of a sheep named Dolly, the fears of human cloning were so prevalent that then U.S. president Bill Clinton called for a ban on the use of federal funds for research that could lead to human cloning. Within days of the announcement of Dolly's cloning, researchers in Oregon announced that they had cloned two rhesus monkeys from embryonic cells.

Cloning is a form of genetic engineering. The term "clone" refers to a group of organisms that are genetically identical. Clones result from asexual reproduction, a process in which a new organism develops from only one parent, and they are exact genetic duplicates of that parent.

From a scientific point of view, Dolly's significance was not that she was a clone. The first experiments with animal clones had begun in the 1950s with tadpoles. Dolly's creation was significant because she was the first cloned animal to be made from a mature cell taken from an adult animal's body. Until then it had been generally assumed that only cells from very early embryos could be used for cloning because in later stages of fetal development, cells become specialized and lose the ability to differentiate into different types of cells. With Dolly, Ian Wilmut and his colleagues at the Roslin Institute in Scotland proved this belief wrong. Scientists at the institute reversed the maturation process by depriving a specialized cell of nutrients, in this case a mature udder cell from a six-year-old ewe. Through a technique called somatic cell nuclear transfer, they put the cell's nucleus into an unfertilized sheep egg cell from which the nucleus had been removed and fused the two with a jolt of electricity.

Dolly was the only successful birth out of 277 attempts. Scientific journals have reported disturbing evidence that Dolly, as well as other adult-cell clones, may age prematurely or suffer from other ailments. In fact, the United States' National Academy of Sciences has cited the high rate of abnormalities and other problems with animals cloned since Dolly as a reason for a legal ban on human reproductive cloning. Cloning is associated with high failure rates and overweight fetuses. According to researchers in Japan who studied a group of twelve cloned mice, cloning results in pneumonia, liver failure, degraded immune systems, and shorter life span. The idea that cloning is a benign process is therefore discredited.

It is possible to distinguish between reproductive cloning used to create human clones and so-called therapeutic cloning that would make an embryo that can supply genetically tailored stem cells via insertion of the DNA of a person's body cell into an enucleated egg. Therapeutic cloning uses stem cells from human embryos (or other sources) and grows them into appropriate body tissue. It has been proposed that this procedure be labeled "nuclear transplantation to produce stem cells" if the blastocyst is not to be implanted in a uterus. Stem cell duplication might be used to provide sources for replacement tissues or organs and could overcome the problems of a limited number of organs available for transplantation and organ transplant rejections.

Cloning has been financed primarily to make animals bigger and better meat machines or laboratory tools. Cloning is a way of making farmed animals more productive and more resistant to disease. Similarly, laboratory animals can be produced with uniform genetic qualities to produce more "pure" data or designed to carry genetic defects to mimic human diseases. In either case, cloning enables the standardization of animals, which is what researchers and meat-producers alike most want. Cloned animals could also be engineered to produce organs for xenotransplantation that might eliminate problems of organ rejection. More far-fetched, some have proposed cloning as a way to save endangered animals or perhaps to resurrect extinct ones, as in the *Jurassic Park* movies. Hundreds of people have expressed interest in cloning their beloved companion animals, following the announcement of the birth of "C.C." ("Copy Cat") at Texas A&M University. Some have difficulty understanding the ethical objections to a technology that produces an endearingly cute result.

The issue of cloning has pitted those who object or raise legitimate ethical and scientific concerns against those who see potential cures for people suffering from Parkinson's, diabetes, leukemia, heart and liver failure, and other diseases. But many of these putative claims for medical advancement are speculative, hypothetical, or as yet untested. Concerns raised by religious groups, ethicists, animal protection groups, and right-to-life followers have included objections to the use of aborted fetuses or the destruction of fertilized eggs to harvest the stem cells. Another objection to animal cloning is the way in which it perpetuates the idea that animals are simply manipulable objects, or commodities, for human advancement, even if that advancement amounts to little more than cheaper meat.

Antivivisectionists have raised concerns that as cloning techniques make it easier to mass-produce genetically engineered animals, there likely will be an increase in the number of animals used in research. This technology could also threaten biodiversity as scientists work to create "perfect" animal specimens at the expense of others. Additional issues raised by animal welfare proponents include, minimally, how to lessen suffering, how to police the production of these genetically engineered animals, and how to amend welfare regulations so as to extend better protection to the animals concerned.

Related articles: Developments in animal law; The ethics of testing; Stem cell research; Transgenic animals; The welfare of sheep

Center for Veterinary Medicine, U.S. Food and Drug Administration, "Animal Cloning: A Risk Assessment," *Washington Post*, January 14, 2008, available at http://www.washingtonpost.com/wp-dyn/content/article/2008/01/14/AR2008011402731.html.

George, Robert P., "Cloning Addendum" [a statement on the cloning report issued by the President's Council on Bioethics], *National Review*, July 15, 2002, available at http://old.nationalreview.com/document/document071602.asp.

Linzey, Andrew, and Barsam, Ara, "Cloning of Animals in Genetic Research: Ethical and Religious Issues," in Cooper, David N. (ed.), *Nature Encyclopaedia of the Human Genome*, vol. 1, Nature, 2003, 830–833.

Pacelle, Wayne, "Is Animal Cloning Ethical?," 2005, available at http://www.SFGate.com.

Pennisi, Elizabeth, and Vogel, Gretchen, "Clones: A Hard Act to Follow," *Science*, September 6, 2000.

U.S. Department of Energy Genome Program's Biological and Environmental Research Information System (BERIS), "Cloning Fact Sheet," 2009, available at http://genomics.energy.gov.

U.S. Food and Drug Administration, "Animal Cloning," 2010, available at http://www.fda.gov.

PEGGY CUNNIFF AND PAMELA OSENKOWSKI

THE ETHICS OF TESTING

The use of animals in testing or experiments (originally known as "vivisection") arouses considerable controversy, particularly between researchers and animal protectionists. On one hand, researchers claim that use of "animal models" is essential to make scientific progress, whereas on the other hand, animal protectionists claim that the infliction of suffering on animals ought never to be countenanced. The range of areas in which animals are used is huge and includes drug testing, product testing, toxicity testing, military experiments, genetic manipulation, and biological and behavioral research as well as medical research. Around 500 million animals worldwide—from primates to rodents—are used and killed annually, representing about 5 percent of all animal deaths caused by humans (Gendin 15).

It is important to establish why animal suffering matters morally. Many people still seem to suppose that how we treat animals is an emotional matter and that there are no objective, rational considerations involved. The term "animal lover" is often used in this respect to imply that concern for animals is only a matter of feeling rather than argument.

In fact, moral concern for animals is undergirded by strong rational considerations, including the fact that animals cannot give or withhold their consent; they cannot represent or vocalize their own interests; they cannot comprehend the harm or captivity that is inflicted on them; they are morally innocent or blameless; and finally, they are relatively vulnerable and defenseless (Linzey, *Why Animal Suffering Matters*). All these considerations are morally relevant in the same way that they are relevant in establishing that children are also a special moral case. Like children, animals are wholly or nearly wholly at the mercy of human adults and require human advocacy to plead their cause.

But what of the possible benefits that animal testing may bring? That there have been some benefits seems impossible to deny (after all, more than 150 years of experimental work involving animals should have produced some results), but two qualifiers are necessary. The first is that a rigorous cost-benefit assessment of these experiments shows that many of these experiments are of doubtful or overstated utility (Knight). The idea that all such experiments contribute directly to advancing specifically medical research is unwarranted since many tests are unrelated to medical research. The second is that the growth of alternatives has gained momentum during the last fifty years, and it is by no means clear that alternatives have been fully utilized or funded.

Nevertheless, there are some animal protectionists who accept that some experiments can be morally justified. For example, Peter Singer maintains that "if one, or even a dozen, animals had to suffer experiments in order to save thousands, I would think it right and in accordance with equal consideration of interests that they should do so." He continues, "That, at least, is the answer a utilitarian must give" (Singer 56). Singer's position is less than satisfactory, however. In the first place, Singer's form of "preference utilitarianism" privileges those adult or more developed beings who have memory, self-awareness, and a high degree of sentiency over others (a position I have elsewhere called "adultism"; Linzey, *Why Animal Suffering Matters* 155) but at the same time neglects those considerations previously outlined here, such as moral innocence, defenselessness, incomprehension, and the inability to represent oneself, which is why Singer also believes that it is permissible to kill newborn babies up to one month old. Second, the problem with all utilitarian ethical theory can be expressed in these questions: what constitutes a utility, and who is to calculate these utilities? Since it is human beings who do the calculations, it is invariably *their* interests that are deemed paramount. In fact, it is less than clear that animal abuse does benefit human beings. The adverse effects of inflicting abuse include desensitization, loss of empathy, and denial (Linzey, "Does Animal Abuse Really Benefit Us?" 6–8), but these factors are seldom, if ever, fully recognized or taken into account.

The third problem is that if utilitarian thinking is sound, then it should equally apply to human subjects. By the same Singerian logic it must also be right for one or even a dozen humans to suffer experimentation in order to save thousands. As I have written previously, "for some of us—unpersuaded that wholly utilitarian considerations should govern our treatment of animals—we would be as disinclined to support painful experimentation on animals as we would be disinclined to support the torture of human subjects, no matter how 'beneficial' the results might be in either case" (Linzey, *Why Animal Suffering Matters* 156). From this perspective then, there are some things that should not be done whatever the consequences, and the deliberate infliction of suffering on innocents, either animals or children, is one of them. There may well be gains, but they are—in the words of Tom Regan—"ill-gotten gains" (Regan 377).

This principled objection is buttressed by a further consideration: that animal testing has become institutionalized and that, like all institutions, it has a tendency to perpetuate itself even and especially in the light of criticism. Animals are *as a matter of routine* subject to scientific procedures and so are treated as means to human ends. As such, testing embodies a historical but unethical view of animals as simply here for our sake without any intrinsic value of their own as individuals. It is difficult to believe that this practice will survive ethical scrutiny of the kind that should be expected during the next few decades.

Related articles: The alternatives; Animal and human violence; Animals used in research; Children's relations with animals; Humane research; Military experiments; Moral anthropocentrism; The moral claims of animals; The moral community; Product testing; Toxicity testing; Transgenic animals

Gendin, Sidney, "The Use of Animals in Science," in Regan, Tom (ed.), *Animal Sacrifices: Religious Perspectives on the Use of Animals in Science*, Temple University Press, 1986.

Knight, Andrew, *The Costs and Benefits of Animal Experiments*, Palgrave Macmillan Series on Animal Ethics, 2011.

Linzey, Andrew, *Animal Theology*, SCM Press/University of Illinois Press, 1994.

———, "Does Animal Abuse Really Benefit Us?," in *The Link between Animal Abuse and Human Violence*, Sussex Academic Press, 2009.

———, *Why Animal Suffering Matters: Philosophy, Theology, and Practical Ethics*, Oxford University Press, 2009.

Regan, Tom, *The Case for Animal Rights*, Routledge and Kegan Paul, 1983.

Singer, Peter, *Practical Ethics*, Cambridge University Press, 1979.

ANDREW LINZEY

FREEDOM OF INFORMATION

Animal experiments are currently excluded within the arrangements for the Freedom of Information Act (FOIA), 2000, in the United Kingdom, preventing a proper scientific scrutiny of proposals to use animals in laboratories. Without access to the technical details of license applications, it is impossible for independent scientists to scrutinize the alleged justification for proposed experiments or recommend non-animal alternatives. The National Anti-Vivisection Society (NAVS, U.K.) argues that a proposal to deliberately inflict pain and suffering surely deserves the widest possible public and scientific scrutiny and that such scrutiny should be carried out before licenses are awarded. After all, if any other member of the community were to inflict such suffering on an animal, they would be liable to prosecution. Holding a license to deliberately inflict pain and suffering on an animal should require the highest, rather than the lowest, level of public accountability.

A huge gap in transparency and public accountability exists at the heart of the United Kingdom's Animals (Scientific Procedures) Act (ASPA) 1986 (EU Directive 86/609/EEC). Section 24 of the ASPA provides a blanket of secrecy over almost all information on animal experiments (ASPA 86). It is widely felt that this undermines regulations designed to safeguard animal welfare.

This was highlighted in 2005 when the Home Office was questioned about regulatory animal testing in one laboratory in Scotland. This is a commercial contract testing company offering its clients dogs, monkeys, rats, mice, rabbits, pigs, guinea pigs, goats, cows, birds, and fishes for experimentation, and at the time it claimed to be responsible for approximately 1 percent of all experiments taking place in the United Kingdom—over 25,000 animals every year.

In 2005, documents and photographs were leaked to Animal Defenders International (ADI) providing a chilling insight into the world of contract research, where laboratories are paid to conduct animal experiments on behalf of manufacturers of products such as drugs, chemicals, and household and industrial substances. ADI's report on the documents highlighted a series of mistakes, inadequacies of scientific protocols, and contradictions in the company's own reports of its experiments, including the following: miscalculations in dosing, resulting in severe suffering, death, and premature termination of studies; researchers running out of the test substance halfway through a study; a test substance passing its expiry date before the end of the experiment, while dosing of the animals continued; animal tests being conducted when human studies were already underway; animal results being ignored, with human studies continuing after bad animal results; and accidentally pumping of chemicals into dogs' lungs instead of their stomachs.

NAVS and ADI submitted freedom of information requests on a number of studies, only to be informed that the information had not been kept. The reason given was that in authorizations for groups of drugs or chemicals (i.e., covering many animal tests for individual products within a group of chemicals or pharmaceuticals), no individual assessments of studies take place, and records of outcomes are not kept. The individual study reports are the property of the client, and the Home Office does not hold copies. In effect, commercial testing laboratories are policing themselves—and in this case, the result was poor practice and little regard for animal welfare.

This secrecy appears to encourage lax enforcement of regulations and a culture of complacency—leading to the poor operation of procedures. The case in question is just one of a number of studies into the day-to-day operations of laboratories using animals in the United Kingdom: undercover investigations, carried out by the NAVS, have repeatedly revealed a ham-fisted approach to regulations and little more than a cursory regard for the current guidelines on animal welfare, the "Code of Practice for the Housing and Care of Laboratory Animals." More than a decade of investigations carried out by the NAVS found an unashamed disregard for animal welfare and the Code of Practice that is designed to safeguard it.

Lack of transparency is undoubtedly a contributing factor to this poor practice. And when in 2009 more than 2.6 million animals were used in U.K. laboratories alone, it is understandable that there is public concern that the researchers carrying out such experiments do not seem to be accountable to the public.

The exclusion of the use of animals in scientific procedures from the Freedom of Information Act is also seen as an obstacle to scientific progress. In the United Kingdom and across Europe, progress on the development and adoption of non-animal replacement techniques has been slow; regulators are used to the data they receive from animal tests, and the law does not have a mechanism to enable a wider critical review of toxicology tests on animals and input from experts on non-animal methodology. Though it is a stated goal in the United Kingdom and Europe that animal experiments be eventually phased out, the blanket of secrecy over all information on animal experiments is preventing this goal from becoming realized.

In reality, there is no workable framework and mechanism within U.K. law to ensure that animal tests are replaced by non-animal alternatives: the validation process is outmoded and currently facilitates easy adoption of animal techniques more readily than the development and validation of alternative methods. Section 24 of the United Kingdom's ASPA only amplifies the problems this brings about. When the validation system is ill-fitted and outdated, it should be even more of a priority to properly scrutinize proposals for animal research before awarding licenses to carry them out. As it stands, all too frequently, animal research is undertaken without the proper consideration of whether there are alternatives available—or whether the research is even necessary.

The U.K. government will be forced to review its legislation to comply with Directive 2010/63/EU on the protection of animals used for scientific purposes, adopted in second reading by the European Parliament in September 2010. This text strikes a better balance between fundamental freedoms and the corporate demands for confidentiality: "to ensure that the public is informed, it is important that objective information concerning projects using live animals is made publicly available. This should not violate proprietary rights or expose confidential information." Although the U.K. government will have some margin of appreciation when transposing the provisions of the directive, article 43 should partly remove the blanket of secrecy covering animal experiments in the United Kingdom.

Thus, project license holders will have to produce "non-technical project summaries" of their experiments on animals, containing "information on the objectives of the project, including the predicted harm and benefits and the number and types of animals to be used" and "a demonstration of compliance with the requirement of replacement, reduction and refinement." These summaries, as well as subsequent updates and retrospective assessments, will then be published by member states but "shall be anonymous and shall not contain the names and addresses of the user and its personnel" and must safeguard "intellectual property and confidential information." This is undoubtedly a step in the right direction. It is being increasingly recognized that if we are to get the best scientific endeavors, we need a raft of different techniques, and we need to constantly develop new technologies—more accurate and more relevant to people.

Related articles: The alternatives; Animal pain; Animals used in research; Humane research; Legal challenges to experiments in the United Kingdom; Primates worldwide; Toxicity testing

Animal Defenders International, National Anti-Vivisection Society, and the Lord Dowding Fund for Humane Research, *Primate Testing in Europe*, 2009.
Animals (Scientific Procedures) Act, U.K., 1986, available at http://www.legislation.gov.uk/ukpga/1986/14/contents.
European Union Council Directive, 86/609/EEC, on the Protection of Animals Used for Experimental and Other Scientific Purposes, November 24, 1986, available at http://ec.europa.eu/food/fs/aw/aw_legislation/scientific/86-609-eec_en.pdf.
Freedom of Information Act, U.K., amended 2000, available at http://www.legislation.gov.uk/ukpga/2000/36/contents.

JAN CREAMER

MILITARY EXPERIMENTS

That the world's military forces rely on animals should be no surprise. We are all accustomed to seeing beautiful horses at the British Trooping of the Colour, regimental billy goats on parade as mascots, and trained dogs sniffing out the presence of unexploded ammunition. Indeed, the Royal Army Veterinary Corps says that its personnel "enjoy a challenging and varied employment role involved in all aspects of the use of animals for military purposes." The Corps states that its Web site "gives advice on how to get the best out of service animals to ensure they are used to full potential." Although the Royal Army Veterinary Corps is not itself involved in experiments on animals for military purposes, and in terms of the numbers of animals in its care, it plays a minor role in global terms, "how to get the best out of service animals" is itself a telling phrase.

However, hundreds of thousands of animals are used annually for military purposes as the subjects of testing and experimentation in laboratories worldwide. Some of the world's military scientists also have not hesitated to use human beings as the subjects of military experiments, especially in connection with nuclear, chemical, and bacteriological weapons. Sometimes the subjects of such experiments have been volunteers unaware of the scale of the dangers to which they were being exposed. Even conscripts have been exposed to nuclear test explosion radiation. Sometimes experiments involving appalling cruelty have been conducted on prisoners and other victims—for example, experiments conducted by the Japanese during World War II.

In short, since it now seems almost normal for the military to experiment on human beings, it should cause little surprise that animals have long been subject to similar cruelties. What will be a surprise to many, and may even cause astonishment, is the sheer number of animals used worldwide, the savagery of the unrelieved pain inflicted on them, and the silence that surrounds the whole issue.

In the United States, it is estimated that twenty million animals are put to death every year in the course of a wide range of experiments, mostly undertaken for commercial purposes. Over 300,000 die specifically as a result of military experimentation. Most of the latter experiments are conducted in Department of Defense laboratories, and some take place in the laboratories of other institutions and universities. These animals die as a consequence of chemical weapons tests, ionizing radiation lasers, high-power microwaves, biological investigations, and gravitational experiments. There are nearly two thousand experiments on primates every year in the United States, with the Department of Defense keeping a special stock of them. Primates are not the only animals involved, however. Sheep, rats, pigs, rabbits, dogs, cats, mice, ferrets, and guinea pigs are regular subjects as well. Rats have even been given implants of depleted uranium to assess the uranium's effects, and monkeys have been deliberately poisoned with nerve gas. Fortunately, such animal experimentation in the United States is now, as a result of public pressure and more openness, on the decline.

It would be quite unfair, however, to suggest or imply that the United States, though responsible for half the world's military expenditure, is the only country to use animals in this way. At least the United States is now more open than most about its activities in this field.

An article in the Israeli newspaper *Ha'aretz* on March 17, 2000, exposed some disturbing experiments. One soldier described the placing of trussed-up but alive and conscious pigs into a trailer that was then blown up in order to simulate the effect of a Scud missile explosion. The soldier had to undergo psychological counseling as a result of the horrors he saw when the trailer was finally opened.

From Britain come regular stories of animal abuse for military purposes. The best-known laboratory is that at Porton Down in Wiltshire, first opened in 1916. It was at Porton Down that scientists worked on the production of anthrax, initially tested on sheep. As long ago as 1936, Beverley Nichols in *Cry Havoc*, a best seller in its day, referred to Porton Down: "Since 1916 to the present day, experiments have been continuously carried out—thousands of animals (horses, cats, rabbits, guinea pigs, rats and mice) have been used and killed by the experiments or have had to be destroyed immediately after" (Nichols 69). That was over seventy years ago, but Porton is still in business. More than 21,000 animals of many species, from ferrets to nonhuman primates, were experimented on in 2005—an increase of 76 percent from 2000.

Among other major powers, the Japanese too have conducted their anthrax experiments on sheep, horses, guinea pigs, and mice. Countries that generally have a better humane record than others—for instance, Sweden and Norway—nevertheless use animals for military experimental purposes too. Both countries in recent years have used fully conscious pigs on firing ranges, so as to be able to assess the impact of live rounds. That other major countries—France, China, and Russia, for instance—are not mentioned here is only because figures are not easily available. Who can forget the Russian dog sent out to his certain lonely death in space, as the space race, which is in fact still largely a military race, started? The French open-air experimental nuclear tests in the Pacific must have resulted in the direct and radiation-caused slaughter of thousands of animals.

Sadly, at the various world summits on environmental policy—Stockholm in 1972, Rio in 1992, Johannesburg in 2002, and Rio again in 2012—the direct use of animals by military entities for research was not discussed, even though much concern was expressed about the damage done to free-ranging animals worldwide as a result of human activity. Those who justify war as a last resort and who think that human beings have needs that entitle them to exploit animals still defend military experimentation and the use of animals for military purposes. A pseudo cult of animal "bravery" is now in vogue. But the new animal war memorial erected in London's Park Lane has on it this honest comment: "They had no choice."

Moralists, religious and otherwise, are now starting to

take this issue more seriously. "It is contrary to human dignity to cause animals to suffer or die needlessly," says the *Catechism of the Catholic Church* (no. 2418). "Needlessly" is the key word and where the argument starts. Many from both religious and secular traditions now believe that no supposed human need can possibly justify the military-inspired cruelty now shown to other species in so many parts of the world. Jilly Cooper in her *Animals in War* says that "man has consistently exploited them, and allowed them to be slaughtered in their millions" (211). She was writing primarily about animals killed in the course of war. But the abuse of animals starts long before war itself, in the research laboratories of the world.

Related articles: Animals used in research; Captive chimpanzees; Catholic teaching; The ethics of testing; Freedom of information; The moral claims of animals; Primates worldwide

Catechism of the Catholic Church, Geoffrey Chapman, 1994.

Cooper, Jilly, *Animals in War*, Corgi, 2000.

Gardiner, Juliet, *The Animals' War: Animals in Wartime from the First World War to the Present Day*, Imperial War Museum, 2006.

Lederer, Susan E., *Subjected to Science: Human Experimentation in America before the Second World War*, Johns Hopkins University Press, 1995.

Morpurgo, Michael, *War Horse*, Egmont Books, 2007.

Nichols, Beverley, *Cry Havoc*, Jonathan Cape, 1936.

"Royal Army Veterinary Corps," 2010, available at http://www.army.mod.uk/army-medical-services/5320.aspx.

Ryder, R. D., *Victims of Science: The Use of Animals in Research*, Davis Poynter, 1975.

BRUCE KENT

PATENTING ANIMALS

Patents protect inventions. They give inventors a monopoly over their invention for a period, usually twenty years. No one can exploit the invention without the patentee's permission during that period. After that, anyone can do so. In return for the protection, a patentee must make his invention public. The history of patents goes back at least to 500 B.C.E., when the Greek city of Sybaris encouraged "all who should discover any new refinement in luxury, the profits arising from which are secured to the inventor by patent for the space of a year" (Anthon 1273).

Patents are granted by governments or international bodies. Many European countries belong to the European Patent Convention (EPC), but national governments can still decide whether to grant a patent on their territory. There is a European Union directive for biotechnological inventions, Directive 98/44, but attempts to harmonize patent law in the EU more generally have so far proved unsuccessful. Under the World Trade Organization's (WTO) Agreement on Trade-Related Aspects of Intellectual Property Rights, patents must be available in WTO member countries in all fields of technology.

Patents are sometimes divided into design patents, plant patents (protecting plant breeders' rights), and utility patents. In the United States, they can extend to research, except for purely philosophical research. The requirements for a patent vary, but typically the invention must be new, non-obvious, and useful or industrially applicable. The invention can be a product or process and can extend to improvements. A patent does not give the holder the right to use the invention—the general law may prevent this—but merely assigns a right to prevent others from doing so.

Many people would be surprised to learn that animals can be patented, but in fact, many jurisdictions have decided that animals can be patentable inventions. This is best illustrated by the famous oncomouse case. The oncomouse was the first animal for which a patent was granted in both the United States and Europe. The animal was created, in the mid-1980s, when oncogenes (cancer genes) were inserted into the genome of two "founder" mice. This markedly increased both their and their descendants' susceptibility to development of cancerous tumors, which of course cause considerable suffering. Oncomice have been used in research, including in the evaluation of highly toxic anti-cancer drugs.

The patentee, Harvard University, obtained a patent at the European Patent Office (EPO) in 1992, as well as in the United States. The EPO patent originally applied to use of the technique in all mammals. This was later reduced to rodents, on the basis that there was no evidence that it worked in other species. A number of organizations formally objected to the patent. These included the British Union for the Abolition of Vivisection (BUAV) and Compassion in World Farming. The proceedings took an inordinately long time and culminated in an appeal by the BUAV and some of the other opponents to the Technical Board of Appeal (TBA) and a cross-appeal by Harvard to the limiting of the patent.

Article 53a of the EPC prevents the grant of a patent where publication or exploitation of an invention would be contrary to public order or morality. Morality exceptions to patentability are found in the laws of China, India, Argentina, the Philippines, Bolivia, Peru, Brazil, and New Zealand, but not, surprisingly, in the laws of the United States, Canada, and Australia. Morality exceptions are not unusual in international law—for example, there are such exceptions to the free trade principle under GATT, one of the WTO agreements, and the Treaty on the Functioning of the European Union. Article 13 of that treaty also recognizes that animals are sentient beings, deserving of full regard in the formulation of relevant policy.

The BUAV had to accept, following an earlier ruling by the TBA in the oncomouse case (T19/90), that the patenting of an animal was not contrary to morality per se. However, it argued that the oncomouse itself should not be patented.

In T 356/93, a case concerning the genetic modification of plants to make them resistant to a particular herbicide, the TBA had given a useful definition of "morality": "the concept of morality is related to the belief that some behavior is right and acceptable whereas other behavior is wrong, this belief being founded on the totality of the accepted norms which are deeply rooted in a particular culture." Also relevant was article 23d(d) of rules implementing article 53a, introduced by the EPO in 1999. This prevents the patenting of "processes for modifying the genetic identity of animals which are likely to cause them suffering without any substantial medical benefit to man or animals, and also animals resulting from such processes." This closely mirrors article 6(2)(d) of the biotechnology patents directive.

The TBA finally gave its ruling in a lengthy judgment in 2005. In large part, it accepted the BUAV's analysis of the correct approach to the public morality exception. Applying rule 23d(d) first, it said that if there is likely to be *any* animal suffering from application of the "invention" and no likelihood of *substantial* medical benefit to people or other animals, the patent must be refused. The anticipated medical benefit must flow from use of particular "invented" animals (the necessary correspondence test).

Where there is a likelihood of substantial medical benefit, one must then consider whether a patent should nevertheless be refused under article 53a viewed in isolation from rule 23d(d). The TBA had earlier in the case—before rule 23d(d) was introduced—posited a cost-benefit test in this regard. The benefit at this stage is usefulness to humans, a lower threshold than substantial medical benefit.

A key question is the time at which morality is to be assessed. The normal rule with patents is that the various tests have to be applied at the "effective date" (either the filing date or the priority date). The BUAV argued that with a wholly new type of invention such as the oncomouse, this was unrealistic. Since the invention process is necessarily secretive, the public could not have formed a view about the morality of this (or any) new type of invention at the effective date—for the obvious reason that it did not know about it. The TBA accepted that one could use hindsight to determine what prevailing moral-

ity would have been at that time had the public had the necessary information.

Applying the legal tests to the voluminous evidence, the TBA upheld the patent but limited it to oncomice (applying the necessary correspondence test). Its reasoning for upholding the patent was not entirely convincing. For example, it claimed that the decision of the Supreme Court of Canada in 2002 (*Commissioner for Patents v President and Fellows of Harvard College*, 2002 SCC 76) to refuse a patent for the oncomouse, based on its interpretation of the word "invention" in the (Canadian) Patent Act 1985, did not establish that animal patents arouse public unease. This runs directly counter to the leading judgment of Justice Bastarache, who referred to the "serious moral and ethical implications of this subject-matter" and recognized that the patenting of higher life forms raised concerns that did not arise in respect of nonliving organisms.

In addition, the TBA focused on public attitudes toward the use of mice in cancer research generally, whereas it should (as it had accepted earlier) have focused on the evidence about attitudes toward the oncomouse (i.e., a genetically modified animal predisposed to suffer cancer) in particular. It was also too dismissive of the value of opinion surveys in gauging public opinion.

However, there is now reasonable clarity about the legal tests to be applied in animal "invention" cases at the EPO. Essentially, a utilitarian cost-benefit test must be applied. Indeed, it was for this reason that Upjohn, the pharmaceutical giant, had earlier failed to obtain a patent for its hairless mouse, designed to advance the cure of baldness ("Transgenic Mice of the Analysis of Hair Growth," European Patent Application 89913146.0, the Upjohn Company of Michigan, filed on November 17, 1989; refused on July 25, 1993, and deemed withdrawn).

Following the TBA decision, there should at least be a limit on the patentability of so-called inventions of animals under the EPC. That might lead to a similar approach in other patent jurisdictions with a morality exception. If research institutions fear they will not be granted a patent on grounds of morality, that is likely to dissuade them from "inventing" the animal in the first place, since it is the prospect of a monopoly for a significant period that acts as the driver for this kind of research. The recent grant of patents by the EPO covering chimpanzees (among other species) in the field of synthetic biology is likely to become another test case (Testbiotech).

Related articles: Animals used in research; The ethics of testing; Freedom of information; Legislation in the European Union; The moral claims of animals; Transgenic animals; The World Trade Organization

Anthon, Charles, *A Classical Dictionary: Containing an Account of the Principal Proper Names Mentioned in Ancient Authors, and Intended to Elucidate All the Important Points Connected with the Geography, History, Biography, Mythology, and Fine Arts of the Greeks and Romans Together with an Account of Coins, Weights, and Measures, with Tabular Values of the Same*, Harper and Bros, 1841.

Dresser, Rebecca, "Ethical and Legal Issues in Patenting New Animal Life," National Agricultural Law Center, University of Arkansas, 1988, available at http://www.nationalaglaw-center.org/assets/bibarticles/dresser_ethical.pdf.

Linzey, Andrew, "Created Not Invented: A Theological Critique of Patenting Animals," *Crucible* (April–June 1993): 60–67.

Linzey, Andrew, and Barsam, Andrew, "Cloning of Animals in Genetic Research: Ethical and Religious Issues," in Cooper, David N. (ed.), *Nature Encyclopaedia of the Human Genome*, vol. 1, Nature, 2003, 830–833.

Macer, Darryl R. J., "Ethical Issues in Patenting Scientific Research," in *Proceedings of the International Conference of the Council of Europe on Ethical Issues Arising from the Application of Biotechnology*, vol. 2, Council of Europe, 2000, 173–181, available at http://www.eubios.info/Papers/PATENT.htm.

Morin, Eileen, "Of Mice and Men: The Ethics of Patenting Animals," *Health Law Journal* 5 (1997): 147, available at https://litigation-essentials.lexisnexis.com.

Testbiotech, "European Patent Office Issues Patents on Chimpanzees," October 2012, available at http://www.testbiotech.org/en/node/721.

DAVID THEW

PRODUCT TESTING

Product testing is one of the most controversial areas of animal use, with opinion polling demonstrating clear public opposition to the practice. Animal tests for cosmetics or household products are not specifically required by law: to market a product a company must demonstrate its safety, but this can be done by using approved non-animal tests and combinations of existing ingredients that have already been established as safe for human use. It has been estimated, for example, that there are over eight thousand ingredients already proven safe for use. More and more companies are saying no to animal testing and still produce safe and effective beauty or cleaning products.

Painful product tests can be carried out on a range of animals, including dogs, rabbits, mice, rats, guinea pigs, fishes, and birds. These includes tests for skin or eye irritation, skin sensitization (allergy), toxicity (poisoning), mutagenicity (genetic damage), teratogencity (birth defects), carcinogenicity (causing cancer), embryonic or fetal genetic damage, and toxicokinetics (to study the absorption, metabolism, distribution, and excretion of the substance). Tests have included controversial and cruel methods such as the Draize test, where substances are poured into the eyes of conscious rabbits.

In 2003, the European Union finally agreed a Europe-wide ban on cosmetics animal testing, which came into effect in 2009. An EU ban on the sale of new animal-tested cosmetics is also set to come into effect in 2013. Around the world animal testing for cosmetics continues, however, as does the testing of household products on animals, with the U.K. government pledging in 2010 to end the practice. Virtually every ingredient, even water, may have been tested on animals in the past. Most consumer products, therefore, may include ingredients once tested on animals. Increasingly, however, companies are responding to pressure to end animal testing in their supply chain.

Methods used in chemical testing are prescribed by a series of global regulations, led largely by the Organisation for Economic Co-operation and Development (OECD), with the regulation and authorization for such tests managed at a national level by member state governments and agencies. Growth in the development of non-animal research methods has been accelerating in recent years, partly because of the deadlines imposed by the European testing and marketing ban. Regional agencies such as the European Centre for the Validation of Alternative Methodologies (ECVAM) and the Interagency Coordinating Committee on the Validation of Alternative Methods (ICCVAM) coordinate the development and validation of such non-animal methods, prior to their eventual adoption by regulatory agencies and global use. Concerns continue to be voiced, however, over the length of time taken to validate such methods and the lack of political will to bring them into widespread use.

Growing criticism of the toxicity tests used to assess chemical ingredients in cosmetics and household products is being voiced on scientific grounds. It is increasingly recognized that the results of animal tests for safety cannot be interpreted with confidence, not least because of the variations in the ways different species react to chemicals. These concerns have lent weight to long-standing moral objections to animal use and have seen increasing urgency in efforts to replace animal use in this area. A report published by the National Research Council of the National Academies (U.S.), commissioned by the U.S. Environmental Protection Agency, concludes that a paradigm shift is necessary and possible in toxicity testing in order to consign animal use to the history books. The European Chemicals Agency, charged with the chemicals management regime for the European Union, has set out its own approach to minimizing animal use in this area.

Sustained consumer pressure, the impact of the EU legislation, action by major corporations, and development of non-animal methods are powerful forces that, when combined, are bringing closer the day when no animal will suffer and die for the development of beauty and household products.

Related articles: The alternatives; Animals used in research; The ethics of testing; Humane research; Legislation in the European Union; The moral claims of animals; Toxicity testing

European Chemicals Agency, _Practical Guide 10: How to Avoid Unnecessary Testing on Animals_ (ECHA-10-B-17-EN), 2010.

European Commission, _Draft Report on Alternative (Non-Animal) Methods for Cosmetics Testing: Current Status and Future Prospects_, 2010.

Interagency Coordinating Committee on the Validation of Alternative Methods, _Test Method Evaluations_, 2010, available at http://iccvam.niehs.nih.gov/methods/methods.htm.

Organisation for Economic Co-operation and Development, _OECD Guidelines for Testing of Chemicals_, 2010, available at http://www.oecd.org/dataoecd/8/11/42451771.pdf.

U.S. National Academy of Sciences, _Toxicity Testing in the 21st Century: A Vision and a Strategy_, 2010, available at http://www.nap.edu/openbook.php?record_id=11970&page=R1.

Zuang, V., et al., _ECVAM Technical Report on the Status of Alternative Methods for Cosmetics Testing (2008–09)_, European Union, 2010.

MICHELLE THEW

STEM CELL RESEARCH

Stem cell research is among the new and controversial frontiers of biomedical research. Respected science journals, as well as the general media, frequently feature reports of successful treatments and promising cures for human diseases using these cells. Some animal welfare proponents have advocated stem cell research as a replacement for research where animals are currently used. But there are skeptics who fear that these claims are exaggerated and others who question the ethics of harvesting cells that may benefit some people at the expense of reducing other lives to the value of "raw material." It is important that the general public understand, at least, the fundamentals of what stem cell research is, so that decisions about if and how this research should be conducted are not the monopoly of the scientific community.

Stem cells are the body's master cells. They can grow into virtually any of the body's cell types. During embryogenesis, humans develop from a single undifferentiated cell called a "totipotent stem cell." Stem cells are unlike any specific adult cell because they have the ability to form any adult cell. Because scientists can culture stem cells in vitro, such cells can potentially provide an unlimited source of clinically important adult cells, if scientists can direct their development in culture into bone, muscle, blood, or liver cells or any of more than two hundred other different kinds of cells in the human body.

Although the term "stem cell" is commonly used to refer to the cells within the adult organism that renew tissue, the most fundamental source of stem cells is the early-stage embryo. These embryonic stem (ES) cells, unlike the more differentiated adult stem cells or other cell types, retain the special ability to develop into nearly any cell type. Embryonic germ (EG) cells, which originate from the primordial reproductive cells of the developing fetus, have properties similar to ES cells.

Human stem cells can be derived from human fetal tissue following elective abortion and also from human embryos that are created by in vitro fertilization and that are no longer needed by couples being treated for infertility. Stem cell research is controversial because cells from fetuses are the beginning cells of a new human life. This controversy principally arises from sharply differing moral views regarding elective abortion and the use of terminated embryos for research. Stem cell research raises the moral dilemma of trying to cure disease yet protect potential life.

Serious ethical discussion will (and should) continue on these issues. The challenge facing society will be how to maintain respect for the human embryo on one hand and the need to pursue the scientific and clinical benefits of stem cell research on the other. It should also be noted that stem cells can be found in bone marrow, umbilical cords, and placentas, and many researchers are limiting their investigations to these sources.

One way to avoid the potential controversy of working with embryonic stem cells is to work instead with induced pluripotent stem cells (iPSCs). These are adult cells that scientists can genetically manipulate back to an embryonic stem cell–like state by altering gene expression in such a way that it mimics properties of embryonic stem cells. This methodology can be used to "de-differentiate" cells to create pluripotent stem cells—cells that have the potential to differentiate into a number of different types of cells to generate all of the cell types in the body. Although much work remains to be done to see whether iPSCs and embryonic stem cells are different in significant ways, researchers are already working with this useful resource to model disease and as a tool for drug development.

Proponents of stem cell research have identified many potential benefits. Physicians can transplant stem cells into children suffering from leukemia, with fewer problems than with bone marrow transplants in regard to matching antigens. Although traditional leukemia therapies include chemotherapy, radiation, and bone marrow transplants, new treatments include stem cell transplants from the patient or a donor. Recent human studies showed that patients who receive stem cell transplants had a 25 percent survival advantage over those who received traditional treatments. Although it was initially thought that only children suffering from leukemia would benefit, it has recently been shown that adults suffering from leukemia can also be treated with umbilical cord–derived stem cells.

Children with sickle cell anemia, immunodeficiency syndromes, and inherited enzyme deficiencies can also benefit from transplantation of stem cells garnered from umbilical cords and placentas. Patients suffering from a broad range of diseases such as juvenile-onset diabetes mellitus and Parkinson's disease can also be treated. Replacing faulty cells with healthy ones offers potential treatment and possibly cures. Likewise, injecting healthy cells to replace damaged or diseased cells could, in theory, rejuvenate failing organs. Already, people with autoimmune diseases, such as multiple sclerosis, scleroderma, juvenile arthritis, systemic lupus erythematosus, and vasculitis/cryoglobulinemia, have been successfully treated using stem cell therapy. About two-thirds of those patients who receive stem cell therapy experience stabilization or improvement in their conditions. Stem cell transplantation has been particularly successful in treatment of persistent systemic lupus erythematosus when combined with chemotherapy.

Advocates of stem cell research point to recent developments that have raised hopes that new therapies will become available that may serve to relieve human suffering. Many argue that instead of funding animal models, we should be conducting research to identify the chemical and molecular pathways that allow stem cells to differentiate into other cells and investigating effective ways to combine gene therapy and stem cell therapy. Given the progress scientists have made in the use of stem cells, animal model–based methodologies seem all the more archaic. Although these exciting developments in stem cell research offer many opportunities, the challenges raised by ethical concerns about the source of stem cells, how the research is conducted, and who will benefit should also continue to be addressed.

Related articles: The alternatives; Animals used in research; The ethics of testing; Humane research; Transgenic animals

Hogan, Pat, "Stem Cell Research: What Progress Has Been Made, What Is Its Potential?," *EurekAlert!*, September 9, 2010, available at http://www.eurekalert.org/pub_releases/2010-09/ehs-scr090910.php.

Knight, Matthew, "Stem Cells Could End Animal Testing," *CNN Health*, December 22, 2008, available at CNN.com.

National Institutes of Heath, "Stem Cell Information," 2012, available at http://stemcells.nih.gov/.

President's Council on Bioethics, "Monitoring Stem Cell Research," 2004, available at http://bioethics.georgetown.edu/pcbe/reports/stemcell/.

Stein, Rob, "Appeals Court Lifts Ban on Stem Cell Funding," *Washington Post*, September 9, 2010, available at http://voices.washingtonpost.com/checkup/2010/09/appeals_courts_lifts_ban_on_st.html.

U.S. Department of Health and Human Services, "History of Bioethics Commissions," available at http://www.bioethics.gov/commissions/.

PEGGY CUNNIFF AND PAMELA OSENKOWSKI

TOXICITY TESTING

The objective of toxicity testing is to develop an adequate database to make reasonable and reliable decisions about the safe use of chemicals in society by testing these chemical agents on living systems. Historically, experimental "animal models" (in vivo) provided the data for making these decisions. However, in vitro models, such as mammalian cells in culture, subcellular and molecular constituents, and knowledge of the chemical structure of the test agent, have gained in prominence because, taken together, this information can provide an insight into the mechanism by which the agent exerts its toxic effect.

In order to reduce or replace animal testing for regulatory purposes, non-animal tests must be independently validated to prove that they can provide information relevant and reliable for hazard prediction in relation to specific types of toxicity. Toxicity testing is used to determine the biological effects of a myriad of substances, including cosmetics, household products, food additives, pharmaceuticals, and pesticides, as well as for environmental testing and monitoring. In addition to growing political and consumer pressure from animal advocates, the impetus toward the change to non–animal model systems has been based on new legislative mandates, the increase in the number of new chemical agents and formulations in the marketplace, the high costs of performing toxicity testing on animals, and the precipitous rise in new and improved testing methods that circumvent the use of whole animals, including the use of human cells. The future challenge in the development and use of non-animal models is the choice of the cell model and the choice of test chemicals on which to make the prediction of toxicity prior to validation of the test system in safety assessments.

Time and time again, scientists have discovered that data obtained from animal studies is unreliable and difficult to extrapolate to people. For example, Pfizer Central Research reported that of nineteen chemicals known to cause cancer in humans when ingested, only seven caused cancer in mice and rats. Despite this low correlation between rodents and humans, mice and rats represent more than 90 percent of all animals used in this kind of research. The significance of the problem of using other species to predict the toxicity of a substance for human beings was again illustrated in a 1994 report that identified more than 100,000 hospitalized patients who had died from toxic reactions to medication. In fact, adverse drug reactions were the fourth leading cause of death that year—more than diabetes, accidents, and HIV/ AIDS. In that same period, more than two million hospitalized patients suffered serious side effects of drugs.

Even the journal *Science* asked in 1992, "Are humans to be regarded as behaving bio-chemically like huge, obese, inbred, cancer-prone rodents?" (Abelson, "Diet"). The journal seemed to answer its own question in 1995: "Chemical risk assessment studies conducted with rodents have helped to justify expenditures of more than a trillion dollars over the past twenty years. Large additional outlays are planned, although it has not been shown that such studies have substantially benefited human health" (Abelson, "Flaws").

Toxicology has traditionally focused on ADMET studies, which identify how a drug is absorbed into the body, how it is distributed, metabolized, and eliminated in the body, and what its toxic effects are (absorption, distribution, metabolism, excretion, and toxicity). Because many different genes influence how a drug is metabolized, slight differences in gene structure will determine significant differences in function. This accounts for different responses to drugs among people and even greater differences between species.

The toxicity testing of chemicals, formulations, and products using whole animal experimentation has long been criticized. Not only do the tests invariably involve suffering and death for the test animals (millions of animals are used, and even those who survive the testing are killed since both dead and surviving animals are necropsied to evaluate gross anatomical evidence of organ toxicity), but also the test results themselves are often questionable in relation to ensuring the health and safety of the general public. In fact, the public perception that animal testing makes products safe is a dangerous fallacy. Oven cleaners, lighter fluids, fertilizers, pesticides, and other products tested on animals and readily available in supermarkets, garden centers, and hardware stores could be fatal in the hands of a child. Some products that can cause harm if used improperly do not feature either a warning label or a childproof cap. No amount of animal testing will prevent serious harm in case of exposure.

In recent years, the development and validation of alternatives to in vivo toxicity testing have significantly reduced the number of animals used. Although noninvasive techniques are growing in use, the scope of information yet to be collected and analyzed includes the development of alternatives to current areas of toxicity testing, including the following:

- Acute toxicity tests—the administration of a single dose of a chemical by injection, inhalation, or force-feeding, at a concentration sufficient to produce toxic effects and death, such as the Lethal Dose 50 (LD50) test in which 50 percent of the test subjects are killed.
- Carcinogenicity—tests that determine the ability of a substance or product to cause cancer.
- Mutagenicity—experiments designed to determine whether a substance or product can cause genetic mutations.
- Phototoxicity—tests in which animals are exposed first to certain chemicals and then subsequently to light/UV radiation to measure effects on skin and other organs.
- Ocular and dermal irritation—tests that traditionally expose the eye or skin of an animal to a substance (Draize eye and skin irritancy tests) and alternative tests that use eye or skin cells, to determine whether exposure causes any degree of irritation.
- Metabolism-mediated toxicity—tests in which animals are exposed first to drugs and then to drug elimination and in which toxic drug reactions are measured via transport through the kidneys and liver.
- Embryotoxicity—tests in which pregnant animals are exposed to chemicals or drugs that may kill the embryo, interfere with embryonic development, retard general growth or organ growth, and/or cause postnatal structural or functional abnormalities in the offspring.
- Reproductive toxicity—tests in which male and female animals are exposed to the test substances to determine adverse effects on the reproductive organs, the endocrine systems, or pregnancy outcomes; the effects measured

include the onset of puberty, gamete production and transport, reproductive cycle normality, sexual behavior, fertility, gestation, and lactation.

▪ Immunotoxicity—tests in which animals are exposed to substances to determine whether immune responses are suppressed that could enhance the risk of disease, or whether inappropriate stimulation of the immune system is induced and could contribute to allergic or autoimmune disease.

Many of the new and improved alternative methods to the use of animals have enhanced a better understanding of the science of the toxic mechanisms and have provided a more humane approach in the development of scientific methods for safety testing. Innovative research in the field of pharmacogenomics and data from in vitro studies, computers, epidemiology, and the analysis of the chemical structure and chemical properties of drugs can predict toxicity better than animal models.

Related articles: The alternatives; Animals used in research; Humane research; Product testing; Stem cell research

Abelson, Philip H., "Diet and Cancer in Humans and Rodents," *Science*, January 10, 1992.

Abelson, Philip H., "Flaws in Risk Assessment," *Science*, October 13, 1995.

Greek, C. Ray, and Greek, Jean Swingle, *Sacred Cows and Golden Geese,* Continuum, 2000.

Lord, Peter G., and Papoian, Thomas, "Genomics and Drug Toxicity," *Science*, October 22, 2004.

National Anti-Vivisection Society (U.S.), "Animals in Product Testing," 2012, available at http://www.navs.org.

———, "Animals in Scientific Research," 2012, available at http://www.navs.org.

———, *The Long and Tragic History of Animal Experimentation: A New Perspective*, 2008.

Shanks, Niall, and Greek, C. Ray, *Animal Research in Light of Evolution*, Rodopi, 2009.

Ward, Sherry L. (ed.), "Toxicity Testing Resource Center," AltTox.org, December 6, 2007, available at http://alttox .org/ttrc/.

JUNE BRADLAW, PEGGY CUNNIFF, AND PAMELA OSENKOWSKI

TRANSGENIC ANIMALS

Transgenic science involves transmitting, through genetic engineering, one or more genes from one species to another. These animals can be manipulated to overexpress specific genes, express human genes, or even express mutated genes. As a result, these animals can produce specific proteins that they normally would not produce. Basic science researchers often use transgenic animals to better understand gene function.

Some researchers generate transgenic animals to study specific diseases because animals can be engineered to express genes implicated in human disease. Scientists can introduce genes implicated in cancer and Alzheimer's disease, for instance, to animals and then study the pathologies that the animals develop as a result.

Other types of transgenic animals have been developed in a new field called "pharming," in which farmed animals are genetically modified to serve as living incubators of certain proteins and other chemical substances that have medicinal value for people. For example, researchers have introduced human genes into cow udders to produce milk that carries human proteins that can be used for medicine, cancer treatment, and even a no-calorie sweetener. Other applications of transgenic farmed animals include modifications that increase an animal's milk production or the nutritional value of milk. Transgenic goats have also been modified to produce milk that contains a protein that regulates blood clotting.

More and more transgenic animals are being used in xenotransplantation experiments. These animals' genes have been manipulated to make their organs more suitable to be transplanted into people. Scientists have recently focused their attention on redesigning and harvesting the organs of pigs because of the suitable size of their organs and because genetic modification of this species has been done for years. However, there are also several problems with using the organs from a pig in xenotransplantation, one of the most important being that the human immune system is designed to attack anything it deems as "foreign"—including pig organs.

Antivivisectionists oppose the development and use of genetically engineered animals from both ethical and scientific perspectives. They believe it is unethical to purposely create mutant animals who are often born sick and deformed and who suffer greatly throughout their lives, strictly for the benefit of humans. For these animals, the disorders, mutations, and deformities represent only the beginning of their suffering. Genetically altered and born with tragic and painful problems, they often spend the remainder of their lives as subjects of highly invasive laboratory experiments.

Some scientists claim that transgenic animals more closely resemble their human counterparts. Others argue that nonhuman animals who have been injected with human genes do not become more "human" in the process because the considerable differences between species cannot be overcome through genetic engineering. Antivivisectionists argue that genetically engineered animals, like their "natural" counterparts, are inappropriate and inadequate models for humans in the laboratory.

Related articles: Animals and public health; Animals used in research; Birds used in food production; Cloning animals; The ethics of testing; The moral claims of animals; Rabbits; The welfare of cows; The welfare of pigs; Xenotransplantation

Glenn, Linda MacDonald, "Ethical Issues in Genetic Engineering and Transgenics," 2004, available at http://ActionBioscience.org.

Greek, C. Ray, "More Transgenic Animals," 2009, available at http://www.navs.org.

Kling, Jim, "First U.S. Approval for a Transgenic Animal Drug," *Nature Biotechnology* (2009).

National Anti-Vivisection Society (U.S.), "Animals and Cross-Species Transplantation," *Expressions* 5 (2002).

———, *Genetically Engineered Animals: A New Perspective*, 2008.

Pary, Leslie, "Recombinant DNA Technology and Transgenic Animals," *Nature Education* (2008).

Warren, Wendelyn Jones, "CVM Participates in PEW Initiative Meeting on Transgenic Animals," 2003, available at http://www.fda.gov.

PEGGY CUNNIFF AND PAMELA OSENKOWSKI

XENOTRANSPLANTATION

With a perceived shortage of human donor organs, the medical community has looked for a new source of organ donors and thinks it has found it in animals. Xenotransplantation, animal-to-human transplant, is being proffered as the ideal solution. The proponents of xenotransplantation want us to envision a world with an unlimited supply of fresh organs, available to anyone in need. What they do not tell us is the downside of xenotransplants—the cost to the animals whose organs are used, to the humans who pay for it financially and ethically, and to all animals (human and nonhuman) who face the real possibility of the catastrophic transmission of a fatal virus.

Is it morally acceptable to use animals as containers of spare parts for humans? Sadly, this question does not ever get serious consideration from the medical community. The animals suggested for xenotransplantation are not regular animals, but transgenic animals, genetically manipulated to be more humanlike. The ethical, moral, philosophical, and religious issues are considerable, but they are seldom given proper consideration.

First, consider the following: about 43 million Americans, almost 16 percent of the American population, are medically uninsured. More than 50 million adults in the United States have difficulties with access to needed medical care and coping with medical bills. Correcting this discriminatory system would save many more lives and reduce more suffering than xenotransplantation, even if xenotransplantation were successful.

Second, costly medical procedures provided to a limited, select group continually raise the overall cost of health care, limit insurance coverages, and increase insurance premiums. Do we save some patients with expensive medical procedures and possibly lose even more patients by denying them access to adequate health care? In countries with universal national health care, new expensive procedures force difficult care choices. Since dollars available for health care are finite, other medical procedures will no longer be provided in order to fund the development of xenotransplantation techniques.

Third, far from assisting human health, xenotransplantation may pose a direct threat to it. Cross-species transplantation enables the spread of infectious agents from animals to human recipients—and subsequently to the public at large. These viruses may remain dormant for long periods of time before causing clinically identifiable disease. The best example of this type of virus is HIV. No surveillance system can screen for unknown viruses.

Is there any alternative to xenotransplantation? The way forward is to reduce the need for transplantation while increasing the supply of human organs to a manageable level. This can be achieved in various ways. The most obvious way is to improve the existing human donor system, which we can do by reevaluating the criteria used for selection of appropriate donor organs and by enacting state-mandated choice laws and/or national presumed-consent legislation, such as has been enacted in many European countries. Not allowing the immediate family to reverse the decision made by the organ donor should be part of any law.

In addition, new surgical techniques, ventricular remodeling, split organ/live donor transplants, artificial organs, cell/tissue engineering, gene therapy, and cloned organs are other medical alternatives being developed. Some of these procedures have their own ethical problems as well. But currently, no system is in place to evaluate the effectiveness and cost-efficiency of xenotransplantation or any of these other experimental procedures.

It is worth bearing in mind that most illnesses are preventable. We know that regular exercise and a plant-based diet have a dramatic effect on reducing incidences of all major chronic diseases. We spend far too much on curing illnesses and not enough trying to prevent them. Prevention is much less expensive and far more effective.

Xenotransplantation, if successful, will generate enormous profits for the pharmaceutical industry, for the bioengineering firms that supply the transgenic pigs for transplant, and for the medical professionals involved. Because of the tremendous private investment from venture capital groups and large drug companies, the pressure to get approval for xenotransplantation is enormous. After all, it is all about money. Good for industry, bad for the consumer. Are we placing profits ahead of public health?

Not least of all, are we again placing profit before animal suffering? Experimental techniques involving interspecies transplantation are just that: experiments. That they carry some risk to the animals is inevitable. Some will say that these risks are small or can be minimized, but it is incontestable that animals will suffer—and have suffered—in the development of these techniques. Xenotransplantation represents a way of understanding animals that is plainly ethically regressive—that is, simply as spare parts or commodities for human beings. Once we go down this road, it will be only a question of time before the similar case is made for using human as well as animal subjects.

Xenotransplantation is not the answer, despite all the rosy pictures that overoptimistic researchers, genetic engineers, and pharmaceutical companies paint of readily available organs. We cannot continue to cure human lives by the wholesale taking of animal lives. We cannot deny health care to others simply because of where they live or because their financial condition prevents them from having access to adequate health care. We must learn to take better care of each other by becoming organ donors and to take better care of ourselves through diet and exercise. It is unethical to suppose that animals should always pay the price of human progress—and in this case, it is more than doubtful whether xenotransplantation will constitute anything like progress in the field of human health.

Related articles: The alternatives; Animal pain; Animals and public health; Animals used in research; Cloning animals; The ethics of testing; The moral clams of animals; Plant-based nutrition; Stem cell research; Transgenic animals; The welfare of pigs

Committee on Xenograft Transplantation, *Xenotransplantation: Science, Ethics, and Public Policy*, Institute of Medicine, National Academy Press, 1996.

Langley, Gill, and D'Silva, Joyce, *Animal Organs in Humans: Uncalculated Risks and Unanswered Questions*, Compassion in World Farming and British Union for the Abolition of Vivisection, 1998, available at http://www.ciwf.org.uk/includes/documents/cm_docs/2008/a/animal_organs_in_humans_1998.pdf.

Nuffield Council on Bioethics, *Animal to Human Transplants: The Ethics of Xenotransplantation*, 1996, available at http://www.nuffieldbioethics.org/xenotransplantation.

Olakanmi, Ololade, and Purdy, Laura, "Xenotransplantation: For and Against," *Philosophy Now* (July/August 2011), available at http://www.philosophynow.org/issue55/Xenotransplantation_For_and_Against.

Stark, Tony, *Knife to the Heart: The Story of Transplant Surgery*, Macmillan, 1996.

Suarex, Anthony, and Huarte, Jaochim (eds.), *Is This Cell a Human Being?: Exploring the Status of Embryos, Stem Cells and Human-Animal Hybrids*, Springer, 2011.

ALAN H. BERGER

ANIMALS IN SPORT AND ENTERTAINMENT

ANGLING FOR SPORT

Angling, also known as sport fishing or recreational fishing, is the catching of fishes for purposes other than commercial gain. The distinction between commercial fishing and angling is blurred by the fact that sport fishing is, in itself, a major commercial enterprise in which over one million people are at least partially employed in the United States alone. For the purposes of this article, angling encompasses any and all catching of fishes by individuals not employed in the commercial fishery industry.

One study estimates that close to 12 percent of the human population worldwide engages regularly in recreational fishing, with a total catch of over 10 million metric tons, or about 55 billion individual fishes. An important difference between recreational and commercial fishing is that whereas almost all of the fishes in the latter category are killed regardless of whether they are targeted species or bycatch, some 60 percent of angled fishes are released. It is unknown how many released die later from trauma caused by hooks (removed or still attached), loss of scales and skin mucus, fin fraying and other damage caused by nets, or prolonged lack of oxygen. The number of fishes killed by recreational fishing is also probably an underestimate, given the numbers of additional fishes commonly used as bait.

The relevance of angling to animal protection revolves around fishes' capacity to experience pain and suffering. Until very recently, fish sentience had not been investigated with much scientific rigor, and it was widely assumed that fishes are not sensitive to pain. But in the past decade a number of studies have been conducted that shine new light on the matter. It should be added that pain perception has been investigated in only a tiny fraction of fish species.

Fishes possess all of the areas of the central nervous system that process pain in mammals. Rainbow trout, for instance, possess similar nerve fibers to those that detect different sources of pain (touch, heat, chemical) in humans. Studies of goldfish and rainbow trout have demonstrated brain activation when these fishes receive noxious stimulation along their flanks. Such studies show that noxious stimuli are registered in fishes by more than a mere reflex response.

Further studies show that these physiological responses to presumptively painful events are accompanied by appropriate behavioral changes. Rainbow trout and zebra fish subjected to painful stimuli show a profound increase in respiration rates (measured by rates at which their gill covers open and close)—a psychologically induced response to pain that is well established in mammals. Trout injected in the lips with noxious substances (bee venom or vinegar) showed increased respiration, rocked their bodies from side to side, rubbed their lips on the substrate or the tank walls, and took longer to resume feeding. Other trout who received the same treatment (netted, anesthetized, handled) but were then either released back into their tanks or first given a small injection of salt water also showed (less pronounced) increase in respiration, but these fishes returned to normal behavior after about one hour, whereas the fishes injected with venom or vinegar took almost three and a half hours to recover. Moreover, treatment with a pain suppressant significantly lowered the effects of the venom/vinegar. Trout exposed to noxious stimulation also failed to show an appropriate fear response to an unfamiliar object (red Lego block), suggesting that the pain was more important and took precedence over the fear; trout who were injected with saline or who received a pain killer (morphine) following a vinegar injection showed an appropriate fear response.

Subsequent studies on goldfish and trout have shown that these fishes quickly learn to avoid swimming in areas of an aquarium tank where they receive an electric shock. Prolonged exposure to aversive conditions also produces stress-related changes in the immune system that make fishes more vulnerable to disease, a phenomenon well established in terrestrial vertebrates.

Together, these and other studies present a quite compelling case that fishes—some at least—are capable of not only registering a noxious stimulus (nociception) but of actually experiencing pain. Although it is impossible to actually feel the pain of another, the evidence for pain and suffering in fishes from studies such as these is leading experts to proclaim that the benefit of any doubt should go to the fishes.

Fish pain has implications for recreational fishing. The simplest way to avoid causing pain to fishes is to cease angling. But assuming this practice will continue at least for some time to come, suggestions have been made to mitigate its negative effects on fishes. Such suggestions include minimizing the time that fishes are subjected to being hooked and brought to land; minimizing air exposure and handling; using equipment that reduces pain, stress, and injury (the most notable example being barbless hooks); and fishing outside the reproductive season.

Related articles: Animal pain; Animals used in research; Cephalopods and decapod crustaceans; The ethics of killing free-living animals; Fish farming; Sea fishes and commercial fishing

Braithwaite, V., *Do Fish Feel Pain?*, Oxford University Press, 2010.
Brown, C., Laland, K., and Krause, J. (eds.), *Fish Cognition and Behavior*, Blackwell, 2006.
Cooke, S. J., and Cowx, I. G., "The Role of Recreational Fisheries in Global Fish Crises," *BioScience* 54 (2004): 857–859.
Cooke, S. J., and Sneddon, L. U., "Animal Welfare Perspectives on Recreational Angling," *Applied Animal Behaviour Science* 104 (2007): 176–198.
Lund, V., Mejdell, C. M., Röcklinsberg, H., Anthony, R., and Håstein, T., "Expanding the Moral Circle: Farmed Fish as Objects of Moral Concern," *Diseases of Aquatic Organisms* 75 (2007): 109–118.
Sneddon, L. U., Braithwaite, V. A., and Gentle, M. J., "Do Fish Have Nociceptors? Evidence for the Evolution of a Vertebrate Sensory System," *Proceedings of the Royal Society of London B* 270 (2003): 1115–1122.

JONATHAN BALCOMBE

ANIMALS IN CIRCUSES

In the first study of its kind, an undercover team from Animal Defenders International (ADI) spent eighteen months investigating conditions in thirteen British and five other countries' traveling circuses and their winter ("permanent") quarters. The team recorded more than 7,200 hours of observation and 800 hours of videotape covering almost every aspect of the lives of circus animals, including daily routines, husbandry, accommodation, exercise, training, health, and psychological well-being. This was combined with a survey of local authorities' performing animal licenses and international animal trafficking evidence. Observations were backed up by academic research.

The data was compiled into a report titled *The Ugliest Show on Earth*, and the videotape evidence was used to produce a film of the same name. The report found that circus animals spend their lives confined in very small spaces, chained, tethered, and restricted in every aspect of their lives. The animals observed spent unbearably long periods on transporters and were rarely unloaded even when they reached their destination. For example, a Shetland pony was left tethered in a transporter for more than twenty-five hours for a five-hour journey (ADI, *The Ugliest Show* 28). Camels likewise spent more than twenty-three hours, and a bear spent thirty-nine hours in his transporter (ADI, *The Ugliest Show* 27).

This study showed that circus animals spend most of their lives on the road, traveling from one makeshift encampment to another, living on the backs of lorries. The report concluded that "severe confinement was not restricted to any particular species but found across the board . . . with the best will in the world, circuses cannot provide the facilities needed for the health and mental well being of their animals" (ADI, *Show* 137). Under these circumstances, it is simply not possible to adequately provide for the welfare of the animals concerned.

This study and the accompanying video were presented to the United Kingdom House of Commons. The videotaped evidence was used by Animal Defenders International and the Crown Prosecution Service to obtain cruelty convictions against two circus trainers and a keeper.

Subsequent data have confirmed the findings of this study. The ADI report *Animals in Traveling Circuses: The Science on Suffering* discusses the scientific evidence of the effects of captivity and transport in a range of species, across different industries. The standpoint of this report is that the welfare of an animal can be assessed on the basis of whether the animal has control over his or her environment and can move about to exercise his or her body and mind. The Farm Animal Welfare Council defines good animal welfare in terms of "five freedoms": freedom from hunger and thirst; freedom from discomfort; freedom from pain, injury, or disease; freedom to express normal behaviors; and freedom from fear and distress. The inherent environment of the circus imposes a restriction on such freedoms.

The traveling environment of the circus restricts animal welfare. Circuses must use portable accommodations and lightweight facilities that are moved on a commonly weekly basis. They also engage in long tours over extended periods of time and spend limited periods in each location; animals spend extended periods in transporters even beyond the length of individual journeys (animals remain in transporters while the circus is dismantled, and then after the journey, they cannot be released until the circus is set up, which can be the next day), and circus staff also face challenges in controlling animals during the move (ADI, *Animals in Traveling Circuses* 10–12). This means that provision of the necessary facilities during travel to maintain animals' optimum health and deliver the five freedoms is not realistic in the circus.

An undercover investigation carried out in a British circus in 2009 confirmed this. The investigation revealed that three elephants living in a tent were kept chained, barely able to move, every night for periods of up to eleven hours. When the circus moved locations, the animals were confined in a metal box in the back of a lorry because one site had to be dismantled and the next built; the animals were stuck there for several hours. It was observed that the circus traveled for five miles, and the elephants were kept locked in the transporter for seven and a half hours (ADI, *Suffering behind the Scenes*). An investigation also showed that lions and tigers live in cages on the backs of lorries known as "beast wagons"; at two and a half meters wide, these are little wider than the length of the animal's body. On average, the large cats spent 75 to 80 percent of their time in these cages (ADI, *The Ugliest Show* 19).

If space permits, "exercise cages" may be provided, but these are smaller than the name implies, they generally lack environmental enrichment, and even access to these cages is restricted. Shared exercise areas generally mean that animals get a short period to exercise; difficult animals, as well as males not allowed to mix with females, may get no exercise at all. A count of the number of animals traveling with a circus and the number of cages available usually indicated to investigators that it was unlikely that all animals would get a turn in the exercise cages. Circus owners often claim that spending a few minutes in the ring provides the animals with stimulation, but most animals plod through the same tricks they learned years earlier.

Investigators have gained access by working behind the scenes inside the industry and have filmed systematic violence and abuse of the animals, particularly during training. Regardless of whether it is the United Kingdom, Europe, South America, or the United States, no other part of the entertainment industry is so routinely associated with violence toward animals. Investigators have witnessed and documented animals being beaten with wooden sticks, metal bars, chains, and golf clubs; punched; poked with iron bars; jabbed with bull hooks; shouted at; and given electric shocks—all in order to train them or to move them into the ring.

Some of the following incidents are examples: An elephant was filmed in a Portuguese circus being jabbed in the face with a metal spike more than twenty times by the presenter, who was trying to force the animal to perform a trick (ADI, "ADI Outraged at Portuguese Circus"). In Colombia a circus trainer was filmed punching and beating a chimp with a metal chain (ADI, *Animales en los Circos*). In Chile several circus tigers were beaten repeatedly and had stage props hurled at them during training (ADI, *Unnatural Acts*). In the United States a circus handler was caught on tape dragging down an elephant with vicious blows and then kicking her in the face as she lay on the ground (ADI, *Animals in Traveling Circuses* 14). In the United Kingdom, an elephant was observed being hit in the face with a broom (ADI, *Suffering behind the Scenes*). And these are only a few of numerous incidents worldwide.

The scientific literature on the effects of captivity, confinement, and transportation of animals in a range of industries such as zoos, farming, and laboratories demonstrates that whether free-living or domesticated species, animals in traveling circuses are likely to suffer from the same effects of travel, poor facilities, and limited provision for their welfare.

For instance, transport has been shown to cause many indicators of stress, including increased heart rate, raised hormone levels, lowered immunity to disease, hormone levels that affect pregnancies, weight loss, aggression, and stereotypic behaviors (ADI, *Animals in Traveling Circuses* 16–20). Isolation or separation from companions leads to complex changes in behavior, including a decreased interest in surroundings, apathy, stereotypies, increased heart rate, vocalizations, and higher levels of physiological stress (*Animals in Traveling Circuses* 30). Limited space and inadequate care make it impossible for animals to express their normal behavior patterns, and this leads to a high number of stereotypies and other abnormal behaviors, increased aggression, increased susceptibility to disease, hormone changes, and increased mortality. Animals forced to live in close proximity with one another show a greater frequency of fighting and competitive behaviors and a greater incidence of stereotypies. When different species are mixed or forced to live in close proximity to one another, they exhibit a range of avoidance behaviors and increases in heart rate and other indicators of physiological stress, including spending more time in a state of alertness. When predators are in close proximity to prey species, the prey animals show anxiety behaviors, changes in their nervous systems, and a suppression of feeding and grooming behaviors (*Animals in Traveling Circuses* 32).

These findings were corroborated in a recent scientific study on animal welfare in circuses that concluded that circuses fail to provide some of the most basic welfare needs of free-living animals, such as space and social groups. The authors found that there was no evidence to suggest that the needs of such animals can be met in circuses because "neither natural environment nor much natural behavior can be recreated" (Iossa, Soulsbury, and Harris 129–140).

In addition, the temporary nature of traveling animal circuses and the close proximity of potentially dangerous animals to the public mean that these shows can never be entirely safe. Animal circuses pose a risk to public safety. In October 2010, an incident in a Ukrainian circus involved lions mauling and seriously injuring a circus trainer during a display. At one point, one of the lions almost leapt out of the net surrounding the ring and into the crowd (ADI, "ADI Encourages Ban"). In April 2010, a startled elephant in a U.S. circus stamped her trainer to death ("An Elephant at the Irem Shrine Circus"), and in February 2010, a zebra escaped from a circus onto a main road and led police and keepers on a forty-minute chase through downtown. The animal was euthanized a few weeks later (Philips).

It is clear from these studies that traveling circuses cannot provide standards of welfare and husbandry that enable animals to adequately express their natural behaviors to the level where optimum physical and psychological health is maintained. Thus, by the most commonly accepted measure of welfare, animal circuses cause suffering.

This evidence has been presented to local and national governments around the world, and there is a strong international trend to put an end to circus suffering. National measures to prohibit or limit the use of animals in circuses have also been adopted in Austria, Belgium, Czech Republic, Denmark, Estonia, Finland, Hungary, Luxembourg, Poland, Portugal, Slovakia, Sweden, Singapore, Bolivia, Costa Rica, India, and Israel. Similar laws are being discussed in Brazil, Chile, Norway, Peru, and Greece. In the United Kingdom, a governmental public consultation showed 94.5 percent of respondents are in favor of a ban on the use of "wild" animals in circuses, and currently the coalition (Conservative–Liberal Democrat) government is considering it.

At a local level, several major European towns and cities have banned all circus animal acts or "wild animal" acts, including Thessaloniki (Greece), Barcelona (Spain), and Cork (Ireland). In the United Kingdom, over two hundred local authorities have bans on animal circuses. In Latin America, such bans are in place in the state of Rio de Janeiro in Brazil and the cities of Buenos Aires

(Argentina) and Santiago (Chile). Parramatta (Sydney) in Australia and Wellington, New Zealand, have local bans on free-living animals in circuses as well.

Related articles: Captive chimpanzees; The ethics of zoos; Live animal exports; Marine mammals in captivity; Roadside zoos and menageries; The scientific claims of zoos

ADI (Animal Defenders International), "ADI Encourages Ban on Use of Circus Animals following Latest Lion Trainer Mauling," 2010.

———, "ADI Outraged at Portuguese Circus Victor Hugo Cardinalli after an Elephant Collapses," 2009, available at http:// www.ad-international.org/animals_in_entertainment/ go.php?id=1546&ssi=10.

———, *Animales en los Circos Itinerantes: La Ciencia del Sufrimiento*, 2009.

———, *Animals in Traveling Circuses: The Science on Suffering*, 2008.

———, *Suffering behind the Scenes in a UK Circus*, 2009, available at http://www.ad-international.org/publications/ go.php?id=1686&si=98.

———, *The Ugliest Show on Earth: The Use of Animals in Circuses*, 1998.

———, "Unnatural Acts: Another Shattering Circus Investigation," 2010, available at http://www.ad-international.org/ publications/go.php?id=1963&si=98.

"An Elephant at the Irem Shrine Circus," *Times Leader*, May 21, 2010, available at http://archives.timesleader. com/2010_60/2010_05_21_Pomicter_column_05–21–2010_ AKDUEIH_-editorial.html.

Farm Animal Welfare Council, press statement, 1979, available at http://www.fawc.org.uk/pdf/fivefreedoms1979.pdf.

Iossa, G., Soulsbury, C. D., and Harris, S., "Are Wild Animals Suited to a Travelling Circus Life?," *Animal Welfare* 18 (2009): 129–140.

Philips, Tom, "Escaped Circus Zebra Caught after Police Chase," *Metro*, February 19, 2010, available at http://www .metro.co.uk/weird/813985-escaped-circus-zebra-caught-after-police-chase.

JAN CREAMER

ANIMALS IN FILM

Taking an overall view of the history of cinema, from its early days in the 1890s to its current state more than a century later, the treatment of animals in film production has improved markedly. However, the narrative of this improvement does not follow a straightforward progression in that there are still plenty of examples in recent years of cruelty to animals during the process of filmmaking. It is also equally the case that there was a strong awareness early on, especially in Britain from the early twentieth century onward, that cruelty should not be a component in the making of films involving animals and that such films should be duly censored.

In 1884, Eadweard Muybridge, whose photographic sequences of moving animals and humans was an important first step on the way to the development of cinematography, set a tiger onto an old buffalo at the Philadelphia Zoo. Indeed, the killing of animals for the purposes of photography has a long pedigree. Sometimes in early films killing was depicted to reinforce the striking novelty of film, such as Thomas Edison's *Electrocuting an Elephant* (1904), or it was presented as part of a natural process, as in the early safari films—for instance, Cherry Kearton's *Lion Hunting in Africa* (1910). At the same time, animal welfare issues in Britain had a high profile, especially as articulated through nineteenth-century legislation, which was particularly concerned with the impact of the mistreatment of animals in visible public contexts, such as city streets. Film came to be included in this concern. In the first annual report of the British Board of Film Censors (BBFC) in 1914, "cruelty to animals" was the first of twenty-two grounds for cuts or rejection. As the BBFC expanded its criteria for excision in subsequent years, it also increased the number of clauses concerning animals and made them more specific. In 1919, these clauses included cock fighting, the branding of animals, and bizarrely, images of animals gnawing men and children. An example of an early film that was censored on grounds of cruelty was *A Spanish Bullfight* (1900).

However, although censorship could cut images of animal cruelty from film, it did not have any further legal powers to stop the mistreatment of animals in filmmaking itself. A campaign was briefly run in the early 1930s, under the auspices of a society called the Performing and Captive Animals Defence League, which resulted in two conferences in London in 1931 and 1934. Many issues were raised, including how to police the treatment of animals in film production; what kinds of international action might be coordinated to control filmmaking in other countries; whether the depiction of killing in nature films was permissible; and whether representatives of animal protection societies should be present during film production. Some of these principles were eventually enshrined in the Cinematograph Films (Animals) Act of 1937, which declared that "no person shall exhibit to the public . . . any cinematograph film (whether produced in Great Britain or elsewhere) if in connection with the production of the film any scene represented in the film was organized or directed in such a way as to involve the cruel infliction of pain or terror on any animal or the cruel goading of any animal to fury."

In the United States, public outrage at a scene of a horse being ridden off a cliff and falling seventy feet in

Jesse James (1939) led to the involvement of the American Humane Association (AHA) in observing the treatment of animals on film sets. A contract between the AHA and the Hays Office, the equivalent of Britain's BBFC, allowed the AHA to review scripts and go on set to supervise filming involving animals. With the dismantling of the Hays Office in the mid-1960s, the AHA lost its influence. However, in 1979 the blowing up of a horse in *Heaven's Gate* (1979) led to the AHA regaining its influence. The Screen Actors Guild (SAG) and the Alliance of Motion Picture and Television Producers agreed to write the AHA into the SAG's film and television contracts. This required producers to notify the AHA prior to beginning any work that would involve the use of animals.

Despite legislation and other measures for animal protection, problems still arise in relation to animals in film production. This is due in part to a lack of resources to observe every film that is made, as well as surrounding issues, such as the fate of screen animals once they have outlived their usefulness. However, there are plenty of grounds for optimism. In the past, as one Hollywood trainer said, "a different type of person was drawn to training animals in show business. It was a heavy-handed business in which people would kill an animal just to get a shot. Animals were just stock or props." Nowadays, the situation is different. In Britain, for instance, animal trainers are very conscious of welfare issues, and many belong to an umbrella organization, the Animal Consultants and Trainers Association, which came into being to provide the industry with a more professional image. Contemporary filmmaking also gets around many of the difficulties presented by animals by using special effects such as animatronic models and computer-generated imagery. Ironically, it may be technology as much as humane sentiment that finally solves the problem of animal mistreatment in filmmaking.

Related articles: Animal protection in Britain; Bull fighting; The ethics of killing free-living animals

Bellow, Raymond, *Le Corps du Cinéma: Hypnoses, émotions, animalitiés*, POL, 2009.

Bousé, Derek, *Wildlife Films*, University of Pennsylvania Press, 2000.

Burt, Jonathan, *Animals in Film*, Reaktion Books, 2002.

Chris, Cynthia, *Watching Wildlife*, University of Minnesota Press, 2006.

Lippit, Akira Mizuta, *Electric Animal: Toward a Rhetoric of Wildlife*, University of Minnesota Press, 2000.

Mitman, Gregg, *Reel Nature: America's Romance with Wildlife on Film*, 2nd ed., University of Washington Press, 2009.

JONATHAN BURT

BLOOD FIESTAS

Spanish blood fiestas center on the torture and death of animals. Many thousands of these fiestas take place in villages throughout Spain each year, the majority in honor of a local saint. There are also blood fiestas in Portugal and Brazil, known as the Farra do Boi, as well as in many Latin American countries, with Mexico being the most prominent.

The vast majority of the animals used are cattle, and blood fiestas with cattle are classified as bull fights. More than 27,000 bulls, cows, and calves—some as young as a few weeks—die and suffer annually. The range of cruelties inflicted on the animals is nothing short of horrific. A cow, calf, or bull may die from stabbing, strangulation, spearing, or multiple injuries. He or she may be deliberately thrown down from a height, repeatedly knocked down by a car or tractor, or drowned. Before the animal dies, he or she may suffer rape by sticks or metal spikes; suffer live castration; have his or her horns, tail, and ears ripped off; be blinded; or be burned. The ordeal can last up to five hours.

Although the suffering of the animals is obvious, political and monetary motives play a part in allowing some fiestas to continue and some to be curtailed. For instance, in Catalonia, where bull fighting was banned in July 2010, a few months later the provincial parliament voted by a large majority to allow the torturing and abuse of cattle in the fire bull and bull rope fiestas (Burladero.com, September 22, 2010). Yet in Extremadura in September 2010 the parliament banned these same fiestas because it recognized the suffering of the animals (Burladero.com, September 25, 2010).

Chickens are the next most used creatures. A few other animals are also used, such as pigs, geese, ducks, donkeys, squirrels, rabbits, and pigeons. With the introduction of animal protection laws in all of the Spanish provinces, even as weak as these laws are, the vast majority of the fiestas involving chickens have stopped. In the past chickens were hung by their feet from a rope, after which they either were decapitated by a sword, often blunted to make it more "fun," or had their heads wrenched off manually. Another variation was to bury the birds in a box or in the earth, with just their heads sticking up; the birds were then beaten to death or had their heads hacked off with swords.

Ducks had their wings clipped and were thrown into a river or the sea, and dozens of swimmers tried to catch them. The birds were pulled apart in the resulting tug-of-war. Geese were normally strung up by their feet, after which their heads were wrenched off manually. Again the animal protection laws have eliminated almost all of these particular blood fiestas.

Pigs are greased and set loose to be caught by crowds of people; the animals are nearly always badly injured, and sometimes they are pulled and crushed so badly that they are virtually dismembered while still alive. Pigeons and squirrels are imprisoned in tiny pots suspended from a very high pole; the pots are stoned until they break, and the animals fall out dead or injured. In the goat fiesta of Manganeses de la Polvorosa, a goat was thrown from a church tower. If the goat survived the ordeal, he or she was killed and eaten afterward. This was banned in January 2000 (Mench).

There are at least ten thousand blood fiestas throughout Spain every year, but the real number could be double that figure. All villages are supposed to obtain a license to hold a fiesta, to ensure compliance with various crowd safety rules and to ensure that the villages have sufficient accident insurance. In fact, such licenses are sometimes not obtained because of the cost. There are, therefore, a great many unlicensed fiestas, and consequently, it is very difficult to get an accurate estimate of the number held. The conservative figure of fifteen thousand has been quoted in the Spanish national press, but it has also been said that there are two thousand fire bulls in the province of Valencia alone.

Blood fiestas take place throughout the year, and almost every month has its share of fiestas, but they peak in late summer. When a village organizes its fiesta, it either buys or rents animals from breeders of fighting bulls. The Ayuntamiento (town hall) pays for most of the animals from public monies, which often include subsidies from regional and national funds. The animals fetch grossly inflated prices, such as Brava cattle; one of these animals sells for three to four thousand pounds. A village of four thousand inhabitants may easily spend sixty thousand pounds of public money on one week's fiesta alone. It is also common for the mayor to receive a kickback from the breeder for putting business his way. This is a very lucrative sideline for the bull breeders; indeed, they brag that there is more money in fiestas than in bull fighting.

In addition to the obvious immediate financial return, there is another, almost equally important advantage for the breeder of fighting cattle and the bull fighting industry. Through the network of bull fighting *peñas* ("supporters") clubs in the villages, the general *afición* is nurtured, sustained, and in some instances, enforced. This helps to guarantee the continuance of the *corrida* (bull fight) at its most grassroots level. In the long term, this garnering of support is probably responsible for more remuneration than the yearly cash income from the animals and paraphernalia used in the fiestas. It ensures constant regeneration and continuance for the bull fight and associated practices, against the possibility of progress and development. The BSE (bovine spongiform encephalopathy) crises had an effect on the fiestas in 2001. Since the meat of fighting bulls could not be sold, some villages could not afford fiestas involving cattle. In August 2001, the town of Viana (Navarra) decided to use an ostrich instead, and the animal was chased up and down the streets and abused by the general public.

Every year, some members of the public are killed and injured in the cattle fiestas, which is becoming an increasing problem for the authorities. Not only is this unacceptable in human terms, but it also has financial implications. The very cost of security and medical services may necessitate change in the fiestas in the long run. In 2001, some villages declared that the participants should themselves bear the costs for medical insurance or assistance.

Fiestas are one of the most outrageous examples of gratuitous cruelty to animals existing in the world today. Their continuance relies on a strange mixture of cultural practice, local tradition, and sheer superstition, buttressed by a deep-seated belief that animals do not really matter morally. But perhaps the most important factor of all is money. Fiestas are in reality a subsidized and hugely profitable business.

Related articles: Animals and public health; Birds used in food production; Bull fighting; Legislation in the European Union; Live pigeon shoots; Live quail shoots; Pig castration; Pigeon racing; Rabbits; South American perspectives on animals; The welfare of cows; The welfare of pigs

Altarriba, Javier, *La Cuestión de los Toros*, Fundación Altarriba, 2007.

Coetzee, J. M., *The Lives of Animals*, St. Edmundsbury Press, 1999.

Cohn, Priscilla N. (ed.), *Ethics and Wildlife*, Edwin Mellen Press, 1999.

Linzey, Andrew, *Why Animal Suffering Matters: Philosophy, Theology, and Practical Ethics*, Oxford University Press, 2009.

Mench, Matilda, *Life on the Line: The Heroic Story of Vicki Moore*, Bluecoat Press, 2007.

de Saldaña, Emma D., *Las Voces del Silencio*, Diseños and Impresion, 2004.

TONY MOORE AND
MECHTHILD MENCH

BULL FIGHTING

Bull fighting is the ritual killing of a bull in a public arena. Bull fighting originated in Spain and spread throughout the Spanish protectorates and still continues in Spain, France, Mexico, Portugal, Colombia, Ecuador, Peru, Venezuela, Bolivia, California, and Costa Rica. So-called bloodless bull fights take place in Portuguese communities in the United States. Early bull fighting was carried out on horseback to celebrate notable occasions, such as royal weddings, military victories, and religious solemnities. Bull fighting on foot came into popular practice in the eighteenth century.

Many of the early bull fighters were slaughtermen. The Seville slaughterhouse was the first official school of tauromachy in Spain. José Rodríguez (Pepete), a well-known nineteenth-century bull fighter, commented that most people of his calling were slaughtermen by trade, and in a letter to a friend he wrote, "What do you expect us people brought up in the slaughterhouse to be like? There's no politeness there, only 'Fling over those innards,' 'Strip off that skin,' 'Cut off the head,' 'Put your feet in those puddles of blood.' We get to know the worst possible side of things" (qtd. in Acquaroni).

In different periods of history, the bull fight has been banned, but it has always been revived. For example, in 1567 a papal bull was issued forbidding clergy from attending under pain of excommunication and denying an ecclesiastical burial to anyone killed as a result of taking part. The papal bull was ignored.

In most bull fights, there are six bulls killed by three matadors. Each matador employs a team of four or five men (cuadrilla) to assist him. When the bull enters the ring, he is caped to gauge his reactions. In the first act, the *tercio de varas*, two picadores (men mounted on horses with spears, the point of which is 8.75 centimeters, or three and a half inches, long) destroy the muscles in the bull's shoulder area, which causes the bull to lower his head, creating considerable loss of blood and consequent weakness. The horses are blindfolded; their ears are blocked with paper; and on occasion, their vocal cords are cut. They are partly protected by padding. Approximately two hundred picador horses are killed every year.

In the second act, the *tercio de banderillas*, up to six banderillas (harpoons), approximately eighty centimeters (thirty-two inches) in length, with a six-centimeter (two-and-a-half-inch) metal end and a three-centimeter (one-and-a-quarter-inch) barb, are thrust into the shoulders of the bull. Further blood loss and pain result. In the final act, the *tercio de muleta y estocada*, the matador performs a number of movements with his cape, to show his domination of the bull. He then attempts to kill the bull by thrusting a sword eighty centimeters (thirty-two inches) in length between the shoulder blades down to the heart. This is very rarely accomplished. Instead, the lungs are usually punctured and the arteries are severed, causing the vomiting of blood, which can be so severe that the animal nearly chokes to death. The matador then uses an *estoque de descabellar* (a sword with a cross-piece near the point that turns the end into a stabbing knife), with which he attempts to sever the spinal cord, behind the head. Then the bull's spinal cord is finally cut through with the *puntilla* (stabbing knife).

If the audience approves of the performance of the matador, the animal's ears and sometimes the tail may be awarded to the matador. The bull is then dragged from the ring. Even at this stage, the animal is seldom completely dead and usually experiences some degree of consciousness.

To minimize the risk to the matador yet keep up the appearance of danger, several manipulations are performed on the bull prior to his entry. The ends of the horns are cut off and reshaped. Behavior-altering drugs are injected. Large quantities of Epsom salts may be administered, to purge and dehydrate the animal, which causes the bull to bloat himself on water.

Although this is the most common form of bull fighting, there are many variations. There is the bull fight without picadores, and there is mounted bull fighting, in both Spanish and Portuguese style (in Portugal without killing the bull in the arena). There is also the *espectáculo taurino cómico* (bull fighting of young animals by clowns), and in the many street fiestas, the general public harass cattle. The street fiestas use the same cattle from the same breeders and are classified under Spanish law as bull fights. In Spain alone, approximately seventy thousand of these cattle are killed in the bullrings and on the streets every year. There are approximately nine hundred registered breeders of fighting bulls in Spain.

Bull fighting is big business. The money accrues not only to the impresarios, top-rate matadors, and bull breeders but also to the many others involved, even in a subsidiary way, in the industry. It is also an international industry, with bull fighters following the seasons around the world. Contrary to popular belief, the meat is not given away to charities but rather is sold at inflated prices. Even with the money that flows into the industry, the bull breeders claim a subsidy paid by the European Union that is intended to support beef producers. In fact, the beef sales are so important that during the 2001 season, the bull-fighting industry threatened to go on strike when meat sales were forbidden as a result of

BSE regulations. For a short time, they even decided to use a captive bolt pistol in the bullring instead of the traditional puntilla.

A modern trend is for new or reconstructed bullrings to be multipurpose, with cinema screens and shopping malls built in. Without these added attractions, the bullrings would not be as profitable. There have been many attempts, some successful, to export bull fighting to countries where there is no bull fighting tradition—for example, Russia, Armenia, Kazakstan, China, Macao, and Cuba.

In the Spanish province of Catalonia, the first animal law in Spain was passed in 1989. This banned the use of traveling bullrings and many of the cattle fiestas. Several bullrings have shut down from lack of business.

The anti–bull fighting movement, after a slow start, is at last beginning to make progress. The most tangible evidence of success is that attendance at bull fights worldwide is declining. Bull fighting appeared to reach its peak in popularity toward the end of the 1990s. Since then the industry has openly complained about lack of attendance. For example, in the Malaga region, a newspaper article noted, "The attendance has decreased more than twenty-two percent in the season of 2001 . . . In more than fifty percent of the cases not even half of the tickets have been sold" (*Diario Sur*). In July 2010, the Catalan parliament voted to ban bull fighting in Catalonia; the ban came into effect on January 1, 2011. As football has become more dominant in the psyche of young people in Spain, the number of live transmissions and the number of bull fights have reduced. For example, in the province of Andalucía in the first half of 2007, the number of bull fights dropped by 32 percent and the number of novilladas (bull fights with inexperienced bull fighters) by 64 percent (*La Vanguardia*, September 23, 2008).

Related articles: Animals and public health; Catholic teaching; The ethics of killing free-living animals; Horses; Legislation in the European Union; Slaughter; South American perspectives on animals; The welfare of cows

Acquaroni, J. L., *Bulls and Bullfighting*, Editorial Noguer, 1964.

Altarriba, Javier, *La Questión de los Toros*, Fundación Altarriba, 2007.

Clavero, Manuel, *La Historia de un Toro*, Ediciones de la Tempestad, 2007.

Hardouin-Fougier, Elisabeth, *Bullfighting: A Troubled History*, Reaktion Books, 2010.

Mench, Matilda, *Life on the Line: The Heroic Story of Vicki Moore*, Bluecoat Press, 2007.

de Saldaña, Emma D., *Las Voces del Silencio*, Diseños and Impresion, 2004.

TONY MOORE AND MECHTHILD MENCH

CANNED HUNTS

A "canned hunt" is a commercial hunt in which the victim is a captive animal. For a sizable fee, usually ranging from several hundred dollars for plentiful game species to several thousand for "exotic" animals and white-tailed deer with trophy-sized antlers, operators of the so-called game ranches and shooting preserves at which canned hunts take place give their customers the opportunity to kill an animal who has no chance to escape. Advertisements often promise "no kill, no bill," a guarantee the operators can afford to make because the animal's death is a virtual certainty.

Because the United States and Canada have long regarded free-living animals as a public resource, canned hunts are a relatively new phenomenon in North America. Historically, animals living in their natural state on private land are not the property of the landowner but are under the control of state, provincial, or federal governments, which generally forbid their capture. Furthermore, North American hunters have typically dismissed canned hunts as a violation of what they consider the foundation of hunting ethics: "fair chase." Jim Posewitz, author and defender of sport hunting, expressed it this way: "Fundamental to ethical hunting is the idea of fair chase [which is] . . . a balance that allows hunters to occasionally succeed while animals generally avoid being taken" (58). Thus, whereas the animal protection community opposes canned hunts because they are an egregious expression of the cruelty that is inherent in all hunting, many hunters oppose them because canned hunts violate their sense of what constitutes an "ethical" hunt.

Canned hunts for mammals take place inside fenced enclosures, which may vary in size from a few square yards or meters to one thousand acres (four hundred hectares) or more. The size of the enclosure makes little difference since canned hunts employ full-time guides who know the land and follow the movements of the animals at all times. Unable to leave the guide's "backyard," the animals are as defenseless in a thousand-enclosure as in a five-acre pasture. A canned hunt on several hundred acres may take longer and be more strenuous than a canned hunt on a few acres, but either way, the outcome is never in doubt; sooner or later, the animal comes up against the fence. Birds, such as pheasants and ducks, are reared in pens and hand-fed until they are released just before the hunt begins.

The first canned hunt was at a cattle ranch in Texas, which in the 1950s began adapting breeding and feeding techniques originally developed for cattle to imported blackbuck antelopes—to whom, because they were an exotic species, the appropriate laws did not apply. When hunts for captive blackbucks proved lucrative, other ranches followed suit. Canned hunting spread to native species, such as white-tailed deer, when game ranchers began purchasing breeding stock from zoos and other legal holders of captive animals, thereby circumventing the laws that forbade landowners from holding free-living animals in captivity.

In fact, many of the animals ultimately killed in canned hunts are born and raised in zoos, which depend on cute and cuddly baby animals to attract paying customers. When the babies grow up, they must be disposed of to make room for a new crop. Since the public would not tolerate zoos killing these animals, the animals are sold to dealers, who in turn often sell them to game ranches. In this way, the zoos can claim to be unaware that the animals they sell are going to canned hunts. Likewise, circus animals who have grown too old to perform may also end their lives as victims of a canned hunt. These are all tame animals who have never learned that they ought to flee a human with a gun.

Another concern occasioned by canned hunts is the increased risk of disease caused by breeding and raising animals in high-density conditions. Outbreaks of chronic wasting disease, a form of mad cow disease, among free-living deer and elk in Wyoming, Colorado, New York, and other states are suspected—though not proved—to be related to game ranching, as is an outbreak of tuberculosis among deer in Michigan.

In an era when small farms are being swallowed up by giant agricultural conglomerates, canned hunts are being promoted by state agricultural agencies as a way to increase the profitability of farms and ranches. The Humane Society of the United States estimates that there are approximately one thousand canned hunts for mammals in the United States and an unknown, but probably larger, number of canned hunts for birds, primarily ducks and pheasants. Ten states have outlawed canned hunts for mammals, and several others have restricted at least some forms. Nevertheless, as traditional hunting in North America continues its decades-long decline, canned hunts are a growth industry in those states where they are legal.

Related articles: Animal protection in Africa; Animals in circuses; Animals and public health; Birds used in food production; Deer hunting; The ethics of killing free-living animals; The ethics of zoos; The humane movement in Canada; Hunting with dogs; Hunting with ferrets; The scientific claims of zoos

Cartmill, Matt, *A View to a Death in the Morning: Hunting and Nature through History*, Harvard University Press, 1991.

Cohn, Priscilla N. (ed.), *Ethics and Wildlife*, Edwin Mellen Press, 1999.

Green, Alan, *Animal Underworld: Inside America's Black Market for Rare and Exotic Species*, Public Affairs, 2006.

Hoyt, John A., *Animals in Peril: How "Sustainable Use" Is Wiping Out the World's Wildlife*, Avery, 1994.

Phelps, Norm, *The Longest Struggle: Animal Advocacy from Pythagoras to PETA*, Lantern Books, 2007.

Posewitz, Jim, *Beyond Fair Chase*, Falcon Press, 1994.

NORM PHELPS

COCK FIGHTING

Humans have staged combat between roosters and gambled on the outcome for thousands of years. Indeed, it has been argued that chickens were originally domesticated from their progenitor, the jungle fowl of Southeast Asia, for fighting rather than for meat or egg production. As a result of centuries of intense selective breeding, modern gamecocks naturally exhibit high levels of intraspecific aggression. Cock fighters have developed hundreds of strains of fighting cocks, each having a different name—for example, roundheads, clarets, Madigan grays, and butchers. Although breeders sometimes cross strains in their search for a more aggressive ("gamer") rooster, great care is taken not to mix game fowl bloodlines with that of domesticated chickens, who are derisively referred to by American cock fighters as "dunghills."

Cock fights are complex affairs. Several weeks prior to a fight, the roosters are put on a "keep" in which they are given special food, dietary supplements, and exercises designed to enhance stamina. If the animal has not been fought previously, his comb and wattles are cut off, and the tail and body feathers trimmed to lighten the bird and reduce overheating. The animal's natural spurs are cut off, leaving stubs to which artificial metal spurs several inches long ("gaffs") are attached just before the match.

The rules of fights vary by subculture and national tradition. In the southern Appalachian Mountains, the cock-fighting "season" extends roughly from October to midsummer. The most common type of fight is the "derby," which is usually staged in a clandestine backwoods arena. Each of the breeders participating in the derby enters a set number of roosters, usually between four and six. The "cocker" pays an entry fee, typically several hundred dollars, which goes into a common pot. The roosters are matched for weight and fought round-robin in a series of individual matches. The cocker whose roosters win the most fights during the course of the derby takes home the pot. Gambling is an inherent part of the sport, and individual side bets are made between the cock fighters and among the spectators.

An intricate set of rules governs the conduct of the matches, which are normally staged in a circular cockpit, roughly fifteen feet in diameter. Just prior to the match, the gaffs are attached to the roosters' feet. Their handlers, who remain in the pit with the birds throughout the fight, then bring the two roosters to the ring. A referee controls the course of the match by instructing the handlers on when to release their birds and when to pull them apart and by timing rest periods between rounds. Fights can last from less than a minute to more than an hour. The winner is determined by a complex system in which the animal who first stops attacking loses. Usually, but not always, the loser dies.

The typical Appalachian cock fighter has a blue-collar or agricultural background. Although cock fighters are often stereotyped as psychosexual sadists, sociological research suggests that this is not the case. Indeed, what is most intriguing about cock fighters is that in many ways their lives are quite conventional except for their involvement in an illegal sport that the larger culture considers brutal. When asked, cock fighters typically claim they are drawn to the activity by their love of competition and their admiration for the bravery of their birds, rather than by its more unsavory aspects, such as its inevitable association with animal cruelty and gambling.

Not surprisingly, cock fighters, as with many people who use animals, construct elaborate justifications for their sport. In the United States, for example, cockers like to point out the historical roots of cock fighting, claiming that great Americans such as Thomas Jefferson, Andrew Jackson, and Abraham Lincoln fought roosters. They also argue that game chickens fight instinctively and do not have to be goaded or trained to kill conspecifics. Some even argue that is in inhumane not to let these animals fight. Cockers tend to view gamecocks as moral exemplars because of their persistence and bravery. Finally, cock fighters point out (correctly) that their animals live much better lives than domesticated chickens whose brief existence on factory farms is characterized by nearly unimaginable squalor.

In the United States, laws against cock fighting have been on the books since 1836. Historically, however, the enforcement of anti–cock fighting statutes has usually been a low priority for local police, and punishments for violations were usually minor. In recent decades, with pressure from animal protection organizations such as the Humane Society of the United States, cock fighting has been banned in every state. In addition, the transport of roosters for the purpose of fighting is a federal felony under the Animal Welfare Act, 1966, as amended in 2002.

It is likely that the cock-fighting subculture will become increasingly marginalized over the next several decades.

Related articles: Animal and human violence; Animals in Asia; Birds used in food production; Bull fighting; Dog fighting; The protection of birds

Dundes, A. (ed.), *The Cockfight: A Casebook*, University of Wisconsin Press, 1994.
Herzog, H., *Some We Love, Some We Hate, Some We Eat: Why It's So Hard to Think Straight about Animals*, Harper, 2010.
Manley, F., *The Cockfighter: A Novel*, Anchor Books, 1999.
Smith, P., and Daniels, C., *The Chicken Book*, University of Georgia Press, 2000.

HAROLD HERZOG

DEER HUNTING

Deer are, it seems, the object of admiration and even affection both by those who want to protect them and by those who want to kill them. Three kinds of deer in the United States are extensively hunted: mule deer, black-tailed deer, and white-tailed deer. Hunting is licensed in almost all states in America. During the 2000s, in Pennsylvania alone, more than half a million whitetails were shot, wounded, and killed. Only the small Florida Key deer is not hunted.

The hunting season for deer overlaps the rut, the breeding season when the males (bucks), treasured for their large antlers (racks), become careless in their pursuit of females (does) and less wary of the hunters pursuing them. Hunting is so intense in Pennsylvania that few bucks reach full maturity. Deer are killed by archers using high-tech bows, by shotguns, by high-powered rifles, and by muskets. Despite the huge numbers killed each year, the herd size has steadily increased from the early 1900s, when there were hardly any deer in Pennsylvania. The herd is now estimated at a million and a half.

With less open space and with suburbs increasing, it is often said there is an overpopulation of deer. This idea is endorsed by game agencies, whose officials, it should be pointed out, have their salaries paid for by the sale of hunting licenses. Many game agencies refer to preestablished "carrying capacity" figures. Above these figures, deer are considered to be overpopulating and to be a threat to human safety, either by increasing deer-vehicle collisions or through an increase of Lyme disease.

These assertions rest on a number of oversimplifications or half-truths. Carrying capacity refers, in theory, to the number of animals that can be sustained in a given area, but this number depends on changing factors, such as the amount of rainfall or snow, the kinds of grasses, insect populations, diseases, the absence or presence of predators, and not least of all, the number of other species competing for the same food source. Carrying capacity is not an unchanging number that can be referred to year after year; it will vary from year to year, or even from season to season.

Similarly, deer have been blamed for incidents of Lyme disease, but ticks carrying this disease can be found on any warm-blooded animal and even on reptiles and birds. Medical authorities have stated that reducing the number of deer will not, by itself, reduce the incidence of Lyme disease. Nor will reducing deer numbers necessarily reduce road kills. Moreover, fewer deer in one area can encourage the migration of deer from another area.

Since the mid-1990s, the battles over the justifiability of hunting have become increasingly fierce, especially in the suburbs. Hunters point to the ancient tradition of hunting, forgetting that their ancestors did not have high-tech bows, sophisticated range finders, listening devices, infrared binoculars, or an array of scents to attract bucks, not to mention camouflaged toilet paper! The number of hunters has steadily decreased, but with one alarming exception—namely, bow hunters. Bow hunting is responsible for a high wounding rate, sometimes estimated as high as 90 percent, and is, incontestably, cruel.

These battles have become fierce when the matter of fertility control is raised. Since deer are classified as food animals, hormonal contraceptives were never seriously considered because people feared ingesting the hormones. With the development of effective immunocontraceptives, however, the assertion that killing is the only way to reduce deer numbers can no longer be sustained. Since they were first tested on deer in the early 1990s, much progress has been made—and continues to be made—with these contraceptive agents.

Paralleling the decrease in hunters has been a growing recognition of the fragile nature of our environment and a strong ethical appreciation of free-ranging animals as valuable in themselves. As a result, a number of products have been developed that go some way toward resolving complaints about deer. There are, for example, innovations in netting and fencing, reflectors to keep deer off the roads, chemical repellents, mechanical repellents aided by motion detectors that squirt water or make noise to frighten deer away, and even nurseries that sell plants that deer are said not to favor.

People are beginning to appreciate that deer cannot multiply indefinitely but are limited by their food supply. In fact, like all mammals, they breed only in relation to the food and environment available. From a scientific point of view, deer are appreciated as extremely adaptable creatures. From an aesthetic and perhaps spiritual point of view, they are admired as graceful animals who, among other things, produce fawns so well camouflaged that one almost steps on the newborn creature before seeing him or her. In other words, deer are not "pests," but rather a wonder of nature.

Related articles: The ethics of killing free-living animals; Hunting with dogs; Hunting with ferrets; Immunocontraception; Living with animal neighbors; The moral claims of animals

Brown, R. D. (ed.), *The Biology of Deer*, Springer-Verlag, 1991.
Cartmill, M., *A View to Death in the Morning: Hunting and Nature through History*, Harvard University Press, 1993.
Kerasote, T., *Bloodties: Nature, Culture and the Hunt*, Kodansha International, 1993.
Ortega y Gasset, J., *Meditations on Hunting*, trans. H. B. Wescot, Charles Scribner's Sons, 1972.
Putman, R., *The Natural History of Deer*, Cornell University Press, 1988.
Swan, J. A., *In Defense of Hunting*, HarperCollins, 1995.
Wemmer, C. M. (ed.), *Biology and Management of the Cervidae*, Smithsonian Institution Press, 1987.

PRISCILLA N. COHN

DOG FIGHTING

Dog fighting is an activity in which two dogs are put into an enclosed area with the aim of attacking and often killing each other. The purpose of this practice is profit and entertainment. Spectators often make bets on which dogs will win. Dogs who have the appearance and characteristics of Staffordshire bull terriers, American pit bull terriers (commonly known as a "pit bulls"), and other large breeds of dogs are frequently used in fighting activities. Dog fighting is illegal in all fifty states of America and, since 2008, is a felony in all of them.

Dogs used in fighting often have observable characteristics, such as short ear crops; recent or long-standing wounds and blisters; scars on the head, throat, legs, and ears; puncture wounds; and lacerations. They frequently wear wide leather or web collars with heavy rings. The dogs actually used in fighting are not the only animals abused. Cats, rabbits, or smaller dogs are used to train the animals to fight. These "bait" animals are often stolen pets or animals obtained through advertisements.

Fighting dogs are often subjected to severe abuse in order to make them vicious. They are brutally trained to develop a taste for blood and flesh and are subjected to exhausting exercise to develop muscle strength. They are often required to hang from tires and swings by their jaws for extended periods and to carry weights around their necks, as conditioning for the impending fight. Even the training techniques are illegal in some places and are regarded as animal cruelty. Dogs who are trained for fighting are often very dangerous to humans. Children are especially at risk because their smaller size often causes the dogs to mistake them for the animals they have been trained to maul and kill.

Dog fights may be part of a highly organized network or simply associated with spontaneous street fight activity. They usually occur at night in empty buildings, barns, and abandoned premises away from or hidden from public view. In an organized fight, the arena is a makeshift ring, usually around fourteen feet in diameter and marked into two halves with a "scratch line" across the middle. Each owner sets his dog into the ring and encourages the dog to attack the other. Fights are grueling and often long (they can last over an hour), and they usually result in serious injuries to one or both dogs. The fight does not end until one of the dogs is unable or unwilling to continue fighting. The loser may be killed outright. A dog who is not killed in a fight may still die of blood loss, shock, infections, or exhaustion after the fight has ended. If the dog lives, the dog may suffer from broken bones and crushed cartilage. Scarring on the face is common.

In a street fight, the arena may be no more than a ring of bystanders; the dogs may be trained for fighting, or the fight may involve a companion animal left unattended in a neighboring yard. Many street gangs have adopted dog fighting as a regular pastime, increasing the frequency and brutality of the fighting in neighborhoods where gangs are prevalent.

In addition to its adoption by gangs in urban areas, there are many other components of dog fighting that can have detrimental effects on the community. It is one of the cruelest forms of animal abuse, and it is usually connected with other criminal activities, such as gambling, gang activity, drug trafficking, child abuse, and domestic violence. Most experts agree that cruelty to animals is a prime indicator of behavior that will most likely lead to acts of violence against humans as well.

One of the most serious obstacles to combating dog fighting is enforcement. For organized fights, which usually involve a great deal of money, substantial thought goes into both the planning of the event and the concealment of the venue. Should the fight location be discovered, either before or during the event, the participants scatter (with or without their dogs), and the event is simply rescheduled for another place and time. There are generally lookouts and a plan for dispersal, and few arrests are made. In the case of gang fights, they are as rapidly dispersed as they are started, and intimidation by gangs in a particular neighborhood may make it difficult for the police to make arrests or make it unlikely that fights will even be reported. Although arrests are made of individuals who have dogs with suspicious injuries, individuals are usually charged with a lesser offense of animal cruelty. In a high-crime area, it may also be difficult to convince the police and the judicial system to treat crimes against animals as seriously as the murders, rapes, and robberies that make up the bulk of their workload.

If dog fighting is suspected in a neighborhood, the police and local humane society should be contacted immediately. To help prevent future dog fights, the community should be made aware of the inherent cruelty involved and the need for humane education. Local citizen groups can be effective "watchdogs" and advocates for strict enforcement of laws prohibiting dog fighting and for the prosecution of offenders.

Related articles: Animal and human violence; Bull fighting; Canine profiling; Cock fighting; Dogs; Humane education

Animal Welfare Institute, *Animals and Their Legal Rights: A Survey of American Laws from 1641 to 1990*, 4th ed., 1990.

Bank, Julie, and Zawistowski, Stephen, "History of Dog Fighting," *ASPCA Animal Watch* (Fall 1997).

Frasch, Pamela D., Wagman, Bruce, A., and Waisman, Sonia S., *Animal Law: Cases and Materials*, Caroline Academic Press, 2006.

Gibson, Hanna, "Dog Fighting Detailed Discussion," *Animal Legal and Historical Center*, Michigan State University College of Law, 2005, available at http://www.animallaw.info/articles/ddusdogfighting.htm.

National Anti-Vivisection Society, *Taking a Bite Out of Breed-Specific Laws: A New Perspective*, 2008.

PEGGY CUNNIFF AND MARCIA KRAMER

GREYHOUND RACING

Pari-mutuel greyhound racing in the United States began over seven decades ago, with the adoption of the mechanical lure. It spread rapidly across the country, reaching a peak in 1991. Since then its popularity has steadily declined. Eleven states and one U.S. territory have banned it since 1993. As of 2013, live racing continues in only seven states. However, among them, those states have twenty-two racetracks. Florida alone has thirteen.

All racing greyhounds are registered with the National Greyhound Association, an industry-controlled, self-regulating body. By the time puppies reach the age of three months, their right and left ears are tattooed with their registration number, date of birth, and place in the litter, a painful introduction to experiences yet to come. An

American greyhound track requires about one thousand dogs to function, but of course this number includes only those dogs who are fast enough and keen enough to race at any given time. It does not include those who are born but never qualify or those who are otherwise rejected. Overbreeding is necessary in an industry where only the fittest earn their keep. Killing ("culling") begins at an early age and continues as the dogs mature. An unknown number of young dogs simply disappear before they reach racing age.

Greyhounds begin racing at eighteen months old. Unprofitable dogs are "graded off"—sent to poorer and poorer tracks until, unable to earn their keep, they are sent to their deaths or to adoption kennels. The survivors are retired at three to five years of age. Some are adopted or sent to breeding farms, but many are "euthanized" in the industry's term.

In the curiously distorted vocabulary of the racetrack, euthanasia simply means a speedy death at the hands of a veterinarian, even if a dog is young and healthy. But as the term implies, this is a fate reserved for the fortunate. Although many discarded greyhounds are killed by lethal injection, significant numbers have suffered agonizing forms of death. In 2002 the remains of at least two thousand greyhounds were discovered on a farm in Alabama. The proprietor, a former security guard at Florida racetracks, had been paid ten dollars apiece over a decade to shoot unwanted dogs.

"Owners" and trainers dispose of unwanted dogs by selling or donating them to medical research laboratories. Untold numbers of greyhounds have endured painful experiments and death at publicly financed institutions, including Colorado State University, where ex-racers were killed in dental experiments in the 1990s.

Life at the track means confinement in a small cage for up to twenty-two hours a day. The standard cage measures thirty-two inches wide, forty-four inches deep, and thirty-four inches high. A large greyhound, standing up, cannot fully raise his head in a cage this size. Bedding consists of shredded newspaper or a bit of carpet. The dogs are taken out for occasional training, and they are turned out in groups a few times a day to relieve themselves. They race about four times a month. Housed by the hundreds in close quarters, they become infested with fleas, ticks, and internal parasites. And because greyhounds are frequently moved from state to state, periodic outbreaks of contagious diseases cause multiple deaths and quarantines.

Injuries are frequent and often severe. In recent years the anti-racing organization GREY2K USA has been able to obtain injury records from several states. These records reveal the true extent of the physical damage inflicted on racing greyhounds—information the industry had managed to keep secret for decades. In Massachusetts, over 800 injuries were reported at two tracks from 2002 to 2008. Nearly 80 percent involved broken legs. In New Hampshire, 716 injuries were reported in 2005 and 2006 at three tracks, one of which did not operate in 2005. West Virginia, with two tracks, reported more than 700 injuries and 62 deaths at one track alone from January 2008 to September 2009, and 1,137 greyhounds were prevented from racing because of lameness, injury, or illness. Similar numbers were reported in Arizona, Iowa, and Texas.

The most commonly reported injuries were broken legs, and other injuries included seizures, paralysis, stroke, head trauma, cardiac arrest, and broken neck. Kennel fires and transportation accidents took an additional toll.

There are hundreds of independent greyhound rescue and adoption kennels in the United States. The American Greyhound Council, an industry group, provides some funding, and many racetracks have established on-site adoption kennels. In the end, though, it is simply not possible to find homes for all the greyhounds rejected by the system. For decades greyhound racing was dear to the hearts of American politicians because it provided jobs and produced tax revenue for the states. The industry once spent millions of dollars annually on political contributions and lobbying. However, increasingly over the last twenty years, animal welfare groups have been able to alert the public to the cruelty of greyhound racing. The Greyhound Protection League, founded in 1991, monitors the industry, publicizes abuses, and organizes rescues.

GREY2K USA, founded in 2001, fights greyhound racing through political action, education, and the media. Recent successes have included a greyhound racing ban passed by popular referendum in Massachusetts, as well as legislative bans passed in New Hampshire, Rhode Island, and the territorial island of Guam. Animal rights advocates continue to defeat legislation that would subsidize greyhound racing through new on-site gambling facilities (slot machines and high-stakes poker). State legislatures have rejected such expansion in Connecticut, Oregon, and Texas. In Arizona, GREY2K USA, in alliance with the Animal Defense League of Arizona and other advocates, helped defeat a referendum that would have legalized racetrack slot machines in that state.

American greyhound racing is a dying industry. As of 2010, greyhound racing commanded less than 1 percent of the entire U.S. gambling market. Even in Florida, considered the heart of the industry, tax revenues to the state have declined 93 percent since 1989. Nevertheless, even in its weakened state, the racing industry remains tenacious and politically powerful. As long as it is allowed to survive, greyhounds will continue to suffer and die.

Related articles: Animals used in research; Dogs; Euthanasia; Jumps racing; Kennels and catteries; Pigeon racing

Benston, Liz, "Has Dog Racing Run Its Course?," *Las Vegas Sun*, March 22, 2010.
Blanchard, Paula, "Greyhounds Win in Massachusetts," *American Dog Magazine* (Spring 2010).
Committee to Protect Dogs (an alliance of GREY2K USA, the Massachusetts Society for the Prevention of Cruelty to Animals, and the Humane Society of the United States), *Commercial Dog Racing in Massachusetts*, 2008.
Dorchak, Christine A., "Greyhound Racing in the United States," *Animals Voice Magazine* (April 2010).
GREY2K USA, *Injuries in Racing Greyhounds: A Report to the New Hampshire General Court*, 2007.
Halbfinger, David M., "Dismal End for Race Dogs, Alabama Authorities Say," *New York Times*, May 23, 2002.

PAULA BLANCHARD

HUNTING WITH DOGS

Although hunting with dogs, especially fox hunting, is usually regarded as an English pastime, hunting packs exist throughout the world, including Belgium, France, Germany, Holland, Italy, Australia, and New Zealand. According to the Masters of Foxhounds Association of America (MFHA), there are 11 fox packs in Canada and 154 in the United States. Fox hunting has evolved its own flavor, with an emphasis on the chase rather than the kill, and "stopping up" (blocking the earth so the foxes cannot go underground) is officially against the MFHA code of practice.

But it is hunting with dogs in the United Kingdom (including fox, deer, hare, and mink hunting and also hare coursing) that has aroused the most controversy. After a long parliamentary battle stretching back many decades, on November 18, 2004, Queen Elizabeth II gave the Royal Assent to the Hunting Act 2004 that two months later criminalized one of the principal leisure pursuits of her eldest son, Charles, and countless numbers of her royal predecessors. Prior to the Hunting Act, an estimated 100,000 free-living animals were hunted and killed by dogs annually (not including rabbits and rodents). Less than one-fifth were foxes killed by Britain's so-called traditional foxhunts—for every fox hounded by "traditional" hunts, another three or four were killed by terriers sent underground to fight or drive out ("bolt") foxes or by fast, powerful lurchers, who attacked foxes flushed out of cover.

When fox hunting with hounds became established some three hundred years ago, foxes were scarce and were imported from the continent to satisfy demand for the new "sport." Thousands of foxes were distributed to hunts in all parts of Britain from London's Leadenhall Market alone. More recently, artificially high fox populations were maintained by building "earths" on land owned by hunt supporters and providing the foxes with food, such as dead poultry.

The fox's reputation as a cunning predator of livestock was, and still is, deeply ingrained in folklore, but four decades of scientific research by both government agriculture departments and the Universities of Oxford, Bristol, Aberdeen, and York reveal, with surprising unanimity, two truths—that fox population densities are unaffected by so-called control and that the impact of foxes on British agriculture is, in the words of the former Ministry of Agriculture, Fisheries and Food, "insignificant."

Despite an 80 percent decline in Britain's hare population over the last century, hares continued to be hunted by approximately one hundred packs of hounds, mostly beagles. Hares were also coursed by greyhounds as a method of testing the speed and agility of competing dogs in events such as the Waterloo Cup, where thousands of spectators watched hares being forced to run, twist, and turn to avoid being killed by pairs of competing greyhounds. The twenty-four coursing clubs in Britain claimed to have killed only 250 hares per season, but since the season ran well into the hares' breeding period, it was inevitable that coursing resulted in young hares (leverets) being orphaned.

Prior to the U.K. hunt ban, there were only three registered packs of hounds hunting deer in England (deer hunting with dogs was already illegal in Scotland). The three remaining deer hunts hunted red deer in Somerset and Devon and killed fewer than two hundred deer annually—less than a fifth of the number killed in the area with rifles.

Unlike the hunting of deer by wolves in times past, deer hunting by humans with dogs, like hunting of foxes and hares, was contrived to entertain followers with a long chase. Strong, fit stags were selected, whereas natural predators pick out the sick and weaker members of a hunted species. The hounds followed the scent of the deer and hounded him for hours before he became exhausted and stood at bay to be either shot with a shortened shotgun or wrestled by hunt supporters and shot with a pistol. Female deer (hinds) were also hunted—sometimes pregnant and handicapped in their flight by having the previous year's calf at foot.

Mink hunting with hounds took place during the spring and summer months. There were around twenty packs of mink hounds, some of them originating from the few packs of otter hounds that remained when otters became protected by law in 1978. Minks, like other North American introductions, suffer a bad press, but scientists have shown that despite breeding in British rivers for fifty years, minks have had little impact on British river life. The only exception may be the water voles, who are made vulnerable by the removal of vegetation in drainage schemes. It is true that minks have few friends, but conservationists were highly critical of mink hunting because of its environmental disruption during the breeding season. Hunts killed only a few hundred minks every year and therefore had no significant impact on mink numbers.

The case against hunting is overwhelming on moral and practical grounds. Morally, it can never be right to chase a creature to death for "sport" and amusement. Hunting mammals with dogs causes prolonged suffering. Moreover, even in practical terms, it is ineffective as a means of control. The Committee of Inquiry set up in 2000 by the then Labour government, chaired by Lord Burns, concluded that the "overall contribution of fox-hunting" was "almost certainly insignificant in terms of the management of the fox population as a whole" (*Report* 89) and concluded similarly with respect to mink and hare hunting. Hunting, therefore, kills too few animals to have any significant impact on actual numbers and in any case fails to distinguish between the "innocent" and "guilty." It also resulted in hounds stampeding and killing livestock and companion animals, damaging crops and gardens, and causing serious road and rail accidents.

Related articles: Conservation philosophy; Deer hunting; Dogs; The ethics of killing free-living animals; Greyhound racing; Hunting with ferrets; Legislation in the European Union; The moral claims of animals; Rabbits; Threats to the brown hare

Bryant, John, *Fettered Kingdoms*, Fox Press, 1982.
Cartmill, Matt, *A View to the Death in the Morning: Hunting and Nature through History*, Harvard University Press, 1991.
Linzey, Andrew, *Christian Theology and the Ethics of Hunting with Dogs*, Christian Socialist Movement, 2003.
———, "Hunting with Dogs," in *Why Animal Suffering Matters: Philosophy, Theology, and Practical Ethics*, Oxford University Press, 2009, 75–96.
Report of the Committee of Inquiry into Hunting with Dogs in England and Wales, chaired by Lord Burns, HMSO, 2000.
Ridley, Jane, *Fox Hunting*, Collins, 1990.

JOHN BRYANT

HUNTING WITH FERRETS

Hunting with ferrets, or "ferreting" as it is sometimes called, is principally a method of chasing and killing rabbits. All entrances and exits to the rabbit's underground burrow are covered with netting (known as "purse nets," which cover each individual hole), and one or more ferrets are placed down the holes to chase rabbits into the nets. After being caught in the nets, the rabbits are usually killed by having their necks broken, though sometimes guns, dogs, falcons, or hawks are used. Hunting with ferrets takes place in many countries in Europe, including the United Kingdom, but it is illegal in some states in the United States.

According to the National Ferret Welfare Society (NFWS), "ferrets are not wild animals; they are domesticated descendants of the wild polecat, members of the Mustelidae family of animals that include the stoat, weasel, otter and badger . . . Ferrets are kept by a wide variety of people, either as working animals or as pets . . . A working ferret is one that is used for flushing wild rabbits out of their burrows, which is a humane and environmentally acceptable means of pest control" (NFWS, Homepage).

Although ferreting is probably more "humane" than other methods of killing, such as snaring and poisoning, it is not free of welfare problems. Since the most aggressive ferrets will invariably be used, it follows that some of the rabbits will end up being mauled, mutilated, or killed in the process of chasing. For example, according to G. A. Cooke, "occasionally the ferret will kill underground, feed on the rabbit and then go to sleep next to it, [and] this is called a 'lay-up.'" Opponents of hunting claim that ferreting invariably causes suffering. Here is one testimony from a hunter: "You have two different types of hunting ferret; you have the 'eye' ferret and you have the 'brain' ferret. An eye ferret in a hole only goes for the rabbit's eye—he blinds him. The 'brain' ferret, he'll bite straight onto the head between the ears" (ICABS).

Since the chase takes place underground, it is difficult to monitor the behavior of the ferrets involved or prevent attacks that may cause suffering. This problem is sometimes overcome by use of a "ferret finder," which consists of a radio transmitter collar attached to the ferret. According to "A Ferreter's Code" published by the NFWS, "if your ferret stays underground you can quickly locate it and dig down to it. An experienced ferreter will follow his/her ferret as it works and note if it stops then moves on as this may indicate a kill below ground to be dug out." But this process is invariably successful only *after* the mauling or killing has taken place.

Some argue that hunting with ferrets is justifiable because the rabbit meat is usually eaten. But this consideration is weakened when it is appreciated that ferreting is widely classed as a rural, country, or field sport and is commended on the grounds that it can provide useful recreation. Indeed, many view it as a "country sport" like coursing or hunting with dogs. Another justification is that rabbits are usually classed as "pests" and need to be controlled. But ferreting, like almost all hunting, does not actually control the species since animals invariably breed in relation to the food and environment available. Killing only dents a particular population in a given area, and in the case of rabbits, it is only a matter of time before others return to repopulate the burrow.

Ferrets are sometimes kept as companion animals. But they require high standards of welfare (NFWS) that are not always met, especially when they are kept purely instrumentally for the sake of hunting.

Related articles: Dogs; The ethics of killing free-living animals; Hunting with dogs; Rabbits; Snares and snaring

Cooke, G. A., "Hunting with Ferrets," National Ferret Welfare Society, 2007, available at http://homepage.ntlworld.com/ferreter/hunting02.htm.
ICABS (Irish Council against Blood Sports), "ICABS Urges Ban on Horrific Ferreting," 2008, available at http://www.banbloodsports.com/ln-0807g.htm#top.
McKay, James, *Complete Guide to Ferrets*, Swan Hill Press, 1995.
NFWS (National Ferret Welfare Society), "A Ferreter's Code," 1997, available at http://host17.qnop.net/~nfws/code.htm
———, Homepage, available at http://host17.qnop.net/~nfws/.
Rickard, Ian C., *Ferrets and Ferreting: Guide to Management*, Crowood Press, 2003.
Siino, Betsy Sikora, *The Essential Ferret*, Wiley, 1999.

ANDREW LINZEY

JUMPS RACING

Jumps racing is a form of thoroughbred horse racing in which horses are made to jump obstacles—"hurdles" or "steeples"—of specific heights over race distances of between three and seven kilometers.

Jumps racing began in England as cross-country contests in which participants would ride from one village church steeple to another over several miles—hence the term "steeplechase." Jumps races are held in dozens of nations around the world, with England, the United States, France, Ireland, Japan, and Australia being major participants. The first jumps race to be held on a specially made racetrack was conducted at Bedlam, England,

in 1810. Because of its high rate of death and the shocking nature of the falls and injuries suffered by horses, this style of racing has been controversial since its beginning. For animal advocates, Bedlam, a name synonymous with chaos and disorder, is an apposite location for jumps racing's inception.

For more than one hundred years rock walls and water obstacles were regular features of jumps races. However, increasing public pressure during the latter half of the twentieth century caused racing authorities to work at improving jumps racing's image and reducing its fatality rate. Rock walls and timber obstacles have been replaced with live hedges and nylon brush jumps. Nevertheless, in spite of these initiatives, the death rate in jumps racing consistently remains around twenty times that of normal racing. For animal advocates this constitutes an unacceptable level of risk to horses.

Jumping a horse, at speed, is inherently dangerous. Speaking of jumps racing, Dr. Thomas Tobin of the Department of Veterinary Science, University of Kentucky, maintains, "To break a normal cannon bone at the start of a race takes around 16,000 foot-pounds of force, but the amount of microcrushing which can take place in a race can reduce this force to about 9000 pounds" (qtd. in Duckworth 115). But fatalities are not the only concern. Jumps racing's fall rate is also up to fifty times higher than that of normal racing. When a 500 kilogram horse falls at thirty kilometers an hour, physical and mental trauma are highly likely, irrespective of whether the fall is fatal. To subject horses to these risks and trauma is to assent to a luck-based approach to the serious health and safety requirements of the animal—and his or her jockey.

The proponents of jumps racing argue that it saves otherwise uncompetitive horses from the slaughterhouse. Animal advocates respond that this is, in fact, an argument against an industry that treats horses as disposable objects, not an argument for jumps racing. It is also true that in comparison to "wastage"—those horses (globally, many tens of thousands each year) who are sent to slaughter either prior to or shortly after beginning their racing careers—the numbers killed in jumps racing are low, perhaps a few hundred per year. But again, animal advocates argue that two wrongs do not make a right, and any abuse is a legitimate area of moral concern. A final defense is that "horses love to jump." However, left to their own devices, horses will do almost anything to avoid jumping. They may be held behind meter-high fences and rarely jump logs or other objects unprompted. For a poor-sighted, stiff-skeleton, plains animal, jumping obstacles creates vulnerability to injury and predation and is therefore always risky.

In Australia the first anti–jumps racing protest was held in Sydney in 1848. During the twentieth century all states other than Victoria and South Australia abandoned jumps racing, and since the early 2000s, anti-jumps protests have been a regular feature of race meetings in both states. If jumps racing ends in the predominant "jumps state" of Victoria, South Australian jumps racing is unlikely to survive. High-profile animal organizations, including the Royal Society for the Prevention of Cruelty to Animals, the Coalition against Jumps Racing, Animals Australia, Victorian Advocates for Animals, and Animal Liberation South Australia continue to campaign to end jumps racing and have achieved some major advances toward this goal. Indeed, following a series of disastrous falls in 2008, Victoria's attorney general and minister for racing Rob Hulls put jumps racing "on notice." In spite of a major review and resultant reforms, racing was unable to improve its safety performance in the 2009 season, and the Board of Racing Victoria publicly announced that the 2010 jumps season would be the last staged in Victoria. Four weeks later, following intensive lobbying by pro-jumps forces, the board modified its decision, saying that if certain key performance measures could be met, jumps racing would be allowed to continue beyond 2010. At the time of this writing, the future of jumps racing in Australia is on a razor's edge.

Around the world jumps racing will remain a source of controversy and concern for animal organizations and for those who believe that animals' lives have a value that is independent of their use value to humans and that they should not used as a disposable means to sundry human ends.

Related articles: Animal advocacy; Animal issues in Australia; Greyhound racing; Horse slaughter; Horses; Japanese attitudes toward animals; The moral claims of animals; Pigeon racing

Animals Australia, "Help End Jumps Racing Carnage," available at http://www.animalsaustralia.org/take_action/jumps-racing-tragedy.
De Grazia, David, *Taking Animals Seriously: Mental Life and Moral Status*, University of Cambridge, 1996.
Duckworth, Jane, *They Shoot Horses, Don't They? The Treatment of Horses in Australia*, Robins, 2001.
Pope, Lawrence, "Grand? Just Horrific," *Herald Sun* (Australia), July 1, 2008.
———, "Horses Can't Jump If They're Dead," *Sydney Morning Herald*, October 10, 2009.
———, "Jumps Era Should Be Long Over," *Herald Sun* (Australia), January 1, 2009.
———, "Jumps Racing Is Simply Indefensible," *The Age*, May 5, 2012.
———, "This Isn't Sport, It's Savagery," *Adelaide Sunday Mail*, May 17, 2009.

LAWRENCE POPE

LIVE PIGEON SHOOTS

A live pigeon shoot is the practice of using live pigeons for target practice. The "sport" appears to have had its origin in Spain, and it was popular during the early twentieth century. Although live pigeon shoots were held at the 1900 Olympics, the so-called sport received a negative reception from the public and was never held again as an Olympic event. However, live pigeon shoots continued to be held in Monaco. The popularity of live pigeon shoots began to decrease, and in the 1960s live pigeons were for the most part replaced with clay pigeons. In the United States many states ban the practice, and in places where it is still legal, such as Texas, the shoots rarely occur. The exception is the state of Pennsylvania, where live pigeon shoots are both legal and still practiced in private gun clubs.

The origin of live pigeon shoots in Pennsylvania can be traced back to a time when pigeons created a nuisance for farmers. Annually, farmers would rid their barns of pigeons and pigeon droppings. The captured pigeons would be taken to the local grange, where they were used for live target practice. During the Depression the birds would sometimes be donated for food. Often the pigeons were fed to barn cats. As the pigeon population decreased, live pigeon shoots at local granges also decreased. However, they continued to be held in private gun clubs in the eastern part of the state and continue to this day. Animal welfare organizations consider eastern Pennsylvania to be the live pigeon shoot capital of the United States.

Because thousands of pigeons are needed for a single shoot, pigeon suppliers cross the border into New York to kidnap pigeons. The pigeons are illegally brought into Pennsylvania and kept in small cages for several days without food or water. This is possible because pigeons are not protected under Pennsylvania animal cruelty laws. On the day of a shoot, animal advocates have reported seeing numerous out-of-state license plates as participants come from surrounding states to engage in a practice that would result in their arrest in their own states.

The pigeon cages are lined up in a semicircle, and the shooters take aim and attempt to shoot the released pigeons within a circle in order to earn points. Often the pigeons are dazed and confused and fail to fly; others have to be forced to leave the cage via a shock from the electric floor. Many birds escape, often injured and unable to fly. The dead and injured birds' necks are wrung and their carcasses placed in fifty-five-gallon drums.

Under U.S. law, animal advocates are prohibited from entering private property. Consequently, on the day of a pigeon shoot, animal advocates are frequently seen standing on public property to observe what they can of the shoots. Observers have attempted to save injured birds whom they can gather up on public property. Protests of live pigeon shoots have been going on in Pennsylvania for a number of years. The Pennsylvania chapter of the Humane Society of the United States (HSUS) has tried unsuccessfully for many years to pass legislation that would outlaw live pigeon shoots. The main opposition to passage of the legislation is the National Rifle Association (NRA), which views the legislation as an assault on America's Second Amendment.

In recent years the HSUS has begun public information campaigns aimed at increasing public awareness of animal cruelty. Such a campaign was successful in creating public awareness of the cruel conditions in Pennsylvania's puppy mills. Public outcry resulted in the passage of a new Pennsylvania dog law aimed at eliminating the inhumane conditions in Pennsylvania puppy mills. The public awareness campaign regarding the pigeon shoots appears to be having a positive effect as well. The HSUS, working with other animal welfare organizations, continues to actively pursue legislation that would outlaw live pigeon shoots in the state of Pennsylvania. Based on the past success of public awareness campaigns, it appears that Pennsylvania is well on its way to losing the title of live pigeon shoot capital.

Related articles: Birds used in food production; Blood fiestas; Developments in animal law; Live quail shoots; Pigeon racing; The protection of birds

Blechman, Andrew, *The Fascinating Saga of the World's Most Revered and Reviled Bird*, Grove Press, 2006.
Brasch, W., "Hunting for Courageous Legislators: Pennsylvania Continues to Lead Nation in Animal Cruelty," 2010, available at http://themoderatevoice.com/85203.
Humane Society of the United States, "Pennsylvania Pigeon Shoots," 2009, available at http://www.humanesociety.org/issues/contest_kills/facts/pennsylvania_pigeon_shoots.html.
Leo, Teresa, "Pigeon Shoot," CrossXconnect, available at http://ccat.sas.upenn.edu/xconnect/v4/i2/t/leo.html.
Prescott, H., "A Cruelty Protected Only in Pa," 2010, available at http://www.philly.com/inquirer/opinion/83523247.html.
Song, Hoon, *Pigeon Trouble: Bestiary Biopolitics in a Deindustrialized America*, University of Pennsylvania Press, 2010.

FAITH BJALOBOK

LIVE QUAIL SHOOTS

Known as *tiradas de codorniz* (throwing of quail), live quail shoots take place regularly in the clay pigeon shooting clubs of Spain. It is normally a monthly event organized as part of the shooting program. *Tiradas de codorniz* are primarily centered in the provinces of Andalucia, Valencia, Murcia, and Castilla Leon, but the practice is spread all over Spain, taking place in purpose-built arenas in the countryside.

In clay pigeon shooting, a disc is thrown into the air by means of a spring-loaded trap or launcher. The disc is shot at, and the shooters are awarded points for their success. The *tirada de codorniz* is performed using a specially adapted, hand-operated clay pigeon launcher. The operator places a live bird into the barrel of the spring-loaded launcher, which then catapults the quail into the air. Some quails are injured as they leave the launcher. Those who survive are usually unable to fly. All of them become targets for the large-caliber shotguns. The area for shooting is usually enclosed by a fence of netting, approximately thirty centimeters high, so that any fallen birds who are still alive cannot escape.

A typical *tirada de codorniz* was one of the events during the fiesta of San Juan de Moró, in the province of Castellon. The "tournament" was open to anyone prepared to pay 1,800 pesetas, just over nine American dollars, to shoot at ten birds. Eighteen crates, containing approximately thirty quails each, were used. The birds were shot into the air, and the pace was nonstop. The arrival of each group of guns was announced by the tooting of a toy rubber horn.

At the end of the shooting, hundreds of bodies lay scattered across the arena. Some of the tiny birds were still alive after this barrage and lay fluttering on the ground. A few hopped through the bodies of their companions, trying to escape. The netting around the area allowed no exit and frustrated these attempts at escape. The escapees were the subject of much laughter and joking and were finally killed by being shot or stamped to death. Prizes were then given, with cash and plastic trophies awarded to the shooter with the highest tally of hits. The birds had all been reared in broiler sheds and supplied by a local breeder a few kilometers away—there is a thriving trade in intensively farmed quail chicks for the purpose of shooting.

The quail is the smallest among common partridges, weighing only one hundred grams, and the only migratory bird among gallinaceous birds. Quails migrate to northern Africa, as far as the equator. The sexes are similar in color, but the cock can be recognized by a black area on his throat. The males and females live together only at the beginning of the breeding season. The breeding period lasts for three weeks, and the chicks are independent after six weeks.

What an irony that a bird who travels great distances and lives a free existence should be bred in close confinement and then, in the last few moments of his or her life, find freedom in the sky, only to become a target for guns.

———————

Related articles: Animal welfare and farming; The ethics of killing free-living animals; Live pigeon shoots; Pigeon racing; The protection of birds

Cavell, Stanley, Diamond, Cora, McDowell, John, Hacking Ian, and Wolfe, Cary, *Philosophy and Animal Life*, Columbia University Press, 2008.

Huggler, Tom, *Live Quail Shooting in America*, Stackpole Books, 1987.

Laney, Dawn (ed.), *Hunting: Opposing Viewpoints*, Greenhaven Press, 2007.

Linzey, Andrew, *Why Animal Suffering Matters: Philosophy, Theology, and Practical Ethics*, Oxford University Press, 2009.

Mench, Matilda, *Life on the Line: The Heroic Story of Vicki Moore*, Bluecoat Press, 2007.

de Saldaña, Emma D., *Las Voces del Silencio*, Diseños and Impresion, 2004.

TONY MOORE

———————

PIGEON RACING

Racing pigeons belong to the species *Columba livia*. What separates these birds from the small colonies who still live free and from feral pigeons, who no longer live under human control, is that they are kept inside the lofts or dovecotes built by humans. Although interest in pigeon racing is declining in many Western countries, it has been reported to be growing elsewhere, particularly in Asia.

In spite of this growth in interest, a topic search using the words "pigeons" and "ethics" in the ISI Web of Science database yields just seven papers. Out of these, only one—a one-page commentary—deals with pigeon racing (MacKenzie 600). Many might think that pigeon racing poses no ethical problems. Pigeon racing is associated with many good things, including the camaraderie that pigeon "fanciers" develop with their birds and with club members, as well as the awe that many experience at the wonders of nature when they see how pigeons manage to return home with great speed, having been released in places where they have never been before and that might be more than six hundred miles away from their lofts.

It must be asked, however, whether these goods outweigh the bads. Killing is part and parcel of how the sport is practiced. Indeed, Charles Darwin was very familiar with the role of killing in the sport, and further reflection on the artificial selection carried out by pigeon racers inspired him to come up with a theory of natural selection that he applied to all organisms (Darwin chap. 1). The reason killing plays such a pivotal role relates to the fancier's desire to breed birds who are faster than the birds of other club members. In order to increase participants' chances of doing well, most races include only relatively young birds. Although domesticated pigeons can live up to twenty-five years, most are no longer used to race beyond the age of five years.

Apart from a few birds who are kept for breeding purposes, most are killed by age five. The questionable good associated with breeding birds who can fly faster than the birds of competitors seems to pale in comparison with the good of allowing pigeons to continue living, at least as long as they are not too ill.

Some pigeon fanciers might respond that a no-killing policy would soon lead to overcrowded lofts because a couple of pigeons can breed up to twelve young birds within a year. The alternative, however, is to separate the sexes, as is done widely already, in the shape of the widowhood system: couples are separated apart from the short times they are allowed to spend together just before and after the race (with one member of each couple being entered in the race while the other awaits the return of his or her partner), in the hope that the prospect of seeing their partner will motivate birds to fly faster. Some might be inspired to consider a system of putative "ethical" pigeon racing: enhance the racing value of old birds by introducing separate races for veterans, prohibit the killing of birds unless it is clearly in their best interests, and breed less.

However, the widowhood system is not free from problems either. Apart from the stress couples may endure as a result of forced separation, cocks tend to become quite excited just before the race and regularly injure each other (mainly by pecking at each other's eyelids) when they are put together with other cocks in baskets—which usually contain up to twenty-five birds—before being transported to the place of release. Even if the sexes were separated permanently, birds still would be bound to harm each other when put together in confined spaces because pigeons are very territorial (normally allowing only their partner and young in their immediate vicinity). Furthermore, even if they do not injure themselves while being transported, many pigeons do not return from the places where they are released, especially in bad weather conditions and when they are released from places in excess of four hundred miles from their lofts. Unlike their free-ranging and feral relatives, racing pigeons do not fare well when they spend more than two consecutive nights outside: their sheer determination to return home drives them to exhaustion, and most lack the skills to fend for themselves.

Even if pigeons could have a good quality of life under human domestication, the question must be asked: who are we to exert such great control over the lives of these animals for the sake of the pleasure we might derive from racing or keeping them? Because pigeons have retained the ability to learn to fend for themselves, they could be weaned off from our control and resume greater control over their own lives. So here is my suggestion to all pigeon fanciers: leave your lofty ambitions and open your lofts! May the future be feral.

Related articles: Animals in Asia; The ethics of killing free-living animals; Greyhound racing; Jumps racing; Live animal exports; The protection of birds

Constantini, D., Dell'Ariccia, G., and Lipp, H., "Long Flights and Age Affect Oxidative Status of Homing Pigeons (*Columba livia*)," *Journal of Experimental Biology* 211.3 (2008): 377–381.

Darwin, C., *The Origin of Species*, Gramercy Books, 1998.

Duchatel, J., Beduin, J., Jauniaux, T., Coignoul, F., and Vindevogel, H., "Premières observations sur l'utilisation des glucocorticoïdes comme agent dopant chez le pigeon voyageur," *Annales de Médecine Vétérinaire* 137 (1993): 557–564.

MacKenzie, P., "Cruelty to Racing Pigeons," *Veterinary Record* 92.22 (1973): 600.

O'Donovan, K., "Pigeon Racing Grows in Popularity Internationally," *BBC News*, April 22, 2010, available at http://news.bbc.co.uk/local/dorset/hi/people_and_places/nature/news-id_8635000/8635315.stm.

Scope, A., Filip, T., Gabler, C., and Resch, F., "The Influence of Stress from Transport and Handling on Hematologic and Clinical Chemistry Blood Parameters of Racing Pigeons (*Columba livia domestica*)," *Avian Diseases* 46.1 (2002): 224–229.

Warzecha, M., "Taubensport und Tierschutz," *Deutsche Tierärztliche Wochenschrift* 114.3 (2007): 108–113.

JAN DECKERS

RODEOS

The word "rodeo" derives from the Spanish word *rodear*, which means "to encircle." The earliest rodeos are reported to have taken place in the 1870s. There are approximately five thousand rodeos annually in the United States. Rodeos also take place in Canada, Mexico, Brazil, Chile, and Australia. In Europe, rodeos take place mostly in Germany, France, Italy, Hungary, Poland, Belgium (American rodeo), and Portugal (Brazilian rodeo). There have also been unsuccessful attempts to introduce it into Spain, Greece, and China.

There are various rodeo disciplines. The most common are as follows: In bareback riding, horses are ridden without saddle, but with a rope halter, for eight seconds, and the cowboy uses blunt spurs to damage and aggravate the animal but draws no blood. In saddle bronc, a saddle is allowed. In "wild horse racing," a team of three cowboys tries to subdue and saddle a horse. Once the saddle has been fixed, one cowboy has to ride the horse to a finish line. In bull riding, a cowboy rides a bull for eight seconds. In team roping, a team of cowboys ropes a calf or steer, and in calf roping, three-month-old calves, running at high speed, are lassoed and slammed to the ground, and then their legs are tied.

In steer wrestling, a steer runs at high speed, and a cowboy leaps from his horse, grabs the horns of the steer, and twists the animal's neck until he is brought down. Steer tripping, or bull dogging, involves a rope being thrown around a steer's horns from the right side while, at the same time, the cowboy's horse turns to the left, and the steer's neck is jerked 180 degrees. The animal falls down and is dragged by his neck until his legs are tied.

Barrel racing is carried out mostly by women. Three barrels are set up in a triangular course, and the horse must go around the barrels without knocking them down. In rescue riding, or buddy pick-up, one man on a horse has to pick up another man who is standing on the ground or on a barrel. "Wild cow milking" involves a cow being thrown to the ground or subdued via one person pulling on the animal's tail and another holding fingers in her nostrils, as a team of cowboys tries to obtain as much milk as possible in a limited period of time. In "mutton busting," children up to the age of six years ride a sheep. There are also rodeo clowns who entertain the audience between breaks by using pigeons and other animals.

There is a constant demand for cattle and horses because cowboys also have to practice prior to the rodeo competitions. In the United States and Canada the majority of the rodeo participants, or "cowboys," are professionals and travel from one event to another for money, in order to accumulate points for the championship. They are organized in professional rodeo cowboy associations. Most of them specialize in one of the rodeo disciplines, and successful competitors are awarded large amounts in prize money. In Europe the participants are amateur weekend cowboys.

Although the rodeo participants bear a certain risk, the risk for the animals—in terms of injury or death—is much higher. Although there is always emergency medical assistance available for the cowboys, it is rare that a veterinarian is available on-site. In fact, most of the time, the animals are not treated at all. They are simply loaded onto a trailer and transported to the next rodeo or taken to the slaughterhouse.

The animals used in rodeos are not free-ranging animals. They are domesticated animals who are forced to behave "wild" by being physically manipulated. The so-called wild mustangs are riding horses in reality. The flank strap, or bucking strap, which is fastened around the horse's body just in front of the hind legs and pulled tight, causes severe pain to the animal, which makes him buck. Tails are intentionally twisted, and mane and tail may be pulled before the animal is released from the chute. The horse is further tormented by the cowboy's spurs and sometimes "runs blind," crashing into the metal bars of the rodeo arena. Serious injury or death may result. Once the flank strap is taken off, the animal immediately ceases to buck.

The bulls have a rope placed around their body in front of the hind legs, which again causes the animal to buck. This rope can also put pressure on the urethra and cause further pain (see the "Expert Opinion" of the Association of Veterinarians for Animal Protection). The use of electric prods on bulls and horses when the animals are confined is very common. Handlers punch calves, scrape them over the rails, and twist their tails to make them fly out of the chute when the gate is opened. The calves who are used in the roping events suffer terribly; they are taken from rodeo to rodeo until they die through physical injury or exhaustion or have grown too large to be useful, in which case they are slaughtered. Often the animals panic and hurt themselves when they try to jump the metal fence. The most frequent injuries include broken backs, broken necks, massive internal injuries, and severe damage to the ligamentum nuchae. When the cattle are slaughtered, some of them cannot go into the food chain because they have been so brutalized. Steers have been known to have as much as three gallons of subcutaneous blood.

Money is obviously a big issue in rodeos. Stock contractors are often also rodeo producers. Corporate sponsorships are the rule, the sponsors being producers and manufacturers of tobacco, alcohol, cars, and jeans. Because of protests by animal advocates, some places have made restrictions, such as banning the use of flank straps, electric prods, spurs, and long trailing ropes or requiring a minimum weight for calves. These restrictions sometimes have resulted in disciplines being abandoned or, in other cases, in no rodeos taking place at all.

Opponents criticize not only the cruelties inherent in rodeo; they also object to the fact that children are exposed to publicly sanctioned animal abuse. Nowadays, audiences appear to approve of calf-roping less and less because this is considered the most brutal. But other disciplines have been criticized too. Even prominent rodeo participants, such as "horse whisperer" Monty Roberts, have spoken out against the "wild horse race" because too many horses die every year.

Rodeo is said to represent ranch work in the "Old West." In fact, although animals occasionally have to be roped on a ranch—for example, for veterinary treatment—ranchers do not treat their animals in the manner the rodeo does. Rodeos have events, such as bull riding, that were never a part of ranching. All these events are meticulously timed, and a split second can make the difference between a large or a small purse. The animals are treated as objects in competitive entertainment. Rodeo has been glorified as an expression of freedom of spirit and all that was good in the "Old West." In reality, it is nothing more, or less, than a callous misuse of animals.

Related articles: Animal advocacy; Animal and human violence; Animal issues in Australia; Bull fighting; Free-ranging horses; Horse slaughter; Horses; The humane movement in Canada; Slaughter; South American perspectives on animals; The welfare of cows

Association of Veterinarians for Animal Protection (Tierärztliche Vereinigung für Tierschutz e.V., Germany), *Expert Opinion regarding Rodeo Events in the Federal Republic of Germany from a Legal, Ethological and Ethical Perspective*, 2005, available at http://www.sharkonline.org/UP0000000419.pdf.

Cotter, Barbara H., *Professional Rodeo: No Room for Cruelty*, Professional Rodeo Cowboys Association, 1986.

Linzey, Andrew, *Why Animal Suffering Matters: Philosophy, Theology, and Practical Ethics*, Oxford University Press, 2009.

Mench, Matilda, *Life on the Line: The Heroic Story of Vicki Moore*, Bluecoat Press, 2007.

Rollin, Bernard E., *Putting the Horse before Descartes: My Life's Work on Behalf of Animals*, Temple University Press, 2011.

de Saldaña, Emma D., *Las Voces del Silencio*, Diseños and Impresion, 2004.

TONY MOORE AND MECHTHILD MENCH

six

CHANGING PERSPECTIVES

The last fifty years have witnessed major changes in the ways humans think about animals.

From a view of them as things, machines, commodities, or resources for humans to do with as they wish, a new conception of animals has emerged—that sentient animals should be regarded as individuals with their own dignity, intrinsic value, and rights. This paradigm change is the result of work by philosophers and ethicists who have challenged the dominant view of animals and is informed by scientific work indicating the extent of animal sentiency and animals' complex systems of awareness.

So huge is this paradigm shift that change is beginning to be felt in almost every area of human life that impacts on animals. This section provides examples of changing perspectives in ethics, law, religion, and science. The section concludes with an account of three declarations on the rights or welfare of animals.

ANDREW LINZEY

CHANGING ETHICAL SENSITIVITY

ANIMAL AND HUMAN VIOLENCE

Historically, violence to animals has been viewed as an issue separate from other forms of family violence. However, in many instances, cruelty to animals, particularly companion animals, is a part of the landscape of family violence and at times shows strong links to interpersonal violence, notably child maltreatment and domestic violence and, to a lesser extent, elder abuse. These links are being examined in a resurgence of popular and interdisciplinary professional interest. A growing and compelling body of research is confirming anecdotal reports—and traditional cultural, ethical, and religious understandings—that acts of animal cruelty (described more contemporarily as animal abuse) may predict serious interpersonal aggression and familial dysfunction.

In the continuum of family violence, an individual or family may manifest any one or any combination of the forms of abuse. Animal abuse is not necessarily a precursor to child maltreatment, domestic violence, or elder abuse. Rather, all four types of abuse are part of the complex constellation of family violence. Human services and animal welfare investigators are not surprised when they see multiple manifestations.

When an individual commits or witnesses acts of abuse against animals, this may lead to a generalized desensitization to violence, which may evolve into acts of interpersonal aggression. Animal cruelty perpetrated by youths has been shown to be not a benign stage of growing up, but rather one of the earliest diagnostic indicators of conduct disorder. A significant number of serial killers and school shooters have had prior histories of abusing animals. People who abuse animals have been found to be significantly more likely to commit violent crimes against people. Several studies have reported that a majority of perpetrators of family violence kill, harm, or threaten companion animals, in order to silence, coerce, and further intimidate other vulnerable family members. The concept of "battered pets" has begun to enter the paradigm of family violence, mimicking earlier terminologies of "battered children" and "battered women."

Advocates of what is often called "the link" espouse three main premises. The first is that since companion animals are more prevalent than children in many Western households, and since they are commonly perceived as members of the family, acts of violence against them should be considered not in isolation but rather within the framework of family violence. Second, since laws prohibiting animal cruelty have historically been enacted not to protect animals' inherent rights, but rather to protect public morals and private property, animal abuse should be seen as a human welfare issue with implications for public health and safety. And the third premise is that interdisciplinary analyses and collaborative social services interventions, utilizing the connections between animal cruelty and interpersonal violence, offer new opportunities for the study of violence and the hope for new insights and preventive solutions.

Professionals are focusing on several programmatic areas of interest:

- Establishing safety plans and emergency housing programs for the companion animals of battered women, in order to remove an obstacle that may prevent them and their children from escaping abusive relationships.
- Coordinating cross-training among the four disciplines that teaches professionals to recognize multiple forms of family violence and to report these findings to appropriate authorities.
- Increasing the criminal penalties for malicious acts of animal abuse; redefining these actions as crimes against public morals, rather than as crimes against property; and authorizing courts to order psychological assessment and anger management treatment for offenders and the inclusion of companion animals in protection-from-abuse orders.

- Including professionals in the four fields among those individuals who are mandated and protected by law to report suspected cases of abuse to appropriate authorities.
- Enhancing empathy and building nonviolent conflict-resolution competencies—for example, in antisocial youths, by helping them utilize humane positive reinforcement techniques for dogs in shelters, thereby making these animals more adoptable.
- Establishing objective diagnostic criteria that will guide veterinarians and animal protection professionals in separating accidental from deliberate injury to animals, thereby facilitating the recognition, treatment, and prosecution of cases of animal abuse.
- Identifying psychological motivators that cause people to mistreat animals, in order to develop effective mental health prevention and treatment strategies.

Although the animal protection community has been generally receptive to undertaking "link" programming, other professions have been somewhat reluctant, citing inadequate training, fear of litigation, economic loss, absence of organizational protocols, professional norms, confidentiality concerns, and inconsistent definitions of "abuse" across disciplinary lines. As professionals address these concerns, public support for a strong and rapid response to animal abuse and its associations with family violence continues to grow.

The origins of violence are exceedingly complex, with no single cause, but rather an accumulation of risk factors. "Link" proponents do not imply that animals are more important than people or that one discipline is more important than others. They believe that when animals are abused, people are at risk, and vice versa. Since no forms of family violence should be tolerated, the four fields should collaborate to reduce family violence in its many forms.

Related articles: Animal-friendly spirituality; Caring for animals and humans; Children's relations with animals; Humane education; The universal charter of the rights of other species

Arkow, P., *Breaking the Cycles of Violence: A Guide to Multi-Disciplinary Interventions. A Handbook for Child Protection, Domestic Violence and Animal Protection Agencies,* Latham Foundation, 2003.
Ascione, F. R., *Children and Animals: Exploring the Roots of Kindness and Cruelty*, Purdue University Press, 2005.
—— (ed.), *International Handbook of Animal Abuse and Cruelty: Theory, Research, and Application*, Purdue University Press, 2008.
Ascione, F. R., and Arkow, P. (eds.), *Child Abuse, Domestic Violence and Animal Abuse: Linking the Circles of Compassion for Prevention and Intervention*, Purdue University Press, 1999.
Linzey, Andrew (ed.), *The Link between Animal Abuse and Human Violence*, Sussex Academic Press, 2009.
Sinclair, L., Merck, M., and Lockwood, R., *Forensic Investigation of Animal Cruelty: A Guide for Veterinary and Law Enforcement Professionals*, Humane Society of the United States, 2006.

PHIL ARKOW

THE FEMINIST ETHIC OF CARE

Within the movement for change in the way humans treat animals, there are many diverse philosophies, including two in particular: the rights theory with justice as its basis and the feminist ethic of care based on caring. Advocates of both philosophies have the well-being of nonhuman animals as their goal, even as they debate how best to change the way animals are treated.

The ethic of care theory is feminist in its modern origins. It dates from Carol Gilligan's 1982 work *In a Different Voice*, in which she reported that women's experience of morality derives from an ethic of care rather than from the more masculine model of rights based on justice. Gilligan points out that the moral problems that arise from the ethic of care come from conflicting responsibilities rather competing rights and that their resolution lies in a mode of thinking that is contextual and narrative rather than formal and abstract. She says that the ethic of care focuses on the understanding of responsibility and relationships, not on the idea of fairness and equal treatment that is required by rights and rules.

Ecofeminists argue that the care theory is more appropriate than the rights theory in dealing with the way humans treat nature and animals. Greta Gaard explains the key elements of ecofeminism in her work *Ecofeminism: Women, Animals, and Nature* (1993), and Marti Kheel pioneered the application of this theory to animals in, among other works, *Nature Ethics: An Ecofeminist Perspective* (2008). In *Beyond Animal Rights: A Feminist Caring Ethic for the Treatment of Animals* (1996), edited by Josephine Donovan and Carol Adams, the theory is treated in detail by several authors.

In *Animals and Why They Matter* (1983), Mary Midgley holds that it is our emotional fellowship with animals, and not their intellectual capacity, that should qualify them for decent treatment. In their concern for animals, many women feel a bond with animals that may stem from their common oppression in patriarchal culture, with its dualistic and hierarchal mode of thinking. Dualism is a way of analyzing various categories of reality by dividing them into opposing and mutually exclusive pairs, such as man or woman, human or animal, masculine or feminine, and so on. Usually, one member of the dyad is considered higher, or of more value, than the other. In patriarchy, that more valued pair member is identified with the masculine in a way that allows for the privilege of the one member of the pair and the oppression or domination of the other. Hence, patriarchy values men over women and humans over animals, allowing for the domination of women, animals, and nature as a result. In a similar way, patriarchy devalues emotion and considers intellectual decision making to be more masculine than and thus superior to any decision influenced by emotion.

Caring, with its emotional undergirding, is often seen as a feminine approach to problems. Some suggest this may be because women have been the nurturers in society. Others hold that it is more a product of socialization. Those opposed to change sometimes show disdain for what they stereotypically consider "feminine" and have often tried to forestall change by ridiculing caring, labeling it "womanish" and "sentimental." This could be one reason some animal rights theorists emphasize a non-emotional approach. Those holding the rights theory argue, for example, that a sentient being is a "subject of a life" or that every being who possesses sentience has inherent value. Such beings should therefore be treated as an end and not a means and should not be exploited by humans. Those holding the ethic of care theory would also say that animals should not be exploited, not because of some characteristic they have but because of a holistic view of life wherein all things are interconnected. This connection gives rise to a feeling of kinship that humans have for animals.

Criticism of a rationalistic view of reality and an overly individualistic ethic has a long history. Adams writes in *The Sexual Politics of Meat* (1992) that many suffragists were vegetarians and antivivisectionists. For example, as reported by Josephine Donovan in *Beyond Animal Rights* (1996), Frances Power Cobbe decried the coldly rational materialism of science that she saw as "freezing sensibility." She saw antivivisection as "shielding the heart and human spirit from heartless cruelty."

Advocates of rights and care theories are engaged in a dialogue that should be enriching to both. Ecofeminist scholars maintain that rights theory denies that feeling should play a role in decision making about animals, whereas the care theory sees "attentive love" and sympathy as its basic operative motives. Proponents of rights theory argue that emotional feelings such as caring are unreliable in moral decision making because, being private, they cannot be universalized. Also, rights theory scholars argue that emotion is anti-intellectual and easily subject to error or volatility. Countering, ecofeminists point to many philosophic writings that show how sympathy often has an intellectual element. In addition, some philosophers contend that all decision making is affected by emotion and that there would not be a claim for rights if one were not moved by sympathy, which is often a basis for moral awareness.

Not all ecofeminists want to discard the notion of rights altogether. Some see a melding, or a more unified approach, as more viable. For example, the rights theory provides useful arguments for the ethical treatment of animals especially in the legal field. Emotion cannot be legislated or regulated by law, but our treatment of animals can be, and the notion of justice is obviously relevant here. Sympathy is nevertheless obviously important because it is one of the mainsprings of moral action. Finally, ecofeminists claim that through our relations and "attentive love" with all beings, we can gain a deeper perception that animals do not want to be treated cruelly or exploited and that this constitutes a "true knowledge" that should guide our treatment of animals.

Related articles: Caring for animals and humans; Moral anthropocentrism; The moral claims of animals; The moral community; The universal charter of the rights of other species

Adams, Carol J., *The Sexual Politics of Meat: A Feminist-Vegetarian Critical Theory*, Continuum, 1992.

Donovan, Josephine, and Adams, Carol J., *Beyond Animal Rights: A Feminist Caring Ethic for the Treatment of Animals*, Continuum, 1996.

Gaard, Greta, *Ecofeminism: Women, Animals and Nature*, Temple University Press, 1993.

Gilligan Carol, *In a Different Voice*, Harvard University Press, 1982.

Kheel, Marti, *Nature Ethics: An Ecofeminist Perspective*, Rowman and Littlefield, 2008.

Midgley, Mary, *Animals and Why They Matter*, University of Georgia Press, 1998.

ELIZABETH FARIANS

MORAL ANTHROPOCENTRISM

Anthropocentrism, or the propensity to interpret things through human-centered values, presents a primary challenge to conceptualizing animals as beings unto themselves, rather than beings who exist for humans to use. Though some contemporary thinkers recognize that animals possess moral standing (e.g., see Singer), the "moral orthodoxy" in Western thought is that any such interest is inferior to that of humans (Garner 8). During the last part of the twentieth century, this orthodoxy—or moral anthropocentrism—has been increasingly challenged by a growing number of leading thinkers. However, moral anthropocentrism, predicated by anthropocentrism, remains firmly entrenched in Western culture.

The supposed inferiority of animals vis-à-vis human beings has its roots in ancient thought—both in early Western philosophy and in the development of Judeo-Christian theology. The position that animals have little or no moral standing springs from anthropocentrism, which rests upon actual or putative differences between humans and animals or upon the belief in a natural hierarchy of beings, with animals in a position inferior to that of humans. Commonly advanced arguments include the assertions that animals are not rational because they cannot engage in human language, that they lack self-consciousness or sentience, and that they lack capacity to reciprocate moral duties and a belief that God granted dominion over animals for humans to use. Steiner, in *Anthropocentrism and Its Discontents*, provides a thorough discussion of the roots of anthropocentrism.

Challenges to moral anthropocentrism spring from an equally rich lineage of thought. A nonexhaustive accounting of historically deep arguments in support of recognizing moral standing of animals on par with that of humans includes the belief in transmigration of souls; belief that animals are rational; and belief that killing animals is contrary to God's will, destroys God's work, or is offensive to gods (e.g., Linzey, *Animal Theology*). Although these positions might still be anthropocentric, they have nonetheless supported practices that sharply mitigate the unchecked consequences of moral anthropocentrism. For example, as understood contemporarily, the transmigration of souls admonishes against harming animals from a human-centered perspective. This is because harming animals will result in distancing one's self from God in the birth-rebirth cycle (Davidson 913–916). Moreover, a belief persists among transmigrationists that the route to God is possible only to those souls currently inhabiting human bodies (e.g., Davidson). This position retains a hierarchy that views humans as superior to (and closer to God than) nonhumans, and it advances a position based on human-centered interests. However, it affords moral standing to animals under what might be called benign anthropocentrism.

The widespread influences of thinkers such as Aristotle, Augustine, and Aquinas in the West—and specifically their writings about animals' relationships to human beings and/or to God—effectively eclipsed non-human-centered viewpoints or benign anthropocentrism in the mainstream. Moral anthropocentrism became so doctrinally entrenched that benign anthropocentric viewpoints were seriously marginalized. In Western thought, for example, moral anthropocentrism is firmly ensconced in law, which regards animals as personal property, allowing humans to own, detain, use, or kill them. Anthropocentrism also drives any legal protection that might be bestowed on animals, in that these laws protect animals whom humans value, rather than the intrinsic value of the animals themselves, thereby allowing for limited protection for certain animals without disturbing the sovereignty that moral anthropocentrism enjoys in Western culture. Such laws create narrowly applied benign anthropocentric approaches, which allow for the protection of a few animals while endorsing the maltreatment of others.

Moral anthropocentrism is pervasive today. Many contemporary arguments advanced in favor of moral standing for animals still concede animals' interests as inferior to those of humans when the choice must be made. Common debates between rights and welfare approaches often, but not always, occur within this realm. For instance, the sentience of animals is often used as a basis to challenge exclusion of their interests, though human interests are considered more important (e.g., Singer).

Some contemporary arguments seek to undermine the concept of presumed inferiority of animals with respect to humans—thereby challenging moral anthropocentrism and advocating a benign anthropocentrism. These arguments include recognition that animals are subjects-of-a-life (Regan), have inherent value (Regan; Nussbaum), and are created by the same God (Linzey, *Creatures of the Same God*). Compelling arguments that question the threshold need for sentience as a condition for moral consideration on par with that of humans have also recently emerged (Steiner; Sorabji).

Serious debates exist regarding whether and how humans could perceive anything—including animals—from anything but a human-centered perspective, thereby challenging the very ability to question anthropocentrism itself. However, contemporary challenges to anthropocentrism do exist, questioning the foundations on which moral anthropocentrism rest. These challenges are found in the works of poststructuralists, who actively seek to decenter the human being as the source of knowledge or "truth." In the context of the animal, language that creates boundaries between human beings and animals is understood as antecedent to an understanding about animals as anything at all, including as beings who are "inferior" or "human property."

To counter the effects of anthropocentrism (and implicitly, moral anthropocentrism itself)—such as the lawful yet wholly unnecessary slaughter of billions of animals each year for food—some efforts have been launched to change the language by which humans conceive of animals. For instance, efforts have been undertaken to change the language used in law to reflect a person's relationship to an animal, so that the person is considered a "guardian" rather than "owner" (Waisman, Wagman, and Frasch 95–96). If poststructuralists are correct, new words or "labels" applied to or about animals will recast concepts about animals. This may allow for the emergence of new understandings that recognize animals as existing for purposes independent from human interests in them.

Related articles: Animal pain; Buddhist attitudes; The complexity of animal awareness; The concept of guardianship; Developments in animal law; Hinduism and animals; The moral claims of animals; Slaughter; The universal charter of the rights of other species; The universal declaration on animal welfare

Davidson, J., *The Gospel of Jesus: In Search of His Original Teachings*, Element Books, 1995.
Garner, R., "Animal Rights, Political Theory and the Liberal Tradition," *Contemporary Politics* 8.1 (2002): 7–22.
Linzey, A., *Animal Theology*, University of Illinois Press, 1995.
———, *Creatures of the Same God*, Lantern Books, 2009.
Nussbaum, M. C., *Frontiers of Justice: Disability, Nationality, Species Membership*, Belknap Press of Harvard University Press, 2006.
Regan, T., *The Case for Animal Rights*, University of California Press, 1983.
Singer, P., *Animal Liberation*, 3rd ed., HarperCollins, 2002.
Sorabji, R., *Animal Minds and Human Morals*, Cornell University Press, 1993.
Steiner, G., *Anthropocentrism and Its Discontents: The Moral Status of Animals in the History of Western Philosophy*, University of Pittsburgh Press, 2005.
Waisman, S. S., Wagman, B. A., and Frasch, P. A., *Animal Law: Cases and Materials*, 2nd ed., Carolina Academic Press, 2002.

LISA JOHNSON

THE MORAL CLAIMS OF ANIMALS

Philosophers who defend the claim that nonhuman animals (hereafter "animals") have rights or that human beings can make moral claims for animals by proxy tend to be reacting, whether explicitly or implicitly, against the thought of the seventeenth-century thinker René Descartes. Descartes thought that reality was made of two radically different sorts of stuff: minds on the one hand and material bodies that worked with machine-like regularity on the other. Although human beings were composed of both sorts of stuff, in his view animals did

not have minds and hence were, strictly speaking, machines. Not only could they not think; they could not experience pain either.

This Cartesian view led not only to the eating of animals with equanimity; it led also to the view that if animals were experimented on in painful ways (see Animals Used in Research), their screams were not *really* indications of pain, but were more like the eerie sounds produced when metal parts in a machine rubbed against each other when not lubricated. That is, the sounds of animal "pain" were more like the screeching of automobile brakes than they were like the auditory evidence received from a human being whose carotid artery has been slit. Unfortunately, Descartes's view was—and is—quite influential, both among scholars and in popular culture.

Contemporary philosophers who defend animal rights have developed at least three different arguments to counteract this influential Cartesian view of animals as machines available for our use. The first and easiest to grasp is the argument from sentiency. A simplified version of this argument goes something like this.

1. Any being who can experience pain or suffer should not have pain or suffering (or death) inflicted on him or her unnecessarily.
2. It is not necessary that we inflict pain or suffering (or death) on a sentient animal in order for us to have a healthy diet or to do science.
3. Therefore, we should not inflict pain or suffering (or death) on sentient animals for the purpose of eating them or experimenting on them.

As Stephen R. L. Clark sums up this argument in the preface to *The Moral Status of Animals*, "this at least cannot be true, that it is proper to be the cause of avoidable ill."

Some philosophers have objected to this argument by claiming that it might be "proper" to kill animals for our purposes, so long as we do so "painlessly" (assuming, for the sake of argument, that painless killing of animals is likely or even possible). An initial response to this objection involves the observation that it is odd to claim that only pain is bad and not premature death as well. But a fuller response is found in a second major argument advanced by philosophers who are animal rightists, the *argument from marginal cases* or *the argument from species overlap*.

Defenders of this argument agree with almost everyone else regarding the criterion that must be met in order to be a *moral agent* (i.e., someone who commits moral or immoral actions and who can be held morally accountable): rationality. It might be difficult to determine whether someone *is* rational, but rationality is the criterion that would be required for an individual to be a moral agent. But what property is required in order to be a moral patient or a moral beneficiary (i.e., someone who can receive immoral treatment from others or who can be treated cruelly or have his or her rights violated)? Here the issue is quite thorny.

The most parsimonious response to this question leads to a type of symmetry that some find appealing: have rationality do double-duty by serving as the standard of moral beneficiary status as well as the standard for moral agency status. However, this leads to frightening consequences because on this basis many human beings (the marginal cases of humanity who are not rational) would not be moral beneficiaries and as a result would not deserve moral respect.

An understandable response to the problems involved in requiring a high standard for moral beneficiary status such as rationality is to lower it dramatically. Some wish to make life the criterion for moral patiency or moral beneficiary status. All life, some say, deserves moral respect. However, this response also leads to dreadful consequences because on its basis we would not be morally permitted to excise cancerous tumors because cancer cells are quite alive and well or even to breathe, in that such activity involves bringing into our bodies living organisms that are killed. It is not clear what one could legitimately eat on a consistent pro-life basis.

Defenders of the argument from marginal cases work their way, both theoretically and practically, to a place in between these two extremes (i.e., rationality and life) in order to find a defensible standard for moral beneficiary status in sentiency. On this standard, all human beings deserve moral respect in that even the most marginal of marginal cases of humanity still have a functioning central nervous system of some sort and are hence sentient. But in order to be consistent, animals with central nervous systems—and hence sentiency—would also deserve moral respect.

A third argument developed by philosophers who are animal rightists involves *a revised social contract*. Historically, social contract theory has involved only rational agents. It is perhaps true that only rational beings can engage in the sort of complex deliberation or calculation that is required in developing a social contract. But one does not need to be rational in order to be affected (whether positively or negatively) by the terms of agreement in a social contract. For example, mentally deficient human beings might not be rational enough to "sign" a social contract, but their situation is greatly affected by what rational beings decide. Likewise, although animals might not be sufficiently rational to be social contractors (this controversial claim can be granted at least for the

sake of argument), they are nonetheless greatly affected by the decisions made by rational human beings. Indeed, in many cases their very lives are at stake.

In conclusion, in the centuries after Descartes, philosophers tended to be anthropocentric. As a result of the arguments presented here and others, however, almost all philosophers now acknowledge that Descartes's legacy regarding animals should be dismantled. In fact, a sizable number of philosophers have been persuaded by the claim that animals have moral rights that should be translated into legal ones (*see* Changing Legal Attitudes).

Related articles: Animal pain; The complexity of animal awareness; Ethical vegetarianism; Moral anthropocentrism; Slaughter; The universal charter of the rights of other species

Clark, Steven R. L., *The Moral Status of Animals*, Clarendon Press, 1977.
Dombrowski, Daniel, A., *Babies and Beasts: The Argument from Marginal Cases*, University of Illinois Press, 1997.
Nussbaum, Martha (ed.), *Animal Rights: Current Debates and New Directions*, Oxford University Press, 2004.
Pluhar, Evelyn, *Beyond Prejudice: The Moral Significance of Human and Nonhuman Animals*, Duke University Press, 1995.
Regan, Tom, *The Case for Animal Rights*, University of California Press, 1983.
Sapontzis, Steve, *Morals, Reason, and Animals*, Temple University Press, 1987.
Singer, Peter, *Animal Liberation*, HarperCollins, 2009.

DANIEL A. DOMBROWSKI

THE MORAL COMMUNITY

At a minimum, full-fledged membership in a moral community entails mutual moral consideration; all members in the community need to take into account the potential impact of their actions on the welfare of others. Unfortunately, history has provided us with many examples of humans self-servingly circumscribing the domain of a moral community. From the ancient Greeks who discounted barbarians to the twentieth-century Nazis who dismissed Jews, cultures have systematically shunned sectors of adult human society from their moral ranks. In our relatively morally enlightened era, we now know that these exclusions had no justifiable basis. Still, haughtiness should be constrained. Although fears of embarrassment and condemnation stymie public pronouncement of racism and sexism, only the most ingenuous would believe that proponents of these attitudes are absent from our ranks.

There is, however, a far more virulent form of bigotry that pervades our moral landscape. It is a type of disenfranchisement that causes much greater pain and suffering than does either racism or sexism. Although pervasive, this exclusionary practice is scarcely noticed, and on the rare occasions that it is discussed, it is typically given short shrift. Virtually all of us are engaged in species chauvinism; we believe and act as if *Homo sapiens* is the only species that morally matters.

Nonhuman animals are the central objects of this marginalization. In addition to the billions who are consumed for their flesh, millions are hunted, experimented on, and used to amuse us. Their interests, if considered at all, are minimized to the point that they cannot affect our deliberations and our resulting actions. Since the only value accorded these creatures is instrumental, the only restrictions on our interaction with them are economic. When chickens are referred to as "egg-laying machines," and animal subjects are labeled "models," we have clear indications of how living, conscious animals are reduced to mere commodities.

Species chauvinists may respond with a shrug. Why do we have any moral reason for including animals in our moral community? Why should we consider their interests as having a moral claim on us? But these very questions contain the seeds of a reply. Once the obvious is admitted—that animals are sentient and therefore have interests in avoiding pain and attracting pleasure—the dialectical burden shifts to those who routinely cause and endorse suffering and death to innocent creatures. The onus is on the exploiters to provide morally compelling reasons for continuing to exclude animals from our moral fraternity.

The challenge has not gone unheeded. Aristotle suggested rationality as the property of demarcation. Descartes forwarded linguistic ability as the attribute that grounds the priority of human interests. But these and other natural offerings such as autonomy and moral agency suffer from a common failing. Even granting the highly questionable assumption that these qualities are possessed by all and only human beings, there is no reason to think that any of these factors are morally relevant. To see the force of this problem, consider the case where two women simultaneously enter a hospital emergency room with equally severe injuries. Suppose, further, that there is only one doctor available to treat them. Surely,

no one would suggest that preference should be given on the basis that one of the women has greater reasoning ability. It is not as though we think that IQ tests should be administered to determine which woman should receive first treatment. Similarly, superior linguistic ability hardly justifies why one person's pain and suffering should take precedence over another's. We do not believe that an English professor should be examined before a construction worker. And the absurdity that attaches to thinking that rationality and linguistic ability are morally relevant criteria applies equally to the criteria of autonomy and the capacity to morally deliberate.

In short, speciesism has never been justified, and the prospects for its support seem bleak. If we take a step back, this conclusion appears less surprising than it otherwise might. We scoff at egoists who believe that their own interests count more than those of others; we censure those who believe that the interests of a particular race or sex should weigh more heavily into a moral calculus than those of another race or sex. Only an ad hoc barrier would stop the natural progression of thought that culminates in the notion that the interests of humans do not necessarily trump those of other animals.

This result is no cause for consternation. On the contrary, in broadening our moral sphere to include those who should have been participants from its inception, we are righting a wrong. This is a good not only for the animals but also for us humans.

Related articles: Animal and human violence; Animal pain; The complexity of animal awareness; Moral anthropocentrism; The moral claims of animals

Bernstein, Mark, *Without a Tear: Our Tragic Relationship with Animals*, University of Illinois Press, 2004.

Kazez, Jean, *Animalkind: What We Owe to Animals*, Wiley-Blackwell, 2010.

Linzey, Andrew, *Why Animal Suffering Matters: Philosophy, Theology, and Practical Ethics*, Oxford University Press, 2009.

Scully, Matthew, *Dominion: The Power of Man, the Suffering of Animals, and the Call to Mercy*, St. Martin's Press, 2002.

Singer, Peter, *Animal Liberation*, rev. ed., HarperCollins, 2002.

Zamir, Tzachi, *Ethics and the Beast*, Princeton University Press, 2007.

MARK H. BERNSTEIN

CHANGING LEGAL ATTITUDES

DEVELOPMENTS IN ANIMAL LAW

Animal law encompasses many different disciplines rather than a single area of law. Based on the common law, which is the root of much of our legal systems, laws regarding animals are founded on the premise that animals are property. As property, they are subject to commercial transactions and, for the most part, treated as fungible commodities, where each individual animal is interchangeable for another of the same specifications.

Even protections at the international level (through international treaties for threatened and endangered species) are concerned with the loss of biological diversity rather than with the fate of individual animals, as witnessed by the issuance of special permits and variances for the export and even killing of protected and endangered animals.

There are many forms of animal protection laws, including anticruelty laws, criminal penalties for abuse, "wildlife" protection legislation for free-living animals, standards for agriculture, and those that require individuals to take responsibility for animals in their care, such as licensing and leash laws. These occur on a national and local level and can vary greatly from region to region. Even within a small geographic region, differences in local laws and law enforcement can have disparate results in the treatment of animals in that area.

Not all animal-related regulations protect or improve the condition of animals. Some seek to diminish existing protections, such as the exclusion of mice, rats, and birds from protection under the U.S. Animal Welfare Act. Other laws exempt certain animals, in particular animals used in agriculture, from protections offered to other species; farmed animals are not covered by most anticruelty legislation. There are even laws that require that animals be subjected to painful testing (often cruel and painful), such as laws governing the development of pharmaceuticals and protection of the environment. Pound seizure laws require that stray animals be donated to research or used for dissection at research institutions or schools.

Laws regarding animals are not designed to protect animals so much as they are designed to protect humans in their relationships with animal use, drawing lines dictated by societal norms as to what is permissible, or impermissible, in a particular relationship. Animals used in agriculture and those bound for slaughter are given a different regard under law, according to historical society norms, than companion animals such as cats and dogs. Even the type of animals valued as companions varies greatly throughout the world, and the protection offered by law largely depends on the value attached to each species.

Animal welfare laws, which have been in existence for more than two hundred years, bring focus to the treatment of individual animals, setting minimum standards of care, by which society can judge what is acceptable in the treatment of animals. These standards, which can range from rules for agricultural use to laboratory standards, vary greatly from country to country and even within countries and provide a wide range of protections to various animal species.

Animal welfare law accepts the premise of animals as property and the propriety of using animals for human benefit. What welfare law addresses is the distinction between an object, such as furniture, and a living creature, and it seeks legal recourse to ensure that animals are not subject to "cruelty" in their servitude. What constitutes "cruel" treatment again varies greatly depending on the use to which an animal is put—for example, different standards apply in biomedical research, agricultural use, and the use of animals as companions. Because animal welfare law seeks to balance the acceptable treatment of animals against the human interest in a particular use, there is no uniformity in the application of standards of animal pain and suffering or in what is permissible in a particular society for all types of animals. An operation performed routinely on a cat in a research laboratory would carry prison time if conducted at home on a companion animal. This dichotomy emphasizes the inequitable results of a subjective system of animal welfare that uses an end/means analysis to formulate how much harm is legally permissible to inflict on animals.

Animal rights law, an emerging field, challenges the basic premise of common law that animals are property. Instead, the animal rights position presumes that an animal capable of sentient life cannot be regarded as the property of another, as slaves were once thought to be the property of their master. It rejects the premise that any justification exists for the exploitation of animals by humans. According to the animal rights movement, animals are entitled to the most basic rights granted to infants and mentally handicapped adults—freedom from torture, the right to bodily integrity, and standing under the law to challenge, on their own behalf, unjust conditions. Because animals lack the voice to speak for themselves on issues of welfare, basic freedoms, and exploitation, humans would be in the position to challenge the treatment of animals—individually and as a species—in ending animal exploitation. As a field of law, animal rights seeks to overturn the basis of the treatment of animals, to provide standing for the animals themselves, and to use the courts to change the foundation on which opinions regarding animals are rendered.

Under current developments in animal law, a field with growing recognition and legitimacy in the legal profession, there are two basic ways of approaching the injustice toward animals in today's society. One approach seeks to establish basic rights for the animals themselves, giving them standing to challenge the status quo and protection from exploitation. The second approach accepts the animals' status as property but seeks to carve out a niche for "sentient property" and, in so doing, to regulate human conduct that causes harm to nonhuman living creatures. The constructive use of the legal system is an effective way to bring about positive and long-term change for animals. Passing animal-protective legislation, stiffening penalties for animal abuse, and mandating the use of non-animal alternatives in the laboratory are all actions within the power of the legal system.

Enforcing already-existing laws, including prosecuting animal abusers, protecting free-living animals from unlawful taking, and forcing regulatory agencies to follow their own directives in dealing with animals represents another challenge in the fight for justice for animals. Under most current legal systems, the protection of animals usually involves regulating human behavior, whether it places leash-law consequences on the human caretaker through fines (or confiscation and destruction of the animal) or prohibits animal transporters from hauling horses for more than twenty-four hours without a stop for water—also subject to a fine or possible (tem-

porary) suspension of license. One difficulty, however, is that the animals suffer the ultimate consequences for human irresponsibility or abuse, without a legal voice in the outcome of enforcement activities.

The challenge for the future is to bring justice into the legal process by establishing a default position that animals are innately entitled to the protection of their bodily and mental integrity. In other words, a presumption that justice is due to the animals themselves, and not merely to the contract under which they are sold or to the criminal justice system punishing the perpetrator of animal abuse, is essential in protecting animals from the humans with whom their lives are so entwined.

Instituting laws that recognize the ability of animals to experience pain and suffering—and effectively enforcing those laws once passed—is the challenge of every country in effecting positive change for animals through the legal system.

Related articles: Animal courses in academia; Legal challenges to experiments in the United Kingdom; Legal protection of animals in China; The legal rights of great apes; Legislation in the European Union; Live animal exports; Moral anthropocentrism; The moral claims of animals

Animal Welfare Institute, _Animals and Their Legal Rights: A Survey of American Laws from 1641 to 1990_, 4th ed., 1990.
Favre, David, _Animal Law and Dog Behavior_, Lawyers and Judges, 2007.
Francione, Gary L., _Animals, Property, and the Law_, Temple University Press, 1996.
Frasch, Pamela D., Wagman, Bruce A., and Waisman, Sonia S., _Animal Law: Cases and Materials_, Caroline Academic Press, 2006.
National Anti-Vivisection Society (U.S.), "Animals and the Law," _Expressions_ 4 (1999).
———, _A New Perspective: Seeking Justice for Animals through the Power of the Law_, 2008, available at http://www.navs.org/document.doc?id=4.
Schaffner, Joan E., _An Introduction to Animals and the Law_, Palgrave Macmillan, 2011.
Sunstein, Cass R., and Nussbaum, Martha Craven, _Animal Rights: Current Debates and New Directions_, Oxford University Press, 2004.

PEGGY CUNNIFF AND MARCIA KRAMER

LEGAL CHALLENGES TO EXPERIMENTS IN THE UNITED KINGDOM

Litigation to maximize the protection animals receive in laboratories under U.K. legislation has historically been underused. There are a number of reasons for this. First is the secrecy that surrounds animal experiments. Short of undercover investigations, which are time-consuming and expensive and can take place only at a handful of laboratories or supply companies, it is very difficult to obtain precise information about what is done to animals and for what purpose, which is often necessary for a legal case. Animal researchers have, for a variety of reasons, traditionally guarded information about what they do jealously, releasing only what they wish to or need to for publication of articles. Some people think that they have found ready allies in successive governments and international institutions.

Second, legal cases in the United Kingdom are very expensive. The normal rule is that the loser has to pay the winner's costs, and this is a major deterrent, given that cases would often be groundbreaking, with no guarantee of success. It is, on occasion, possible to get costs protection at an early stage of a case through an order limiting the costs liability that a nongovernmental organization (NGO) bringing the case in the public interest may ultimately face. The British Union for the Abolition of Vivisection (BUAV) was successful in obtaining one of these orders in the judicial review arising out of its undercover investigation into neuroscience research on marmosets at Cambridge University in 2001–2002 (*R [BUAV] v. Secretary of State for the Home Department*, 2006; EWHC 250 (Admin), January 31, 2006). The order enabled it to continue with a case it otherwise would have had to withdraw from. Nevertheless, costs explain why the BUAV, for example, has brought many fewer cases than it would have liked to and why litigation is used far less in the United Kingdom than in the United States.

It is fair to say, as well, that the animal protection movement has not woken up to the full potential of using the law to further its campaign objectives, in the way that, for example, the antislavery and the environmental movements have done.

However, the BUAV has brought a couple of judicial reviews against the home secretary in recent years. In the first (*R [BUAV] v. Secretary of State for the Home Department*, CO/264/2001), there were two issues related to the rules about alternatives under section 5(5) of the Animals (Scientific Procedures) Act 1986 (ASPA), section 5(5) being based on articles 7(2)–(3) of European Directive 86/609 (now replaced by Directive 2010/63). The BUAV contended that where the home secretary concluded that the scientific objective could be achieved without using animals, or by using fewer animals or causing less suffering than proposed (collectively "alternatives"), he was prohibited from licensing a proposed animal experiment, irrespective of whether regulators in other countries required that experiment for safety data. The BUAV also contended

that where the home secretary came to accept that there was an alternative, he could not allow the original animal experiments to continue, even if the license had not yet expired (licenses are usually granted for five years).

The home secretary conceded both points just before the full hearing. However, there are grounds—including from a BUAV undercover investigation at Wickham Laboratories in 2009—for believing that the Home Office has continued to pay unlawful heed to the wishes of international regulators. That should, in any event, change under the new directive.

On a similar issue, in the late 1990s the Home Office conceded, under threat of a judicial review by the BUAV, that it could no longer license the notorious oral Lethal Dose 50 test, given the availability of alternatives.

In the Cambridge judicial review referred to previously, there were two main issues. First, had the home secretary acted irrationally in concluding that none of the experimental protocols would cause "substantial" rather than "moderate" suffering to the marmosets? The high court judge ruled that he had (EWHC 1964 [Admin], July 27, 2007), but the court of appeal disagreed (EWCA Civ 417, April 23, 2008). The court of appeal suggested that a high degree of deference should be given to the judgment of the home secretary on such matters. The court did not say that the home secretary's assessment was right, but simply that it could not be sure that he was wrong.

The correct assessment of suffering is crucial to the cost-benefit test that lies at the heart of the ASPA—under section 5(4), the home secretary has to weigh the suffering of the animals against the expected benefit. Importantly for operation of the regulatory scheme more generally, the court of appeal agreed with the judge that a "relative" approach to the assessment of suffering was wrong—the home office had said it reserved the "substantial" category for a small subset of experiments causing the most severe suffering that it licenses. The correct approach, the high court said, was simply to ask whether the experiments would cause a major departure from an animal's usual state of health or well-being, the main definition of "substantial" in Home Office guidance.

The second issue related to the researchers' care arrangements for the animals, particularly postoperatively. Marmosets were routinely left overnight very soon after brain surgery, even if they were having persistent seizures. Some were found dead in the morning. Again, the court was not willing to second-guess the Home Office. The high court also had ruled that death was not an "adverse effect" in the context of the ASPA and could therefore be left out of the cost-benefit assessment.

The ASPA has been amended to reflect the new directive, which sets rules for all twenty-seven EU countries.

Bringing cases about animal experiments directly to the European courts is extremely difficult for NGOs because of the restrictive rules on standing (the right to sue). It remains to be seen how much difference the relaxation of these rules by the Lisbon Treaty has made. The Lisbon Treaty amended both the Treaty of Rome, now called the Treaty on the Functioning of the European Union (TFEU), and the Treaty of the European Union. The new rule on standing is in the fourth paragraph of article 263 of the TFEU. A case at the Court of Justice of the European Communities involving a challenge to the EU regulation banning the marketing of seal products may clarify the rules on standing in public interest challenges. Judgment is expected in 2013.

It is possible to complain to the European Commission about the alleged failure by a member state to accurately reflect ("transpose") the directive in its national law, and the commission can bring proceedings against the member state in the (European) General Court if it cannot persuade it to toe the line. The BUAV has, with some success, used this device—for example, against Belgium in relation to the use of stray cats and dogs in experiments.

In addition, the European coalition that the BUAV leads has been given permission to intervene in three appeals before the Board of Appeal of the European Chemicals Agency (ECHA). ECHA is a key regulator of REACH (EU Regulation 1907/2006), which sets out the information that chemical companies must hold about the safety of their substances. REACH will generate millions of animal tests. The appeals relate to whether ECHA was entitled to order particular animal tests.

It is important to understand that in a campaigning context, it is not just direct legal challenges to application of the legislation that are important. There are a number of ancillary types of legal challenge too. In the field of animal experiments, probably the most important is challenging refusals by public authorities—mainly, in the United Kingdom, the Home Office and universities—to disclose information under the Freedom of Information Act 2000. The BUAV has brought a number of cases (e.g., *BUAV v. Home Office and Information Commissioner*, EWCA Civ 870, July 30, 2008—see also the Information Tribunal decision in the same case, EA/0059/2007, January 30, 2008; *University of Newcastle-upon-Tyne v. Information Commissioner and BUAV*, UKUT 185 [AAC], May 11, 2011; and various Information Commissioner decisions). PETA brought a case against Oxford University (EA/2009/0076, April 13, 2010). The record of success has been mixed.

Protecting the right of peaceful protest is also key, in a climate some people see as increasingly intolerant of protest. The BUAV overturned injunctions obtained by Huntingdon Life Sciences (HLS) and Hillgrove Farm that would have severely curtailed its right to protest against them (*Huntingdon Life Sciences v. Curtin and others*, 1997 [unreported]). In addition, challenges can be made to animal patents, such as the oncomouse.

Preserving the right to publish information obtained via undercover investigations, or following leaks, is also crucial. Some years ago, Uncaged Campaigns obtained a favorable settlement in relation to documents leaked to it about Imutran's xenotransplantation research at HLS, and in 2004 the BUAV investigator at Covance in Germany overturned an injunction prohibiting him from using the footage and images he had obtained. In 2005, following proceedings, PETA retained the right to publish in the United Kingdom material obtained during its undercover investigation of a Covance laboratory in the United States (*Covance Laboratories Ltd and another v. the Covance Campaign and others*, Claim No. 5C-00295 [2005]).

Similarly, a number of "soft law" vehicles can be very useful in the battle for hearts and minds. These include complaints to the Press Complaints Commission (sometimes a threat of a complaint suffices to persuade a newspaper to give a right to reply following inaccuracies), to the Parliamentary Commissioner for Administration or European Ombudsman (who investigates allegations of maladministration by public bodies), to the Advertising Standards Authority (it may be necessary, instead, to defend a complaint made by an opponent), or to the Market Research Society (as the BUAV did in relation to Mori's survey about public opinion on animal experiments in 2002). It may also be necessary to bring or defend defamation proceedings, to preserve reputation or the right to express one's opinion.

Finally, legal argument, outside the context of actual or contemplated court proceedings, can prove very effective. One example: in 2002, the BUAV was able to persuade members of the European Parliament that, contrary to the views of the European Commission and many member states (including the United Kingdom), a ban on the import into the European Union of cosmetics tested on animals need not fall foul of free trade rules under the World Trade Organization. There is a public morality exception, which the European Union has subsequently used in legislating in several animal protection areas.

Related articles: The alternatives; Animals used in research; Developments in animal law; Freedom of information; Legislation in the European Union; Patenting animals; The World Trade Organization

Dolan, Kevin, *Laboratory Animal Law*, Wiley-Blackwell, 2000.
Favre, David S., and Loring, Murray, *Animal Law*, Greenwood Press, 1983.

Palmer, Julian, *Animal Law: A Concise Guide to the Law Relating to Animals*, 3rd ed., Shaw and Sons, 2011.

Schaffner, Joan E., *An Introduction to Animals and the Law*, Palgrave Macmillan, 2011.

DAVID THOMAS

LEGAL PROTECTION OF ANIMALS IN CHINA

In the long history of human activities in China, animals have occupied a very important place. They have been used for their practical roles in animal husbandry, hunting, transport, and human consumption and healing; as victims in religious and ritual sacrifices; as symbols and metaphors in everyday life (e.g., in the Chinese zodiac, in which the personality and other character traits of animals are used to describe people and vice versa); and as symbols of authority (e.g., an imaginary one-horned animal called *xie zhi* was used in traditional China as a symbol of law and justice). In traditional China, animals were also considered part of the social order, subject to bureaucratic management and control in the form of legal regulation in the service of government and emperors (Cao, "Visibility and Invisibility").

According to studies, China has some of the earliest decrees and official regulations on the protection of animals in human history (Cao, "Animal Law")—for example, around 2100 B.C.E., Emperor Da Yu decreed that "for three months in summer, fishing nets must not be cast into the rivers and streams so as to ensure the thriving of fish and turtles."

Around 1100 B.C.E., the Xi Zhou Dynasty had an official order called "Tree Felling Decree," stipulating that at certain times of a year, one must not destroy houses, fill wells, cut trees, or harm six types of farmed animals. In the Han Dynasty (206 B.C.E.–220 C.E.), there were official orders and decrees that limited and controlled the killing of young animals. Another regulation at the time was that deaths of cattle must be reported to the authorities, and if the death rate exceeded a certain percentage, the owners or officials in charge would be punished. Animal management was an essential part of government, with "animal officers" appointed, including herdsmen, stable and park attendants, keepers of sacrificial meats, animal physiognomists, healers, and trainers.

Significantly, there were provisions on animal protection in the imperial codes in traditional China. The Tang Code enforced during the Tang Dynasty (618–907 C.E.) introduced provisions on animal treatment used for official purposes, including public stables and sacrificial animals (Johnson; Cao, "Visibility and Invisibility"). There were provisions in the code for such circumstances as the examination of the conditions of domesticated animals not reported truthfully; persons in charge of government animals who became sick; use of sacrificial animals in ways not conforming to the rules; use of government animals in a manner where their backs were laid bare or their throats were worn through by the harness; and intentional killing of government or private horses or cattle. These provisions were retained with minor variations in all the succeeding imperial codes from the Tang Dynasty onward to the end of imperial China in the Qing Dynasty (1644–1911). Thus, working animals were considered valuable property warranting legal protection, and people in charge of the government animals assumed certain responsibilities for their well-being and would be punished for failure.

Since the founding of the People's Republic of China in 1949, a number of laws and provisions concerning animal protection have been passed. The Chinese Constitution, originally promulgated in 1954, made no mention of animals. The 1982 Constitution still in force states in article 9 that "the State ensures the rational use of natural resources and protects rare and valuable animals and plants." The most important laws related to animals are the Law on the Protection of Wildlife (1988) and the Environmental Protection Law (1989) with subordinate regulations and measures involving protection, health, and quarantine for free-living animals. The Regulation on the Management of Laboratory Animals (1988) was made for the purpose of strengthening the management of animals used for research. Additionally, the Criminal Code (1997) has a provision on "wildlife protection" and penalties for killing certain endangered animals. China is a signatory to the Convention on the International Trade in Endangered Species of Wild Fauna and Flora.

So far, China's animal-related laws are limited to "wildlife protection." China does not have any law for domesticated animals used for various purposes, and thus, most animals—including companion animals, farmed animals, and even free-living animals used for entertainment—have no protection. In late 2008, a team of Chinese legal scholars (including this author) led by Professor Chang Jiwen started to work on a proposed law for protecting and improving the treatment of domesticated animals in China with support from international animal welfare organizations. The first draft, titled "Animal Protection Law of the People's Republic of China (Experts' Draft Proposal)," was released for public comment in September 2009. Many thousands of comments were received from across China, from individuals and animal welfare organizations and other volunteer organizations. Heated debates were staged in national television shows, newspapers, and internet forums as a result. A revised proposal was released in March 2010 titled "The Law for the Prevention of Cruelty to Animals of the People's Republic of China (Experts' Draft Proposal)." It was submitted to the Chinese national legislature and central government later in the year, but so far there has been no official response despite persistent calls for such a law from animal advocates and some legislators in recent years. It may take many years before any such law is enacted (Cao, "Towards Legal Protection").

Related articles: Animals in Chinese culture; Confucianism and Daoism

Cao, Deborah, "Animal Law and Other Matters: The Need for Intellectual Debates about the Status of Animals in China," in Chang, Jiwen, and Littlefair, Paul (eds.), *Animal Welfare Law: Focal and Difficult Issues*, China Law Press, 2008, 19–38 (in Chinese).
———, "Towards Legal Protection of Animals in China," *Australian Animal Protection Law Journal* 5.2 (2011): 76.
———, "Visibility and Invisibility of Animals in Traditional Chinese Philosophy and Law," *International Journal for the Semiotics of Law* 24.3 (2011).
Chang, Jiwen, *A Comparative Study of Animal Welfare Law in China and the European Union*, Kexue huanjing chubanshe, 2000 (in Chinese).
———, "The Expert Proposal for the Law of Prevention of Cruelty to Animals Is Not a Foreign Import," *Jingji cankao bao* (Economic Reference News), March 3, 2010 (in Chinese).
Johnson, Wallace, *The T'ang Code: Volume II, Specific Articles*, Princeton University Press, 1997.

DEBORAH CAO

THE LEGAL RIGHTS OF GREAT APES

Apes, including great apes, are members of the Hominoidea superfamily of the biological order primates. The term "great apes" typically includes eastern and western gorillas, chimpanzees, bonobos, Sumatran orangutans, and Bornean orangutans. The first four species are found exclusively in Africa, and the last two are found only in Southeast Asia. All of these species of great apes fall into the endangered or critically endangered categories of the Red List gathered by the International Union for Conservation of Nature.

Although great apes are ethologically known to be sentient, cognitively complex, communicative, and self-aware, no legal system recognizes them as legal "persons," in contrast to corporations and some other nonhuman entities, which are so recognized. Great apes, humans' closest biological relatives, are rather regarded as legal "things." They are therefore not regarded as legitimate holders of legal rights. In most Western societies, the fundamental premise of current legislation concerning animals (including great apes) is that they are the property of humans. The property status of great apes makes it legal to treat them as objects for sale, experimentation, entertainment, and various other exploitative uses.

The property status of animals has been increasingly contested since at least 1992, when Switzerland amended its constitution to change the legal status of animals from "things" to "beings." In 2002, Germany's parliament followed suit and voted to grant animals a constitutional right to be protected by the state. The implications of this amendment to the German Basic Law remain to be determined, but the courts are likely to rule that it creates a legal right for animals to be protected from unnecessary pain and experiments.

Furthermore, a mounting number of legal systems impose limits on what humans can do to great apes. In this way, the ownership rights of humans over their great ape property are restricted. These legal restrictions vary depending on the country but are rarely wide-ranging. Since 1997, a growing number of national parliaments have enacted legislation to ban or severely restrict invasive experiments on great apes. The United Kingdom (since 1997), New Zealand (since 1999), Sweden (since 2003), the Netherlands (since 2004), and Austria (since 2006) have banned the use of great apes in research and testing laboratories. These bans effectively ended the practice in Europe. In Australia, great ape experimentation is forbidden by policy unless it is in the interests of the individual animal or species. Some countries have enacted less inclusive bans: in 2006 Japan ceased only invasive research on chimpanzees. Other countries have enacted more inclusive bans: a policy of the Republic of Ireland prohibits the use of any primate species in research, and the Principality of Liechtenstein banned all animal experiments in 1989.

In September 2007, 433 members of the European Parliament signed the Declaration of the European Parliament on the use of primates in scientific experiments, which calls for an end to the use of apes and "wild caught" monkeys in scientific experiments and for the setting of a timetable for the end of all primate experiments. In 2008 the executive body of the European Union, the European Commission, proposed that scientific experiments with great apes be officially banned in the European Union, except when necessary to preserve the species or protect the public from an unexpected outbreak of life-threatening disease. In September 2010, the European Parliament adopted Directive 2010/63/EU, which will make this ban legally binding in all of the member states of the European Union. However, scientific experiments conducted on primates other than great apes will continue to be legal, even if now strictly restricted.

The United States of America is where the largest number of great apes are kept in captivity. More than one thousand great apes (mostly chimpanzees) are enslaved in the United States for use in invasive biomedical research (including drug and vaccine testing), zoological parks, and public entertainment. The most ambitious legal initiative to protect great apes in the United States has been the Great Ape Protection and Cost Savings Act, which was introduced in Congress in April 2011. This bill was never debated or voted on and never became law. It expired with the end of the 112th Congress in January 2013. If it had been enacted, this bill would have forbidden the performance of invasive research on great apes as well as the transport and breeding of great apes for this purpose. It would have also retired the federally owned great apes to permanent sanctuaries. A similar bill was introduced twice previously in Congress, in April 2008 and March 2009, but was never voted on and never became law.

The most ambitious campaign to grant basic legal rights to all great apes worldwide has been promoted by an organization called the Great Ape Project. The Great Ape Project's main goal is international in scope. It aims at convincing the United Nations to adopt the Declaration on Great Apes, which in turn should persuade national governments to change their laws accordingly. It is true, however, that this international campaign has influenced politicians and activists in a small number of countries (e.g., Spain and New Zealand) to campaign for the adoption of the Declaration of Great Apes by their national legislatures. The Declaration on Great Apes was initiated by the 1993 publication *The Great Ape Project: Equality beyond Humanity*, edited by philosopher-activists Peter Singer and Paola Cavalieri. The signatories of this declaration argue that our recently acquired knowledge of the rich social and emotional lives of great apes requires a reassessment of their moral status. All great apes, not just humans, should be included in the "community of equals" within which all members are protected by enforceable basic rights, including the rights to life, to individual liberty, and to be free from torture (*see* Declarations for Animals).

In February 2007, the parliament of the Balearic Islands, one of Spain's autonomous communities, became the world's first regional parliament to approve the legislative propositions of the Declaration on Great Apes. The great apes living in the Balearic Islands are now regarded as legitimate holders of a small number of basic legal rights. Legal guardians can be appointed to these great apes in order to ensure that they are free from unwarranted death, arbitrary imprisonment, and unnecessary pain.

The Spanish Parliament was the first national parliament to give its support to incorporating the Declaration on Great Apes into its domestic law. On June 25, 2008, the Environment Commission of the Spanish Parliament voted in favor of a nonlegislative motion urging the government to harmonize the country's laws with the Declaration on Great Apes. If the Spanish government were to do so, gorillas, chimpanzees, bonobos, and orangutans, in addition to Homo sapiens, would have their sentience and agency legally recognized. Such beings would be accorded certain rights, including the right to life, the right to liberty, and the right not to be tortured. Thus, Spain's penal code is expected to outlaw experiments on great apes, as well as the great apes' use in zoos, circuses, films, and television commercials. However, amid public opposition, the Spanish government has so far failed to act on this motion; Spain's laws have not been harmonized with the Declaration on Great Apes.

Related articles: Animals in circuses; Animals in film; Animals used in research; Captive chimpanzees; CITES and international trade; Developments in animal law; The ethics of zoos; Free-living chimpanzees; The future of free-roaming orangutans; Legislation in the European Union; Primates worldwide; Roadside zoos and menageries; The trade in primates for research; The universal charter of the rights of other species

Caldecott, J., and Miles, L. (eds.), *World Atlas of Great Apes and Their Conservation* (prepared at the UNEP World Conservation Monitoring Centre), University of California Press, 2005.

Cavalieri, P., and Singer, P. (eds.), *The Great Ape Project: Equality beyond Humanity*, St. Martin's Griffin, 1993.

Directive 2010/63/EU of the European Parliament and of the Council on the Protection of Animals Used for Scientific Purposes, September 22, 2010, *Official Journal of the European Union L* 276/33, available at http://eur-lex.europa.eu/LexUriServ/LexUriServ.do?uri=OJ:L:2010:276:0033:0079:EN:PDF.

Knight, A., "The Beginning of the End for Chimpanzee Experiments?," *Philosophy, Ethics, and Humanities in Medicine* 3 (2008), available at http://www.peh-med.com/content/3/1/16/.

Pozas Terrados, P., *Voces del Planeta*, Aebuis, 2009.

Rook, D., "Should Great Apes Have 'Human Rights'?," *Web Journal of Current Legal Issues* 1 (2009), available at http://webjcli.ncl.ac.uk/2009/issue1/rook1.html/.

U.S. Congress, *Great Ape Protection and Cost Savings Act of 2011*, SB 810, 112th Congress, 1st sess., 2011, available at http://www.govtrack.us/congress/bills/112/s810.

Wadman, M., "Animal Rights: Chimpanzee Research on Trial," *Nature* 474.7351 (2011): 268–271.

Wise, S. M., "The Entitlement of Chimpanzees to the Common Law Writs of Habeas Corpus and De Homine Replegiando," *Golden Gate University Law Review* 37 (2007): 219–280.

———, *Rattling the Cage: Toward Legal Rights for Animals*, Perseus, 2000.

CARL SAUCIER-BOUFFARD

LEGISLATION IN THE EUROPEAN UNION

The European Economic Community, or Common Market, was created by the Treaty of Rome in 1956. As the name implies, the main purpose of the treaty was to encourage trade between member states by harmonizing rules and removing obstacles. There was no mention of animals, let alone animal welfare. Farmed animals came under the heading of agricultural products. It was no surprise, therefore, to find that in such a treaty there was no legal basis under which legislation for the specific purpose of protecting animals could be drawn up.

It is remarkable that there is any European animal welfare legislation at all in such circumstances and that, furthermore, there is now legislation that has led to significant improvement in the well-being of animals. It is true that there have been major changes to the treaty since 1956, most particularly at Maastricht (1992) and Amsterdam (1997); these changes have broadened the scope of the treaty, created the European Union, and laid the basis for more political, economic, and social integration. However, there is still no legal basis that would permit animal welfare legislation, per se, to be drawn up. The protocol on animal welfare agreed on at Amsterdam was nevertheless a significant step forward because it stated that animals are "sentient beings" and also placed a legal obligation on the community institutions (the European Commission, Parliament, and Council) to pay full regard to animal welfare when formulating policies on research, transport, agriculture, and the internal market. However, it still does not make animal protection a basic principle of the European Union alongside, for example, protecting the environment or conserving free-living "wildlife" and habitats.

The story of how the European Union has pioneered Europe-wide legislation is itself revealing. Much of the credit for these achievements is owed to the animal welfare movement's willingness to cooperate and collaborate in order to bring pressure to bear on—and provide information for—the legislators, including commissioners, commission officials, members of the European Parliament, civil servants, and ministers in member states. Furthermore, this is not just a story of powerful and wealthy animal welfare organizations in northern member states doing all the work. Animal welfare organizations in all member states have played their part and, in spite of inadequate resources, have brought pressure on their governments through campaigning.

In the 1970s, there were only two pieces of European law concerned with animal protection: a directive (1974) on slaughter, which made pre-slaughter stunning obligatory, and another on international transport (1977), although this applied only to animals being transported in or out of the European Union or from one member state to another, and its enforcement depended on checking transport at border posts.

It was in this legislatively barren environment that the European animal welfare movement had to begin its work. In 1980, the majority of member states were skeptic of animal welfare, and there was apathy, even a degree of hostility, in most parts of the European Commission.

It was, and still is, in the European Parliament that support was found for animal welfare in general and also concern about the problems caused to farmed animals in intensive farming, transport, and slaughter, in particular. This support came mostly from northern members of the parliament (predominantly British, Dutch, and Danish), but it also included members from all member states and crossed political and party boundaries. We in animal welfare used this parliamentary support to bring pressure on the commission to do something to improve the situation for farmed animals in particular. Sympathy and support for our point of view was not enough; we had to back up our demands for legislative change with good scientific and veterinary evidence. There was no scientific veterinary committee at this time, and the veterinary section in the commission's Directorate-General for Agriculture was occupied with animal health issues.

The first priority was to get the commission (Directorate-General of Agriculture) to accept that farmed animal welfare deserved attention. In 1986 several important events occurred:

- The Parliament produced a comprehensive "own-initiative" report on farmed animal welfare policy, which demanded action from the commission.
- The directive laying down standards for hens in battery cages was referred to the European Court of Justice. The court's verdict (in 1998) was that the commission was legally entitled to draw up minimum standards for the rearing of farmed animals because these would help to prevent any distortion of trade.
- The Single European Act was passed, and therefore, borders (and border checks) between

member states would have to be removed by January 1, 1993.

■ A directive regulating animal experiments was agreed on by council and came under the responsibility of another part of the commission, the Directorate-General for the Environment.

Therefore, the commission was forced to take action. A veterinarian was appointed in the Directorate-General for Agriculture to have responsibility for animal welfare, with the immediate task of drawing up directives on minimum standards for calves and pigs. The removal of borders and border checks meant that a new directive laying down transport rules had to be in place by 1993. In the Directorate-General for the Environment, a section was established to oversee the implementation of the directive on animal experimentation. Suddenly, animal welfare was recognized as an important issue in all the European institutions. More progress followed when the commission set up the Scientific Veterinary Committee, which has since been retitled the Scientific Committee on Animal Health and Animal Welfare. Scientific evidence, comprehensively summarized by this committee in a series of reports over several years, has always supported most of the demands of the animal welfare movement, particularly as they relate to farmed animal welfare.

As a consequence of all these events, together with active lobbying and campaigning by animal welfare advocates, there is now European legislation in place, which

■ phases out keeping calves raised for veal in small individual pens;
■ phases out keeping pregnant sows in individual stalls;
■ phases out the battery cage system for egg production;
■ lays down high standards for slaughterhouses and the slaughter process;
■ requires inspections and licensing of zoos;
■ lays down detailed rules for the transport of animals throughout the European Union; and
■ requires animal experimentation to be properly regulated.

None of these directives solves all the problems of animal welfare, but because they are all regularly reviewed, amendments are possible. Enforcement can also be a problem, varying from one member state to another. Only pressure from within a member state will bring about improvement because enforcement is left entirely to the competent national authorities and is not a function of the European Commission.

There is still much animal suffering in Europe, not all of which can be stopped through legislation. There is a long way to go, but much has been achieved in the last twenty years, not least because animal welfare organizations have been willing to work together.

Related articles: Animal advocacy; Animal welfare and farming; Animals used in research; Birds used in food production; Developments in animal law; The ethics of zoos; Live animal exports; Slaughter; The welfare of cows; The welfare of pigs

Appleby, Michael C., Cussen, Victoria, Garces, Leah, Lambert, Lesley A., and Turner, Jacky (eds.), *Long Distance Transport and Welfare of Farm Animals*, CAB International, 2008.
"European Council Regulation (EC) No.1/2005 on the Protection of Animals during Transport and Related Operations," *Official Journal of the European Union L* 3 (2005): 1–44.
Moss, R., "Welfare in National and International Legislation" in Moss, R. (ed.), *Livestock Health and Welfare*, Longman, 1993.
Radford, M., "Animal Passions, Animal Welfare and European Policy Making," in Craig, P., and Harlow, C. (eds.), *Law Making in the European Union*, Kluwer Law International, 1998, 412–432.
Wilkins, David B. (ed.), *Animal Welfare in Europe* (European Legislation and Concerns), Kluwer Law International, 1997.

DAVID B. WILKINS

PROGRESS IN ANIMAL WELFARE

There have been significant legislative initiatives in many countries since the 1980s that have improved the position of animals, although much remains to be done. What is allowed, for example, in laboratories varies widely throughout the world. Even in the developed world, some countries, such as Spain and Portugal, have initiated very little legislation of their own, whereas others, such as Britain, Holland, Denmark, and Germany, have detailed statutes.

In Britain, the 1986 Animals (Scientific Procedures) Act requires all animal researchers to hold a license that attests to their fitness to conduct such work, in addition to project licenses for the specific work they do. Proposals are assessed by Home Office inspectors according to a utilitarian, cost-benefit analysis in which the severity of the procedures proposed, coupled with the number of animals used, has to be balanced against the likely benefit that may result.

The legislation has not resulted in a significant reduction in the number of animals used for scientific procedures, although some of the most trivial and extreme procedures have been disallowed. Arguably of greater importance was the creation of the Animal Procedures Committee (APC) in the 1986 Act. The APC, whose membership includes animal welfare as well as commercial and scientific representatives, is a useful forum for the discussion of the ethics of animal experimentation. Moreover, the British government has adopted a number of its proposals, including a ban on the use of "wild caught" primates and the ending of toxicity testing for cosmetics.

Federal legislation in the United States regulating scientific experimentation is less stringent than in Britain and a number of other European countries. This is primarily because the legislation originally passed in 1966, and amended several times since, is not concerned with animal procedures so much as where animals come from and how well they are kept before and after use. In addition, mice and birds are excluded, and the legislation applies only to those institutions that receive federal funding. One positive development has been that the 1985 amendments have required institutions using animals in research to establish "ethics committees," which are supposed to consider the ethical aspects of experimentation and even to limit or prohibit certain kinds of animal work being performed in the host institution.

More animals are used to produce food than for any other purpose. As with experimentation, legislative progress has been varied, although the target is uniform. The development of intensive forms of animal husbandry in the post-1945 period has entailed considerable suffering for animals, and legislative progress can be measured by the degree to which these systems of "factory farming" have been dismantled. Some European countries have done better than others. In Britain, for instance, the veal crate has been prohibited, as have pig stalls and tethers. Significantly, the battery cage is being phased out throughout the European Union, but nonveterinary mutilations, such as the tail docking of pigs and beak trimming of poultry, remain.

Of all the developed countries, the United States has the worst legislative record as far as restrictions on factory farming are concerned. There are no laws on farmed animal welfare at the federal level, and there is only one relatively weak statute on slaughtering. All the states have general anticruelty statutes that can provide some protection for farmed animals, but state legislatures—under enormous pressure from agribusiness interests—have increasingly removed farmed animals from legislative protection.

The European Union has been involved increasingly in both farmed animal and laboratory animal welfare but tends to appeal to the lowest common denominator of animal welfare standards. It is rare, too, for the EU to act unless a significant number of member states have already indicated their agreement—as witnessed by the directives phasing out the testing of cosmetics, battery cages, and pig stalls and tethers.

Measures to protect free-living animals, or "wildlife," in the past fifteen years have been mostly concerned with conserving particular species rather than individual animals. Much of the action taken has also been precipitated by international treaty obligations, whether to do with whaling, international trade, or biodiversity. One important development in the United Kingdom has been the closing of the loophole in the 1911 Protection of Animals Act, which until 1996 denied protection to those animals not regarded as captive at the time an act of cruelty took place.

In conclusion, two general points about legislative progress should be borne in mind. First, statutory developments are not, of course, the only way of measuring progress. In animal welfare terms, for instance, the changing of individual behavior is also important. In this context, since the 1980s there has been an increasing number of people who are not prepared to eat meat, or factory-farmed food products, as well as a growing market in "cruelty-free" products, such as cosmetics. Second, legislative action is obviously important, but without effective enforcement, it is all but useless. One of the big challenges for animal advocates is to ensure not only that legislative improvements continue but also that existing legislation is more rigorously enforced.

Related articles: Animal advocacy; Animal welfare and farming; Animals used in research; Birds used in food production; Caring shopping; CITES and international trade; Commercial whaling; Cruelty-free labeling; Ethical vegetarianism; Humane education; Legislative changes in the European Union; Pig castration; Primates worldwide; The protection of birds; Slaughter; Toxicity testing; The welfare of pigs

Garner, Robert, *Animals, Politics and Morality*, 2nd ed., Manchester University Press, 2004.
———, *Political Animals: Animal Protection Politics in Britain and the United States*, Macmillan, 1998.
Gluck, John, DiPasquale, Tony, and Orlans, Barbara (eds.), *Applied Ethics in Animal Research*, Purdue University Press, 2002.
Radford, Mike, *Animal Welfare Law in Britain*, Oxford University Press, 2001.
Webster, John, *Animal Welfare: A Cool Eye towards Eden*, Blackwell, 1994.
———, *Animal Welfare: Limping towards Eden*, Blackwell, 2005.

ROBERT GARNER

CHANGING RELIGIOUS PERSPECTIVES

ANIMAL-FRIENDLY SPIRITUALITY

Many religious traditions are known for being anything but animal-friendly. The dominant voices—and the dominant practices—within almost all traditions often appear antithetical to progressive positions on animal protection. It is important to understand why this is the case. There are broadly three reasons: In the first place, almost all religious traditions are anthropocentric in orientation; that is, they center on human beings and their nature, welfare, and destiny. This means that animals get little attention; indeed, concern for animals is frequently regarded as marginal in religious thought and practice. Second, most religious traditions exhibit hierarchical thinking in which humans are placed as the most important concern just below concern for the deity itself. This emphasis inevitably means that animals are relegated to a secondary moral status or sometimes no status at all. The third reason is that most religious traditions see animals in an instrumental light, as either made for human use or subservient to human needs. This means that they often see utility for human beings as the only purpose or *telos* of animals. How often we hear that animals are "made for our use" or that we are given "dominion" over them. Although these are not exclusively religious views, religious traditions have at various times validated and buttressed them.

Together, anthropocentrism, hierarchy, and instrumentalism in their varying forms hold such a grip over religious thought that it is common within religious circles for animals to be automatically regarded as beings without intrinsic value, without moral status or rights, and as an utterly marginal concern for theology and religious ethics. In the light of these factors, the prospect of progressive concern emanating from these traditions might appear slight, but it is important to recognize that the dominant views and practices are not the only ones. In fact, many religious traditions also have substrands or subtraditions that are animal-friendly or that contain very positive insights about animals and how humans should relate to them.

Jainism here has pride of place as the one tradition that has advanced respect for all life (even vegetable and insect life) and has seen acts of animal protection as meritorious. "For there is nothing inaccessible for death. All beings are fond of life, hate pain, like pleasure, shun destruction, like life, long to live. To life all life is dear." These words of the venerable Mahavira found in the Acaranga Sutra are some of the profoundest in all religious scripture. Out of this tradition emerged an emphasis on ahimsa, a doctrine of nonviolence or causing no harm, which has also influenced other Indic religions, especially Hinduism and Buddhism. The Krishna movement within Hinduism has reaffirmed the sacredness of life and supported vegetarian and vegan initiatives within India. Buddhism, too, takes as its first precept respect for life, which has inspired a long tradition of vegetarianism. Also in Buddhism are the noble boddhistvas, the enlightened ones, who defer their ultimate enlightenment to help other creatures reach enlightenment. Of course, the doctrine of reincarnation, or *samsara*, is not animal-friendly in some of its versions since those who incur bad karma are invariably relegated to an animal or insect status, but at least it emphasizes the commonality of all migrating souls. Although these traditions (with the exception of Jainism) remain firmly anthropocentric in practice, there are insights concerning peaceableness, respect, and nonviolence that can inform and vitalize animal-friendly spirituality.

Within monotheistic traditions (often apparently least animal-friendly), notably Judaism, Christianity, and Islam, there are also positive teachings. Within the Jewish tradition, many rabbis, including no less a person than Moses Maimonides (one of the greatest legal codifiers and philosophers of the Middle Ages), assumed that the concept of *tsar baalei hayyim* (generally, the obligation not to cause pain to other creatures) was biblically ordained. Judaism arguably taught the impermissibility of cruelty to other monotheistic religions. This is reflected in Islam, especially in the hadith in which Muhammad says that "kindness to any living creature will be rewarded." In addition, according to the Qur'an, animals are created by the same God and form their own "communities" under God (Q 6:38).

Even in Christianity (arguably the most anthropocentric of all religions), there are neglected subtraditions offering positive perspectives on animals. Based on the gospel stories of Jesus and animals (especially Jesus dwelling with the beasts in Mark 1:12–13), a voluminous amount of early apocryphal literature (Linzey, *Creatures of the Same God*) arose from the fourth to the eighth centuries that comprised many stories of Jesus and the apostles befriending and protecting animals. That tradition seems to have continued in the many lives of the canonized saints, both East and West, who also befriended animals and enjoyed respectful, convivial relations with them. Although Saint Francis of Assisi is often remembered in this regard, there are countless other examples in hagiography.

This subtradition arguably made possible the formation of the world's first national animal protection society in the world—namely, the Society for the Prevention of Cruelty to Animals (SPCA—later to become the Royal Society for the Prevention of Cruelty to Animals, or RSPCA) in 1824. An Anglican priest, Arthur Broome, gave up his London church to devote himself full-time to becoming its first secretary, and the first Minute Book of the Society records that it was "a Christian Society based on Christian principles" (Linzey, *Animal Theology*). Thus, a subtradition within Christianity helped to crystallize the organized worldwide movement for animal protection. The organization took its inspiration from the Anglican divine Humphry Primatt, who wrote *The Duty of Mercy and the Sin of Cruelty* in 1776. He famously wrote, "We may pretend to what religion we please, but cruelty is atheism. We may make our boast of Christianity, but cruelty is infidelity. We may trust to our orthodoxy, but cruelty is the worst of heresies" (288).

The challenge, then, for scholars and theologians is to articulate these neglected positive teachings within world religions. It is not that they are not there so much as that they have not been looked for. Even from this brief summary, it is clear that there are alternative and authoritative voices for celebrating, befriending, and protecting animals (Linzey and Cohn-Sherbok). The work of animal theology (Linzey, *Animal Theology*)—and more generally, animal religious studies—is essential in order to help religious believers reconnect with the fullness of their own traditions and reclaim, and even embody, those traditions' more positive features in relation to other creatures.

Related articles: Animals in the Bible; Animals in Jainism; Buddhist attitudes; The Buddhist case for vegetarianism; Catholic teaching; Ethical vegetarianism; Hinduism and animals; Islam and animals; Judaism and animal life; Moral anthropocentrism; The moral claims of animals; The treatment of animals in India

Linzey, Andrew, *Animal Gospel: Christian Faith As If Animals Mattered*, Hodder and Stoughton/Westminster John Knox Press, 1999.

———, *Animal Rites: Liturgies of Animal Care*, SCM Press/Pilgrim Press, 1999.

———, *Animal Theology*, SCM Press/University of Illinois Press, 1994.

———, *Creatures of the Same God: Explorations in Animal Theology*, Winchester University Press/Lantern Books, 2007.

Linzey, Andrew, and Cohn-Sherbok, Dan, *After Noah: Animals and the Liberation of Theology*, Mowbray/Continuum, 1997.

Primatt, Humphry, *The Duty of Mercy and the Sin of Cruelty*, T. Constable, 1776.

ANDREW LINZEY

ANIMAL SACRIFICE

"Animal sacrifice" is frequently used as a euphemism for killing other-than-human animals for human purposes, particularly in scientific research, "wildlife" management (*see* Preservation and Killing), and the like. Less misleadingly, but not less commonly, it denotes the process of killing for religious or cultural reasons—for example, in the service of one or multiple deities or ancestors. These practices usually follow precise instructions as to how the animal's life ought to be taken, who may do the killing, what instruments should be used, and what incantations must accompany the ritual. The reasons for a particular practice vary, ranging from making amends, seeking forgiveness or reconciliation, enlisting the deities' or ancestors' blessings and goodwill, and securing good fortune (for a new professional venture, moving house, or a football match or other competitive encounter) to celebrating and giving praise and thanks.

Historically, the sacrifice involved "offering" (Latin *operari*: to serve the godhead through one's offerings) part of one's initial harvest or herd of animals, literally surrendering a crucial source of income and means toward one's livelihood—an expression of renunciation and devotion. In recent times, however, many of these practices have come under attack for being outdated, based on ancient superstition, and for failing to reflect an appreciation of findings in evolutionary theory, ethology, and cognitive neuroscience, let alone ethical coherence and consistency.

It is with regard to animal sacrifice that a significant clash between two competing moral imperatives occurs: preservation versus change (of culture and tradition). Toward the end of every year, the Ukweshwama ritual takes place in KwaZulu-Natal, South Africa, during the First Fruits Festival. The ritual, which involves the barehanded killing of a bull by a group of young Zulu warriors, is traditionally performed to ensure that the Zulu nation has a strong army to defend the king and his subjects. It is defended, further, in terms of upholding culture and traditions. By killing the bull, a symbol of power, with their bare hands, the modern-day warriors gain a bond with forefathers who ruled the region.

The ritual begins with a call by an *induna*, or warrior chief, for the brave among them to enter the fifty-meter-diameter kraal to face the bull amid chanting and singing. Scores do so, some in tribal garb but most in long pants and tennis shoes or barefoot. The bull starts running around the perimeter and continues until slowed by the crowd and finally stopped. For forty minutes, dozens trample the bellowing, groaning bull; wrench his head around by the horns to try to break his neck; pull his tongue out; stuff sand in his mouth; and even attempt to tie his penis in a knot. Gleaming with sweat, they raise their arms in triumph and sing when the bull finally succumbs. Although some observers acknowledge that the requirement of warriors to use their bare hands might be seen as cruelty, it is believed by the participants that one cannot change one's culture—and that its dictates ought to be obeyed.

Apart from referring to the protracted fear, suffering, and indignity experienced by the animal, objections include the following considerations: Since there is no Zulu army and South Africa is not at war, and all South Africans are protected by the National Defence Force and the police, and since the Zulu king is protected by personal bodyguards provided by the government via taxpayers' money, the rationale for this particular cultural practice has all but disappeared. In addition, it might be argued that violence breeds violence, and violence against animals and violence against humans, especially women and children, are demonstrably interlinked. Finally, given that traditions and cultural practices are by their very nature fluid, dynamic, and ever-evolving, it might be emphasized that a particular ritual does not solely define "traditional" identity and culture, nor does it define royal authority: ruling from 274 to 232 B.C.E., Indian emperor Ashoka forbade the killing of animals, without suffering a corresponding loss in popularity and esteem. It is worth noting, in this regard, that acceptable "warrior" attire includes long trousers, socks, and running shoes. "Culture," by definition, is not something that is static. It implies ongoing growth and development—and occasionally even progress.

A related ritual is that of stabbing a bull, cow, goat, or sheep with the family spear before the animal is slaughtered, as part of a cleansing ceremony at the family home. The response from animal protection societies, which usually consider legal prosecution, is countered by the claim that this goes much deeper than so-called cruelty to animals. Commonly emphasized is the constitutional right of all indigenous families and groups to perform rituals that they believe reconnect them to their ancestors, and attention is drawn to the consideration that the ritual in question is intended to promote peace of mind and harmonious existence in the lives of the family. Considering that Muslim and Jewish rituals around the slaughter of animals are not considered abnormal, and the respective communities' right to engage in their rituals is rarely questioned, it is argued that condemnation of these kinds of indigenous African rituals betrays "selective racism."

Another response cautions against adopting a simplistic approach of dealing with allegations of cruelty to animals by employing criminal law. According to this line of thinking, animal sacrifice goes to the very heart of how people define themselves and how they construct their identity. If the principle of cultural diversity were properly understood, the contention goes, the merits of one group's spirituality could not reasonably be challenged. In particular, the singling out of historically disadvantaged people or groups amounts to selective treatment. People ought to be permitted to practice their own spirituality; one ought to give them credibility and trust that they practice their culture responsibly. Commentators state that white South Africans who engage in legalistic complaining should perhaps try to reach the ears of those they are trying to convert because their dedication to the animals' cause indicates insensitivity to black South Africans and African history; their objections come across as inspired by the colonial desire to educate the brutish natives. Among black Africans, there has commonly been a perception that whites care more about animals than about black people.

In response, one might ask whether objection to cultural practices such as "virginity testing," "dry sex," and female genital excision would also make a person guilty of "selective racism." Is this also a manifestation of a "colonial desire to educate"? Not obviously, one could argue. The moral disvalue of killing and causing suffering trumps "cultural" considerations—and is indivisible across sex, race, and species.

Related articles: Animal-friendly spirituality; Animal protection in Africa; Animals used in research; Caring for animals and humans; Developments in animal law; The ethics of killing free-living animals; Hinduism and animals; Islam and ani-

ANC Daily Press Briefings, December 11, 1995, available at http://70.84.171.10/~etools/newsbrief/1995/news1211.

Burbidge, M., "The Big Beef: Tony Yengeni Stabbing a Bull Has Reignited the Debate around the Sacrificial Slaughtering of Animals," *Mail and Guardian* (South Africa), January 26–February 1, 2007: 10.

Horsthemke, K., *The Moral Status and Rights of Animals*, Porcupine Press, 2010.

———, "Rethinking Humane Education," *Ethics and Education* 4.2 (October 2009): 201–214.

Moya, F.-N., "SPCA Needs to Work with Black People," *Mail and Guardian* (South Africa), January 26–February 1, 2007: 10.

Pickover, M., "Human Rites and Wrongs: Ukweshwama, Culture and Compassion" (opinion piece), Animal Rights Africa online, 2009, available at http://www.animalrightsafrica.org/news/blog1.php/2009/12/18/human-rites-and-wrongs-ukweshawama-culture-and-compassion.

KAI HORSTHEMKE

ANIMALS IN THE BIBLE

The biblical view of animals is distinctive for what it does not say as well as for what it does. That is, the Bible does not divinize or demonize animals. The Bible contains no animal magic, animals are not messengers of the gods, and animals do not directly influence human affairs. Although we can learn from them, we are not to worship animals or treat them as a part of divinity. In a word, the Bible is more realistic than romantic about the world of animals. The Bible treats animals as creatures who are rather different from us and yet sufficiently similar to merit kindness and compassion.

Because the Bible does not have a romantic view of animals, it is often criticized for justifying human dominion over them. It is true that the Bible does not treat animals as equal to humans. According to the Bible, humans clearly are superior to animals, not only in intelligence but also in their divinely given place in the cosmos. The biblical world is an ordered world, and humans have the most important role to play in that order.

Nevertheless, humans are not given absolute power over animals. Instead, humans are given certain basic responsibilities toward animals because animals too are loved by God and have a special role to play in God's good creation. Humans are God's representatives on earth, put here for a variety of purposes, one of which is to mediate to animals God's original purposes and intentions.

Of course, God's plan for the animals, like God's plan for humans, has been savagely compromised by what theologians call "the Fall." Christian theology teaches that nature, whether human or animal, is not currently what God meant it to be. This means that Christians cannot look at nature as something that is completely good in its present state. The world is good because God created it, but much that happens within the world, including within the animal world, is far from good. This is why nature needs human intervention, not in terms of exploitation and abuse for economic and personal gain, but in terms of management and care, in order to become a reflection of God's original intentions. Humans cannot save the world, but we can be good stewards of God's many gifts.

The Bible places the harmony of humans and animals both at the beginning and at the end of time. In between, it allows for the use of animals, even as it considers them worthy of God's justice and mercy. Only after the flood are humans permitted to kill and eat animals. Restrictions on the killing and eating of animals are clearly stated in the Mosaic covenant between God and the Israelites, where many of the laws concern animals—for example, the Sabbath was meant to be a day of rest for animals as well as humans.

Although the Bible teaches that God cares about all life, the Israelites were asked to worry more about domesticated than free-living animals. Animals who worked for humans were to be treated with special care. Sheep play a particularly important role in the Bible. In fact, God is often portrayed as a shepherd who loves his flock dearly. The New Testament continues this focus on domesticated animals by favoring animals such as the dove and the lamb, not the eagle or the lion. God descends as a dove at Jesus's baptism, and Jesus is portrayed as the "Lamb of God." Animals also gather to witness and rejoice in Jesus's birth. Jesus tells many stories about animals. He portrays God as a feeder of birds and compares himself to a hen gathering together her brood under her wings. In one story, he imagines dogs tenderly attending an otherwise abandoned poor man by licking his sores.

Overall, the Bible appears to tell two stories about animals at the same time—God's divine plan and human use and abuse. The Hebrew prophets insist that in the end God will restore the world to its original peace and harmony, a vision confirmed by the message of the New Testament. If God's ultimate plan for animals is not kept in mind, then the Bible can seem to legitimate all sorts of practices that many would find abhorrent today.

Related articles: Animal-friendly spirituality; Catholic teaching; Ethical vegetarianism; Judaism and animal life; The welfare of sheep

Boroski, Oded, *Every Living Thing: Daily Use of Animals in Ancient Israel*, AltaMira Press, 1999.

Kowalski, Gary, *The Bible according to Noah: Theology As If Animals Mattered*, Lantern Books, 2001.

Petropoulou, Maria-Zoe, *Animal Sacrifice in Ancient Greek Religion, Judaism, and Christianity, 100 BC to AD 200*, Oxford University Press, 2008.

Simkins, Ronald A., *Creator and Creation: Nature in the Worldview of Ancient Israel*, Hendrickson, 1994.

Webb, Stephen H., *On God and Dogs: A Christian Theology of Animal Compassion*, Oxford University Press, 1998.

———, *Good Eating*, Brazos Press, 2001.

STEPHEN H. WEBB

ANIMALS IN JAINISM

Jainism, a minority religion practiced in India and around the world, is particularly well known for its advocacy for animals. The Jain faith arose more than 2,500 years ago on India's northern Gangetic plain. Its founding figures, Parshvanatha (ca. 850 B.C.E.) and Mahavira (ca. 500 B.C.E.), are regarded as the twenty-third and twenty-fourth of a long line of spiritual teachers (*tirthankaras*). They taught and lived a way of life that emphasizes the practice of nonviolence (ahimsa). This commitment to nonviolence, which includes vegetarianism and rejection of occupations that involve the harm of animals, is designed to release the fettering karmas that occlude the luminous nature of the soul (*jiva*). Because of violence committed in this life and in past lives, dimly colored karmas have cloaked one's innate pure consciousness with ignorance and desire. By the careful application of the Jain vows of nonviolence, truthfulness, not stealing, sexual restraint, and non-possession, one expels these afflicted karmas, advancing toward a state of liberation, known as *kevala*.

For two reasons, animals play an important role in the Jain religion. First, each human person has endured countless lives as a nonhuman animal. The Jain teaching of reincarnation (*punarjanma*) specifies that unpurged karma in this life will carry over to shape one's future life. Hence, all people have a history that intertwines animal narratives with one's current human narrative. The second reason animals are important relates to ethics. Ethical behavior, particularly as listed in the previously listed vows, determines the course of present and future life. One way to improve one's ethical and future ontological status is to treat animals with benevolence. Acts of kindness toward animals can help release the binding karmas that otherwise would cause an inauspicious rebirth. From a Jain perspective, all humans have been nonhuman animals, and good treatment of animals can help improve one's lot both in this life and in the next.

In Jainism, all animals possess consciousness. Jains identify ascending gradations of consciousness, beginning with a consciousness that arises with the sense of touch. Jains attribute consciousness even to entities that in Aristotelian thought are inanimate. For instance, rocks are said to possess the sense of touch and hence hold their own consciousness. The same is true for water, whether droplets or oceans, and for fire, gusts of wind, and the innumerable microorganisms that pervade each and every environment and every plant, large and small. Most cultures would not consider rocks or lumps of ice or palm trees to be "animals." For Jains, they merit recognition for their ability to touch and, presumably, their ability to convey certain moods. Perhaps J. R. R. Tolkien, in his rendering of the Ents, was somewhat familiar with Jain ontology.

Recognizable animals appear at the next level of the Jain categorization of reality. Dwelling within the earth and within various decaying or diseased bodies are worms, gnawing and tunneling though their environments. According to the Jain worldview, these worms possess both the sense of touch and the sense of taste. They are considered higher-level beings and must be spared from harm. Whereas it is permissible to walk on the earth and breathe air and make food from plants, it would not be acceptable to cause harm to worms because such harm would further deepen the karma that shrouds the soul. Higher than worms, insects such as crawling bugs and ants are said to possess the sense of smell. They also merit protection. The next station in Jain taxonomy names butterflies, bees, flies, and moths as having the sense of sight atop the foundations of touch and taste and smell. Water snakes also have the sense of hearing. All mammals, reptiles, and birds fall under the highest category—those beings who possess all six senses, including the ability to think.

This worldview is reinforced in the daily life of Jains and also can be seen as somewhat reflected in the overall attitude toward animals in India, where animals are part of daily life, with cows, goats, elephants, and camels spilling into the streets and sidewalks. The Jains assiduously, for more than 2,500 years, have advocated against animal sacrifice and for vegetarianism. They influenced the practices of Buddhism and Hinduism and successfully appealed to the Mughal rulers for increased regard for animals. Jains have opened and maintained thousands of shelters throughout the subcontinent for the protection of animals; these shelters, known as *pinjrapoles*, provide food and water to hundreds of thousands of ill or unwanted animals each year throughout all parts of India. In the recent Jain diaspora, they have lent support to animal shelters and to various causes that work for the protection of animals worldwide.

The stories of animals include a famous tale about King Yasodhara, who—because of anger and jealousy and maltreatment of a rooster made of flour—is reborn in turn as a peacock, a mongoose, a fish, a goat, and a chicken, enduring difficult lives and gruesome deaths, before regaining human form and taking up the religious life. Sixteen of the twenty-four great teachers, or *tirthankaras*, can be identified by their companion animal. Parshvanatha is always seen with a snake; Mahavira, with a lion.

Animals are said to possess an ethical compass, and animals who perform evil deeds can earn a birth in hell. The *Tattvartha Sutra* (ca. 400 C.E.) states that "birds can be born no lower than the third hell, quadrupeds not below the fourth, and snakes not below the fifth; only fish and human males are able to be born in the seventh hell" (Jaini, *Jaina Path* 174), in a commentary on the ability of humans to commit incredible acts of cruelty and on the murderous capacity of predatory fishes such as sharks.

The oldest text of Jainism, the Acaranga Sutra (ca. 300 B.C.E.), gives Mahavira's foundational teaching on animals and the need for their protection:

> Some slay animals for sacrificial purposes, some slay animals for the sake of their skin, some kill them for the sake of their blood; others for the sake of their heart, their bile, the feathers of their tail, their tail, their big or small horns, their teeth, their tusks, their nails, their sinews, their bones; with a purpose and without a purpose. Some kill animals because they have been wounded by them or are wounded or will be wounded. He who injures these animals does not comprehend and renounce these sinful acts; he who does not injure these, comprehends and renounces these sinful acts. Knowing them, a wise man should not act sinfully towards animals, or cause others to act so, nor allow others to act so. (Jacobi 12)

According to Jainism, by refraining from cruelty to animals, the human being can elevate himself or herself, recognizing that when we hurt other beings, human or nonhuman, we ultimately hurt ourselves.

Related articles: Animal advocacy; Animal and human violence; Animal sacrifice; Animals in Hinduism; Buddhist attitudes; The Buddhist case for vegetarianism; The complexity of animal awareness; Ethical vegetarianism; Humane education; Moral anthropocentrism; Sanctuaries and rehabilitation; The treatment of animals in India

Chapple, Christopher Key, "Inherent Value without Nostalgia: Animals and the Jaina Tradition," in Waldau, Paul, and Patton, Kimberley (eds.), *A Communion of Subjects: Animals in Religion, Science, and Ethics*, Columbia University Press, 2006.

———, *Nonviolence to Animals, Earth, and Self in Asian Traditions*, State University of New York Press, 1993.

Jacobi, Hermann, *Jaina Sutras Translated from the Prakrit*, Clarendon Press, 1884.

Jaini, Padmanabh S., "Indian Perspectives on the Spirituality of Animals," *Collected Papers on Jaina Studies*, Motilal Banarsidass, 2000.

———, *The Jaina Path of Purification*, University of California Press, 1979.

Lodrick, Deryk O., *Sacred Cows, Sacred Places: The Origin and Survival of Animal Homes in India*, University of California Press, 1981.

Wiley, Kristi, "Five-Sensed Animals in Jainism," in Waldau, Paul, and Patton, Kimberley (eds.), *A Communion of Subjects: Animals in Religion, Science, and Ethics*, Columbia University Press, 2006.

CHRISTOPHER KEY CHAPPLE

BUDDHIST ATTITUDES

Among political, social, economic, and artistic achievements, sixth to fifth century B.C.E., India is distinguished by the propagation of the Buddhist religious tradition. The founder of this widespread and diverse tradition is generally known as the Buddha, a descriptive title meaning "Enlightened One," though his given name was actually Siddhartha Gautama.

The life of Siddhartha Gautama (ca. 563–483 B.C.E.) is known only through his followers and has become immersed in legend. According to tradition, at his birth sages recognized in him the marks of a great man with the potential to become either a ruler or a sage. Four signs, it was foretold, would guide him to his proper path. At the age of twenty-nine, despite his father's best efforts to make him a ruler, Siddhartha finally saw the four signs: old age (a decrepit old man), sickness (a man ailing from disease), death (a corpse), and serenity (a wandering religious mendicant). The belief that all birth leads only to suffering and death and that the succession of births is endless led Siddhartha to renounce earthly attachments that his father had cultivated. He embarked on a quest for peace and enlightenment, seeking release from the universal impermanence and sorrow (*dukkha*) in the world and from the endless cycle of rebirths (*samsara*).

As Siddhartha meditated under a bo tree, he rose through a series of higher states of consciousness until he attained the enlightenment that he was seeking. The Buddha began to preach, gathering a body of disciples and organizing them into a monastic community known as the *sangha*. In this way he spent the rest of his life. Because the Buddha was an oral teacher, his teachings were gathered into canonical collections by his followers. The teaching of the Buddha is broadly summarized in the Four Noble Truths (the truth of *dukkha* and how to escape it) and the Eightfold Path (the route to enlightenment or escape).

From the standpoint of ethical sensitivity to animals, there are three key aspects of the Buddha's teaching that deserve particular attention. The first concerns the ethic of ahimsa, or nonviolence to sentient life as the central moral imperative. Both Buddhism and Jainism rejected as cruel the practice of animal sacrifice, which had played an important role in the religious rites in India from ancient times. Although many Buddhists accept the inviolability of life, the destruction of life is morally wrong for them only when it is caused intentionally or as a result of negligence. As such, although many Buddhists have a profound respect for all living beings, it must be said that (in sharp contrast to Jainism, for example) vegetarianism is by no means universally practiced, and animals have not always received a prominent place in most Buddhist ethical teachings.

Although the central ethical precepts in Buddhism are expressed in negative wording, as an abstention, each has a positive counterpart. The second teaching concerns the positive counterpart to ahimsa: the principle of universal compassion (*karuna*). Rebuking those who mistreat others, the Buddha says, "As a mother cares for her son, all her days, so towards all living things a man's mind should be all-embracing." The moral claim is that it is evil to cause suffering to others and good to alleviate and prevent their sufferings. This moral outlook developed in some forms of Buddhism into the ideal of the *bodhisattva*: one who has reached the verge of *nirvana* (liberation from the process of rebirths), but who out of limitless compassion renounces final liberation until all sentient beings have been raised to the same level. The bodhisattva's vow is one of self-sacrifice: "All creatures are in pain . . . I take upon myself the burden of sorrow . . . Assuredly I must bear the burdens of all beings . . . for I have resolved to save them all." This passage encapsulates the attitudes that underlie much of the morality taught by the Buddha, capturing the positive spirit that is to accompany the negative injunctions.

The third teaching concerns "exchanging self and others"—that is, the view that all are equal, in that all beings desire happiness and the avoidance of suffering. With understanding of the extent of *dukkha* in one's own life, the importance of "comparing oneself with others" is stressed: "since the self of others is dear to each one, let him who loves himself not harm another." The basis of ethical action is that it is wrong to inflict on other beings what you yourself find unpleasant. Notwithstanding these exhortations, a "speciesist" moral hierarchy is evident in Buddhist teachings. For example, it is considered more serious to kill a human than an animal, and it is worse to kill a large animal than a small one. But although humans are seen as superior to animals, this is only a matter of degree and not an absolute moral distinction. Humans are to show their superiority by using their freedom of choice to treat animals well, not by maltreating them.

Buddhist ethical teachings concerning animals are likely to become increasingly important as the tradition continues to spread. The Buddha's ethical teachings regarding ahimsa and karuna—when actualized in life ethics—have the capacity to radically reshape present attitudes toward animals. Such a transformation of thought and action was inevitably one of the Buddha's goals, and we would do well to make it ours too.

Related articles: Animal sacrifice; Animals in Hinduism; Animals in Jainism; The Buddhist case for vegetarianism; Ethical vegetarianism; Moral anthropocentrism

Barsam, Ara Paul, *Reverence for Life: Albert Schweitzer's Great Contribution to Ethical Thought*, Oxford University Press, 2008.
Gombrich, Richard, *What the Buddha Thought*, Equinox, 2009.
Harvey, Peter, *An Introduction to Buddhism: Teachings, History and Practices*, Cambridge University Press, 1990.
Keown, Damien (ed.), *Contemporary Buddhist Ethics*, Routledge, 2000.
———, *The Nature of Buddhist Ethics*, Macmillan/Palgrave, 1992.
Rahula, Walpoloa, *What the Buddha Taught*, Grove Press, 1974.

ARA PAUL BARSAM

THE BUDDHIST CASE FOR VEGETARIANISM

There are many compelling reasons to refrain from eating animals, but the central one for Buddhists is to not be complicit in harm. The first of the Five Grave Precepts in Buddhism is "not to kill but to cherish all life." Each and every creature, in his or her own unique way, manifests Buddha Nature, an ultimate completeness, or perfection, with which nonhumans are endowed as much as humans. This essential wholeness, common to all sentient beings, is both a reality and a potentiality: it is intrinsic to us, and it is our nature to actualize this perfection. Thus, to unnecessarily take the life of any living being is to disrupt his or her potentiality and deny that being's fundamental bond with us.

To eat flesh foods is to participate in killing, for in doing so we indirectly inflict suffering, as well as death, on animals by sustaining a market for the slaughter industry. Emerson recognized this when he said, "However scrupulously the slaughter-house is concealed in the graceful distance of miles, there is complicity" (Emerson 7). The complicity, moreover, is in not only the killing itself but also the wholesale cruelty that leads up to it. Multinational corporations for which animals are merely commodities to be exploited largely control the modern business of animal husbandry. In their rearing, pigs, chickens, cattle, calves used for veal, and other animals are subjected to brutal overcrowding and painful procedures to make them more profitable. In their transportation to slaughter, which often involves long journeys without food or water, they endure further miseries through inhumane treatment, exposure to weather extremes, and injury. And then the slaughterhouses themselves are hellishly violent and messy. Furthermore, large-scale meat production has been linked to severe erosion, destruction of rainforests, and staggering pollution from animal waste; research by the Union of Concerned Scientists showed that household meat and poultry consumption alone is responsible for about a quarter of threats to natural ecosystems and free-living animals. In supporting the animal husbandry industry by eating meat, Buddhists betray their highest aspiration: to relieve suffering and liberate all sentient beings.

But indeed, surprisingly, not all people who consider themselves Buddhists refrain from eating meat. Buddhism is an immensely diverse religion, with many differences in how it has been taught and practiced by the peoples who have embraced it. Moreover, not since the Buddha has there been any one master or religious body recognized worldwide as Buddhism's ultimate authority. In determining what the Buddha's position on meat eating was, we have to rely on the Buddhist scriptures (sutras), his purported words. The two main streams of Buddhist teaching that flowed out of the Buddha's native India are the Mahayana (literally, "great vehicle") and the Theravada ("the way of the elders"). Each has its own body of sutras, and they present different versions of what the Buddha taught on meat eating. Several major Mahayana sutras, which are revered in China, Japan, Tibet, and Korea, have the Buddha clearly and unequivocally condemning it. The Lankavatara Sutra devotes a whole chapter to the evils of eating meat (Suzuki chap. 8).

The Surangama Sutra poses the question, "How can a bhikshu [monk], who hopes to become a deliverer of others, himself be living on the flesh of other sentient beings?" (Goddard 205). The Mahaparinirvana Sutra flatly states, "The eating of meat extinguishes the seed of great compassion" (Kapleau 34). It is not surprising, then, that by all accounts flesh foods have always been prohibited in Buddhist monasteries in China, Korea, and until fairly recently, Japan. Even in Tibet, where non-flesh foods are extremely limited, many lamas entirely abstain from animal food, and according to Alexandra David-Neel, who spent many years living there, even those who do eat meat believe that meat eating "creates a deleterious psychic atmosphere in places where it is habitually eaten" (158).

In the countries of Southeast Asia, however, Buddhist monks found a yawning loophole in the prohibition against meat eating. They cite Theravadan sutras that have the Buddha allowing the eating of meat in three cases: "if you have neither seen, heard, nor suspected that it was killed on purpose for you" (Nikaya 55). It is hard to imagine the Buddha laying down such permissive guidelines, which would have effectively removed all restrictions on animal consumption for his monks. This was a man renowned for his compassion toward not only humans but also all creatures, and even the Theravadins do not dispute that he condemned "the bloody trades of slaughtering, hunting, and trapping" (Horner).

Assuming then that the Buddha never granted the exceptions on meat eating that are attributed to him in the Theravada sutras, how might those references have gotten into those texts? First, the Buddha's teachings were not recorded until some two hundred years after his passing. Until then they were handed down orally. The Buddhist canon, like that of other ancient religions, developed gradually, and leading Buddhist scholars maintain that when the sutras were finally written down, through the work of three Buddhist councils over one hundred years, the old material was still so unsettled that it was common among Buddhist elders of the time to add to and alter it. Furthermore, changes easily could have crept in later at the hands of monk scribes, either inadvertently or to suit their own biases. Revisions inevitably occurred in the anti-meat-eating Mahayana texts as well, but all evidence points to the Buddha holding to the ancient doctrine of ahimsa, non-injuriousness toward living beings, which has always been widely accepted in India.

Many vegetarians grow accustomed to hearing this philosophical challenge: "you abstain from eating meat to avoid participating in killing, but in eating vegetables you are also taking life." The charge of hypocrisy implied in this refrain holds water only as an abstraction. In the real world, no living thing can survive without taking life, and eating animal flesh involves a different order of violence than eating plant foods. Drawing on this principle, some Buddhists simply decline to eat anything or any being they would not be willing to take the life of themselves.

Monks who eat meat as part of the alms they accept from lay supporters insist that tradition obliges them to eat whatever food is offered, without discrimination. There is truth in this, and some lay Buddhists cite a similar excuse for eating meat in others' homes: "Dinner guests should just accept what the host serves and bow with gratitude." In fact, the Buddha died from upholding this principle, having eaten a poisonous mushroom served inadvertently at the house of a devotee. One version of the story claims that the food was a piece of pork, but the weight of scholarship favors the translation of the word as "truffles." In any case, it is a simple matter, whether monk or lay person, to get the word out to the community that you do not eat flesh foods, after which such offerings will cease.

One of the fundamental tenets of Buddhism is the law of causation, which on a moral plane is known as karma. Our actions carry consequences, or karmic implications, and in eating meat we are perpetuating our bondage to suffering. Fortunately, there are few places in the world where a hostile climate requires meat eating, and most of us living in modern, industrial countries have an abundance of non-flesh foods available that can keep us robustly healthy our whole lives. Recognizing this, the Dalai Lama XIV has noted that "we have the capacity and the responsibility to save billions of lives" (20) by refraining from eating meat.

No matter what the record shows in Buddhism as to the importance of abstaining from flesh foods, ultimately each individual must look to himself or herself in settling the matter. The Buddha urged this approach in all matters in one of his most famous utterances: "Do not believe solely because the written testimony of some ancient wise man is shown you . . . and don't believe anything on the mere authority of your teachers or priests. What you should accept as true, and as the guide to your life, is whatever agrees with your own Reason and your own experience, after thorough investigation, and whatever is helpful both to your own well-being and that of other living beings." The essential truth to which Buddhism points is beyond prescribed conduct, and one need not become vegetarian to practice it. But in recognizing our kinship with animals and refusing to be party to their unnecessary suffering, we honor our innate compassion and aim for the greater good.

_____

Related articles: Animal agriculture and climate change; Animal-friendly spirituality; Animal welfare and farming; Animals in Asia; Animals in Chinese culture; Animals in Jainism; Buddhist attitudes; Ethical vegetarianism; Hinduism and animals; Japanese attitudes toward animals; Live animal exports; Slaughter; The treatment of animals in India

Dalai Lama XIV, *Worlds in Harmony: Dialogues on Compassionate Action*, Parallax Press, 1992.

David-Neel, Alexandra, *Buddhism: Its Doctrines and Its Methods*, Avon Books, 1977.

Dharmasiri, Gunapala, *Fundamentals of Buddhist Ethics*, Golden Leaves, 1992.

Emerson, Ralph Waldo, "The Conduct of Life," in *The Complete Works of Ralph Waldo Emerson*, Houghton Mifflin, 1904.

Goddard, Dwight (ed.), "The Surangama Sutra," in *A Buddhist Bible*, Beacon Press, 1994.

Horner, I. B., *Early Buddhism and the Taking of Life*, Buddhist Publication Society, 1967.

Kapleau, Philip, *To Cherish All Life: A Buddhist Case for Vegetarianism*, the Zen Center, 1986.

Nikaya, Majjhima, *Further Dialogues of the Buddha*, trans. Robert Chalmers, Sri Satguru, 1988.

Phelps, Norm, *The Great Compassion: Buddhism and Animal Rights*, Lantern Books, 2004.

Suzuki, D. T., *The Lankavatara Sutra: A Mahayana Text*, Routledge and Kegan Paul, 1956.

BODHIN KJOLHEDE

CATHOLIC TEACHING

For Catholics, the animal world is a sign of God's creative power, his wisdom, and his goodness. God made every living thing and delights in the abundance and the variety of life. "The Lord's is the earth and the fullness thereof" (Psalm 24)—all exists to give glory to the God who created it. As the *Catechism of the Catholic Church* states, all human beings "must therefore respect the particular goodness of every creature, [and] avoid any disordered use of things which would be in contempt of the Creator and would bring disastrous consequences for human beings and their environment." Cruelty to animals is considered to be a sin (a fault against God's law) because it is contrary to God's care for them. God cares for "every sparrow that falls to the ground" (Matthew 10:29) and has the supreme right to have all his creatures treated with proper respect.

Catholic tradition has exhibited several ways of looking at our relationship with animals. One ancient tradition put more emphasis on spiritual concerns than on bodily matter—and because animals are not known to be spiritual, they were not considered to be very important. Such people would not be actually cruel to animals, only indifferent. Another tradition valued the innocence of animals and efforts to live in harmony with them. Examples of this tradition are the many Celtic saints whose close fellowship with animals resembled the Garden of Eden (paradise before the Fall) restored and the Kingdom of God already here. Some medieval Christian writers and artists used animals (real and imaginary) allegorically—as can be seen in the sculptured decorations in many old churches and cathedrals. The pelican, for instance, thought to feed her young by her own blood, stood for Christ's sacrifice. Some even thought animals capable of committing crimes and even put them on trial.

Whatever the various theological views, over the Christian centuries, most ordinary people lived closely with their animals. They tended to treat well the ones who were useful to them and, after heavy work in the fields, had little energy or resources left over to spend on other animals. They ate a largely lacto-vegetarian diet and kept intact the natural balance of the environment. It was after the eighteenth-century Enlightenment, when people became largely urbanized, that they increasingly lost respect for nonhuman life and began to treat animals as if they were unfeeling things. Although the Church constantly taught that cruelty was wrong (although, by today's standards, Christians in previous centuries have been mercilessly cruel, not only toward animals but also toward other people), it also maintained that animals were created for the service of people—who had been created "in the image of God." Today, however, being made in God's image is understood by many to mean that human beings should treat animals as God would, and that would not involve making animals suffer for the sake of people.

Since 1929, Catholic Concern for Animals (formerly the Catholic Study Circle for Animal Welfare) has been helping Catholics reflect on their use of animals and recover some of the more positive traditions and wholesome ways of thinking about them. Some of the worst deliberate cruelties seem to happen in Catholic countries, such as bull fighting and abusing animals in fiestas, but these cultural events have pagan or superstitious origins and are often maintained to attract the tourist trade. Although many young people in those countries, as in others, reject these instances of obvious and unnecessary cruelty, they may still patronize other institutions that engage in abuse, such as fast-food outlets serving factory-farmed chicken. Much of the harm to animals is done out of sight, so that raising awareness and encouraging reflection is central to the work of Catholic Concern.

It is important that animals be treated according to their real nature and not judged as though they were people. At the same time, it is wrong to call people "animals" when they behave in a less-than-human manner. Animals never behave sinfully, as people do. The only true human being, in Catholic belief, was Jesus of Nazareth—he is the measure of being human. And he was a person of infinite compassion. To become like him is the goal of the Christian life, and the way to follow him is to live a virtuous life, with God's help. Nobody can do that overnight—it takes a lifetime to cultivate the virtues. The cardinal ones are, traditionally, prudence, justice, fortitude, and temperance. Temperance includes such dispositions as gentleness and compassion, which must be exercised toward all sentient creatures. All were loved into being by God, for whose sake they exist. Catholic tradition affirms that truth, and the Church celebrates God's loving kindness in daily acts of devotion.

Related articles: Animal-friendly spirituality; Animals in the Bible; Birds used in food production; Blood fiestas; Bull fighting; Ethical vegetarianism; Moral anthropocentrism

Clark, Stephen R. L., *Animals and Their Moral Standing*, Routledge, 1997.

Jones, Deborah M., *The School of Compassion: A Roman Catholic Theology of Animals*, Gracewing, 2009.

Linzey, Andrew, *Why Animal Suffering Matters: Philosophy, Theology, and Practical Ethics*, Oxford University Press, 2009.

Linzey, Andrew, and Cohn-Sherbok, Dan, *After Noah: Animals and the Liberation of Theology*, Mowbray (Cassell), 1997.

Midgley, Mary, *Animals and Why They Matter: A Journey around the Species Barrier*, University of Georgia Press, 1983.

Scully, Matthew, *Dominion: The Power of Man, the Suffering of Animals, and the Call to Mercy*, Souvenir Press, 2011.

DEBORAH M. JONES

CONFUCIANISM AND DAOISM

The Chinese people and Chinese culture have had a long-standing and ambivalent interest in animals. Chinese culture, both ancient and contemporary, has always been human-centered, but animals have also been very important to Chinese life. In traditional Chinese philosophy, animals are considered part of the moral cosmos, as in Confucianism and Daoism (Taoism), in search of the betterment of life and society. In traditional Chinese thought, humans and animals are part of the moral universe of the exemplary humans, who should be models of benevolence and compassion, and such compassion and benevolence extend beyond humans to other life forms in nature. There is no strict delineation to distinguish animals and humans because both are considered part of the cosmos (Cao).

Specifically, in early China, animals were considered signifying exponents of a larger cosmic pattern rather than creatures conceived as a purely biological species (Sterckx 241), a contrast to mainstream Western philosophy (Cheng, "On the Environmental Ethics"; *New Dimensions*). One of the most important and enduring ideas in traditional Chinese philosophy is the notion of *ren tian he yi* (humans and heaven as one, or humans and nature as one). Human and animal worlds lie in a continuum, with no firm or essential divisions between the two. It is believed that the human world and the natural world are interconnected in that they accord with the same normative patterns of the universe (Tu).

It follows that in the Chinese mapping of the universe, mountains, rivers, and animals as well as humans are legitimate beings in this great cosmos and great transformation (Tu 73). Humans are organically connected with rocks, trees, and animals. Human life is only part of a continuous flow of the vital energy that constitutes the cosmic process. In Chinese popular and elite culture, the notion of humans forming one body with the universe is widely accepted. So is the notion of the transformation between animals and humans. Rocks, trees, animals, humans, and gods represent different levels of spirituality based on varying compositions of vital energy (Tu). They are differentiated but organically connected, integral parts of a continuous process of cosmic transformation, and humans are considered the most sentient beings of all (Tu 75). The uniqueness of humans lies in our consciousness of being human (Tu 76).

In addition, classical Chinese philosophy recognizes that because the physical and psychic aspects of existence of beings are construed as a continuum, consequently, all beings have varying degrees of sensitivity or awareness (Hall and Ames 189). Everything in the classical Chinese world is considered to be "alive" or even aware in some degree, and the animate/inanimate distinction is absent (Hall and Ames 188). This is true for both Confucianism (and neo-Confucianism) and Daoism. The Confucianists find *li* or rationality in all things. With Daoists, *dao* (*tao*) or "the way"—that is, the concrete, universal creative and transformative power of the universe—can be found in anything and everything, including both humans and nonhumans. If nothing in the world is without value or without an inner reason for existence, then one could interpret this to mean that both humans and nonhumans have their own existential value—that is, intrinsic values of their own. However, at the same time, animals are assumed to have value and be worthy of interest relative to humans and others, and they are resources or serviceable for human needs and enterprises (Blakeley 139).

By and large, in traditional Chinese thought, animals hold normative standing. Literally everything under the sun and beyond has a place or role in the ongoing process of nature, and both humans and animals are part

of the productivity, richness, diversity, and beauty that are central features of this Chinese conception of Heaven and Earth (Blakeley 153). Nevertheless, the instrumental view and the use of animals have always prevailed in Chinese culture and on the Chinese landscape (Cao).

Related articles: Animals in Chinese culture; The complexity of animal awareness; Legal protection of animals in China; Moral anthropocentrism

Blakeley, Donald N., "Listening to the Animals: The Confucian View of Animal Welfare," *Journal of Chinese Philosophy* 30.2 (2003): 137–157.

Cao, Deborah, "Visibility and Invisibility of Animals in Traditional Chinese Philosophy and Law," *International Journal for the Semiotics of Law* 24.3 (2011).

Cheng, Chung-ying, "On the Environmental Ethics of the Tao and the Ch'i," *Environmental Ethics* 8.4 (1986): 351–370.

——, *New Dimensions of Confucian and Neo-Confucian Philosophy*, State University of New York Press, 1991.

Hall, David L., and Ames, Roger T., *Anticipating China: Thinking through the Narratives of Chinese and Western Culture*, State University of New York Press, 1995.

Sterckx, Roel, *The Animal and the Daemon in Early China*, State University of New York Press, 2002.

Tu, Weiming, "The Continuity of Being: Chinese Visions of Nature," in Callicott, J. B., and Ames, Roger T. (eds.), *Nature in Asian Traditions of Thought: Essays in Environmental Philosophy*, State University of New York Press, 1989, 67–78.

DEBORAH CAO

HINDUISM AND ANIMALS

The Hindu religion, the product of five thousand years of socioreligious development, has no founder. It is the reflection of a cultural ethos that is closely associated with the ethnic traditions spawned by the distinct cultural life of India. It possesses an ancient literature that is eminently religious and reflects a philosophic tradition that exemplifies its perceptions of all existence. The foundational scriptures are the Vedas, followed by a litany of other works that reflect Hindu theological and, above all, religio-philosophical conceptions on God and life in its many forms.

Ancient Hindu cosmology, like the cosmology of the ancient Greeks, posited air, water, fire, earth, and ether as the primordial elements out of which the rich biodiversity of the world is composed. Cosmic forces arise from the infinite. The spiritual principle called Brahman-Atman is the ground of the universe of animate and inanimate things, including humans, animals, and plants. One eternal element, called Akasha, closely akin to the ether of modern science, combines with Prana, or primal energy. The combination and recombination of Prana and Akasha form the external elements in an endless cyclical process without a known first beginning.

Just as there is natural law in cosmic order, so is there moral governance in human affairs. Nature reveals at all times the dichotomy of justice and injustice. The occurrence of mixed fortunes is traced to causes in this life and previous ones. The law of karma, with its corollary—reincarnation—matches consequences to deeds. The criteria determining reward and punishment depend on intent or motive. Since animals act subconsciously, they are exempt from the law. In the Hindu worldview there is progression from one form of life to another. Because dharma denotes the law of moral responsibility, the Hindu ethical ideal is not to despoil the natural environment. All life is sacred because it is the manifestation of the divine.

The Hindu relationship with animals began with the holistic view of life adopted in the Vedas. There are therefore numerous references to plants and animals in almost all of Hindu literature. Archaeo-zoological studies show that India has been home to a vast array of free-living animals for thousands of years. The domestication of many of them began with the horse, followed by the elephant. Silhouetted representations of animals on seals have been found in the Indus Valley. What best typifies the Hindu view of animals is the status accorded them. An avatar is God incarnate in human form. Rama and Krishna are to Hinduism what Jesus is to Christianity or Buddha is to Buddhism, and although Hindu tradition recognizes numerous beings, both real and mythological, the conception of God in human form is, strictly speaking, reserved for such beings as Rama, Krishna, Buddha, and Jesus. However, the concept of avatar in Hindu mythology extends to animals as well—hence, the descent of God in the form of Matsya the fish, Varaha the boar, Kurma the tortoise, and Narasimha the man-lion. Such birds as the eagle and the peacock are also accorded the status of sacredness. So are elephants, bulls, tigers, snakes, and deer. The ever-popular Ramayana, which tells the story of Rama and his consort Sita, mentions several animals, who form an important part of the epic. Numerous too are the animals mentioned in a series of works called the Puranas. Much of Hindu religious literature is replete with references to animals, many of them holding speaking parts in the dialogues. This would not have been possible if there was no love of animals or consideration of them as very much a part of creation. Hence, the speaking parts given to them indicate a love for animals and thereby accord them a status very close to that of humans.

The concept of ahimsa, or non-killing, also known as nonviolence, is found in the Bhagavad Gita, one of several Hindu scriptures. It is well known that, of all the religions of the world, it is Hinduism (together with Jainism and Buddhism, which have stemmed from it) that lays the greatest emphasis on nonviolence. However, of the three religions that had their birth in India, it is Jainism more than the others that adhered to the principle of nonviolence to its ultimate, logical conclusion. The most natural extension of this principle is found in the concept of vegetarianism. Vegetarianism is essentially a Jain ethical principle that found a natural home in both Hinduism and Buddhism. Most Hindus, however, approximate to the ideal. It is impossible to say what percentage of Hindus are vegetarians. Many compromise the stand on vegetarianism by confining the practice to specific days of the week and special religious occasions. Although several scriptures raise the status of animals in the social hierarchy, Hinduism recognizes that no animal seeks knowledge of any kind, including the spiritual objective humans aspire to. Jainism extends the principle of nonviolence, or non-killing, to all of creation, including animals—even insects. The bird hospital in New Delhi is a Jain institution. Hinduism says that if God is all, all is sacred. And no injury should be caused to any of God's creation. Total nonviolence is the ideal, and it is the endeavor of Hindus, Jains, and Buddhists to approximate to this.

The best known proponent of nonviolence is Mahatma Gandhi, who extended the application of the principle of ahimsa from the individual to the nation. Other teachers of great prominence within the Hindu community, such as Ramana Maharishi, emphasized the principle of reverence for all creatures. Of all the religious institutions found within the Hindu tradition, it is the International Society for Krishna Consciousness (ISKCON), better known as the Hare Krishna movement, that makes the care and love of animals a cardinal principle. Its cow protection program is now well known. The killing of animals, it says, violates karmic laws, creating collective and individual reactions in human society.

Related articles: Animal-friendly spirituality; Animals in Jainism; Buddhist attitudes; The Buddhist case for vegetarianism; Ethical vegetarianism; Perceptions of elephants; Sanctuaries and rehabilitation; The treatment of animals in India; The welfare of cows

Morgan, Kenneth, W., *The Religion of the Hindus*, Ronald Press, 1953.
Naidoo, Thillayvel, *Long Walk to Enlightenment*, RoseDog Books, 2010.
Prabhavananda, Swami, *Spiritual Heritage of India*, Sri Ramakrishna Math, 1977.

Prabhupada, Swami, *Krsna*, Bhaktivedanta Book Trust, 1986.
———, *Srimad Bhagavatam*, Bhaktivedanta Book Trust, 1973.
Radhakrishnan, S., *Radhakrishnan Reader—An Anthology*, Bharatiya Vidya Bhavan, 1969.
Vivekananda, Swami, *Complete Works, Volume I*, Advaita Ashrama, 1960.

THILLAYVEL NAIDOO

ISLAM AND ANIMALS

In current English usage, a Muslim is an adherent of Islam, the religion founded by Muhammad, who was active in Mecca and Medina between 610 and 632 C.E. and who claimed that he received divine revelations known as the Qur'an. However, in Arabic the word Islam means "submission" or "surrender," and the term Muslim denotes a person who has surrendered himself or herself to God by entering into his peace. The Qur'an teaches that the prophets who preceded Muhammad, including Noah, Abraham, Moses, and Jesus, were all Muslims and that Islam is the primordial religion of humankind. In keeping with this, Muhammad said that all human beings are born Muslims and that it is their parents who turn them into Jews, Christians, or Zoroastrians. Then, in order to drive the message home, he likened the parents' action to the mutilation of animals who are born whole—"for have you ever seen one born with its ears clipped?" This article draws principally on the Qur'an and to a lesser extent on the sayings of Muhammad, the so-called hadiths. The reader should bear in mind, however, that there is a good deal of regional and sectarian variation in Islamic belief and practice.

According to the Qur'an, there is only one God, the sole Creator (Q 2:29) who has created every living thing (Q 21:30). He has, however, submitted the creation to humankind (Q 45:13). Hence, humans use animals and animal products for food, transport, clothing, and adornment and take aesthetic pleasure in them (Q 16:5–8). Nevertheless, the various species of animals resemble human beings in so far as they have their own languages (Q 27:16–18) and form communities that will be gathered at the resurrection (Q 6:38). Islam therefore forbids needless destruction of even the lowliest of God's creatures. There is a hadith in which Muhammad relates how God chided an earlier prophet for destroying a colony of ants: "Just because you were bitten by a single ant, you have destroyed a whole community who sing my praise!" Other hadiths mention Muhammad's kindness to a cat and his condemnation of people who were cruel to dogs and birds. He also instructed his followers to kill "pests"

with as few blows as possible and to use a sharp blade when slaughtering animals for food.

The Qur'an summons us to recognize that the universe contains a whole host of signs that point to the Creator's beneficence and power. Correctly interpreted, these signs should evoke our gratitude and result in its expression through worship of him alone and right conduct. They should also lead us to believe in his ability to resurrect us to face the judgment. This is the context of many of the Qur'an's references to animals. For example, it urges us to reflect on the Creator's beneficence in feeding us with milk from the herds and in creating the bee whose honey has curative properties (Q 16:66–69). Similarly, it invites those who doubt that he has the power to re-create them on the Day of Resurrection to contemplate the marvels of his first creation, including the birds, whom he holds in flight (Q 67:19), and the camel (Q 88:17).

The Qur'an also contains a number of stories that feature animals: Salih's camel who was hamstrung by his impious people (Q 7:73–9), the raven who showed Cain how to bury his brother (Q 5:31), the wolf who Joseph's brothers alleged had eaten Joseph (Q 12:13), the heifer whom Moses's people were told to sacrifice (Q 2:67–71), the termite who gnawed through Solomon's staff (Q 34:14), the fish who saved Jonah by swallowing him and spewing him out on dry land (Q 37:139–145), and the elephant used by invaders of Mecca in the year traditionally held to be that of Muhammad's birth (Q 105:1). There are two further stories that call for comment. The Qur'anic version of the legend of the seven sleepers of Ephesus depicts their dog stretching out his paws over the threshold (Q 18:18). However, although Muslims use dogs for shepherding and hunting, they generally shrink from keeping them as domestic companions because the Prophet said that angels do not enter houses where there are dogs or pictures. The Qur'anic version of the apocryphal story of Jesus's creation of birds from clay (Q 3:49 and 5:110) marks him out as unique among human beings because God has never permitted anyone else to endow inanimate objects with life. However, the Qur'an stresses that this was something Jesus did with God's permission and is not proof of his divinity, for elsewhere it categorically denies that he was God's son.

Despite Islam's generally enlightened and humane attitude toward animals, it presents three problems for those who are concerned about animal welfare:

The Qur'an contains several apparently disparaging remarks about animals. The Sabbath breakers in ancient Israel are turned into apes (Q 7:166). The Jews who do not understand or obey the Torah are like an ass carrying books (Q 62:5). Unbelievers are like a dog who growls whether or not you attack him (Q 7:176); they are even further astray than cattle (Q 7:179). Those who are deaf to the preaching of Islam are "the worst of beasts" (Q 8:22). And so on.

The Qur'an urges believers to eat the excellent foods that God has declared licit for them and not to transgress by declaring them illicit (Q 5:87f). Therefore, because the only species of animal whose consumption the Qur'an explicitly forbids is the pig (Q 5:3), Muslims generally assume that vegetarianism is wrong.

In the early days of Islam, the number of animals sacrificed at the culmination of the annual pilgrimage rarely exceeded a few hundred. In recent years this has increased to over half a million. Most of the animals have to be imported from abroad and the meat re-exported.

These are difficult and controversial issues that merit detailed discussion. Here there is only space for a few brief reflections. It is not really animals that the Qur'an disparages, but disobedient and unbelieving human beings. Nor is it vegetarianism that it criticizes, but rather the human-created dietary prohibitions of Jewish rabbis and Christian ascetics. Thus, although Islam rejects doctrinaire vegetarianism, individuals are in principle free to choose to avoid meat. Before the advent of factory farming and commercial abattoirs, religious slaughter solemnized the taking of animal life. Now that the majority of Muslims neither rear nor slaughter the animals whose meat they consume, that safeguard is no longer present. In the case of the annual sacrifices, because of the logistic problems caused by the increase in numbers, very few pilgrims even see the victims they have paid for or distribute the meat to the poor in person. These radically changed circumstances raise the question of whether these Islamic institutions still fulfill their original intentions.

Related articles: Animal-friendly spirituality; Animal sacrifice; Animal welfare and farming; Animals in the Middle East; Ethical vegetarianism; Judaism and animal life; Live animal exports; The protection of birds; Religious slaughter; Slaughter

Masri, Al-Hafiz Basheer Ahmad, *Animal Welfare in Islam*, Islamic Foundation (Leicester), 2009.

Rafeeque, Ahmed, *Islam and Vegetarianism*, published privately, available for order at http://www.viva.org.uk/vivashop/productlist.php?category=27.

Robinson, Neal, *Discovering the Qur'an: A Contemporary Approach to a Veiled Text*, 2nd ed., Canterbury-SCM Press/Georgetown University Press, 2003.

———, *Islam: A Concise Introduction*, Georgetown University Press, 2000.

———, *The Sayings of Muhammad*, selected and translated from the Arabic, Eco Press, 1998.

Schimmel, Annemarie, *Islam and the Wonders of Creation: The Animal Kingdom*, al-Furqan, 2003.

NEAL ROBINSON

JUDAISM AND ANIMAL LIFE

The first volume of the *Encyclopedia Judaica*, under "Animals, Cruelty to," provides a summary of the moral and legal Jewish rules regarding the animal world: "Moral and legal rules concerning the treatment of animals are based on the principle that animals are part of God's creation toward which man bears responsibility. Laws and other indications in the Pentateuch make it clear not only that cruelty to animals is forbidden, but also that compassion and mercy to them are demanded of man by God" (Roth 6).

Although Genesis 1:27 seemingly awards superiority to humans in the statement that we are "made in God's image," as Elijah Schochet points out in his monumental book, *Animal Life in Jewish Tradition*, that superiority is "in image," but not "in substance." Both humans and animals are created from the earth and are subject to the same fallibilities of the natural process. Both have soul (*nefesh chaya*) breathed into them, and both, as Schochet points out, "possess the divine quality of life" (10).

Moreover, the covenantal statements specifically include animals and reflect the centrality of animals within the divine plan. It is worth recalling the precise formulation in Genesis: "'As for me,' says the Lord, 'I will establish my Covenant with you and with your seed after you, and with every living creature that is with you, the fowl, the cattle, and every beast of the earth with you; all that go out of the ark, even every beast of the earth'" (Genesis 9:9–10). And also in Hosea: "And in that day I will make a covenant for them with the beasts of the field and with the fowls of the heaven, and with the creeping creatures of the ground. And I will break the bow and the sword and the battle out of the land and I will make them to lie down safely" (Hosea 2:20).

Biblical people felt a kinship with animals that is wonderfully reflected in the endearing story wherein the prophet Nathan chastises King David for his adulterous affair with Bathsheba (Samuel 11:12). Nathan compares David's theft of Bathsheba to the theft of a little ewe lamb who had been brought up in the bosom of a poor person's family "and grew up together with his children, ate of his own morsel, and drank of his own cup and lay in his bosom and was unto him as a daughter."

Evidence of an underlying sense of a kinship or bond between animals and humans is documented by Noah Cohen in his work *Tsa'ar Ba'ali Hayim: The Prevention of Cruelty to Animals*. He writes that "the Hebrew sages considered the wall of partition between man and beasts as rather thin." Specifically, he maintains that "the Jew was forever to remember that the beast reflects similar affections and passions as himself ... Consequently he was admonished to seek its welfare and its comfort as an integral part of his daily routine and instructed that the more he considers its well-being and comfort, the more would he be exalted in the eyes of his maker" (1).

Animals were used and sacrificed during biblical times, as was then common throughout the ancient world, but a strong legal system evolved in Judaism that attempted to protect the animals' comfort and welfare and to minimize the harm that would be done to animals in people's use of them. This principle came to be known as *tsa'ar ba'alei chayim*: "you may not cause sorrow to living creatures." It comprised such injunctions as "you may not muzzle the ox when he treads out the grain in the field" (Deuteronomy 25:4). The point of the prescription was to allow the ox to satisfy his appetite as he worked—with the implication that he was not there only to satisfy human need. Again the command that "you may not yoke an ox and an ass together" (Deuteronomy 22:10) was designed to protect the weaker animal, who would otherwise be hurt by the pulling strength of the stronger animal. These are only two of the many positive prescriptions found in the Hebrew Bible. Their meaning is best summed up in the verse in Proverbs 12:10—"the righteous person regards the soul of his animal."

Related articles: Animal-friendly spirituality; Animal sacrifice; Animals in the Bible

Bleich, J. David, "Judaism and Animal Experimentation," in Regan, Tom (ed.), *Animal Sacrifices: Religious Perspectives on the Use of Animals in Science*, Temple University Press, 1986, 61–114.
Cohen, Noah, *Tsa'ar Ba'ali Hayim: The Prevention of Cruelty to Animals—Its Bases, Development and Legislation in Hebrew Literature*, Feldheim, 1976.
Kalechofsky, Roberta (ed.), *Animal Suffering and the Holocaust: The Problem with Comparisons*, Micah, 2003.
——, *Haggadah for the Liberated Lamb: A Haggadah for a Vegetarian Seder*, Micah, 1988.
——, *Judaism and Animal Rights: Classical and Contemporary Responses*, Micah, 1992.
—— (ed.), *Rabbis and Vegetarianism: An Evolving Tradition*, Micah, 1995, reprinted 2002.
——, *Vegetarian Judaism—A Guide for Everyone*, Micah, 1998, reprinted 2006.
Roth, Cecil (ed.), "Animals, Cruelty To," *Encyclopedia Judaica*, Keter, 1976.
Schochet, Elijah Judah, *Animal Life in Jewish Tradition: Attitudes and Relationships*, Ktav, 1984.

ROBERTA KALECHOFSKY

CHANGING SCIENTIFIC ATTITUDES

ANIMAL AGRICULTURE AND CLIMATE CHANGE

The sixth mass extinction

Evidence from the fossil record demonstrates five mass extinctions in which over 50 percent of animal species died within the past 540 million years. Prior to this time animals with hard body parts—and hence, significant fossilization—had not evolved.

Four of these extinctions corresponded to global temperature peaks (Mayhew, Jenkins, and Benton). Contemporary climate change now poses the greatest threat to most animal species since the last mass extinction, some 65 million years ago. Since 1970, the earth's average surface temperature has increased by 0.6 degrees Celsius, and the Intergovernmental Panel on Climate Change projects temperature rises of up to 6 degrees Celsius this coming century. Although partially caused by habitat destruction and other human activity, the current rate of animal extinctions has rapidly risen to at least one hundred times the background rate typical of Earth's long-term history. Less conservative estimates place the rate far higher.

Nonhuman animals will not be the only ones severely affected in coming years. Expected melting of the Greenland and West Antarctic ice sheets, combined with thermal expansion of the oceans, could raise sea levels by up to six feet. Rises of half this level would devastate the rice-growing river deltas and floodplains of Asia, on which hundreds of millions of people depend for food.

Similarly, the Himalayan and Tibetan glaciers that sustain the major rivers of India and China during the dry season—and thus also sustain the grain irrigation systems that depend on the rivers—are rapidly melting. The vast populations dependent on these glaciers make this melting the greatest threat to food security ever faced by humanity. Crop-destroying climatic events such as droughts and floods are now increasing in frequency, with subsequent rises in global food prices, hunger, and malnutrition.

Impacts of animal agriculture

In 2006, the United Nations Food and Agriculture Organization (Steinfeld et al.) calculated that when measured as carbon dioxide (CO_2) equivalents (CO_2e), 18 percent of worldwide greenhouse gases (GHGs)—totaling 7.5 billion tons annually—result from the production of cattle, buffalo, sheep, goats, camels, horses, pigs, and poultry. These emissions result from land-clearing for feed crop production and grazing, from the animals themselves, and from the transportation and processing of animal products. In contrast, all forms of transportation combined were estimated to produce around 13.5 percent of global GHGs.

The GHGs produced by animal production are composed of CO_2, methane, nitrous oxide, and ammonia. Steinfeld and colleagues calculated that the livestock sector is responsible for 9 percent of anthropogenic CO_2 emissions—that is, those attributable to human activity—which mostly arise from deforestation caused by the encroachment of feed crops and pastures. Animal production occupies some 30 percent of the Earth's land surface and is increasingly driving deforestation, particularly in Latin America. Seventy percent of previously forested Amazonian land has now been converted to pastures, with feed crops covering a large part of the remainder.

Animals kept for production emit 37 percent of anthropogenic methane—which has been calculated as exerting seventy-two times the global warming potential (GWP) of CO_2 over a twenty-year time frame, mostly from gastrointestinal fermentation by ruminants (particularly, cows and sheep). They also emit 65 percent of anthropogenic nitrous oxide—with 296 times the GWP of CO_2, the great majority of which is released from manure. Finally, they emit 64 percent of anthropogenic ammonia, which contributes significantly to acid rain and ecosystem acidification.

However, in 2009 Goodland and Anhang calculated that at least 22 billion tons of CO_2e attributable to animal production were not counted, and at least 3 billion tons were misallocated, by Steinfeld and colleagues. Uncounted sources included livestock respiration, deforestation, and methane underestimates. They concluded that animal production actually accounts for at least 51

percent of worldwide GHGs, and probably significantly more. Although the precise figures remain under study, it is nevertheless clear that the GHGs resulting from animal production are one of the largest contributors to modern climate change.

Reducing impacts

Strategies to reduce methane emissions from ruminants through dietary management, to reduce nitrous oxide emissions through manure management, and to decrease deforestation and encourage carbon sequestration through improved pastoral management are all important in combating climate change. However, marked population increases and attempts by increasingly affluent developing-world consumers to adopt the lifestyles of richer countries are jointly expected to double global meat and dairy consumption by 2050. Hence, the elementary conclusion noted by Steinfeld and colleagues is that "the environmental impact per unit of livestock production must be cut by half, just to avoid increasing the level of damage beyond its present level." Yet climate scientists believe significant reductions in present GHG levels are actually necessary to offer realistic hope of avoiding catastrophic climate change, rather than simple maintenance of the status quo.

Hence, mitigation of emissions resulting from existing patterns of consumption will be far from sufficient. Considerable changes in consumption patterns are also required. As concluded by Goodland and Anhang as well as Stehfest and colleagues, replacing animal products with alternatives is the best strategy for reversing, or even slowing, climate change. This would have far more rapid effects on GHG emissions than the replacement of fossil fuels by renewable energy sources. Decreasing animal production would bring the most immediate benefits for the lowest cost and would not require substantial development of new technologies. As Stehfest and colleagues observed, a diet low in animal products would also provide profound benefits for public health, public finances, and global land availability. The solution to our problems could hardly be simpler; it is the wisdom required to implement it that appears beyond our collective reach.

Related articles: Animals in Asia; Animals in Chinese culture; Birds used in food production; Ethical vegetarianism; Horses; Live animal exports; Slaughter; South American perspectives on animals; The treatment of animals in India; The welfare of cows; The welfare of pigs; The welfare of sheep

Brown, L. R., *Plan B 4.0: Mobilising to Save Civilisation*, Norton, 2009.

Goodland, R., and Anhang, J., "Livestock and Climate Change," *World Watch* (November–December 2009): 10–19, available at http://www.worldwatch.org/files/pdf/Livestock%20 and%20Climate%20Change.pdf.

Knight, A., "Livestock Casts Long Shadow over Climate Debate," *Veterinary Times* [U.K.] 40.18 (2010): 17, 20, available at http://www.andrewknight.info/publications/vegetarianism/ climate_change.html.

———, "Livestock and Climate Change," *Veterinary Times* [U.K.] 40.23 (2010): 26, 28–29, available at http://www. andrewknight.info/publications/vegetarianism/climate_ change.html.

Mayhew, P. J., Jenkins, G. B., and Benton, T. G., "A Long-Term Association between Global Temperature and Biodiversity, Origination and Extinction in the Fossil Record," *Proceedings of the Royal Society B: Biological Sciences* 275.1630 (2008): 47–53, available at http://rspb.royalsocietypublishing.org/content/275/1630/47.full.

Stehfest, E., Bouwman, L., van Vuuren, D. P., den Elzen, M. G. J., Eickhout, B., and Kabat, P., "Climate Benefits of Changing Diet," *Climatic Change* 95 (2009): 83–102.

Steinfeld, H., Gerber, P., Wassenaar, T., Castel, V., Rosales, M., and de Haan, C., *Livestock's Long Shadow: Environmental Issues and Options*, Food and Agriculture Organisation of the United Nations, 2006, available at http://www.fao.org/ docrep/010/a0701e/a0701e00.HTM.

ANDREW KNIGHT

ANIMAL PAIN

David Hume (1711–1776), arguably the greatest skeptic in modern philosophy, affirmed, despite his skepticism, "No truth appears to me more evident, than that beasts are endowed with thought and reason, as well as men. The arguments . . . are so obvious, that they never escape the most stupid and ignorant." That animals feel pleasure and pain would, for Hume, be an even more obvious conclusion. Nonetheless, the obviousness of animal pain clearly escaped René Descartes (1596–1650), who asserted that animals, lacking language, are just sophisticated pieces of machinery, exhibiting pain behavior but feeling nothing. This ideology was embraced in France and elsewhere in Europe and served to remove moral compunctions about animal experiments involving pain—for example, literal vivisection ("cutting alive") experiments undertaken by Cartesians.

would be reasonable to believe that such an implau-
losophy would have been forever laid to rest by
f Darwinism. After all, Charles Darwin him-
evolutionary continuity from animals
of morphological and physiological
logical ones, a position elegantly

elaborated in a number of his works as well as books by his student and secretary George Romanes. Unfortunately, a new ideology was developed in the early twentieth century that again served to deny the reality of felt pain in animals.

This ideology, which served to banish untestable concepts, demanded an empirical correlate for every meaningful concept used in science. In addition to eliminating legitimately suspect concepts, such as "life force" and "absolute space," the philosophy that pressed verifiability denied the relevance to science of ethical and other value judgments and, in the psychological realm, dismissed talk of subjective experiences such as pain as illegitimate, to be replaced in British and American psychology by behaviorism, which allowed only descriptions of learned behavior. Even among European ethologists who stressed the evolution of behavior as opposed to learning, thought and feeling were denied a place in science.

A major victim of this ideology was the notion of felt pain in animals. No doubt, this denial, as in Descartes's time, served to assuage the consciences of those engaged in invasive animal research. But its primary role was preserving alleged scientific objectivity. When scientists talked of pain in animals, they totally ignored any subjective dimension of feeling and dealt only with the neurological and chemical substratum, the "plumbing" of pain.

Animal anesthesia was known as "chemical restraint" throughout most of the twentieth century, and the first textbook on veterinary anesthesia, published in the United States in the middle of the 1970s, does not list control of felt pain as a reason for anesthetic use. ("Legitimate" reasons were to keep the animal still, to avoid injury to scientists and veterinarians, and so on.) Anyone doing a literature search on animal analgesia in the late 1970s would have found literally no journal articles on the topic, and such theoretical lack of concern was replicated in laboratories and in veterinary practice. And despite the fact that literally all human analgesics were tested on animals in the United States, the official story was that no knowledge of analgesia in animals existed, since one could not even know "scientifically" that animals felt pain.

Many arguments in favor of the claim that animals felt pain were marshaled in an attempt to circumvent the foregoing ideology. These included citing physiological, neurological, and behavioral analogues between animals and humans in the area of pain; pointing out that if animals did not feel pain, they could not be deployed as research "models" for human pain; reminding researchers that animals learn by positive and negative reinforcement; affirming that humans who cannot feel pain do not survive; and calling attention to the fact that anesthetics and analgesics work in animals as they do in humans. Although the research community did not refute these arguments, it continued to ignore felt pain in animals in accordance with its ideology.

In the end, it was public awareness in the United States, Britain, and elsewhere that animal pain was being untreated that led to legislation legally mandating the control of pain by anesthesia and analgesia in animal uses in science. The ideology that had been immune to rational argument crumbled in the face of law presupposing that animals felt pain. As researchers scurried to obey, research interest turned to animal pain for its own sake, veterinary schools made pain control a major concern, and the resulting knowledge spread to veterinary practices as well as to research laboratories. One can now find thousands of articles on animal pain, and the same U.S. veterinary anesthesia textbook that had ignored pain in the 1970s is now replete with examples of how pain control causes animals to heal faster and avoids stress that compromises research results.

Ideology, however, dies hard. The International Society for the Study of Pain, the world's largest organization of pain researchers and clinicians, until very recently maintained a definition of pain that made the possession of language a necessary condition for experiencing pain, and it resisted all efforts to have that definition revised, despite the fact that the old ideology was eroding in most quarters. Eventually, the definition included a footnote allowing the possibility of other evidence for pain.

Related articles: Animals used in research; The complexity of animal awareness; Developments in animal law; European animal protection; Moral anthropocentrism; Veterinary ethics

Darwin, C., *The Expression of the Emotions in Man and Animals*, Greenwood Press, 1969, first published 1872.

Rollin, B. E., *Animal Rights and Human Morality*, 3rd ed., Prometheus Books, 2006.

———, "Pain and Ideology in Human and Veterinary Medicine," *Seminars in Veterinary Medicine and Surgery (Small Animal)* 12.2 (May 1997): 56–60.

———, "Pain, Paradox, and Value," *Bioethics* 3 (July 1989): 211–225.

———, *Science and Ethics*, Cambridge University Press, 2006.

———, *The Unheeded Cry: Animal Consciousness, Animal Pain and Science*, Oxford University Press, 1989.

BERNARD E. ROLLIN

ANIMALS AND PUBLIC HEALTH

If we were to take a good look at the top news stories worldwide over the past ten years, we would notice an interesting trend: more and more of these stories concern animal welfare. What is perhaps even more interesting is that a significant number of these stories reveal just how intricately connected the welfare of nonhuman animals is to public health. Consider the following examples.

In 2003, avian influenza (H5N1) spread swiftly across poultry farms in Asia and jumped the species barrier to infect humans, causing alarm to be raised about the potential for the next pandemic to originate from animal farms. When in 2009 swine flu (H1N1)—although relatively mild—swept across the globe, it was confirmed that animal agriculture can play a significant role in the emergence of new strains of flu viruses. Animals raised for food are now ubiquitously crammed into intensive animal operations, or "factory farms", living in profoundly filthy and cruel conditions. Their resultant reduced immunity, resulting from prolonged stress and high crowding, creates perfect breeding grounds for new, deadlier diseases.

In 2005, Hurricane Katrina's onslaught against the Louisiana coast forced many animal caregivers to make a life-threatening choice: evacuate their homes, abandoning their companion animals (who were not welcome in rescue shelters) to the rising tides, or risk death themselves. As a result, many refused to evacuate. This was a wake-up call for public health and rescue agencies throughout the world to take the human-animal bond seriously and incorporate animal rescue into their emergency plans.

In 2009, Bolivia made international precedent by becoming the first country to ban the use of nonhuman animals in circuses. Although the focus of the ban was the immense cruelty toward animals involved when they are forced to perform and kept in captivity, humans also benefit from the ban. As demonstrated by the numerous reports of humans being maimed or killed by nondomesticated animals used for "entertainment," including circuses, marine "amusement parks," private collections, and zoos, such forms of entertainment pose significant danger to the public.

Almost every issue that concerns the welfare of nonhuman animals has a public health implication. Here are some additional examples:

Medical studies demonstrate positive effects of the human-animal bond, including how healthy companion animals help lower blood pressure and cardiovascular disease risk, improve our mental and physical health, help us combat grief, and assist autistic children in socialization. By treating our companion animals well, we also help ourselves.

Up to two-thirds of those who commit cruelty against other animals also commit at least one other criminal offense, including violence toward other humans, particularly women and children.

Our unprecedented worldwide demand for meat, eggs, and dairy products is proving to be hazardous—both to other animals and to us. In the United States alone, over nine billion land animals are slaughtered annually for meat—that is about one million animals per hour—and world meat production is expected to double by 2020. With this demand comes intensification of animal agriculture and the suffering of more animals than ever seen before in human history. And our meat addiction is literally killing us. It is now known to be a major player in the deadly rise in obesity, chronic diseases such as heart disease and stroke, climate change, and the emergence of new infectious diseases. So the next public health step is to figure out how to kick the meat habit.

In the past few decades, the world has witnessed an alarming surge in new infectious diseases. Evidence now points to the hunting (*see* Animals in Sport and Entertainment) and trading of nondomesticated or "exotic" animals for meat, fur, skins, "pets," "entertainment," biomedical research, and traditional medicines as a key factor in the emergence of some of the most profound infectious diseases we have so far encountered. In addition to causing tremendous torment and misery in animals, HIV/AIDs, Ebola, severe acute respiratory syndrome (SARS), and monkey pox, to name a few, can also be blamed on this trade.

Every year, millions of animals are experimented on and killed in the name of science or human health. However, evidence is mounting that non-animal testing methods are more accurate and better at predicting human outcomes. In 2007, a landmark report by the National Research Council in the United States largely called for the replacement of animal experiments in toxicity testing with cheaper, more efficient, and far more accurate human in vitro testing methods. The public health impact of transforming the toxicology field as envisioned by this report is tremendous. This is just one example of how replacement of animal experiments with other testing methods is a public health boon, not only because more sophisticated testing methods will better collective health, but also because the saved can be redirected toward tackling health priority.

treatment of nonhuman animals and human health and dis-

ease, animal welfare issues have been notoriously absent from the public health dialogue. Discussions concerning other animals in medicine and public health have usually revolved around their potential to pass infections to humans or cause human injuries. However, there has been almost no discourse about the fact that *the way in which we treat* other animals is often central to how and why humans are injured or catch infections from other animals and to a number of other public health concerns.

This is starting to change. With reports such as those from the National Research Council exploring alternatives to animal experiments and the Pew Charitable Trust detailing animal agriculture's impact on climate change, public health and medical professionals are starting to take notice. The time is now for a new paradigm in public health and medicine—one that encompasses both human and nonhuman animal welfare and health. Under this new paradigm, a radical shift of perspective will occur, so that the welfare of other animals will be seen not as separate from but as integral to the welfare of humans.

Related articles: The alternatives; Animal agriculture and climate change; Animal and human violence; Animal welfare and farming; Animals in circuses; Animals used in research; Disaster planning; The ethics of zoos; The fur trade; Humane research; Live animal exports; Meatout; Shelters and sanctuaries; Slaughter; Stem cell research; Toxicity testing; The trade in primates for research; The trade in reptiles

Akhtar, A., *Animals and Public Health: Why Treating Animals Better Is Critical to Human Welfare*, Palgrave Macmillan, 2012.
———, "Flu Farms?," *Science Progress*, April 29, 2009, available at http://www.scienceprogress.org/2009/04/flu-farms/.
Akhtar, A., Greger, M., Ferdowsian, H., and Frank, E., "Health Professionals' Role in Animal Agriculture, Climate Change, and Human Health," *American Journal of Preventive Medicine* 36 (2009): 182–187.
Arluke, A., and Luke, C., "Physical Cruelty towards Animals in Massachusetts, 1975–1996," *Society and Animals* 5 (1997): 195–204.
Greger, M., "The Human/Animal Interface: Emergence and Resurgence of Zoonotic Infectious Diseases," *Critical Reviews in Microbiology* 33 (2007): 243–299.
National Research Council, *Toxicity Testing in the 21st Century: A Vision and a Strategy*, National Academy Press, 2007, available at http://www.nas.edu.
The Pew Charitable Trusts and Johns Hopkins Bloomberg School of Public Health, "Putting Meat on the Table: Industrial Farm Animal Production in America," Pew Commission on Industrial Farm Animal Production, 2008, available at http://www.ncifap.org/.

AYSHA AKHTAR

THE COMPLEXITY OF ANIMAL AWARENESS

Do animals suffer? Do animals know who they are? Do animals enjoy a good belly rub? Do animals think about what they will do next? Intuitively, you would likely answer, "Yes, of course animals feel and think." Spend one day with a dog or watch a squirrel interact with another squirrel, and you would be hard-pressed to deny them these basic capacities.

But deny them we have. Our use of nonhuman animals for experimentation and for other purposes that compromise their welfare is in need of justification. Often enough, that justification has come from scientists who have argued that nonhuman animals lack sentience or cognitive sophistication. By concluding that animals do not have the ability to sense or think in the way humans do, these arguments have provided what was needed, for many, to deny other animals any moral relevance. Together, these positions have prevailed over our commonsense view toward nonhuman animals.

Our commonsense view is now returning to favor, and it is science, ironically, that is providing the impetus. Behavioral, psychological and neurological studies are revealing what we already knew: not only are nonhuman animals indeed sentient, but they also experience a wide range of emotional and cognitive capacities previously attributed only to humans.

For instance, it appears that rhesus monkeys know how to play dumb. When given tests in front of dominant rhesus monkeys, subordinate monkeys performed poorly (Drea and Wallen). But when given those same tests apart from higher-ranking conspecifics, the subordinate monkeys performed well. Just as humans might choose to hide their intelligence in response to social pressure, it is theorized that subordinate monkeys chose to hide what they knew in front of dominant animals, perhaps to avoid any social repercussions. Captive beavers alter their dam-building behaviors to build dams around a pole in order to reach food that is placed on the top of the pole (Griffin 101). Jaybirds deceive other birds, employing deceptive tactics to hide food when they know that other birds are watching them (Clayton).

In a widely publicized study, researchers injected painful irritants into mice and then watched them writhe in pain (Langford). When other mice witnessed this, they showed heightened sensitivity to pain themselves. In other words, the observer mice reacted to the pain being experienced by other mice, but mostly only to the pain of mice they knew. This demonstrated that their response was more than simply an automatic fear reaction and that it was a form of empathy (which was apparently lacking in the researchers). Rub a rat's belly, and he will

emit an ultrasonic sound, believed to have the same neural underpinnings as human laughter (Panksepp). This raises the question: do rats laugh when tickled?

Many of the medical experiments conducted on other animals in attempts to understand human disease reveal how similar they are to us cognitively. We have intentionally caused nonhuman animals, including mice and rats, to display symptoms remarkably similar to human forms of chronic depression, posttraumatic stress disorder, schizophrenia, and dementia. If they exhibit the symptoms, then isn't it logical to surmise that these animals do indeed experience chronic depression and the like?

Each time we develop a standard by which we think only humans are capable, we prove ourselves wrong. Like humans, other animals also experience empathy, altruism, sadness, anger, loneliness, depression, pain, anxiety, joy, and pleasure. Other animals use tools, anticipate and plan for the future, deceive, add numbers, demonstrate culture, learn, and some may even possess the capacity for language. Emotionally and cognitively, humans share a wide range of capabilities with other animals. This makes evolutionary, biological, and neurological sense. The ability to think about and adapt to changing circumstances and to experience emotions such as fear and pleasure is useful for survival. Neurological and neuroimaging studies demonstrate that basic neurophysiologic mechanisms are similar across animal species, even species considered far removed from humans in the phylogenetic tree. It would be unscientific to believe that although other animals largely share the same evolutionary history and fundamental neurological underpinnings as humans, they are nevertheless inherently different from humans in their basic emotional and cognitive capabilities.

There is evolutionary and biological continuity across species. No longer can we claim that that there exists any true dichotomy between humans and other animals. Of course, this is not to say that the cognitive and emotional capabilities of nonhuman animals are exactly the same as those of humans. But as Darwin argued, the differences in our capabilities are differences in degrees, not in kind.

We cannot continue to hide behind the veil of science to justify our exploitation of other animals, particularly for medical experiments. Though nonhuman animals share many of the same neurophysiological processes and cognitive abilities as humans, these similarities do not imply that other animals make good models for human disease. Medicine now deals with the subtle nuances of physiological mechanisms in order to precisely target an intervention, such as a drug to boost or inhibit a specific cellular process. The more we study other animals, the more we learn how species and even individuals differ in these subtle mechanisms.

Science is revealing how other animals are unlike humans in *medically* relevant ways but are like us in *morally* relevant ways. Now that we are acknowledging and proving that other animals are indeed sentient beings with complex and rich emotional and cognitive lives, it is time for a changed moral view that dictates a more just approach to our treatment of nonhuman animals.

And perhaps most importantly, even when the scientific evidence for certain forms of cognitive sophistication in nonhuman animals is lacking, there is enough evidence in general to dictate that ethical concerns should trump the scientific lapses. There is substantial evidence to clearly conclude that all mammals, birds, and reptiles and some invertebrates feel pain, and evidence demonstrates that most vertebrates can suffer. With newborn infants and with severely mentally incapacitated humans, it is their ability to experience pain and to suffer and not their possession of any other cognitive capacity that guides our ethical conduct toward them. Ultimately, our ethical conduct toward other animals should be guided by the same general principle: one based on the ability to feel pain and suffer.

Related articles: The alternatives; Animal pain; Animals used in research; Moral anthropocentrism; The moral claims of animals; The moral community

Clayton, N. S., Dally, J. M., and Emery, N. J., "Social Cognition by Food-Caching Corvids: The Western Scrub-Jay as a Natural Psychologist," *Philosophical Transactions of the Royal Society B* 362 (2007): 507–511.

Drea, C. M., and Wallen, K., "Low-Status Monkeys 'Play Dumb' When Learning in Mixed Social Groups," *Proceedings of the National Academy of Sciences* 96 (1999): 12965–12969.

Griffin, D. R., *Animal Minds: Beyond Cognition to Consciousness*, University of Chicago Press, 1992.

Langford, D. J., Crager, S. E., Shehzad, Z., et al., "Social Modulation of Pain as Evidence for Empathy in Mice," *Science* 312 (2006): 1967–1970.

Panksepp, J., "Neuroevolutionary Sources of Laugher and Social Joy: Modeling Primal Human Laughter in Laboratory Rats," *Behavioural Brain Research* 182 (2007): 231–244.

AYSHA AKHTAR

HUMANE RESEARCH

The field of non-animal or replacement research emerged as a response to both ethical and scientific imperatives. Recognition of the capacity of other animals to experience pain and distress or well-being shaped a desire to end their suffering in the world's laboratories. Equally, as evidence has accrued that the results of animal experiments predict human responses only imperfectly, the need to develop more reliable and reproducible research and testing methods has grown.

Recognition of animal sentiency underpins the European Union goal to fully replace animal experiments with non-animal alternatives. Achieving this is also seen by the EU as a means of promoting scientific excellence and the safety of consumers. The route to widespread adoption of this goal began in Britain in the 1960s, when antivivisection organizations first established humane research charities funding scientists to develop non-animal methods. At the time the concept was both novel and visionary. For many years the research and toxicology communities were largely dismissive, but the approach quietly gained impetus, as well as support from a number of individual scientists—although there was targeted resistance from others who actively promoted animal experimentation.

Since 1986, European legislation has required that, where available, non-animal techniques must be used instead of experiments on animals. In the United States a similar imperative operates at the institutional level. Non-animal science is now mainstream and is widely considered—in research, toxicological, regulatory, and political circles—as an advanced approach that can overcome many of the limitations of animal experiments.

Non-animal research and testing techniques include molecular approaches (e.g., receptor studies or DNA microarrays using human tissues); use of nonsentient organisms (e.g., bacteria) where appropriate; use of human cells and tissues in vitro (i.e., in the test tube); computer modeling, analysis, and simulations; sensitive analytical technologies, including those that enable safe human volunteer studies (e.g., high-performance liquid chromatography or accelerator mass spectrometry); human postmortem tissue research; ethical studies with volunteers (such as brain imaging or genetic analysis); and population-level research.

Since 1991, the European Centre for the Validation of Alternative Methods (ECVAM) has successfully validated more than eighteen full or partial replacement tests in the safety testing arena, many of which have already gained regulatory acceptance. Satisfying regulatory authorities that a non-animal test method can substitute for an established animal assay has proved as time-consuming as the method development and validation stages. However, the need for improved relevance, precision, sensitivity, range, and reproducibility has continued to drive the initiative. Animal tests have been replaced by in vitro methods for predicting whether chemicals and drugs will penetrate the skin or cause skin irritation, severe eye irritation, skin corrosion, or light-induced irritation. The safety of injectable drugs (pyrogenicity) can now be assessed more rapidly, sensitively, and effectively using human cells in vitro, replacing many thousands of rabbits. Biological medicines such as digitalis, insulin, and several vaccines are safer and better standardized since less reliable animal tests have been replaced by colorimetric assays, high-performance liquid chromatography, and cell assays. Over the years it is likely that millions of animals have been spared by all these advances.

In fundamental medical research and drug development, a long-standing but unproven confidence in animal "models" of human conditions has been a barrier to more rapid progress. Major scientific uncertainties in the use of animals in medical research include widespread species differences (such as between mice and humans) in physiology, biochemistry, and responses to medicines. Additionally, the artificial nature of disease conditions inflicted on animals, along with their limited resemblance to the range of human disease characteristics, has curtailed the value of the animal-based results. Evidence-based systematic reviews of the concordance between animal research and subsequent clinical benefits in a range of illnesses have revealed disturbingly low success rates, averaging less than 50 percent. These analyses, revealing the need for disease models that are more relevant and reliable, provide a strong scientific impetus for developing replacement, non-animal techniques.

Studies with human volunteer patients and with human tissues avoid the problem of species differences and accurately represent target illnesses and so can significantly increase the relevance and reliability of research while also replacing experiments on animals such as primates, dogs, rodents, and rabbits. Examples include human neurological research with techniques such as magnetic resonance imaging and transcranial magnetic stimulation; molecular-level analysis of tissue donated by patients to identify genes that influence disease (e.g., asthma); and in vitro research into new drug targets using human cells. Computer simulations based on human data are enabling virtual experimentation in fields as varied as heart disease, dental treatments, pregnancy, and the efficacy of new medicines. These approaches, combined with cell- and molecular-level research, have replaced many animal experiments.

Leading scientific organizations are developing a new vision for safety testing that would massively reduce animal use: in the United States, for example, the National Research Council has recommended that chemical testing for environmental safety adopt novel techniques such as toxicogenomics, bioinformatics, systems biology, epigenetics, and computational toxicology and thus move away from whole-animal testing to methods primarily using cells and cellular components, preferably of human origin. Recent international cooperative work—particularly between the United States, Canada, the European Union, and Japan —to develop and validate non-animal methods more effectively is likely to accelerate progress.

Related articles: The alternatives; Animal pain; Animals used in research; The humane movement in Canada; Japanese attitudes toward animals; Legislation in the European Union; Primates worldwide; Stem cell research; Toxicity testing

Bekoff, M., *The Animal Manifesto: Six Reasons for Expanding Our Compassion Footprint*, New World Library, 2010.

Gordon, N., and Langley, G. (eds.), *Replacing Primates in Medical Research: An Expert Report by the Dr Hadwen Trust/FRAME/St Andrew Animal Fund*, 2008, available at http://www.frame.org.uk/dynamic_files/foa_replacingprimates.pdf.

Langley, C. K., Aziz, Q., Bountra, C., Gordon, N., Hawkins, P., Jones, A., Langley, G., Nurmikko, T., and Tracey, I., "Volunteer Studies in Pain Research—Opportunities and Challenges to Replace Animal Experiments: The Report and Recommendations of a Focus on Alternatives Workshop," *NeuroImage* 42 (2008): 467–473.

Langley, G. (ed.), *Animal Experimentation: The Consensus Changes*, Macmillan, 1989.

Langley, G., Evans, T., Holgate, S. T., and Jones, A., "Replacing Animal Experiments: Choices, Chances and Challenges," *BioEssays* 29.9 (2008): 918–926.

Wise, S. M., *Drawing the Line: Science and the Case for Animal Rights*, Perseus Books, 2002.

GILL LANGLEY

VETERINARY ETHICS

Veterinary ethics is the field of study that examines issues of right and wrong, good and bad, and justice and injustice that arise in veterinary medicine. Conceptually, much of veterinary ethics is structurally similar to human medical ethics in that the same sorts of conflicting obligations arise. After all, veterinarians, like physicians, have clear-cut moral obligations to their clients, to society, to their peers, and to themselves, some of which may conflict with each other.

What makes veterinary ethics more philosophically interesting is a fifth ethical dimension—the question of moral obligation to the patient, which, in the case of veterinary medicine, is the animal. Whereas social ethics, as codified in law, makes clear the ethical primacy of the human patient, this is not the case with animals. Legally, animals are viewed as property and may be dealt with—

and disposed of—as owners see fit, the only traditional constraint being a prohibition against sadistic, deliberate, intentional cruelty.

This lack of a clear-cut social ethic for animals often creates a dilemma for veterinarians, which has been called the "fundamental question of veterinary ethics"— do veterinary practitioners owe a primary obligation to caregivers (who pay their fees) or to the animals, who are directly in need of their care? The problem can be put more starkly: Is the veterinarian comparable to a garage mechanic, so that, if the car owner says, "The problem is too expensive to fix—dispose of the vehicle," the veterinarian is obliged to acquiesce? Or is he or she more like a pediatrician, who has a primary responsibility to the child and feels under no obligation to follow parental demands to ignore medical treatment?

The majority of veterinarians accept the pediatrician model. But unlike the pediatrician, the veterinarian cannot rely on clear social and legal norms in support. This creates major tensions for veterinarians on a regular basis. What ought a veterinarian do when an owner brings in a healthy animal for "convenience" euthanasia —for example, for a trivial reason such as that the animal no longer matches the color scheme in the home? How does a veterinarian respond to a caregiver's insistence on painful cosmetic surgery, such as ear cropping or tail docking? What about caregivers who seek to manage unruly animal behavior by declawing a cat, or devocalizing a dog? How does the responsible equine veterinarian deal with a situation where a racehorse keeper wants the veterinarian to mask the pain of injury so that the animal can continue to run (and, most likely, further injure himself)? What ought a veterinarian do about dog breed standards that perpetuate genetic diseases? How should a veterinarian specializing in farmed animals respond to factory farming situations, or to farmers who will kill an animal if the cost of remedying a treatable disease exceeds the economic value of the animal? Should veterinarians control procedural or the other pain in animals even when keepers appear unconcerned about such control?

Confronting such situations can cause a great deal of stress in veterinary practitioners and erode job satisfaction. In light of this, one might expect veterinarians to be longtime leaders in changing social ethics in the direction of animal protection and in raising the moral and legal status of animals. Such an expectation would be erroneous, however. Until very recently what was traditionally called veterinary ethics was concerned with little more than intra-professional etiquette, involving such questions as whether it is "ethical" to advertise or to send Christmas cards to clients!

The reason for the traditional eschewal of concern for genuine veterinary ethics was that veterinary medicine, like human medicine, saw itself as part of science, which in turn was grounded in an unshakable ideology affirming that science was "value-free" in general and "ethics-free" in particular, since value judgments cannot be empirically verified. (The same ideology denied the reality of felt pain in animals, and thus veterinarians ignored pain control.) This ideology has only recently begun to crumble and to be replaced by an admission that science is grounded in, and fraught with, value judgments in general and ethical judgments in particular. Only very slowly has veterinary medicine begun to realize the moral requirement for pain control.

The result is that genuine veterinary ethics is still comparatively new, with the world's first course being offered at Colorado State University as late as 1978. Since then, as society as a whole has grown increasingly concerned with animal welfare, animal rights, and creation of new legal protections for animals used in science, agriculture, entertainment, and elsewhere, veterinary medicine has slowly begun to concern itself with the study of the moral aspects of veterinary practice. Although most veterinary schools offer a number of lectures in veterinary ethics, few offer full systematic courses, and none teach ethics throughout the entire program of veterinary training. Nevertheless, given society's concern with ethics in general and with animal ethics in particular, as well as expanding student interest in animal treatment, veterinary ethics is likely to become a major topic in the future.

Related articles: Animal pain; Animal welfare and farming; Cosmetic surgery; Developments in animal law; Euthanasia; Moral anthropocentrism; The moral claims of animals; The moral community; Selective breeding

Legood, Giles, *Veterinary Ethics: An Introduction*, Continuum, 2000.
Rollin, B. E., *Animal Rights and Human Morality*, 3rd ed., Prometheus, 2006.
———, *An Introduction to Veterinary Medical Ethics*, 2nd ed., Blackwell, 2006.
———, "Updating Veterinary Medical Ethics," *JAVMA* 173.8 (October 15, 1978).
Tannenbaum, J., *Veterinary Ethics*, Williams and Wilkins, 1989.
Wilson, J., Rollin, B. E., and Garbe, J. L., *Law and Ethics of the Veterinary Profession*, Priority Press, 1988.

BERNARD E. ROLLIN

DECLARATIONS FOR ANIMALS

THE DECLARATION OF THE
RIGHTS OF CETACEANS

One of the most significant areas in which scientific discoveries are revealing unethical treatment of nonhumans is the study of cetaceans. Modern marine science has shown that whales and dolphins have sophisticated cognitive and affective abilities, possess self-awareness, manage complex social relationships, and can even use tools. The ethical implication of such findings is that cetaceans should be regarded as nonhuman persons, not as economic resources.

Accordingly, in May 2010, a select group of scholars and scientists met at the Helsinki Collegium for Advanced Studies at the University of Helsinki to consider the question of whether the scientific findings about cetaceans were sufficient for the attribution of basic moral and legal rights. The experts included Chris Butler-Stroud, Paola Cavalieri, Sudhir Chopra, Nicholas Entrup, Matti Häyry, Lori Marino, Thomas White, and Hal Whitehead (for speaker biographies and presentation abstracts, see http://www.cetaceanconservation.com.au/cetaceanrights).

The findings of the conference resulted in the following "Declaration of Rights for Cetaceans: Whales and Dolphins."

- Every individual cetacean has the right to life.
- No cetacean should be held in captivity or servitude; be subject to cruel treatment; or be removed from their natural environment.
- All cetaceans have the right to freedom of movement and residence within their natural environment.
- No cetacean is the property of any State, corporation, human group or individual.
- Cetaceans have the right to the protection of their natural environment.
- Cetaceans have the right not to be subject to the disruption of their cultures.

- The rights, freedoms and norms set forth in this Declaration should be protected under international and domestic law.
- Cetaceans are entitled to an international order in which these rights, freedoms and norms can be fully realized.
- No State, corporation, human group or individual should engage in any activity that undermines these rights, freedoms and norms.
- Nothing in this Declaration shall prevent a State from enacting stricter provisions for the protection of cetacean rights.

From philosophical and ethical perspectives, the most significant feature of the declaration is the claim that cetaceans have moral standing as individuals. This means that the death or injury of a cetacean is the moral equivalent of the death or injury of a human. This immediately suggests that most human dealings with cetaceans are ethically indefensible: the captivity of cetaceans in oceanariums and other entertainment facilities; the deliberate killing of cetaceans, whether for economic or cultural reasons; and the deaths of approximately 300,000 cetaceans as the result of bycatch.

From a legal perspective, Sudhir Chopra argues that the main issues are the scope and validity of various provisions of the original treaty that established the International Whaling Commission and the legal arguments advanced by the small group states that want to end the moratorium on commercial whaling (D'Amato and Chopra). The range of questionable behaviors toward cetaceans means that it will take a variety of solutions to ensure global protection of cetaceans, including cases before the International Court of Justice, negotiation of a new global treaty regarding the treatment of cetaceans, political and economic pressure against states that continue to harm cetaceans, political pressure by citizens against elected officials who refuse to act to protect cetaceans, legislation that outlaws harming whales and dolphins or keeping cetaceans captive, and a greater commitment by the corporations involved to operate in a more ethical fashion.

Related articles: Commercial whaling; Intelligence in whales and dolphins; Marine mammals in captivity; The moral claims of animals; Sea fishes and commercial fishing; The universal charter of the rights of other species

Cavalieri, Paola, *The Animal Question: Why Nonhuman Animals Deserve Human Rights*, Oxford University Press, 2004.

D'Amato, Anthony, and Chopra, Sudhir K., "Whales: Their Emerging Right to Life," *American Journal of International Law* 85 (1991): 21–62.

Marino, Lori, Lilienfeld, Scott O., Malamud, Randy, Nobis, Nathan, and Broglio, Ron, "Do Zoos and Aquariums Promote Attitude Change in Visitors? A Critical Evaluation of the American Zoo and Aquarium Study," *Society and Animals* 18 (2010): 126–138.

Reiss, Diana, and Marino, Lori, "Mirror Self-Recognition in the Bottlenose Dolphin: A Case of Cognitive Convergence," *Proceedings of the National Academy of Sciences* 98.10 (May 8, 2001): 5937–5942.

White, Thomas I., *In Defense of Dolphins: The New Moral Frontier*, Blackwell, 2007.

Whitehead, Hal, Rendell, Luke, Osborne, Richard W., and Würsig, Bernd, "Culture and Conservation of Non-Humans with Reference to Whales and Dolphins: Review and New Directions," *Biological Conservation* 120 (2004): 427–437.

THOMAS I. WHITE

THE UNIVERSAL CHARTER OF THE RIGHTS OF OTHER SPECIES

When we hear of an individual being deprived of his or her "basic human rights," we normally understand that the person has been wronged in a serious way. Usually the person has been unjustly deprived of something that is essential to the person's thriving and well-being. It may be education, fresh drinking water, food and shelter, or the freedom to express his or her views without fear of punishment. To be unjustly deprived of one's conscious life, to be killed, is generally regarded as the most severe form of rights violation because it deprives one of that upon which all else of value depends—namely, life itself.

Although the concept of human rights can be traced back many centuries, the 1948 United Nations Declaration of Human Rights saw the birth of a new rights era. Since that time, international conventions have been reached on the rights of children, the rights of refugees, and the rights of prisoners. However, until recently, no attempt was made to reach an agreement on, or even to promote, the idea that species other than human beings could have rights. A growing number of people believe that the members of numerous other sentient species equally qualify for—and are often in dire need of—the advocacy and protection that should follow from a recognition of their rights. The Universal Charter of the Rights of Other Species is one such document reflecting this position.

The Universal Charter shares many similarities with other rights documents. It seeks to state as clearly and unambiguously as possible what our duties to other sentient beings are. In its foreword, preamble, and nineteen articles, the charter asserts the rights of other species and calls for the reform of our relations with them in a way that reflects contemporary advances in our ethical, philosophical, and scientific understanding of animals. It also seeks to reflect a growing awareness that killing or harming other species for reasons of tradition, profit, or amusement is morally wrong.

Although the first anticruelty laws in Western society appeared in England in 1822, improvements in animal welfare have been painfully slow. Many species have suffered extinction in the twentieth century, and worldwide, billions of individual animals continue to suffer at the hands of human beings each year.

The Universal Charter and its endorsing organizations and persons believe that the time for rationalizing or excusing the harsh and unjust treatment of animals is over and that the time to state clearly our proper relations with other species has arrived. The core intuition of the charter is that animals are not "objects" or "commodities" for our use and that we are morally culpable in continuing to act against their serious welfare interests.

The charter states, without qualification, that it is wrong to kill or otherwise harm an animal for sport or amusement (*see* Animals in Sport and Entertainment), for unnecessary food (*see* Animals in Farming), or for experimentation (*see* Animals in Research). It states that industries and human activities that routinely violate the lives of other species should be prohibited. It calls for, among other things, an end to habitat destruction and harsher sanctions for those who commit crimes against other species. It further argues that each country should provide adequate funding, resources, and powers to agencies responsible for investigating cases of abuse or should establish such agencies where none exist. There should be a recognition that all sentient species have a prima facie right to live their lives free from human-caused harm. In sum, the charter seeks the legal and sociocultural enactment of its maxim: "an end to harming."

The Universal Charter aims to do the following:

- Educate the public as to the rights of other species through the distribution of the charter as a wall poster to schools and organizations and via the media.
- Formally represent the charter by way of submissions to ethics committees attached to international organizations, such as UNESCO's International Bioethics Committee.
- Act as a support for organizations and individuals working to end the abuse of the rights of other species.
- Provide a means whereby diverse organizations can be seen to speak together on the issue of our treatment of other species.
- Assist campaigns fighting against specific forms of abuse, including factory farming, whaling, and steel-jawed trapping.

Many international animal welfare and rights organizations, such as the Australian and New Zealand Federation of Animal Societies, the International Fund for Animal Welfare Australia, and Advocates for Animals, as well as prominent individuals, including His Holiness the Dalai Lama, endorse the Universal Charter of the Rights of Other Species. The charter's patron is Professor Andrew Linzey, an Oxford theologian and author of many books and articles on animals, religion, and ethics. The charter is available at http://www.kindnesstrust.com/Universal-CharterRightsOtherSpecies.pdf

---

Related articles: Animal advocacy; Animal protection in Britain; Animal welfare and farming; Animals used in research; Commercial whaling; Conservation philosophy; Developments in animal law; Ethical vegetarianism; The fur trade; Humane education; Moral anthropocentrism; The moral claims of animals; The moral community

DeGrazia, David, *Taking Animals Seriously: Mental Life and Moral Status*, Cambridge University Press, 1996.

Linzey, Andrew, *Animal Gospel: Christian Faith As if Animals Mattered*, Hodder and Stoughton, 1996.

———, *Why Animal Suffering Matters: Philosophy, Theology, and Practical Ethics*, Oxford University Press, 2009.

Midgley, Mary, *Animals and Why They Matter*, University of Georgia Press, 1983.

Pope, Lawrence, *Non-Harming in a Hard World*, Tirralirra, 2003.

Rollin, Bernard E., *The Unheeded Cry: Animal Consciousness, Animal Pain, and Science*, Oxford University Press, 1990.

Singer, Peter, *Animal Liberation: A New Ethics for Our Treatment of Animals*, Thorsons, 1983.

LAWRENCE POPE

THE UNIVERSAL DECLARATION ON ANIMAL WELFARE

The campaign for the Universal Declaration on Animal Welfare (UDAW, awaiting adoption by the United Nations) was launched in 2000 by the World Society for the Protection of Animals (WSPA) and partners. The Philippines hosted an intergovernmental conference agreeing to the principles in Manila in 2003, and in 2005 Costa Rica held a follow-up meeting with representatives from five countries. Forty-three countries from the developed and developing world have declared their interest in supporting a declaration, as has the World Organization for Animal Health (the OIE, comprising the chief veterinary officers of 169 countries). An expert meeting report from the UN Food and Agriculture Organization noted the UDAW as "a valuable guiding philosophy."

The UDAW, agreed on by governments, would recognize that animals are sentient beings, deserving respect and consideration; acknowledge that human beings share the planet with other species, in an interdependent ecosystem; note that animals should be treated in a humane manner; and establish the welfare of animals as a common objective for all states. It would cover all sentient animals, including animals used in farming (*see* Animals in Farming), companion animals (*see* Companion Animals), animals used in scientific research (*see* Animals in Research), draft animals, free-living animals (*see* Free-Living Animals), and animals in recreation (*see* Animals in Sport and Entertainment).

Such a declaration would raise the status of animals as an international issue, encourage governments to implement and improve national legislation, provide a basis for legislation where none exists, help establish animal welfare as a factor in environmental and humanitarian policy-making, and add to the pressures on industry to take animal welfare into consideration.

Apart from the moral aspects of preventing cruelty to animals and reducing their suffering, the UDAW would produce tangible benefits for animals, people, and the environment because

- good animal care reduces the risk of food poisoning and of diseases transmissible to humans;
- responsible animal management affects land use, climate change, pollution, water supplies, habitat conservation, and biodiversity for the better and should play a role in disaster preparedness and response;

- looking after animals properly improves their productivity and helps farmers to provide food for their families and their communities; and
- people's attitudes and behavior toward animals overlap with their attitudes and behavior toward each other, and the human-animal bond has important therapeutic benefits.

Related articles: Animal agriculture and climate change; Animal and human violence; Animals and public health; Conservation philosophy; Developments in animal law; Disaster planning

World Society for the Protection of Animals, "Animal Welfare Matters to Animals, People and the Environment: The Case for a Universal Declaration on Animal Welfare," available at http://media.animalsmatter.org/media/resources/en/en_brochure.pdf.

———, "Provisional Draft Text 2007," available at http://media.animalsmatter.org/media/resources/en/en_draft.pdf.

———, "The Value of Declarations," available at http://media.animalsmatter.org/media/resources/en/en_valueofdec.pdf.

DAVID MADDEN

seven

ANIMAL-FRIENDLY LIVING

The final section details those projects—both personal and social—that we need to consider in order to make a difference for animals worldwide.

Although it may seem that individuals are powerless in the face of institutional abuse and cruelty, the reality is that we have great power as consumers, as investors, as educators, and as voters to effect change for animals. Even in apparently small matters, such as the products we buy or the way we teach our children, can make a big impact. The cause of animal protection needs thoughtful people who shop, buy, invest, teach, and vote—with the animals in mind.

One area of interest is the increasing number of institutes of higher education that are offering courses in such subjects as animal law, animal ethics, human-animal studies, animals in philosophy, animals in literature, animals and political theory, and animal theology—all of which include discussion of our human obligations to animals. Now hundreds, even thousands, of students worldwide have to think about animal ethics in the courses they study in colleges and universities.

So enormous is the suffering we inflict on animals that an increasing number of people are now considering reducing their intake of meat or adopting vegetarianism or veganism. The final subsection provides essential information about the ethics of vegetarianism, plant-based nutrition, how to garden ethically, and how to create meat-free meals.

ANDREW LINZEY

ACTION FOR ANIMALS

ALTERNATIVES TO DISSECTION

Dissection is the cutting open and studying of dead animals (*see* Animals in Research). The dissection of human and nonhuman animals has a long history dating back at least two thousand years. As a method for teaching biology in schools, however, it became common only from the twentieth century onward. Some ten million vertebrate animals—and many more invertebrates—are dissected yearly in classrooms worldwide. Frogs, rats, fetal pigs, cats, snakes, turtles, birds, bony fishes, and sharks are among the commonly used vertebrates; earthworms, crayfish, clams, sea stars, and grasshoppers are commonly used invertebrates.

There are two main arguments—one moral and the other practical—against animal dissection or any exercise that inflicts intentional harm on animals in schools. The moral argument is that dissection causes unnecessary animal suffering and death and reinforces the human-centered view that animals are of no moral consequence. The practical argument is that dissection is inferior to alternative learning methods, such as computer simulations, which cause little or no harm to animals.

The dissection supply trade undoubtedly causes much animal suffering. Investigations in North America have documented routinely inhumane conditions of capture, transport, housing, and killing. A 1990 undercover investigation of the largest supplier of animals to classrooms in the United States documented many abuses, including video footage of traumatized domesticated cats crowded into wire cages and roughly prodded into gas chambers to be killed. In 1994, another investigation described the rounding up of domesticated cats (including people's companion animals) from Mexican streets, after which their captors killed them by either drowning them or cutting their throats and then shipped them to a distributor in the United States. Frogs, practically all of whom are taken from free-living populations, are collected in sacks of one hundred or more live frogs. Survivors are killed by immersion in an alcohol solution, a process that takes ten to twenty minutes. Animal protection laws, where

they exist, are too weak to halt such practices, and abuses will likely continue for as long as schools keep supply companies profitable by purchasing their products.

In addition to the humane problems, dissection may also corrupt young people's attitudes toward animals and nature. Insisting that children cut up dead animals and then put their bodies in a dustbin or a hazardous waste repository is thought by many to undermine the development of attitudes of caring for others and stewardship toward nature. The behavior of many students toward the animals they dissect has been observed to follow a three-phase pattern. At first, the student is hesitant to cut into a once-living creature, but as the dissection proceeds, most students begin to show confidence in performing dissection. In the final phase, some students—usually boys—often begin to act callously toward the animal, during which time acts of mutilation are commonplace. This pattern suggests a dulling of the child's initial concern for the animal, a form of desensitization.

Most surveys find that half or more of a typical student population do not want animals to be hurt or killed for their education. However, vastly fewer students—perhaps one in twenty—will resist a teacher who expects his or her students to dissect animals. Conscientious objectors risk possible confrontation with a teacher or the school, deductions in marks, and/or ridicule from less sensitive students. Nevertheless, as public awareness of animals as thinking, feeling creatures grows, more and more students are objecting to dissection.

Dissection and live animal experimentation in schools have begun to decline, and the advancement of alternative learning methods is probably most responsible for this trend. Many thousands of alternatives are now available, ranging from simple plastic models to highly sophisticated computer simulations. Computer programs in particular have many advantages. They allow the student to dictate the pace and direction of the lesson; to view microscopic structures and animations unobservable in a dissection; to interact with the program through quizzes, hints, and feedback; and to repeat the exercise as many times as the student wishes. More than thirty published studies have shown that students learn as well using alternatives as they do using live or dead animals, if not better. These studies span a broad range of disciplines, including general biology, physiology, pharmacology, psychology, nursing, veterinary medicine, and medicine. The use of animals in medical training has been outlawed in the United Kingdom since 1876, and 152 of the 159 American medical schools—including the most prestigious ones—have eliminated the "animal labs" they once conducted. If it is better to train medical doctors without harming animals, then surely the same can be said of the other life sciences.

Related articles: The alternatives; Animal and human violence; Caring for animals and humans; Cephalopods and decapod crustaceans; Children's relations with animals; Developments in animal law; Humane education; Moral anthropocentrism; Stray animals; Understanding amphibians; The welfare of pigs

Balcombe, J. P., *The Use of Animals in Higher Education: Problems, Alternatives, and Recommendations*, Humane Society Press, 2000.

Downie, R., and Meadows J., "Experience with a Dissection Opt-Out Scheme in University Level Biology," *Journal of Biological Education* 29.3 (1995): 187–194.

Francione, G. L., and Charlton, A. E., *Vivisection and Dissection in the Classroom: A Guide to Conscientious Objection*, American Anti-Vivisection Society, 1992.

Jukes, N., and Chiuia, M. (eds.), *From Guinea Pig to Computer Mouse*, 2nd ed., InterNICHE, 2003.

Pedersen, H., *Humane Education—Animals and Alternatives in Laboratory Classes: Aspects, Attitudes and Implications*, MA thesis, Stockholm University, 2000.

Tasto, J. L., and Balcombe, J. P., "Medical Simulation: Current Uses and Future Applications," in Simoff, M. J., Sterman, D. H., and Ernst, A. (eds.), *Thoracic Endoscopy: Advances in Interventional Pulmonology*, Blackwell, 2006, 76–87.

JONATHAN BALCOMBE

ANIMAL ADVOCACY

We can become animal-friendly in many ways. Animals suffer pain, fear, and discomfort in farms, transport vehicles, abattoirs, laboratories, circuses, their natural environments, and our homes. Unlike us, however, they cannot organize themselves into protest groups or trade unions in order to campaign for their rights. Therefore, we have to do this for them. We can try to improve the laws protecting animals.

In the nineteenth century, it was quite common to send boys up chimneys to clean them, to capture Africans and force them to be slaves, and to send women and children to work sixteen hours a day in dangerous factories and mines. Then came along people such as William Wilberforce and Thomas Fowell Buxton, who successfully campaigned in the British Parliament against the slave trade, and the Earl of Shaftesbury, who amended the laws controlling the conditions of workers in factories. It is sometimes forgotten that Wilberforce and Buxton were also founders of the Royal Society for the Prevention of Cruelty to Animals (RSPCA) in 1824 and that Shaftesbury led the campaign to legislate to protect laboratory animals in 1876. These great philanthropists were also animal welfare pioneers. They used politics to achieve reforms. By persuading Parliament to pass new laws, they saved thousands of humans and nonhumans from further suffering.

In a democracy, we can all have a role in the creation of new laws. We can try to become members of the legislature ourselves, or we can, as voters, attempt to persuade politicians to legislate for the causes we believe in. If good laws against cruelty to animals already exist, then we can campaign to have these laws properly enforced. In other words, we can become advocates or campaigners for animals.

How then should we campaign against cruelty? Here are a few rules of thumb as to how we can campaign both legally and effectively (I do not advocate violence because this is morally unacceptable and often counterproductive).

We can start with a statement of moral principle: we believe it is wrong to cause suffering and distress to nonhumans for the same reasons that we believe it is wrong to cause suffering to humans. We are all (human and nonhuman) capable of experiencing pain and distress. A difference in species does not affect the moral issue any more than do differences in race or gender.

Now to proceed to practical matters:

1. Collect reliable evidence of specific examples of cruelty to animals in laboratories, farms, circuses, traps, or elsewhere.
2. Present this evidence to the media, to those in positions of political and other influence, and to the public.
3. Call for specified and attainable actions, such as new legislation or standards.
4. Focus public outrage on those who can achieve reforms—for example, politicians, company directors, or government officials can be contacted.
5. Back up demands with good scientific and legal opinions.
6. Persevere over many years, if necessary, until the goals are achieved and made secure.

7. Remember that the public will invariably support a campaign once it sees evidence of cruelty.

Generally, photographs (or film) of cruelty will have a far greater impact than words alone. Urge members of the public, once they are aroused, to write to one clearly identified person—for example, a prime minister, a president, or a managing director. They should also contact their local media. In order to attract media attention, it may be necessary to devise some novel, amusing (but not violent) protest action or other event. The media are constantly hungry for news. The media need campaigners as much as campaigners need the media. Television is the most effective medium, but it needs good pictures. Think of what would make a good television story—for example, the use of celebrities, of glamour, or of other visual excitement.

Campaigners and advocates often form themselves into pressure (or interest) groups and spend time trying to establish effective channels of communication with those in power. In some countries (for example, Britain) power lies not in the parliament, but with government ministers and their close advisers. In the European Union, the government ministers of each member state hold the ultimate power. It is their Council of Ministers that finally decides legislation. However, the other parts of the European Union—the European Parliament and the officials who form the Commission—should also be lobbied. In Washington, DC, it is the members of Congress, rather than the White House, who decide on legislation. Where political parties or individual politicians can legitimately seek funding, then donations of money are an obvious method of establishing contact.

In democracies, votes matter. Elected politicians are therefore especially receptive to pressure from interest groups just before elections. Ask them for written promises of action and for new statements of policy to be published officially. It is important to be knowledgeable about the issue and to back up requests with the latest scientific and legal advice. However, above all, elected politicians respond to public opinion. People can use the evidence of commissioned opinion polls here to indicate that the politicians will pick up some extra votes if they support an anticruelty campaign. Try to establish relations of friendship and trust with media people and politicians. Meet them socially and give them hospitality. Politicians receive so much negative criticism that they often respond well to public gratitude and praise.

Of course, it is increasingly big national and international corporations, such as the World Trade Organization (WTO), that hold power. The heads of these organizations, however, can be approached in the same way.

Campaigners can threaten organized boycotts of their goods or buy a few company shares and so speak at their company meetings. Ultimately, all such businesses will listen to public opinion. Nevertheless, it is up to people to raise public awareness of cruelty to animals and to focus it on those who can alter the system. It is important not to fight others in the movement who may have slightly differing aims. Join forces with other lobbying groups. However, one does not have to be part of a big organization in order to be effective—determined individuals have achieved some of the greatest successes in the animal movement.

Related articles: Animal pain; Animal protection in Britain; Animals in circuses; Animals in farming; Animals and the major media; Animals in politics; Animals used in research; Developments in animal law; The fur trade; Legislation in the European Union; Live animal exports; Slaughter; The universal charter of the rights of other species; The World Trade Organization

Ryder, Richard D., *Animal Revolution: Changing Attitudes towards Speciesism*, Basil Blackwell, 1989, rev. ed. Berg, 2000.
———, *Painism: A Modern Morality*, Opengate Press, 2001.
———, *The Political Animal: The Conquest of Speciesism*, McFarland, 1998.
———, *Putting Morality Back into Politics*, Imprint Academic, 2006.
———, *Speciesism, Painism and Happiness: A Morality for the Twenty-First Century*, Imprint Academic, 2011.
———, *Victims of Science: The Use of Animals in Research*, Davis-Poynter, 1975.

RICHARD D. RYDER

ANIMAL COURSES IN ACADEMIA

Animal studies courses are no longer just for veterinarian students. Colleges and universities around the globe are adding animal courses across multiple disciplines.

Human-animal studies (HAS) represents the broadest and most rapid interdisciplinary expansion of courses addressing animals in academia. Sometimes referred to as critical animal studies, the wide purview of HAS could encompass all of the other categories of animals studies that are detailed separately in this article. The U.S.-based Animals and Society Institute offers an extensive database of HAS course offerings throughout the world involving disciplines as varied as agricultural science, art, gender and cultural studies, child development, posthumanities, media studies, literature, environmental sciences, humane education, political and postcolonial theories, sociology, and women's studies, to name a few.

Human-animal studies critically explores the intersection of animal and human life in any of its manifestations, while probing the various foundations that obscure and make possible these interactions. Scholars in these fields approach the question of the "animal" from multiple angles, often deconstructing or experimentally dispensing with taxonomic or linguistic categories that enable distinctions between species. HAS courses are offered in the United States, Canada, Australia, New Zealand, the United Kingdom, Israel, Poland, Finland, Germany, and Sweden. Online courses, previously offered only through the Humane Society University, are also on the rise. At this point, there is a dearth of academic courses in Central America, Southeast Asia, Asia, the Middle East, Eastern Europe, and Africa, though legal protections, animal welfare policies, and education are taking place globally.

Animal philosophy and ethics. Since the publication of Peter Singer's *Animal Liberation* in 1975, numerous professors have devoted class time, if not entire courses, to analyzing the ethical dimensions of animal use, exploitation, and suffering. Courses in animal philosophy, animal rights, the ethics of eating, and ecofeminist and environmental philosophy, as well as historical surveys of "animal" across cultures and time periods, are standard fare either as stand-alone courses or as modules within broader disciplinary perspectives.

Animals in religion. The critical examination of animals within religious or spiritual traditions is a relatively new development in academic and theological education. Courses in Asian studies as well as naturalist philosophies and theologies have typically made mention of animal life because of the metaphysical suppositions within these traditions that value other-than-human organisms. However, courses that explicitly address the position of animals in sacred texts, rituals, or orthodox practice, either within a single tradition or comparatively across traditions, are novel—but increasing with regularity. In the United Kingdom, noted animal theologian Andrew Linzey held the first academic post in ethics, theology, and animal welfare from 1992 to 2000 and is currently director of the Oxford Centre for Animal Ethics. Harvard University is now offering a course called Animals and Religion. The American Academy of Religion recently added a program unit for Animals and Religion. Animal chaplaincy education is also on the rise, with courses and avenues for certification for those wanting to formally include animals in spiritual community and ritual.

Animal behavior and assisted therapy. Animal behavior studies have always been a part of biology and veterinary academic programs. This methodology has also extended into the sectors of agriculture, zoology, and biomedical experimentation, often with the purpose of improving, but not necessarily challenging, animal use and confinement. Today, however, many animal behavior courses reflect the broader discourse on animal welfare that has developed in response to data revealing the social organization, tool and language use, emotions, sentiency, intelligence, and virtues expressed by land, air, and aquatic creatures, as well as the damaging effects captivity has on their well-being. The Universities of Edinburgh and Dublin are but two among many schools that offer degrees in animal behavior and welfare. Purdue University in the United States also runs the Center for the Human-Animal Bond, which makes classes and animal behavior training available to students, professionals, and the public.

Two emergent fields of study within animal behavior are anthrozoology and zoosemiotics. The former is the interdisciplinary study of human-animal interactions, for which numerous major or minor degrees are currently offered in conjunction with psychology, anthropology, and sociology curricula. The latter involves the study of animal communication and is a derivation of biosemiotics, meaning the study of the production, action, and interpretation of signs within biological evolution.

Finally, based on the last two decades of behavioral neuroscience data that posit human health benefits derived from companion animals, students now have access to innovative courses in animal-assisted therapy within fields such as social work and psychology. These programs include degrees, online courses, and certifications.

Animal law and policy. Animal law works to advance the interests of animals in the legal sphere. This work includes passing anticruelty legislation, filing lawsuits on behalf of animals, prosecuting animal abuse or neglect, and developing social networks and educational resources for lawyers and law students interested in adding animal law to their practice. According to the Animal Legal Defense Fund, 121 law schools in the United States and Canada offered animal law courses in 2010. Over a dozen universities throughout Australia and New Zealand boast animal law courses, as do universities in Spain, Austria, China, Israel, and the United Kingdom.

Activism, networks, and journals. In addition to coursework, numerous schools have student-run groups that provide avenues for education, collective protest, activism, research, and policy changes within and outside the university setting.

Networks for animal studies that link scholar-activists around the world include the Nordic Human Animal Studies Network, the Animals and Society Study Group of Australia, the Oxford Centre for Animal Ethics, and the H-Animal Discussion Network, which also offers a syllabus exchange program. Other organizations such as Animals and Society Institute and CENSHARE offer grants to support the innovative research of scholars, students, and artists, as well as further development of animal studies curricula, conferences, and publications.

Finally, a number of interdisciplinary academic journals now exist online and in print. Among them are *Society and Animals: Journal of Human-Animal Studies*, *Anthrozoos: A Multidisciplinary Journal of the Interactions of People and Animals*, *Between the Species: A Journal for the Study of Philosophy and Animals*, the *Journal of Animal Law*, the *Journal of Applied Animal Welfare Science*, and the *Journal of Animal Ethics*.

Related articles: Animal advocacy; Animal and human violence; The complexity of animal awareness; The ethics of zoos; Humane education; Veterinary ethics

Colonius, Tristan, and Swoboda, Jamie, "Student Perspectives on Animal-Welfare Education in American Veterinary Medical Curricula," *Journal of Veterinary Medical Education* 37.1 (2010): 56–60.

De Mello, Marge (ed.), *Teaching the Animal: Human–Animal Studies across the Disciplines*, Lantern Books, 2010.

Hurn, Samantha, "What's in a Name? Anthrozoology, Human-Animal Studies, Animal Studies or . . . ?," *Anthropology Today* 26 (June 2010): 27–28.

Sankoff, Peter, and White, Steven (eds.), *Animal Law in Australasia*, Federation Press, 2010.

Wolfe, Cary, *What Is Posthumanism?*, University of Minnesota Press, 2009.

BRIANNE DONALDSON

ANIMALS AND THE MAJOR MEDIA

It is only in recent decades that animal abuse has become visible. What happened to animals in the past invariably happened in the dark, behind closed doors. People simply did not stop to think where their hamburgers came from; they did not know the gruesome story behind every fur coat, that the makeup they wore was cruelly tested on animals, that animals led impoverished and derelict lives in zoos and endured inhumane treatment in circuses, or that millions of animals suffered relentless pain in laboratories. They were unaware because the major media paid scant attention to these issues, and even to this day, if an issue fails to attract mainstream media coverage, for many, it is as though it does not exist.

Times and the media landscape have changed. Furthermore, the animal protection movement has evolved into an effective communicator, raising the exploitation

and abuse of animals to an issue of social concern, and the news and entertainment media are taking notice. Thanks to a voracious twenty-four-hour news cycle; the explosion of cable television networks, such as National Geographic Channel and Animal Planet; the influence of talk show hosts such as Oprah Winfrey and Ellen DeGeneres; popular reality shows such as *Whale Wars*; and the vast, unprecedented reach of the internet, more and more people now know what factory farms (*see* Animals in Farming) and puppy mills are. There is an awareness of the continuing slaughter of whales, of the decimation of the planet's free-living animals, and of the fundamental principle of easing companion animal overpopulation by adopting from shelters and rescue groups.

In recent years animal protection–related stories have been big news. In 2008, California's Chino slaughterhouse exposé hit the headlines in the United States, resulting in the largest meat recall in the country's history. The undercover investigation by the Humane Society of the United States (HSUS) revealed the inhumane practice of dragging injured and diseased cattle ("downers") to slaughter and showed that these animals were the probable source of the contaminated meat. Although consumers were clearly alarmed about the dangers to human health, they were also disturbed by footage of injured cows being brutalized and bulldozed. The public had reason to question the way in which animals raised for *their* food were treated, and soon thereafter a ban was implemented, banning adult "downer" cows from entering the food supply.

Substantiating the impact of media coverage, Farmgate.illinois.edu, an online agribusiness trade publication, concluded, "When media attention is given to animal welfare issues, regardless of the production practices involved, consumer demand softens not only for that particular meat, but for all meats" (September 16, 2010). Evidence indeed has shown that when the public is informed about the inhumane treatment of animals, consumer habits change. Another issue that dominated the news for several months and provided the public with a crash course on a different form of animal cruelty was the Michael Vick dog-fighting scandal. Vick was convicted of torturing and killing a number of his fighting dogs, and the NFL footballer's celebrity no doubt helped catapult this "below the radar" blood sport into the public consciousness, but the media went deeper into the backstory. It examined the culture that fosters the "sport," the abusive techniques used to train the dogs, and most importantly, the physical and mental toll taken on the surviving animals. It was a story that saturated all media, leaving few people still in the dark about the brutality of dog fighting.

"The power of the media is awesome. The media tell society what is hot, what is hip, what matters," writes Karen Dawn in her book *Thanking the Monkey: Rethinking the Way We Treat Animals* (318). And so it follows that social issues find their way into the entertainment media, where popular narrative films and dramatic TV and comedy series reflect societal and cultural concerns. In 1995, millions of people all around the world watched the remarkable episode of the animated comedy series *The Simpsons* called "Lisa the Vegetarian," in which Bart's spunky sister, Lisa, converted to ethical vegetarianism. In one shining moment of moral illumination, Lisa made the connection between the lamb chops on her dinner plate and the lamb she had befriended earlier in the day at a petting zoo.

"The past two decades have seen an upsurge in the use of entertainment programming for the dissemination of pro-social messages . . . [because] of the truism that people learn from the programming they watch," states Mandy Shaivitz in a report to the Carnegie Foundation on Media, Citizens and Democracy titled *How Pro-Social Messages Make Their Way into Entertainment Programming* (Shaivitz 4). If this is the case, then primetime TV dramas such as *Grey's Anatomy*, *CSI: Crime Scene Investigation*, *Bones*, and *Law and Order* have contributed to the education of their considerable audiences with storylines that have touched on topics as diverse as medical research (*see* Animals in Research), factory farming (*see* Animals in Farming), exotic animal trafficking (*see* Trade), and dog fighting.

Although Walt Disney may have been among the first in the movie world to recognize the appeal of the anthropomorphized animal hero, in recent years animated feature film characters have evolved beyond simply being cute to become "poster animals" for their cause. In *Babe* (1995) and *Charlotte's Web* (2006), young pigs are shocked to discover they are destined for slaughter. Not only do these characters succeed in putting a face on pork, but they also call for respect for all animals raised for food. The eponymous mustang in *Spirit: Stallion of the Cimarron* (2002) wants the right to live free, as nature intended, as does Nemo the clown fish in *Finding Nemo* (2003), and even the dancing penguin in *Happy Feet* strives to protect his natural habitat.

The animal protection message is echoed in live-action films, too. From *Free Willy* (1995), which leaves its audience questioning whether it is humane to keep orca whales captive for our entertainment, to *Gorillas in the Mist*'s (1988) dire warning of the human threat to mountain gorillas, to the comedy *Legally Blonde 2: Red, White, and Blue* (2003), which condemns animal testing, there has been a shift toward presenting animals as sentient beings invariably exploited by humans. Even the documentary medium, the traditional home of free-living "wildlife" and animal conservation topics, boldly took on Japan's shameful dolphin slaughter and its connections to the marine park industry in *The Cove* (2009). Offering a thrilling new approach to documentary filmmaking, *The Cove* won critical acclaim and an Academy Award, while thrusting the issue of the annual dolphin massacre into the public eye as never before.

The signs are encouraging. Animal protection issues are firmly enshrined in the social agenda and are frequently cast in the media spotlight. However, the harsh reality is that millions of animals still suffer in factory farming, fur farms, medical research, circuses, and puppy mills, although thanks to the media, the world now knows of their plight. And with awareness comes change, albeit gradual. The media has the power to shape, as well as reflect, public opinion for good and for ill. It can help propel important legislation and influence societal behavior. It serves to organize, summarize, simplify, and dramatize the key elements of common values and culture that we must all share in order to survive and to communicate.

The digital age may have brought about a media revolution in that no single print outlet or major TV show can reach a vast audience in the way that was once possible, but now the internet can communicate information to millions at the click of a mouse. YouTube videos can go viral in a matter of hours, and in the blogosphere anyone with a computer can make their opinions heard. In this brave new media environment, it is surely easier to get the word out about a multitude of animal issues, but it is still important for traditional media to take up the story.

Established in 1986, the annual Genesis Awards event, now presented by the Humane Society of the United States, has always recognized the power of the media in raising public consciousness of animal issues. Born of the credo that "cruelty can't stand the spotlight," each year the event honors outstanding coverage of animal protection concerns by the news and entertainment media. By monitoring this output, the awards provide a valuable reading of the growth and scope of the media's attention to the animal cause. From a mere handful of entries in 1986, the number of candidates has risen to an estimated 250–300 annually, a true indicator of the place animal protection concerns now occupy in the media arena.

But although animal abuse and exploitation have more difficulty hiding in the dark, behind closed doors, the abuse and exploitation continue. It is therefore vital to keep the media's spotlight trained on the issues because when the media lose interest, so often does the public.

Animals need all the good friends they can get, and with its vast power to move hearts and change minds, the media is one of their most powerful and effective allies.

***

Related articles: Animals in circuses; Animals and public health; Caring shopping; Commercial whaling; Conservation philosophy; Dog fighting; Ethical vegetarianism; The ethics of zoos; Fur farming; The fur trade; Intelligence in whales and dolphins; Neutering and spaying; Primates worldwide; Product testing; Puppy mills; The rehabilitation of dolphins; Roadside zoos and menageries; Shelters and sanctuaries; Slaughter; The welfare of cows

Abbott, Sam, "Animals, Too, Are Movie Stars," *Billboard*, April 7, 1951.
Bousé, Pierre, *Wildlife Films*, University of Pennsylvania Press, 2000.
Dawn, Karen, *Thanking the Monkey*, HarperCollins, 2008.
Ellis, Stu, "The Farm Gate" (blog), University of Illinois, September 16, 2010, available at http://www.farmgate.illinois.edu/archive.
Molloy, Claire, *Popular Media and Animals*, Palgrave Macmillan, 2011.
Shaivitz, Mandy, *How Pro-Social Messages Make Their Way into Entertainment Programming*, USC Annenberg Norman Lear Center, 2001.

GRETCHEN WYLER, SUE BLACKMORE,
AND BEVERLY KASKEY

ANIMALS IN POLITICS

Political parties and animal policies

Animal protection issues are a mainstream public concern (Garner, *Animals, Politics and Morality*), and in some countries, constituents send members of the parliament (MPs) and other governmental representatives more mail on animal-related issues than on most other issues. Yet concern for animals is poorly reflected in most political party policies. Initiatives to improve the legal status and protection of animals are usually taken by the same few animal-friendly politicians who often struggle to recruit support from additional MPs for these causes.

It is understandable that many pressing social issues require urgent action; however, ample examples demonstrate that animal and environmental issues affect many other important social issues. The economic crisis, the fuel crisis, the food crisis, animal disease crises, loss of biodiversity, animal welfare, and climate change are all interconnected (e.g., Loewenberg; Campbell, Conder, and Marchiondo). Animal and environmental protection, therefore, should be a mainstream political priority in a world aspiring to be sustainable.

Lobbying by the third sector: industry and nonprofit

Politicians are regularly approached by lobbyists from industry or pressure groups representing nonprofit organizations, including animal protection organizations. Agribusiness and pharmaceutical industry representatives are organized, are generally well resourced, and usually represent the majority public opinion (e.g., food or fossil fuels should be cheap). Leaning toward the needs of the industry rather than toward those of minority groups on sensitive issues will increase MPs' chances of being reelected. This partly explains why bad practices, such as intensive farming (*see* Animals in Farming), continue to exist, despite clear scientific evidence regarding detrimental effects on animals, the environment, and people.

Many nongovernmental organizations track politicians' parliamentary voting records on animal issues, make recommendations for supporting humane candidates, and organize political campaigns to change legislation (Garner, *Political Animals*). Although these initiatives are vital to advance animal protection politically, a new movement emerged recently, adding further pressure to political parties to seriously consider animal welfare and protection.

Parties for animals worldwide

In 1993, the Animal Protection Party (Tierschutzpartei) was established in Germany, but the concept of a dedicated party for animals really took hold in the Netherlands, where the Party for the Animals (Partij voor de Dieren) was established in October 2002 and gained electoral representation (two MPs) in 2006. By 2010 the number of representatives had increased to twenty-six, including one senator and twenty-three local and regional representatives. The party maintained its two parliamentary seats in the June 2010 and September 2012 general elections.

From 2007 to 2010, Marianne Thieme MP (leader of the Dutch Party for the Animals) asked the largest number of parliamentary questions of any Dutch MP, most of which were related to animal issues. This ensured that animal welfare was always on the political agenda and encouraged other political parties and MPs to think about animal issues and support animal protection initiatives. With support from other MPs, the Party for the Animals achieved a number of political changes for animals, including bans on the enriched (laying hen) cage, on down plucked from live geese, and on mink farming; improved measures in the animal husbandry sector; required consideration of fish welfare in innovation subsidies in the fishery industry; doubling of the budget for research using alternative methods; and a reduction in the use of primates in research and testing (Partij voor de Dieren).

By 2010 political parties for animals existed in more than a dozen countries, including European countries, Canada, and Australia. In the United Kingdom, for example, Animals Count was modeled on the Dutch Party for the Animals and contested three elections from 2008 to 2010 (Animals Count). Although in countries with proportional-representation voting systems, animal parties are more likely to gain electoral success, in other countries they may contribute to raising awareness among the public and politicians and may influence other parties to adopt more animal-friendly policies. In many countries green parties—which usually include progressive policies on animal issues—are on the rise too.

Animal parties are at the leading edge of politics in this field. They seek to encourage other parties to make animal welfare a higher priority. It is unlikely that they will become mainstream or form part of any government within the next few years. They usually have a general outline of non-animal policies in their manifestos as well, given that they would be required to vote on these issues in the parliament. They normally place themselves in the center or center-left of the political spectrum and are guided by values such as compassion, environmental protection and sustainability, personal responsibility, and personal freedom.

Engaging citizens, political parties, and nonprofit organizations in the political process

To ensure long-term achievements for animals and the planet, it is of vital importance that constituents organize themselves and support animal protection initiatives aimed at their local MPs or representatives, whatever political party they represent. It may be hoped that, during election times, constituents will give increasing consideration to animal and environmental protection and focus less on issues of short-term benefit to themselves.

Although animal protection can be achieved through a number of ways and methods, the power, potential, and implications of legislation for animals are significant. Citizens, organizations, political parties for animals, and other animal-friendly politicians can play a valuable role in shaping the development of legislation that impacts animals (*see* Changing Legal Perspectives).

Related articles: The alternatives; Animal agriculture and climate change; Animals and public health; Birds used in food production; Fish farming; Fur farming; Humane research; Legislation in the European Union; Primates worldwide

Animals Count, "Elections," 2010, available at http://www. animalscount.org/elections/.

Campbell, W. C., Conder, G. A., and Marchiondo, A. A., "Future of the Animal Health Industry at a Time of Food Crisis," *Veterinary Parasitology* 163.3 (2009): 188–195.

Garner, R., *Animals, Politics and Morality*, 2nd ed., Manchester University Press, 2004.

———, *Political Animals: Animal Protection Politics in Britain and the United States*, Macmillan, 1998.

Loewenberg, S., "Global Food Crisis Looks Set to Continue," *The Lancet* 372.9645 (2008): 1209–1210.

Partij voor de Dieren, "Successen," 2010, available at http:// www.partijvoordedieren.nl/departij/successen.

JASMIJN DE BOO

REPORTING CRUELTY IN THE UNITED KINGDOM

Hundreds of successful Royal Society for the Prevention of Cruelty to Animals (RSPCA) prosecutions are made each year in the United Kingdom, and thousands of animals are saved from further suffering as a direct consequence of action by members of the public.

Witnessing, or even suspecting, that an animal is being cruelly treated can be very distressing. It is important to assess the situation calmly and consider your own safety before acting. Then take a note of what you have seen and phone the RSPCA's twenty-four-hour national cruelty and advice line—0300-1234-999. This number takes all calls and refers the details to a local RSPCA officer to respond as appropriate.

Remaining calm while giving a detailed description of what you saw or heard will help you to remember everything that happened. The RSPCA control center operator is likely to want to know the following information:

- The name and telephone number of the person reporting the incident. This is necessary for recording purposes and will be used by the RSPCA officer if he or she is requested to update the caller with the result of the investigation. It is RSPCA policy to treat all complaints in the strictest confidence. Callers' names are not disclosed without their permission.
- The date, time, and place of the incident. If it has been possible to take any photographs, please let the RSPCA know because they may help provide vital evidence in any prosecution.

- The name(s) and address(es) of the person(s) involved, if known.
- The name(s) and address(es) of any witnesses.
- The registration number and description of any vehicle involved.
- Whether you would be prepared to testify in court if necessary. The RSPCA always aims to prevent cruelty through education and opts for court proceedings only as a last resort.

The work of the RSPCA extends to caring for all animals in all situations. In the spring and early summer, the RSPCA is contacted by thousands of people who find what they think is an abandoned young bird or other orphaned animal. In most cases these animals have not been abandoned, and "rescuing" them may do more harm than good. Their mother is usually close by and looking out for them. Human interference can lessen a young animal's chances of survival.

If you find a young bird out of his or her nest, the bird is probably a fledgling. Fledglings of garden birds usually leave their nests about two weeks after hatching, just before they can fly. They will have most of their feathers and can walk, run, and hop onto low branches. A fledgling should not be returned to his or her nest because this may disturb other young birds.

Fledglings are fed by their parents, who are rarely far away and will encourage the young bird to stay in cover. If worried, go right away from the site and return in an hour or so. You will almost certainly find that the natural parents have taken care of the young bird. Young animals in immediate danger from a predator or traffic should be placed out of harm a short distance away. If you find an unfeathered bird who has fallen out of the nest (probably by accident), contact the RSPCA national advice line, and someone there will be able to advise you on the best course of action.

If the animal is obviously sick, injured, or distressed, please contact the RSPCA national advice line immediately. If you feel that you must take the animal from the area yourself, keep handling to a minimum, making a note of exactly where the animal was found.

It is not uncommon for four-week-old fox cubs to be seen outside their earth. It is a normal part of a fox's growing-up process to spend his or her days alone in or around patches of cover above ground. If after twenty-four hours the cub is still in the same spot, it is still often better to leave the cub in the "wild." Leaving some food, such as meat bones, household scraps, bread soaked in fat, carcasses of road-killed birds, and perhaps some tinned dog food, and placing a bowl of water nearby may help.

If in doubt always telephone the RSPCA advice line and set your mind at rest; remember—you might be saving an animal's life.

———

Related articles: Animal pain; First aid; Humane education; The protection of birds

RSPCA, "Help and Advice," 2011, available at http://www.rspca.org.uk/allaboutanimals/helpandadvice.
———, "Measuring Animal Welfare in the U.K., 2005–2009," 2011, available at http://www.animalwelfarefootprint.com.
———, "Reporting Animals in Distress," 2010, available at http://www.rspca.org.uk/allaboutanimals/helpandadvice/reportinganimalsindistress.
———, "Rescue," 2011, available at http://www.rspca.org.uk/in-action/aboutus/whatwedo/rescue.
———, "Seasonal Advice," 2011, available at http://www.rspca.org.uk/allaboutanimals/helpandadvice/seasonal/.

NIGEL YEO

REPORTING CRUELTY IN THE UNITED STATES

Reporting and responding to animal cruelty in the United States presents special challenges. Most companion animal cruelty is addressed under state laws. Every state law defines "animal" and "animal cruelty" in its own way. This presents the public and law enforcement officials with the task of determining which acts against which creatures are to be addressed by these laws. Some states apply their anticruelty statutes only to mammals; others limit them to vertebrates other than humans. Some states specifically remove certain animals from consideration, such as Delaware's exclusion of "fish, crustaceans or molluska" from its criminal code.

The specific acts or omissions of care that are covered by these laws also vary widely across states. Some laws are brief and nonspecific, such as Wisconsin's law, which simply states, "No person may treat any animal, whether belonging to the person or another, in a cruel manner." Others provide a lengthy collection of prohibited actions, some of them reflecting the origins of these laws in the mid-nineteenth century as a way of protecting working animals from overdriving, overloading, and overworking. Most states further complicate the reporting of cruelty by including specific exemptions for certain socially accepted practices, even if they might result in pain or death. Such exemptions usually include hunting, trapping, pest control, humane euthanasia, rodeo, farmed animal husbandry and slaughter, scientific research, and the practice of veterinary medicine.

This variability means that members of the public, as well as law enforcement professionals, need to have a basic understanding of state and local laws. In some cases you may feel that the care and treatment of an animal is inadequate or cruel, but it might not rise to the level of an offense that authorities can respond to.

An additional challenge to reporting suspected animal cruelty is knowing the appropriate authorities to contact. In the United States, this varies across different cities and counties. Reports of animal cruelty are usually investigated by a government animal care and control agency. In many areas a private nonprofit humane society or society for the prevention of cruelty to animals may be under contract to provide animal control or cruelty investigation services. Your telephone directory will usually provide contact information for the appropriate agency to call to report animal-related problems.

In areas where there are no special animal protection organizations or resources, cruelty complaints are the responsibility of the local police or sheriff's office. If you witness an animal being abused or other acts of intentional cruelty, such as dog fighting, you should contact the police emergency number (911 throughout most of the United States).

Simple animal neglect (failure to provide basic needs) is not always considered a criminal act and can often be resolved by the intervention of local animal care and control or humane agencies, which may be able to offer resources and educate offenders on how to provide proper care for their animals. However, many states make a distinction between simply failing to take adequate care of animals and intentionally or knowingly withholding sustenance. Accordingly, "willful" neglect is considered a more serious, often prosecutable offense. Neglect can also be an indicator of animal hoarding, the accumulation of large numbers of animals in extremely unsanitary conditions, often resulting in the death of many animals and potentially serious health consequences for the people who are living with them. Such cases often require the cooperation of many local agencies, including adult protective services, animal care and control, and mental health as well as police and fire departments.

Once you have found out which law enforcement agency you should speak to, it is important to provide a concise, written, factual statement of what you observed, giving dates and approximate times whenever possible. If at all feasible, try to photograph the situation and date your pictures. When you call to report animal cruelty, always make sure to keep a careful record of exactly whom you have contacted, the date of the contacts, and the content and outcome of your discussion. Make it clear to the agent that you are concerned about the case and that you are willing to lend whatever assistance you can. You can file an anonymous report of animal cruelty, but the case is more likely to be pursued when there are credible witnesses willing to stand behind the report and, if necessary, testify in court about what they may have witnessed.

If you do not receive a response from the officer assigned to your case within a reasonable length of time, do not be afraid to present your information to his or her supervisor and, if necessary, to local government officials, such as the county commissioner, and ask them to act. Please keep in mind that most law enforcement agencies operate with limited personnel and resources. Most of these agencies are doing their best to conduct timely and efficient investigations. Be respectful of the challenges they face. Giving them the benefit of the doubt when appropriate will likely get you much further than premature complaints to their superiors.

Reporting animal abuse and neglect is an important part of maintaining a safe and humane community. Without tips from the public, many animals would remain in abusive circumstances, mute and unable to defend themselves. It all starts with you—that is why it is so important to learn how to recognize and report crimes against animals.

Related articles: Animal pain; Animal welfare and farming; Animals and public health; Animals used in research; Deer hunting; Developments in animal law; Euthanasia; First aid; The fur trade; Humane education; Living with animal neighbors; Rodeos; Slaughter; Societies against cruelty in the United States; Veterinary ethics

Ascione, F. R., and Lockwood, R., "Animal Cruelty: Changing Psychological, Social and Legislative Perspectives," in Salem, D., and Rowan, A. (eds.), *State of the Animals 2001*, Humane Society Press, 2001, 39–53.

Lockwood, R., *Animal Cruelty Prosecution: Opportunities for Early Response to Crime and Interpersonal Violence*, American Prosecutors Research Institute, 2006.

———, "Counting Cruelty: Challenges and Opportunities in Assessing Animal Abuse and Neglect in America," in Ascione, Frank R. (ed.), *International Handbook of Theory and Research on Animal Abuse and Cruelty*, Purdue University Press, 2008, 87–110.

Lockwood, R., and Ascione, F. (eds.), *Animal Cruelty and Interpersonal Violence: Readings in Research and Application*, Purdue University Press, 1998.

Merz-Perez, L., and Heide, K. M., *Animal Cruelty: Pathway to Violence against People*, Altamira Press, 2003.

Sinclair, L., Merck, M., and Lockwood, R., *Forensic Investigation of Animal Cruelty: A Guide for Veterinary and Law Enforcement Professionals*, Humane Society Press, 2006.

RANDALL LOCKWOOD

COMPASSIONATE LIFESTYLE

CARING FOR ANIMALS AND HUMANS

Animal protectionists living in South Africa are sometimes asked whether ethical concern for animals is really a luxury, even an indulgence. Dare we, in Africa, care about the well-being of animals while so many of our people are dying of hunger, of AIDS, or in violent civil conflict? It is certainly a question worth pondering.

The statistics of abuse and violence in South Africa are staggering. The murder rate is the highest in the world. A rape occurs every twenty-five seconds. One in three girls and one in four boys will be sexually molested before adulthood. In some communities, drive-by shootings and gang warfare in the streets have become a daily hazard. To care about animals in this context might appear misplaced and unbalanced, even antihuman.

And yet there is a growing awareness that animal abuse and cruelty, far from being peripheral to the problem, might actually be linked to the problem of violence against humans. Consider, for example, the impassioned plea of Wikus Gresse, chairman of the parole board at Pollsmoor Prison near Cape Town, featured in a 2001 documentary: "Teach people how to care" (*Caring Classrooms*). Gresse's words are telling because he is the founder of one of the most successful criminal rehabilitation projects in the world today. Gresse has seen firsthand the healing power inherent in the gentle art of caring for animals. "The Bird Project," as it is known, enables prisoners to hand-rear lovebirds, cockatiels, and parrots for ultimate sale to avid bird-keepers. Of course there is much irony in prisoners receiving benefit from perpetuating the imprisonment of other species, but the therapeutic value of learning to care is noteworthy. Gresse is unequivocal: "If these people [the inmates], as youngsters, had been given the chance of humane education, of learning how to care—some of them would most probably not be here today."

Neither is his a lone voice. Professor Sean Kaliski, head of forensic psychiatry at Valkenburg hospital in Cape Town, goes as far as to say that the entire nation's mental health is diminished by the ubiquitous evidence of animal neglect and cruelty. "The link is there," says Kaliski. "Someone who is cruel and violent to animals will also be so to people. We need to sensitise a desensitised nation and the younger we start, the better" ("Domestic Violence" 3). One insight into the interrelationship between one form of violence and the other is provided by Rosemary Cox, manager of the Saartjie Baartman shelter for battered women and their children, near Cape Town. She comments, "Sometimes a man will use an animal as a weapon against his wife. If he sees that she loves her little dog, for instance, he will hurt it in order to hurt her. In cases like this, the trauma for the wife is more severe than if he had simply beaten her up" ("Domestic Violence" 3).

In the last quarter of the year 2000, the Humane Education Trust was given the opportunity to rekindle a spirit of care and respect for life in eleven of the Western Cape's most disadvantaged and violence-torn schools. The Western Cape Education Department agreed that humane education, as a pilot project, would get a three-month opportunity to establish its value and benefit to schoolchildren. P. W. Roux, a clinical psychologist with six years' experience in the rehabilitation of criminals, was chosen to assess the impact of the project on a scientific basis. He concluded that humane education was an "overwhelmingly positive" influence in the lives of the learners (*Caring Classrooms*).

Most noteworthy to those involved in the project, however, was the obvious sense of self-worth that the project generated among the children themselves. In learning to care about the well-being of animals, they also learned to care more about each other, and most importantly, they developed a sense of their own individual value. One boy, Brendan, in grade ten, gave this positive evaluation: "Humane education gave me a new pair of eyes. Everything I look at now, I see differently. Nowadays, I don't throw stones at stray dogs anymore, and I give that thief-cat, that always hangs at our door, our leftover food . . . I feel really proud about it" (*Caring Classrooms*).

These programs show that there is a much deeper link between animal and human abuse than even many animal protectionists had anticipated. We know that abuse often arises out of early abusive relationships and especially a sense of low self-esteem. Caring for others—including other living creatures—can help combat such deep-seated feelings of lack of worth. As one of the educators involved in the project perceptively remarked, "a sense of self-worth and pride in being human is diametrically in opposition to acts of crime and violence" (*Caring Classrooms*).

Ethical concern for animals—for the way in which they are regularly beaten, tortured, and killed—cannot then be regarded as incidental in a world in which humans likewise are often casually beaten, tortured, and killed. We do not yet fully know, nor have we invested the necessary resources in order to know, the precise mechanisms that trigger abuse both to animals and to humans, but we can be sure—at least, surer than we have ever been—that in victimizing animals, we also become the victims.

Frank Meintjies, change management specialist on the reconstruction of post-apartheid South Africa, was invited by a national Sunday newspaper to advise the nation on how best to proceed, in a climate so fraught with violence and crime. He said, "South Africa is struggling to put together a platform of values to guide the building of a new society . . . If we don't organise the new society on the basis of values, the entire project falls flat" (Meintjies 24). One of those values, which so urgently needs to be championed, is the care of and respect for other living beings. Animal protection, with its central message of humane education, far from being peripheral, may well be central to the moral reconstruction of the country we love.

Related articles: Animal and human violence; Animal protection in Africa; Humane education; Moral anthropocentrism; The moral claims of animals; The moral community; The protection of birds

Balcombe, Jonathan, *Pleasurable Kingdom*, Macmillan, 2006.
Caring Classrooms (documentary), the Humane Education Trust, South Africa, 2001; see http://www.humane-education.org.za.
"Domestic Violence—The Missing Link!," *Humane Education News*, South Africa, Summer 2003–2004.
Horsthemke, Kai, *The Moral Status and Rights of Animals*, Porcupine Press, 2010.
Meintjies, Frank, "Opinion," *Sunday Times*, June 25, 2000.
Pickover, Michele, *Animal Rights in South Africa*, Double Storey, 2005.

Van der Merwe, Louise, *Goosie's Story*, Gecko Books, 1998.
——, *Heroes and Lionhearts*, Gecko Books, 1996.
——, *Magnificent Boy and the Spirit of the Grey Hare*, Humane Education Trust, 2007.

LOUISE VAN DER MERWE

CARING SHOPPING

Not quite ready to give up animal products but concerned about the ways animals are reared and killed? That makes you a very powerful person, among those most able to change intensive farming methods for kinder systems. Every time you step inside a supermarket or shop, look at a mail order catalog, or buy through a Web site, you can help bring about a kinder world for animals. Here is how animal-loving omnivores can shop for change. Although most of my examples come from the United Kingdom, some are relevant to other countries as well.

Every supermarket and most retailers in the United Kingdom now offer more humanely produced alternatives to almost every animal product displayed. These carry special labels and cost at least a little extra. If you and other caring consumers seek out and buy such products, retailers will stock more. This way, you and they will steer the farming industry toward more animal-friendly rearing systems. Nowadays, informed consumers have more power than governments. By supporting the most humane rearing systems, you can use your power for the animals' cause:

Organic products carrying the Soil Association label

The Soil Association label offers the safest guarantee of humane rearing systems. Britain's Soil Association sets stringent and well-inspected welfare standards governing such things as the provision of straw bedding and adequate space. Most animals in Soil Association systems are reared free-range.

Other organic products

Organic welfare standards vary. Not all are quite as high as those of the Soil Association, but the vast majority of animal products labeled organic will come from kinder systems than non-organic products. Drugs used by factory farmers to keep animals alive in otherwise unendurable systems are banned from all organic farms. This means the animals must be given more space and better conditions in order to thrive. Even buying organic vegetables ultimately helps animals by turning the tide against intensive farming.

Free-range

This is certainly a label to support. Do not let agribusiness spokesmen fool you into thinking that animals reared in barren indoor systems are content as long as they are well fed and warm. Outdoors, animals occupy all of their waking hours in exploratory and social behavior. Indoors, often kept on metal slats between concrete walls, they feel just as frustrated as you would if confined in a small space with absolutely nothing to do. Neither do they "get used to it." If released outdoors from lifelong incarceration in factory farms, hens and pigs who have never even seen the color green will eagerly forage, root, play, exercise, dust-bathe, or wallow, just like their free-living ancestors. When products from large animals such as pigs and meat from poultry are labeled free-range, you can feel reassured—even more so if the label is "organic free-range." Free-range eggs are more contentious. They might have been laid by hens kept in ideal small flock conditions or by those housed overnight in such huge numbers that some never find their way out to the light of day. Again, the label organic free-range offers additional assurances, as does buying eggs from a small see-for-yourself local supplier. But nothing is quite as cruel as the battery cage. So whether you seek the extra reassurances or not, opt for free-range.

RSPCA Freedom Food in the United Kingdom

This is another label to support, even though it does not necessarily represent perfect rearing conditions. This scheme is a realistic attempt by the RSPCA to raise standards, step by step, for many farmed animals, rather than setting the very highest standards for a few. Again, it adds extra welfare assurances to the free-range label and helps to move agriculture in the right direction.

We're-out-to-fool-you labels

"This product comes from rural Dorset," the label proudly reveals. So what? An intensive pig or poultry farm in Dorset is just as horrible for the animals incarcerated in it as would be one in Hackney. Watch out for weasel words on labels designed to lull you into thinking this poor creature enjoyed life among the buttercups.

"Traditionally cured" does not mean traditionally or outdoor-reared. "Farm-fresh" means fresh from the factory farm. "Grain-fed" or "corn-fed" simply means this cruelly incarcerated creature was fed grain or corn. That is why it is so important to look carefully at labels.

Nonspecific labels

Safely assume the worst unless the label specifically promises a better standard or rearing. For instance, the word "eggs" among any list of ingredients means eggs from caged hens. If the manufacturer has gone to the expense of using free-range eggs, the company will be sure to let you know. Products, such as mayonnaise, containing free-range eggs are now appearing in stores. It is particularly important to support them to encourage this trend.

Pig products are also worthy of special attention. Pig farming in Europe, the United States, and most other countries is highly intensive. These very intelligent animals (more intelligent than dogs!) endure wretched lives, in most cases on metal slats in totally barren environments. Your bacon or sausages almost certainly come from animals reared like this unless they carry a better-welfare label.

Economy or low-cost

The cheaper the product, the more cruel the system. That is a good rule of thumb for judging animal products—unless they happen to be organic or free-range reduced to clear by a sell-by date. It costs less to keep laying hens in cages, pigs on metals slats, birds raised for meat crammed in vast sheds, and beef cattle indoors. Shoppers pay less—"and that's all they really care about," claim producers. Sadly, they are right in far too many cases. And that makes you, the caring consumer, particularly precious. Health experts advise that we eat fewer animal products. Use less, and pay more for those animal foods you choose, and both you and the animals benefit. Regard the extra cost on any item as a donation to animal welfare. There is no more effective way of giving to support this cause.

Related articles: Animal welfare and farming; Animals and public health; Birds used in food production; Cruelty-free labeling; Pig castration; The welfare of pigs

Body, Richard, *Our Food, Our Land*, Rider, 1991.
Eyton, Audrey, *Kind Food Guide*, Penguin, 1991.
Harrison, Ruth, *Animal Machines*, Vincent Stuart, 1964.
Rifkin, Jeremy, *Beyond Beef*, Penguin, 1992.

Robbins, John, *Diet for a New America*, Stillpoint, 1987.
Sainsbury, David, *Farm Animal Welfare*, Collins, 1986.
Webster, John, *Animal Welfare: A Cool Look towards Eden*, Blackwell Science, 1994.

AUDREY EYTON

CRUELTY-FREE LABELING

Consumers care about animal testing for cosmetics and household products, and increasing numbers of people wish to shop with compassion. According to the Co-operative Bank's Ethical Consumerism Report, ethical spending in 2008 in the United Kingdom alone amounted to 36 billion pounds, with spending on humane cosmetics rising.

An opinion poll commissioned by the British Union for the Abolition of Vivisection (BUAV) and the Royal Society for the Prevention of Cruelty to Animals (RSPCA) found that 96 percent of women thought there should be compulsory labeling of animal testing for cosmetics. Furthermore, in a BUAV poll conducted by Opinion Research Business, 79 percent of people said they would be likely to swap to a brand that was not animal-tested if they discovered that their existing brand was tested on animals.

In response to such public concern, many consumer product companies have ended animal testing for products and ingredients. Rightly, these companies wish to celebrate and promote their ethical credentials and encourage the public to buy their products as a result. So a plethora of statements and logos have appeared.

A company itself may very well not test; it may not even commission testing on its behalf. However, testing may occur by its ingredient suppliers, and a company may purchase ingredients with a "don't ask, don't tell" philosophy. The testing may be done by a parent company, even if the subsidiary company has actually done "no testing." In such cases, the product is simply packaged and labeled by the smaller subsidiary company but tested by the parent. Unfortunately, some companies have exploited this complex situation and the growth in the ethical marketplace by encouraging consumers to purchase products with mere final-product claims—with a potentially deceptive "not tested on animals" label. Truthful in the literal sense, this may well hide the fact that the ingredients were tested on animals.

What all of this means is that the statements on packaging may be literally correct—enough to shield the company from accusations of legal breaches or public relations problems—but also quite disingenuous. As a consequence, animals could still suffer and die to make these products given that virtually all testing is done at the ingredient level.

In response to growing consumer confusion around different claims and labels, and keen to support those companies that had taken genuine steps to end animal testing, fifty leading animal protection organizations on both sides of the Atlantic developed the Humane Cosmetics Standard in 1998.

The Humane Cosmetics Standard is the only internationally recognized scheme that enables consumers to easily identify and purchase cosmetic and toiletry products that have not been tested on animals. The Humane Household Products Standard is a sister program for household products.

To be approved a company must no longer conduct or commission animal testing and must apply a verifiable, fixed cut-off date—an immovable date after which none of the products or ingredients have been animal-tested. It is the only scheme that requires each company to be open to an independent audit throughout the supply chain, to ensure that the company adheres to its animal testing policy and the Humane Cosmetics Standard's strict criteria.

The program promotes one standard and one logo across the world for all cosmetics and household products. Any number of lists are promoted by various individual animal groups and organizations. The Humane Cosmetics Standard, however, offers not just a list, but an internationally recognized standard.

The program currently operates in the United Kingdom, the United States, Canada, and Europe and is spreading globally. In Europe the scheme is managed by the European Coalition to End Animal Experiments. In the United States and Canada it is managed by the Coalition for Consumer Information on Cosmetics, as the Corporate Standard of Compassion for Animals, and is signaled by the Leaping Bunny logo. It is the only scheme that the BUAV, one of the leading international organizations campaigning to end animal testing, recommends.

The Humane Cosmetics Standard is also recognized by industry and the media as the international benchmark for products claiming to be free of animal testing. Leading global companies, such as the Body Shop, Method, Marks and Spencer, and Liz Earle, have met the standard's criteria, and many carry the bunny logo on their products.

Many ingredients have been tested on animals in the past. The Humane Cosmetics Standard is designed to prevent future animal testing and eventually drive such testing out of the industry completely. Over time, more companies are committing to join the program and implement a fixed cut-off date. This global effort—combined with regional animal testing bans, such as that in the European Union for cosmetics—will, it is hoped, reduce and eventually eliminate animal testing from the cosmetics and household products industry (*see* Animals in Research).

Related articles: Animal protection in Britain; Caring shopping; The humane movement in Canada; Legislation in the European Union; Product testing; Societies against cruelty in the United States

Body Shop International, *Living Our Values: Values Report*, 2009, available at http://www.thebodyshop.com/values-campaigns/assets/pdf/Values_report_lowres_v2.

British Union of the Abolition of Vivisection, *The Little Book of Cruelty Free*, 2010, available at http://www.gocrueltyfree.org/consumer/get-involved/lbcf-request.

Consumer Reports, *Label Report Card for the Leaping Bunny Logo*, 2010, available at http://www.greenerchoices.org/eco-labels.

The Cooperative, *Ten Years of Ethical Consumerism: 1999–2008*, 2009, available at http://www.goodwithmoney.co.uk/assets/Ethical-Consumerism-Report-2009.pdf.

European Commission, *Guidelines for the Interpretation of the Cosmetics Directive*, 2010, available at http://ec.europa.eu/consumers/sectors/cosmetics/documents/guidelines/.

Opinion Research Business, *Market Research on Consumer Attitudes to Animal Testing: Report for the BUAV*, 2004.

MICHELLE THEW

ETHICAL FINANCE

Individuals often feel powerless in the face of large corporations that support or gain financially from animal exploitation and abuse. What can the individual do, apart from write to his or her governmental representative, join an organization, or sign a petition? In fact, individuals (as well as charities and other organizations) can have an enormous impact if they are careful to ensure that their money is not invested in companies involved in unacceptable activities, such as animal experiments, the fur trade, or intensive farming. By applying ethical criteria to the use of your money within the system, you can make a stand for change.

Thankfully, there is a move globally for funds to be made available for those wishing to avoid investment in companies involved in animal abuse. Be aware, however, that ethical funds have different criteria. Some are stricter than others, and some hardly cover animal issues at all. Most will avoid companies involved in cosmetics research, but others will invest generally in, for example, pharmaceutical companies. Ethical investment came of age with boycotts against companies involved in the South African apartheid regime and the Vietnam War in the 1960s. Some funds incorporate positive as well as negative criteria. Consideration of negative criteria refers to avoidance of companies involved in certain activities. Consideration of positive criteria means that they will seek to invest in companies involved in desirable activities, such as environmental protection, waste management, and sustainable forestry.

Some funds utilize "engagement" criteria. This means that they utilize their shares to bring pressure to bear on companies—for example, by seeking to commit companies to policies of "reduction and eventual elimination of animal testing." Engagement criteria would not be suitable for those investors who wish to avoid investing in any companies involved in, for example, animal experiments.

Most banks lend to companies involved in animal exploitation unless they have a specific policy to invest ethically. It is worth searching out the small number of banks that operate on appropriate ethical criteria.

Ethical Investors Group established the concept of "cruelty-free money," which is now gaining traction globally. When the group was founded in 1989, there were no cruelty-free investment funds available. The Ethical Investment Research Service (EIRIS) carries out research into ethical issues and provides information for ethical investors. EIRIS has a global network of research partners to further extend its research coverage (http://www.eiris.org).

Australia's first animal-friendly superfund was launched in 2010. Ethical Money's "Cruelty Free Super" has been designed for anyone wishing to screen for animal exploitation, such as intensive farming, the export of live animals, and animal testing, as well as broader ethical values, including issues related to environment, human rights, armaments, and tobacco (see http://www.crueltyfreesuper.com.au/?pg=Cruelty+Free+Money). In the United States, PETA (People for the Ethical Treatment of Animals) also provides advice for those wishing to invest "cruelty-free." The Global Reporting Initiative (GRI) is a network-based organization that has pioneered the development of the world's most widely used sustainability reporting framework and is committed to its continuous improvement and application worldwide (http://www.globalreporting.org).

The Social Funds Web site features over 10,000 pages of information on SRI mutual funds, community investments, corporate research, shareowner actions, and daily social investment news (http://www.SocialFunds.com).

Related articles: Animal welfare and farming; Animals used in research; The fur trade; Live animal exports; Product testing

Fehrenbacher, Scott, *Put Your Money Where Your Morals Are: A Guide to Values-Based Investing*, B and H, 2001.
Fung, Hung-Gay, Law, Sheryl A., and Yau, Jot, *Socially Responsible Investment in a Global Environment*, Edward Elgar, 2010.
Landier, Augustin, and Nair, Vinay B., *Investing for Change: Profit from Responsible Investment*, Oxford University Press, 2008.
Sparkes, Russell, *Socially Responsible Investment: A Global Revolution*, Society of Investment Professions, Wiley, 2002.

CHRIS DEACON

HUMANE EDUCATION

Instinctively, we know that kind children become kind adults. Statistics bear out that the opposite is also true. Children who learn to ignore the feelings of others—or even take delight in someone else's pain or distress—grow up to be, at best, unhappy adults and, at worst, sociopaths with whom society must grapple on a number of legal, social, and emotional levels. Whenever confronted by the abhorrent acts of such disturbed individuals, our leaders stumble to provide answers, or at least to develop the questions, that will allow us all to rest easier and believe that this could not happen to us, in our neighborhood, with our children.

However, in these discussions, one significant clue to the violence puzzle is left out—that is, that promoting kindness in children needs to be extended beyond kindness to their parents, their teachers, their church, and their peers. This foundation in compassion must be laid in a child's first encounter with those beings who are most at his or her mercy. We need to develop and nurture in children a feeling of empathy for all sentient individuals, including animals with whom we share this planet.

This is not just a measure of teaching civility. It is a necessary component of developing a social consciousness that will translate into socially responsible adulthood. Virtually every serial killer in recent memory had a history of torturing and killing animals. The United States' Federal Bureau of Investigation (FBI) has added cruelty to animals as one of the factors it uses in developing a profile of behavior patterns in violent criminals. A 1985 study showed that 25 percent of aggressive criminals incarcerated in federal penitentiaries had committed five or more acts of animal cruelty during their childhood, compared to only 6 percent of nonaggressive inmates. None of the noncriminals interviewed as a control group reported any childhood cruelty to animals. In an FBI study of thirty-six convicted multiple murderers, conducted in 1970, 46 percent confessed to acts of animal torture during their adolescence.

Even more frightening is the fact that a seemingly growing number of children who routinely abuse animals are crossing the species barrier long before reaching adulthood. Children who had a previous history of animal cruelty perpetrated nearly all of the mass school shootings in recent years. In fact, guidelines published in response to these shootings by the American Psychological Association, the National School Safety Center, the National Crime Prevention Council, and the U.S. Department of Education all list early acts of cruelty to animals as indicators that a child may be in imminent danger of directing his or her violent impulses toward human victims.

How can we effectively nurture the natural feelings of empathy in most children, even when they face ridicule by their peers and some adult role models, and how can we bring children without that natural empathy into a circle of compassion? Although very few of us will ever have contact with kids who later go on to become nationally infamous for their inhumanity, most adults will interact with a child or two who goes on to torture a cat or hit a dog and then his or her partner or child. These are the kids who need to have a strong role model who states unequivocally that harming others is not acceptable.

The correlation between childhood cruelty and adult violence is an emerging area of psychological study, and the lines are not clear. For example, many of us who grew up with and developed empathy for animals nevertheless set an ant on fire or pulled the wings off a fly as a child. We have not grown up to be disturbed adults, and there is no reason to believe our children will be any different. However, since none of us knows exactly where that line between innocent child curiosity and intentionally cruel behavior lies in an individual mind, it would seem incumbent on us to stay far away from that line, in terms of the messages we send to children.

The appropriate ethical relationship between humans and other animals is not an issue that can or will be addressed in the isolation of the education community. But members of that community are in a unique position to explore this subject with children. Someone who is trying to do just that is Susan Carr Grant, who has taught prekindergarten and kindergarten at All Saints School in Buffalo Falls, New York. Long before becoming aware of any organized humane education movement, she was improvising her own exercises to teach compassion in the classroom. Grant has found that using the example of animals children encounter in everyday life may provide educators with the best tool to expand their students' circle of compassion. A picture of her dog, Bonnie Prince, adorns her classroom, and he is a frequent topic of conversation. At the end of the year, she brought Bonnie Prince to school and taught the children how to treat him gently and respectfully: "They recognized his intelligence, and they understood that he was family to me, in the truest sense of the word. We talked about other animals in this sense as well. It was something I am sure they will never forget."

We must teach our children that even if our society is not always kind, we should all strive to be. Just as most teachers would never allow a racist comment or a violent act toward another child to go unaddressed, we need to be equally vigilant when witnessing—or hearing of—so-called pranks played out at an animal's expense. These actions, unchallenged, can only encourage the development of an unhealthy sense of power that will be increasingly difficult to curb. We need to look to a day when the saying "boys will be boys" means curiosity, not cruelty, and respect, not ridicule.

Related articles: Animal and human violence; Animal pain; Children's relations with animals; The moral community; Teaching animals humanely

Arluke, Arnold, *Just a Dog: Understanding Animal Cruelty and Ourselves*, Temple University Press, 2006.

Ascione, Frank R., *Children and Animals: Exploring the Roots of Kindness and Cruelty*, Purdue University Press, 2005.

———— (ed.), *The International Handbook of Theory, Research, and Application on Animal Abuse and Cruelty*, Purdue University Press, 2009.

Ascione, Frank R., and Arkow, Phil (eds.), *Child Abuse, Domestic Violence and Animal Abuse: Linking the Circles of Compassion for Prevention and Intervention*, Purdue University Press, 1998.

Linzey, Andrew (ed.), *The Link between Animal Abuse and Human Violence*, Sussex Academic Press, 2009.

Lockwood, Randall, Sinclair, Leslie, and Merck, Melinda (eds.), *Forensic Investigations of Animal Cruelty: A Guide for Veterinary and Law Enforcement Professionals*, Humane Society Press, 2006.

HOLLY HAZARD

LIVING WITH ANIMAL NEIGHBORS

To get an idea of the size of the "pest control" industry in the United Kingdom alone, one need only look in the *Yellow Pages* directory. In the southeast London edition alone, there are more than fifty companies competing to kill nuisance animals, including mammals, birds, and insects, in an area of little more than 250 square kilometers. Agencies offer the "eradication" of pigeons, rats, mice, squirrels, foxes, wasps, beetles, flies, cockroaches, and ants.

This is not an isolated example. All over the world countless companies are engaged in nothing less than a war against free-living animals. Millions of gallons of toxic chemicals and tons of poisons are discharged into our environment annually, and as soon as one toxin is invented, the search begins for the next to combat the eventual immunity. The negative environmental impact of the use of deadly pesticides such as DDT (dichlorodiphenyl-trichlorethane) and dieldrin are well documented.

In addition to guns and poisons, devices such as traps and snares destroy a wide variety of free-ranging animals, and they also maim or kill nontarget domesticated animals. The suffering to sentient creatures involved in the apparently innocuous term "pest control" is colossal. Snaring, for example, can involve both target and non-target animals being caught around their stomach by an ever-tightening steel wire snare for hours, even days. And "glue traps" for rats and mice involve the creatures being literally stuck fast by their feet to a glue board until the human being concerned returns (assuming he or she does) to end the animal's misery.

However, over recent years there have been some, albeit embryonic, indications of a change in attitude—some of them originating in unlikely places. The price paid by fur-bearing animals in the history of Canada is legendary. Yet times are changing. Every year, polar bears arrive at the Manitoba town of Churchill to await the freezing of the Hudson Bay and the chance to hunt seals. Up until a few years ago, these powerful and potentially dangerous bears were shot dead on sight. Now the worst they can expect is a tranquilizer dart and a sleepy ride slung under a helicopter thirty miles along the coast. In the Rocky Mountains, where grizzly and black bears occasionally threaten walkers, mountain bikers, and other tourists, almost no one now expects or demands their immediate death in reprisal.

When Calgary in Alberta found that its beautiful city park was being badly fouled by huge numbers of Canada geese, an intelligent plan of action was devised. First, a public education campaign was devised to inform the public that feeding the geese bread and cake did the birds no favors. Second, a watch was kept on the nests and the eggs collected—not for destruction, but for incubation, so that the goslings could be later transferred to a lake outside town, upon which they would imprint. Then, finally, when the adult birds molted their flight feathers, they were rounded up and taken in air-conditioned trucks to be reunited with their young on the distant lake. The plan was a complete success.

Similarly, the Swiss city of Basle solved a significant feral pigeon problem with a scheme that satisfied both the pro- and anti-pigeon lobbies. Several sites were established where people could feed pigeons, but strict bylaws were enacted to forbid feeding anywhere else. At the feeding sites, pigeon lofts were built so that the birds had somewhere to congregate, roost, and nest. The birds' eggs were regularly removed with the result that, over subsequent years, the pigeon population was dramatically reduced without the need for killing adult birds. The idea is now being promoted, with some success, to British local authorities by the Pigeon Control Advisory Service. Hitherto, many local authorities have unthinkingly conducted culls with guns, traps, and poisons, causing widespread suffering and miserably failing to achieve a permanent solution. The Fox Project, based in Tonbridge, Kent, has developed an effective system of humane deterrence that, over the last decade, has led to virtually all local councils abandoning the destruction of nuisance foxes.

Already, there are signs that industry is beginning to respond to the increasing demand for the humane, nonlethal control of nuisance species. Many garden centers display safe chemical repellents that were designed originally to repel nuisance domesticated animals but that are also effective against some other animals. There are also ultrasonic sound devices (with varying degrees of efficacy) and even a device (again of Canadian origin) that detects intruding animals and repels them with squirts of

water! A current company even produces tethered helium kites that replicate hovering birds of prey, which deter unwanted birds from feeding or settling below. And there are many humane live-capture traps available for the relocation of nuisance animals, especially rats and mice.

It is hoped that exciting new technologies will help deliver us from the old view that we have to live in a state of war with animals. New techniques, based on knowledge of the relevant species, common sense, and compassion, could bring about a future where all people, whether they live in town or in the country, resolve their conflicts with free-living creatures without resorting to killing and cruelty.

Related articles: Animals and public health; The ethics of killing free-living animals; Moral anthropocentrism

Bryant, John, *Animal Sanctuary*, Centaur Press, 1999.
——, *Fettered Kingdoms*, Fox Press, 1982.
——, *Living with Urban Wildlife*, Centaur Press, 2002.
Harris, Stephen, and Baker, Phil, *Urban Foxes*, Whittet Books, 1986.
Humane Society of the United States, *Wild Neighbors*, Fulcrum, 1997.
Roots, Clive, *Animal Invaders*, David and Charles, 1976.

JOHN BRYANT

VEGETARIAN LIVING

ETHICAL VEGETARIANISM

Vegetarianism is the practice of not eating the flesh of animals, including fishes and birds as well as red meat. Vegans do not eat any animal products, including eggs and dairy products, and some of the ethical reasons for being a vegetarian also apply to veganism. Ethical arguments for vegetarianism focus on two issues: the suffering inflicted on animals in the production of meat and the value of conscious life itself, which is, of course, destroyed when animals are killed for food.

Both arguments presuppose that animals can feel pleasure and pain, fulfillment and frustration, and contentment and fear or have similar experiences, making life better or worse for them. This may not be true of simpler life-forms in the animal kingdom, including some that are routinely eaten, such as clams and oysters, but many animals who are used for human food are clearly

capable of all these experiences. This awareness that animals, like us, are also sentient, self-conscious, and complex beings is important because preserving and enhancing the lives of beings who possess such qualities should be one of the goals of ethics.

One of the most widely accepted ethical principles is that we should not make others suffer unnecessarily. If making someone suffer is in the best interests of that individual—for example, in a medical procedure designed to restore health—and is the only means available, then that may justify the infliction of suffering in that case. But if there are other, less hurtful ways of attaining the good result, then causing the extra pain is unjustified, as with cruel or excessive punishments. Also, if the good attained is less significant than the suffering caused, as with cruel entertainments, such as dog and cock fighting, then causing that pain is also unjustified. Another issue is fairness: when one group is made to suffer so that another group may prosper, as with slavery and other forms of exploitation, then causing that suffering is also unethical.

These considerations mean that contemporary animal husbandry practices called "factory farming," where animals are kept indoors, closely confined, and on artificial diets, are to be condemned. They inflict a great deal of suffering on millions of animals annually. Causing this suffering is not justified by the production of plentiful, nutritious, tasty food because we can reach that goal without factory farming. Since a vegetarian diet can be both nutritious and tasty, and since plant agriculture produces more food than animal husbandry, the suffering inflicted on animals in meat production is unnecessary. The same is true for eggs and dairy products, where, for example, hens live their lives in cramped conditions, which denies fulfillment of their basic behavioral needs. Increasing efficiency and profit cannot justify factory farming since these economic goals are ethically insignificant in comparison to the lifelong pain and suffering caused. Moreover, it is unfair that animals endure the suffering of living in small cages, crates, and stalls; having many of their instincts frustrated; being fed poor, unsatisfying food; and other miseries so that humans can have extra food choices.

The second argument concerns the value of life and specifically the destruction involved in killing animals. Even if animals do not reflect on the significance and value of life and death, they still have an interest in their continued life, since death terminates all experiences. If an animal is suffering from a painful, incurable illness, then death can be a blessing, but for a healthy animal in an environment that can support his or her normal way of life, depriving the animal of all future opportunities for happiness, fulfillment, excitement, or other sorts of positive experiences is the most devastating loss we can inflict on him or her. An ethical justification for inflicting this catastrophic loss on another would have to be similarly weighty. Self-defense or survival could qualify, as when people who must live in a climate that cannot support a vegetarian diet hunt animals for food. But there is no such justification for the mass slaughtering of animals by people who can lead high-quality lives without destroying the lives of animals.

The ethical fault with eating meat, eggs, or dairy products lies not in consuming these items as such, but in the cruel processes employed in making them available for us to eat (where "cruel" refers to causing unjustified suffering). Since some animals, such as clams and oysters, probably lack feelings, killing and eating them is probably as ethically unobjectionable as harvesting potatoes. Eating eggs laid by chickens we protect and nurture,

as loving caregivers do their companion animals, would probably be a fair exchange. Harvesting the corpses of animals who have lived normal lives and died of natural causes and then using them for food or nutrients would not run afoul of these arguments, though we might find being scavengers distasteful.

However, by unjustifiably causing animals suffering and loss of life, most animal husbandry, hunting, fishing, and trapping is ethically deplorable, and meat or other animal products produced in these ways should not be eaten. This would produce a diet far closer to vegetarianism and veganism than the diets currently followed by the vast majority of people. Acknowledging our ethical duties to animals could even expand our sense of community with them, so we could join George Bernard Shaw in saying, "Animals are my friends, and I don't eat my friends."

Related articles: Meatout; The moral claims of animals; Vegan living

Dombrowski, Daniel A., *The Philosophy of Vegetarianism*, University of Massachusetts Press, 1984.
Fox, Michael Allen, *Deep Vegetarianism*, Temple University Press, 1999.
Mason, Jim, and Singer, Peter, *Animal Factories*, Crown, 1988.
Preece, Rod, *Sins of the Flesh: A History of Ethical Vegetarian Thought*, University of British Columbia Press, 2008.
Sapontzis, Steve F. (ed.), *Food for Thought: The Debate over Eating Meat*, Prometheus Books, 2004.
———, *Morals, Reason, and Animals*, Temple University Press, 1987.

STEVE F. SAPONTZIS

MEATOUT

Originally a modest effort, with a couple dozen events in 1985, Meatout has grown into the world's largest annual grassroots diet education campaign. On or about March 20 each year, caring people in a thousand communities in all fifty states and twenty other countries welcome spring with colorful educational events. France, Germany, and Spain have even launched their own Meatout Web sites. The purpose is to help consumers evolve to a wholesome, nonviolent, plant-based diet.

The events range from simple information tables, exhibits, food samplings, and cooking demonstrations to elaborate receptions, street theater, and festivals. Visitors at each event are asked to "kick the meat habit on March 20 (first day of spring) and explore a wholesome, nonviolent diet of grains, vegetables, and fruits." The Meatout message is further propagated by a dozen billboards, hundreds of bus display cards, TV ads, and scores of letters to the editors of local newspapers. Dozens of governors and mayors of large cities issue special proclamations.

Meatout's most effective strategy for promoting a plant-based (vegan) diet has been distributing samples of meat and dairy analogs—veggie burgers, dogs, and lunch meats and soy and rice ice cream. Sales of these items have been doubling each year, and 22 percent of American consumers buy them regularly. Several major manufacturers of meat and dairy foods, such as Kraft, Kellogg, and ConAgra, have responded to this development by buying out analog manufacturers or launching their own analog product lines.

In 2003, realizing that Meatout pledge signers needed continuing support, we launched "Meatout Mondays," a free, colorful weekly e-newsletter to support prospective or new vegans. Each issue, going to 60,000 subscribers, contains a recipe, a product or book review, a health/nutrition news item, and an inspirational story. Meatout draws broad public support from animal, environment, and consumer protection advocates, meatless food manufacturers and retailers, health care providers, educators, public interest advocates, and mass media, as well as public officials and celebrity entertainers. Most are moved by a concern for the devastation to consumer and environmental health wreaked by intensive meat production and consumption. Some feel that providing a contrasting view to the relentless barrage of meat industry propaganda will allow consumers to reach more informed food-selection choices.

A number of U.S. health advocacy organizations have followed the Meatout lead:

- The American Cancer Society, National Cancer Institute, and American Heart Association have launched their own campaigns promoting consumption of plant-based foods.
- Johns Hopkins University has launched a program promoting Meatless Mondays.
- Paul McCartney credits Meatout for his own recent Meatfree Mondays campaign.

The Meatout campaign has been organized each year by FARM (Farm Animal Rights Movement), a national nonprofit public interest organization headquartered in Washington, DC. Local events are planned, promoted, and executed by grassroots animal, environment, and consumer protection advocates, using local volunteers.

Related articles: Animal advocacy; Caring shopping; Ethical vegetarianism; Plant-based nutrition; Vegan living; Vegetarian cooking; Vegetarianism in Britain and America

Berry, Rynn (ed.), *Food for the Gods: Vegetarianism and the World's Religions*, Pythagorean, 1998.

Connelly, Joseph, "The Brains behind the Great American Meatout," *VegNews*, March 20, 2012, available at http://vegnews.com/articles/page.do?pageId=4331&catId=2.

Hsu, Tiffany, "More Vegans, Vegetarians Fuel Meatless Market: Soy Burger Anyone?," *Los Angeles Times*, March 20, 2012, available at http://www.latimes.com/business/money/la-fi-mo-meatless-vegans-vegetarians-20120320,0,3945988.story.

Iacobbo, Karen, and Iacobbo, Michael, *Vegetarian America: A History*, Greenwood Press, 2004.

Kanner, Ellen, "Meatless Monday: Great American Meatout Puts Kindness on the Menu," *Huffington Post*, March 15, 2010, available at http://www.huffingtonpost.com/ellen-kanner/meatless-monday-great-ame_b_496508.html.

"'Michigan Meatout Day' Draws Scorn," UPI, March 17, 2010, available at http://www.upi.com/Odd_News/2010/03/17/Michigan-Meatout-Day-draws-scorn/UPI-52021268854066/.

Norman, Meaghan M., "PETA: Go Green, Go Vegan", WILX, March 19, 2010, available at http://www.wilx.com/news/headlines/88689702.html.

Puskar-Pasewicz, Margaret (ed.), *Cultural Encyclopedia of Vegetarianism*, Greenwood Press, 2010.

Sapontzis, Steve F. (ed.), *Food for Thought: The Debate over Eating Meat*, Prometheus Books, 2004.

Schonholz, Stephanie, "MARS Celebrates Great American MeatOut Day," *Michigan Daily*, April 11, 2011, available at http://www.michigandaily.com/content/mars-celebrates-great-american-meatout-day.

Tuttle, Brad, "The Meatless (and Less Meat) Revolution," *Time*, March 22, 2012, available at http://business.time.com/2012/03/22/the-meatless-and-less-meat-revolution/.

ALEX HERSHAFT

PLANT-BASED NUTRITION

It is the position of the American Dietetic Association that appropriately planned vegetarian diets, including total vegetarian or vegan diets, are healthful, nutritionally adequate, and may provide health benefits in the prevention and treatment of certain diseases. Well-planned vegetarian diets are appropriate for individuals during all stages of the life cycle, including pregnancy, lactation, infancy, childhood, and adolescence, and for athletes. . . . A vegetarian diet is associated with a lower risk of death from ischemic heart disease. (Craig and Mangels)

A central piece of evidence underpinning the preceding conclusions from the American Dietetic Association (ADA) is the collaborative analysis of five separate studies of vegetarians in the United States, the United Kingdom, and Germany (Key et al.). This analysis showed a moderate advantage for vegetarians compared with meat-eaters in terms of lower death rates both from heart disease and from all causes combined.

This has been confirmed by some more recent studies. The longest-living group of people in the world are U.S. Seventh Day Adventists. U.S. Adventist vegetarians who drink milk live about two years longer than non-vegetarians, and U.S. Adventist vegans (who use no animal products at all) have slightly lower death rates than other vegetarians (Fraser 238). This observation is sufficient to show that animal foods are not required for excellent health.

It is noteworthy that this health *advantage* for vegetarian and vegan diets is more apparent in studies in the United States than in the United Kingdom or Germany. The reasons for this difference continue to be debated and explored (better B12 intakes for U.S. vegetarians, higher intake of red meat by U.S. nonvegetarians, and so on), but overall there is good evidence that vegetarians are at no disadvantage compared with meat-eaters.

However, any diet can be rendered unhealthy by poor choices, and common weaknesses in vegetarian diets differ from common weaknesses in Western omnivorous diets. For instance, a vegan is much less likely than a meat-eater to consume excessive saturated fat but more likely to get too little vitamin B12. It is therefore important to set out specific guidelines for the "appropriately planned" diet referred to by the ADA. Although some vegetarians may include milk, eggs, or honey in addition to plant-derived foods in their diet, the following guidelines provide a foundation for good health for all types of vegetarians, including vegans.

- Eat a wide variety of whole, lightly processed foods.
- Include plenty of brightly colored fruits and vegetables—ideally five hundred grams (about a pound) or more per day. Oranges, berries, apricots, cherries, nectarines, tomatoes, green leafy vegetables, beetroot, carrots, and sweet potatoes all count.
- Eat regular small amounts of nuts and oils, preferably those rich in monounsaturates, such as almonds, cashews, hazels (filberts), and macadamias, and olive and rapeseed oil. (Use more of these foods if you tend to be underweight.)
- Limit use of highly processed foods, particularly those containing hydrogenated fats or a lot of salt.
- Get at least three micrograms of vitamin B12 per day from fortified foods or supplements.
- Include a good source of plant omega-3s, such as

a teaspoon of flaxseed oil or two tablespoons of ground flaxseed or two tablespoons of rapeseed oil per day.
- Get at least 500 milligrams of calcium per day from calcium-rich foods or supplements (together with calcium in other foods, this should give an adequate intake).

Ensure an adequate amount of the following:

- Selenium (if local crops are low in selenium, take ten Brazil nuts per week or a supplement providing about fifty micrograms per day)
- Iodine (if local crops are low in iodine, eat fifteen grams of kelp *per year* or two kelp tablets per week or take a supplement providing about 150 micrograms per day)
- Vitamin D (from sunlight when the sun is more than forty degrees above the horizon or from a supplement if this is not possible for more than a few months of the year)

The example of iodine illustrates the need for care in setting guidelines for vegetarian diets in different countries. Plants will grow even if soil iodine levels are low, but animals need iodine for healthy growth and reproduction, and plants grown in low-iodine soils contain little iodine. Many countries compensate for low soil iodine by iodizing salt, but this is a blunt instrument, given both the variability of salt intakes and the widespread recommendation to reduce use of salt. In the United Kingdom, salt is not iodized, but iodine supply relies critically on iodine added to cattle feed concentrates, making dairy products the main source of iodine in the U.K. diet.

Vitamin D is mainly provided by sunshine, but synthesis requires wavelengths that are filtered out when the sun is low on the horizon or when sunblock is used heavily. Dark-skinned people living far from the equator are at particularly high risk if dietary supply is low. Cow's milk is sometimes perceived as a good source of vitamin D, but this depends not on naturally occurring vitamin D in milk but on whether the vitamin D is added (this varies by country and is very common in the United States but rare in the United Kingdom).

Some people may be surprised to see no mention of protein in these recommendations, but almost any reasonably varied diet with sufficient calories will meet protein needs. Similarly, iron is generally no more (or less) an issue for vegetarians than for omnivores.

Appropriate planning therefore involves some guidelines specific to vegetarians and in some cases specific to particular countries and particular types of vegetarianism. Such guidelines are easily implemented, though unfortunately not all vegetarians follow them. Wider adoption of the aforementioned healthy choices could improve the good health already observed still further.

Related articles: Ethical vegetarianism; Vegan living; Vegetarianism in Britain and America; The welfare of cows

Craig, W. J., and Mangels, A. R. (for the American Dietetic Association), "Position of the American Dietetic Association: Vegetarian Diets," *Journal of the American Dietetic Association* 109.7 (2009): 1266–1282, available at http://www.eatright.org/WorkArea/DownloadAsset.aspx?id=8417.

Davis, B., and Melina, V., *Becoming Vegan*, Book Publishing Company, 2000.

Fraser, G., *Diet, Life Expectancy and Chronic Disease*, Oxford University Press, 2003.

Key, T. J., et al., "Mortality in Vegetarians and Nonvegetarians: Detailed Findings from a Collaborative Analysis of 5 Prospective Studies," *American Journal of Clinical Nutrition* 70 (1999): 516S–524S, available at http://www.ajcn.org/content/70/3/516S.full.pdf.

Messina, V., Mangels, R., and Messina, M., *The Dietitian's Guide to Vegetarian Diets*, Jones and Bartlett, 2004.

Norris, J., and Messina, V., *Vegan for Life*, Da Capo, 2011.

Walsh, S., *Plant Based Nutrition and Health*, the Vegan Society, 2003.

STEPHEN WALSH

VEGAN LIVING

What do the following everyday items have in common: a pair of shoes, a paintbrush, a roll of photographic film, and a glass of wine? Chances are that they have all been manufactured using products derived from animals. In some cases, the connection is obvious: the shoes will probably be made of leather, and the paintbrush from animal bristles. In others, less so: photographic film is coated in gelatin (derived from animal bones and skins); most wines are cleared using a variety of animal-derived substances. The good news for vegans and others who prefer to avoid products derived wholly or partly from animals is that animal-free alternatives are available for all of these items.

Vegans are vegetarians who, recognizing the cruelties inherent in the farming of animals, choose not to consume any animal foods, including meat, poultry, game, fishes, shellfishes, dairy products, eggs, and honey. At first sight this might appear to leave little to choose from. However, a healthy vegan diet is based on whole grains, beans, fruits, vegetables, nuts, and seeds. That is a lot of foods to choose from, and with the year-round availability of fruits and vegetables and the widespread introduction of alternatives to animal foods, the choices are growing daily. Many readers will be familiar with, for example, vegetarian burgers and soy milks, but did you know that you can now buy animal-free versions of haggis or even caviar? This is not to characterize vegan cooking, which draws inspiration from a wide range of international cuisines, as a pale imitation of "meat and two vegetables," but it is reassuring to know that you can still enjoy the taste of animal foods if you want to without contributing to the suffering that their production entails.

Around sixty billion birds and mammals are slaughtered for food in the world each year: roughly nine animals for every man, woman, and child on the planet (fish catch is measured in tonnage, so numbers are almost impossible to estimate). Many of these animals are reared intensively in farming systems that deny some of their most basic behavioral needs. Most are killed at an early age, as soon as they have reached slaughter weight, or when their productive capacity declines. Vegans reject the view that farmed animals are mere commodities to be traded, exploited, slaughtered, and butchered. If animals are to be granted rights, the right to life itself is fundamental, and if this sounds hopelessly idealistic, consider the alternative. With the human population expected to exceed nine billion by the middle of the twenty-first century, can we really afford to continue feeding one-third of the world's grain harvest to farmed animals? Should we continue to cut down tropical rainforest for cattle ranching, plunder the world's oceans, and destroy the habitats of free-living animals merely to satisfy a craving for animal food? Or should we adopt a varied plant-based diet instead, a truly sustainable diet that promotes both human health and the health of the planet?

Buying animal-free food is relatively easy, especially if you base your diet on whole foods. A varied vegan diet can provide all the nutrients that the human body needs at all stages of life. Indeed, because vegans tend to be slimmer and have lower cholesterol levels than either meat-eaters or vegetarians, you might enjoy better health than previously. The resources listed in the reference list will help you plan a nutritious vegan diet. But what about those shoes and other everyday items normally derived from animals? Vegans may "tread lightly on the earth," but must they walk barefoot? Fortunately not! Publications such as the Vegan Society's *Animal Free Shopper*, which lists animal-free foods, drinks, household and garden products, toiletries and cosmetics, footwear, and clothing, make vegan living a practical as well as a compassionate alternative.

Related articles: Animal welfare and farming; Animals and public health; Birds used in food production; Caring shopping; Cruelty-free labeling; Ethical vegetarianism; The ethics of killing free-living animals; Fish farming; Meatout; The moral claims of animals; Plant-based nutrition; Sea fishes and commercial fishing; Slaughter; The universal charter of the rights of other species; Vegetarian cooking; Vegetarianism in Britain and America

Cook, Liz, *So, What Do You Eat? A Practical Guide to Healthy Animal-Free Nutrition and Easy Family Meals*, Liz Cook, 1999.

Davis, Brenda, and Melina, Vesanto, *Becoming Vegan*, Book Publishing Company, 2000.

Davis, Brenda, Melina, Vesanto, and Berry, Rynn, *Becoming Raw: The Essential Guide to Raw Vegan Diets*, Book Publishing Company, 2010.

Masson, Jeffrey Moussaieff, *The Face on Your Plate*, Norton, 2009.

The Vegan Society, *Animal Free Shopper*, 8th ed., 2008.

Walsh, Stephen, *Plant Based Nutrition and Health*, the Vegan Society, 2003.

PAUL APPLEBY

VEGANIC GARDENING

Many animal advocates, including vegetarians and vegans, enjoy growing their own fruits and vegetables. For those who shun animal products for ethical, health, and environmental reasons, the idea of growing their own organic foods makes perfect sense and gives peace of mind about their food supply. Although gardening organically means avoiding harmful synthetic chemicals, many instructions for organic gardening include the use of animal-based products, such as bone meal, blood meal, fish emulsion, and manure—all of which involve killing more than just your appetite.

Thankfully, vegetarians can have their kale and eat it too if they follow the principles of veganic gardening and use only plant-based materials to prepare soil and nourish crops. The basics of successful gardening include preparing and maintaining healthy soil, fertilizing plants with the right combination of nutrients, and protecting crops from "pests" and disease. All of this can be accomplished without employing the animal by-products that unfortunately often link the organic and animal agriculture industries.

The leftover blood, bone, offal, hooves, horns, and feathers not directly processed by slaughterhouses are taken by rendering companies to be turned into material sold to commercial farms and gardening supply companies. Blood is spray-dried and turned into meal, which is used as a fertilizer; bones are steamed to separate out any remaining collagen and flesh before being ground into a meal that is spread on fields to add nitrogen. Fish-processing plants sell "squid juice" and other remains, which are processed with sulfuric or phosphoric acid to create liquid emulsions or are dried into meals for supplemental nitrogen.

In addition to the ethical implications of using slaughterhouse by-products, there are concerns about human health and safety; it is possible that contaminants from factory farms can be spread to products derived from such facilities. For example, the use of cow and poultry manure as fertilizer is questionable because of the fear of E. coli, staphylococci, and enterococci bacteria being spread onto crops. There are few regulations on the processing or sale of manure, and degrees of processing (such as heating or aging) vary.

Plant-based materials offer the same nutrients as animal-based products and are as easy, if not easier, to obtain and use. The compost concept dates back to Sir Albert Howard (1873–1947), a British botanist and governor in India who helped pioneer the "Indore method" of layering green (freshly cut) vegetation with brown (dead leaves and so on) to create an organic mix that is eaten by bacteria, which in turn are consumed by protozoa that excrete nitrogen, to create nature's perfect plant food. Earthworms, who eat the protozoa, improve soil by virtue of their waste as well as their natural aeration.

When gardening veganically, use compost derived from dead leaves, grass clippings, and other organic matter to create a healthy environment for cultivation; a soil test can determine the health of the plot. Next, sow plants based on their suitability to the soil and climate, to reduce the need for maintenance. Nitrogen is a key nutrient that can be supplied by adding so-called green manure, plant-based sources of nitrogen. Planting peas, beans, barley, buckwheat, rye, clover, or alfalfa alongside regular crops, but turning them into the soil while they are at the flowering (and most nitrogen-producing) stage, increases soil fertility. Seaweed meal is another plant-based form of fertilizer, as are comfrey and nettles.

A variety of techniques and materials can control weeds, "pests," and diseases. Mulching with straw, grass clippings, wood bark, or even newspaper (without colored ink) is highly effective in blocking weed growth. For natural "pest" control, gardeners can make their plots hospitable to the snakes, toads, birds, and other animals who normally feed on insects that can threaten crops. For example, ladybugs (also called "ladybird beetles") eat aphids, and hedgehogs consume slugs and snails. Planting small trees or shrubs near a garden offers shelter to birds and natural predators. Marigolds are among the plants that attract beneficial nematodes to thwart certain "pests." Sprays containing horticultural oil or insecticidal soaps (often with pyrethrins, a natural pesticide derived from chrysanthemums) can be applied directly to plants. Netting and plant collars can be used as physical barriers. Diseases should be handled on an individual basis with advice from Web sites or gardening manuals.

As concern for the Earth and its inhabitants grows, so does the availability of vegan organic gardening products and information. With the right amount of preparation and supervision, plus a holistic approach to cultivation and replenishment, a safe and savory harvest awaits.

Related articles: Animals and public health; Birds used in food production; Ethical vegetarianism; Living with animal neighbors; Plant-based nutrition; The protection of birds; Slaughter; Understanding amphibians; Vegan living; Vegetarian cooking; Vegetarianism in Britain and America; The welfare of cows

Church, Jill Howard, "Veganic Gardening," *The Animals' Agenda* 20.4 (2000).

Coleman, Elliot, *The New Organic Grower*, Chelsea Green, 1995.

Flowerdew, Bob, *Bob Flowerdew's Organic Bible: Successful Gardening the Natural Way*, Kyle Cathie, 2003.

Hall, Jenny, and Tolhurst, Iain, *Growing Green—Organic Techniques for a Sustainable Future*, Chelsea Green, 2007.

O'Brien, Kenneth Dalziel, *Veganic Gardening—The Alternative System for Healthier Crops*, Thorsons, 1986.

Vegan Organic Network, "Vegan Organic Growing—The Basics," available at http://www.veganorganic.net/information-sheets/4-vegan-organic-growing-the-basics.

JILL HOWARD CHURCH

VEGETARIAN COOKING

It is not as difficult to move toward a plant-based diet as many suppose. There are many good cookbooks readily available and many large searchable Web archives—for example, from the International Vegetarian Union. Many communities and grocery stores offer vegetarian cooking classes. Following are a few foods that you may want to incorporate into your kitchen and several quick ideas of how you can create simple, but very appealing dishes.

In terms of staples, try soy products such as tofu and tempeh. Tofu is soybean curds pressed into a block; tempeh is fermented whole-bean soy, often with other grains added. Buy water-packed tofu for main-course dishes and aseptically packaged silken tofu for desserts (try blending silken tofu with chocolate, jam, or preserves and a little sweetener such as brown rice syrup for a yummy pudding!). A trick for water-packed tofu is to put it, unopened, in the freezer and then defrost it. The tofu gains a nice spongy texture and an increased ability to soak up marinades and flavors of food it is cooked with. Try adding medium-cubed tofu to stir-fries or mashing it and making scrambled tofu with turmeric, sautéed onions, mushrooms, and bell peppers. Tempeh is delicious sliced thinly and then sautéed till both sides are golden brown. I love the simple but tasty dinner of a quick pasta served next to tempeh sautéed with onion and shiitake mushrooms, along with crusty bread and a salad.

Lentils are heavily used in Indian cooking (among other culinary traditions), and there are a wide variety of lentil soups (dhals) that one can make. South Indians make a tremendous range of rice dishes, including one of my favorites, dosa, which consists of fermented rice and lentils made into a thin crepe and filled with a savory potato-onion mixture. There are many other interesting pastas and grains, such as buckwheat, couscous, and quinoa; in general, they can be prepared as part of sophisticated delicacies or simply simmered in water or vegetable broth for texture and to complement a main course.

One thing that can mark out someone as a good cook is the use of slightly different ingredients. Bell pepper? Use a pretty purple or bright yellow one—color and presentation definitely count, even when cooking for oneself. Want to use an onion? Try a (well-cleaned) leek or several shallots instead. Add fresh herbs to recipes. Peanut butter? Try other nut butters, such as cashew, almond, macadamia nut, or pistachio—often available freshly ground in fine stores. Or even substitute sesame paste (tahini), the base for the wonderful Middle Eastern dips hummus and baba ghanoush (the basic hummus recipe calls for a can of chickpeas, several cloves of garlic, a scallion, a few tablespoons of lemon juice, a little salt, and a few tablespoons of tahini blended to a thick paste and then seasoned with a little bit of cayenne and cumin and possibly thinned with some of the liquid the chickpeas were canned with; baba ghanoush is prepared similarly, but use roasted eggplant instead of chickpeas). The best popcorn I have ever tasted is one I make with gourmet red "strawberry" popcorn kernels popped in rosemary-infused grapeseed oil and served with a nondairy, nonhydrogenated butter-like spread, with salt and optional nutritional yeast.

It is also possible to embrace vegetarianism while beginning with the "standard" ingredients you already have. Warm some tortillas; stuff them with vegetables, including lettuce and tomatoes, and maybe fresh oregano; and top with your favorite salsa. Invest in an inexpensive electric grater and make hash brown potatoes that your friends will request over and over again—and make them special by including gourmet mushrooms, onions, and a dash of hot sauce. Sweet potatoes are nutritional and tasty; try making mashed sweet potatoes—or for that matter, add fun color to your dishes by looking for (natural) blue or purple potatoes.

If you are a pizza fan, find or make a crust that you like, and cut ripe, but firm roma tomatoes into quarter-inch slices. Overlap the slices on the shell, spray a little olive oil on top, sprinkle on a pinch of salt, and bake at a moderate temperature (350 degrees Fahrenheit) in the oven for about eight to ten minutes, until the tomatoes start to melt and become sauce-like. Serve with fresh basil and oregano—and you will love it without any toppings.

As you explore vegetarian cooking, you will find it offers endless varieties. Food preparation can be simple, or you can explore truly gourmet ideas and make complex meals. There is a wide range of vegetarian burgers, hot dogs, and cold cuts and of dairy-free ice creams and frozen dinners, for those who seek convenience without sacrificing taste. In helping the animals, there is no reason to sacrifice your taste buds.

Ethical vegetarianism; Meatout; Plant-based nutrition; Veganic gardening; Vegetarianism in Britain and America

Brown, Sarah, *Vegetarian Kitchen*, BBC Books, 1984.

Fraser, Gary E., et al., "Ten Years of Life: Is It a Matter of Choice?" *Archives of Internal Medicine* 161 (2001): 1645–1652, available at http://www.inlandempireonline.com/de/metro/vegetarian.

Iacobbo, Karen, and Iacobbo, Michael, *Vegetarians and Vegans in America Today*, Greenwood, 2006.

Kesteloot, H., "Dietary Fat and Health: The Epidemiological Evidence," *Acta Cardiologica* 44.6 (1989): 446–448.

Moskowitz, Isa Chandra, and Romero, Terry Hope, *Veganomicon: The Ultimate Vegan Cookbook*, Perseus Books, 2007.

Robertson, Robin, and Robertson, Jon, *The Sacred Kitchen*, New World Library, 1999.

Towns, Sharon, and Towns, Daniel, *Voices from the Garden: Stories of Becoming a Vegetarian*, Lantern Books, 2001.

DILIP BARMAN

ABOUT THE EDITOR

ANDREW LINZEY is director of the Oxford Centre for Animal Ethics and a member of the Faculty of Theology in the University of Oxford. He is also honorary professor at the University of Winchester, special professor at Saint Xavier University in Chicago, and the first professor of animal ethics at the Graduate Theological Foundation in Indiana. He has written or edited more than twenty books, including *Animal Theology* (SCM Press and University of Illinois Press, 1994); *Animal Gospel* (Hodder and Stoughton and Westminster John Knox Press, 1999); *Animals on the Agenda: Questions about Animals for Theology and Ethics* (SCM Press and University of Illinois Press, 1999); *Creatures of the Same God* (Winchester University Press and Lantern Books, 2007); and *Why Animal Suffering Matters* (Oxford University Press, 2009). With Priscilla N. Cohn, he edits the *Journal of Animal Ethics* published by the University of Illinois Press and also the Palgrave Macmillan book series on animal ethics.

ABOUT THE CONTRIBUTORS

AYSHA AKHTAR is a double board–certified neurologist and public health specialist with the U.S. Food and Drug Administration and a fellow of the Oxford Centre for Animal Ethics. She is the author of *Animals and Public Health: Why Treating Animals Better Is Critical to Human Welfare* (2012). The opinions expressed in her articles are solely her own.

LIBBY ANDERSON is the policy director of the U.K. animal welfare charity OneKind.

PAUL APPLEBY was secretary of Oxford Vegetarians from 1983 to 2008 and has also served as a trustee of both the Vegetarian Society and the Vegan Society in the United Kingdom.

PHIL ARKOW is cofounder of the National Link Coalition and chairs the Latham Foundation's Animal Abuse and Family Violence Prevention Project. He has served with the National Animal Control Association, the American Veterinary Medical Association, the Delta Society, and the American Association of Human-Animal Bond Veterinarians. He teaches animal-assisted therapy at Harcum College and Camden County College.

GWEN BAILEY was head of animal behavior for the Blue Cross for twelve years and now organizes Puppy School, which runs positive training classes for puppy caregivers in the United Kingdom.

JONATHAN BALCOMBE is an ethologist based in Washington, DC. He is the author of numerous books, including *Second Nature* (2010), *Pleasurable Kingdom* (2011), and *The Exultant Ark* (2007).

DILIP BARMAN is an author, the president of the Triangle Vegetarian Society, and the vice president of the Vegetarian Union of North America.

ARA PAUL BARSAM is an associate professor at Arizona State University in the School of Politics and Global Studies and a founding fellow of the Oxford Centre for Animal Ethics.

JANET E. BAYNGER has researched the humane movement in Canada and is author of *Fanbelt Freddie and Friends: The History of the Kingston Humane Society* (2000).

DOROTHY BEESON is the founder of the Swan Sanctuary, which is the largest facility dedicated to swan and waterfowl welfare in the United Kingdom.

MARC BEKOFF is a professor emeritus of ecology and evolutionary biology at the University of Colorado.

ALAN H. BERGER served as the executive director/CEO of the Animal Protection Institute from 1994 to 2003.

ALEXANDRA BERNSTEIN is studying law at the University of Pace Law School with a concentration on environmental law and animal law.

MARK H. BERNSTEIN is a professor of philosophy and holds the Joyce and Edward E. Brewer Chair in Applied Ethics at Purdue University. He is also a fellow of the Oxford Centre for Animal Ethics.

FAITH BJALOBOK is a professor of philosophy at Duquesne University and West Virginia University and a fellow at the Oxford Centre for Animal Ethics. She is the founder of Fluffyjean Fund for Felines and the outreach program director for Hog Heaven Rescue Farm.

SUE BLACKMORE is the director of marketing and development in the Hollywood office of the Humane Society of the United States and a former entertainment industry publicist and marketer.

PAULA BLANCHARD is an author and biographer. She was a cochairperson of the Committee to Protect Dogs (Massachusetts, 2007–2008) and currently serves on the board of directors of the GREY2K USA Education Fund.

JASMIJN DE BOO is the chief executive officer of the Vegan Society (U.K.) and founded the political party Animals Count (U.K.) in 2006.

JUNE BRADLAW was a research biologist with the U.S. Food and Drug Administration whose work led to test tube alternatives to using animals in laboratory testing. She has served as a scientific adviser to the National Anti-Vivisection Society in the United States and the International Foundation for Ethical Research.

PHIL BROOKE is the welfare and education development manager for Compassion in World Farming, a leading farm animal welfare organization.

SHARON TAYLOR BROWN is a biologist with the U.S.-based educational nonprofit Beavers: Wetlands and Wildlife.

JOHN BRYANT was formerly vice-chair of the council of the Royal Society for the Prevention of Cruelty to Animals and manager of the Ferne Animal Sanctuary in Somerset. Since 1998, he has been director of a professional humane urban wildlife deterrence service.

JONATHAN BURT is a writer, the author of *Animals in Film* (2002), and the editor of the Reaktion Animal Series.

SAMANTHA JANE CALVERT recently completed her PhD at the School of Philosophy, Theology and Religion, University of Birmingham, England, and is an associate fellow of the Oxford Centre for Animal Ethics.

DEBORAH CAO is a professor of Griffith University, Australia, and a linguist, legal scholar, and animal advocate. She is also a fellow of the Oxford Centre for Animal Ethics.

CHRISTOPHER KEY CHAPPLE is the Doshi Professor of Indic and Comparative Theology at Loyola Marymount University in Los Angeles.

HOLLY CHEEVER is a veterinarian, a member of the Leadership Council of the Humane Society Veterinary Medical Association, and the vice president of the New York State Humane Association.

JILL HOWARD CHURCH is a writer, editor, and photographer and is the communications director for the Animals and Society Institute.

BARBARA CLARKE is cofounder and executive director of the DreamCatcher Wild Horse and Burro Sanctuary.

PRISCILLA N. COHN is a professor emeritus of philosophy at Abington College, Pennsylvania State University, and the associate director of the Oxford Centre for Animal Ethics.

ANDREW CONSTANT is the founder, a trustee, and a behavior coordinator of Animals in Mind (U.K.).

JAN CREAMER is the chief executive of the National Anti-Vivisection Society (U.K.) and the Lord Dowding Fund for Humane Research, a post that she has held since 1986. In 1990, she cofounded Animal Defenders International.

PEGGY CUNNIFF has been the executive director of the National Anti-Vivisection Society in the United States since 1987 and serves as the president of the International Foundation for Ethical Research.

KAREN DAVIS was professor of English at the University of Maryland and is now president of United Poultry Concerns, which she founded in 1990 to promote the compassionate and respectful treatment of domesticated fowl.

CHRIS DEACON is a consultant with the U.K.-based company Ethical Investors.

JAN DECKERS is a lecturer in health care ethics in the Institute of Health and Society at Newcastle University.

DANIEL A. DOMBROWSKI is a professor of philosophy at the University of Seattle and a fellow of the Oxford Centre for Animal Ethics.

BRIANNE DONALDSON is a professor and the director of the Center for Jain Studies at Claremont Lincoln University.

JOYCE D'SILVA is the ambassador and former CEO of Compassion in World Farming, a leading farm animal welfare organization.

DEBORAH ELLSWORTH helped run Redwings Horse Sanctuary for ten years and cofounded DreamCatcher Wild Horse and Burro Sanctuary.

AUDREY EYTON is a best-selling writer on food, diet, and animal welfare.

CHRISTOPHER FAIRFAX is a lawyer and the director of Animal Friends Insurance.

ELIZABETH FARIANS is a pioneer woman theologian, lifelong feminist, and animal activist who created a course on animal theology at Xavier University in Cincinnati, Ohio.

JOANNE FIELDER is a veterinarian and has worked with farmed, companion, and free-living animals—notably through the Orangutan Foundation International in Borneo and the International Fund for Animal Welfare, serving as global emergency relief veterinarian with the latter. She is currently a trustee for the British Veterinary Association Animal Welfare Foundation.

DEBORAH FOUTS is the cofounder and codirector of the nonprofit organization Friends of Washoe and directs the Chimpanzee and Human Communication Institute, a sanctuary located on the campus of Central Washington University.

ROGER FOUTS is the dean of graduate studies and research at Central Washington University and is a cofounder and codirector of the nonprofit organization Friends of Washoe.

JO-ANN FOWLER is director of the Society for Companion Animal Studies.

CAMILLA H. FOX is the founding executive director of Project Coyote and a wildlife consultant with the Animal Welfare Institute.

LYNDA FREEBREY served as the press officer of the International League for the Protection of Horses, now World Horse Welfare.

BIRUTÉ MARY GALDIKAS is a full professor at Simon Fraser University in British Columbia, Canada, and the president of Orangutan Foundation International in the United States.

ROBERT GARNER is a professor of politics at the University of Leicester and a fellow of the Oxford Centre for Animal Ethics.

JULIET GELLATLEY is a nutritional therapist and the founder and director of Viva!—Europe's largest campaigning group on vegetarian and vegan issues—and of the Vegetarian and Vegan Foundation, a U.K. charity specializing in health and nutrition.

MARK GLOVER is the director of Respect for Animals and a recipient of the Lord Erskine award from the Royal Society for the Prevention of Cruelty to Animals.

JANE GOODALL is a conservationist and animal advocate famous for her research on chimpanzees at Tanzania's Gombe national park. She is the founder of the Jane Goodall Institute and currently serves as a National Geographic Society Explorer-in-Residence. In 2004, Dr. Goodall was made a dame of the British Empire.

MARSHA L. GREEN is a professor at Albright College and the founder and president of the Ocean Mammal Institute.

ELEONORA GULLONE is an associate professor of psychology at Monash University in Victoria, Australia, and a fellow of the Oxford Centre for Animal Ethics.

CELIA HAMMOND, one of the supermodels of the 1960s, gave up her modeling career to devote her life to animal welfare and is now director of the Celia Hammond Animal Trust (U.K.).

STEPHEN HARRIS is a professor of environmental sciences at the University of Bristol.

HOLLY HAZARD is the chief innovations officer at the Humane Society of the United States, where she leads a variety of programs, including the Humane Society Veterinary Medical Association, the HSUS Direct Care Centers, the equine program, and humane wildlife services.

ALEX HERSHAFT is the founder and president of Farm Animal Rights Movement. He launched World Farm Animals Day in 1983, the Great American Meatout in 1985, and Gentle Thanksgiving in 1990.

HAROLD HERZOG is a professor of psychology at Western Carolina University.

SIDNEY J. HOLT is a marine biologist who has served as director of the Fisheries Resources and Operations Division of the Food and Agriculture Organization of the United Nations and as scientific adviser to the International Fund for Animal Welfare.

KAI HORSTHEMKE is an associate professor in the Wits School of Education, University of the Witwatersrand, South Africa, where he teaches philosophy.

CAROL B. JOHNSON is a private investigator licensed by the State of Alabama and the president of Critter Haven, Inc.

LISA JOHNSON is an associate professor at the University of Puget Sound and a fellow of the Oxford Centre for Animal Ethics.

DEBORAH M. JONES is the general secretary of Catholic Concern for Animals and a fellow of the Oxford Centre for Animal Ethics.

DENA M. JONES is the farm animal program manager at the Animal Welfare Institute in Washington, DC.

W. J. JORDAN is a veterinarian and has taught at Pretoria University in South Africa. He received an Order of the British Empire from the Queen and the highest award from the Royal Society for the Prevention of Cruelty to Animals for animal welfare and conservation.

ROBERTA KALECHOFSKY is a fiction writer, speaker, and essayist and the publisher of Micah Publications.

BEVERLY KASKEY is the senior director of the Hollywood office of the Humane Society of the United States and the executive producer of the annual Genesis Awards. She was formerly director of special projects for Metro Goldwyn Mayer.

ELLIOT M. KATZ is a veterinarian and the founder and president of In Defense of Animals.

HILDA KEAN was until recently the director of public history and dean of Ruskin College, Oxford.

BRUCE KENT is the chair of the Movement for the Abolition of War, founded in 2000. He is also a vice president of Pax Christi UK and the British Campaign for Nuclear Disarmament.

ELAINE KING is a zoologist and former chief executive of the Badger Trust (U.K.).

STEPHEN G. KING is a dog behavior specialist and a founding member of the Association of Pet Dog Trainers, whose code of practice allows only kind, fair, and force-free methods of training.

SARAH KITE is director of special projects for the British Union for the Abolition of Vivisection and has been investigating the international trade in primates for research for the past twenty years.

BODHIN KJOLHEDE completed a fifteen-year course of residential training under Roshi Philip Kapleau, who ordained him as a Buddhist priest in 1976, and in 1987, he became Kapleau's dharma successor and abbot of the Zen Center, New York.

LIVE KLEVELAND is the legal adviser for the Norwegian Animal Protection Alliance and has been a practicing lawyer with the Norwegian Food Safety Authority.

ANDREW KNIGHT is a European veterinary specialist in welfare science, ethics, and law and a fellow of the Oxford Centre for Animal Ethics. He has authored around 100 publications on animal issues, including *The Costs and Benefits of Animal Experiments* (2011).

ANTON KRAG is a biologist and scientific adviser to the Norwegian Animal Protection Alliance.

MARCIA KRAMER is an attorney and works as the director of Legal and Legislative Programs for the National Anti-Vivisection Society in the United States.

ROB LAIDLAW is a biologist and the executive director of Zoocheck Canada.

GILL LANGLEY is a scientist who for thirty years played a key role in the development of non-animal science, mainly through her work as science director at the Dr Hadwen Trust for Humane Research.

DAVID M. LAVIGNE, a former zoology professor at the University of Guelph, is currently science adviser to the International Fund for Animal Welfare.

CHIEN-HUI LI is an assistant professor of history at the National Cheng Kung University, Taiwan.

RANDALL LOCKWOOD is the senior vice president of forensic sciences and anticruelty projects with the American Society for the Prevention of Cruelty to Animals. He provides training in the investigation and prosecution of animal cruelty for law enforcement, veterinary, and animal care and control professionals worldwide.

PHILIP LYMBERY is the chief executive of Compassion in World Farming, a leading international farm animal welfare organization.

ALASTAIR MacMILLAN is the chief veterinary officer of the Royal Society for the Prevention of Cruelty to Animals.

DAVID MADDEN is a retired British diplomat, a former ambassador to Greece, and a consultant to the World Society for the Protection of Animals.

RANDY MALAMUD is Regents' Professor and chair of English at Georgia State University in Atlanta and the author of *Reading Zoos: Representations of Animals and Captivity* (1998) and *Poetic Animals and Animal Souls* (2003). He is a patron of the Captive Animals' Protection Society and a fellow of the Oxford Centre for Animal Ethics.

BRUNO MANZINI is a worker-student of veterinary medicine at the University of Parma and has written and broadcast on the welfare of stray dogs.

SUSAN MARINO is a registered nurse and a specialist in many forms of holistic therapy. She is the founder of Angel's Gate Hospice and Rehabilitation Centre for Animals.

CHRISTOPHER F. MASON was formerly professor of ecology at the University of Essex.

ELLY MAYNARD is the founder and president of Sirius Global Animal Charitable Trust.

PERRY McCARNEY formerly worked as an information technology specialist and is now a writer with Helium.com.

SHIRLEY McGREAL founded the International Primate Protection League in 1973 and continues to run the organization from its headquarters in Summerville, South Carolina.

MECHTHILD MENCH is the chairman of Initiative-Anti-Corrida in Germany and vice president of Animal 2000—Menschen fuer Tierrechte Bayern e.V. She has worked against bull fighting, blood fiestas, and rodeos since 2000.

ROSS MINETT has a master of science degree in applied animal behavior and animal welfare and previously held the position of "knowledge builder" for OneKind (U.K.).

LES MITCHELL is the director of the Hunterstoun Centre of the University of Fort Hare, South Africa.

TERRY MOORE is the director of the Cat Survival Trust for endangered species.

TONY MOORE cofounded Fight Against Animal Cruelty in Europe (FAACE) in 1987 to work against animal cruelty in Europe.

ELIZABETH MURDOCK is a wildlife conservationist and organizational development consultant based in San Francisco. She has worked on avian, marine, and predator conservation issues with a number of non-profits, including as executive director of the Golden Gate Audubon Society and as the shark-conservation program manager for WildAid.

CARLOS M. NACONECY is a Brazilian ethicist, independent researcher, and author. He was a visiting scholar at the University of Cambridge and is a fellow of the Oxford Centre for Animal Ethics.

THILLAYVEL NAIDOO was formerly senior lecturer in the Department of Science of Religion at the University of Kwazulu-Natal.

STEPHEN V. NASH works for the CITES Secretariat, which is administered by the United Nations Environment Programme (UNEP) and is located at Geneva, Switzerland. Its role is fundamental to the Convention on International Trade in Endangered Species, and its functions are laid down in Article XII of the text of the convention. His article is written on behalf of the CITES Secretariat.

PETER F. NEVILLE is a referral companion animal behavior consultant and currently a clinical professor at the Department of Veterinary Medicine at Miyazaki University, Japan, with an adjunct position at Ohio State University in the United States.

JEAN-CLAUDE NOUËT is a professor of medicine and biology and emeritus vice-dean in the Faculty of Medicine, Pierre et Marie Curie, Paris, and founder of the French League for Animal Rights.

IRINA NOVOZHILOVA is the president of the VITA Animal Rights Center in Moscow and a member of the Russian Union of Journalists.

RICHARD O'BARRY made a radical transition from training dolphins in captivity to opposing the captivity industry soon after Kathy, one of the *Flipper* dolphins, died. In 1970, he founded the Dolphin Project, a group that aims to educate the public about captivity and, where feasible, free captive dolphins.

PAMELA OSENKOWSKI is the director of science programs at the National Anti-Vivisection Society in the United States and is an instructor in the biology department at Loyola University Chicago.

SIOBHAN O'SULLIVAN is a research fellow in the School of Social and Political Sciences at the University of Melbourne.

ANDY OTTAWAY is the founder and director of Campaign Whale and the Seal Protection Action Group.

NORM PHELPS is an author and a member of the North America Committee of the Institute for Critical Animal Studies.

LAWRENCE POPE is an author and campaigner and the head of the Victorian Advocates for Animals in Victoria, Australia.

KURT REMELE is an associate professor of ethics and Catholic social thought at Karl-Franzens-University in Graz, Austria, and a fellow of the Oxford Centre for Animal Ethics. He was a Fulbright Scholar at the Catholic University of America in 2003 and a visiting professor at the University of Minnesota in 2007 and at Gonzaga University in 2011–2012.

SALLIE K. RIGGS worked for eight years as the deputy director and then president and executive director of the National Marine Life Center in Bourne, Massachusetts.

JOANNE RIGHETTI is an animal behavior consultant, educating, researching, and communicating the pleasures and problems of the human–companion animal relationship.

JILL ROBINSON is the founder and chief executive officer of the Animals Asia Foundation.

NEAL ROBINSON is a professor of Arab and Islamic studies at the Australian National University and was formerly professor of Islamic studies at Sogang University in Seoul, Korea.

BERNARD E. ROLLIN is a university distinguished professor, professor of philosophy, professor of biomedical sciences, professor of animal sciences, and university bioethicist at Colorado State University, Fort Collins.

JOHN ROLLS is the director of policy at the Royal Society for the Prevention of Cruelty to Animals.

SANDY ROSS is a research fellow at the School of Social and Political Sciences, University of Melbourne.

RICHARD D. RYDER created the term "speciesism" in 1970 and has been chair of the council of the Royal Society for the Prevention of Cruelty to Animals, director of the Political Animal Lobby, and Mellon professor at Tulane University.

STEVE F. SAPONTZIS is a professor emeritus of philosophy at the East Bay campus of the California State University.

CARL SAUCIER-BOUFFARD is a professor in the Department of Humanities at Dawson College in Montreal, Canada, where he teaches courses in environmental and animal ethics. He is an associate fellow of the Oxford Centre for Animal Ethics.

J. G. G. SAXTON is an English veterinary surgeon, international homeopathic teacher, and writer.

JOAN E. SCHAFFNER is an associate professor of law at the George Washington University Law School and a fellow of the Oxford Centre for Animal Ethics.

DEREK SCHUURMAN specializes in nature-based tourism to Madagascar for Rainbow Tours (U.K.) and has worked with nongovernmental organizations, including the Missouri Botanical Gardens, on a lengthy campaign against illegal logging.

B. K. SHARMA is an associate professor and the head of zoology at R. L. Saharia Government P.G. College in Kaladera, which is affiliated with the University of Rajasthan in Jaipur, India. Recipient of the British Council's coveted Commonwealth Academic Staff Fellowship, he is also a former member of Britain's prestigious Royal Society.

SHAILJA SHARMA is a student of international business and management at Manchester Business School, the University of Manchester (U.K).

MARK PETER SIMMONDS is a biologist specializing in the effects of environmental changes on cetaceans and is the international director of science at the Whale and Dolphin Conservation Society.

JOHN SIMONS is the executive dean of the Faculty of Arts at Macquarie University in Sydney, Australia, and a fellow of the Oxford Centre for Animals Ethics.

ABBEY ANNE SMITH is a doctoral student, a veterinary anesthetist, and a canine behaviorist. She has a practical involvement in animal welfare, assessing and fostering rescued Great Danes with behavioral and/or physical problems.

DAVID SPRATT is a chartered biologist and a chartered scientist. He has worked in the zoo industry and has practical experience in fields of conservation and ecotourism. He is also a fellow of the Oxford Centre for Animal Ethics.

MARY F. STEWART is a veterinarian and honorary senior research fellow at the University of Glasgow Veterinary School. She is a veterinary adviser to the Pet Loss Befriender Service run jointly by the Society for Companion Animal Studies and the Blue Cross.

DEBORAH TABART is the chief executive officer of the Australian Koala Foundation.

ALI TAYLOR is the head of canine welfare training at the Battersea Dogs and Cats Home in London.

ANNE KENT TAYLOR is a National Geographic grantee and the founder of the Anne K. Taylor Fund, which seeks to conserve, protect, and restore biodiversity through sound economic activities that are ecologically sustainable.

KATY TAYLOR has a doctorate in animal behavior and medical statistics and is the senior science adviser at the British Union for the Abolition of Vivisection.

MICHELLE THEW is the chief executive of the British Union for the Abolition of Vivisection and the European Coalition to End Animal Experiments.

DAVID THOMAS is a lawyer, specializing in U.K. and international animal protection and human rights law. He is the legal adviser to the British Union for the Abolition of Vivisection and past chair of the council of the Royal Society for the Prevention of Cruelty to Animals.

SABRINA TONUTTI is a cultural anthropologist and a fellow of the Oxford Centre for Animal Ethics and was formerly a researcher at the University of Udine, Italy.

KATIE TRIPP is the director of science and conservation at Save the Manatee Club in Maitland, Florida.

JACKY TURNER has worked as a university researcher and teacher in physical science, was formerly the education and research director at Compassion in World Farming, and is now an independent writer on farmed animal welfare.

LOUISE VAN DER MERWE is the editor of the quarterly publication *Animal Voice*, the South African representative for Compassion in World Farming, and the managing trustee of the Humane Education Trust.

LILY THERESE VENIZELOS is an IUCN (World Conservation Union) Marine Turtle Specialist Group member and the founder and president of MEDASSET, the Mediterranean Association to Save the Sea Turtles.

STEPHEN WALSH is the author of *Plant Based Nutrition and Health* (2003) and a nutrition and health spokesperson for the Vegan Society in the United Kingdom.

NIGEL K. WALTON is the founder of the Poffins Company Limited and a fellow of the Institute of Sales and Marketing Management.

CLIFFORD WARWICK is an independent consultant biologist and medical scientist. He is an adviser to many animal welfare, conservation, and human health organizations, and he researches, writes, and broadcasts on biology and medicine.

VICTOR WATKINS is a wildlife adviser to the World Society for the Protection of Animals and has specialized for the past twenty years in international bear protection issues.

STEPHEN H. WEBB is a professor of religion and philosophy at Wabash College in Crawfordsville, Indiana.

TREVOR P. WHEELER is the Middle East programs director for the World Society for the Protection of Animals.

THOMAS I. WHITE holds the Conrad N. Hilton Chair in Business Ethics at Loyola Marymount University in Los Angeles, California, where he is the director of the Center of Ethics and Business. He is also a fellow of the Oxford Centre for Animal Ethics.

DAVID WILKINS is a veterinarian who served as chief veterinary officer of the Royal Society for the Prevention of Cruelty to Animals and director of Eurogroup for Animal Welfare.

GEORGE WITTEMYER is a professor in the Department of Fish, Wildlife and Conservation Biology at Colorado State University. He began working with elephants in 1997 when he individually identified the Samburu elephant population of northern Kenya.

GRETCHEN WYLER was a Broadway headliner, animal advocate, and founder of the Ark Trust and the annual Genesis Awards.

NIGEL YEO is the director of operations of the Royal Society for the Prevention of Cruelty to Animals.

STEPHEN L. ZAWISTOWSKI is the science adviser for the American Society for the Prevention of Cruelty to Animals, an adjunct professor in clinical medicine at the University of Illinois College of Veterinary Medicine, and an adjunct professor in the Animal Behavior and Conservation Program at Hunter College in New York City.

sensory perception, 47
sentience, 43, 68, 244, 246; argument from, 227; scientific attitude regarding animals', 259–260
sentiocentric ethics, 68
September 11, 2001, 127
serial killers, 30
setts (badger lairs), 91
Seventh Day Adventists, 291
severe acute respiratory syndrome (SARS), 258
Sexual Politics of Meat, The (Adams), 225
Shaftesbury, Earl of, 272
Shaivitz, Mandy, 276
sharks, 48, 51–52, 181; finning of, 49, 51, 52
Shaw, George Bernard, 289
sheep, 22, 42, 96–97, 171, 243; cloning, 181, 183–184; free-range, 163; lambs, 177; live exportation of, 104–105; in New Zealand, 176, 177; welfare of, 176–177
shehita slaughter, 171–172
Sheldrick Wildlife Trust (Kenya), 79
shells, 33
shelters. *See* animal shelters; evacuation shelters
Shintoism, 29, 30
Sho-Ban Indians (Shoshone-Bannock Tribes), 100
shopping, caring, 282–283
show dogs, 156
shrimp, 110
Siddhartha Gautama (Buddha), 245–246
Sierra Leone, 93
sight, sense of, 244
silkworms, 25
Simian AIDS retrovirus, 84–85
Simpsons, The, 276
Singapore, 94
Singer, Peter, 14, 68, 185, 236, 274
Single European Act (1986), 237–238
skates, 181
skin, of animals, 33; of birds, 94; of kangaroos and wallabies, 96; of reptiles, 108
skin irritation tests, 178, 179, 191, 194, 261
slaughterhouses, 12, 22, 105–106, 150–151, 238; bull fighting and, 204; "factory" ships and, 42; in India, 34, 35; media exposés of, 10, 275; total number of animals kills in, 172
slaughtering, 171–173; of animals in India, 34, 35; on "factory" ships, 42; of fish, 166; of horses, 86, 167–168; live animal exports for, 104–106; of pigs, 172, 173, 175–176; public health and, 258; religious methods for, 21,

22, 171–172, 173, 202–203, 243, 252, 253; as religious or cultural sacrifice, 241–242; transportation of animals for, 14, 27, 35, 104–106, 172, 176–177; of whales, 42. *See also* cattle; factory farming; meat; meat-eating; meat/slaughter/farmed animals legislation
sloth bears, 83
smell, sense of, 47, 244
smuggling animals. *See* animal trade, illegal
snakes, 32, 108
snare traps, 79–80, 287; in Africa, 22–23, 70–71, 79; badgers and, 91, 92; beavers and, 100; chimpanzees and, 79, 84; fur trade and, 104. *See also* hunting/trapping
snipes, 95
Snohomish County Public Works Department, 100
snow crabs, 39
snow leopards, 80, 81, 102
social behavior, 152; of beavers, 259; behaviorism and, 256; breed-discriminatory laws and, 148; of cats, 115–116, 136; of cephalopods and decapod crustaceans, 40–41; of cetaceans, 43–44; of chimpanzees and humans, 85, 182; contraceptives and, 74, 75; courses in, 274–275; of dogs, 116–118, 129–130, 132, 135–136, 136–137, 148; of elephants, 90–91; euthanasia and, 140; of gerbils, 118; of guinea pigs, 119; of mute swans, 101; of pigs, 175; of rabbits, 123; in zoos, 66–67
social behavior deviations: of cats, 115, 132; of cetaceans in captivity, 63; circus animals and, 200; of dogs, 129–130, 132, 134, 156; euthanasia and, 140; of farmed animals, 163, 167, 175, 200, 283; of zoo animals, 65, 83, 200
social contract theory, 228
Social Funds, 285
Società fiorentina per la protezione degli animali (SPA in Florence) (Italy), 13
Società Protettrice degli Animali contro i mali trattamenti che subiscono dai guardiani e dai conducenti (SPA) (Italy), 12
Société contre la vivisection (France), 13
Société protectrice des animaux (France), 13
societies for the prevention of cruelty to animals: in Africa, 20, 22; in Australia, 18–19, 96, 214; in Canada, 14–15; in Europe, 12–13; in U.S., 15–16,

168. *See also* Royal Society for the Prevention of Cruelty to Animals (RSPCA) (Britain)
Society for the Prevention of Cruelty to Children (U.S.), 16
Soil Association, 282
sonar technology, 39
song thrushes, 95
sound, and aquatic animals, 39–40, 50 51, 64
South Africa, 281–282; animal protection in, 20, 21–22, 23, 24; animal sacrifice in, 242; apartheid protests in, 285; humane education in, 281–282; Treasure oil spill in, 78; whaling in, 30
South America, 31–33, 55, 92, 93, 97. *See also specific countries*
South Carolina, U.S., 154
Southeast Asia, 105
southern elephant seal (*Mirounga leonina*), 44
South Korea, 89
sow stalls, 163, 175, 176
Spain, 104, 105, 148, 176, 236; blood fiestas in, 202–203; bull fighting in, 202, 203, 204–205; fish farming in, 166; live pigeon shoots in, 214; live quail shoots and, 215
Spanish Bullfight, A (film), 201
Spanish explorers, 85
Spanish lynxes, 80
sparrows, 95
spaying, 75, 146–147, 152, 154; trap-neuter-release (TNR) projects, 24, 25, 153. *See also* neutering
species chauvinism, 229
species endemism, 76
speciesism, 32
Species Survival Plan (SSP), 69
spider monkeys, 93
spiny dogfish sharks, 52
Spirit: Stallion of the Cimarron (movie), 276
sports. *See* entertainment and sport, animals for; hunting/trapping
Spurgeon, Charles, 139
squids, giant, 39
squirrel monkeys, 93, 106
squirrels, 71, 103, 203
Staffordshire terriers, 148, 208
Stahler, Charles, 18
starlings, 95
Stehfest, E., 255
Steiner, G., 226
Steinfeld, H., 255
stem cell research, 178, 184, 192–193

Wang Yangming, 25

Washington, D. C., 154

Wasserman, Debra, 18

water quality in cetacean-housing aquariums, 64

West Indian manatees, 55–56

Westminster Parliament, 167

West Virginia, U.S., 154, 210

wetlands, 99–100

whales, 152, 263–264; breeding of, 64; food supply of, 42; intelligence of, 43–44; lifespan of, 44; sonar and, 39; stranding of, 53. *See also* cetaceans

whale sharks, 51, 52

whaling, 49, 263; in Australia, 19; commercial, 41–43; in Greenland, 28; in Japan, 30, 41, 42; in Norway, 28

Wheeler, Etta, 16

whiskers, 33

White, Caroline Earle, 16

White, Thomas, 263

Whitehead, Hal, 263

white lemuroid ringtail possums, 19

white-tailed deer, 205, 206, 207

Whole Foods supermarket chain, 41

widowhood system of separating pigeons by sex, 216

Wilberforce, William, 272

wildcats, African, 153

Wild Free Roaming Horse and Burro Act (U.S., 1971), 86

"Wild Horse Annie," 86

Wildlife (Protection) Act (India, 1972), 33

Wildlife and Countryside Act (U.K., 1981), 94

Wildlife Institute of India, 33

wildlife liaison officers (WLOs), 92

Wildlife Protection Society of India (WPSI), 33

"wild" turkeys, 164

Wilmut, Ian, 183

Winter, Anna, 12

Wisconsin, U.S. ., 279

wolves, 75, 82, 211; reintroduction of, 72, 73, 74

women, 14–15, 16; feminism, 224–225, 274; suffrage reforms for, in U.S., 17

woodcocks, 95

wool, 177

woolly monkeys, 93

working animals, 27, 151, 212, 234, 279

World Animal Net Directory, 20

World Health Organization (WHO), 154

World Horse Welfare (WHW), 121

World Organisation for Animal Health (OIE), 21, 109, 166, 173, 265

World Small Animal Veterinary Association, 150

World Society for the Protection of Animals (WSPA), 20, 83–84, 265

World Trade Organization (WTO), 109–110, 189

World Vegetarian Congress (1975), 18

World War I, 86

World Wide Fund for Nature (WWF), 33

worms/parasites, 122, 142, 165, 177, 210

Wright, Belinda, 33

WSPA (World Society for the Protection of Animals), 20, 83–84, 265

WTO (World Trade Organization), 109–110, 189

Wu, emperor of Liang, 26

xenotransplantation, 181, 182, 196–197; cloning and, 184; ethics of, 196; transgenic animals and, 195, 196, 197

Yemen, 27

Zakynthos National Marine Park (Greece), 51

Zambia, 21, 79, 93

zebra fish, 181, 198

zebras, 79

Zimbabwe, 20, 23, 79

zoo animals: bears, 83; breeding of, 62–63, 65; canned hunting of, 206; chimpanzees, 61, 85; contraceptives for, 74; primates, 61, 85, 93; reptiles, 108; rescue of, 78

Zoo Licensing Act (U.K., 1981), 66

zoos, 24, 29, 61; arguments against, 67; conservation claims by, 62–63, 65, 67; ethics of, 62–63; laws regarding, 65–66; public perceptions of, 65; roadside, 65–66; scientific claims of, 66–67; veterinary medicine in, 66

zoosemiotics, 274

Zulu nation, 242

ss

e

iversity Presses.

n Pro

ress
ooks, Inc.